MODERN STRATEGY

MODERN STRATEGY

COLIN S. GRAY

OXFORD
UNIVERSITY PRESS

OXFORD

UNIVERSITY PRESS

Great Clarendon Street, Oxford OX2 6DP

Oxford University Press is a department of the University of Oxford.
It furthers the University's objective of excellence in research, scholarship,
and education by publishing worldwide in

Oxford New York

Auckland Bangkok Buenos Aires Cape Town Chennai
Dar es Salaam Delhi Hong Kong Istanbul Karachi Kolkata
Kuala Lumpur Madrid Melbourne Mexico City Mumbai Nairobi
São Paulo Shanghai Taipei Tokyo Toronto

Oxford is a registered trade mark of Oxford University Press
in the UK and in certain other countries

Published in the United States
by Oxford University Press Inc., New York

British Library Cataloguing in Publication Data

Data available

Library of Congress Cataloging in Publication Data
Gray, Colin S.
Modern strategy / Colin S. Gray.
Includes bibliographical references and index.
1. Strategy. I. Title
U162.G694 1999   355.4—dc21   99-32729

ISBN 978-0-19-878251-3

13 15 17 19 20 18 16 14 12

Typeset in OUP Swift
by RefineCatch Limited, Bungay, Suffolk

To Valerie, my inspiration

FORETHOUGHTS

'The political object—the original motive for the war—will thus determine both the military objective to be reached and the amount of effort it requires.'

Carl von Clausewitz, *On War* (1976)

'I may be permitted to call attention to the fact that my work furnishes for the first time a comprehensive review of the development of strategical science in the past century; but that it tries, besides, to give scientific reasons for the standpoint from which strategy is to be viewed at the present and in the near future ... Theory is not dangerous in itself but it is the tabulating system which presses the spirit into a Spanish boot, instead of making it freer and stronger. There may certainly be doubts among clever and highly cultured men as to the boundary between legitimate theory and the illegitimate tabulated system, but any one who adopts Clausewitz as the true master and guide in his theoretical studies will surely never go grievously wrong.'

Lt.-Gen. Rudolf von Caemmerer, *The Development of Strategical Science during the 19th Century* (1905)

'Prudence is the statesman's supreme virtue.'

Raymond Aron, *Peace and War: A Theory of International Relations* (1966)

'Theory cannot be accepted as conclusive when practice points the other way.'

Charles E. Callwell, *Small Wars* (1906)

'Strategy is not, however, the final arbiter in war. The battle-field decides.'

Charles E. Callwell, *Small Wars* (1906)

'[I]f any young soldiers of today should read this book, they may understand that while the face of war may alter, some things have not changed since Joshua stood before Jericho, and Xenophon marched to the sea.'

G. MacDonald Fraser, *Quartered Safe Out Here: A Recollection of the War in Burma* (1995)

'Arms create permanent risk, not permanent war. It is men not weapons that start wars.'

Raymond Aron, *Clausewitz: Philosopher of War* (1983)

'As in any field that straddles science, policy, and politics, the temptation to overreach is considerable. High demand for unwaffled answers creates a market for study products that package immature theories as final easily digestible truth.'

Bruce G. Blair, *The Logic of Accidental Nuclear War* (1993)

'There is no hierarchy among the elements of war; one cannot pretend that one is more important than another.'

J. Colin, *The Transformations of War*, trans. L. H. R. Pope-Hennessy (1912)

'That Clausewitzian world, which has endured for three thousand years of recorded history, will also hold sway in the next century. It is not that the entire weight of the past says so: everything we know about the nonlinear, incalculable world indicates that we will not ever achieve predictability given natural phenomena.'

Williamson Murray, 'The 1996 RMA Essay Contest', *Joint Force Quarterly* (1997)

'Anyone who produces a book on strategy in this day and age may seem bold to the point of foolhardiness. No one today believes in strategic genius. Great strategists have been swept away by the cataclysm of two world wars and the pressure of day-to-day events; they have gone the way of the old coloured prints with their naïve simplicity and strong colours, pictures of an ancient civilization in process of disintegration.'

A. Beaufre, *An Introduction to Strategy* (1963)

PREFACE

It is immodest and self-indulgent to use the personal pronoun in a work with pretensions to scholarship. That said, *Modern Strategy* is well sown with personal pronouns. This book is not an intellectual autobiography, but for me it is a landmark work that represents my best effort to share understanding of my chosen field of scholarly interest at the thirty-year point in my career. *Modern Strategy* does not purport to present modern strategy historically, but it does suggest ways to approach the subject.

My approach to strategy is captured in the questions and themes of the book. The master theme is the claim that there is a unity to all strategic experience: nothing essential changes in the nature and function (or purpose)—in sharp contrast to the character—of strategy and war. The significance of this theme to the understanding of modern strategy is reflected in the title assigned to the concluding chapter, 'Strategy Eternal'. The more widely I have visited the training-grounds and killing-fields of strategy, the more impressed I have been with the essentially unitary nature of the subject. The master theme here of the unity of strategy and strategic experience is employed and developed to counter a widespread error. That error is the tendency to confuse tactics with strategy and, as a consequence, to mistake changes in the character of events with changes in their nature.

Definition of key terms is critically important. Readers are advised, therefore, that the deliberately few definitions that this book offers are presented neither as a matter of pro forma scholarly duty, nor are they a demonstration of scholarly rigour. Above all others, my preferred definition of strategy, which is strictly Clausewitzian, is vital to understanding of the subject. I do not claim that Clausewitz's definition of strategy is correct; indeed, a definition cannot be so described. But I do claim that Clausewitz's definition provides the path for superior strategic understanding to those wise enough to adopt it.

This book is not presented over-ambitiously as a definitive guide to modern strategy, as a point of view on the course and ever-dynamic outcome of that strategy, still less as a 'cookbook' so that reader-chefs might 'do' strategy better. My purpose is simply to help readers better to understand modern strategy. The basis for this text is my rather unusual, not to say eccentric, career as a strategic thinker. I might say 'defence intellectual', but a British pen cannot quite cope with that concept.

Depending upon one's point of view, the course of my career is either a net asset or a liability for the central purpose of this book. Bracketed by stints as a university teacher in Britain and Canada (1968–73, and from 1993 to the present), I was for nearly twenty years a strategic theorist, defence analyst, and policy adviser in the United States. Those twenty years included five as a part-time member of the US government—I held a presidential appointment from 1982 to 1987—and involved me personally in many of the topics treated here. In a more or less classified form, I have written reports for the US government on a wide range of topics that includes nuclear strategy, arms control, the defence of NATO's then Central Front, ICBM basing, maritime strategy, strategy for airpower, space strategy, strategic defence, and special operations. In addition to my activities as an adviser to government, I have accumulated an extensive record of unclassified publications on matters both policy-oriented and scholarly but policy relevant.

The advantages of a long and varied career for a book such as this are unambiguous. I have known and worked with many of the leaders in the field. Furthermore, my knowledge of some strategic issues is a knowledge informed by prolonged and close association with those who must 'do' strategy, as policy-maker, senior official, or warrior. The potential disadvantages that flow from my career are probably equally unambiguous. On most of the topics treated here I have a published track record, and in some cases a controversial track record. I can assure readers that it is no part of my ambition to use this book to refight old battles over policy, let alone engage in extensive retrospective self-justification. In some passages, however, especially those devoted to nuclear questions, some readers might believe that I appear to have re-entered the lists of strategic controversy. Given my intent, such an impression would be false. There is much about the nuclear history of the Cold War that awaits better understanding. I do not try to argue that I—and theorists, officials, and soldiers who thought like me—was correct in my advice and theorizing about, say, nuclear strategy, in the 1970s. But I do believe that many academics, particularly the younger ones, are apt to lack empathy with the policymakers of the superpowers who had to respond to the novelty of the nuclear challenge to strategy as best they could. Readers are not asked to agree with my exploration in nuclear strategic history, but they are invited to question their own beliefs.

As well as requesting readers to tolerate the occasional personal pronoun, I ask also that they accept a modest approach to references. Although everything that needs reference is duly supported, I do not believe that after thirty years of professional life I need burden this book, and the reader, with demonstration of a heroic mastery of the relevant literature. The footnotes and bibliography could be as extensive as the publisher would allow. Given that my mission is to help improve understanding of modern strategy, and that I do not see important differences among ancient, medieval, and modern strategy, which books, studies, and real-world experiences should not add to that understanding?

In a characteristically trenchant manner, Ken Booth has written pejoratively, 'This is not to say that there is any shortage of nineteenth-century minds at the end of the twentieth century.'[1] It may well be that mine is one of those nineteenth-

[1] Ken Booth, 'Dare Not to Know: International Relations Theory versus the Future', in Booth and Steve Smith (eds.), *International Relations Theory Today* (Cambridge, 1995), 343.

century minds. Indeed, given my insistence upon the unity of all historical strategic experience, mine could well be portrayed as a twelfth-century, or a fifth-century BC, mind. Professor Booth might be both appalled and amused to learn that in one of my finer moments as a government adviser in the United States I wrote a brief commentary on Byzantine strategy for the Defense Nuclear Agency, on the general theme of strategic defence as exemplified by the strategic effect of the walls of Constantinople. If Professor Booth and other right-thinking folk are correct, then it may well be that people like me, who like to flatter ourselves with the belief that we are part of the solution, turn out to be part of the problem. Plainly, nineteenth-century mindsets miseducated by Clausewitz and Jomini, as well as Metternich and Bismarck, are unlikely to prove suitably flexible and adaptive to the challenges of the twenty-first century.

In the writing of this book as honestly as I knew how, I found that while over thirty years I may sometimes have reached the wrong conclusions, and at other times sought to achieve the wrong objectives, the reasons for those errors were honourable. Despite my record as a policy analyst and strategic debater, *Modern Strategy* is not designed to advance any policy agenda, or indeed anything beyond better understanding of the subject of modern strategy. Although I claim that strategy and war are eternal in their essentials—hence their persisting dimensions, as described in Chapter 1—my analysis still could stand as valid interpretation of strategic history until the end of the twentieth century, even if the strategic thread to history were to end abruptly tomorrow. This is not a work of futurology. I believe we can understand the broad character of future strategic history on the basis of comprehension of past strategic history. Nonetheless, *Modern Strategy* is about exactly what it claims, and no more. To predict rather than understand the future, buy a crystal ball—if you can find one.

Much of whatever merit this book may have is attributable to the educational effect of the writings of Carl von Clausewitz. Whether I have been studying nuclear targeting, the leverage of seapower, or the strategic utility of special operations, Clausewitz's *On War* has been my constant companion and by far the most heavily used book in my library.[2] On a more personal note, I owe great professional debts to Donald G. Brennan and Herman Kahn. Those two scholar-controversialists set standards of personal integrity, courage, and intellectual breadth and depth that shine down through the years. In different ways, two other strategic theorists that I came to know also set professional standards that I respect: namely Bernard Brodie and Albert Wohlstetter.[3] I am not uncritical of either of those scholars—any more than I am uncritical of Clausewitz, Brennan, and Kahn—but, again, each in his way was a giant in the field and a source of personal inspiration.

[2] Carl von Clausewitz, *On War*, trans. Michael Howard and Peter Paret (Princeton, NJ, 1976).
[3] I was probably ungenerous to Albert Wohlstetter in 'The Holistic Strategist', *Global Affairs*, 7 (1992), 171–82.

It is sad but true to record that honest professional disagreements can translate into personal antipathies, just as personal antipathies can translate into somewhat less honest professional disagreements. I have learnt a great deal from scholars with whom I disagreed. In fact, sometimes had they not written in professionally so disagreeable a way, I would not have known what my views really were. I am indebted especially to five scholars with whom I have crossed pens, but never exchanged cross words: Ken Booth, Lawrence Freedman, Sir Michael Howard, Robert Jervis, and Martin van Creveld. With each of these scholars I have had my professional differences, and in each case I have emerged wiser, if not always thoroughly persuaded.

I wish to acknowledge the support I have received over many years from three personal and professional friends with whom usually I find myself in substantive agreement. Williamson Murray, Keith B. Payne, and William R. Van Cleave are special people whom I am privileged to know.

Modern Strategy has been a long time in the making. Pieces of the argument have been exposed informally to the outstanding group of doctoral students associated with the Centre for Security Studies at the University of Hull, and somewhat more formally to the students at the National War College in Washington, DC, and to the students with the Center for Defense and Strategic Studies at Southwest Missouri State University in Springfield, Missouri. In particular, I thank my doctoral students at Hull, and especially James Kiras, for their help with this difficult manuscript.

After myself and Carl von Clausewitz, the person most responsible for the shape and even some of the detail of this work is my very good friend James Wirtz of the Naval Postgraduate School, Monterey, California. Jim performed the scholarly equivalent of a Medal of Honor mission for this book. To say that I am grateful would be an absurd understatement.

My editor at Oxford University Press, Tim Barton, kept the faith when this project might have faltered—to him I say, thank you, and I hope you believe that your confidence has been rewarded.

I cannot express adequately my gratitude to Sue Wiles of the Department of Politics and Asian Studies at the University of Hull, who laboured without complaint—to me, at least—to produce a miracle of word-processing. Also I am much indebted to my assistant, Ernest Garcia, who saved me on the bibliography.

I am grateful to Cambridge University Press for granting me permission to deploy as Chapter 5 a text that they have published in slightly different form in the *Review of International Studies* (25 [1999]).

Finally, I thank my wife and closest friend, Valerie, and my daughter, Tonia, for their unfailing support.

Hull   C.S.G.
April 1999

CONTENTS

INTRODUCTION: THE EXPANDING UNIVERSE OF STRATEGY

Poor strategy is expensive, bad strategy can be lethal, while when the stakes include survival, very bad strategy is almost always fatal. *Modern Strategy* is about the theory and practice of the use, and threat of use, of organized force for political purposes in the twentieth century. My concern is to advance the understanding of strategy by exploring the relationship between the ever-growing complexity of modern war and a general theory of war and strategy that, when properly formulated, is indifferent to the specifics of history. Proliferation in the forms of war should be explicable in theory. *Modern Strategy*, following Carl von Clausewitz in *On War*[1] and Admiral Sir Reginald Custance in his *A Study of War*,[2] joins the short column of books that represent the 'historical', rather than the 'materialist', school of strategic thought. Followers of the historical school believe that there are elements common to war and strategy in all periods, in all geographies, and with all technologies. War remains war despite the many different forms that it can assume in distinctive political or technical-tactical contexts.

These pages bear the stamp of the pervasive organizing idea that *there is an essential unity to all strategic experience in all periods of history because nothing vital to the nature and function of war and strategy changes.* Strategy rules over every chapter, and every page of this book, regardless of the immediate subject. Chapter 1, on 'The Dimensions of Strategy', presents a theory of strategy that allows us to make sense of all strategic experience, regardless of the diversity of tactical forms it may assume; it provides a general theory of strategy. The twentieth century has donated us an appallingly rich collection of strategic experiences; although the century has added some new character to matters strategic, it has not, and could not, alter the nature of strategy. The intellectual integrity of this book rests upon the validity of the claim that a single framework of strategy's dimensions can explain all strategic phenomena, of all kinds and in all periods. For example, J. F. Verbruggen usefully reminds us that '[m]edieval wars present the same diversity as wars in other times. Commanders and learned chroniclers knew the various possibilities of strategy. They made plans for a crusade and several treatises on war.' He advises that the 'knowledge of strategy [by medieval leaders] left nothing to be desired, but the practical means for large-scale operations were almost entirely

---

[1] Carl von Clausewitz, *On War*, trans. Michael Howard and Peter Paret (Princeton, NJ, 1976).

[2] Reginald Custance, *A Study of War* (Boston, 1924); see esp. 'Barfleur' (pseud. for Custance), *Naval Policy: A Plea for the Study of War* (Edinburgh, 1907), pp. vii–ix.

lacking'.[3] Simple theories can simply be wrong, or at least misleading. For example, three ambitious books in the field of strategy have each fixed upon a different, but single, guiding light. In one case the author explains the nature of strategy with reference to its inherently paradoxical logic, in another the author follows the lead of German military historian Hans Delbrück and requires the distinction between strategies of annihilation, or prompt overthrow, and strategies of attrition to provide the key to understanding. In the final case, in a monumental work a military historian lays extravagant emphasis upon an insistence that the art of war reduces essentially to a choice between persisting and raiding strategies. These three books, respectively by Edward N. Luttwak, John J. Weltman, and Archer Jones, are of exceptional merit.[4] In each case, however, a central organizing idea is overtaxed.[5] Readers of this book, in contrast, are not invited to believe that a paradoxical logic, a choice between annihilation and attrition, or a decision to persist or to raid, captures the key to understanding. Instead, I claim only that strategy has a complex nature and a function that is unchanging over the centuries.

A book which aspires to explain strategic phenomena from the relief of Mafeking on 17–18 May 1900 to the Balkan wars of the 1990s has to steer a careful passage between two extreme views of theory. One view, as expressed by Alex Danchev, is that '[p]aradigms are not politics. They are merely the pets and playthings of political scientists.'[6] The other view is presented in these words of F. A. Hayek: '[w]ithout a theory the facts are silent.'[7] Big ideas are helpful in the ordering and comprehension of a messy historical reality. For example, Jonathan Bailey's proposition that the twentieth century has registered a single military revolution—the one that introduced what he calls 'the modern style of warfare', led by the vast improvement in artillery in 1916–18—is a powerful idea indeed.[8] Even if Bailey's idea is judged unduly heroic in sweep, it is not self-evident that a

---

[3] J. F. Verbruggen, *The Art of Warfare in Western Europe during the Middle Ages: From the Eighth Century to 1340*, 2nd edn. (Woodbridge, 1997), 276, 349.

[4] Edward N. Luttwak, *Strategy: The Logic of War and Peace* (Cambridge, Mass., 1987); John J. Weltman, *World Politics and the Evolution of War* (Baltimore, 1995); Archer Jones, *The Art of War in the Western World* (Urbana, Ill., 1987). See Hans Delbrück, *History of the Art of War*, iv: *The Dawn of Modern Warfare* (Lincoln, Neb., 1985), 439–44, for the inspiration for Weltman's organizing distinction. Delbrück had made himself thoroughly unpopular in the German Army of his day by arguing that Frederick the Great had been an exponent of a strategy of attrition rather than annihilation. This claim was viewed by many Germans as a slur upon a national hero. See Arden Bucholz, *Hans Delbrück and the German Military Establishment* (Iowa City, 1985,), 35–9.

[5] Some big ideas do work well enough. Brian Bond, *The Pursuit of Victory: From Napoleon to Saddam Hussein* (Oxford, 1996).

[6] Alex Danchev, 'On Specialness', *International Affairs*, 72 (1996), 746.

[7] Quoted in John Keegan, *A History of Warfare* (London, 1993), 6.

[8] Jonathan Bailey, *The First World War and the Birth of the Modern Style of Warfare*, Occasional Paper 22 (Camberley, 1996). Scholars are ever liable to locate the most momentous of changes in the period of their special expertise. For example readers unpersuaded by Bailey that modern war began in 1916–18, could consider the argument of Robert M. Epstein that it first appeared in the Franco-Austrian war of 1809. Whereas Bailey keys his notion of a modern style of war to the perfection of predicted artillery fire in a combined arms team, Epstein highlights the appearance of 'distributed maneuver' for an

more inclusive approach to the idea of military revolution necessarily has merit. Is it helpful to interpret strategy in the twentieth century primarily with reference to one or several revolutions in military affairs (RMAs)? To emphasize great discontinuities—*revolutions* in military affairs—is to risk undue de-emphasis of continuities. Whether historical continuities or discontinuities are more import-ant is an empirical matter calling for careful judgement; it is not a question whose answer should be conceptually preordained.

I am a social scientist with a deep respect for history, but this work is neither a strategic history of the twentieth century nor a history of strategy in the twentieth century—rather, *Modern Strategy* is principally about characteristically 'modern' expression of the ageless phenomena of strategy. It has been my intention to write a book that combines strategic history and policy science. Strategic history refers to a view of history, in this case of the twentieth century, that focuses upon efforts to secure political ends through the threat or use of force. Policy science refers to identification and examination of the structure of the problems and opportun-ities perceived, or perhaps missed, by policymakers, strategists, military com-manders, and attentive publics as the universe of strategy and war has expanded with new layers of complexity.

QUESTIONS

In support of the master theme which argues that there is a permanent unity to strategy and strategic experience, six major questions shape the design of this book.

HOW DO THE THEORY AND PRACTICE OF STRATEGY INTERACT?

What is the relationship between strategic ideas and strategic behaviour? The most respected American strategic theorist of the nuclear era, Bernard Brodie, commented that strategy pre-eminently 'is nothing if not pragmatic. . . . Above all, strategic theory is a theory for action.'[9] Thinking along similar lines, Raymond Aron once observed that '[s]trategic thought draws its inspiration each century, or rather at each moment of history, from the problems which events themselves

operational level of war. He requires 'modern' war to show such symptoms as 'a strategic war plan that effectively integrates the various theaters of operations; the fullest mobilization of the resources of the state . . . and the use of operational campaigns by opposing sides to achieve strategic objectives in the various theaters of operations'. *Napoleon's Last Victory and the Emergence of Modern War* (Lawrence, Kan., 1994), 6. If neither the operational artistry discernible in 1809 nor the artillery-led combined arms of 1916–18 is judged satisfactory as the marker for 'modern war', readers can split the difference chrono-logically and vote for Edward Hagerman's view that 'the American Civil War ushered in a new era in land warfare'. *The American Civil War and the Origins of Modern Warfare: Ideas, Organisation, and Field Command* (Bloomington, Ind., 1988), p. xi. Hagerman finds 'the origins of modern warfare' in the tactics, operations, and organisational responses of both sides in the Civil War to the challenges posed by the products of the Industrial Revolution. All three scholars are correct.

[9] Bernard Brodie, *War and Politics* (New York, 1973), 452.

pose'.[10] Scholarly strategic theorists can forget that their professional world, the world of ideas, is not itself a world that can test strategic ideas. Charles E. Callwell, Britain's leading theorist on 'small wars' (wars wherein regular troops fight irregulars), was very much on the mark when he suggested ironically that '[t]heory cannot be accepted as conclusive when practice points the other way'.[11] The authority of practice over theory is akin to the practical authority of tactics over strategy;[12] higher direction always can be thwarted by adverse local conditions or by troops incapable of doing what strategic guidance requires. The relationship between strategic theory and the practice and malpractice of strategy pervades every chapter here. From the logistical nightmares of the German Army in 1914 and 1941 as respectively it invaded France and Russia,[13] to the tactical, operational, and political problems of the US Army in Vietnam in 1965–71,[14] this analysis seeks to confront ideas with facts 'from the field'. Nonetheless, ideas help shape behaviour, even as they are shaped in their turn by behaviour.

WHAT HAS THE GROWING COMPLEXITY OF DEFENCE PREPARATION AND WAR MEANT FOR STRATEGY?

The text emphasizes the expanding complexity of war in the twentieth century, and hence the growing complexity both of peacetime defence planning and of the wartime problems faced by strategists. As Chapter 1 explains, strategy is strategy regardless of historical, geographical, or technological context. Nonetheless, in 1900 the strategists of the British Empire operated in a strategic universe that was geographically only two-dimensional. Despite more than a century of military experience with both lighter-than-air craft (balloons) and experimental submarines, and the recent demonstration of radio communications, the military commander in 1900 lived in a strategic world that comprised only operations on land and the surface of the sea. By contrast, a century later the 'battlespace' of interest to the military commander includes land, sea, air, and space. Moreover,

[10] Raymond Aron, 'The Evolution of Modern Strategic Thought', in Institute for Strategic Studies (ed.), *Problems of Modern Strategy*, pt. i: Adelphi Paper 54 (London, Feb. 1969), 7.

[11] Charles E. Callwell, *Small Wars: A Tactical Textbook for Imperial Soldiers*, repr. of 1906 [3rd] edn. (London, 1990), 270.

[12] Cyril Falls, *A Hundred Years of War* (London, 1953), 18–19.

[13] Martin van Creveld, *Supplying War: Logistics from Wallenstein to Patton* (Cambridge, 1977), chs. 4–5. Van Creveld's arguments are examined critically in John A. Lynn, 'The History of Logistics and *Supplying War*', in Lynn (ed.), *Feeding Mars: Logistics in Western Warfare from the Middle Ages to the Present* (Boulder, Colo., 1993), 9–27. Thomas Kane, 'Getting It There: The Relationship Between Logistics and Strategy' (Ph.D. thesis, Hull, 1998), is also critical of van Creveld's view.

[14] Especially useful are Harry G. Summers, Jr., *On Strategy: A Critical Analysis of the Vietnam War* (Novato, Calif., 1982); Andrew F. Krepinevich, Jr., *The Army and Vietnam* (Baltimore, 1986); Robert Buzzanco, *Masters of War: Military Dissent and Politics in the Vietnam Era* (Cambridge, 1996); Robert D. Schulzinger, *A Time for War: The United States and Vietnam, 1941–1975* (New York, 1997); H. R. McMaster, *Dereliction of Duty: Lyndon Johnson, Robert McNamara, the Joint Chiefs of Staff, and the Lies That Led to Vietnam* (New York, 1997); Jeffrey Record, *The Wrong War: Why We Lost in Vietnam* (Annapolis, Md., 1998).

today there are overhead (air and space) complications for the land, and sub-surface and overhead (air and space) complications for the sea. As if all that were not enough to cause strategic indigestion, today's commander must plan to fight, and defend, across the electromagnetic spectrum (EMS), which includes 'cyber-space'. (The EMS ranges from radio, to radar, through infrared, ultraviolet, and X-rays, to gamma rays.) Proficiency on the EMS has increasingly enabled higher prowess in land, sea, air, and, putatively, space warfare. If the world just identified were not complicated enough, one needs also to factor in weapons of mass destruction and irregular warfare as distinctive forms of conflict, and even as forms of warfare that could conflate as 'catastrophe terrorism'.

Detail matters less than principle. The point is that no matter how many vari-ants of conflict one elects to recognize, the strategic world of the year 2000 is much more complex in structure than was the strategic world of 1900. This reality has implications which identify the next general question. As for all six of these broad organizing questions, the text below is shaped to find plausible answers. At this juncture, it suffices to identify problems in need of investigation.

WHY IS STRATEGY SO DIFFICULT?[15]

Although modern technology is wonderful and many military establishments are characterized by a sophisticated professionalism, superior strategic perform-ance is as difficult to achieve today as it was in 1900. Clausewitz comments:

It might be thought that policy could make demands on war which war could not fulfil; but that hypothesis would challenge the natural and unavoidable assumption that *policy knows the instrument it means to use*. If policy reads the course of military events correctly, it is wholly and exclusively entitled to decide which events and trends are best for the objectives of war.[16]

Policy, or politics—depending upon which translation of *Politik* one favours—generally does not know the military 'instrument it means to use'. Strategy is about the use of military power in support of political goals, but statesmen in peacetime, and even generals and admirals in peacetime, can rarely be confident about the probable performance of their military instrument in war. Armed forces do not wage war in a political vacuum. Against whom is their net performance to be measured? Early in the twentieth century the conscript armies of continental Europe were strategically ill-understood by their political owners. In 1990–1 neither the US-led coalition nor Iraq completely understood how well or poorly its military machine would function in war. At the close of the twentieth century, debate in the US defence community was joined on the question of what quality of strategic performance the United States could anticipate from its increasingly

[15] I am grateful to David Jablonsky, 'Why Is Strategy Difficult?', in Gary L. Guertner (ed.), *The Search for Strategy: Politics and Strategic Vision* (Westport, Conn., 1993), 3–45.

[16] Clausewitz, *On War*, 607 (emphasis added).

information-rich armed forces. The United States might achieve what the then Secretary of Defense William J. Perry referred to as 'an "unfair" competitive advantage over its opponents',[17] but that advantage is likely to be at a severe discount in conditions either of irregular or of very high intensity conflict when the enemy declines to accept battle with regular conventional forces.[18]

After a century of periodically intensive development of military, and militarily exploitable commercial, technology, the problems of the strategist have not been much eased. War is still a gamble. Whether one is anchored temporally in the 1900s or the 2000s, one cannot take exception to Clausewitz's observations that '[n]o other human activity [than war] is so continuously or universally bound up with chance. And through the element of chance, guesswork and luck come to play a great part in war.'[19] The more simple-minded strategist is ever in search of that Eldorado, that golden city of guaranteed strategic riches which lures Americans today in the guise of the promises of 'dominant battlespace knowledge' and force dominance in order to achieve swift victory through 'shock and awe'.[20] Alas, quality of strategic performance does not lend itself to reliable sustainable improvement by applying science, technology, and engineering. Better weapons always are preferable to worse weapons—provided large opportunity costs are not incurred—but tactical and operational military prowess is easily squandered if battles are ill-chosen, campaigns are wrongly pointed, and war is ill-conceived. This is not to deny that for people at risk at the sharp end of strategy there is everything to be said in favour of tactical excellence. For example, the abundant use of helicopters was essential to the American style of war in Vietnam in the 1960s. US rotary-wing airpower performed tactically superbly. What was wrong with the American conduct of the war in South-East Asia, however, could not be corrected by an excellence in helicopters.

SINCE STRATEGY AND WAR HAVE MANY DIMENSIONS, IS IT PROBABLE THAT SUPERIORITY IN ONLY ONE OR EVEN SEVERAL SUCH DIMENSIONS CAN DELIVER VICTORY?

The complexity of strategy and war—conflict on land, at sea, in the air, and in space and cyberspace—is modest compared with the complexity of the dimensions,

---

[17] William J. Perry, 'Defense in an Age of Hope', *Foreign Affairs*, 75 (1996), 76.

[18] Lawrence Freedman, *The Revolution in Strategic Affairs*, Adelphi Paper 318 (London, Apr. 1998); Lloyd J. Matthews (ed.), *Challenging the United States Symmetrically and Asymmetrically: Can America Be Defeated?* (Carlisle Barracks, Pa., July 1998). Notwithstanding its subtitle, the Matthews collection comprises essays of exceptional interest and sophistication.

[19] Clausewitz, *On War*, 85.

[20] Harlan K. Ullman and James P. Wade, *Shock and Awe: Achieving Rapid Dominance* (Washington, DC, 1996); Joseph S. Nye, Jr., and William A. Owens, 'America's Information Edge', *Foreign Affairs*, 75 (1996), 20–36; Perry, 'Defense'; James R. Blaker, *Understanding the Revolution in Military Affairs: A Guide to America's 21st Century Defense*, Progressive Policy Institute Defense Working Paper 3 (Washington, DC, 1997); John Arquilla and David Ronfeldt (eds.), *In Athena's Camp: Preparing for Conflict in the Information Age* (Santa Monica, Calif., 1997).

factors, or elements that interactively comprise their nature. Does the strategic history of the twentieth century suggest plausibly that superior weapons guarantee success? Perhaps the more just cause is wont to triumph, but who is to judge the justice of a motivating cause? The strategic literature is awash with studies which, at least by plain implication, suggest that a particular favoured dimension of strategy and war is the key to victory. Technology, generalship, economic strength, logistic competence, political popularity, to cite but a few of the dimensions treated in Chapter 1, have all been promoted as the golden key to strategic success. *Modern Strategy* examines this question to see if indeed there is one, or perhaps several, of strategy's dimensions on which superiority would all but guarantee success. American readers should not be surprised to learn that technology and political ethics have tended to be the panacea dimensions in their country's approach to strategic problems.[21] Armed with a just cause and better equipped than any foe, how could American soldiers not prevail?

If any questions can open historical doors to strategic understanding, it is this one and the next (what has changed and what has not). This question, about possible 'golden keys' to strategic victory, penetrates to the heart of many strategic policy debates. The strategic world is perennially beset with salespersons for this or that magical elixir, or 'golden key' (or 'silver bullet'). That key may be the insight and willpower of a leader believed by the credulous to be touched by God or history; it may be the presumed justice of a cause; it may be the economic strength of the polity; it may be the applied military-technological prowess of friendly and Allied armed forces. The point is that prowess on one or two of strategy and war's dimensions are credited with cure-all qualities. Does the strategic history of the twentieth century demonstrate that a particular kind of competence delivers victory? That question pervades this text.

WHAT HAS CHANGED FOR STRATEGY IN THE TWENTIETH CENTURY AND WHAT HAS NOT?

This question at least opens the possibility that nothing essential to the nature of statecraft and war has changed in this century, or perhaps even in all of history. Before readers condemn this book as reactionary, I would hasten to mention that in its earliest stage my professional career focused on the Eisenhower administration's policy, strategy, and force-structural adjustment to military-technological change.[22] Subsequently, most of my work was keyed to the military, strategic, and political implications of new weapon technologies (especially in the ICBM and

---

[21] A. J. Bacevich and Brian R. Sullivan (eds.), *The Limits of Technology in Modern War*, forthcoming, is path-breaking.

[22] Colin S. Gray, 'The Defence Policy of the Eisenhower Administrations, 1953–1961' (D.Phil. thesis, Oxford, 1970).

space systems realms).[23] In short, I should not be a person inclined professionally either to cling romantically to the past or to undervalue the significance of technological change.

This book analyses strategy for a century wherein the lamps of civilization were kept lit through the waging of three world wars that were waged to satisfactory conclusions. For those among us reared on Clausewitz and his emphasis upon the role of chance in war, it is impressive to be reminded that Western civilization has recorded no fewer than three great successes in the twentieth century: against Wilhelmine Germany, against Nazi Germany, and against the USSR. It is as likely as not that ten or twenty years into the twenty-first century, the leading polity for the West will be contending at least in cold war with another worthy superstate foe, possibly a selectively modernized China. Whether the future holds a Chinese or a resurgent Russia as such a foe, the story-line of strategic history is probably the same.[24] History, including strategic history, does not end.

There appears to be a unity to all strategic experience, regardless of period, polity, or technology. The need to use or threaten force for political objectives, the need to behave strategically, is perennial and universal. John Keegan is not persuasive when he argues that premodern warfare really was cultural in most senses, rather than what today we mean by political.[25] Readers impressed by Keegan's intriguing and infuriating book *A History of Warfare* could do a lot worse than consult J. F. Verbruggen's classic work on *The Art of Warfare in Western Europe during the Middle Ages*, Richard A. Gabriel and Donald W. Boose, Jr.'s study of *The Great Battles of Antiquity*, and Lawrence H. Keeley's *War Before Civilization*, as healthy antidotes.[26] Keegan is correct in asserting that war is a cultural activity. That good idea, however, should not obscure the fact that war is always influenced by cultural, political, economic, and human factors. Strategic performance serves all masters and all 'political' purposes. Strategic effect is the currency that produces political change, it matters little to the strategic theorist how that effect is generated. Columns of British imperial mounted infantry chasing Boer commandos on the high veldt of South Africa, RAF Lancaster bombers wielded by the leadership

---

[23] e.g. Colin S. Gray: *The Future of Land-Based Missile Forces*, Adelphi Paper 140 (London, winter 1977); id., *The MX ICBM and National Security* (New York, 1981); id., *American Military Space Policy: Information Systems, Weapons Systems, and Arms Control* (Cambridge, Mass., 1982).

[24] The case is overstated in Richard Bernstein and Ross H. Munro, *The Coming War with China* (New York, 1997), but there is a case to state.

[25] John Keegan, *A History of Warfare* (London, 1993).

[26] Verbruggen, *Art of Warfare in Western Europe*; Richard A. Gabriel and Donald W. Boose, Jr., *The Great Battles of Antiquity: A Strategic and Tactical Guide to Great Battles That Shaped the Development of War* (Westport, Conn., 1994); Lawrence H. Keeley, *War Before Civilization* (New York, 1996). See also Arthur Ferrill, *The Origins of War: From the Stone Age to Alexander the Great* (London, 1985); Barry S. Strauss and Josiah Ober, *The Anatomy of Error: Ancient Military Disasters and Their Lessons for Modern Strategists* (New York, 1990). Victor Davis Hanson, 'The Status Of Ancient Military History: Traditional Work, Recent Research, and On-going Controversies', *Journal of Military History*, 63 (1999), 379–413, is a first-rate historiographical review.

of Bomber Command in some expectation that World War II could be won in the night sky over Berlin late in 1943, and search and destroy sweeps by the US Army in Vietnam in 1966-7—all can be assessed in the coinage of 'joint'—which is to say, inter-service or even trans-service—strategic effect.

This question—about continuity and change, and about the possible unity of strategic experience across boundaries of time, place, and technology—highlights the thought that, although tactical forms of war alter with political, economic, social, and technological change, war and strategy retain their integrity as distinctive phenomena.

WHAT DOES THE STRATEGIC EXPERIENCE OF THE TWENTIETH CENTURY TELL US ABOUT WHAT IS PROBABLY TO COME IN THE TWENTY-FIRST CENTURY?

Must bad times return to world politics? Could it be that we are witnessing today the end of bad old strategic history? Or is there realism in pessimism? Writing only a year after the formal demise of the USSR, Bruce Russett ventured the optimistic judgement that a window of opportunity was open briefly for the benign reordering of world polities.

The conjunction of these few major changes in the world—changes not just since Thucydides' time, but within the past decade—provide the basis for constructing a different kind of international order. The end of a great war and the consequent opportunity for reforming the order, the end of bipolar hostility and insecurity, the new space for international organizations to act by wide agreement and not single-power dictate, and the spread of democratic norms and institutions together provide this opportunity.[27]

Neoclassical realists know—certainly we believe we know—that there is not, and can never be, such an opportunity to improve the nature, as contrasted with the temporary functioning, of world politics.[28] One of the merits in old-fashioned narrative history is that that history shows how today's problems and opportunities are rooted in prior conditions. Focus upon the narrative flow of events tends to show how choices are constrained rather than open. 'Nothing comes from nothing, nothing ever could' is a familiar lyric from *The Sound of Music*. World politics seems to remain locked into a recurring interwar–war–interwar cycle. With reference only to unquestionably major wars, the twentieth century witnessed no fewer than four interwar (which include postwar and prewar elements) periods (1871-1914, 1918-39, 1945-7, 1989–present), and three episodes of great war (World War I, World War II, and the Cold War—a virtual World War III). Modern history

[27] Bruce Russett, *A Post-Thucydides, Post-Cold-War World*, Panteoin University Institute of International Relations, Occasional Research Papers Special Issue (Athens, Dec. 1992).
[28] Benjamin Frankel (ed.), 'Roots of Realism', *Security Studies*, 5 (1995), and Frankel (ed.), 'Realism; Restatements and Renewal', *Security Studies*, 5 (1996), offer unduly exhaustive analyses. My favourite classical realist text is Raymond Aron, *Peace and War: A Theory of International Relations* (Garden City, NY, 1966).

has had a cyclical character. The cycle is irregular, and no doubt the material from which history is shaped could allow a variety of alternative futures. Nonetheless, one should be impressed by the ways in which the past shapes the future and by the recurrence of the threat or actuality of large-scale violence. It is no central mission of this book to explore the possibilities, let alone prescribe, for a twenty-first century notably more peaceful than the twentieth. It is heroic task enough to make sense of the century now past. Readers are at liberty to conclude, however, that a theorist who sees continuities rather than discontinuities in strategy from, say, Greece in the fifth-century BC until today is not a person inclined to believe that the immediate future will register radical demotion of the relevance of strategic issues.

As a leading theorist in the new approach called 'critical security studies',[29] Ken Booth is on the mark when he writes of a band of theorists that includes myself:

From the dominating realist theoretical perspective, reinventing the future has never been the issue, since the game of states does not change. Asking realists to reinvent the future would be like asking Brian Johnston to reinvent cricket. For realists, like revered cricket commentators, reinvention is unthinkable: the task is to tell the story of reincarnation. The game (whether cricket or international relations) is endlessly replicated, in different circumstances and forms, but its soul remains the same. So does the script. This timeless present is seen as both natural and the best of all possible worlds.[30]

Booth overreaches in his final sentence, but overall he offers fair comment. We neoclassical realists stand 'guilty as charged'; we believe in the realism of pessimism.[31] To those afflicted with the virus of hope for systemic improvement in international security conditions, one must recommend Hedley Bull's observation that 'the lessons of the realists have to be learnt afresh by every new generation'.[32] With regard to the question of whether bad times will return to world politics, there have been at least two approaches adoptable by scholars. Moreover, for powerful reasons these approaches tend to be incompatible. On the one hand is the tradition of the scholar who struggles to reform, or revolutionize, the war-prone, semi-anarchic world system of international relations. On the other hand is the tradition of the scholar who tries to work with that war-prone system, and who seeks to improve the performance of 'his side'. Empirically, the two traditions do not disagree notably: they concur on the reality of a war-prone world system. Where they differ is both in their attitude towards the scope for international reform and in their analysis of how world politics works.

[29] Ken Booth, 'Security and Self: Reflections of a Fallen Realist', in Keith Krause and Michael C. Williams (eds.), *Critical Security Studies: Concepts and Cases* (London, 1997), 83–119.

[30] Ken Booth, 'Dare Not to Know: International Relations Theory versus the Future', in id. and Steve Smith (eds.), *International Relations Theory Today* (Cambridge, 1995), 332.

[31] Aron, *Peace and War*, 585, is particularly penetrating.

[32] Hedley Bull, 'The Theory of International Politics, 1919–1969', in Brian Porter (ed.), *The Aberystwyth Papers: International Politics, 1919–1969* (London, 1972), 39.

One can respect a scholar like Ken Booth who believes that world politics can be altered radically for the better, but one need not share his apparent optimism. Indeed, one should be fearful lest lack of attention to strategic fundamentals could lead to a future wherein world politics altered radically for the worse. Awful though the twentieth century was, it could have been much more awful still. It was not foreordained by some hidden hand of history that the countries most representative of Western civilization had to win the three great conflicts of the century. The title of a revisionist study of deterrence, *We All Lost the Cold War*,[33] expresses a minor truth at the expense of suppressing a major one. Yes, there are senses in which 'we all lost the Cold War'; but the USSR lost the Cold War in a way that the Western coalition did not, and that distinction is of historic significance. Scholars can be so clever that they are blind to obvious, and important, points.

Beyond the general questions posed thus far lies yet another: whether projects for peace with security can be soundly conceived only when the most powerful state is prepared to defend the existing international order. Statement of this belief should not be misunderstood. Strategic logic is value-neutral. Fortunately, however, tendencies in relative strategic performance are much less value-neutral, because strategy is not a theoretical exercise, but a practical activity involving human beings. Strategic behaviour that offends the sense of justice of key constituencies will meet with more resistance than will behaviour that is not ethically so challenged.

The most powerful country in the twentieth century was the United States of America. In 1918 and in 1942 the most powerful state on earth might have been Germany. As Richard Overy reminds us in *Why the Allies Won*, in 1942 World War II apparently was Germany's to lose.[34] The point is that the maintenance of a particular 'order' of world politics may require active guardianship by the leading, militarily most potent, state. The argument would not be that international order is necessarily just or politically stable, or ought always to be defended and preserved. The importance of international guardianship, self-interested of course, is well stated by Donald Kagan. Writing about the conditions for peace, if not always justice, Kagan observes: 'What seems to work best, even though imperfectly, is the possession by those states who wish to preserve the peace of the preponderant power and of the will to accept the burdens and responsibilities required to achieve that purpose.'[35] One needs to remember that the states in question with the preponderant power might embody and advance values profoundly hostile to Western civilization.

---

[33] Richard Ned Lebow and Janice Gross Stein, *We All Lost the Cold War* (Princeton, NJ, 1994).

[34] Richard Overy, *Why the Allies Won* (London, 1995).

[35] Donald Kagan, *On the Origins of War and the Preservation of Peace* (New York, 1995), 570.

APPROACHES

The whole of this book is an extended exploration and test of the proposition that there is a unity in essentials among all strategic phenomena in all forms and in all periods. This organizing proposition is explored and tested via a narrative and analytical trajectory that proceeds from the nature of strategy to consider political direction and moral constraints, strategic ideas, strategic culture, strategic history, regular warfare in each of the distinctive geographical environments, irregular conflict, nuclear weapons (and other weapons of mass destruction), and which concludes with answers to the six broad questions posed above.

Chapter 1 explains why strategy has many dimensions, why all of those dimensions always are in play, and why superiority in one or two dimensions does not guarantee success. Chapter 2 explores the political and ethical dimensions of strategy and finds that politics (or policy), in Clausewitz's sense, is eternal, as is strategy. The discussion explains why strategy is more than just 'a continuation of political intercourse, with the addition of other means',[36] and ventures into a land where Clausewitz did not tread—the friction that can impede relations between the realms of policy and war. Chapter 2 also develops the argument that whereas strategy is simple but not easy, ethics tend to be complicated but easy to accommodate in practice.

Chapters 3 and 4 examine critically the Clausewitzian legacy of strategic theory, with particular reference to the proposition that Clausewitz should retain the title of First Theorist of War. Chapter 3 argues that, although the exceptionally violent twentieth century has bequeathed us many notable works of strategic importance, the continuing intellectual supremacy of *On War* is not hard to demonstrate. The chapter proceeds to identify the distinctive strengths and weaknesses of *On War*, concluding that the great Prussian's achievements hugely outweigh his limitations. Chapter 4 advances and discusses many possible reasons for the relative (to *On War*) poverty of modern strategic theory worthy of the name. The claim that modern strategy is too complex to be encompassed by a single general theory is considered and rejected. The discussion is more respectful of the view that it is too soon to judge which of the strategic theorists of the twentieth century wrote truly classic works, and which did not. Chapter 4 speculates that in some ways Clausewitz probably tackled an easier set of tasks in his dedication of *On War* fairly strictly to the nature and higher conduct of 'war proper' than would have been the case had he addressed rigorously the connections between the causes and the conduct of war, and the course and outcome of war.

Chapter 5 explains how every human agent and organization must function within a cultural context. This chapter explores the pervasiveness of culture in ideas and ideals, in iconic texts and symbols, and in behaviour. Culture, though identified as a distinctive dimension to strategy, is actually manifested in all

---

[36] Clausewitz, *On War*, 605.

dimensions. Chapter 5 lays to rest some recent controversies over whether strategic culture is strictly ideational, or whether it encompasses patterns of behaviour, and over a possible distinction between culturalist and realist views of security and world politics. All strategic behaviour is cultural, which is to say that it is effected by encultured people, and every realist perspective has such people as its agents.

Chapters 6 and 7 provide complementary interpretations of modern strategic experience. Chapter 6 explains the importance of strategic history and shows how every conflict can be analysed on a range of criteria, here termed 'windows', each of which explores different aspects of the struggle in question (e.g. commitment, scale, environment, period, duration). Chapter 7 pursues the idea that there are several, perhaps many, complementary strategic histories of the twentieth century. If authors are most interested in major wars, or technological innovation, for example, they will develop different strategic chronologies from those favoured by, say, students of Jewish history or of the liberation of formerly colonized peoples.

Chapters 8 and 9 treat the grammar—if you will, the reality—of modern war in each physical geographical dimension. Chapter 8 affirms that nothing can occur 'beyond geography', and that each particular geography has its own terms and conditions (or grammar) for conflict. Also, Chapter 8 explains that it is a golden rule of classical strategy that environmentally specialized military forces—e.g. armies or navies—have to be successful within their own geographical environment if they are to operate very usefully 'jointly' (with other geographically specialized kinds of forces). This chapter argues that although the land must matter most—it is the only environment in which man can live—the armed forces specialized for distinctive geographies contribute distinctively, but 'jointly', to overall strategic effect. Chapter 9 continues the analysis of geographically focused military power into the air, space, and cyberspace. The chapter argues that airpower has been cursed by the repeated determination of its advocates to achieve independent—often termed 'strategic' by strategic illiterates—decision in war. The author contends that war is a 'joint' endeavour and that nothing in modern strategic history seriously contests that belief, except perhaps only for the 'virtual' history of a World War III of comprehensive annihilation. In addition to consideration of the promise in, and performance of, airpower, Chapter 9 also reviews arguments about so-called revolutions in military affairs (RMAs). The author is under-impressed with the strategic potential of 'cyberspace', while recognizing the value both of superior information and of the ability to exploit that information for command and targeting. The author is impressed with the strategic potential of spacepower. If an RMA is under way today, most probably it is in spacepower.

Chapter 10 provides a unified view of irregular warfare in the twentieth century, in contrast to the regular activities of armies, navies, air and space forces treated in Chapters 8 and 9. This chapter puts the spotlight of strategy on 'small wars'—which is to say wars between regular and irregular combatants of all kinds—explaining that the domain of strategy does indeed include this particular zone of frequently hugely savage violence. The discussion emphasizes the contrasting tactical and strategic dilemmas of regulars and irregulars. In modern strategy, as in all strategic experience, the overwhelming challenge to the regular combatant force is the difficulty of bringing the irregular foe to battle for destruction. Chapter 10 also explains how 'small wars' tend to be political in a way that is not conveyed adequately by the Clausewitzian formula which informs us that conflict is about politics, or is guided by policy. The political—as contrasted with criminal—status itself of some combatants typically is a stake in the fighting. This chapter also explores the significance of the invention in the early years of World War II of those 'regular' special operations forces created to wage war irregularly. In addition to filling out the whole of modern strategic experience, this analysis of 'small wars' and other savage violence shows the pervasive authority of strategy in conflicts of all kinds.

Chapters 11 and 12 have in common with Chapter 10 the mission of demonstrating the practical authority of strategic reasoning over regions often dismissed as comprising phenomena that are inherently astrategic or even anti-strategic. Whereas Chapter 10 demonstrates that terrorist and counter-terrorist, insurgent and counter-insurgent, are all subject to the rules of strategy, so Chapters 11 and 12 brave scholarly orthodoxy in explaining why the idea, and practice, of strategy for nuclear weapons are not oxymorons. These chapters show how the near-universally accepted hypothesis of a nuclear revolution fuelled the creation and growth of the profession and industry of modern strategic studies; they show why and how nuclear weapons are not 'beyond strategy'; they argue that enough of what the Western extended defence community in the Cold War believed about the USSR was true to provide sufficient justification, even in retrospect, for most of Western nuclear policy and strategy; and they advance the proposition that both sides in the great Cold War, on balance, behaved with notable military prudence. Chapter 11 argues that both sides typically performed responsibly, to the point where even when they behaved in ways which today, in hindsight, appear dangerous, they tended to behave dangerously for the right reasons.

Overall, Chapters 11 and 12 reaffirm the hegemony of strategy, even over the most unpromising of military terrain. Chapter 12 notes the permanence of the nuclear condition, though recognizes a historical succession of distinct nuclear ages. The chapter recognizes the limitations to the strategic utility of nuclear weapons, but underlines the potency of those few, truly vital missions that these weapons can perform. Together, Chapters 11 and 12 cast an empathetic, and on balance sympathetic, eye upon our strategic experience with weapons of mass destruction.

Chapter 13 provides direct answers to the broad general questions posed in this

Introduction and employed to help guide analysis throughout the book. Above all else, the final chapter argues that strategy is eternal. This claim means both that the demand for strategy endures and that the nature and function of strategy does not change from one period to the next.

THE WHOLE CENTURY

With only a few exceptions, each topic treated here, and the perspectives adopted, apply to the whole of the twentieth century. Nuclear weapons, spacepower, and cyberpower, are, of course, noteworthy exceptions. As a working hypothesis, I judge understanding of all the strategic experience of the century to be of equal significance for the advancement of scholarship and for the improvement of future strategic performance. Indeed, this hypothesis is really a restatement of the master theme of the book. If there is an essential unity to all strategic experience, it follows that all conflicts and preparations for conflicts have to be made from the same ingredients, from the same dimensions of strategy. It is with this hypothesis in mind that historical illustration of the argument draws from all of modern strategic experience.

This book is about modern strategy: the use or threat of military power for political purposes. The discussion is not cast as a cookbook or manual aspiring to instruct readers directly in the making of better strategy. For the intention behind this book, the Franco-German competition in land armaments prior to 1914 is quite as salient as was the competition in long-range nuclear armed forces between the superpowers in the 1970s and 1980s. Even for people most interested in policy today, the relevance of historical example does not decline arithmetically, geometrically, or indeed at all with time.

Chapter 1

THE DIMENSIONS OF STRATEGY

Carl von Clausewitz was persuasive when he wrote: 'Everything in strategy is very simple, but that does not mean that everything is very easy.'[1] Key relationships among policy, strategy, and tactics are simple and can be expressed in simple terms. Often in practice, however, the noun and the adjective, 'strategy' and 'strategic', are purloined by the unscrupulous or misapplied by those who are careless or ignorant. Such sins, or errors can have dire consequences in practice for a realm of behaviour that is, after all, about life and death, victory or defeat. This chapter describes the nature of strategy, identifies its principal dimensions, and explores the reasons why it is important. The discussion explains why a postulated unity to all strategic experience, in all periods, is the principal theme of this book. After presenting Clausewitz's definition of strategy as the one preferred as the basis for a new, albeit only broadened and restated, formulation, the analysis moves on to show what strategy 'is made of', what its dimensions are. The nature and purpose, or function, of strategy are invariable throughout all strategic history. The dimensions of strategy presented here pertain to every conflict everywhere. This chapter explains that the multidimensionality of strategy limits the potential for superiority in one or even several of those dimensions to deliver success. Truly poor performance in any of strategy's dimensions has the potential to offset excellence elsewhere. Similarly, a selective excellence, earnt or fortuitous—in strategic geography, for example, think of Britain in May–June 1940—may well offset inferior performance in other dimensions. In general, the analysis finds that there is no single 'master' dimension of strategy, though people, politics, and time are strong candidates. Performance in all but one of strategy's dimensions— politics, ethics, military preparation, technology, and so forth—can be improved. The sole exception is the dimension of time. Time lost is literally irretrievable. A belligerent polity may be enabled by an insular geography to use time to raise new armies. But no one can rerun the temporal tape to 'play it again' in strategic history.

Finally, in this chapter I show how strategic effect is unavoidable, which is to say that means and ends will conduct a strategic discourse whether or not a polity has an explicit strategy (in the sense of plan). It should be clear that this analysis addresses each of the six broad questions posed in the Introduction above. In particular, holistic discussion of strategy's many dimensions helps explain why

[1] Carl von Clausewitz, *On War*, trans. Michael Howard and Peter Paret (Princeton, NJ, 1976), 178.

strategy is so difficult to do well; why the growing complexity of strategic phenomena does not affect strategy's nature and function; and why the changes in the military and other referents for strategy in the twentieth century simply provide more diverse data for strategic theorists to master, not a fundamental challenge to their intellectual grip on the subject.

DEFINITIONS

Strategy is the bridge that relates military power to political purpose; it is neither military power *per se* nor political purpose. By strategy I mean *the use that is made of force and the threat of force for the ends of policy*. This is an adaptation from Clausewitz, though certainly not an adaptation of his plain intent. In *On War*, Clausewitz provides an admirably tight and terse, yet apparently narrow, definition: 'Strategy [is] the use of engagements for the object of the war.'[2] Clausewitz's definition is a superior one. His definition has an operational, even battlefield orientation, that suggests a restrictive focus upon combat. But his definition has a more than compensating virtue in clarity on the core of the matter. If one can think expansively about what should be encompassed by the idea of 'engagements', the merit in Clausewitz's approach is overwhelming. Freely translated, he tells us that strategy is the use of tacit and explicit threats, as well as of actual battles and campaigns, to advance political purposes. Moreover, the strategy at issue may not be military strategy; instead it may be grand strategy that uses 'engagements', meaning all of the relevant instruments of power as threat or in action, for the objectives of statecraft.

Both Clausewitz's original definition and my adaptation of it easily lend themselves to expansion of domain so as to encompass policy instruments other than the military. The cardinal virtue of the Clausewitzian definition of strategy is that it separates those things that must be separated. Anyone who reads, understands, and accepts the Clausewitzian definition will never be confused about what is strategic and what is not: 'tactics teaches the use of armed forces in the engagement.'[3] Armed forces in action, indeed any instrument of power in action, is the realm of tactics. Strategy, in contrast, seeks to direct and relate the use of those instruments to policy goals. Clausewitz, therefore, is crystal-clear in distinguishing between action and effect and between instrument and objective. To illustrate: 'strategic airpower' is a hideous misnomer because it confuses capability with effect. In contrast, to refer to the 'strategic effect of airpower' correctly distinguishes cause from consequence. Whatever the form, or quantity, of military power at issue, that power does not have inherent strategic—or tactical, or operational—characteristics. Armed forces, and the consequences of the use or threat of armed forces, are different in kind and it is a difference that matters greatly. If ever there

[3] Ibid. 128.   [2] Ibid.

was a field of human behaviour about which people should be encouraged to think consequentially, it is the strategic.

A second narrow definition, offered by J. C. Wylie, corresponds usefully to much commonsense usage of 'strategy'. Wylie suggests that strategy is '[a] plan of action designed in order to achieve some end; a purpose together with a system of measures for its accomplishment'.[4] He prefers this definition because it accommodates times of peace as well as war, and because it embraces both ends and means. On balance, the prominence Wylie accords to 'a plan of action' risks distraction from the instrumental and consequentialist character of strategy—as emphasized by Clausewitz—but still he captures much of what needs to be captured.

Another, now classic, definition of strategy is the one offered by Basil H. Liddell Hart. Strategy is 'the art of distributing and applying military means to fulfil the ends of policy'.[5] Liddell Hart suggests that 'the role of grand strategy—higher strategy—is to coordinate and direct all the resources of a nation, or band of nations, towards the attainment of the political object of the war—the goal defined by fundamental policy.'[6] Definitions of strategy abound, but there is no good reason to look far beyond Clausewitz and Liddell Hart for inspiration on the heart of the matter.

It does not matter precisely which form of words are preferred for a working definition, but the essence of strategy must be identified unambiguously. That essence lies in the realm of the consequences of actions for future outcomes. Any military activity is inherently tactical. The consequences of all military activity is the realm of strategy: the clearer that distinction, the better the definition.[7]

Clausewitz's and Liddell Hart's definitions of strategy can be augmented usefully by the view of General André Beaufre. He insists that strategy 'is therefore the art of the dialectic of force or, more precisely, *the art of the dialectic of two opposing wills using force to resolve their dispute*'.[8] Notwithstanding the opacity of this Gallic definition, Beaufre adopts as his centrepiece the duelling character of strategic behaviour which Clausewitz probably treats at insufficient length. Although *On War* identifies brilliantly the enemy's 'power of resistance . . . as the product of two inseparable factors, viz. *the total means at his disposal* and *the strength of his will*',[9] strategic history demonstrates the prevalence of the error of

---

[4] J. C. Wylie, *Military Strategy: A General Theory of Power Control*, ed. John B. Hattendorf, repr. of 1967 edn. (Annapolis, Md., 1989), 14.

[5] Basil H. Liddell Hart, *Strategy: The Indirect Approach* (London, 1967), 335.

[6] Ibid. 335–6.

[7] Judy M. Graffis, 'Strategic: Use with Care', *Airpower Journal*, 8, special issue (1994), 4–10, is commendable. Capt. Graffis, USAF, will have noticed that for the past 40 years her service has typically employed so-called 'strategic' aircraft on 'tactical' missions, and so-called 'tactical' aircraft frequently on 'strategic' missions. She argues, admirably, that 'strategic' should label 'effect' and not things.

[8] André Beaufre, *An Introduction to Strategy*, trans. R. H. Barry (London, 1963), 22 (emphasis original).

[9] Clausewitz, *On War*, 77 (emphasis original).

neglect of the enemy, and especially of the enemy's will. In adition, there is some merit in the relaxed wording offered by Gregory D. Foster, 'strategy is ultimately about effectively exercising power',[10] and with the metaphor that strategy is the bridge that relates military power to political purpose. Foster's formula harbours the disconcerting implicit question: what if strategy in practice is often about exercising power ineffectively? He points correctly and usefully to the pragmatism of the world of strategy, and writes with insight from within the US defence community. Of course, every polity seeks to exercise power 'effectively'. However, many polities and political groups, functioning in a consciously strategic way, exercise power ineffectively. To be a strategic player is not necessarily to be a successful one.

This brief survey of useful definitions of strategy is complemented by suggestions from Martin Edmonds and from Williamson Murray and Mark Grimsley. Neither definition challenges the Clausewitzian formula for authority, but each yields a distinctive orientation that rounds out understanding. Edmonds tells us that 'strategy refers to the conduct of a war as a whole',[11] a definition that for all its indiscriminate compounding of statecraft, grand strategy, and military strategy, still has a kind of rough and ready merit. Murray and Grimsley, as befits the editors of a path-breaking book on the making of strategy, offer a dynamic process definition: 'Strategy is a process, a constant adaptation to shifting conditions and circumstances in a world where chance, uncertainty, and ambiguity dominate.'[12] This definition is not parsimonious and fails to capture the instrumental kernel of strategy, but it offers powerful insight. Specifically, the process of strategy-making can be critical to the quality of strategic performance. Intellectual historians, even those in the field of war and strategy, are not apt to see strategy expressed in organization and process.

The concepts of strategic effect and strategic performance, which are required to perform hard duty in this text, flow from the nature and function of strategy as defined by Clausewitz. Strategic effect is the impact of strategic performance upon the course of events. The concept of strategic performance, logically, can be employed both descriptively and judgementally. The sum total of strategic effect achieved by the United States in Vietnam from, say, 1965 until the spring of 1973 amounted to an appallingly poor overall strategic performance. The fall of Saigon in April 1975, following an arguably decent interval after the cease-fire agreement of 23 January 1973, provides conclusive comment upon US strategic performance in the war as a whole.

[10] Gregory D. Foster, 'Research, Writing, and the Mind of the Strategist', *Joint Force Quarterly*, 14 (1996–7), 111.

[11] Martin Edmonds, 'Land Warfare', in Roger Carey and Trevor C. Salmon (eds.), *International Security in the Modern World* (London, 1996), 200. Strategy's domain is not confined to time of war, as Edmonds implies.

[12] Williamson Murray and Mark Grimsley, 'Introduction: On Strategy', in Murray, MacGregor Knox, and Alvin Bernstein (eds.), *The Making of Strategy: Rulers, States, and War* (Cambridge, 1994), 1.

How are the concepts of strategy, strategic effect, and strategic performance given reality in the field? Who and what are the agents of strategy? Furthermore, it is necessary to look above and beyond strategy in order to probe what is meant by 'the object of the war' and 'political purpose'.

As Wayne Hughes observes, '[s]trategists *plan*, tacticians *do*'—you have a strategy, but you do tactics.[13] Strategy, military strategy at least, is 'done' by tactics and by operations. Tactics, as Clausewitz insists, is 'the use of armed forces', while operations—a concept he did not employ—is the use of armed forces in campaigns to achieve military and political results in a distinctive geographical theatre. Strategic performance in war as a whole is generated by the strategic effect of the net costs and gains of the campaigns of which the war consists. Clausewitz generally denies his readers the convenience of being able to ignore the enemy, though his treatment of the discourse in violence between adversaries is not among the stronger features of his work.[14] People unfamiliar with the arcane world of defence analysis might be surprised to learn just how common it is for imaginative, energetic, and determined strategic thinkers and defence planners to forget that the enemy too has preferences and choices. Strategic effect for strategic performance should be treated as composite measures, albeit not usually lending themselves to exact computation, that can provide net assessment. The course and outcome of a period of competition, crisis, or war itself are the products of the net strategic performance of the contending parties. Fighting power and military effectiveness are concepts derived from the same concern to find a currency common to different kinds of armed forces.[15]

As operations and tactics are the instruments of military strategy, so strategy should serve policy goals which are instrumental in relation to a polity's broad vision of the desirable. Conditioned by ethical traditions, culture, and the consequentialist reasoning that balances means with ends, policy choice should express an idea of the international political equivalent to the good, or at least a tolerable, life. For example, behind the grand strategic choices of the day made on behalf of Britain lie the policy goals that yield political guidance, while behind those policy goals is a vision of the country's role in the world.

Even if there is widespread agreement on a vision of the polity's role in the world, controversy over policy is not necessarily precluded. In the late 1940s, most Americans could agree that the USSR needed 'containing'. Also they could agree that only the United States could organize and lead the 'posse' for such containment. But need the containment be military in character? Should military policy

---

[13] Wayne P. Hughes, Jr., 'The Strategy–Tactics Relationship', in Colin S. Gray and Roger W. Barnett (eds.), *Seapower and Strategy* (Annapolis, Md., 1989), 54; id., *Fleet Tactics: Theory and Practice* (Annapolis, Md., 1986), is a gem.

[14] Clausewitz, *On War*, 75.

[15] For an earlier effort to clarify conceptual usage, see Colin S. Gray, *War, Peace, and Victory: Strategy and Statecraft for the Next Century* (New York, 1990), ch. 1.

constitute the leading edge of US-led containment policy?[16] For a more recent case, Americans have little difficulty agreeing upon the desirability of the emergence of a global political system supported by a truly global and liberal trading system which is enabled by a global march of democracy.[17] But to identify an attractive vision of fairly free-trading democracies, effecting the end of ideological or strategic history,[18] is not necessarily to provide a guiding light for policy. If future history is to be more than the chronicle of 'the crimes, follies and misfortunes of mankind',[19] does the United States have to play the role of global policeman, the provider of SWAT teams for international order? Or should US policy seek to build conditions for regional order so that only minimal demands are placed upon US military power?[20] Questions abound at every level of analysis. If US policy requires the projection of military power, does that power have to be American, can it take the form strictly of sea, air, missile, and spacepower, or do American soldiers have to be seen to proceed in harm's way on the ground?

A problem with popular formulas can be that their familiarity breeds an unwarranted confidence in interpretation. Clausewitz and other theorists are entirely right to capture the relationship between military power and political purpose within their definition of strategy. That granted, however, there is much about strategy that requires further elucidation if strategic ideas are to be helpful in practical application. In the domain of statecraft, motives typically are distinctly mixed, of variable weight, and prove less than durable in the face of developments.

Although it is apparently sensible to approach vision, policy, grand strategy, military strategy, operations, and tactics (with administration, logistics, and technology as major contributors) as comprising a descending hierarchy of realms of behaviour, there is a strong argument for regarding these realms as being very substantially interdependent. This means that these realms need to be viewed as mutually dependent partners, related essentially horizontally, as well as on a ladder of subordination.[21] The hierarchical view, with its inevitable implication of a descent from matters of greater to lesser importance, can conceal the interdependencies that give integrity to the whole. Recognition of these complex interdependencies underlies the emphatically non-hierarchical concept of

[16] Melvyn P. Leffler, *A Preponderance of Power: National Security, the Truman Administration, and the Cold War* (Stanford, Calif., 1992).

[17] Janne E. Nolan (ed.), *Global Engagement: Cooperation and Security in the 21st Century* (Washington, DC, 1994).

[18] Francis Fukuyama, *The End of History and the Last Man* (New York, 1992).

[19] Edward Gibbon, *The History of the Decline and Fall of the Roman Empire*, ed. J. B. Bury (7 vols., London, 1909), i. 84.

[20] John J. Kohout III et al., 'Alternative Grand Strategy Options for the United States', *Comparative Strategy*, 14 (1995), 361–420; Barry R. Posen and Andrew L. Ross, 'Competing Visions for U.S. Grand Strategy', *International Security*, 21 (1996/7), 5–53.

[21] Michael I. Handel favours a non-hierarchical 'complex model of interaction' among strategy, operation, and tactics. *Masters of War: Classical Strategic Thought*, 2nd edn. (London, 1996), 57, fig. 6. 1.

strategy's many vital dimensions that occupies most of the remainder of this chapter. T. E. Lawrence made the relevant point with exemplary clarity when he confronted the practical challenge of the Arab Revolt in the somewhat dim light of the military classics he had read years before at Oxford. Lawrence considered

the whole house of war in its structural aspect, which was strategy, in its arrangements, which were tactics, and in the sentiment of its inhabitants, which was psychology; for my personal duty was command, and the commander, like the master architect was responsible for all. The first confusion was the false antithesis between strategy, the aim in war, the synoptic regard seeing each part relative to the whole, and tactics, the means towards a strategic end, the particular steps of its staircase. They seemed only points of view from which to ponder the elements of war, the Algebraical element of things, a Biological element of lives, and the Psychological element of ideas.[22]

Lawrence is persuasive. Strategy and tactics, and, one should add, policy, operations, and logistics, can be regarded more as distinctive points of view of a single complex phenomenon than as discrete subjects—the whole house of strategy. Tactical success does not have to yield successful strategic performance, while even tactical failure paradoxically can have positive strategic effect.[23] Nonetheless, it is only in very special circumstances that a military record of all but unrelieved tactical failure will prove compatible with strategic success. A leading example is in 'small wars'—wars between regular and irregular forces—where the irregular forces may need only to remain selectively active in the field to wear down the political will of the more regular belligerent. Both Vietcong Main Force units and the North Vietnamese Army fought competently, yet they registered few tactical successes against a tactically adequate US Army that was taking most of the strain from 1966 until 1970.

In conditions of more symmetrical war, which is to say when the course of military events is likely to dominate, success in combat is generally the only sound currency reliably able to provide strategic effect. Battles, even campaigns, can be lost, but ultimately the enemy has to be beaten by somebody somewhere. It is an error to believe that tactics are more important than strategy; in fact such a claim is an absurdity. But, tactical competence is the material of which strategic effect is made. Such competence is not the only material of which strategic effect consists, because quality of strategic performance requires assessment in the light of the often shifting demands of policy or politics.[24] Policy is not an absolute, a 'given' handed to military commanders on tablets of stone. Just as there is in practice a

---

[22] T. E. Lawrence, *Seven Pillars of Wisdom: A Triumph* (New York, 1991), 191–2.

[23] Consider the examples of the tactically successful but strategically irrelevant British commando raid on the Normandie dock at St Nazaire on 27–8 Mar. 1942, and the tactically unsuccessful but strategically outstanding Anglo-Canadian raid on Dieppe on 19 Aug. 1942. See Colin S. Gray, *Explorations in Strategy* (Westport, Conn., 1996), 141–2.

[24] Clausewitz's *Politik* can mean policy, the carefully considered outcome of a rational weighing of costs and benefits, or it can mean politics, in the sense of an outcome to a process of contention that may have witnessed little, if any, careful weighing of means and ends.

constant dialogue between strategy and tactical performance, as plan meets action, so there is a constant dialogue between strategic performance and policy demand. If the troops cannot do it, the politicians should not require it: this was the German, French, and British dilemma in World War I. Charles E. Callwell was to the point when he wrote: 'Strategy is not, however, the final arbiter in war. The battlefield decides.'[25]

The meaning of strategy is both clear and important. It is essential that military (and diplomatic, economic, and so forth) behaviour should not be confused with the consequences of that behaviour. This is why Clausewitz's definition of strategy, for all its apparently narrow focus upon the battlefield—a focus easily broadened, as in my adaptation of his words—has overwhelming merit. A firm conceptual grip on the meaning of strategy enables appreciation without confusion that strategy both comprises many activities (strategy is effected on and off the field of battle), and conducts continuous dialogues with politics and tactics.

THE DIMENSIONS OF STRATEGY

Strategy can be analysed with reference to the geographical environments to which it is specifically applied (i.e. land, sea, air, space, cyberspace). Alternatively, one can dissect the character and working of strategy with regard to weapons or technologies (the strategic consequences of armoured forces, or nuclear weapons, or computers), or with a focus upon different levels of violence or character of wars (general war, limited war, irregular conflict and terrorism). A further way into the maze of strategic phenomena is via what Michael Howard called the dimensions of strategy.[26] He identified four dimensions in a brilliant analysis designed to demonstrate an unwise focus upon weaponry in American strategic debate. Howard's dimensions were the social, the logistical, the operational, and the technological. Sir Michael's 1979 argument about allegedly 'forgotten dimensions of strategy' is primarily of historical and cultural interest, but his basic concept is well worth pursuing. The inspiration for Michael Howard's analysis, and indeed for my own, as usual belongs to Clausewitz. In a chapter titled 'The Elements of Strategy', we are told:

The strategic elements that affect the use of engagements may be classified into various types: moral, physical, mathematical, geographical, and statistical.

The first type covers everything that is created by intellectual and psychological qualities and influences; the second consists of the size of the armed forces, their composition, armament and so forth; the third includes the angle of lines of operation, the convergent and divergent movements wherever geometry enters into their calculation; the fourth

---

[25] Charles E. Callwell, *Small Wars: A Tactical Textbook for Imperial Soldiers*, repr. of 1906 edn. (London, 1990), 90.

[26] Michael Howard, 'The Forgotten Dimensions of Strategy', *Foreign Affairs*, 57 (1979), 976–86.

comprises the influence of terrain, such as commanding positions, mountains, rivers, woods and roads; and, finally, the fifth covers support and maintenance. [27]

Following Clausewitz and Howard, therefore, strategy can be thought of usefully as having many broad, pervasive, and interpenetrating dimensions. Seventeen such dimensions are preferred here, but the precise number does not matter so long as everything of importance is properly corralled. These dimensions affect all strategic performance fundamentally. My seventeen dimensions are clustered into three categories. The first category, 'People and Politics', comprises: people; society; culture; politics; and ethics. Category two, 'Preparation for War', includes: economics and logistics; organization (including defence and force planning); military administration (including recruitment, training, and most aspects of armament); information and intelligence; strategic theory and doctrine; and technology. The final category, 'War Proper', is composed of: military operations; command (political and military); geography; friction (including chance and uncertainty); the adversary; and time. These pervasive dimensions are not presented in order to capture literally every ingredient from which strategy is made, as in an inclusively encyclopedic exercise. Nonetheless, these dimensions are selected because they encompass most of what contributes to the making and execution of strategy. Six of the seventeen provide distinctive organizing foci for chapters (the political and ethical in Chapter 2, the strategic theoretical in Chapters 3 and 4, the cultural in Chapter 5, and the geographical and military-operational in Chapters 8 and 9), while the remaining eleven are too ubiquitous to be confined to particular chapters.

When one talks about the dimensions of strategy, it is sometimes difficult to convey the proposition that these are only distinctive dimensions of a whole entity. Strategy is seriously incomplete if considered in the absence of any of them. After the fashion of Lawrence's 'whole house' of strategy, the notion here is holistic. As an exercise in what social scientists call pre-theory, one could conduct comparative research on particular conflicts employing these dimensions as the principal methodological architecture. Every dimension discussed here will always be relevant in principle to a case of strategy for investigation, but the distinctive rankings in relative significance must be ever variable from instance to instance. The approach adopted here is intended, at least, to express the sense in Clausewitz's good advice:

It would however be disastrous to try to develop our understanding of strategy by analyzing these factors [the 'five elements'] in isolation, since they are usually interconnected in each military action in manifold and intricate ways. . . . We shall continue to examine the picture as a whole, and take our analysis no further than is necessary in each case to elucidate the idea we wish to convey, which will always have its origins in the impressions made by the sum total of the phenomena of war, rather than in speculative study.[28]

---

[27] Clausewitz, *On War*, 183.   [28] Ibid.

Because the dimensions, factors, or elements are distinctive aspects of a whole entity, they cannot be rank-ordered for relative importance in a general theory of strategy.[29] This is akin to the conundrum of hierarchy or non-hierarchy among strategy, operations, and tactics, to which reference has already been made. Tactical achievement has meaning only in terms of operational intention and strategic effect. Nonetheless, without positive tactical achievement the operational intention and the desired strategic effect are strictly moot.

These dimensions are not wholly distinctive, because each influences the others (e.g. ethical attitudes may influence military operations and technological choices). Some dimensions could also be interpreted as more fundamental than others; and some possible dimensions of strategy are too imperial to use. In explanation, I have, for example, rejected identification of historical experience as a distinctive dimension of strategy, notwithstanding the strong preference in its favour expressed by Williamson Murray and Mark Grimsley.[30] Paradoxically, the very strength of historical experience also is its weakness. What has been experienced and who has experienced it? The objective consequences of that experience are captured in other dimensions (e.g. social, geographical, economic-logistical), while historical experience as interpreted by and for the present day is probably best considered in the dimension of (strategic) culture. For example, while US strategy today can be said in part to be the product of American historical experience, that strategy is also the product of how Americans today choose to interpret their country's historical experience.[31]

My argument is that strategy has many dimensions, each of which is always in play to a greater or lesser extent. Strategy, by analogy, is like a racing car that has, *inter alia*, an engine, gears, brakes, tyres, and a driver; strategic performance is secured against the will and capabilities of other racers. Incompetence or ill fortune on any of strategy's seventeen dimensions might prove fatal for the whole enterprise. In practice, no polity will be equally excellent, or awful, on each of the seventeen. But, there are limits to tolerable lack of excellence on any of strategy's many dimensions. To pursue the mechanical analogy just mentioned, a vehicle does not have to be excellent in all its mechanical, electrical, and human dimensions in order to perform well. Nonetheless, a superior engine, gears, steering, and brakes will prove a cause more for sorrow than celebration if the driver lacks the skills to control the machinery and exploit its technical superiority. In the realm of strategy, this sounds very much like the German armed forces which, in two world wars, were very good at fighting but were heroically incapable of waging war successfully.

Even dramatic improvement in one or two dimensions—say in technology,

[29] I develop this idea in 'RMAs and the Dimensions of Strategy', *Joint Force Quarterly*, 17 (1997–8), 50–4.
[30] Murray and Grimsley, 'Introduction: On Strategy', 10–12.
[31] Colin S. Gray, 'Strategy in the Nuclear Age: The United States, 1945–1991', in Murray et al., *Making of Strategy*, 579–613.

quality of command, or access to military intelligence information—carries no guarantee of excellent strategic performance overall. 'Great captains' may lack troops who can perform on the battlefield, technically superior weapons are only as tactically effective as the soldiers who must use them, and military intelligence is useful operationally only if there are forces willing and able to use it as a basis for action. Of course, there is room for some compensation across dimensions. Hannibal's operational and tactical genius provided huge compensation for Rome's superiority in numbers and, indeed, in basic economic assets. Notwithstanding the possible fungibility among dimensions, the argument holds that genuine major weakness in *any one* of the seventeen dimensions (or however many the reader prefers) can prove fatal to the whole enterprise of strategy.

PEOPLE AND POLITICS

Human beings live in societies which educate and train them, and behave strategically for political purposes in ways they deem ethically tolerable.

People

The human dimension of strategy is so basic and obvious that it often escapes notice by scholars with a theoretical bent. At all relevant levels of analysis strategy is done by individuals. Strategy is 'done' by tactics; tactics is 'done' by combat forces, *inter alia*; and the most important element in combat and support forces is people. To be yet more precise, the people in question come down to individuals.[32] When, as in this book, an author is sweeping over the strategic history of a whole century and employs such collective concepts as landpower, seapower, airpower, spacepower, and cyberpower, it is not difficult to forget that real people must execute and do strategy.

Policy and strategy will propose, but ultimately it is tactics, which is to say people in combat, which must dispose. People matter most,[33] and people differ. The political context of the Weimar Republic, and the myth of a German army undefeated in the field but stabbed in the back at home, undoubtedly provided the opportunity for the political genius of Adolf Hitler. Opportunity, though, is not everything; the genius of Hitler also was necessary.[34] The Napoleonic wars in general, and especially the experience of crushing national defeat at Jena–Auerstadt in 1806, provided much of the fuel for the intellectual fire that was to burn so brightly in Clausewitz's *On War*.[35] Nonetheless, *On War* was not a book waiting to be written by somebody, who just happened to be a certain Major-General Carl Maria von Clausewitz who had the leisure of dignified, protracted underemploy-

[32] John Keegan, *The Face of Battle* (London, 1976); Victor Davis Hanson, *The Western Way of War: Infantry Battle in Classical Greece* (London, 1989); Paul Addison and Angus Calder (eds.), *Time to Kill: The Soldier's Experience of War in the West, 1939–1945* (London, 1997).

[33] With gratitude I acknowledge inspiration from Hughes, *Fleet Tactics*, 26–8.

[34] John Lukacs, *The Hitler of History* (New York, 1998), is outstanding.

[35] Peter Paret, *Clausewitz and the State* (New York, 1976), ch. 7.

ment in which to play out his historic intellectual role. Instead, Clausewitz had a unique talent.

The discussion below of the geographical dimension of strategy will refer to the demodernization of the *Wehrmacht*, specifically the *Östheer*, (the army in the East), in Russia during World War II. 'Demodernization' refers to a process with the most direct of human consequences.

Material and mentality were closely related matters in the *Östheer*. As the number of the tanks diminished, the troops had to dig in and revert to trench warfare; as the trucks broke down and the trains failed to arrive, provisions of ammunition, food, and clothes decreased. The demodernization of the front was thus a process whereby the disappearance of the machine forced the individual soldier into living conditions of the utmost primitiveness.[36]

A regimental doctor wrote as follows about living conditions for the German soldiers trapped in the 'Demyansk pocket' in northern Russia early in 1942:

The men are greatly overstrung. This is becoming more visible every day, in loss of strength, loss of weight, and increasing nervousness, and has a progressively negative effect on battle performance with the accompanying appearance of friction, breakdowns, and failures on the part of commanders and men as a result of over-fatigue and overstrain of the nerves.[37]

The doctor's report attests to an extreme variant of the human condition at the sharp end of war in all periods and geographies. There is much more to strategy than its human dimension alone, though whether or not there should be is, of course, an ethical as well as a political matter. Strategy has a human dimension: the face of battle, broadly understood, includes a human face. If war and strategy had only a human dimension, then those activities might have been discontinued long ago; alternatively, they might not. We should not confuse the human race with the humane race. Ralph Peters reminds us of the awful truth that 'there is at least a minority of human beings—mostly male—who enjoy killing'.[38] Probably it is true, if unpopularly pessimistic, to argue that our very humanity is more the problem than the solution as far as the persistence of violence is concerned.

Society

The social dimension of strategy can be hard to find in major bodies of strategic analysis. Bernard Brodie, Ken Booth, and John Keegan, among others, are correct in their claims that mastery of sociology, anthropology, and, indeed, local or regional knowledge are not general strengths among strategists, or at least

---

[36] Omer Bartov, *Hitler's Army: Soldiers, Nazis, and War in the Third Reich* (New York, 1991), 17.

[37] Ibid. 19.

[38] Ralph Peters, 'Our New Old Enemies', in Lloyd J. Matthews (ed.), *Challenging the United States Symmetrically and Asymmetrically: Can America be Defeated?* (Carlisle Barracks, Pa., July 1998), 230. See Michael Ignatieff, *The Warrior's Honor: Ethnic War and the Modern Conscience* (London, 1998), for a more optimistic view.

American strategists.[39] Appreciation of the social dimension of strategy requires recognition that strategy is made and executed by the institutions of particular societies in ways that express cultural preferences. In modern times, societies as a whole have prepared for, and made, war. The master concept in Clausewitz's theory of war is not strategy; rather it is the 'remarkable trinity—composed of primordial violence, hatred, and enmity . . . the play of chance and probability . . . and [the] element of subordination, as an instrument of policy'.[40] Clausewitz associated these three elements respectively primarily with the people, the commander and his army, and the government. He was most definite, however, in asserting that the three primordial 'tendencies' of war—passion, chance, and reason—are 'variable in their relationship to one another'.[41]

Culture

Culture is a deeply contested concept. Chapter 5 explains the importance of the concept of strategic culture, and discusses relevant conceptual and method-ological issues. There is always a cultural dimension to strategic behaviour. By strategic culture I mean both the assumptions that lie behind strategic behaviour and the manifestation of such assumptions in behaviour. In an influential work on popular culture in early modern Europe, social historian Peter Burke defined culture as 'a system of shared meanings, attitudes and values, and the symbolic forms (performances, artefacts) in which they are expressed or embodied'.[42] That is almost good enough, notwithstanding the ambiguity over whether the term 'performances' strays from the realm of ideas into that of action. Strategic culture consists of the socially constructed and transmitted assumptions, habits of mind, traditions, and preferred methods of operation—that is, behaviour—that are more or less specific to a particular geographically based security community.[43] A security community may not be monolithic and can have several strategic (and military) cultures—a case of multiple personalities—and it or they will be challenged constantly to adapt to new conditions. Strategic culture is likely to manifest itself in strategic behaviour, though certainly not in a mechanistic or deterministic way. Every person who 'does' strategy in some sense or other is himself or herself a person affiliated with one or more culture(s). No one exists beyond culture. Strategic culture provides the context for events and behaviour, a context meaning not only something 'beyond', 'out there', but also a framework of beliefs, attitudes, and habits, of which human beings are an integral part.

---

[39] Bernard Brodie, *War and Politics* (New York, 1973), esp. 332; Ken Booth, *Strategy and Ethnocentrism* (London, 1979), *passim*; John Keegan, *A History of Warfare* (London, 1993), esp. 92. A great strength of Harry G. Summers, Jr., *On Strategy: A Critical Analysis of the Vietnam War* (Novato, Calif., 1982), is that it emphasizes the vital importance of the social dimension of war.

[40] Clausewitz, *On War*, 89.

[41] Ibid.

[42] Peter Burke, *Popular Culture in Early Modern Europe* (Aldershot, 1994), p. x.

[43] Colin S. Gray, *Nuclear Strategy and National Style* (Lanham, Md., 1986), ch. 2.

Sociologist Raymond Williams argued that '[t]here are three general categories in the definition of culture'. He identified, first, an 'ideal' category, 'in which culture is a state or process of human perfection, in terms of certain absolute or universal values'; second, he located a 'documentary' category of 'intellectual and imaginative work'; and, third, he specified a 'social' category, 'in which culture is a description of a particular way of life, which expresses certain meanings and values not only in art and learning but also in institutions and ordinary behaviour.'[44] Williams's supremely intelligent, even commonsensical, tripartite definition guides the discussion of strategic culture in this book.

Anyone doubtful about the potency of culture for strategy should reflect upon what McGregor Knox has written about the influence of Nazi racial ideology upon the Third Reich's prospects for victory in war. Tersely put, '[f]orcibly uniting most of them [the Soviet peoples, who Germany might have set against each other, as had been achieved in 1914–18] with Stalin cost Hitler the war'.[45]

Culture is not everything, even though some of its scholarly devotees affirm that '*all* history is cultural history, since there can be no processes, whether economic, social or political, which are not mediated through ideas, concepts, theories, images or languages'.[46] A cultural dimension to strategy does not stand in stark opposition to a process of strategic calculation that seeks rational choices to the problems of the moment. On the contrary, when security communities exercise strategic choice they do so not with a completely open, or blank, mind on strategic ideas, but rather with values, attitudes, and preferences through which they filter new data, and in terms of which they judge among alternative courses of action.[47] These values, attitudes, and preferences derive from a typically national, or tribal, process of historical education.

Politics

The political dimension of strategy is the one that gives it meaning. John Keegan and Martin van Creveld would probably disagree with me.[48] Keegan, for example, argues that in most historical experience war is a cultural activity rather than a rational instrument of policy or politics. He is correct in his argument, but his understanding of what is cultural, as opposed to political, is distinctly contestable.

---

[44] Raymond Williams, 'The Analysis of Culture', in John Storey (ed.), *Cultural Theory and Popular Culture: A Reader* (New York, 1994), 56. Williams' analysis was first published in 1961. See also id., *Culture and Society: 1780–1950* (New York, 1983), pp. xvi–xviii.

[45] MacGregor Knox, 'Conclusion: Continuity and Revolution in the Making of Strategy', in Murray et al., *Making of Strategy*, 636.

[46] Ludmilla Jordanova, quoted in Tim Harris, 'Problematizing Popular Culture', in Harris (ed.), *Popular Culture in England, c.1500–1850* (London, 1995), 11 (emphasis original).

[47] It is unsound to suggest, as does Michael C. Desch, 'Culture Clash: Assessing the Importance of Ideas in Security Studies', *International Security*, 23 (1998), 141–70, that realist and culturalist explanations can be contrasted. Gideon Rose, 'Neoclassical Realism and Theories of Foreign Policy', *World Politics*, 51 (1998), 144–72, helps explain why such a contrast is illusory. See the analysis in Ch. 5 below.

[48] Keegan, *History of Warfare*; Martin van Creveld, *The Transformation of War* (New York, 1991).

It can be difficult to defend the integrity of politics and the political as a dimension of strategy, without as a consequence appearing to be willing to defend a witless interpretation of Clausewitz's most famous dictum: 'war is simply a continuation of political intercourse, with the addition of other means.'[49] That judgement was dubious, at least incomplete, at its date of birth; today it is close to absurd unless commentary is added. The fact that this happens to be the best known of Clausewitz's opinions is unfortunate but unavoidable. Although Clausewitz was more wise than foolish in this dictum, the wisdom in the formula is hostage to the folly.

Clausewitz's critics suggest that politics tends to become an instrument of war and that policy is often captured by the dynamics of conflict, rather than vice versa. Also, Clausewitz lends himself to the convenient role of surrogate target when the conduct of war fails to advance political purpose noticeably. The too familiar, if still ambiguous, Clausewitzian dictum in praise of the political direction of war is a counsel of perfection. In practice, the 'grammar' of war and strategy shows policy what is, and what is not, possible.[50] Although the political dimension of strategy necessarily is logically superior to the operational military dimension, the latter field-tests the viability of the goals generated by the former.

The political dimension of strategy has the rich ambiguity of Clausewitz's text. First, insistence upon preeminence for this dimension affirms the importance of political purpose for defence preparation and the use of force in war. Armed forces and their use cannot produce their own justification. War, let alone military glory, does not provide its own reward in the West. There is a great deal to be said in favour of viewing military power of all kinds as an instrument of political purpose. However, social, cultural, and political reality may be more complicated than the simple formula stipulates. The idea of force as an agent of political purpose is generally persuasive. Second, it is useful to retain the ambiguity from Clausewitz's German original and regard strategy as the product and agent not only of political purpose, or policy, but also of political contention, or policy process. If strategy is the agent of policy, so policy is the product of an ongoing political process, just as strategy itself is the product of an ongoing strategy-making process. The political (and ethical) dimension of strategy is explored in Chapter 2.

Ethics

The theory and practice of strategy do not require their human agents to be either immoral or amoral. Moral discourse often tends to be missing in action—more accurately, perhaps, locked away for the duration of hostilities with regard to the musings and deeds of strategists. Ethics is a formally neglected dimension of strategy. That is not to say, however, that strategists in practice neglect ethics. Theorists and practitioners of strategy tend to internalize one or more ethical

---

[49] Clausewitz, *On War*, 605.   [50] Ibid.

traditions, and only rarely are obliged to trade moral arguments in the company of professional moral philosophers.[51]

Questions of justice can be hugely relevant to strategic performance. At minimum, those questions reduce to the need to recognize the occasional tension between fighting well in an ethical sense and fighting effectively in pursuit of an economical victory. Even though soldiers at maximum risk will often fight effectively though nominally in aid of a poor political cause, there is little doubt that an unmatched sense of the justice of one's cause yields notable strategic advantage. It is open season for debate over the strategic value of moral superiority in war. Richard Overy is plausible, but no more than plausible, in his argument that '[w]hatever the rights and wrongs of the Allied cause [in World War II], the belief that they fought on the side of righteousness equipped them with powerful moral armament'.[52] Overy concludes his chapter on 'the moral contest' with the rhetorical question: 'can there be any doubt that populations will fight with less effect in the service of an evil cause?'[53] It may be needless to add that strategic history is not in the habit of serving up adversary pairs and groups wherein the villain is quite so unambiguously evil as was the Führer of the Third Reich. Contrary to Overy's interpretation of history, it is not quite persuasive to argue that the moral iniquities of the Third Reich had fatally limiting consequences for that polity's strategic effectiveness. The *Landsers* of the *Östheer*, for a leading case, were fighting for their lives and their variably beloved Führer; they were not obviously militarily impaired by being caught on the disadvantaged end of some implicit moral discourse.[54]

PREPARATION FOR WAR

The economic resources of a polity supply and move a military machine that is directed by a strategy-making organization, recruited, armed, and trained by military administration, ordered in accordance with intelligence information, educated and drilled respectively by strategic theory and doctrine. Economic resources are also expressed in the military fruits of technology.

Economics and Logistics
Strategy requires the use or development of scarce economic resources. It rests

[51] Terry Nadin and David R. Mapel (eds.), *Traditions of International Ethics* (Cambridge, 1992). For rare cases of attempted collaboration between strategic theorists and moral philosophers, see Russell Hardin et al. (eds.), *Nuclear Deterrence: Ethics and Strategy* (Chicago, 1985); Henry Shue (ed.), *Nuclear Deterrence and Moral Restraint: Critical Choices for American Strategy* (Cambridge, 1989).

[52] Richard Overy, *Why the Allies Won* (London, 1995), 312.

[53] Ibid. 313.

[54] Bartov, *Hitler's Army*, offers a controversially ideological explanation of the fighting power of German soldiers in the East (the *Östheer*). There can be little doubt that Bartov is right in claiming that Nazi ideology was important for the combat prowess of the *Östheer*; the question remains, how important? In *Frontsoldaten: The German Soldier in World War II* (Lexington, Ky., 1995), Stephen G. Fritz offers some corrective to Bartov's thesis.

completely upon economic activity, and relies entirely upon logistical performance, i.e. the supply and movement of armed forces. In short, strategy has an economic-logistical dimension that is fundamental, enduring, comprehensive, and inescapable.[55] There is much more to strategy than economics and logistics, but strategy attempted heedless of their discipline is wont to founder at the operational and tactical levels of war. One thinks of the negatively instructive examples provided by the Germans in 1914 in France and in Russia in 1941. Field Marshal Lord Wavell advises that the most important mental quality of a general

is what the French call *le sens du praticable*, and we call common sense, knowledge of what is and what is not possible. It must be based on a really sound knowledge of the 'mechanism of war', *i.e.*, topography, movement, and supply. These are the real foundations of military knowledge, not strategy and tactics as most people think. It is the lack of this knowledge of the principles and practice of military movement and administration—'the logistics' of war, some people call it—which puts what we call amateur strategists wrong, not the principles of strategy themselves, which can be apprehended in a very short time by any reasonable intelligence.[56]

The economic and logistical dimension of strategy has a subordinate but enabling role *vis-à-vis* the political and operational military dimensions. Generals, no matter how gifted as operational commanders, are constrained by the resources—human and material—available to them and their foe at the operational level of war. Almost every campaign and war is shaped in its course and at least influenced in its outcome by the economic-logistical dimension. Many campaigns and wars illustrate the salience of economic-logistical matters: the campaigns in Burma in 1942–5,[57] in North Africa in 1941–2,[58] and the war to retake the Falklands in 1982,[59] for example. Even when the economic-logistical dimension is thoroughly permissive for one belligerent, such as the United States in Vietnam, notwithstanding the trans-oceanic distance,[60] one finds that material abundance and its consequent logistical bloat itself has a negative influence upon the conduct of war.

Defence and force planning conducted in peacetime against the possibility of armed conflict always has a strong economic dimension. There is an uneasy

---

[55] George C. Thorpe, *Pure Logistics: The Science of War Preparation*, repr. of 1917 edn. (Washington, DC, 1986); Julian Thompson, *The Lifeblood of War: Logistics in Armed Conflict* (London, 1991).

[56] Archibald Wavell, *Generals and Generalship* (New York, 1943), 10.

[57] Viscount Slim, *Defeat into Victory* (London, 1986), 115, 209–10, 291, 380, 539.

[58] Gerhard Schreiber, Bernd Stegemann, and Detlef Vogel, *Germany and the Second World War, iii: The Mediterranean, South-East Europe, and North Africa, 1939–1941* (Oxford, 1995), pt. 5.

[59] Thompson, *Lifeblood of War*, ch. 8.

[60] Albert Wohlstetter, 'Illusions of Distance', *Foreign Affairs*, 46 (1968), 242–55. Contrast Wohlstetter with the idea of the 'loss-of-strength gradient' (LSG), which holds that power diminishes with distance. See Kenneth Boulding, *Conflict and Defense: A General Theory* (New York, 1962), 242–7, 262–4. Classic illustration of the LSG in action was provided in 1812 by Napoleon. The Grande Armée entered Russia with approximately 422,000 men, reached Moscow with 100,000, and returned to Poland with barely 10,000. See the classic graphical depiction, 'Napoleon's Russian Campaign (1812)', by Charles Joseph Minard, reproduced facing p. 120 in Handel, *Masters of War*.

relationship among the economic, the political, and the operational military dimensions of strategy. How should one resolve disputes between those who urge defence preparation according to threat-based military analysis of what the polity allegedly needs to be secure and those who assert that the polity can only afford to spend so much on defence functions? Strategy is not only an economic problem; *inter alia* it is also an economic problem. There is more to war than logistics, but those disdainful of logistics can run out of water in the desert or find themselves fighting in summer uniforms near Moscow in December. Wars are not won directly by logisticians, but poor logisticians make it all but impossible even for operational military genius to exercise its talent effectively.

Organization

The organizational dimension of strategy finds historical expression as a continuum of competence extending from Wilhelmine and Nazi Germany at the lower extremity to Britain in World War II at the higher.[61] Superior organization for strategy cannot offset monumental operational incompetence or inadequate training of the troops—for example, as revealed in the Anglo-French performance in the campaign in France and Belgium in May 1940[62]—and is not entirely proof against fools in high places. Such organization, however, does provide institutional safeguards that help offset individuals' failings. By analogy, technically 'safe' cars do not guarantee safety on the road, because the road is used by unsafe drivers. Nonetheless, the driver of a large, solidly built Swedish vehicle is more likely to walk away from a collision than is the driver of a Gallic 'hot hatch'.

Strategy is a process. If the process that makes, executes, and monitors the consequences of the execution of strategy is best described as the intuition of the warlord, then national security is hostage to that warlord's genius, sanity, sobriety, energy, industry, and judgement. Both historical experience and common sense suggest strongly that such a personal process of strategy-making is unwise; even genius needs assistance. Strategic ideas need to be staffed and coordinated, priced, and critically reviewed at the grand strategic level of assay. On the evidence of comparative strategic performance in the twentieth century, only a fairly complex organization is able to make, execute, and constantly review strategy. Scholars recognize in principle the organizational demands of practicable strategy, but in practice they often proceed to discuss strategy as though the

---

[61] Dominick Graham and Shelford Bidwell, *Coalitions, Politicians and Generals: Some Aspects of Command in Two World Wars* (London, 1993), is exemplary.

[62] Robert Allan Doughty, *The Breaking Point: Sedan and the Fall of France, 1940* (Hamden, Conn., 1990); Eugenia C. Kiesling, *Arming against Hitler: France and the Limits of Military Planning* (Princeton, NJ, 1997). James S. Corum has explained how a 'German military tradition [which] gave top priority to the thorough training of troops' was an enduring source of military advantage. *The Roots of Blitzkrieg: Hans von Seeckt and German Military Reform* (Lawrence, Kan., 1992), 10–13. In May 1940, German operational tempo in the march through the Ardennes to the Meuse crossing at Sedan, and the subsequent thrust to the coast, was at least as much of a problem for French and British forces as was the lingering doubt over identification of the German Schwerpunkt.

subject were simply a matter of contending ideas. Just as strategy is 'done' by tactical activity, also it is, or should be, 'done' by a bureaucratic organization that staffs alternatives critically, coordinates rival inputs, and oversees execution and feedback on the effect of execution. This is neither exciting nor heroic, but it is absolutely essential for superior strategic performance.

Military Administration

Between the resources of a polity and the science of supply and movement known as 'logistics' lies a large and complex zone that can simply be termed 'military administration'.[63] By administration we mean the activities of military preparation that eventually provide suitably armed forces ready to be moved by the logisticians so that the generals can exercise command. Those activities must include all aspects of military recruitment, training, and armament. Sometimes scholars claim that great state bureaucracies, military services, and industrial interests all but capture the strategy of a polity.[64] Occasionally, those scholars will be correct. For example, there is persuasive evidence to suggest that the surging, broad-fronted procurement of 'strategic' armaments in the USSR in the 1970s and early 1980s was attributable far more to a party–industry alliance for self-interested institutional, and personal, reasons than it was to any drive to meet strategic requirements.[65]

The demand for administrative skill in military preparation is as easily demonstrated by the record of Albert Speer as Hitler's Minister of Armaments as by the dilemmas facing imperial Spain in the late 1580s. With respect to the latter case, an historian has noted: 'By the end of 1587 the Armada was slipping rapidly into chaos, and the whole project was in crisis . . . In this desperate situation, with the future strategy and present reputation of the Spanish empire in the balance, the most urgent requirement was administrative skill.'[66] It so happens that the Duke of Medina Sidonia had to command the expedition whose military and naval preparation he rescued, but such need not be, indeed usually is not, the case. When we read about the triumphs and disasters of great and not so great captains, the strategic effect they can extract from their forces often derives from the activities of military preparation pursued over decades. If troops are poorly equipped — as with the British for the conditions of siege warfare that set in on what became the Western Front during the autumn of 1914 — or are inadequately trained — as were the French and the British in 1940 — then even skilled generalship will not

---

[63] A study that captures most of what I mean by the administrative dimension of strategy is H. J. Hewitt, *The Organization of War under Edward III, 1338–62* (Manchester, 1966).

[64] Theo Farrell, *Weapons Without a Cause: The Politics of Weapons Acquisition in the United States* (London, 1997).

[65] John G. Hines, Ellis M. Mishulovich, and John F. Shull, *Soviet Intentions, 1965–1985* (2 vols., McLean, Va., 1995).

[66] N. A. M. Rodger, *The Safeguard of the Sea: A Naval History of Great Britain, i: 660–1649* (London, 1997), 258.

yield sufficient compensation. This is another example of how every one of these dimensions of strategy always operates in war.

Information and Intelligence

Sun Tzu advises: 'Warfare is the Way [Tao] of deception.'[67] To deceive, one must first penetrate the cultural veil to comprehend an adversary's world-view so that one can feed his expectations. Since people tend to believe what they want to believe, deception requires an empathy with their adversary's expectations. But deception, surprise, or stratagems have a mixed and controversial past in strategic history. There can be no question but that information and intelligence qualify as a dimension of strategy, statecraft, and war.[68] The prospective strategic effect likely to be harvested from superior information and intelligence, however, has varied radically with the salient technologies, politics, geographies, and logistics of war. If war can be prepared and launched with scant detectable evidence, then strategic surprise should be achievable, if rarely achieved. If, in contrast, war can be prepared and launched only in a manner that must yield massive signatures for enemy intelligence-gatherers, then operational or tactical surprise must constitute the outer bounds of prudent ambition. Historically, opinions by military experts on the value of deception, surprise, and intelligence have tended to reflect their actual, if transitory, circumstances.[69] For example, Sun Tzu in the fifth century BC and many American theorists at the close of the twentieth century agree on the primacy of information as a factor that helps enable superior strategy and facilitates victory in war. It must be noted that even when the military preparations for a great offensive cannot be concealed comprehensively, strategic surprise is still possible. If the victim polity can be induced politically to persuade itself that the military evidence of major danger should be discounted, then strategic surprise can be achieved. This was the Soviet experience in 1941.

Strategic Theory and Doctrine

One could elect to subsume strategic theory in strategic culture, understanding the realm of strategic ideas to refer only to the first of Williams's three categories of cultural evidence, the 'ideal'. In a book which identifies the complex relationship between theory and practice as a major theme, however, there is merit in treating the world of strategic ideas as a distinctive dimension to strategy. There is so much more to strategic culture than just ideas that one needs to guard against the possibility that the latter somehow may be lost or underappreciated when discussed with the former. Although the development of strategic theory is driven by the needs of strategic practice, its ability to capture the minds of supposedly practical people should never be underestimated. Wherever one looks in modern strategic history one finds testimony to the influence of ideas. Many members of

---

[67] Sun Tzu, *The Art of War*, trans. Ralph D. Sawyer (Boulder, Colo., 1994), 168.

[68] Michael Herman, *Intelligence Power in Peace and War* (Cambridge, 1996), is superior.

[69] Handel, *Masters of War*, ch. 12.

the Western arms control community, for example, have believed for decades that the deployment of ballistic missile defences (BMD) would detract from the stability of deterrence by menacing the adversary's ability to retaliate massively.[70] In the 1930s, for another example, Britain's Royal Air Force, and some British politicians, were convinced by the theory of strategic airpower that bombers could deter, and if need be win, wars, without much assistance from other military elements.[71] Of recent years, some of the more innovative people in the US armed forces have toyed with the strategic idea that American 'information warriors' will be the midwives of victory by providing a dominant battlespace knowledge.[72] Examples abound. But no matter how firmly sets of strategic ideas are anchored in the realities of yesterday's strategic history or in anticipated strategic realities, there is always a strategic theoretical dimension to the making, execution, and doing of strategy.

If strategic theory educates the mind by providing intellectual organization, defining terms, suggesting connections among apparently disparate matters, and offering speculative consequentialist postulates, strategic (and operational, and tactical) doctrine states beliefs. Doctrine teaches what to think and what to do, rather than how to think and how to be prepared to do it. Academic scholars of strategy and war are apt to forget about the vital intermediary function that doctrine plays between ideas and behaviour. Scholars write theory, they do not write doctrine. Military organizations have to develop and employ doctrine—whether written, or culturally transmitted orally and by example—if they are to train large numbers of people with equipment in sufficiently standard modes of behaviour for them to be predictable instruments of the commander's will.

Although doctrine is an organization's credo on the subject at hand, it does not have to be tightly restrictive of lower-level initiative. Doctrine *per se* is a box empty of content until organizations decide how much of it they want, and how constraining they wish it to be. Because doctrine lends itself to many definitions, there is much to be said for Theo Farrell's view that 'a more fruitful' approach than trying to decide what is doctrine and what is not doctrine

might be to concentrate on the purpose of doctrine as opposed to its meaning. Essentially, *service doctrine explains the goals, identifies the tasks, and shapes the tools of the organization.* Furthermore, it does so to three distinct audiences—the members of the organization,

[70] The debate over BMD became noticeably theological, with advocates advancing arguments that in actuality were closer to beliefs. Useful works include Craig Snyder (ed.), *The Strategic Defense Debate: Can 'Star Wars' Make us Safe?* (Philadelphia, 1986); Keith B. Payne, *Strategic Defense: 'Star Wars' in Perspective* (Lanham, Md., 1986); Edward Reiss, *The Strategic Defense Initiative* (Cambridge, 1992).

[71] George H. Quester, *Deterrence before Hiroshima: The Airpower Background to Modern Strategy* (New York, 1966), chs. 5–6; Uri Bialer, *The Shadow of the Bomber: The Fear of Air Attack and British Politics, 1932–1939* (London, 1980); Malcolm Smith, *British Air Strategy between the Wars* (Oxford, 1984).

[72] Martin C. Libicki, *The Mesh and the Net: Speculations on Armed Conflict in a Time of Free Silicon* (Washington, DC, 1995); Stuart G. Johnson and Martin C. Libicki (eds.), *Dominant Battlespace Knowledge* (Washington, DC, 1996).

sister military services, and policymakers—and for three distinct reasons. Directed at organizational members, doctrine helps a military organization maintain internal cohesion in how it prepares for, and prosecutes, military operations. Directed at sister services, doctrine facilitates joint and combined operations. Directed at policymakers, doctrine enables a military organisation to maximise its autonomy and resource base.[73]

Technology

Technology is of permanent significance as a dimension of strategy. The difficulty lies with generic critics who always champion the virtues of the warrior over the purported power of machines, and generic enthusiasts who discern the solution to every human—including strategic, operational, and tactical—problem in new marvels of science and engineering. There has long been a strain of theory, commentary, and military practice inclined to accord sovereign status to technology in war.[74] To discuss the nonsense that has been written about new weaponry could easily require book-length treatment. Technology, as weaponry or as equipment in support of weaponry, does not determine the outbreak, course, and outcome of conflicts, but it constitutes an important dimension. The most modern military technology will avail little if the human operators of weapons are poorly drilled in their use, or if they decline to fight. Moreover, Janus-like, each new generation of weapons technology has its own set of technical and tactical vulnerabilities. Those who would emphasize the importance of the human being in the person–machine combination that forms a weapon system need to recognize that the human requirement is different for the warrior who must dispatch his enemy within arm's length, as extended by an edged or pointed weapon, and the 'warrior' who 'wields' a keyboard to dispatch an unmanned cruise missile to its target.

The technological dimension of strategy as registered here inherently carries no baggage of argument as to its relative significance. The claim simply is that strategy, in all periods, at all levels, and among any sets of adversaries, must have a technological dimension. Technology is important. But historical evidence suggests that the outcomes to none of the wars in modern history among the great powers have plausibly been determined by superiority in weapons technology. One might argue about the atomic bomb in August 1945, but even in that case one could claim that the defeat of imperial Japan was overdetermined by Allied success at sea, in the air, and even, through amphibious assault, on land.

Because technology is but one dimension of the essential unity of strategy, some

---

[73] Theo Farrell, 'Making Sense of Doctrine', in Michael Duffy, Theo Farrell, and Geoffrey Sloan (eds.), *Doctrine and Military Effectiveness*, Strategic Policy Studies, i (Exeter, 1997), 2 (emphasis original). Historical windows on doctrine are opened in John Gooch (ed.), *The Origins of Contemporary Doctrine*, Occasional Paper 30 (Camberley, Sept. 1997).

[74] e.g. J. F. C. Fuller, *Armament and History: A Study of the Influence of Armament on History from the Dawn of Classical Warfare to the Second World War* (London, 1946). Useful wide-ranging commentaries include Bernard Brodie, 'Technological Change, Strategic Doctrine, and Political Outcomes', in Klaus Knorr (ed.), *Historical Dimensions of National Security Problems* (Lawrence, Kan., 1976), 263-306; Martin van Creveld, *Technology and War: From 2000 B.C. to the Present* (New York, 1989).

compensation from other dimensions can be provided when it is in short supply or of poor quality. For example, on the Eastern Front in World War II, Nazi Germany was quite successful in substituting culture, in this case ideology, for technology as the *Ostheer* demodernized precipitately in 1941-2 under the pressures of unfriendly geography and intense combat.[75] By contrast, as the cultural dimension of the American war in Vietnam faltered both politically and operationally, sheer technological muscle proved tactically effective in the avoidance of defeat in combat.

WAR PROPER

Military operations present problems of command which are influenced pervasively by distinctive geographies, are beset by the workings of friction, may be thwarted by an intelligent adversary, and are subject to an often severe discipline of time.

Military Operations

There is an operational military dimension to strategy that can be neglected because it is so obvious. That which is taken for granted is scarcely worthy of extensive discussion. Fashionable studies in the mode of 'war and society' often underplay the importance of the brute combat of tactical history.[76] Military history and strategic studies have come a long way from Edward Creasey's strategically reductionist classic study, *The Fifteen Decisive Battles of the World*,[77] but it is possible to shift the decent, liberal, and scholarly focus in strategy and security too far from the battlefield (or should one say battlespace to modernize the concept?). Merit remains in Clausewitz's famous dictum that

The decision by arms is for all major and minor operations in war what cash payment is in commerce. Regardless how complex the relationship between the two parties, regardless how rarely settlements actually occur, they can never be entirely absent.[78]

This dimension of strategy expresses the reality of the relationship between strategy and tactics. Strategy, no matter how apparently brilliant, is moot until somebody does it. It must use the threats and actions of organized bodies of warriors. To record operational military activity as a pervasive dimension of strategy is like reminding readers that intelligence success *per se* accomplishes nothing. The Ultra intelligence derived from the prompt decoding of German operational message traffic processed by Enigma coding machines, was a priceless

---

[75] Bartov, *Hitler's Army*; Fritz, *Frontsoldaten*.

[76] This complaint pervades Hanson, *Western Way of War*; Paddy Griffith, *Battle Tactics of the Western Front: The British Army's Art of Attack, 1916-18* (New Haven, Conn., 1994), esp. 201-3; Alan B. Lloyd (ed.), *Battle in Antiquity* (London, 1996).

[77] Edward Creasey, *The Fifteen Decisive Battles of the World: From Marathon to Waterloo*, repr. of 1851 edn. (Royston, 1996).

[78] Clausewitz, *On War*, 97.

Allied asset in World War II, but Ultra itself could sink no U-boats.[79] U-boats were sunk at the sharp end of the war at sea by Allied personnel on ships and aircraft.

The operational military dimension may refer only to the agents of higher strategic direction in pursuit of political advantage, but those agents, logically subordinate though they are to strategy, are essential if strategy is to be more than just aspiration. Even if the cause is plausibly just, society supports the war effort, political goals are well chosen, the military effort is well supplied, and the weapons and other military equipment are good enough, troops still have to fight. Errors in the conduct of the fighting, at the level either of campaign or of tactical engagement, can offset almost any set of net strengths on the other dimensions of strategy. Although there was much to criticize about Anglo-French readiness for war in 1939–40, the expulsion of the bulk of the British Expeditionary Force (BEF) from Dunkirk and the collapse of France were attributable primarily to the fact that British and French forces were outmanoeuvred by a German army that had innovated radically in the 1920s in its method of war, and which had trained hard under the guidance of a sound doctrine.[80] Below the operational level of war, however, there is always the question of how well do the troops actually fight. Field Marshal William Slim recognizes the core of the strategy–operations–tactics nexus when he writes:

There comes a moment in every battle against a stubborn enemy when the result hangs in the balance. Then the general, however skilful and far-sighted he may have been, must hand over to his soldiers, to the men in the ranks and to their regimental officers, and leave them to complete what he has begun. The issue then rests with them, on their courage, their hardihood, their refusal to be beaten either by the cruel hazards of nature, or by the fierce strengths of their human enemy.[81]

At the end of the day military operations is the dimension of strategy that poses the brutally direct question, 'How good are the belligerents at actual fighting?'

Command

'Command' refers to the quality of military and political leadership. A huge amount of the literature on military history is about military command. Whether or not the musings of historians and strategic theorists on 'great captains' have been unduly dominant,[82] political and military 'captaincy' still matters. Quality of command invariably makes a strategic difference, which is to say it is a dimension of strategy contributing to overall strategic effect. Whether or not one believes

---

[79] John Winton, *Ultra at Sea* (London, 1988); Overy, *Why the Allies Won*, ch. 2; Ralph Bennett, *Behind the Battle: Intelligence in the War with Germany, 1939–45* (London, 1994).

[80] Archer Jones, *The Art of War in the Western World* (Urbana, Ill., 1987), 510–44; and esp. Corum, *Roots of Blitzkrieg*, ch. 4.

[81] Slim, *Defeat into Victory*, 551.

[82] B. H. Liddell Hart, *Great Captains Unveiled* (Freeport, NY, 1967). Baron Antoine Henri de Jomini, *The Art of War*, repr. of 1962 edn. (London, 1992), is very much a manual on generalship.

that Generals Montgomery, Rommel, and Patton are serious candidates for the 'most overrated' category of commanders,[83] or that Stonewall Jackson's tragic death at Chancellorsville had the ultimate consequence of Confederate defeat in the American Civil War,[84] commanders are significant in their capacity to do harm or find and exploit advantage. Modern strategic studies, in its fascination with technology, its newly fashionable attraction to the face of battle at the sharpest end of war, and with its focus on broad social forces, often forgets the commanders behind the mask of command.[85] Readers may care to ponder the merit, or otherwise, in the Arab proverb that 'an army of sheep led by a lion will defeat an army of lions led by a sheep'.[86]

Geography

The geography relevant to conflict has expanded in this century from the land and the surface of the sea to encompass the domains of air and space, as well as the electromagnetic spectrum (EMS), including today the virtuality of cyberspace.[87] There is always a geographical dimension to conflict. Geography, in common with history and culture, is one of those candidate imperial dimensions that can be treated in so inclusive a way that it begins unduly to dominate theory, analysis, and explanation. Near-constant though physical geography has been, its significance can alter with technology. That significance does not alter with technology alone, because technology cannot be treated in isolation as the arbiter of strategic history. A particular terrain, climate, and sheer distance—Russian geography, for example—in principle can be reduced in strategic significance by modern means of transport and supply. In practice, however, in 1941–2 a Russian military effectiveness born of ideology, desperation, growing skill, and depth of resources so blunted the cutting edge of the German Wehrmacht that physical geography could play fully as a net asset for the USSR. Together, the Soviet defender and Russian geography actually imposed a massive technological demodernization upon all but the élite units of the German army. The German vehicle park, with its inventory critically dependent upon the unduly

---

[83] John Ellis, 'Reflections on the "Sharp End" of War', in Addison and Calder, Time to Kill, 13.

[84] William C. Davis, The Cause Lost: Myths and Realities of the Confederacy (Lawrence, Kan., 1996), esp. 174. A recent enthusiastic presentation of the myth is Bevin Alexander, Lost Victories: The Military Genius of Stonewall Jackson (Edison, NJ, 1996). The modern biography is James I. Robertson, Jr., Stonewall Jackson: The Man, The Soldier, The Legend (New York, 1997). Jackson's death was compounded in its strategic consequences by the overconfidence that the Chancellorsville victory bred in Robert E. Lee. As James M. McPherson has commented, '[b]elieving his troops invincible, Lee was about to ask them to do the impossible'. Battle Cry of Freedom: The Civil War Era (New York, 1988), 645.

[85] John Keegan, The Mask of Command (New York, 1987). Michael R. Gordon and Bernard E. Trainor, The Generals' War: The Inside Story of the Conflict in the Gulf (Boston, 1995), is also useful.

[86] I am grateful to Professor Stephen Cimbala of Pennsylvania State University for bringing this glorious proverb to my attention.

[87] Martin Libicki, 'The Emerging Primacy of Information', Orbis, 40 (1996), 261–74; which is challenged in Colin S. Gray 'The Continued Primacy of Geography', Orbis, 40 (1996), 247–59, 274–6.

diverse mechanical spoils of the easy victories of 1938–41, did not fare well in Russian conditions.[88]

Though in an obvious sense a constant, geography is anything but constant in its influence upon history as a dimension of strategy for all belligerents at all times. There are claims, hopes rather, to the effect that geography is in the process of being dismissed as a dimension with much ability to constrain. Who cares about 'mere' geography when intercontinental ballistic missiles (ICBMs) can deliver weapons of mass destruction, or small conventional explosives, essentially with perfect accuracy (a zero circular error probable, CEP)[89] at ranges in excess of 7000 miles? What significant influence can brute geography possibly have when human beings are exploiting cyberspace, which is potentially everywhere and therefore is so well distributed as effectively to be nowhere? The geographical dimension of strategy is ubiquitous and permanent, yet varied in its specific influence upon particular conflicts at particular times.[90]

Friction, Chance, and Uncertainty

This unholy trinity, lifted gratefully from Clausewitz,[91] constitutes a compound dimension of strategy and war that can prove lethally disabling. The would-be rational and prudent defence planner lives in a world of uncertainty. Chance does not quite rule but is always a player, and friction can impede cumulatively the smooth performance of anything and everything. It would be absurd to elevate this dimension of strategy to master status, but still it would be difficult to over-estimate its salience. From the pattern of untimely rainfall in autumn 1917 that drowned out General Douglas Haig's Passchendaele offensive,[92] through the Belgian (then the Allied) capture in January 1940 of the initial German plan (Plan Yellow) for attack in the West,[93] to the anxieties about surprise attack against their ICBMs which drove the superpowers to devise potentially perilous tactics of launch under attack (LUA),[94] the unholy trinity of friction, chance, and uncertainty figures on every page of strategic history.

[88] Albert Seaton, *The Russo-German War, 1941–45* (New York, 1971); David M. Glantz and Jonathan House, *When Titans Clashed: How the Red Army Stopped Hitler* (Lawrence, Kan., 1995); Rolf-Dieter Müller and Gerd R. Ueberschär, *Hitler's War in the East, 1941–1945, A Critical Reassessment* (Providence, RI, 1997); Horst Boog et al., *Germany and the Second World War, iv: The Attack on the Soviet Union* (Oxford, 1998).

[89] Circular error probable is a measure of missile accuracy keyed to the principle that there is a 50% probability of ordnance striking within a circle of a specified radius.

[90] Gray, 'Continued Primacy of Geography'; John M. Collins, *Military Geography for Professionals and the Public* (Washington, DC, 1998); and esp. Harold A. Winters, *Battling the Elements: Weather and Terrain in the Conduct of War* (Baltimore, 1998).

[91] Clausewitz, *On War*, 85–6, 101–2, 119–21, 140; Katherine L. Herbig, 'Chance and Uncertainty in *On War*', in Michael I. Handel (ed.), *Clausewitz and Modern Strategy* (London, 1986), 95–116.

[92] Griffith, *Battle Tactics*, 88; Robin Prior and Trevor Wilson, *Passchendaele: The Untold Story* (New Haven, Conn., 1996), ch. 10, 'Rain'; John Hussey, 'The Flanders Battleground and the Weather in 1917', in Peter H. Liddle (ed.), *Passchendaele in Perspective: The Third Battle of Ypres* (London, 1997), 140–58.

[93] Doughty, *Breaking Point*, 23–4; Klauss A. Maier et al., *Germany and the Second World War, ii: Germany's Initial Conquests in Europe* (Oxford, 1991), 245–6.

[94] Bruce G. Blair, *The Logic of Accidental Nuclear War* (Washington, DC, 1993), esp. ch. 6.

Adversary

Strategy is not a game played against nature. Instead, it is activity geared to secure advantage over, or deny advantage to, an adversary who is motivated, and not infrequently able, to thwart you. Because strategy is always devised 'at home'—nationally or within a coalition—through the workings of a process beset with myriad domestic difficulties, the enemy is often neglected in deliberations. In fact, from the peacetime point of view of the strategic planner, the adversary is actually the easiest variable to manipulate. The real enemy of a new scheme of defence planning will be the treasury, the arms control agency, and so forth; it will not be the Soviet Union, or China, or some other adversary who truly will 'play' beyond convenient assumptions only in time of crisis and particularly in war itself. In war, the adversary speaks through action in a manner that commands attention by its actual strategic effect. Speculation about the net worth of Hitler's army, the merit in the Maginot Line, and so forth is simply swept aside when proof is provided by worth in battle.

Strategy is so difficult to design and do well that consideration of an intelligent and self-willed foe is frequently a complication too far. Many are the studies on modern strategy that impress in all regards—especially their promise of devastating military performance—save that of coping with the malign machinations of a dedicated, competent, and devious foe. Not for nothing is one of the few great books of modern strategic theory—that by Edward N. Luttwak—organized around the proposition that strategy is fundamentally, perhaps uniquely, paradoxical in nature.[95] Strategy is paradoxical in that what works well today will not work well tomorrow, precisely because it worked well today. Mount Everest cannot plan and act deliberately to defeat assaults that already have 'shown their hand'; strategic adversaries will do exactly that. The problem for strategy, as Luttwak outlines persuasively, is that every cunning plan has to succeed against, not blind nature, but rather an adversary with whom you conduct a permanent tactical, operational, strategic, and political-moral dialogue.

Time

The final dimension to be introduced, the temporal is, again, so obvious that it invites neglect by theorists.[96] Every military plan at every level of war is ruled by the clock; defence planning is governed by annual, biannual, or quinquennial budget cycles. Geographical distance, and terrain, translate inexorably into time that must elapse if they are to be crossed. Peter Wilson argues that strategic ideas can be categorized in three ways that are temporally commanded.[97] An idea can be

---

[95] Edward N. Luttwak, *Strategy: The Logic of War and Peace* (Cambridge, Mass., 1987).

[96] Harold Nelson, 'Space and Time in *On War*', in Handel, *Clausewitz*, 134–49; Laure Paquette, 'Strategy and Time in Clausewitz's *On War* and in Sun Tzu's *The Art of War*', *Comparative Strategy*, 10 (1991), 37–51; Ajay Singh, 'Time: The New Dimension in War', *Joint Force Quarterly*, 10 (1995–6), 56–61.

[97] Peter Wilson, 'The Transformation of Military Power, 1997-2027', paper presented at the 1997 Pacific Symposium, Honolulu, Hawaii, 28–9 Apr., 1997, 21–4.

advanced too soon, too late, or at the right time. As a significant overlay to timeliness, one then has to consider whether the idea is right or wrong. On the virtual battlefield of cyberspace, electronic warfare is apt to mock geography, and therefore time. But in all forms of combat for which the speed of light cannot govern time and eliminate space, time will rule tactically and operationally (politically and strategically, the significance of time cannot be diminished by technical advances). Characteristically, time is an ally of the sea power and of the irregular warrior, neither of whom can secure victory by swift decision. The former needs time in which to translate advantage at sea into success on land, while the latter can win only by avoiding 'decisive' battle and attriting the political will of the enemy. Whether it was the British in 1940–1 waiting for Nazi Germany—following in Napoleonic France's bootsteps—to make strategically fatal errors,[98] or whether it was North Vietnam in 1968–9 waiting for the United States politically and morally to tire of war,[99] modern strategy all but commands the theorist to recognize the importance of its temporal dimension.

Although I risk providing what may seem merely a listing of the obvious, in fact I am capturing the whole nature of strategy for all periods. To organize the dimensions into more, rather than fewer, items helps convey the true complexity of the subject. Presented here is a general theory of strategy which specifies seventeen still quite broad dimensions. This analysis argues, further, that every one of these dimensions is always a player in conflict, albeit sometimes only weakly. Every belligerent will score variably in merit across these dimensions and may find compensation for areas of weakness in particular areas of strength.

The holistic principle which guides this analysis must deny imperial master status to any one dimension of strategy, but three dimensions contend plausibly for extraordinary notice. Politics may seem to be the master, in that it is the only realm that provides meaning to strategy. Alternatively, or perhaps in addition, the influence of people has a strong claim to be the most pervasive element in strategic activity of all kinds. Finally, as noted earlier, 'time' is undoubtedly the least forgiving of error among strategy's dimensions. The precise relationships among the dimensions must always be in some measure uncertain, because there are no hard boundaries among them.[100] However, this general theory of strategy lends itself to application to any conflict in strategic history. A general theory of strategy, such as this, which explains the nature of the subject and at least suggests how the subject 'works', cannot itself explain particular strategic experience. Rather, this theory educates strategic analysts so that when they look at the Battle of Britain in 1940,

[98] Paul Kennedy, *The Realities Behind Diplomacy: Background Influences on British External Policy, 1865–1980* (London, 1981), 345–50.

[99] Ronald H. Spector, *After Tet: The Bloodiest Year in Vietnam* (New York, 1993).

[100] For example, decisions on how to use new technology are influenced by military service culture, while geographical circumstances both help shape national culture and imply priorities among technologies.

or the Soviet adventure in Afghanistan in the 1980s, for example, they know what their strategic subject is made of.[101] The approximate relative net worth of technology, geography, and command for belligerents can be calculated only on a historical case-by-case basis, in a way totally respectful of historical evidence. The theory of strategy developed here has the purpose of helping historians make better sense of their research while enabling strategic theorists to relate the historically unique to more general patterns in strategic experience.

WHY STRATEGY MATTERS

To neglect strategy in defence planning or the conduct of war would be like trying to play chess without kings on the board; there would be no point. Failure of strategy, however, does not always flow from neglect of strategy. The problem can lie with policy. A strategist can only orchestrate engagements purposefully for the political objective of the war if the war has a clear political objective. Strategic performance either in defence planning in peacetime or in war itself will be harmed if policy is vague, if its objectives are ephemeral, or if it sets political constraints upon military activity that prevent generation of sufficent strategic effect to produce success. However, even when policy is plainly at fault, the military strategist is not thereby exonerated from responsibility. In his Maxim LXXII, the Emperor Napoleon dictated a decision rule:

A general-in-chief has no right to shelter his mistakes in war under cover of his sovereign, or of a minister, when they are both distant from the scene of operation, and must consequently be either ill informed or wholly ignorant of the actual state of things.

Hence it follows that every general is culpable who undertakes the execution of a plan which he considers faulty. It is his duty to represent his reasons, to insist upon a change of plan; in short to give in his resignation rather than allow himself to become the instrument of his army's ruin. Every general-in-chief who fights a battle in consequence of superior orders, with the certainty of losing it, is equally blamable.[102]

Napoleon's words could have been written for the US Joint Chiefs of Staff, and Secretary of Defence Robert S. McNamara, in 1965-7.[103] No level of responsibility can afford to treat superior direction as absolute authority. The tactician must be prepared to explain battlefield realities to the theatre commander at the latter's

---

[101] I have applied this theory of strategy to a wide range of historical case studies in my essay 'Fuller's Folly: Technology, Strategic Effectiveness, and the Quest for Dominant Weapons', in A. J. Bacevich and Brian R. Sullivan (eds.), The Limits of Technology in Modern War, forthcoming.

[102] David G. Chandler, The Military Maxims of Napoleon, trans. Lt.-Gen. Sir George C. D'Aguilar, repr. of 1901 edn. (New York, 1988), 79.

[103] Robert S. McNamara, In Retrospect: The Tragedy and Lessons of Vietnam (New York, 1995); H. R. McMaster, Dereliction of Duty: Lyndon Johnson, Robert McNamara, the Joint Chiefs of Staff, and the Lies That Led to Vietnam (New York, 1997); Lewis Sorley, Honorable Warrior: General Harold K. Johnson and the Ethics of Command (Lawrence, Kan., 1998).

operational level of war; the operational commander may need to educate his country's strategist, or strategists, about the bounds of the practicable in his theatre of operations; and the strategist must always be willing to speak the truth to politicians and advise them that their war aims are unduly heroic or overly modest.

Responsibility for strategy is so far above the pay grade of more than 99.9 per cent of the personnel in any army that one might expect awareness of its ramifications scarcely to intrude upon the awful business of fighting, or on the perilous lives of soldiers on the battlefield. In practice, though, soldiers in combat can be acutely sensitive to strategic-level concerns. The strategic and the human psychological connection between the soldier whose life is on the line and his country's military strategy lies in the soldier's personal cost–benefit analysis. A study of the US Army in Vietnam provides convincing oral historical evidence from combat veterans of the 25th Division, to the effect that their political morale was almost extinct because they sensed the strategic futility of their tactical performance. For example, Jerry Headley of the 3/4th (third squadron, fourth troop) Armored Cavalry, 25th Division, inadvertently offered this strategic judgement upon his personal experience in Vietnam:

There wasn't anything different in Vietnam from the day I arrived to the day I left. We were still fighting over the same terrain, the same areas [Tay Ninh and Hau Nghia provinces]. Where an ambush or a fight had been a month before, you were fighting again. You never, never held anything. You'd fight in an area one day and come back again and fight on another. It was very frustrating to know that it didn't matter what you did or how many of the enemy you killed or how many you captured. He was going to be there again tomorrow. And so the more you did this, you kept wondering, what the hell am I doing here? I'm not getting anywhere. It's just the same thing over and over again.[104]

This testimony does not prove that the US Army in Vietnam lacked strategic guidance. It does suggest, though, that at least the junior officer just quoted could not relate purposefully his daily tactical activity to any strategic purpose. Although the concerns of people in combat focus upon survival, the political morale that can buttress field morale requires an army to explain to its endangered warriors how their daily behaviour relates to the likelihood of victory. In addition, it is important for morale for soldiers to be persuaded that victory matters. The US military performance in Vietnam, especially after spring 1968, is testimony to just how well soldiers will fight for themselves and their immediate group, even when they have been all but abandoned by strategy and policy. Had the US Army faced a tactically and operationally more formidable foe than the North Vietnamese Army (NVA) in 1969–70, in a generally symmetrical regular conflict, then recognition of futility of risk and sacrifice at the tactical level could have had catastrophic strategic consequences.

---

[104] Eric M. Bergerud, *Red Thunder, Tropic Lightning: The World of a Combat Division in Vietnam* (New York, 1994), 267.

Some readers may wonder why it is that soldiers can fight so well in defence of a cause that they do not value highly. The reason is not hard to find. War is about personal survival. As public international law separates the rights and duties of individual combatants from issues pertaining to just war (i.e. judgements as to *jus ad bellum* do not reach out to influence opinion about *jus in bello*), so the harsh realities of combat leave individuals with a clear choice only between effective and ineffective military behaviour. When troops are threatened in the most personal of ways, their behaviour is likely to express the competence of necessity. Without sound strategic direction that competence may not translate into superior strategic performance, but in many wars, especially when the foe is believed to be ignorant or uncaring of Geneva and Hague niceties, soldiers have little prudent choice other than to fight hard. While the US government may have believed somewhat inchoately that its soldiers in Vietnam were 'protecting the process of modernization'[105] — or some similarly hubristic pseudo-social scientific cliché—American soldiers, more prosaically, were trying to survive their one-year tour of duty 'in country' and return home, to the 'world' safely. Perspective commands attitude.

Strategy should give meaning to the tactical behaviour of the 'grunts' in the field for their country.[106] In *The Art of War* Sun Tzu warns: 'Warfare is the greatest affair of state, the basis of life and death, the Way (Tao) to survival or extinction. It must be thoroughly pondered and analyzed.'[107] Also he notes: 'Anger can revert to happiness, annoyance can revert to joy, but a vanquished state cannot be revived, the dead cannot be brought back to life.'[108] Strategy bears directly upon the first duty of the polity: the duty to provide security. Security, like strategy, has different dimensions—military, political, economic, societal, and environmental[109]—but the military is the fundamental enabler for the others. If a society is not physically secure against military depredation, the other kinds of security are likely to prove short-lived.

Strategy has both extrinsic and intrinsic value. The extrinsic merit in strategy lies in its utility for keeping the military assets (*inter alia*) of a particular security

---

[105] On which worthy aspiration see Samuel P. Huntington, *Political Order in Changing Societies* (New Haven, Conn., 1968).

[106] Charles R. Anderson, *The Grunts* (San Rafael, Calif., 1976), is classic, as of course is S. L. A. Marshall, *Men Against Fire: The Problem of Battle Command in Future War* (New York, 1967); Stanley Whitehouse and George B. Bennett, *Fear Is the Foe: A Footslogger from Normandy to the Rhine* (London, 1995); Gerald F. Linderman, *The World Within War: America's Combat Experience in World War II* (New York, 1997); Samuel Hynes, *The Soldier's Tale: Bearing Witness to Modern War* (New York, 1997).

[107] Sun Tzu, *Art of War*, 167.

[108] Ibid. 228.

[109] Barry Buzan, *People, States and Fear: An Agenda for International Security Studies in the Post-Cold War Era*, 2nd edn. (Boulder, Colo., 1991), 19; Barry Buzan, Ole Waever, and Jaap de Wilde, *Security: A New Framework for Analysis* (Boulder, Colo., 1998); and for a characteristically robust and unflattering review of modern security studies as strategic studies, see Gwyn Prins, 'The Four-Stroke Cycle in Security Studies', *International Affairs*, 74 (1998), 781–808.

community, or coalition of communities, roughly in balance with the demands and opportunities that flow as stimuli from the outside world. The means and ends that grand and military strategy balance and direct are means and ends connected by the threat or use of the instrument of force. The intrinsic merit in strategy resides in its role as conductor of the orchestra of military and other assets so that they can be applied economically to serve political objectives. Strategy transforms tactical performance into strategic effect for strategic performance in the service of policy.

Although the explicit adoption of a strategy, in the sense of a plan, is an optional extra for a country, net (positive or negative) strategic performance is not such an extra. Tactical activity influences the course and outcome of war, whether or not that activity is subject to guidance from higher command that merits the description 'strategic'. States may blunder to victory as a result of the piling up of tactical success after tactical success by their armed forces. There might be no one functioning as a strategist who asks, 'Which engagements should we wage in order to win the war as a whole?' Instead, after the fashion of General Ulysses S. Grant in 1864–5, strategy can amount to little more than resolute application of the principle that hard fighting by the bigger battalions should eventually lead to victory.[110] Even attrition is strategy of a sort, albeit a grim sort; certainly it generates strategic effect, if bloodily and cumulatively.

Field Marshal Helmuth Graf von Moltke (the Elder), the victor of Sedan in the Franco-Prussian War, was in no doubt both that '[t]he demands of strategy grow silent in the face of a tactical victory and adapt themselves to the newly created situation' and that '[s]trategy is a system of expedients'.[111] Epitaph material indeed for German strategic performance in the twentieth century. Germany's *de facto* ruler in the last two years of World War I, General Erich Ludendorff, was a pragmatist very much in the Moltkeian tradition, albeit with a less happy outcome. When asked about the operational objective of his 1918 spring offensive, the warlord commented, 'I object to the word "operation". We will punch a hole in [their line]. For the rest, we shall see.'[112] Although admirably flexible, such an approach translates in practice into pure expediency, tactical pragmatism innocent of strategic command.

One can choose to devote more or less time to strategic calculation and speculation. One cannot choose to evade the strategic effect of tactics and operations, no matter how ill directed those activities may be.

---

[110] Ulysses S. Grant, *Personal Memoirs* (2 vols., New York, 1994); Russell F. Weigley, *The American Way of War: A History of United States Military Strategy and Policy* (New York, 1973), ch. 7; Herman Hattaway and Archer Jones, *How the North Won: A Military History of the Civil War* (Urbana, Ill., 1983).

[111] Daniel J. Hughes (ed.), *Moltke On the Art of War: Selected Writings*, trans. Hughes and Harry Bell (Novato, Calif., 1993), 47.

[112] Quoted in Murray and Grimsley, 'Introduction: On Strategy', 3.

Chapter 2

STRATEGY, POLITICS, ETHICS

Although this chapter is fundamental, its content is neither basic nor familiar. Because everyone agrees that military power is instrumental for, and therefore subordinate to, politics, and also that ethics should be important to statecraft and strategy, the subjects of this discussion ought to be already well mapped. In practice, nothing could be further from the truth. The vocation of a strategist is not well appreciated; the relationship between politics and war is not clearly delineated. Furthermore, the role of ethics in the bridge of strategy between politics and war, though much discussed, is rarely considered from a strategically prudential standpoint.

The strategic history of the twentieth century illustrates the master theme of this book all too clearly. Politically and ethically viewed, strategy and war do not alter significantly from period to period. This chapter probes the qualities desirable in a strategist, and finds them to be broad rather than narrow. The discussion pursues a thread of modern criticism of Clausewitz and explores the possibility that politics, or policy, in Clausewitz's sense, has had a historically limited writ—perhaps from 1648 to 1945 (or 1989)—only to find the suggestion without merit.[1] Policy and strategy are judged here to be eternal phenomena, albeit with some sharply different characteristics on both sides of the means–ends equation over the centuries.

Even though the Clausewitzian approach to war, strategy, and politics is judged sound, this analysis is not content with the view that 'war is simply a continuation of political intercourse, with the addition of other means'.[2] The undoubted truth in that Clausewitzian dictum today is all but overwhelmed by the need to record caveats. No matter how neatly Clausewitz appears to dispatch the potential difficulties in policy–war relations, modern history alerts us to the problems that arise over policy guidance for strategy. Recognition of that inescapable fact leads the discussion into the troubled waters of the relations between politics and war, or between policy and policy instrument. Again the point is developed that one reason why strategy is so difficult to do well is because it requires expert two-way translation between the realms and currencies of the politician and the warrior.

The chapter moves from a focus upon politics and strategy to consider how, or

---

[1] Martin van Creveld, 'What Is Wrong with Clausewitz?', in Gert de Nooy (ed.), *The Clausewitzian Dictum and the Future of Western Military Strategy* (The Hague, 1997), 7–23, is an impressive, if ultimately unpersuasive, critique.

[2] Carl von Clausewitz, *On War*, trans. Michael Howard and Peter Paret (Princeton, NJ, 1976), 605.

indeed if, ethics affect strategic behaviour. The argument suggests that, for all the theoretical complexity of ethical considerations, in practice modern strategy has scarcely been troubled by matters of conscience. Also, the text notices that, far from recording moral improvement in man's behaviour towards man, the strategic history of the twentieth century has shown, if anything, a 'return to barbarism'. I note that crimes against humanity—judged so both legally and morally—have increased approximately, though of course only incidentally, in parallel with the burgeoning of the 'war convention' that should constrain human beastliness. Ethical influences upon behaviour are internalized and learnt socially as a part of political and strategic culture. Futhermore, national culture tends over-whelmingly to prove superior in leverage to the writ of potentially contrasting application of ethical principles. Security communities persuade themselves with scant difficulty that what they believe they need to do is always right enough.

With respect to the broad questions that guide this entire enquiry, Chapter 2 provides answers on the relationship between theory and practice that are not encouraging for those who expect progress in the human condition. Ethical ideas are regularly drilled into line with what are believed to be the prudent needs of states. The moral of this chapter, perhaps, is that we learn from history both that we cannot learn from history and that human beings continue to be literally capable of anything. The sadness of strategic history that sparks sentimental popular songs with rhetorical lines such as 'when will they ever learn?' promotes the hard-nosed question, 'learn what?' The horror of war has been known to mankind for ever. If full recognition of that horror were all that we humans had to learn, then the social institution of war might have been long banished. Unfortunately, things are not quite that elementally simple.

STRATEGISTS

With characteristic wit and literary felicity, Fred Charles Iklé observes that 'strategy is not a vocation for stunted minds'.[3] That wise judgement merits expansion with the complementary thought that strategy should not be a vocation for stunted consciences. He proceeds to advise:

To do good work on national strategy almost demands a rotund intellect, a well-rounded personality. He whose vocation it is to work on these issues of war and peace cannot suffer from intellectual poverty. His soul must be in harmony with this world of ours. He must not only appreciate different cultures and good art, but also find nourishment in things that are beautiful and be endowed with a sense of humor. He might have, perhaps, an eye for architecture or painting, an ear for the best music; he must have a broad understanding of

[3] Fred Charles Iklé, 'The Role of Character and Intellect in Strategy', in Andrew W. Marshall, J. J. Martin, and Henry S. Rowen (eds.), *On Not Confusing Ourselves: Essays on National Security Strategy in Honor of Albert and Roberta Wohlstetter* (Boulder, Colo., 1991), 315.

philosophy, literature, and, of course, history. And—why not?—let me have men about me that are sophisticated epicures.[4]

Iklé is writing in praise of the co-doyen of modern American strategic studies, Albert Wohlstetter (his adversary-partner and co-doyen was Bernard Brodie). Whether or not Wohlstetter fitted Iklé's mould of Renaissance Person with strategic interests, the mould errs on the side of accuracy in requiring a whole, balanced human being as an exemplary strategist, rather than a narrowly military professional or a 'cybernerd' whose strategic vision is blinded by the glow of a computer monitor's screen. General Alfred Graf von Schlieffen, for example, was about as far removed from Iklé's idea of the 'rotund intellect' as one could imagine.[5] Carl von Clausewitz, in sharp contrast, was a person with inclinations, interests, and accomplishments that at least approached the ideal specified by Iklé.[6] The good strategist requires a breadth of mind that does not compromise depth on those subjects that demand no less than expert mastery if they are to be treated competently.

Who is a strategist? In theory, at least, each polity or coalition can have only one strategist. If strategy is, as Clausewitz insists, 'the use of engagements for the object of the war',[7] each belligerent can afford only one person, institution, or process, acting as strategy-maker. Strategy abhors a vacuum: if the strategic function is lacking, strategic effect will be generated by the casual cumulation of tactical and operational outcomes. Germany in World War I is the classic example in the twentieth century of an appalling lack of purposive strategic grip upon a conflict. US performance in Vietnam from 1965 to 1973 appears a close rival for poor strategic direction.[8]

German military—one should not dignify it with the description 'strategic'—planning in the quarter-century preceding *der Tag* on 1 August 1914, and performance in the world war itself instructs by negative example on the nature of a truly strategic outlook.[9] The Germans were without equal in the grim trade of fighting, but they were fatally weak in the waging of war. The reason is not hard to find, at least for the Wilhelmine period. Germany's limited succession of 'strategists' was allowed by German statecraft to approach its task as a mindlessly literal applica-

[4] Fred Charles Iklé, 'The Role of Character and Intellect in Strategy', in Andrew W. Marshall, J. J. Martin, and Henry S. Rowen (eds.), *On Not Confusing Ourselves: Essays on National Security Strategy in Honor of Albert and Roberta Wohlstetter* (Boulder, Colo., 1991), 315.

[5] Alfred Graf von Schlieffen has been described by Gordon A. Craig as a 'pure technician': *Germany, 1866–1945* (New York, 1978), 316. See Arden Bucholz, *Moltke, Schlieffen, and Prussian War Planning* (New York, 1991), ch. 3.

[6] Peter Paret, *Clausewitz and the State* (New York, 1976).

[7] Clausewitz, *On War*, 128.

[8] Bruce Palmer, Jr., *The 25-Year War: America's Military Role in Vietnam* (Lexington, Ky., 1984), and John Prados, *The Hidden History of the Vietnam War* (Chicago, 1995), are particularly thought-provoking.

[9] Bucholz, *Moltke, Schlieffen*; Holger H. Herwig, *The First World War: Germany and Austria-Hungary, 1914–18* (London, 1997).

tion of the Clausewitzian definition of strategy. Clausewitz's claim that strategy is 'the use of engagements for the object of the war' lends itself to encouragement of an unhealthy fixation upon the battlefield. Hew Strachan speaks convincingly for recent scholarship:

Admirers of German military prowess have to confront the conundrum that in the First World War, as in the Second, Germany lost. It did so because its definitions of strategy were too restricted for the scale of war that confronted it. The army made operational solutions do duty for problems that were as much economic as political.[10]

Much of the structure of the problem is explained by the familiar aphorism, 'where you stand depends on where you sit'. If a theatre military commander is allowed by lack of superior direction or pressing advice to control the country's war effort, he will deliver operational-level military solutions to the problems of the day. It is all too appropriate that Schlieffen should design his campaign plan against France upon the hope that tactical and operational success *somehow* would translate as a strategic victory.[11]

The principal German problem in both world wars was that the country lacked a competent strategy-making, and strategy-reviewing, body. In World War I, and in the immediate prewar decades, Germany did not have an effective institution located between the Kaiser as head of state (and nominally commander-in-chief) and the Chief of the General Staff to oversee strategy (there was a war minister, but his influence was unremarkable). If the Kaiser of the day is not a person with a broad grasp of statecraft, together with a mastery of the strengths and limitations of his military and naval instruments, or if he is unwilling to seek expert advice, then subsequent policymaking is likely to be narrowly conceived. The problem was bad enough at the turn of the century when there was perilously little to save Germany and Europe from the consequences of the relationship between Kaiser Wilhelm II and Schlieffen as Chief of the General Staff, but that problem was to grow still worse.

If it was difficult for strategic considerations to make other than a guest appearance in German statecraft early in the century, consider the impediments to superior strategic performance in Nazi Germany. The author of the vision of the Thousand-Year Reich was nothing if not long-term in his approach to statecraft. Moreover, unlike Kaiser Wilhelm, Adolf Hitler functioned as grand and military strategist. The problem was that the Führer was not competent as a strategist and he lacked that 'rotund intellect' to which Iklé refers. Above all else, after 1940

[10] Hew Strachan, 'Germany in the First World War: The Problem of Strategy', *German History*, 12 (1994), 249.

[11] Bucholz, *Moltke, Schlieffen*, 156–7; id., *Hans Delbrück and the German Establishment* (Iowa City, 1985), 63–4 and Gerhard Ritter, *The Schlieffen Plan: Critique of a Myth* (London, 1958), present the orthodox view of the so-called 'Schlieffen Plan'. Recently revealed archival sources show clearly that the Schlieffen Plan believed in by scholars for eighty years never existed. See Terence Zuber, 'The Schlieffen Plan Reconsidered', *War in History*, 6 (1999), 262–305. Every book about 1914 will have to be rewritten!

Hitler lacked 'what the French call *le sens du praticable*, and we call common sense, knowledge of what is and what is not possible'.[12]

A person could easily lose his grip on strategic reality when in little more than a decade, apparently by an effort of will, he had transformed himself from the status of a marginal figure in German politics to being the ruler of most of Europe. On the evidence of 1933–40, Hitler believed that his will could dictate the course of history.[13] The malign effect of the belief that one is blessed by the gods (or by history, or whatever) has by no means been confined recently to the person of Adolf Hitler. US policy and military endeavour—one hesitates to say 'strategy'—in Vietnam in the mid-1960s, as with German policy in 1941–3, suffered fatally from the malady known as 'victory disease'. In strategy nothing fails like success, not only because enemies adapt to your methods,[14] but also because you become unduly persuaded of your genius or of the favour of the gods.

A strategist worthy of the name is a person who sees, even though he or she cannot possibly be expert in, all dimensions of the 'big picture' of the evolving conditions of war. Defence preparation and the conduct of war involve an array of resources, even though those resources are unlikely to be committed totally. Strategic expertise has to imply educated familiarity with each of the dimensions of war. Prominent among the several reasons why strategy is so difficult is the sheer diversity of subjects that the strategist must understand. More challenging still is understanding the complexity of the relationships among the dimensions. The strategist does not have to be an engineer, logistician, sociologist, moral philosopher, politician, or outstanding combat commander. But he does need to understand enough about each of those areas of specialization, and especially about their interrelationships, to be able to use, or advise on the use of, force as an instrument of policy. Quality of strategic performance must ever be at risk if, for example, the strategist is ignorant of logistical constraints, fails to provide field commanders capable of leading troops, or neglects to consider how apparent ethical weakness with regard either to *jus ad bellum* or to *jus in bello* reduces political support at home for a war, or morale among the soldiers themselves.

The strategist is not concerned *per se* with the military effectiveness of landpower, seapower, airpower, spacepower, or cyberpower. Rather, the strategist must orchestrate the threat and use of armed forces, in all geographical environments, across all dimensions, and in all character of conflicts. The job description for the strategist is exceedingly demanding. Even when national war colleges attempt to teach grand strategy, they are constrained by the fact that strategy is an art. By analogy, art schools teach technical competence, but they cannot teach

---

[12] Archibald Wavell, *Generals and Generalship* (New York, 1943), 10.

[13] Joachim C. Fest, *Hitler* (New York, 1975); Gerhard L. Weinberg, *Germany, Hitler, and World War II* (Cambridge, 1995); Sebastian Haffner, *The Meaning of Hitler* (London, 1997); John Lukacs, *The Hitler of History* (New York, 1998).

[14] Edward N. Luttwak, *Strategy: The Logic of War and Peace* (Cambridge, Mass., 1987).

competent artists how to be great. Fortunately, countries have few employment opportunities for strategists, so the acute shortage in supply of strategic genius is typically less than fatal for national security performance. No less fortunately, competence in strategy is all that a country or coalition needs to achieve. After all, it is unlikely, though not impossible, that the enemy of the day will enjoy the services of an inspired strategist. Even a poor strategist may perform well enough, if the enemy is worse. Because the practical realm of strategy is a relational one, strictly the need is to do better than the foe. There is no requirement to perform elegantly.

It is precisely because a Marlborough or George Washington cannot be summoned reliably in time of dire national need, that genius is sought in the system of strategy-making and strategic execution rather than in the person of an outstanding strategist. War cabinets, general staffs, and chiefs of staff committees were invented to function as a surrogate for individual strategic genius. If the chief executive in an authoritarian polity believes himself to be a strategist of genius, then the institutional buffers of a general staff and other advisory bodies will be bypassed or, more likely, employed as passive administrative agents of the executive will.[15] Even genuine genius has its limitations: health, time, and focus, for example. By almost any method of assay, Napoleon Bonaparte ranks prominently among the most competent leaders in all of history.[16] The fact remains that Napoleon's long and bloody bid for dynastic empire failed catastrophically. As with assessment of the German bids for greater empire in this century, one is unsure whether to be amazed by the scope of the temporary success achieved or impressed by the fact of ultimate failure. A competent strategist, such as Frederick the Great of Prussia, balances means with ends and understands that lasting success requires the definition of an international order which erstwhile foes find

[15] Walter Goerlitz, *History of the German General Staff, 1657–1945* (New York, 1953), chs. 12–16; Walter Warlimont, *Inside Hitler's Headquarters, 1939–45*, repr. of 1962 edn. (Novato, Calif., n.d.); Charles Burdick and Hans-Adolf Jacobsen (eds.), *The Halder War Diary, 1939–1942*, abridged version of 1962–4 edn. (Novato, Calif., 1988). Admittedly, the story of 'Hitler and his generals' became an extreme case of absence of genuine dialogue after the near-catastrophe in Russia in December 1941 (see Horst Boog et al., *Germany and the Second World War, iv: The Attack on the Soviet Union* (Oxford, 1998), esp. 707–25). Even in the different context of a popular democracy with a mature policy- and strategy-making organization, a strong enough political will at the top shapes military advice and strategic decisions, regardless of professional military misgivings. Anglo-American history shows that over Suez in 1956, Vietnam in 1964–5, the Falklands in 1982, and Iraq in 1990–1, and Kosovo in 1999, the military instrument in a democracy did what it was told to do by determined political leaders, notwithstanding military reservations. For the Vietnam case, for example, see Robert Buzzanco, *Masters of War: Military Dissent and Politics in the Vietnam Era* (Cambridge, 1996). For a classic case of the reverse phenomenon, of politicans lacking the moral courage to overrule overconfident generals, see David R. Woodward, *Lloyd George and the Generals* (Newark, Del., 1983); Robin Prior and Trevor Wilson, *Passchendaele: The Untold Story* (New Haven, Conn., 1996). In 1917 Prime Minister Lloyd George failed Britain and the British Army by declining repeatedly to act on his conviction that Sir Douglas Haig's protracted offensive at Passchendaele was hurting the Allies more than it was damaging the Germans. Lloyd George knew what he should do, but he decided not to do it for fear of adverse domestic political consequences.

[16] Martin van Creveld, *Command in War* (Cambridge, Mass., 1985), 64.

tolerable. An incompetent strategist, such as Napoleon Bonaparte, fails to define and settle for such an order. Military victories, no matter how dazzling, tend to promote further cycles of war if they are not allowed to promote political outcomes acceptable to most interested polities.[17]

I use the label 'strategist' flexibly. Strictly speaking, the word should be reserved to describe a person who makes and 'executes' strategy. By 'executes' I mean the person or persons who direct either all the assets of a polity (grand strategy) or all the military assets of a polity (military strategy). In a Western state, the strategist function at its lesser military, rather than grand strategic, level is exercised by some combination of the following: a minister of defence; a chairman of a chiefs of staff committee; a chiefs of staff committee functioning collectively; and, an inner war cabinet or national security council chaired by the head of government (and possibly by the head of state).

It is expedient also from time to time to refer to strategists in the same sense in which it is commonplace to refer, say, to economists. Relatively few scholars of economics actually 'do' the economics at which they profess to be expert; instead, they theorize and advise. Economics and strategy share the property of being practical disciplines.[18] It can be ponderous to write constantly of strategic theorists rather than strategists. A strategist is both a person who 'does' strategy and a person who advises on the 'doing'. The former should not be confused with the sense in which strategy is 'done' tactically by tacticians. Strictly speaking, strategists do not 'do' any action; it is the military instrument that 'does' strategy at the operational and tactical levels of war.

In the closing decades of the twentieth century, ever fewer theorists of strategy had 'done' strategy themselves in any sense other than strictly with brain, pen, and word-processor. This professional and sociological trend has had implications for problems in communication between the realms of theory and practice. Readers might care to consider the implications of J. F. Lazenby's concluding paragraph in his valuable study of Hannibal.

But, in the end, it is, perhaps, almost an impertinence for an armchair historian who has never experienced a battle, and never commanded anything more than a patrol of Scouts, to assess one of the great commanders of history, and Hannibal himself is said to have had little patience with amateur critics. According to Cicero (de Oratore, 2.75), the great general, when in exile in Ephesus, was once invited to attend a lecture by one Phormio, and after being treated to a lengthy discourse on the commander's art, was asked by his friends what he thought of it. 'I have seen many old drivellers', he replied, 'on more than one occasion, but I have seen no one who drivelled more than Phormio'. I cannot help but wonder what he would have thought of this book.[19]

---

[17] These and related points are made superbly in Brian Bond, *The Pursuit of Victory: From Napoleon to Saddam Hussein* (Oxford, 1996).

[18] Bernard Brodie, 'Strategy as a Science', *World Politics*, 1 (1949), 476–88.

[19] J. F. Lazenby, *Hannibal's War: A Military History of the Second Punic War* (Warminster, 1978), 257.

POLITICS AND WAR

It is a cliché to assert that history is not a morality tale; but the cliché is partly wrong. The course and outcome of historical processes does provide shifting definition of a just international order—witness the change of opinion in this century over the legitimacy and justice of colonial rule by 'civilized' nations as imperial powers.[20] History's winners, which means preeminently history's strategic winners, are the ones who decide what is just and what is not. Justice is always an important concept; its exact meaning, however, is ever in contention on the playing-field of politics.

As Clausewitz appreciated so clearly, politics is what war is all about. Some recent commentators evince difficulty understanding what is political,[21] but such difficulty yields rapidly to common sense. Nonetheless, the concept of politics lends itself to sundry interpretations. Different cultures invest the idea of politics with distinctive emphases. In Greek, for example, the idea is dignified by its close linguistic association with the *polis*, or (city-)state. In English, 'politics' carries less elevated association and often refers to the process of struggle over the right, or authority, to govern the 'body politic', and hence decide on the distribution of civic burdens and rewards ('who gets what, when, and how').[22]

Politics produces policy which may require the services of strategy. Force distinguishes the realm of strategy, so organized violence is one key to a definition of war. The other, more contentious key to a satisfactory definition of war is the requirement that the violence be organized for political purposes.[23] Given that the dimensions of war and strategy look remarkably stable throughout history, it is wise to be relaxed about, and empathetic to, the exact meaning of 'political' over the centuries.

Politics, implying the processes that yield policy, and policy itself is the dominant reason for the reality of our subject. Modern strategy ultimately derives its significance from the realm of politics. If this is not true, what else was the strategic history of the twentieth century about? Although war and its strategic conduct is an economic activity, engages our moral judgement, and consists at its brutal core of combat of various kinds, war is not 'about' economics, morality, or fighting. Instead, it is about politics. Some modern critics of this notably Clausewitzian point question the historical authority of the claims for periods outside the bounds of the Westphalian western world of 1648 to 1945, or perhaps 1989. Some of the criticism of Clausewitz's famous dictum about the instrumental relationship of war with political intercourse is rooted in a fundamental misreading of *On War*, especially with regard to Clausewitz's conception of the 'remarkable

---

[20] Gerrit W. Gong, *The Standard of 'Civilization' in International Society* (Oxford, 1984).
[21] John Keegan, *A History of Warfare* (London, 1993).
[22] Harold D. Lasswell, *Politics: Who Gets What, When, How* (New York, 1950).
[23] Hedley Bull, *The Anarchical Society: A Study of Order in World Politics* (New York, 1977), 184.

trinity' of violence, chance, and reason.[24] When simplified to correspond neatly with people, army, and government, Clausewitz's trinity can appear to be a framework with only limited historical writ.[25]

Warfare in medieval Europe frequently appeared to be about rights rather than what the modern world understands by state policy, but that apparent fact does not render such warfare any the less political, properly translated by an historic-ally empathetic common sense. Similarly, after the Cold War a notable fraction of conflict is prosecuted by agents other than formally constituted governments. The Palestinian conduct of its *intifada*, or the terrorist campaigns of the Irish Repub-lican Army (IRA)–Sinn Fein, are entirely as political as was US or Soviet conduct of the Cold War. War has been waged, strategy has been devised and implemented, and tactics have been 'done', for a host of diverse motives over the centuries. The explicit or implicit dialogue between war (and strategy) and 'politics' is permanent.

PERILOUS ESSENTIALISM

Three problems shape the terms of the war–politics relationship. First, although there is truth in Clausewitz's assertion that 'war is simply a continuation of political intercourse, with the addition of other means', the essentialism in the assertion obscures necessary qualifications. Security communities sometimes do resort to the organized violence that we define as war when other avenues appear less promising. Although some individuals enjoy fighting, some institu-tions anticipate benefit from hostilities, and the community as a whole finds the condition of war in some ways pleasurably thrilling, the decision to fight will be political, intended by its immediate authors to yield net advantage to the polity. Clausewitz is right to identify war as a condition chosen for political reasons to advance political ends. Whether or not some individuals, groups, and institutions anticipate benefit of a non-political kind from a condition of belli-gerency may be interesting, but is not relevant to the merit in Clausewitz's argument.

Beyond the truth that war is waged, and strategy is effected, for political ends, lies the scarcely less basic truth that war, and hence much of the realm within which strategy seeks to be authoritative, is preeminently the zone of passion and of chance.[26] War, therefore, is an instrument of policy, but it is an instrument ever liable both to capture by feeling and to diversion and negation by what would

---

[24] Martin van Creveld, *The Transformation of War* (New York, 1991); id., *Nuclear Proliferation and the Future of Conflict* (New York, 1993), chs. 1–3; id., 'What Is Wrong with Clausewitz?'; Keegan, *History of Warfare*; id., *War and Our World* (London, 1998), ch. 3. Although van Creveld and Keegan both criticize Clausewitz, the former, unlike the latter, regards the Prussian 'apart perhaps from Sun Tzu, [as] by far the greatest writer on war of all times' ('What is wrong with Clausewitz?', 7).

[25] Clausewitz, *On War*, 89; Edward J. Villacres and Christopher Bassford, 'Reclaiming the Clausewitz-ian Trinity', *Parameters*, 25 (1995), 9–19.

[26] Clausewitz, *On War*, 85, 101.

amount to bad luck. Clausewitz equated war with a game of cards.[27] The challenge is to see the world of war and strategy in the round, as did Clausewitz. It is necessary to recognize the politically instrumental nature of war, while also acknowledging the existence and influence of the reasons why even a deliberate decision to fight is akin to a roll of the dice.

POLITICAL OBJECTIVES CAN BE ELUSIVE

Second, although there are many kinds of grit that create friction in the relationship between politics and strategy, by far the most pernicious is an absence of appropriate political objectives. The defence planner, the strategist, and the military field commander are disarmed by the absence of clear political guidance. This second basic problem in the nexus between politics and war and strategy appears historically in four guises.

1. Defence planners and military commanders can be charged to accomplish objectives beyond the military means available. Notwithstanding the temporal geostrategic sequencing intended, Hitler's political ambitions encompassed what would amount to achievement of a global hegemony, and required the military ability to defeat all challenges to the establishment of such a hegemony.[28]

2. Political guidance to the military commander may direct him to be more restrained in what he chooses to accomplish by force of arms than the political aim really requires. The military operational goal should match the political goal. The Gulf War of 1991 stands as a classic example of what happens when ill-informed political guidance meets friction and the fog of war in a campaign that appears to be a stunning success.[29] In 1991 the coalition's military commander, General Norman Schwartzkopf, lacked a real grip on operational happenings and believed that his forces had inflicted a more conclusive defeat on the enemy than in fact was the case.

3. The political guidance that should inform and shape strategy may be missing in action. A general may be dispatched, as was Erwin Rommel in 1941, with only vague political guidance, though Hitler's limited and generally defensive intent was clear enough. Rommel's task was to help stabilize the Italian front in North Africa and prevent North Africa, and the Mediterranean more broadly, from becoming a dangerous distraction from the invasion of the Soviet Union that was scheduled for the early summer of 1941. In the best, or worst,

---

[27] Ibid. 86.

[28] Williamson Murray, *The Change in the European Balance of Power, 1938–1939: The Path to Ruin* (Princeton, NJ, 1984); Gerhard L. Weinberg, *A World at Arms: A Global History of World War II* (Cambridge, 1994).

[29] Lawrence Freedman and Efraim Karsh, *The Gulf Conflict, 1990–1991: Diplomacy and War in the New World Order* (Princeton, NJ, 1993); Jeffrey Record, *Hollow Victory: A Contrary View of the Gulf War* (Washington, DC, 1993); Michael R. Gordon and Bernard E. Trainor, *The Generals' War: The Inside Story of the Conflict in the Gulf* (Boston, 1995).

German tradition, Rommel created dazzling strategic possibilities out of tactical and operational success.[30]

4. The final problem in the politics–war nexus takes the form of objectives that cannot be operationalized in military terms. For example, US political goals in Vietnam could not be expressed plausibly in identifiable, achievable objectives for the armed forces.

It is easy to slip into counselling what amounts to strategic perfection. Because the art of strategy is so difficult, there is an abundance of explanation as to why politics and war often march out of step. Who knows for certain what an army can accomplish until it tries? Flexibility on the part of the policymaker need not be evidence of incomprehension, indecision, or cynical opportunism; it may simply indicate a willingness to adjust policy ambition to the demonstrated prowess of the nation's arms on the battlefield. The impediments to successful strategic performance are so substantial that one should be generous in the distribution of praise, sparing in the apportionment of blame, and empathetic in considering the problems of the strategist. The curse of hindsight for fair historical appraisal is under-recognized.

DIALOGUE IS DIFFICULT BETWEEN POLITICS AND WAR

The third general problem to beset the relationship between war and politics is the difficulty of establishing and sustaining a genuine dialogue between warriors and politicians. Unless a state approximates the condition of an army with a country, as was said of eighteenth-century Prussia, and of Wilhelmine Germany after the fall of General Erich Graf von Falkenhayn in August 1916, civil–military relations will prove a rich source of tension for strategy-making and strategy execution. Scholarly discussion of the value of dialogue between policymaker and military commander is apt to forget that ideal types can creep subversively into the analysis. Although there often is a problem of mutual ignorance in the politics–war nexus, that problem is by no means the only source of difficulty for civil–military relations.

Politicians and generals tend to lack understanding of, and empathy for, each other's roles. It is not so commonplace to notice that politicians and generals are often less than competent in their own sphere of responsibility, let alone in the sphere of the other. There will always be mediocre politicians and generals, and they will be promoted to a level of responsibility for which they are not competent. What often appears to be professional incompetence is really nothing more sinister than ignorance. In Europe in 1914, for example, neither the leading

---

[30] B. H. Liddell Hart (ed.), *The Rommel Papers* (London, 1953), pts. 1–3; David Fraser, *Knight's Cross: A Life of Field Marshal Erwin Rommel* (London, 1993), pt. 4; Gerhard Schreiber, Bernd Stegemann, and Detlef Vogel, *Germany and the Second World War, iii: The Mediterranean, South-East Europe, and North Africa, 1939–1941* (Oxford, 1995), pt. 5.

politicians nor the designated field commanders understood their own mission in a great war, let alone the mission of the other occupational group. Some individual wars can share characteristics, but more often than not the challenge in each conflict is sufficiently novel for both politician and general to have major difficulty adapting expertise to the case specifically at hand. Lord Kitchener, the principal arbiter of British strategy in 1914–15,[31] had seen a considerable amount of war. Unfortunately, perhaps, he had never seen a war such as that which erupted in August 1914.

Four reasons in particular stand out as major contributors to the friction that is wont to impair the fruitful dialogue between politics and war, policymakers and generals, that is so self-evidently desirable.

Culture Clash

The culture, ethos, and skills most typical respectively of politicians and generals work systemically to impair genuine communication between them. Character tends to fade into caricature all too easily. Words are the stock-in-trade of the politician. In addition, political leaders, especially war leaders, are likely to lean on the side of undeniable eloquence. There have been eloquent generals, but eloquence *per se* is not highly regarded in the military profession. Generals are liable to find their political masters to be glib windbags, able to argue persuasively for whatever is the latest strategic idea to come their way. Politicians are liable to find generals both inarticulate and hence presumably intellectually limited and therefore to be despised or patronized, as well as focused upon narrowly military matters. The historical exemplar of this phenomenon in the twentieth century was the appallingly poor relationship in 1917–18 between the British Prime Minister, David Lloyd George, and the Commander-in-Chief of the British Expeditionary Force, General Sir Douglas Haig.[32] Lloyd George was no William Pitt the Elder, and Douglas Haig was no Marlborough, but each was the best available from his particular realm. Viewed in long retrospect, the high quality of each is beyond reasonable doubt. No less obvious is the inevitability of what amounted to a cultural clash between an over-articulate Welsh politician and a tongue-tied Scottish soldier. Gratuitous misunderstanding and lack of mutual esteem was present in their relationship from the outset. To the one, the other appeared as a rigid and mindlessly unimaginative 'butcher'; while to the other the one was plainly a crafty politician with a silver tongue and no principles.

Reciprocal Ignorance

The next problem with constructive dialogue between politics and war is

---

[31] Paul Guinn, *British Strategy and Politics, 1914–1918* (Oxford, 1965), pt. 1; John Gooch, *The Plans of War: The General Staff and British Military Strategy, c.1900–1916* (London, 1974), ch. 10; David French, *British Strategy and War Aims, 1914–1916* (London, 1986).

[32] Woodward, *Lloyd George and the Generals*; David French, *The Strategy of the Lloyd George Coalition, 1916–1918* (Oxford, 1995).

reciprocal ignorance. Politicians are promoted to the stratosphere of senior policymaking, membership in war cabinets, and the like for many reasons, but demonstrable skill in strategy is unlikely to be prominent among them. Politicians may know too little, if not of war *per se*, at least of the probable character of war today, to know what to demand or expect of their generals. Similarly, professional soldiers may know, perhaps choose to know, so little about the world of politics that they genuinely do not comprehend the policymaker's world-view. Unfortunately, the problem in civil–military relations is not just mutual ignorance. The malign effect of that ignorance can be multiplied by an all-too-personal human dimension which adds unhealthily to the brew, when individual politicians and soldiers distrust, despise, and dislike people whom they do not understand. Scholarly strategic theorists and sociologists of civil–military relations cannot afford to forget that theirs is a practical subject wherein real people attempt to conduct the strategic dialogue between politics and war. In modern times, there are few politicians who understand what Clausewitz called the 'grammar' of war,[33] how war works as war, or even how war works at the preparatory stage of defence mobilization. Also, there are few generals who understand what Clausewitz called the policy 'logic' of war.

Distinctive Responsibilities

Distinctive responsibilities complicate the process of orchestrating the 'grammar' and 'logic' of war through constructive dialogue. Legends of callous, bloodthirsty generals confronting militarily unworldly, casualty-shy politicians who are always searching for the strategic 'free lunch' often are exactly that — legends. Nonetheless, the aphorism that 'where you stand depends on where you sit' contains more than a grain of truth. With the exception of execution of a nuclear war plan, the responsibility of a military commander will be more restricted than is that of the policymaker. The policymaker wages war, while the military commander fights battles or conducts campaigns; between those realms, though drawing from them both, lies the 'bridging' zone of strategy. Though eloquent on the subject of the political instrumentality of war, Clausewitz offers little to help educate the policymaker and military commander for their critical mutual dealings.

The politician is an expert generalist. His or her role in national security is to articulate a suitable vision of security, to select attainable policy goals in pursuit of that vision, and to act as competent broker among the interests that beg for preeminent consideration. The political war leader has to choose among competing military demands and apparent opportunities, including economically rival capabilities in the near term versus medium term. In addition, the politician may have to strike a balance between commitment to military and to civil purposes, and temporally between the needs of war today and the assets preserved to be

---

[33] Clausewitz, *On War*, 605.

productive in peace tomorrow.[34] The general who needs reinforcements and new equipment now, lest his army invite defeat through numerical and material weakness, is unlikely to empathize with the choices facing the policymaker who must decide among all theatres of operation, between civil and military demands, and between the needs of today and the probable needs of the future. The activity of the policymaker belongs in the realm of statecraft.

If it is essential for the statesman to act as broker for all interests, and if the military commander is to rely upon the world of statecraft to fulfil that function, it follows that the military profession has to be true to its expertise. The military commander, or perhaps senior military adviser to the government, has responsibility both upwards and downwards. He is responsible to his polity for the military integrity and strategic effectiveness of the armed forces. He is responsible, also, to those armed forces for the military integrity of the missions they are assigned as an instrument of state policy. Above all else, the professional military person must be viewed by politicians and military subordinates as a repository of sound military advice. Politicians and the country as a whole have a right to expect senior military professionals to speak military, and hence probably strategic, truth to political power. If politicians demand the militarily impossible, then the military adviser or commander must call political fantasy what it is, in military terms, and—if necessary—resign. Similarly, the rank and file of the armed forces have every right to require of their military leaders that militarily futile operations should not be undertaken, at least not without some overwhelmingly powerful political reason. Occasionally, and for excellent military reasons, the tactical and operational levels of war are obliged to provide what amounts to suicidal rearguard actions. More controversial are military operations designed, if not to fail, at least to make the point that that kind of operation is unlikely to succeed (Dieppe, August 1942, springs to mind, as does the US attempt to rescue its hostages in Iran in April 1980).[35] Statecraft and war have several levels: preeminently the political, strategic, operational, and tactical. It can be difficult to explain to people who might die at the tactical level of war that the tactical failure of their mission can translate as operational, strategic, and political success. Infrequently, strategists need to demonstrate that something is impracticable.

Hindsight is a leading difficulty with this topic of distinctive civil and military responsibilities. There was a lack of genuine dialogue between the leadership of the British army and the government throughout World War I, but neither side was trying to mislead the other. Both military people and civilians were striving as best they knew how to address modern mass warfare. The difficulties in transforming a 'break-in' into a 'breakthrough' into a 'breakout' on the Western Front

---

[34] Paul Kennedy, *The Rise and Fall of the Great Powers: Economic Change and Military Conflict from 1500 to 2000* (New York, 1987).

[35] Colin S. Gray, *Explorations in Strategy* (Westport, Conn., 1996), 177.

by and large were not withheld from politicians; rather, the facts about these difficulties emerged only slowly from a long process of bloody experimentation.[36] Similarly, the truth about the military-operational perils of nuclear alerts in the Cold War was not withheld from US or Soviet civilian policymakers, who blithely played at crisis management with the assumption that their military tools would not themselves inadvertently become catalysts of war.[37] That truth was that operational crisis stability was always less reliable than policymakers assumed. There is some evidence to suggest, for example, that in neither of the nuclear crises over Cuba in October 1962 and Israel in October 1973 did American policymakers worry as seriously as perhaps they should have done about the possibility that technical or operational instabilities might trigger a war that neither side intended.[38]

With hindsight, one can identify mismatches between military instruments and policy reach; in World War I and II on the Anglo-French, then on the German, side, in Korea for the United States in the autumn of 1950, and in Vietnam again for the United States in the 1960s. With hindsight it is obvious that military professionals on both sides from 1914 until mid-1918, in Germany in 1940–1, and in the United States in September–October 1950 and 1964–5, tended to an undue optimism. Today, many scholars believe that they know what British, French, German, Austro-Hungarian, and Russian generals should have said to the realm of high policy in 1914, what German generals should have said in 1940–1, and what American generals should have said in 1950, 1962, 1964–5, and 1973. But such scholarly judgements can be profoundly unhistorical. The real difficulty is that even the best professional military advice frequently will be wrong.

Although Clausewitz warns of the risks in war that should have a sobering effect upon a politician inclined to gamble upon a quick military solution to a political problem, he does not really alert the politician to the perils in military advice. Those perils take some of their fuel from the difficulty found by military experts in understanding their technically dynamic trade well enough. War is highly variable in at least two principal ways. On the one hand, the grammar of war changes with technology, *inter alia*. On the other hand, the grammar is always local and individual to the particular conflict at issue. With reference to the historical scope of this book, the wars of 1900–10, apart from the significant exception of

---

[36] Robin Prior and Trevor Wilson, *Command on the Western Front: The Military Career of Sir Henry Rawlinson, 1914–18* (Oxford, 1992); id., *Passchendaele: The Untold Story* (New Haven, Conn., 1996); Paddy Griffith (ed.), *British Fighting Methods in the Great War* (London, 1996), esp. chs. 1, 2, 7.

[37] Scott D. Sagan, 'Nuclear Alerts and Crisis Management', *International Security*, 9 (1985), 99–139; Bruce G. Blair, *Strategic Command and Control: Redefining the Nuclear Threat* (Washington, DC, 1985); Ashton B. Carter, John D. Steinbruner, and Charles A. Zraket (eds.), *Managing Nuclear Operations* (Washington, DC, 1987).

[38] Bruce G. Blair, *The Logic of Accidental Nuclear War* (Washington, DC, 1993); Richard Ned Lebow and Janice Gross Stein, *We All Lost the Cold War* (Princeton, NJ, 1994).

submarine mines,[39] were all geographically two-dimensional on the land and the surface of the sea. In contrast, such interstate war as occurred in the 1990s was geographically at least five-dimensional (land, sea, air, space, EMS-cyberspace).[40] Each conflict in the 1900s and 1990s was unique, but still it was shaped by the technological (*inter alia*) parameters of its period.

Strategy is Difficult

The final source of friction in the interface between politics and war is the inherent difficulty in relating military action and intended political consequences. I have been a civilian strategic theorist for thirty years; for nearly twenty of those I had regular dealings with (American) military professionals, and yet I remain genuinely undecided as to how best a polity can educate people in strategy. It is the beginning of wisdom to grasp that military action has political meaning only through its strategic effect. But between policymakers who must be competent domestic politicians and military commanders and advisers who must be successful soldiers, a systemic cultural inclination to miscommunicate is all but foreordained.

To the politician, the soldier is focused upon battlefield success as an end in itself. To the soldier, the politician is insensitive to the human cost of strategic advantage; a person who regards the warrior merely as an instrument of policy, as an agent of his or her will. Scarcely more conducive to constructive dialogue between politics and war is the historically deviant phenomenon of politicians so fearful of casualties that they demand bloodless victories. American generals have long favoured sending steel, rather than men, to perform military tasks.[41] It is not the case, however, that American generals from the Civil War years until the 1980s have been unusually careful with the lives of their men. Indeed, it was a frequent American complaint in World War II that British politicians and generals tended to be casualty-averse to the point of military ineffectiveness. In the 1940s, Americans attributed that particular British disease to the trauma of the Western Front in the Great War.[42] It is ironic that

---

[39] Newton A. McCully, *The McCully Report: The Russo-Japanese War, 1904–05*, repr. of 1906 report (Annapolis, Md., 1977), 248; Philip Towle, 'The Evaluation of the Experience of the Russo-Japanese War', in Bryan Ranft (ed.), *Technical Change and British Naval Policy, 1860–1939* (London, 1977), 65–79; Richard Connaughton, *The War of the Rising Sun and Tumbling Bear: A Military History of the Russo-Japanese War, 1904–5* (London, 1988).

[40] Bruce W. Watson (ed.), *Military Lessons of the Gulf War* (London, 1991); Jeffrey McCausland, *The Gulf Conflict: A Military Analysis*, Adelphi Paper 282 (London, Nov. 1993). Domestic rather than inter-state quarrels dominated the 1990s, as was noted suitably in Steven R. David, 'Internal War: Causes and Cures', *World Politics*, 49 (1997), 552–76.

[41] Russell F. Weigley, *The American Way of War: A History of United States Military Strategy and Policy* (New York, 1973); Reginald C. Stuart, *War and American Thought: From the Revolution to the Monroe Doctrine* (Kent, OH, 1982); Geoffrey Perrett, *A Country Made by War: From the Revolution to Vietnam—the Story of America's Rise to Power* (New York, 1989); Allan R. Millett and Peter Maslowski, *For the Common Defense: A Military History of the United States of America*, rev. edn. (New York, 1994).

[42] G. D. Sheffield, 'The Shadow of the Somme: The Influence of the First World War on British Soldiers' Perceptions and Behaviour in the Second World War', in Paul Addison and Angus Calder (eds.), *Time to Kill: The Soldier's Experience of War in the West, 1939–1945* (London, 1997), 29–39.

that British disease appeared in the United States in virulent form in the 1990s.[43]

The United States can employ information-led weaponry that increasingly consists of unmanned machines for terrestrial bombardment. Such 'post-heroic warfare' is occasionally feasible for some polities.[44] But, is 'post-heroic warfare' conducted so as to minimize friendly casualties a strategically effective form of war? Particularly in circumstances of highly asymmetric conflict, as with the United States in Vietnam, a failure by civilians to understand the requirements, including the human costs, of war leaves the military commander in a terrible dilemma. Few military professionals have built successful careers by resolutely saying 'no' to superiors. Furthermore, because in asymmetric conflict straight-forward military—as contrasted with political—defeat is not a plausible outcome, the consequences of military ineffectiveness are likely to be neither readily appar-ent nor even thoroughly intolerable. The US Army waged its preferred style of war in South Vietnam, albeit with ambitions constrained by policy, but could not deliver operational, let alone strategic, level success.[45]

It is appallingly difficult for politicians and warriors—the realms of policy and military command—to conduct a genuine dialogue so that the two stay in step. Politicians may ask too much, or too little, of their military instrument. That military instrument may be so professional in its determination to provide the military effectiveness that policy demands that its leaders resist what they judge to be political measures likely to impair that effectiveness. For example, if a German army general, a British admiral, or a US air force general believes that he holds in trust the military crown jewels of the country, he is not likely to be cooperative when politicians make demands which affront his responsibility to be ready to fight. In the cases just cited, there could be demands that mobilization should be directed against only Russia (rather than Russia and France) in 1914,[46] that major detachments should be effected from the Grand Fleet in 1914-15,[47] and that most of the Strategic Air Command (and submarine-based strategic missile force) should be withheld from an initial nuclear strike in the 1970s and 1980s.[48] Each of these demands appear to contradict the 'principles of war' that insist upon concentration of effort for true economy of force.[49]

[43] John Mueller, 'The Perfect Enemy: Assessing the Gulf War', *Security Studies*, 5 (1995), 77–117.

[44] Edward N. Luttwak, 'Toward Post-Heroic Warfare', *Foreign Affairs*, 74 (1995), 109–22; id., 'A Post-Heroic Military Policy', *Foreign Affairs*, 75 (1996), 33–44; id., 'From Vietnam to Desert Fox: Civil-Military Relations in Modern Democracies', *Survival*, 431 (1999), 99–112.

[45] Andrew F. Krepinevich, *The Army and Vietnam* (Baltimore, 1986).

[46] Herwig, *First World War*, 58.

[47] Winston S. Churchill, *The World Crisis* (2 vols., London, 1938), i. 371, 384.

[48] Lawrence Freedman, *The Evolution of Nuclear Strategy*, 2nd edn. (London, 1989), ch. 25.

[49] John I. Alger, *The Quest for Victory: The History of the Principles of War* (Westport, Conn., 1982); id., *Definitions and Doctrine of the Military Art: Past and Present* (Wayne, NJ, 1985), 8–11.

A Case in Point: Britain and the Continental Commitment, 1905–1915

The proposition that strategy is an art and not a science, a proposition that even Jomini formally endorsed,[50] pervades these pages. The dedicated pursuer of strategic wisdom is occasionally able to close with significant strategic argument. Readers can supply their own favourite examples, but the case of the British Empire from 1905 until late 1915 provides an unusually rich source of arguments, principles, dilemmas, and indeed everything that makes life interesting for the strategist. A discussion of this period illustrates the claim that it is difficult for the worlds of politics and war to establish and sustain the kind of constructive dialogue that Clausewitz all but takes for granted as a factor in success in war.

It is all very well to say that 'war is simply a continuation of political intercourse, with the addition of other means'. How does this aphorism, even definition, translate into actual strategic choices? For Britain in 1905, what kind of war, against whom, for which objectives, should be the focus of military planning by the new general staff? The dominant problem was how best to balance power in Europe. The authoritative principle was to join, or at least behave in support of, the second strongest state or coalition. Practical difficulties, however, then intruded.

As a consequence of the first Morocco crisis in 1905, British military planners, for the first time in several generations, discerned the strong possibility of a continental alliance. The terms of the strategic problem for London improved radically, from consideration of how Britain might unilaterally wage war against Germany to how Britain might wage war as an ally of France.[51] Political guidance to the British armed forces, save in the form of budgetary constraints and a persisting unwillingness to adopt continental style conscription, was less than useful. British policy, though periodically alarmed by the apparent strategic implications of German naval construction and generally determined to do what was needed to deny an emerging European hegemony to imperial Germany,[52] was less than firm on key matters. The British government repeatedly refused actual alliance with France, declined to make definitive and specific military promises of contingent continental intervention, and did not decide in advance just what would constitute a *casus belli*.

Thanks to the scholarship of such historians as Samuel R. Williamson, Jr. and John Gooch, the facts of British military planning and the dialogue between that planning and policy are now well established.[53] If, as I believe, Britain was wise to

[50] Antoine Henri de Jomini, *The Art of War*, repr. of 1862 edn. (London, 1992), 321–3.

[51] The most relevant archival documents are reproduced in Charles E. Callwell, *Military Operations and Maritime Preponderance: Their Relations and Interdependence*, ed. Colin S. Gray, repr. of 1905 edn. (Annapolis, Md., 1996), app. 1.

[52] Paul Kennedy, *The Rise of the Anglo-German Antagonism, 1860–1914* (London, 1980).

[53] Samuel R. Williamson, Jr., *The Politics of Grand Strategy: Britain and France Prepare for War, 1904–1914* (Cambridge, Mass., 1969); Gooch, *Plans of War*. In addition, see Neil W. Summerton, 'The Development of British Military Planning for a War Against Germany, 1904–1914' (Ph.D. thesis, London, 1970);

oppose the erratic German bid for continental hegemony in the early decades of the twentieth century,[54] did British statecraft and strategy perform as well as anyone empathetic to what was known at the time could expect?

In 1905 the British General Staff was asked to consider what the British field army (approximately 120,000 available men) might achieve in a war with Germany. General Staff memoranda dated 28 August and 3 October 1905 argued respectively for an amphibious diversion in the Baltic and for inserting what was to become the British Expeditionary Force (BEF) into the main theatre of operations. In the words of Colonel Charles E. Callwell of the General Staff:

An efficient army of 120,000 British Troops might just have the effect of preventing any important German successes on the Franco-German frontier, and of leading up to the situation that Germany, crushed at sea, also felt herself impotent on land. That would almost certainly bring about a speedy, and from the British and French point of view satisfactory, peace.[55]

Britain had to decide (i) whether and over what issue to fight, (ii) where to fight (in the Baltic, or from Antwerp, or from the Franco-Belgian, or even Franco-German, border), (iii) under whose control to fight (distinctively from the French, or independently though with the French, or actually under French command), and (iv) how hard to fight. Unlike the US challenge in Vietnam in 1964-5, Britain in 1914, and again in 1939-40, at least had a clear policy goal; in the vernacular, it was simply to 'stop Germany' and restore the *status quo ante*.

Whether or not the temporary victory achieved in autumn 1918 was worth its human and other costs to Britain is best viewed as an irrelevant issue. British leaders and society did what they had to do to stop Germany, and the bill was not calculable in advance. From the viewpoint of grand strategy, the British war effort was masterful indeed; readers who doubt that judgement are invited to compare the lists of allies and co-belligerents for the *Entente* with the list for the Central Powers. At the level of military strategy, courtesy both of its imprudently far-forward assembly area around the French frontier fortress of Mauberge and of the unexpected extent of the westward sweep of the Germans across the Meuse and Sambre rivers,[56] the BEF found itself in a blocking position astride the invasion

Michael Howard, *The Continental Commitment: The Dilemma of British Defence Policy in the Era of the Two World Wars* (London, 1972), chs. 1-2; C. J. Lowe and M. L. Dockrill, *The Mirage of Power: British Foreign Policy, 1903-22, iii: The Documents* (London, 1972); David French, *British Economic and Strategic Planning, 1905-1915* (London, 1982).

[54] For a contrasting view, see Niall Ferguson, 'The Kaiser's European Union: What if Britain Had "Stood Aside" in August 1914?', in Ferguson (ed.), *Virtual History: Alternatives and Counterfactuals* (London, 1997), 228-80; id., *The Pity of War* (London, 1998). Contrary to Ferguson, I believe Britain had no prudent choice other than to join the anti-German coalition in 1914. Had Britain stood aside, Germany would have defeated France and Russia. Britain then would have been deservedly friendless, facing a hegemonic Germany with an undamaged—indeed probably augmented—High Seas Fleet.

[55] Callwell, *Military Operations*, 454.

[56] Williamson, *Politics of Grand Strategy*, 122, 169-70, 176.

route of General Alexander von Kluck's First Army. Alone among the great powers, Britain's military plans in 1914 produced their long-advertised strategic effect; as forecast on 3 October 1905 by Callwell,[57] it is plausible to argue that the BEF from August to November 1914 made a decisive impact upon the course and outcome of a continental war. At the price of its own destruction in the First Battle of Ypres, the BEF of 1914 yielded a leverage in strategic effect out of all proportion to its modest size.

Given German dependency on the Swedish economy in a long war, it is possible that there may have been more to recommend Baltic schemes for British strategy early in the twentieth century than policymakers at the time, or most historians since, have allowed.[58] Furthermore, the long-term strategic cost of sacrificing a small professional army in the first campaign of the war was a heavy one.[59] Nonetheless, if British policy to prevent German hegemony was correct in the period 1905–18, given that nobody knew for certain about modern continental-scale warfare, how much better a performance could be asked of British statesmen and strategists? In World War II, the abrupt German demolition of the first British alliance system and continental commitment in 1939–40 indefinitely postponed renewal of that commitment, pending the commission by Germany of grand strategic errors. In World War I, notwithstanding the apparent strategic flexibility accorded by a workable maritime superiority, the vital role of the French alliance locked British military effort into Belgium and northern France, *faute de mieux*.

The chief problem with Clausewitz on the instrumentality of force is that his magisterial analysis and dicta inadvertently obscure the true difficulty of the subject. As the great man said, 'Everything in strategy is very simple, but that does not mean that everything is very easy.'[60] Even if one is clear enough about policy goals, or war aims, every war is distinctive in the detail of *all* its dimensions. Policy may be certain (e.g. in 1914 for Britain, to stop Germany, or in 1982, again for Britain, to retake the Falkland Islands), but the capabilities of one's armed forces in combat against an actual enemy must be less certain (e.g. in 1914, can the British army make a strategic difference in a continental war? Or, in 1982, can British forces retake the Falkland Islands at a cost that British society will deem bearable and proportionate to what is at stake?). The problem most essential to strategy as contrasted with the other levels of conflict is the sheer complexity of its domain. Having grasped the central Clausewitzian truth about war as an instrument of politics, one then has to consider how to make strategy work well enough in the face of probably inconstant politicians, variably competent armed forces,

[57] Callwell, *Military Operations*, 454.

[58] I am grateful to Dr Andrew Lambert of King's College, London, for his intriguing, and decidedly revisionist, thoughts on this subject.

[59] Anthony Farrar-Hockley, *Death of an Army* (London, 1967).

[60] Clausewitz, *On War*, 178.

unreliable allies, and an enemy who is planning to do his best to thwart our efforts at all levels.

THE FORCE OF ETHICS: OR, THE DOG THAT DOES NOT BARK

The claim, or hope, for *Gott mit uns* that long embellished the belt-buckle of the *Landser*, the German soldier, expressed a universal human psychological need. Soldiers and their strategic directors may not care much about doing good, but they are not comfortable with the idea that they are doing harm. Fortunately for the mental health of soldier and strategist, though unfortunately for the authority of moral analysis and discourse, the ethical dimension to war and strategy is as indeterminate as it is real; there is always scope for local interpretation. That is not to deny the burgeoning fact of what Michael Walzer has usefully called the 'war convention';[61] rather, in application important elements of that convention are subject to rival interpretations. In Walzer's words, the war convention comprises 'the set of articulated norms, customs, professional codes, legal precepts, religious and philosophical principles, and reciprocal arrangements that shape our judgments of military conduct'. The convention provides a rich argument for convenient deployment by those in need.

ETHICS ARE EASY, BUT NOT SIMPLE

Ethics have a practical character exactly the reverse of strategy. Whereas strategy, following Clausewitz, is simple but not easy, ethics are easy but not simple. Important though ethics are and should be as a guide to behaviour, on the historical evidence there is less to this topic than meets the eye. Ethics is a dimension of war and strategy wherein arguments that are massively dubious in theory nonetheless seem to work well enough in practice. Many war cabinet rooms, ships' bridges, aircraft cockpits, and soldiers' camp-fires ought to resonate with arguments about justice and war, ends and means, but they do not. Although Walzer informs us that '[n]uclear weapons explode the theory of just war',[62] to date that claim has failed to register to notable effect among the shapers and executive agents of nuclear war plans, world-wide.[63]

Ethics are important—at least, so almost everybody claims, and there are grounds for believing them. People care about right conduct. Ethics are fundamental in a sense in which politics are not. In principle, political action is subject

[61] Michael Walzer, *Just and Unjust Wars: A Moral Argument with Historical Illustrations* (New York, 1977), 44.
[62] Ibid. 282.
[63] The pertinent issues are aired in Russell Hardin et al. (eds.), *Nuclear Deterrence: Ethics and Strategy* (Chicago, 1985); Joseph S. Nye, Jr., *Nuclear Ethics* (New York, 1986); Henry Shue (ed.), *Nuclear Deterrence and Moral Restraint: Critical Choices for American Strategy* (Cambridge, 1989).

to ethical assay, whereas ethically driven action should not be subject to authoritative political judgement. In the practical world of strategic effect, however, a consequentialist logic rules. The justice of behaviour is weighed in the light of its intended, anticipated, and actual, effect. Form follows function. The 'war convention' that is our living and dynamic heritage does not operate as a distinctive source of difficulty for strategy, at least not in the connection between politics and war.

Even in the world of strategy, ethical concerns are so internalized by individuals and social organizations that explicit treatment of topics about justice are exceedingly rare. Ethics, as a distinctive source of constraint or encouragement bearing upon strategic behaviour, remain of trivial significance. This is to claim neither that ethical beliefs have been unimportant nor that modern strategic history lacks an ethical dimension. The point is that, although a library of philosophical and psychological speculation has been written about ethics and modern war, and although there is now a legal library on the subject of war crimes, no sound strategic history of the twentieth century would spend many pages on ethics as an independent shaper of strategic behaviour. Subject to the admittedly proliferating laws of war,[64] soldiers and strategists have been inclined to view the claims of justice as translated by the perceived needs of their particular polity, civilization, or ideology, and as mediated by the political-military necessities of the moment.

'ADVANCE TO BARBARISM' IN AN EVER MORE REGULATED WORLD?

The second general observation about the force of ethics in modern strategy reflects the proliferation since the 1850s of legal guidance for behaviour bearing upon war, and of the practical dominance of culture over legal duty. Many authorities have noted what has been called an 'advance to barbarism' temporally coincident with the proliferation of solemn international commitments in the field of the laws of war.[65] The prudential strategic choices exercised in the twentieth century were little encumbered by explicit ethical constraint. For nearly a century and a half multiplying conventions, treaties, protocols, and declarations have endeavoured to build a 'convention' for the greater humanization of war (preeminently the Treaty of Paris, 1856, the Geneva Conventions, 1864, 1906, 1929, 1977, the Geneva Gas Protocol, 1925, the St Petersburg Declaration, 1868, the Hague Conventions, 1899, 1907, the Nuremberg Judgments of 1947, and the UN Charter and the UN's Universal Declaration of Human Rights, 1948). These modern efforts to provide a positive law of war may well have saved many thousands of lives. The central problem with the authority of this expanding body of law and quasi-law, however, has been its apparent inability to provide humane discipline

---

[64] Geoffrey Best, *Humanity in Warfare* (New York, 1980); id., *War and Law since 1945* (Oxford, 1994); Michael Howard, George J. Andreopoulos, and Mark R. Shulman (eds.), *The Laws of War: Constraints on Warfare in the Western World* (New Haven, Conn., 1994).

[65] 'A. Jurist' (pseud. for F. J. P. Veale), *Advance to Barbarism* (London, 1948).

in the truly hard cases when the cultural dimension of war and strategy threatens to overwhelm the ethical.

Although the history of the twentieth century could record a myriad of decisions by individual soldiers to eschew strict military prudence in favour of ethically more right conduct, that history does not record major cases wherein a distinctively ethical, as contrasted with a bluntly prudential, reasoning shaped statecraft and strategy. The fact that many belligerents wage war as they must, and not as they might choose, flags the elasticity in the principle of military necessity. This ethically perilous doctrine found honest expression in these words by Britain's Chief of the Imperial General Staff, Sir John Dill, on 15 June 1940: 'At a time when our National existence is at stake when we are threatened by an implacable enemy who himself recognizes no rules save those of expediency, we should not hesitate to adopt whatever means appear to offer the best chance of success.'[66] This decent English officer and gentleman spoke for the reality of strategic history. In practice, often it would be strategically imprudent and therefore inexpedient to adopt a lawless approach to conduct in war. Nonetheless, while granting that just conduct can avoid strategic disadvantage, polities and would-be polities often believe that military necessity has a superordinate ethic all its own.

WAR CRIMES, OR THE CRIME OF WAR?

Observation number three on ethics in twentieth-century warfare is a question that points to a persisting unease about the proper object for treatment. If war is an inevitable feature of the human condition, then there is much to be said in praise of its limitation and 'humanization': but, is war inevitable? Do efforts to humanize war help legitimize what should be regarded as the worst crime of all, war itself, and to impose opportunity costs significant for the prospects for war's abolition? Following the horrors of the 'Great' war of 1914–18, a war that on land, though not at sea, by and large was conducted justly according to the war convention of the period, many people sought to slay war rather than tame it. This belief that war should be regarded as inherently beyond the pale of 'civilized' behaviour, though shaken by the rematch of 1939–45, was naturally reinforced by the implications of nuclear facts after 1945. As a practical matter, however, the nexus between politics and war has not been severed by the ethical dilemmas posed either by modern war itself or even by prospective choices over its conduct. It might be said that ethics is akin to the dog that does not bark in the night.[67] One might believe that the ethical dimension to war and strategy should have posed individual and collective crises of conscience fatal for continuation of the familiar course of strategic history, but that subversive thought has no place in this text.

---

[66] Quoted in Edward M. Spiers, *Chemical Warfare* (London, 1986), 67.
[67] Arthur Conan Doyle, *Sherlock Holmes: The Complete Short Stories* (London, 1928), 326–7.

The concern here is to aid understanding of modern strategy, not to suggest alternative strategic, or anti-strategic, histories.

THE ROAD TO HELL IS MADE AND USED BY HIGH TECHNOLOGY

The fourth general observation on the force of ethics is to claim that there are no technological passports out of ethically troubling terrain. Adam Roberts suggests persuasively 'that new weaponry ... has perhaps been overrated as a cause of barbarism in two world wars'.[68] But in emphasizing culture, Roberts falls into the trap of misreading the technical history of World War II. He advises that

the lists of names on war memorials in England, the United States, and many other countries are far shorter for 1939–45 than they were for 1914–18. This fact was not due to the laws of war, but rather to developments in military technology (especially the tank) and strategy (the blitzkrieg and its variants) which tended to favour decisive action rather than a war of attrition.[69]

Roberts is correct when he argues that the barbarity of World War II in Eastern Europe and in Asia had political, social, and especially cultural, rather than military-technical, roots.[70] He is not correct, however, in his argument that new military technology for strategic decision lowered casualty rates in the wars of 1939–45. The Eastern Front of World War II was analogous—and then some, given its character as a *Kulturkampf*—to the Western Front of World War I. Moreover, even for Anglo-American forces, casualty rates for the principal continental campaign of 1944–5,[71] as well as in the air war,[72] were entirely in line with the levels of 1914–18.

Necessity requires that polities make the ethical best of the hands that they are dealt, or that they have little practicable option other than to deal themselves. Following its continental operational failures in 1914–16, imperial Germany was desperate to identify a theory of victory in the war. The ethical case against unrestricted submarine war upon Allied trade was overborne by the quasi-ethical notion of reprisal against Allied (indiscriminate) economic warfare,[73] and the balance of prudential logic which suggested that Britain would be obliged to cease hostilities before US intervention could have decisive effect. Operationally speaking, Germany employed U-boats against Allied trade in the only way practicable, given the nature of submarines—which is to say that the U-boats sank their victims without warning.

---

[68] Adam Roberts, 'Land Warfare: From Hague to Nuremberg', in Howard et al., *Laws of War*, 138.

[69] Ibid. 130.

[70] John W. Dower, *War Without Mercy: Race and Power in the Pacific War* (New York, 1986).

[71] Sheffield, 'Shadow of the Somme', 35–6.

[72] John Terraine, *A Time for Courage: The Royal Air Force in the European War, 1939–1945* (New York, 1985), 682.

[73] A. C. Bell, *A History of the Blockade of Germany and of the Countries Associated with Her in the Great War, Austria-Hungary, Bulgaria, and Turkey, 1914–1918* (London, 1937).

Until the summer of 1944 at least, night bombing, or bombing in bad weather, could not achieve precise discrimination of military from civilian targets. The ethical argument levelled against the Royal Air Force's Bomber Command in World War II is not that it was an inherently indiscriminate instrument of destruction, a charge that by and large was technically accurate only until mid-1944. Rather, it is the charge that the Command persisted, in the absence of a truly compelling strategic rationale, with 'area' attacks long after a significant measure of discrimination in bombardment was technically feasible.[74] Ironically, perhaps, whereas RAF Bomber Command technically speaking had a broad choice between area and precision bombing in 1944–5, the United States Army Air Forces' (USAAF) Twentieth Air Force had no practicable choice in 1945 between the precision or the area bombing of Japan.[75] In the absence of target intelligence about the exact location of what amounted to Japan's highly dispersed cottage industry of defence subcontractors, General Curtis LeMay could only attack Japanese war-supporting industry by attacking Japanese urban areas *per se*. One may be morally appalled at such a rationale, but it reflected the strategic reality of the specific case.

For a more recent twist to this story, although there are more and less careful ways to target a nuclear-armed force of bombers and ballistic and cruise missiles, it is a technical fact for statecraft and ethics that nuclear weapons derive their value for strategic effect from their exceptionally high ratio of energy yield released to weight of explosive device. It can be misleading to assert that nuclear weapons are inherently indiscriminate, because alternatives among targeting schemes could be significant. Nonetheless, there was never even a remote prospect of the ethical dimension to strategy denying the contingent use of nuclear weapons to the realm of politics. If nuclear weapons are inevitable, a necessary evil if one prefers, can a polity prudentially do other than seek to tame those weapons for strategic purposes? A different view is advanced by those who believe that nuclear weapons can be tamed by the same kind of 'taboo' that has long inhibited strategic exploitation of chemical weapons.[76]

Although culture can dominate the influence of technology on war, one should not dismiss as trivial what amounts to the military necessities commanded by contemporary weaponry. Scholars of strategy and international relations today, people generally lacking personal military experience as well as technical educa-

---

[74] Charles Webster and Noble Frankland, *The Strategic Air Offensive against Germany, 1939–1945* (4 vols., London, 1961); Max Hastings, *Bomber Command* (New York, 1979); Martin Middlebrook and Chris Everitt, *The Bomber Command War Diaries: An Operational Reference Book, 1939–1945* (London, 1985); Horst Boog (ed.), *The Conduct of the Air War in the Second World War: An International Comparison* (New York, 1992).

[75] Ronald Schaffer, *Wings of Judgment: American Bombing in World War II* (New York, 1985), chs. 6–8; Michael S. Sherry, *The Rise of American Air Power: The Creation of Armageddon* (New Haven, Conn., 1987); Conrad C. Crane, *Bombs, Cities, and Civilians: American Airpower Strategy in World War II* (Lawrence, Kan., 1993), ch. 9.

[76] Richard M. Price, *The Chemical Weapons Taboo* (Ithaca, NY, 1997).

tion, are inclined to be unduly dismissive of the world of military necessity, of the 'grammar' of war.

JUST BEHAVIOUR PAYS BEST

Notwithstanding the apparently dismissive judgements registered above about the typical absence of ethical effect upon strategic choice, this analysis advises adherence to plausible definitions of just conduct.[77] In human affairs, including statecraft and strategy, might is not right, and those who would play the Athenian role of arrogant hegemon in the Melian dialogue can discover that right has a consequential might all its own.[78] However, the might of right is not reliable, which is why the forces of justice are well advised to be heavily armed.

Much more often than not, *Gott mit uns*, or *deus vult*, is believed by both sides to a conflict to bless their belligerent effort. In those normal cases the ethical equation should yield no advantage to either side, except that potential friends and allies may find the claims of one more just than the claims of the other. Those potential friends and allies will not be moved to act by considerations of justice alone, but such considerations can ease the path for action taken for prudential motives. The grimy reality of personal careerism and perfidious state opportunism may suggest otherwise, but plausible claims for just policy goals and right conduct have a value for popular political mobilization that is wont to embarrass the cynical. In all three great wars of this century—1914-18, 1939-45, 1947-89—the ultimately victorious parties enjoyed the advantages of an ethically compelling story. Soldiers can fight well even without intense political belief in their cause, as witness the French Colonial Army in Indochina and Algeria in the 1950s, and the US Army in Vietnam in 1968-70. To fight bereft of ideological support, however, is to fight with a self-inflicted wound. Just causes do not triumph because they are just, but belief that one's cause is just is a useful flak-jacket against the systemically unfriendly grammar of war.

STRATEGIC ETHICS

The approach taken in this chapter to politics and ethics in their connection with war and strategy will not find universal favour. This discussion of ethical considerations finds that typically they play scant explicit role in the processes of strategy-making and strategy execution, though of course every individual and organization has internalized some notion of a (or the) moral universe. In practice,

[77] Robert E. Osgood and Robert W. Tucker, *Force, Order, and Justice* (Baltimore, 1967); Morton A. Kaplan (ed.), *Strategic Thinking and Its Moral Implications* (Chicago, 1973); Terry Nardin and David R. Mapel (eds.), *Traditions of International Ethics* (Cambridge, 1992); Colin S. Gray, 'Force, Order, and Justice: The Ethics of Realism in Statecraft', *Global Affairs*, 8 (1993), 1–17.

[78] Robert B. Strassler (ed.), *The Landmark Thucydides: A Comprehensive Guide to 'The Peloponnesian War'*, trans. Richard Crawley, rev. edn. (New York, 1996), 351–6.

it is hard to locate many unambiguous historical cases wherein prudential strategic logic was challenged from within the relevant defence community by people wielding explicitly ethical principles. The elastic realm of military and strategic necessity, even mere prudence, has a powerful ethic all its own. Ethics functions as the dog that does not bark and sound a moral alarm in strategic decisionmaking. The reason is because the ethical dimension to statecraft and strategy is already integral to the human and bureaucratic instruments that decide upon strategic issues. Far from providing the solution to the organized violence that is war, ethical ideas, well integrated into particular strategic cultures, are part of the problem. Within living memory millions of highly civilized Europeans in uniform were persuaded that it was not only a pleasure to slaughter the *Untermenschen*, it was also a moral duty owed to *Volk*, Führer, and the future of Western civilization. More recently still, the 'ethnic cleansers' in the former Yugoslavia in the 1990s provided further demonstration of the sad truth that cultural preference can shape ethical judgement.

In practice, strategic performance is exceedingly difficult to effect well in relation to politics, but generally is not hampered by ethical considerations. My analysis presents a contrast. Strategy is simple, but not easy; ethics is complex, but easy to manage in strategic practice. Strategic ethics do not act distinctively as a brake upon strategic (mis)behaviour.

Chapter 3

THE STRATEGIST'S TOOLKIT: THE LEGACY OF CLAUSEWITZ

Most of what we need to know in order to understand modern strategy is on offer to the careful reader of Carl von Clausewitz's *On War*.[1] Richard K. Betts is correct in his claim that '[o]ne Clausewitz is still worth a busload of most other theorists'.[2] John Keegan could hardly be more in error than when he judges Clausewitz to have promulgated 'the most pernicious philosophy of warmaking yet conceived'.[3] Whether or not readers share my enthusiasm for Clausewitz, it is notable that an incomplete book manuscript first published in 1832 can inspire opinions today as diverse as those just quoted.

This chapter is devoted to the ideas of Carl von Clausewitz for the practical reason that he provides most of the conceptual tools needed for the strategist's toolkit. I explain the reason why the argument in *On War* remains the gold standard for theory about war and strategy. Clausewitz bequeathed to posterity a body of thought on war that is more persuasive by far than is any body of thought by a rival theorist, or even rival camp of theorists. There can be no last word on war and strategy; certainly there can be no sacred texts. Clausewitz, simply, is more persuasive than other theorists.

Clausewitz's *On War* organizes the analysis here. The discussion opens with consideration of the sources of inspiration for strategic theory. While respectful of the dependence of Clausewitz upon such recent exemplars of strategists as Frederick the Great and especially Napoleon, I am not convinced that that kind of personalized inspiration is a necessary spark if genius in theory is to flower. The argument continues with a broad explanation of why *On War* speaks so powerfully to us. Next, the possible successors to Clausewitz as theorists of war are weighed in the balance and are all found wanting, notwithstanding the merit in some of their strategic writing. (Chapter 4 is devoted to understanding why Clausewitz's possible successors have failed to make the grade.) The remainder of the chapter, indeed its principal focus, consists of a critical celebration of the ideas in *On War*. Back-to-back analyses are offered respectively of the strengths and limitations of Clausewitz as a theorist of war. Overall, the chapter argues that Clausewitz uniquely laid bare the nature of war and strategy, and that his virtues vastly

---

[1] Carl von Clausewitz, *On War*, trans. Michael Howard and Peter Paret (Princeton, NJ, 1976).
[2] Richard K. Betts, 'Should Strategic Studies Survive?' *World Politics*, 50 (1997), 29.
[3] John Keegan, *War and Our World* (London, 1998), 41–2.

outweigh his weaknesses. Those limitations, or weaknesses, most typically stem from influences particular to his time and place in history and geography. Clausewitz needs to be amended and augmented because strategic theory is a living tradition, which is one reason why this book has been written.

My principal theme, that there is an essential unity to all strategic experience, both in its many dimensions working contemporaneously and across all historical periods, derives directly from *On War* — as we shall see — and four of the six broad questions that weave through the text are also addressed quite directly by Clausewitz. He analyses the relationship between ideas and practice; indirectly at least, he settles the issue of what a growing complexity in strategic phenomena means for the character and nature of the subject; he debates majestically the matter of why strategy is so difficult and, incomparably, he donates the compound concept of 'friction' to us as a large part of his answer; and indirectly he advises as to the virtues in a balanced approach to war, one that does not seek victory in a reductionist way relying only upon the genius of a commander or in cunning plans. Judgement on what has changed about war and strategy since Clausewitz wrote *On War* in the 1820s, and what those changes may mean for the strategic history of the twenty-first century, are our calls to make. The first of those questions is tackled in the section here on the limitations of *On War*, while the second must await direct answer in the last chapter.

ON INSPIRATION

Scholars a hundred years hence may disagree, but the twentieth century produced no truly great book on war or strategy. The multidimensional convulsions in war and strategy of 1914–18, 1939–45, and even the potential convulsions of 1947–89, were at least as traumatic as the changes between 1792 and 1815. Yet the wars of the French Revolution and Empire yielded in Clausewitz's *On War* a great work on war and strategy, as well as in Jomini's *Art of War* a text of unquestionably classic status.[4] Clausewitz has no modern rival among theorists of war. The nature of modern war and strategy is best explained in the somewhat fractured and incomplete writings of a Prussian major-general who died in 1831. In common with the rest of us who venture into military theory, Clausewitz was a person of his time, place, and culture.[5] Also in common with the rest of us, Clausewitz was merely human and could err. The argument, therefore, is that, errors notwithstanding, Clausewitz continues to stand head and shoulders above possible rival theorists of war.

[4] Antoine Henri de Jomini, *The Art of War*, repr. of 1862 edn. (London, 1992).

[5] Peter Paret, 'The Genesis of *On War*', in Clausewitz, *On War*, 3–25; id., *Clausewitz and the State* (New York, 1976); id., 'Clausewitz', in Paret (ed.), *Makers of Modern Strategy: From Machiavelli to the Nuclear Age* (Princeton, NJ, 1986), 186–213, 887–9; Michael Howard, *Clausewitz* (Oxford, 1983), ch. 1; Azar Gat, *The Origins of Military Thought: From the Enlightenment to Clausewitz* (Oxford, 1989).

If there was no close rival to Clausewitz in the twentieth century, the explanation is unlikely to lie in lack of need. One might explore the idea of correlating great theorists with the dominating inspiration of great practitioners: specifically Clausewitz (and Jomini) interpreted the Napoleonic way of war.[6] Clausewitz, as a Prussian veteran of Jena–Auerstadt, Russia in 1812, the Ligny–Waterloo campaign, and much else *en route*, was more than simply a celebrant of Napoleon's military genius (the 'God of War').[7] Clausewitz could hardly help but notice that the great captain, for all his undoubted military and administrative genius, ultimately lost.

None of the great wars of the twentieth century produced a 'great captain' analogous to Napoleon Bonaparte. Douglas Haig and Ferdinand Foch were competent, though even that minimal claim is controversial, while the German–Austro-Hungarian side yields only one semi-serious candidate, Erich Ludendorff, whose record of responsibility for strategic effect in 1917–18 is persuasively damning.[8] Ludendorff had a domain of high command far exceeding that of Haig or Foch.

If the political-military role of generalissimo as fused in Napoleon was

---

[6] Following a line of thought suggested by H. Camon early in the twentieth century (in *Clausewitz*, Paris, 1911), Gat suggests dubiously that 'Clausewitz's conception of the Napoleonic art of war was largely a myth, born out of Prussia's traumatic experience and reflecting the prevailing emphasis on moral energies': *Origins*, 209. Although he is right in pointing to some frailty in Clausewitz's analysis of Napoleonic warfare, Grat appears to have succumbed to the French conceit that no Prussian (e.g. Clausewitz) could possibly appreciate the genius of Napoleon. At the beginning of the twentieth century, French writers like Camon were as protective of the Napoleonic legend, and also of the superiority of Jomini as the most authoritative interpreter of the master, as German writers were protective of the reputation of Clausewitz. Writing in 1905, a lieutenant-general on the German General Staff wrote as follows: 'A young French field-officer, Camon, in the *Journal des sciences militaires* of 1900, in a study of Clausewitz, has once more furnished a proof how difficult it is for our neighbours to understand another nation. According to his version, Clausewitz not only did not comprehend the Emperor [Napoleon] in any way, but seems to be a perfect muddle-head, whom it is impossible to take seriously. We ought really to be glad, after all, if the sources of our strength remain for the French a sealed book also in the future': Rudolf von Caemmerer, *The Development of Strategical Science during the 19th Century*, trans. Karl von Donat (London, 1905), 109, n. 2. Of course, von Caemmerer is partisan towards Clausewitz, but so were his French contemporaries towards Jomini and, indeed, towards the Napoleonic way in war writ large. Aside from the minor fact that Clausewitz was not reliable in his judgement on Napoleon's battlefield generalship, it is ironical that the great theorist did not choose to employ Napoleon—his exemplar as 'God of War'—as proof by negative example of his pervasively political theory of war. Napoleon proved systematically incapable of turning success in war into a lasting peace with security for imperial France.

[7] Jay Luvaas, 'Student as Teacher: Clausewitz on Frederick the Great and Napoleon', in Michael I. Handel (ed.), *Clausewitz and Modern Strategy* (London, 1986), 150–70; Gat, *Origins*, ch. 7, s. I.

[8] Keith Simpson, 'The Reputation of Sir Douglas Haig', in Brian Bond (ed.), *The First World War and British Military History* (Oxford, 1991), 141–62; Stefan T. Possony and Etienne Montoux, 'Du Picq and Foch: The French School', in Edward Mead Earle (ed.), *Makers of Modern Strategy: Military Thought from Machiavelli to Hitler* (Princeton, NJ, 1941), 206–33; Holger H. Herwig, *The First World War: Germany and Austria-Hungary, 1914–18* (London, 1997). Allan R. Millett and Williamson Murray (eds.), *Military Effectiveness* (3 vols., Boston, 1987), is useful, as are the twentieth-century topics in Paret, *Makers of Modern Strategy*, and in Williamson Murray, MacGregor Knox, and Alvin Bernstein (eds.), *The Making of Strategy: Rulers, States and War* (Cambridge, 1994).

approximated in World War I only by Ludendorff, in World War II it had three full-throttle candidates in Adolf Hitler, Winston Churchill, and Joseph Stalin. Of the three, only Hitler sustained the fused Napoleonic political and military command roles. Interesting though it is to compare the political and strategic performances of Hitler, Churchill, and Stalin, none of them, and none of their subordinate generals, emerged in 1945 with an unquestionable 'great captain' sticker on their résumé. The greatest of military names in the Grand Alliance, those of Marshal of the Soviet Union Georgi Zhukov, General Dwight D. Eisenhower, and even General Douglas MacArthur, were all but dwarfed by their obvious subordination to political authority, as well as by the sheer complexity, even near-totality, of modern war.[9]

For the third great war of the twentieth century, the cold conflict of 1947–89, the absence of military victories means the absence of military victors. If a would-be Clausewitz of the nuclear age were to seek to interpret the genius of his historical model, who would provide the Napoleonic inspiration? Who were the heroes or heroines of statecraft and strategy in the Cold War? Do Harry S. Truman, Dwight D. Eisenhower, John F. Kennedy, Richard M. Nixon, Ronald Reagan, or George Bush qualify for the short list of candidates, or just for honourable mention? If there is something to be said in favour of those American statesmen, should one proceed one step down and consider the claims of Dean Acheson, John Foster Dulles, Robert S. McNamara, and Henry Kissinger? In addition, given that deterrence presumably was mutual, is there not some case for seeing merit in the actions, and particular the inaction, of Joseph Stalin, Nikita Khrushchev, Leonid Brezhnev, and Mikhail Gorbachev? From superpower terrain, one can move out in search of inspiration for authors of potential strategic classics to the ranks of the allies and friends of the USSR and United States, and even to non-aligned observers. Alas, the search yields no unquestionable vein of pure gold.

Scholarship on the Cold War does not suggest that the absence of nuclear disaster primarily should be attributed either to genius in high office or to genius in the whole system of mutual deterrence. It is not even certain that rival theories and systems of deterrence were actually tested from 1947 to 1989:[10] the theories and systems were present, but did they really affect political outcomes?[11] Indeed, the more that we learn from archives and oral history about the surrogate battles, which is to say the crises and the competition in armaments, of the third great conflict of the century, the more prescient does Clausewitz appear in his insistence upon the centrality of chance, risk, and uncertainty to war. While it would

---

[9] e.g. D. Clayton James, 'American and Japanese Strategies in the Pacific War', in Paret, *Makers of Modern Strategy*, 73. James pursues MacArthur's problems with the political sphere to their bitter conclusion in *Fighting the Last War: Command and Crisis in Korea, 1950–1953* (New York, 1993), esp. ch. 2.

[10] See the discussion in Chs. 11 and 12 below.

[11] Fred Charles Iklé, 'The Second Coming of the Nuclear Age', *Foreign Affairs*, 75 (1996), 119–28; Keith B. Payne, *Deterrence in the Second Nuclear Age* (Lexington, Ky., 1996).

probably be an exaggeration to attribute the absence of a violent conclusion to the East–West Cold War simply to a fortunate series in the 'drop of the cards', such an assertion would be no more of an oversimplification than would be a bold claim for the efficacy of deterrence.

Inspiration can be contextual (e.g. an appalling looming threat) as well as personal. It is probable that the inspiration of strategic context most typically triggers an applied level of strategic study more likely to produce texts of immediate interest than true classics. If the barbarians are approaching the gates of the city, profound study of the nature of war will be judged a luxury by most people.

CLAUSEWITZ AND MODERN STRATEGY

An appraisal of Clausewitz cannot explain as much about war and strategy in the twentieth century as the quality of the great man's theory suggests should be the case. The century was 'Clausewitzian' only in the senses that his subject remained all too important, and his theoretical writings reigned supreme, though not unchallenged. It is possible that *On War* had an influence upon the process of strategic thought of a politician and general here and there, but the mark of general theory upon behaviour is always difficult to demonstrate. It is quite possible that modern strategic history has been entirely untouched by the consequences of people reading and misreading *On War*. Strategic behaviour can flow from the interaction of many factors, among which a particular book of general strategic theory, almost no matter how diffuse its educational impact, is never likely to rank high. Even when strategic theorists are known or believed to be players in a particular defence community—as with Albert Wohlstetter in the United States, Marshal V. D. Sokolovskiy in the USSR, and General Pierre Gallois in France[12]—it is often unclear whether their studies and writings are independently influential or whether they simply express attitudes and opinions already extant.

Clausewitz earns the extensive attention he receives in this book primarily because his theoretical writing on war and strategy yields the most powerful of conceptual tools available to understand the course and outcome of conflict. Also, he attracts notice because his ideas appear (certainly are claimed) to have influenced strategic behaviour. Clausewitz's alleged influence has periodically been the subject of unfavourable comment. Today the relevance of *On War* to future conflict is under theoretical assault at least as spirited as were the claims recorded much earlier for his purportedly dangerous irrelevance to the real strategic

---

[12] A. J. Wohlstetter et al., *Selection and Use of Strategic Air Bases*, R–266 (Santa Monica, Calif., Apr. 1954); id., 'The Delicate Balance of Terror', *Foreign Affairs*, 37 (1959), 211–34; V. D. Sokolovskiy, *Soviet Military Strategy*, ed. Herbert Dinerstein, Leon Gouré, and Thomas Wolfe (Englewood Cliffs, NJ, 1963); Pierre Gallois, *The Balance of Terror: Strategy for the Nuclear Age* (Boston, 1961).

challenges posed by, first, industrial-age mass warfare and, second, nuclear weapons.[13]

As social scientists are discovering in their pioneering exploration in the murky waters of strategic culture, the connections between strategic ideas and behaviour are difficult to conceptualize, research, and demonstrate. Ideas and behaviour interpenetrate to a degree that can thwart even the most careful social scientist in quest of reliable theory.[14] It does not diminish the esteem in which we should hold Clausewitz, to observe that his theory of war and strategy is inductive, explaining as it does the historically enduring nature of his subject. He invented his theory of war and strategy much as Mahan invented his more restricted theory of seapower. Both of these historian-theorists 'discovered' what human beings have practised for millennia.

If Clausewitz interpreted Napoleonic practice, he interpreted also the practice of war by Marlborough, Turenne, Henry V of England, Basil II 'Bulgaroctonus' of the Byzantine Empire, Julius Caesar, and Alexander of Macedon. What Clausewitz, Mahan, and Corbett, *inter alia*, discovered in more (Clausewitz and Corbett) or less (Mahan)[15] theoretical terms was the nature of war and strategic behaviour and the identity of those practices and kinds of behaviour likely to promote strategic success or strategic failure. Specific strategic advice is absent from *On War*, but nonetheless the book yields a daunting set of implied recommendations. For example, strategic genius is not required for one to translate the following point by Clausewitz into an educational recommendation for statesmen: 'War in general, and the commander in any specific instance, is entitled to require that the trend and designs of policy shall not be inconsistent with these [military] means.'[16]

Although Clausewitz discovered what human beings always had been doing, the discovery was necessary. He may have been, as it were, the Copernicus of strategy, but he did not discover the political context and function for strategic behaviour. There may have been few great works on war and strategy written before, or after, *On War*, but—with minor assistance from Sun Tzu (and the remainder of China's

---

[13] B. H. Liddell Hart, *Strategy: The Indirect Approach* (London, 1967), 352–7; Martin van Creveld, *The Transformation of War* (New York, 1991), ch. 2; id., *Nuclear Proliferation and the Future of Conflict* (New York, 1993), ch. 2; id., 'What Is Wrong with Clausewitz?', in Gert de Nooy (ed.), *The Clausewitzian Dictum and the Future of Western Military Strategy* (The Hague, 1997), 7–23.

[14] Strategic behaviour both expresses and fuels strategic ideas. The problem for the methodologically ambitious social scientist is that strategic culture is expressed in strategic behaviour.

[15] Although there is an abundance of strategic theory informing the voluminous writings of Alfred Thayer Mahan, only ch. 1 of *The Influence of Sea Power upon History, 1660–1783*, repr. of 1890 edn. (London, 1965) is explicitly theoretical. Philip Crowl suggests that 'the argument [in *Influence of Sea Power*, ch. 1] is tangential to the main line of his thought, and the outline of six "general conditions" can best be understood simply as an artful device for exposing America's woeful backwardness': 'Alfred Thayer Mahan: The Naval Historian', in Paret, *Makers of Modern Strategy*, 463. In point of fact, ch. 1 of *Influence of Sea Power*, 'Discussion of the Elements of Sea Power', was a last-minute and not particularly original addition to the text, upon which Mahan's publisher insisted for commercial reasons.

[16] Clausewitz, *On War*, 87.

Seven Military Classics),[17] Thucydides, Vegetius,[18] the Emperor Maurice,[19] and Machiavelli[20] — statesmen and commanders often behaved strategically in a purposeful way and with intended political consequences. But, prior to the availability of *On War*, there was no coherent general theory of war and strategy which people with particular military needs or interests could consult. Admiral Custance made the point when he advised:

> The reader is to remember that Mahan and [Admiral P. H.] Columb were pioneers [on the subject of seapower] with no reasoned theory of war behind them, when they began to discuss the facts of past wars. They were in a like case to men who started to inquire into the motions of heavenly bodies without any knowledge of the laws of motion.[21]

So familiar is the strategic theorist and defence planner of today with the conceptualizations that are scattered profusely throughout the text of *On War*, and so habituated have we become to reaching for the great book when we are in need of conceptual assistance, that life without Clausewitz is all but unimaginable. Much of what is most penetrating in *On War* can be located also in Sun Tzu's *Art of War*,[22] while Thucydides' immortal history and the Emperor Maurice's manual on the conduct of war are both rich sources for strategic education. Clausewitz's *On War*, however, is unique in the combination of sheer number, as well as quality and, with reservations, overall coherence, of insights. He provides a system of thought on war and strategy, not merely maxims or isolated points, even though his writing lends itself to selective quotation.

It can be difficult to convey to those who are not strategic theorists a full appreciation of the true monumentality of Clausewitz's achievement. Strategic thought in the twentieth century, as well as some strategic practice and malpractice, in the Western world and the Eastern (including the USSR and China), was shaped pervasively by ideas presented, and sometimes explained, in *On War*. It is a book that can be used to help elucidate almost any problem in strategy, regardless of time, place, and technology; it is not a book to be revered, but kept unopened as the tactical character of warfare, driven by technological change, evolves further and further away from the Napoleonic world of the great theorist.

Strategic cultures are constantly being altered as succeeding generations of strategic thinkers reinterpret the past in light refracted by a dynamic prism of contemporary perspective and values. For example, consider how British attitudes towards their imperial political-military behaviour have shifted over the course of

---

[17] *The Seven Military Classics of Ancient China*, trans. Ralph D. Sawyer (Boulder, Colo., 1993).

[18] Vegetius, *Vegetius: Epitome of Military Science*, trans. N. P. Milner (Liverpool, 1993).

[19] Emperor Maurice, *Maurice's Strategikon: Handbook of Byzantine Military Strategy*, trans. George T. Dennis (Philadelphia, 1984).

[20] Niccolò Machiavelli, *The Art of War*, trans. Ellis Farnsworth (Indianapolis, 1965). Sebastian de Grazia, *Machiavelli in Hell* (New York, 1994), is an outstanding intellectual biography.

[21] Reginald Custance, *A Study of War* (Boston, 1924), 101.

[22] Michael I. Handel, *Masters of War: Classical Strategic Thought*, 2nd edn. (London, 1996), ch. 2.

a hundred years, or how radically American views of their past political-military behaviour towards native peoples on their internal frontier have altered. Without apology we should take from Clausewitz what we find useful. He intended his book to be used for the education of policymakers and military commanders. Indeed, his self-confidence, though occasionally severely dented, was such that he intended to compose the most useful book ever written on war. While we should try to understand Clausewitz on his own terms, a concern that obliges us to probe the sources of his education, broadly his 'life and times', a quest after truly faithful interpretation of *On War* is essentially a sterile scholastic mission.

For students of intellectual history it is important to close with the real Clause-witz.[23] However, for those of us who wish to use Clausewitz to help shine light in dark strategic places today, what we need is a comprehension of his theory that does full justice to his insights so that we do not use *On War* to mislead. The book should not be raided for the decorative quotation or the impressive axiom, according to contemporary taste and debating requirement. But one should not be afraid to treat *On War* much as innovative actor-directors handle Shakespeare when they present the bard in modern dress.

It is commonplace to warn against back-fitting—or conceptual reverse engineering—modern ideas on strategy into interpretations of yesterday's texts on theory, or into the minds of yesterday's politicians and generals. The warning is sound, provided one is concerned with being historically faithful. The warning is less sound if one is a working strategist or strategic theorist who needs to use *On War* as a tool of the pragmatic trade of strategy. Clausewitz would have understood and approved this point. Strategy is an applied art or social science, and theory about it has merit in the measure of its value to those who must meet the practical challenges of strategy. Clausewitz knew that when one writes a tract for the ages, theorists in different times will interpret the work for their own purposes. Given the magnetic pull of the Napoleonic style of war upon the structure and content of Clausewitz's theory, he was excellently placed to recognize the attractive power of contemporary events. The yardstick by which he judged when war was most truly war was, unsurprisingly, the experience of his own times. It is a common conceit for theorists to find in their own day the behaviour that, as it were by historical accident, allegedly provides the key to general understanding. Temporal location, as well as cultural and other affiliation, fuels the content for the axiom long favoured by theorists of bureaucratic politics that 'where you stand depends on where [in this case *when*] you sit'.[24] Clausewitz gives an impression of intellectual uneasiness when treading the marches between particular periods and universal experience. After a speedy review of military history from earliest times to his time of writing, a survey plainly shaped to demonstrate contrasts with the near-perfection of absolute war achieved between 1792 and 1815, Clausewitz offers a

---

[23] As, persuasively, does Gat, *Origins*, for example.
[24] Graham T. Allison, *Essence of Decision: Explaining the Cuban Missile Crisis* (Boston, 1971), 176.

penetrating explanation of how the historically particular should relate to the universal. In order not to miss important nuances and qualifications, the quotation has to be extensive.

At this point our historical survey can end. Our purpose was not to assign, in passing, a handful of principles of warfare to each period. We wanted to show how every age had its own kind of war, its own limiting conditions, and its own peculiar preconceptions. Each period, therefore, would have held to its own theory of war, even if the urge had always and universally existed to work things out on scientific principles. It follows that the events of every age must be judged in the light of its own peculiarities. One cannot, therefore, understand and appreciate the commanders of the past until one has placed oneself in the situation of their times, not so much by a painstaking study of all its details as by an accurate appreciation of its major determining features.

But war, though conditioned by the particular characteristics of states and their armed forces, must contain some more general—indeed a universal element with which every theorist ought above all to be concerned.

The age in which this postulate, this universally valid element, was at its strongest was the most recent one, when war attained the absolute in violence. But it is no more likely that war will always be so monumental in character than that the ample scope it has come to enjoy will again be severely restricted. A theory, then, that dealt exclusively with absolute war would either have to ignore any case in which the nature of war had been deformed by outside influence, or else it would have to dismiss them all as misconstrued. That cannot be what theory is for. Its purpose is to demonstrate what war is in practice, not what its ideal nature ought to be. So the theorist . . . must always bear in mind the wide variety of situations that can lead to war. If he does, he will draw the outline of its salient features in such a way that it can accommodate both the dictates of the age, and those of the immediate situation.

We can thus only say that the aims a belligerent adopts, and the resources he employs, must be governed by the particular characteristics of his own position, but they will also conform to the spirit of the age and to its general character. Finally, they must always be governed by the general conclusions to be drawn from the nature of war itself.[25]

This long passage states clearly enough Clausewitz's view that the warfare waged recently by the French, *inter alia*, nation in arms most closely resembles the tendency towards 'the absolute in violence' that is the very epitome of war. In addition, he claims promptly that wars in the future are no more likely to have such a 'monumental character' than they are to return to their erstwhile 'restricted' form. What had happened was that Clausewitz effected a late (mid-1820s) shotgun marriage of necessity between his lifelong theme of fighting and battle with a tendency towards absolute violence (though, as Azar Gat insists, 'absolute war' is a formula applied only very late in the development of *On War*)[26] and the new theme of limited aims in war that must govern the style of warfare conducted. Although Clausewitz appears uneasy with his parallel recognition of absolute and real, or limited, war, and although his explanation of the relations

---

[25] Clausewitz, *On War*, 593–4 (emphasis added).   [26] Gat, *Origins*, ch. 7.

between the two falls short of crystal clarity, the conceptual marriage is nonethe-less a happy one. The strategic history of the past two centuries supports the proposition that Clausewitz's twin-focused general theory of absolute and limited war works much better in practice than probably he anticipated. The fear of nuclear escalation that loomed over the theorizing in the nuclear age about limited war provides a perfect illustration of the uneasy relationship one finds in Clause-witz's writings between real and an apparently idealized notion, which actually is a real-world tendency towards absolute war.[27] When it seems that all too real, albeit still only potential, war approaches the absolute level of violence—arguably the East–West strategic condition of the late 1950s and after—the theorists and policymakers rummage in *On War* to find the Clausewitz that they need—that is, the Clausewitz of real, which is to say limited, war, and of war as a political instrument. The neo-Clausewitzian strategists, as critics have termed some of the strategic theorists of the nuclear age,[28] by and large elected to ignore the darker side of *On War* that expressed the lifelong 'battle Clausewitz' who saw in fighting the epitome of warfare.

SUCCESSORS TO CLAUSEWITZ?

To quote Bernard Brodie, 'Clausewitz's book [*On War*] is not simply the greatest but the only truly great book on war'.[29] His judgement is widely shared among the strategic theorists of many countries today, and indeed endured for much of the twentieth century.[30] This is a book about modern strategy, not about Clausewitz. Nonetheless, whatever one's view of the quality of *On War*, or its relevance to modern strategy, Clausewitz enjoys an intellectual near-hegemony as the leading general theorist of war and strategy. Sun Tzu is the only possible competitor, but that competition would be ill-matched, as *Art of War* provides cook-book guid-ance for statecraft, rather than a comprehensive theory of war.[31]

Clausewitz's greatness as a general theorist with a continuing relevance has been contested by such modern writers as Basil Liddell Hart, Martin van Creveld, and John Keegan.[32] In my view there is no worthy contest over the merit in

---

[27] Stephen J. Cimbala, *Clausewitz and Escalation: Classical Perspective on Nuclear Strategy* (London, 1991), is a brave venture into opaque water.

[28] Raymond Aron, *Clausewitz: Philosopher of War*, trans. Christine Booker and Norman Stone (London, 1983), pt. 5.

[29] Bernard Brodie, 'The Continuing Relevance of *On War*', in Clausewitz, *On War*, 53.

[30] Handel, *Clausewitz*, pt. 3; Christopher Bassford, *Clausewitz in English: The Reception of Clausewitz in Britain and America, 1815–1945* (New York, 1994).

[31] Sun Tzu, *The Art of War*, trans. Ralph D. Sawyer (Boulder, Colo., 1994); Handel, *Masters of War*, ch. 2.

[32] Liddell Hart, *Strategy*; van Creveld, *Transformation of War*; id., *Nuclear Proliferation*; John Keegan, 'Peace by Other Means?', *Times Literary Supplement*, 11 Dec. 1992, 3–4; id., *A History of Warfare* (London, 1993); id., *War and Our World* (London, 1998). Van Creveld does not question Clausewitz's greatness as a theorist, only his continuing relevance: 'What is Wrong with Clausewitz?', 7.

Clausewitz's theory of war. Paradoxically, he is a theorist whose reputation tends to grow when under challenge.

To argue for the greatness of Clausewitz and for his continuing relevance is not necessarily to suggest that he has been notably influential. Great books need not be read; if read they need not be understood; and even if understood, they may not be allowed to help guide strategic behaviour. Clausewitz has not been as influential as he should have been, notwithstanding his intellectual preeminence. Just how far strategic practice can stray from the education available in superior strategic theory can be gauged from Harry Summers's controversial study of the American war in Vietnam, *On Strategy*.[33] Summers oversimplifies the Vietnam war, and his retrospective strategic advice is not to all tastes, but his explicit and pervasive employment of Clausewitz's ideas yield a persuasive indictment of US strategic behaviour.

The claim for the unique superiority of Clausewitz as a general strategic theorist points to both the quality and the quantity of his insights. *On War* is close to unreadable from beginning to end, given its lack of coherent intellectual or narrative trajectory, but it rewards browsing readers with gemlike insights at almost any random opening of its pages. Clausewitz provides uneasily both an Old Testament and a New Testament in *On War*. An intellectual crisis in 1827 obliged him to begin to write-in the revelation that political guidance ensures that real, which is to say limited, war almost always dampens the prospect for war to proceed to exhibit its ideal, absolute character.[34] Not for nothing is the comment often made that *On War* is copiously quoted but much less frequently read, let alone read from cover to cover. It provides a general and considerably but still incompletely unified theory of war and strategy unmatched by the works of other theorists before or since. Furthermore, the partial theories of seapower, airpower, and nuclear strategy, all of which could draw upon the strengths of Clausewitzian general theory, have failed to come within close reach of Clausewitz's standard of excellence. Despite the problem of trying to compare unlike efforts at general strategic theory with geographically, functionally, or weapon specific theory, still one can at least conceive of a category of works that might be judged to have members as good as *On War*, though in their own more restricted way. For example, Corbett's *Some Principles of Maritime Strategy* is a lone, albeit unsuccessful, nominee for that underpopulated club.[35]

[33] Harry G. Summers, Jr., *On Strategy: A Critical Analysis of the Vietnam War* (Novato, Calif., 1982). Clausewitz is also allowed a leading role in some of Summers's other books: *On Strategy, ii: A Critical Analysis of the Gulf War* (New York, 1992); *The New World Strategy: A Military Policy for America's Future* (New York, 1995).

[34] Gat, *Origins*, ch. 7.

[35] Julian S. Corbett, *Some Principles of Maritime Strategy*, ed. Eric Grove, repr. of 1911 edn. (Annapolis, Md., 1988). The leading limitation of *Some Principles* is that, for all its excellent, if complex, strategic reasoning, it is tied too closely to British experience (necessarily) prior to the great wars of the twentieth century. One cannot criticize a strategic theorist for not knowing what could not be known at the time of composition. However, theorists can be criticized legitimately if they aspire to write 'for the ages', but to a significant measure are overtaken by strategic history. With the end of the Cold War

By far the most persuasive way to register the superiority of Clausewitz is to consider the merit in his general theory as compared with the merit in the theories of possible successors or rivals. Few theorists aspire to write truly general theory that transcends particular temporal, geographical, or technological contexts. It would not be true to claim that Clausewitz is unique in transcending distinctive categories of wars, geographies, and weapons. His uniqueness, rather, lies in the range and quality of his transcendence.

It is instructive to consider the contributions of seven general strategic theorists of the twentieth century. These seven are not unarguably the best that the century could offer, but my assessment of descending order of merit of achievement *in general theory* ranks these authors as follows: J. C. Wylie, Edward N. Luttwak, Bernard Brodie, Basil Liddell Hart, and Raoul Castex . Aside from these author-theorists, Reginald Custance and John Boyd also warrant honourable mention. Each of these writers pitched their theories to transcend limitations of time, geography, and technology. A case can be made for an eighth entry, Mao Tse-tung. Two drawbacks, however, must lower the mark given to Mao's *Selected Military Writings*. First, his theorizing is heavily indebted intellectually to Sun Tzu; second, it focuses narrowly upon a particular form of war (people's revolutionary).[36] Nonetheless, *Selected Military Writings* and closely associated texts—*On Guerrilla Warfare*, for example[37]—if less than Clausewitzian, are still of star quality in offering a superb, if only partial, theory of strategy and war.

Admiral Wylie's modest little book—with an original text of only 108 pages—is by far the best of the 'successor' works considered here. In *Military Strategy*, Wylie provides a powerful central organizing concept or 'fundamental theme':

The primary aim of the strategist in the conduct of war is some selected degree of control of

marking the demise, for a while at least, of the prospects for major continental war, Corbett today appears more contemporary than he has for many decades. The same can be said for Charles E. Callwell, *Military Operations and Maritime Preponderance: Their Relations and Interdependence*, ed. Colin S. Gray, repr. of 1905 edn. (Annapolis, Md., 1996). In both the US and Britain, sea-based expeditionary warfare is back in vogue. For the American side, Jay L. Johnson, 'The Navy in 2010: A Joint Vision', *Joint Force Quarterly*, 14 (1996–7), 17–19; Roger W. Barnett, 'Grasping 2010 with Naval Forces', *Joint Force Quarterly*, 17 (1997–8), 25–31; F. G. Hoffman, 'Joint Vision 2010: A Marine Perspective', *Joint Force Quarterly*, 17 (1997–8), 32–8. For the British, Robert Fry, 'End of the Continental Century', *RUSI Journal*, 143 (1998), 15–18; Jock Slater, 'The Maritime Contribution to Joint Operations', *RUSI Journal*, 143 (1998), 20–4.

[36] Mao Tse-tung, *Selected Military Writings* (Peking, 1967). It is encouraging to note that Eliot A. Cohen lists *Selected Military Writings* among his 6 choices of 'most significant' books in the military field over the last 75 years: *Foreign Affairs*, 76 (1997), 219–20.

[37] Mao Tse-tung [attrib.], *On Guerrilla Warfare*, trans. Samuel B. Griffith (New York, 1961). Notwithstanding Griffith's belief in Mao's authorship of this work, it is now clear enough that it was written by 'Chu Te, P'eng Te-huai and others': Stuart Schram, *The Thought of Mao-Tse-tung* (Cambridge, 1989), 52–3. This, however, constitutes a distinction without a difference. *On Guerrilla Warfare* is from the same intellectual and strategic historical stable as *Selected Military Writings*, and is so treated in the discussion of irregular warfare presented in Ch. 10 below.

the enemy for the strategist's own purpose; this is achieved by control of the pattern of war; and this control of the pattern of war is had by manipulation of the center of gravity of war to the disadvantage of the opponent.[38]

Along the way, Wylie makes points of exceptional interest and persuasiveness about the world-views of those who fight on land, at sea, and in the air. He discusses how one might proceed from inherently limited and partial maritime, air, and continental theories towards the higher reaches of general theory. Wylie is no Clausewitz. Much of his insight is derivative, especially from the great Prussian theorist himself. Nonetheless, Wylie has written the best book of general theory on war and strategy to appear for more than a century.

Wylie's work lacks the originality and sheer quantity of powerful insights of Clausewitz, but when he scores he scores heavily. Two maxims in particular illustrate the quality of his thought: 'But planning for certitude is the greatest of all military mistakes, as military history demonstrates all too vividly';[39] 'The ultimate determinant in war is the man on the scene with the gun. This man is the final power in war. He is control. He determines who wins.'[40] It would be difficult to exaggerate the authority of these propositions. Both maxims are of outstanding relevance as caveats to be included with contemporary arguments over the implications of information-led warfare.

Edward N. Luttwak's intellectual *tour de force*, *Strategy*, is generally successful in its rigorous and relentless intellectual harrying of a *'paradoxical logic'* that pervades *'the entire realm of strategy'*.[41] On the first page of his preface, Luttwak leaves readers in no doubt about the heroic domain of his theoretical mission. 'No strategies are suggested here for the conduct of the United States on the world scene, or for the employment of its armed forces in war. My purpose, rather, is to uncover the universal logic that conditions all forms of war as well as the adversarial dealings of nations in peacetime.'[42] Luttwak's brilliant explanation of how what works today in strategy may not work tomorrow, precisely because it worked today[43]—though there could be surprise in repetition tomorrow of what has failed many times in the past—is persuasive, but limited in its explanatory power. He has written a classic treatment of the logic of paradox in conflict and strategy. Unfortunately, there is more to conflict and strategy than either the 'horizontal' dimension of adversarial relations that promotes paradoxical logic or the 'vertical' problems and opportunities created by the different levels of

---

[38] J. C. Wylie, *Military Strategy: A General Theory of Power Control*, ed. John B. Hattendorf, repr. of 1967 edn. (Annapolis, Md., 1989), 77.

[39] Ibid. 72.

[40] Ibid.

[41] Edward N. Luttwak, *Strategy: The Logic of War and Peace* (Cambridge, Mass., 1987), 4 (emphasis original).

[42] Ibid. p. xi.

[43] Ibid. ch. 2.

conflict.[44] What Luttwak attempts he achieves very well, but he does not attempt enough.[45]

Bernard Brodie, among all the strategic theorists of the twentieth century, was probably the best equipped by education, professional experience, range of interests, and opportunity to write a landmark text on the theory of war and strategy.[46] In the context of an enormous number of influential writings over the course of three-and-a-half decades, his mature work, *War and Politics*, published five years before his death in 1978, has to constitute his principal bid for status amongst the immortals of strategic theory.[47] The two long chapters on 'The Weapon' in the 1946 book, *The Absolute Weapon*, the four chapters on 'The Origins of Air Strategy', comprising part 1 of his 1959 book, *Strategy in the Missile Age*, and the two essay contributions to the edition of Clausewitz's *On War* translated by Michael Howard and Peter Paret, also warrant inclusion in the *corpus classicus* of Brodie's more theoretical writings.[48]

War and Politics is a wide-ranging book, packed with insight, which in some ways vitally augments *On War*. For example, Brodie has important arguments to make about the identity of national interests, the causes of wars, the selection of war aims, and social attitudes towards war; all of these are subjects omitted or neglected by Clausewitz, albeit generally for good reason, given his focus on the nature and conduct of 'war proper'. In addition, Brodie has insights to offer on the theory of strategic practice and the practice of strategy theory that are as penetrating as one would hope to read from a person whose career included advisory roles to government for nearly thirty years. Brodie's lifetime contribution to understanding the meaning of nuclear weapons for war and strategy—summarized as the subtitle to chapter 9 of *War and Politics*, 'Utility in Nonuse', and in a journal article published in 1978[49]—enjoy classic status.

Unfortunately, *War and Politics* comprises a loose collection of quite powerful essays masquerading as a book. That is not in itself a fatal disqualification for election to the premier league of strategic theory; after all, Clausewitz's *On War* merits its lonely five-star status despite its unfinished character, less than ideal internal organization, uncertainties in translation of some key concepts, and the

[44] Edward N. Luttwak, *Strategy: The Logic of War and Peace* (Cambridge, Mass., 1987), 4 (emphasis original), p. xii.

[45] Gregory D. Foster, 'On Strategic Theory and Logic: Review of Edward N. Luttwak, *Strategy: The Logic of War and Peace*', *Strategic Review*, 15 (1987), 75–80, scores some important hits.

[46] Barry H. Steiner, *Bernard Brodie and the Foundations of American Nuclear Strategy* (Lawrence, Kan., 1991); Ken Booth, 'Bernard Brodie', in John Baylis and John Garnett (eds.), *Makers of Nuclear Strategy* (New York, 1991), 19–56.

[47] Bernard Brodie, *War and Politics* (New York, 1973).

[48] Bernard Brodie, 'War in the Atomic Age', and 'Implications for Military Policy', in Brodie (ed.), *The Absolute Weapon: Atomic Power and World Order* (New York, 1946), 21–69, 70–107; id., *Strategy in the Missile Age* (Princeton, NJ, 1959), pt. 1; id., 'The Continuing Relevance of *On War*', and 'A Guide to the Reading of *On War*', in Clausewitz, *On War*, 45–68, 641–711.

[49] Bernard Brodie, 'The Development of Nuclear Strategy', *International Security*, 2 (1978), 65–83.

hallmark of its time, place, and strategic cultural context of creation. Classic though it is, *War and Politics* still falls short of the major work that this author believes Brodie could have written on the enduring fundamentals of his subject. *War and Politics* lacks coherence in trajectory, and is unduly personal and contemporary in much of its analysis, examples, and judgement.

At a lower level of performance, one must cite the interesting writings of the British strategic theorist Basil Liddell Hart and the French theorist Raoul Castex. They earn their place in this short short list of great strategic theorists because they each sought, and believed they had identified, keys to success in the general conduct of strategy in war. Even if they failed, as I believe they did, they failed in interesting ways. Unlike Corbett, Mahan,[50] and Douhet,[51] to each of whom analytical focus upon a particular geographical environment was the boundary of his theory, Liddell Hart and Castex sought to provide general theories of strategy.

Liddell Hart's discovery and claim that 'throughout the ages, effective results in war have rarely been attained unless the approach has such indirectness as to ensure the opponent's unreadiness to meet it',[52] though perilously tautological and unfalsifiable, is not bereft of merit. Albeit in a different league (i.e. belonging to a general, rather than geographically partial, category of theorist) from Mahan, Liddell Hart shares with the American admiral the distinction of having been unduly criticized.[53] Liddell Hart's favoured idea of an 'indirect approach', allegedly the conceptual philosopher's stone for the strategist, is as difficult to corral intellectually as it is to locate historically. Nonetheless, it constitutes a valuable if elusive theoretical insight.

Raoul Castex is noted here not because he has been influential—he has not—but

---

[50] Mahan, *Influence of Sea Power upon History, 1660–1783*, esp. ch. 1; id., *The Influence of Sea Power upon the French Revolution and Empire, 1793–1812* (2 vols., Boston, 1892), esp. vol. ii, ch. 19; id., *Mahan on Naval Strategy: Selections from the Writings of Rear Admiral Alfred Thayer Mahan*, ed. John B. Hattendorf (Annapolis, Md., 1991). Jon Tetsuro Sumida, *Inventing Grand Strategy and Teaching Command: The Classic Works of Alfred Thayer Mahan Reconsidered* (Washington, DC, 1997), is a welcome major revisionist study that ably defends the admiral against many of the charges levelled at him.

[51] Giulio Douhet, *The Command of the Air*, trans. Dino Ferrari, repr. of 1942 edn. (New York, 1972).

[52] Liddell Hart, *Strategy*, 25.

[53] John J. Mearsheimer, *Liddell Hart and the Weight of History* (Ithaca, NY, 1988), is a severe critique. Brian Bond, *Liddell Hart: A Study of His Military Thought* (New Brunswick, NJ, 1977), is more generous. Azar Gat, 'Liddell Hart's Theory of Armoured Warfare: Revising the Revisionists', *Journal of Strategic Studies*, 19 (1996), 1–30; id., 'British Influence and the Evolution of the Panzer Arm: Myth or Reality?', in 2 parts, *War in History*, 4 (1997), 150–73, 316–38, adds new detail to assist a more balanced view, as, especially, does Gat, *Fascist and Liberal Visions of War: Fuller, Liddell Hart, Douhet, and Other Modernists* (Oxford, 1998), pt. 2. Alex Danchev, *Alchemist of War: The Life of Basil Liddell Hart* (London, 1998), is a most literate, even literary, empathetic biography, while Brian Holden Reid, *Studies in British Military Thought: Debates with Fuller and Liddell Hart* (Lincoln, Neb., 1998), like Gat (*Fascist and Liberal*), breaks new ground in looking at Liddell Hart in intellectual historical context. Although Liddell Hart's reputation as a grand general theorist suffers quite justly from critical recognition of the circularity in his concept of the 'indirect approach', he was capable of extraordinary prescience and insight. For example, his small book *The Revolution in Warfare* (London, 1946) anticipates much of the American theory of limited war in the nuclear era that was composed in the 1950s.

rather because he had a clear understanding of general strategy for joint warfare. Similarly, his large ideas about the centrality of *manoeuvre* (in French, the quest for advantage, rather than manoeuvre, narrowly, in English) the persisting appearance of *perterbateurs* (dissatisfied, revolutionary, predatory, or rogue political actors) in European politics, and of a geostrategic pattern in conflict between Europe and Asia, serve to render his prolific writings on *Théories stratégiques* more interesting than their maritime focus might otherwise suggest.[54]

This brief discussion of the successors of Clausewitz as general theorists of strategy cannot be complete without mention of two additional authors fifty years and more apart; Admiral Sir Reginald Custance (RN), and Colonel John Boyd (USAF). In *A Study of War*, with praiseworthy directness and brevity (few books can boast a first chapter consisting of only one page), Custance restates and clarifies what many readers of Clausewitz, especially in Germany, apparently had missed:

Whatever be the form of Government and whatever be the internal political dissensions, each side starts, consciously or unconsciously, in every war with an object, which may be called National or Political, and with an aim, which may be called Military, to use the armed force to attain the National or Political object. Hence, the idea of war as a political act includes both the National or Political object and the Military aim.[55]

It is particularly refreshing to find in Custance's *A Study of War* a recognition of the critical importance of battle that is thoroughly Clausewitzian. Civilian scholars of strategy today are wont to find in the writings of Clausewitz and other preferred practitioners of strategic theory (Sun Tzu especially) a politically correct disdain for battle. Custance reminds his readers:

It is the province of strategy to attain the national object through the complete, partial or threatened achievement of the military aim under the existing political, economic and military conditions. The underlying assertion is that when armed force is used instead of moral suasion security is reached through battle or the threat of battle.[56]

In no sense does Custance rival Clausewitz as a strategic theorist, but as a disciple with a gift for clear thinking, economy of expression, and reliable grasp of most of the master's teachings, the admiral performed usefully. He tended to take his enthusiasm for offensive action to imprudent lengths, especially in opposition to a Corbettian insistence upon the primacy of the control of maritime communications by means other than decisive battle. This aggressive urge on Custance's part, however, is irrelevant to the overall merit of *A Study of War*.

Finally, if Edward N. Luttwak warrants high praise for his rigorous examination of the workings of paradox as key to 'the universal logic that conditions all forms of war', John Boyd deserves at least an honourable mention for his discovery of the 'OODA loop'. The loop specifies a process of Observation–Orientation–Decision–

---

[54] Raoul Castex, *Strategic Theories*, trans. and ed. Eugenia C. Kiesling (Annapolis, Md., 1994).
[55] Custance, *Study of War*, 1.
[56] Ibid. 94.

Action, allegedly comprising a universal logic of conflict.[57] As a fighter pilot and subsequent investigator of the reasons why USAF F-86 Sabre jets achieved such remarkably favourable kill ratios in combat against MiG-15s over North Korea (10 to 1), Boyd found in the OODA loop the essential logic of success in battle.[58] Just as Luttwak's logic of paradox permeates all levels and kinds of conflict, so Boyd's loop can apply to the operational, strategic, and political levels of war, as well as to tactics for aerial dogfights. Boyd's theory claims that the key to success in conflict is to operate inside the opponent's decision cycle. Advantages in observation and orientation enable a tempo in decisionmaking and execution that outpaces the ability of the foe to react effectively in time. This seemingly simple tactical formula was duly explained and copiously illustrated historically by Boyd in many briefings within the US defence community over the course of twenty years. The OODA loop may appear too humble to merit categorization as grand theory, but that is what it is. It has an elegant simplicity, an extensive domain of applicability, and contains a high quality of insight about strategic essentials, such that its author well merits honourable mention as an outstanding general theorist of strategy. The ambitious reach of Boyd's insight is conveyed by this briefing note:

Strategy
Penetrate adversary's moral–mental–physical being to dissolve his moral fiber, disorient his mental images, disrupt his operations, and overload his system, as well as subvert, shatter, seize, or otherwise subdue, those moral–mental–physical bastions, connections, or activities that he depends upon, in order to destroy internal harmony, produce paralysis, and collapse adversary's will to resist.[59]

The strategic theorists discussed here are representative of the best of their breed in the twentieth century. Possible reasons why general theory on war and strategy since Clausewitz has failed to match the standard of excellence that he set are identified and discussed in the next chapter.

THE STRENGTHS OF *ON WAR*

What follows constitutes my view of the extraordinary conceptual contributions on offer in *On War*.

Clausewitz characterizes war as a 'Remarkable Trinity'.[60] His trinity comprises 'primordial violence, hatred, and enmity', 'the play of chance and probability

---

[57] John R. Boyd, 'A Discourse on Winning and Losing' (MS, Aug. 1987). I am grateful to Barry D. Watts of the Northrop Corporation for supplying this rare classic. 'Discourse' comprises a set of richly annotated briefings. The 'OODA loop' also is known as the 'Boyd theory' and the 'Boyd cycle'.

[58] David S. Fadok, *John Boyd and John Warden: Air Power's Quest for Strategic Paralysis* (Maxwell AFB, Ala., Feb. 1995).

[59] Boyd, 'Patterns of Conflict', 134, in 'Discourse'.

[60] Clausewitz, *On War*, 89.

within which the creative spirit is free to roam', and instrumental rationality. Although he associates the first of these aspects mainly with the people, the second with the commander and his army, and the third with the government, his genius discerns that these aspects interpenetrate each other and cannot have fixed relationships. He specifies that '[o]ur task therefore is to develop a theory that maintains a balance between these three tendencies [passion, chance, rationality], like an object suspended between three magnets'. Clausewitz leaves this brilliant formulation under-explored, but he provides navigation aids of incomparable worth to those who would follow.

Clausewitz advises that war is an instrument, or act of policy.[61] Errors in comprehension of this fundamental point are strategically irredeemable, at least in a current conflict, as Germany demonstrated twice in the twentieth century, and as the United States learnt by bitter experience in Vietnam, yet needed to learn again if the outcome to the Gulf War of 1991 is admitted as evidence. The power of Saddam Hussein's Iraq was reduced, but it was not reduced as much as the US-led coalition believed in early 1991. The coalition believed that it had won a war; in fact it had won a campaign. Clausewitz advised that '[s]ubordinating the political point of view to the military would be absurd, for it is policy that creates war', while 'at the highest level the art of war turns into policy'.[62]

On War insists that policymakers must understand the military instrument that they intend to use.[63] The statesman does not have to be a soldier, but 'a certain grasp of military affairs is vital for those in charge of general policy'.[64] Earlier, Clausewitz offers the luminous explanation:

War plans cover every aspect of a war, and weave them all into a single operation that must have a single, ultimate objective in which all particular aims are reconciled. No one starts a war—or rather, no one in his senses ought to do so—without first being clear in his mind what he intends to achieve by that war and how he intends to conduct it. The former is its political purpose, the latter its operational objective.[65]

Here Clausewitz probes the core meaning of strategy. The use of force and the political consequences of that use—this is the real stuff of strategy. For reasons that Clausewitz did not explore, it can be difficult for policymakers to understand their military instrument. Indeed, in most wars one or even both sides have to learn just what their military instruments are capable of achieving. This argument by Clausewitz is fundamental to all strategic performance. No one has expressed the matter better than he.

War is subordinate to policy but remains distinctive. *On War* tells us that war's 'grammar, indeed, may be its own, but not its logic [in policy]'.[66] Because of the context of this quotation, in book VIII, chapter 6, 'B. War Is an Instrument of Policy', commentary often focuses unduly upon the policy 'logic' of war, and not

---

[61] Clausewitz, *On War*, 605–10.   [62] Ibid. 607.   [63] Ibid.
[64] Ibid. 608.   [65] Ibid. 579.   [66] Ibid. 605.

sufficiently upon the distinctive integrity of war's 'grammar'. To my mind, no commentary on Clausewitz as yet has accorded his conceptual opposition of war's policy 'logic' and 'grammar' the celebration that it merits. What Clausewitz is saying is that the threat and use of force is not a self-validating exercise. Admittedly proceeding somewhat beyond what Clausewitz wrote, I am moved by his writing to claim that he insists upon a 'grammar', a distinctive character and dynamic, of war that is inalienable, though it lacks any policy 'logic' of its own. To illustrate, whatever the political intention, the policy logic of biological weapons in modern war, there is a 'grammar', a set of physical conditions and tactical challenges, that must constrain the effectiveness of the employment of those weapons. The point is really obvious, but it needs to be made, and Clausewitz made it superbly.

With brutal clarity and elegant parsimony Clausewitz tells us: 'War is thus an act of force to compel our enemy to do our will.'[67] When Hedley Bull insists that war is 'organised violence carried on by political units against each other',[68] it is not obvious that he offers a superior definition, notwithstanding the intrusion of the 'political' qualifier, which in the modern world distinguishes 'war' from crime or other private violence. Clausewitz tells us that 'to impose our will on the enemy is its [war's] object', while the 'character of war must be determined by policy'.[69] None of this is earth-shattering, but it is an elementary wisdom that policymakers frequently ignore in practice.

Many so-called strategic studies are partial in their focus and treatment of war. Clausewitz warns, in the first paragraph of book I, chapter 1 of *On War*, that 'in war more than in any other subject we must begin by looking at the nature of the whole; for here more than elsewhere the part and the whole must always be thought of together.'[70] As warfare has become ever more complex in its elements, so Clausewitz's insistence upon holistic analysis becomes yet more salient. He is advising that an advancing complexity in the phenomena of strategic experience should not confuse us as to the nature and function of strategy and war. New environments and new weapons will add to the pile of matters needing attention by strategists, but the nature of war and strategy, and the relationship between policy and military instrument, endure.

Clausewitz's resolution of his intellectual crisis in 1827 by roughly marrying his concepts of absolute, or decisive, war to a newly recognized notion of real war, or war for limited aims, helps policymakers and would-be successor theorists to appreciate the full spectrum of possible war.[71] More by historical-intellectual accident than grand design, *On War* describes total warfare and warfare somewhat

[67] Ibid. 75.
[68] Hedley Bull, *The Anarchical Society: A Study of Order in World Politics* (New York, 1977), 184.
[69] Clausewitz, *On War*, 75, 606.
[70] Ibid. 75.
[71] Gat, *Origins*, ch. 7.

tamed as a rational instrument of policy pursued in restrained ways for limited aims. Although Clausewitz does not reconcile the ideas of absolute and limited war, there is no essential contradiction between the two. It is important for policymakers and strategic theorists to grasp the whole of his understanding of the spectrum of war. Limited though real conflicts tend to be, war is 'an act of force to compel our enemy to do our will'. The competitive application of force can cease to be an instrument of policy, let alone 'simply a continuation of political intercourse, with the addition of other means'. We need to remember that it is the Janus-like nature of war to be both a process of violence that will tend to escalate in the heat and passion of the doing, and an instrument of policy.

If Clausewitz had written only about friction in war, his place among the heroes in the Valhalla of strategic theory would be secure for all time. What is friction? 'Friction, as we choose to call it, is the force that makes the apparently easy so difficult.'[72] Clausewitz notes: 'Action in war is like movement in a resistant element.'[73] Earlier, he advises that in war 'the difficulties accumulate and end by producing a kind of friction that is inconceivable unless one has experienced war'.[74] In general, he comments, 'Friction is the only concept that more or less corresponds to the factors that distinguish real war from war on paper.' Barry Watts, the most careful modern interpreter of Clausewitz's ideas on friction, argues that *On War* suggests the malign, ubiquitous possibilities of operation both of a narrow friction that impedes the smooth functioning of people and machines and of a more general friction deriving from danger, exertion, uncertainties, and chance, in short from characteristic conditions of war.[75] These two sources of friction can interact to hinder military performance and hence strategic effectiveness. An ill-coordinated complex military instrument will find its weaknesses mercilessly exposed by those circumstances of 'war proper' that cannot be replicated for training purposes adequately in peacetime exercises. In addition, the more general causes of friction in war—generically, the unparalleled danger, the extreme exertion, and so forth—will reveal real-time fragilities in the armed forces that previously had barely even been suspected. While everyone knows about 'friction', Clausewitz is unique in emphasizing its power to frustrate. Strategic theorists usually dwell on how to perform well in war, if only their advice is followed. Clausewitz may be unique in the persuasiveness of his writing on the subject of how and why things can go very wrong.

Not content to warn of the perils to good performance posed by friction, *On War* advises also: 'War is the realm of uncertainty; three quarters of the factors on which action in war is based are wrapped in a fog of greater or lesser uncertainty.'[76] This thought complements Clausewitz's earlier observation that

[72] Clausewitz, *On War*, 121.
[73] Ibid. 120.
[74] Ibid. 119.
[75] Barry D. Watts, *Clausewitzian Friction and Future War*, McNair Paper 52 (Washington, DC, Oct. 1996).
[76] Clausewitz, *On War*, 101.

'[i]n the whole range of human activities, war most closely resembles a game of cards'.[77] Commonplace though emphasis upon the role of chance in war may appear, such emphasis is highly unusual among strategic theorists, a rare exception being Thucydides, who shared Clausewitz's view about the unpredictability of war. In one guise or another, most strategic theorists have been retailing alleged keys to strategic success: it follows that those theorists would be unlikely to emphasize the uncertainties of war. If Clausewitz warned that war is the realm of chance, Baron Antoine Henri de Jomini believed that much of the risk of failure in war could be eliminated—always provided one embraced the Baron's theory.

It is true that theories cannot teach men with mathematical precision what they should do in every possible case; but it is also certain that they will always point out the errors which should be avoided; and this is a highly-important consideration, for these rules thus become, in the hands of skilful generals commanding brave troops, means of almost certain success.[78]

Notwithstanding a superficially narrow battlefield focus (upon the 'engagement'), Clausewitz's definitions of, and distinction between, strategy and tactics are the clearest and most useful. His definition of strategy, 'the use of engagements for the object of the war',[79] may read like operational art but transfers readily to a higher level of effort. If proof is needed of the superiority of his distinction between strategy and tactics, one need only reflect upon the infrequency with which the distinction is observed. How can a country's policymakers think properly instrumentally about their armed forces when, for example, they label a part of their arsenal 'strategic forces'? In its 1998 *Strategic Defence Review* —one wonders what a non-strategic defence review might be—the British government refers to the possibility of 'strategic attack on NATO', to 'strategic transport', and, for maximum opacity, even to a ' "sub-strategic" role' for Trident missiles.[80] If 'strategic' is allowed to mean long-range, or most important, then how can one protect a clarity of distinction between means and ends? The Clausewitzian formula prevents confusion on that score. Given the now longstanding availability of a good English translation of *On War*, there is no excuse for confusing today what Clausewitz explained correctly in the 1820s.

In sharp distinction to Sun Tzu and to many of the optimistic would-be information warriors of today, Clausewitz warns of the poverty of reliable information available to a commander in war: 'the general unreliability of all information presents a specific problem in war: all action takes place, so to speak, in a kind of twilight, which, like fog or moonlight, often tends to make things seem grotesque

---

[77] Ibid. 86.

[78] Jomini, *Art of War*, 323.

[79] Clausewitz, *On War*, 128.

[80] George Robertson, Secretary of State for Defence, *The Strategic Defence Review* (London, July 1998), 16, 24, 18.

and larger than they really are.'[81] He might have modified his negative attitude towards intelligence had he been granted some foresight about technological developments in information-gathering (e.g. from space, from unmanned aerial vehicles, and generically from exploitation of the electromagnetic spectrum). It seems most probable, however, that he would have remained sceptical about the ability of technology to conquer friction. Periodic celebration of the concept of the fog of war can serve as a healthy corrective to those who are unduly credulous about the prospects for achieving total transparency over a battlespace of 40,000 square miles.[82]

As befitting a continental theorist inspired by his interpretation of the Napoleonic example, Clausewitz advised that in war

one must keep the dominant characteristics of both belligerents in mind. Out of these characteristics a certain center of gravity develops, the hub of all power and movement, on which everything depends. That is the point against which all our energies should be directed.[83]

He reasoned that 'by constantly seeking out the center of his power, by daring all to win all, will one really defeat the enemy'.[84] The concept retains its utility, even if one rejects Clausewitz's preference for applying strength against strength. The US Marine Corps, for example, in their doctrinal manual on *Warfighting*, note that 'we have since come to prefer pitting strength against weakness. Applying the term to modern warfare, we must make it clear that by the enemy's center of gravity we do not mean a source of strength, but rather a critical vulnerability.'[85]

The idea of centre of gravity can apply to all levels and kinds of conflict, and can accommodate a wide range of 'targets'. Clausewitz himself offered, in descending order of general attractiveness, the following possible centres of gravity: the enemy's army, his capital city, his principal ally, the enemy's leader, and enemy public opinion.[86] In the US phase of the Vietnam War, North Vietnam correctly identified American public opinion as their enemy's most critical centre of gravity. In the Gulf War of 1991, US political and military leaders focused upon the person of the enemy leader, Saddam Hussein, and that fraction of his army used to support his deeply personal regime, the Republican Guard. Application to particular cases is rarely easy, but this simple idea of a centre of gravity is essential, helping a defence community avoid the error of merely being active in war, rather

---

[81] Clausewitz, *On War*, 140. See David Kahn, 'Clausewitz and Intelligence', in Handel, *Clausewitz and Modern Strategy*, 117–26; Handel, *Masters of War*, ch. 12; Watts, *Clausewitzian Friction*.

[82] James R. Blaker, *Understanding the Revolution in Military Affairs: A Guide to America's 21st Century Defense*, Progressive Policy Institute Defense Working Paper 3 (Washington, DC, Jan. 1997), 9. The title tells all in Joseph S. Nye, Jr., and William A. Owens, 'America's Information Edge', *Foreign Affairs*, 75 (1996), 20–36.

[83] Clausewitz, *On War*, 595–6.

[84] Ibid. 596.

[85] The US Marine Corps, *Warfighting* (New York, 1994), 107, n. 28.

[86] Clausewitz, *On War*, 596. For the contrast with Sun Tzu, see Handel, *Masters of War*, 47, table 5.1.

than purposefully active. Whether one interprets the idea of a centre of gravity as an enemy strength to be overthrown, or an enemy vulnerability to be exploited, in either case a candidate theory of victory in war is identified. Centre of gravity is key to strategic thinking because its translation for a particular case—for the British and Sinn Fein–IRA in Northern Ireland, or for Iraq and the United States– United Nations over inspection for weapons of mass destruction—organizes the bridge between means and ends that truly is the realm of strategy.

On War declares that although 'war . . . is an act of policy',[87] it is nonetheless war and war has a necessary tactical level that is about fighting. Even though war is a 'true political instrument', '[t]he decision by arms is for all major and minor operations in war what cash payment is in commerce. Regardless how complex the relationship between the two parties, regardless how rarely settlements actually occur, they can never be entirely absent.'[88] From theories of naval strategy to nuclear and space strategy, modern scholars have struggled in vain to sidestep the logic in Clausewitz's insistence upon the permanent salience of the possibility of combat.[89]

As well as emphasizing the significance of actual combat, Clausewitz was not confused on the point that moral forces really matter. A weapon can be no more effective than the person who uses it. Technology is important, but in war and strategy people matter most. Clausewitz understood this and stated it clearly: 'Theory becomes infinitely more difficult as soon as it touches the realm of moral values.'[90] Also he reminds all who need reminding that '[m]ilitary activity is never directed against material force alone; it is always aimed simultaneously at the moral forces which give it life, and the two cannot be separated.'[91] The human dimension of war and strategy has a way of triumphing over technology and cunning plans.

Though perilously close to tautology, Clausewitz offers universal strategic wisdom when he states that '[t]he best strategy is always *to be very strong*; first in general, and then at the decisive point.'[92] This thought is of course simple, but in true Clausewitzian fashion it is not easy to realize in practice. How can one identify a 'decisive point'? Is such a 'point' determined by our, or the enemy's, concentration of effort? Notwithstanding the difficulties in application, the principle of concentration of effort has merit across the entire spectrum of conflict, from special operations by handfuls of heroes to nuclear bombardment. For example,

---

[87] Clausewitz, *On War*, 87.

[88] Ibid. 97.

[89] Jan S. Breemer, *The Burden of Trafalgar: Decisive Battle and Naval Strategic Expectations on the Eve of the First World War*, Newport Paper 6 (Newport, RI, Oct. 1993); Michael Howard, *The Causes of Wars and Other Essays* (London, 1983), 133–50; Gerald Segal (ed.), *New Directions in Strategic Studies: A Chatham House Debate*, RIIA Discussion Paper 17 (London, 1989), 7–8.

[90] Clausewitz, *On War*, 136.

[91] Ibid. 137.

[92] Ibid. 204 (emphasis original).

readers of a recent study of special operations are told: 'Relative superiority is a concept crucial to the theory of special operations.' The study proceeds to claim: 'Relative superiority is achieved at the pivotal moment in an engagement.'[93] 'Decisive points' and 'pivotal moments' are not, of course, objectively contextual features in geography and history, but rather are created by successful applications of Clausewitz's dictum as just quoted. The fact that this is hard to do helps explain why some generals succeed but many do not.

Clausewitz offers a superior analysis of the proper and improper uses of strategic theory. His observations on the proper role of theory offer insights literally unique in strategic literature. 'Theory should cast a steady light on all phenomena so that we can more easily recognize and eliminate the weeds that always spring from ignorance; it should show how one thing is related to another, and keep the important and unimportant separate.'[94] He lit a beacon for future generations of strategic theorists by claiming:

Theory cannot equip the mind with formulas for solving problems, nor can it mark the narrow path on which the sole solution is supposed to lie by planting a hedge of principles on either side. But it can give the mind insight into the great mass of phenomena and of their relationships, then leave it free to rise into the higher realms of action.[95]

Clausewitz understood the educational, rather than directive, role of strategic theory much more clearly than did many defence analysts in the 1960s and 1970s.[96] As John Shy has noticed, modern strategic thought can be criticized for its Jominian positivist characteristics, and particularly for its tendency to 'reduce war to an operational exercise, transforming it thereby into an unrealistic but extremely dangerous game'.[97] Strategy is a practical subject, but strategic theory cannot yield a field manual for action.

Of all the theorists of war and strategy, Clausewitz best identifies the mixture of qualities necessary in the good general. Above all else, he explains that the key element of 'determination proceeds from a special type of mind, from a strong rather than a brilliant one'.[98] He is apt to praise intuition, the *coup d'œil*, more than is prudent, but he is right to emphasize the importance of moral qualities, which amount approximately to genius, in the direction of war. There is no virtue in stupidity; Clausewitz's thoughts on command do not include celebration of ignorance in any of its forms. The point is that, while generals need to be clever enough

---

[93] William H. McRaven, *SPEC OPS, Case Studies in Special Operations Warfare: Theory and Practice* (Novato, Calif., 1995), 4.

[94] Ibid. 578.

[95] Ibid.

[96] American theorists on strategic stability are among the worst offenders against Clausewitz's judgement, e.g. Jerome H. Kahan, *Security in the Nuclear Age: Developing U.S. Strategic Arms Policy* (Washington, DC, 1995).

[97] John Shy, 'Jomini', in Paret, *Makers of Modern Strategy*, 183.

[98] Clausewitz, *On War*, 103.

to grasp what they need to grasp, intellectual cleverness *per se*, of the kind highly prized by scholars, is of little, and probably would be of negative, value. When one considers what might have made Sir Douglas Haig or Dwight D. Eisenhower better generals, the most plausible answers lie in the regions of different operating styles and job definitions—both of which are really critically matters of character—not of better intellect or professional education.[99]

With the powerful concept of the culminating point of victory, Clausewitz warns about the perils of apparent success.[100] The paradoxical logic of conflict, operating at all levels from high statecraft down to tactics, suggests that success can lure the victor down the road to eventual disadvantage and even destruction. At the level of statecraft, it is apparent that France in 1807 after the Treaties of Tilsit with Prussia and Russia, Germany in 1940, Japan early in 1942, and the United States in the 1990s all succumbed to a 'victory disease' that disinclined their leaders to recognize the contexts and consequential terms of engagement that had yielded each of them such stunning successes.[101] As with so much in Clausewitz, the concept—in this case, translated into general advice, of knowing when to stop—is as commonsensical as its application is frequently ferociously difficult. Williamson Murray and Mark Grimsley express the nub of the problem: 'Like politics, strategy is the art of the possible; but few can discern what is possible.'[102] Moreover, how can one know what is possible, unless one tries? Clausewitz alerts his readers that beyond a certain point apparent strength is actually a growing weakness (e.g. the nominal occupation of more and more enemy territory). Strategic success can fuel a political ambition for empire that exceeds the scale of mobilizable, or seizeable, resources, while it triggers the creation or augmentation of a hostile coalition. At the operational level of war, this observation yields a cautionary insight for those who see a quick offensive as the cure for their strategic difficulties. Just as endeavours to defend everything can result in nothing being defended well enough, so more definitely can be less when it comes to extending the operational offensive.

Apart from the short intervals in every campaign during which both sides are on the defensive, every attack which does not lead to peace must necessarily end up as a defense.
  It is thus defense itself that weakens the attack. Far from being idle sophistry, we consider

[99] Dominick Graham and Shelford Bidwell, *Coalitions, Politicians and Generals: Some Aspects of Command in Two World Wars* (London, 1993), is especially persuasive.

[100] Ibid. 566–73.

[101] John W. Dower, *War Without Mercy: Race and Power in the Pacific War* (New York, 1986), 260–1. Also, Robert Epstein's careful study of Napoleon's campaign against Austria in 1809 shows how even the great French 'God of War' could mistake the reach of his undoubted genius, forgetting how dependent he was for success upon the cooperative folly of previously hapless foes. *Napoleon's Last Victory and the Emergence of Modern War* (Lawrence, Kan. 1994).

[102] Williamson Murray and Mark Grimsley, 'Introduction: On Strategy', in Murray et al., *Making of Strategy*, 22.

it to be the greatest disadvantage of the attack that one is eventually left in a most awkward defensive position.[103]

With the exposed salients that they created, the German armies that failed to reach Paris in March–July 1918, that were halted in the first week of December 1941 in Moscow's outer suburbs, and that were trapped in the Stalingrad pocket from November 1942 to the denouement on 2 February 1943, provided textbook illustration of Clausewitz's warning.

Finally, among the gems selected here from the Clausewitz collection, he advises: 'It is easier to hold ground than take it. It follows that defense is easier than attack, assuming both sides have equal means.'[104] This proposition is reflected in the tactical rule of thumb that specifies a 3:1 ratio as the manpower advantage required for an attack to succeed against a continuous and cohesive defence.[105] This general wisdom offered by Clausewitz is, of course, vulnerable in any particular case. Defence may be the stronger form of waging regular war on land, but even with approximately 'equal means' it is not proof against operational incompetence on the heroic scale demonstrated, for example, by the French high command in 1940, or the Soviet high command in the summer of 1941.[106]

THE LIMITATIONS OR WEAKNESSES OF *ON WAR*

Copernicus, Shakespeare, Newton, and Adam Smith are not beyond all criticism, and the products of their genius are not entirely beyond the possibility of benefit by amendment. To allow that general strategic theory is a dynamic subject is not to allow that Clausewitz had feet of clay, let alone that he wrote a book that is fatally flawed. One can argue that he left much work to be done. In some ways, progress can be made in areas that he did not address, precisely because he laid so well the foundations of a general theory of war and strategy. Paradoxically, it is abundant testimony to the power of his writing that so many gifted critics, so long after his death, find inspiration in his work. There is honour to the great theorist even in a

---

[103] Clausewitz, *On War*, 572.

[104] Ibid. 357.

[105] 'Where the ratio of force to space is high enough to provide a continuous defensive front, with a properly woven network of fire and mobile reserves, the attacking side requires about a three to one superiority—measured in weapon power—to achieve more than a local and momentary effect. That conclusion was drawn from the experience of the last war [1914–18]; although disputed in many quarters during the peace interval and the early stages of the present war [1939–45], it has come to be recognized authoritatively as experience has extended': Liddell Hart, *Revolution in Warfare*, 21–2.

[106] Robert Allan Doughty, *The Breaking Point: Sedan and the Fall of France* (Hamden, Conn., 1990); Andrei Mertsalov, 'The Collapse of Stalin's Diplomacy and Strategy', in John Erickson and David Dilks (eds.), *Barbarossa: The Axis and the Allies* (Edinburgh, 1994), 134–49.

'grand tradition of trashing Clausewitz'.[107] After all, it is better to be criticized than ignored.

The discussion that follows of possible limitations and weaknesses is not presented to defend Clausewitz. However, many of the points advanced in criticism of him in the twentieth century are pertinent to practical problems in the making and execution of strategy. Most of these points, therefore, should be considered as part of the dynamic development of a general theory of strategy.

Clausewitz's trinitarian view of war as the keystone piece of conceptual architecture requires more analysis. In part it requires modernization of emphasis in his claims that passions emanate mainly from the people, chance is characteristic principally of the realm of the commander and the army, while rationality resides mainly with the government that would use the army as an instrument of policy. Clausewitz's 'remarkable trinity' also needs to be rescued from careless scholars who believe incorrectly that he identified passion, chance, and rationality, neatly and discretely, with the people, the commander and the army, and the government.[108] The communications revolution of modern times that now, for example, allows a country's political leaders to watch television pictures of war nearly in real time means that the temptation to play general, captain, or even sergeant is likely occasionally to prove irresistible. Moreover, if the whole world is watching military events in a fairly direct technical sense, political sensibility to the brutalities of war is certain to place a novel and heavy strain on the relations that Clausewitz envisaged between army and government. This is not to claim that technology has overtaken Clausewitz's view of war as a 'remarkable trinity', but it is to recognize that his subtle, though still somewhat idealized, notion of this trinity requires heavy elaboration in augmenting and explanatory detail on the character of war that changes with technology and society.

It is one thing to grasp the importance in Clausewitz's insistence that 'war . . . is an act of policy' and not even 'a mere act of policy but a true political instrument';[109] it is quite another to know how to go about reconciling the two, let alone effecting such reconciliation. In what sense should policy direct war as its instrument? Furthermore, might policy, or politics, or perhaps culture, sometimes be an instrument of war, rather than vice versa? Clausewitz has little to say about policy. Although in principle allowing in his 'remarkable trinity' for some penetration by passion into the realm of policy, his 'policy' is still quintessentially rational. One might have expected a close observer of Napoleon's operational brilliance, yet

---

[107] Christopher Bassford, 'John Keegan and the Grand Tradition of Trashing Clausewitz: A Polemic', *War in History*, 1 (1994), 319–36; id., 'Landmarks in Defense Literature: *On War*, by Carl von Clausewitz', *Defense Analysis*, 12 (1996), 267–71.

[108] Edward J. Villacres and Christopher Bassford, 'Reclaiming the Clausewitzian Trinity', *Parameters*, 25 (1995), 9–19.

[109] Clausewitz, *On War*, 87.

political and 'strategic lunacy', to have been more probing of the quality of policy.[110] There is, of course, the partial excuse, or explanation, that Clausewitz was exploring the nature of, not the reasons for or goals of, war. The treatment in *On War* of the nexus that binds war and policy is exemplary in its logic and its clarity. Clausewitz leaves no room for doubt that, logically, policy has to be the master, ends must control means. He allows, also, that what is feasible for the military instrument must be permitted 'to affect political aims in a given case' though 'it will never do more than modify them'.[111] Beyond the rigorous world of politico-military logic, however, lies a real zone of uncertainty over what is and what is not policy. Moreover, there is extensive historical experience of the fortunes of 'war proper' in effect directing policy goals. *On War* is justly celebrated for the rigour of its exposition of the character of the relationship between war and policy, but unwary readers might be so impressed by what Clausewitz achieves that they fail to notice what he neglects to attempt. That neglect extends to the meaning of policy, the strategic fact of historical experience that once the dice of war are rolled, policy achievement is largely hostage to military performance, and the all too obvious practical difficulty of actually coordinating the conduct of war with the pursuit of particular policy goals. History is generous with illustration of the problems not addressed in *On War*.

As just one example, over Korea between 1950 and 1953 the United Nations shifted policy from the modest goal of repelling North Korea's invasion and restoring the *status quo ante* to unifying all of the Korean peninsula, and then back to approximate restoration of the *status quo ante*, and all for reason of the dynamic verdict of the battlefield.[112] The Clausewitzian formula on war and policy is not wrong, far from it, but it is seriously incomplete in that it is not augmented by the explanation necessary to alert readers to the major difficulties that in practice often govern the relationship between military instrument and political purpose.

Jessica Mathews tells us that '[t]he steady concentration of power in the hands of states that began in 1648 with the Peace of Westphalia is over, at least for a while'.[113] The political culture assumed in *On War* is state-centric. In Clausewitz's European order, states with governments had armies with commanders, and the people, if mobilized politically, could provide some healthy passion in the national cause—albeit under state direction. Some of those theorists and historians of the late twentieth century who discerned a decline in the authority of the state decided that Clausewitz, as a theorist for a world of states, had been

[110] MacGregor Knox, 'Conclusion: Continuity and Revolution in the Making of Strategy', in Murray et al., *Making of Strategy*, 616.

[111] Clausewitz, *On War*, 87.

[112] Rosemary Foot, *The Wrong War: American Policy and the Dimensions of the Korean Conflict* (Ithaca, NY, 1985); T. R. Fehrenbach, *This Kind of War: The Classic Korean War History* (Washington, DC, 1994).

[113] Jessica T. Mathews, 'Power Shift', *Foreign Affairs*, 76 (1997), 50. See also Martin van Creveld, 'The Fate of the State', *Parameters*, 26 (1996), 4–18.

overtaken by events.[114] *On War*, however, lends itself to application to any period. But there is a small but noisy body of opinion which claims that Clausewitz cannot apply to worlds that are pre-, or post-, Westphalian. With his focus on recent military history for illustrative examples, Clausewitz himself appeared to lend support to this charge of limited temporal (and hence political-order) domain. A more serious point is that Clausewitz, for all his good intentions to write a universal theory that would endure, nonetheless could not help but be a Prussian of his time. Aside from what one might make of the effects of the Enlightenment and German Romanticism upon his world-view,[115] there can be little doubt that some of the potentially significant decisions on omission and commission in *On War* were influenced by the author's time, place, and culture. In itself this is not a criticism; it is simply a fact about the human dimension of war and strategy. Although Clausewitz sought to write a lasting work of universal character, the recent past pervades *On War* and limits some of the confidence we can repose in it. Paradoxically, the trigger for Clausewitz's theorizing, his extensive experience of a Napoleonic war which had been of a decisive kind until 1807, can be judged to have been so overwhelming that he was unable to gain perspective and fully recover historical balance.[116] The power of inspiration he drew from Napoleon's career, though in a sense a most vital source for Clausewitz's greatness, also necessarily had a biasing, indeed a limiting, effect. The high and enduring quality of the incomplete manuscript that is *On War* attests, not to Clausewitz's ability to be impervious in his general theorizing to the prejudicing effect of the pull of recent events, but rather to his ability largely to transcend the constraints of that 'pull'.

Clausewitz advises that 'in the whole range of human activities, war most closely resembles a game of cards',[117] but the other players do not come in for close scrutiny in *On War*. We are told persuasively that 'war is nothing but a duel on a larger scale',[118] a thought that leads us to expect careful treatment of interaction among calculating adversaries. In fact, *On War* says much more about how 'to impose our will on the enemy'[119] than it does about the perils posed by the enemy's will. *On War* insists properly from the outset on recognition that war is

---

[114] Preeminently, Martin van Creveld, *The Transformation of War* (New York, 1991); id., *Nuclear Proliferation and the Future of Conflict* (New York, 1993); id., 'Fate of the State'; id., 'What is Wrong with Clausewitz?'

[115] Paret, *Clausewitz and the State*; id., *Understanding War: Essays on Clausewitz and the History of Military Power* (Princeton, NJ, 1992), ch. 7; Gat, *Origins*.

[116] There is merit in Robert M. Epstein's view that 'neither Napoleon, the Allied commanders who fought him, nor the theorists Clausewitz and Jomini were able to articulate the way warfare had changed since 1809'. *Napoleon's Last Victory and the Emergence of Modern War* (Lawrence, Kan., 1994), 179. As Napoleon's foes modernized in the late 1800s, so the possibility of victory via a single decisive battle became less and less likely.

[117] Clausewitz, *On War*, 86.

[118] Ibid. 75.

[119] Ibid.

not a unilateral exercise. Nonetheless, the book is weaker than it should be in the analysis of 'the enemy'. This is not a matter of marginal note. It is in the nature of war and strategy for their dynamic and variable characters to be influenced significantly by the more or less distinctive cultures of belligerents acting upon the strategic conditions in which they find themselves. Unwillingness or inability to comprehend the foe on his own terms, and to assess his choices as he should be expected to define and make them, is a principal source of poor performance in the conduct of war.[120] Of course, Clausewitz knew this, but he did not write about it in a way that accorded with its importance.

It can be argued that Clausewitz offers a narrowly military definition of strategy that encourages precisely the kind of obsession with decision by battle (or single campaign) that undid Germany twice in the twentieth century and that, indeed, has been all too characteristic of a 'Western way of war'.[121] The absence of grand strategic sense, or indeed of state machinery for strategy-making that could discover such sense, was fatal for Germany in both world wars. *On War* directs strategic attention to the battlefield. The charge that Clausewitz is thinking at the operational, even the tactical, level of war is not warranted. He insists logically, as well as for reason of his experience, upon battle—'engagements'—as the currency of strategy, but the sharp clarity of his distinction between tactics and strategy rescues him entirely from this charge. Although Clausewitz insists upon the importance of battle, he insists no less plainly that war is a political instrument and that battle has value precisely because of the use made of its outcome. This is not an iconic devotion to battle.

As one would expect of a Prussian—i.e. Central European continental—theorist, Clausewitz's thoughts on the objectives in war tend to be military-operational in character. Because Germany often has provided the battlefield, and has actual or potential foes on her borders, and because Berlin is unprotected by geography, Clausewitz suggests that one should seek swift decision in war by means of menacing his 'center of gravity, the hub of all power and movement'.[122] This approach pits strength against strength, and encourages one to roll the dice in the riskiest of ways (e.g. Robert E. Lee's direct assault on Cemetery Ridge on the third day at Gettysburg). Such advice might make sense for a continental power confronting a hostile coalition around its borders, but as general strategic wisdom it is a prescription for impatience, high casualties, and a fair chance of defeat. In addition, though he cannot be faulted for this, Clausewitz's discussion of centres of gravity has licensed lesser minds to apply his rather mechanistic Newtonian idea in a somewhat mindless manner. *Caveat emptor* is a reasonable defence of *On War*, but nonetheless the concept of centre of gravity, as Clausewitz treats it, should come

[120] Robert B. Bathurst, *Intelligence and the Mirror: On Creating an Enemy* (London, 1993).

[121] Victor David Hanson, *The Western Way of War: Infantry Battle in Classical Greece* (London, 1989); John Keegan, *A History of Warfare* (London, 1993).

[122] Clausewitz, *On War*, 595.

with a public health label attached. As an idea it does helpfully encourage policy-makers to seek focus in strategic endeavour. In addition, though, centre of gravity lends itself to simplistic application in a reductionist exercise that neglects true complexity. A strategic planner equipped with the powerful idea of centre of gravity can sometimes be likened to a medieval alchemist seeking earnestly but hopelessly for the base material that can be transmuted into gold.

The concepts of absolute and real war are not as well reconciled as they ought to be, given their centrality to the subject of *On War*. Clausewitz added the distinc-tion between 'real war' and 'absolute war' in the late 1820s to an already unwieldy manuscript, and the incompleteness of the fusing of the logic that should bind the two concepts is all too apparent. Nonetheless, the awkwardness of the juxta-position of absolute and real war does not offset the high value of an argument so richly comprehensive in analytical reach. That granted, Clausewitz is not as clear as he should be, and probably would have been had he lived longer, on the rela-tionship between absolute and real (limited) war. A terrifyingly apt illustration of the merit in his twin focuses may be found in the practice of nuclear strategy. Nuclear-armed states have the strongest of motives—self-preservation—to pre-pare plans and equip and train forces to conduct nuclear war only in a hugely self-restrained manner. If governments are rational, and can control their military instruments, any real nuclear war will be very limited nuclear war indeed. The policy logic for operational limitation is as unarguable as it is crystal-clear. In practice, however, which is to say in the practice of bilateral (or more) nuclear war, the ability of centralized politico-military command to insist upon tight limita-tion of nuclear effort could be desperately fragile. Moreover, even paradoxically, there is probably some merit for deterrent effect in the suspicion harboured by all parties that nuclear war would most likely escape policy constraint and assume an absolute character. When Thomas C. Schelling wrote in the 1950s about 'the threat leaves something to chance', and in the 1960s about 'the manipulation of risk', he was exploiting for nuclear-age strategic theory and policy exactly that dualism in the absolute and the real (limited) nature of war, as well as the sover-eign possibility of chaos, which Clausewitz sought to explain.[123]

Clausewitz could seriously miseducate the modern strategist on intelligence, deception, and surprise. *On War* teaches that strategic and operational—unlike tactical—surprise generally is infeasible in war.[124] It follows that intelligence typ-ically is unimportant, because it is unreliable, and that therefore efforts to deceive and surprise the enemy are not worth the effort. This is not to say that com-manders are not surprised at the operational level in war, but practical command and logistical (*inter alia*) problems in Clausewitz's time rendered deception and surprise all but forlorn hopes. He was correct with reference to warfare in the

[123] Thomas C. Schelling, *The Strategy of Conflict* (Cambridge, Mass., 1960), ch. 8; id., *Arms and Influence* (New Haven, Conn., 1960), ch. 3.
[124] Clausewitz, *On War*, 117–18; Handel, *Masters of War*, ch. 12.

early nineteenth century, at least for land warfare; he was emphatically wrong with reference to the evidence of the twentieth century. Germany achieved operational surprise in 1914, 1918, and 1940, and strategic surprise with Operation Barbarossa on 22 June 1941.[125] Clausewitz is not wrong about intelligence, deception, and surprise, but the validity of his negative judgement on their significance is limited to his time and continentalist frame of reference. It is because of limitations like these that *On War* needs to be treated with respect rather than veneration. Information and intelligence constitute a permanent dimension of strategy, but their technical feasibility is not constant across all periods, at all levels of war, and in all kinds of conflicts. Some of Clausewitz's wisdom is more timeless than others.

There is little or nothing in *On War* on the causes of war, the political goals of policy in war, or on statecraft in general. We know that these omissions were deliberate, but once Clausewitz attempted to back-fit 'real war' for limited aims into his manuscript, the rationale for the exclusions is seriously weakened. Although the principal claim to theoretical fame of *On War* reposes in its insistence upon the political context for military action, the book constitutes a study of 'war proper' and strategy that is all but naked of political content. If readers are careful and follow, as it were, the stage directions, they will know that 'war proper' is all about serving the ends of policy. If readers are less careful, they will notice that most of *On War* is almost all about the military conduct of war. Clausewitzian scholars have yet to address the implications of this omission, and arguable limitation, convincingly. War is about policy, but *On War* is not. The extent to which this matters is debatable, but it does need to be debated.

Clausewitz certainly had ethical views, but they played no formal role in the development of his general theory of war and strategy.[126] This fact, attributable to Clausewitz's strategic culture, actually to the culture of his period rather than his nationality, should be recorded as a limitation upon the universal and enduring merit in his writing. This omission is as significant and regrettable as it is understandable in historical context. It is worth mentioning, however, that Clausewitz the soldier-theorist provides a healthy antidote to sentimentality and hypocrisy about war. As a man of his times, Clausewitz questioned neither the social institution of war nor its inescapable brutalities and occasional atrocities. He did not glorify war, but neither did he shed tears for its horrors. The author of *On War* accepts war as a fact, a necessity, perhaps (though not very persuasively) as a regrettable necessity. It is a limitation upon his enduring value that Clausewitz's culture cannot recognize war itself as an ethical question. More empathetically,

[125] Barton Whaley, *Codeword Barbarossa* (Cambridge, Mass., 1973); Richard K. Betts, *Surprise Attack: Lessons for Defense Planning* (Washington, DC, 1982); Michael I. Handel (ed.), *Intelligence and Military Operations* (London, 1990); Walter T. Hitchcock (ed.), *The Intelligence Revolution: A Historical Perspective* (Washington, DC, 1991).

[126] Gat, *Origins*, 236 ff.; Paret, *Understanding War*, 96–7.

given his added focus in the late 1820s upon real, or limited, war, it is unfortunate that he did not consider ethical issues in relation to the conduct of war in such a way as to help keep combat limited. After all, the passion of 'the people', a fact that Clausewitz recognized explicitly in his trinitarian reading of war's structure, is likely to be inflamed by a sense that unjust deeds have been done. For a parallel thought, demands for justice by military action are likely to promote demands, and an excuse, for commission of bloody deeds.

Chapter 14 of book V of *On War*, on 'Maintenance and Supply', although historically dated, if read for its general implications for the relationships among logistics, strategy, and the political purposes of war, provides powerful and persuasive analysis. Nonetheless, the fact remains that, apart from that single chapter, there is little discussion in *On War* of what General Wavell called the 'mechanism of war',[127] which is to say economics, logistics, administration, and technology. There is no question about the importance of these matters. There is some question, however, about their proper place in a general theory of war and strategy. Clausewitz recognizes the strategic significance of logistics ('supply'):

Of the items wholly unconnected with engagements, serving only to maintain the forces, supply is the one which most directly affects the fighting. It takes place almost every day and affects every individual. Thus it thoroughly permeates the strategic aspects of all military action.

He distinguishes firmly, however, between the activities 'that are merely preparation for war and war proper'.[128] His focus is upon '[t]he theory of war . . . the use of those means, once they have been developed, for the purposes of the war'.[129] One might dismiss Clausewitz's apparent neglect of logistics as an expression of a continental, indeed Central European, strategic culture to which supply and movement inherently were less problematical than they were to, say, Anglo-American culture.[130] Also, one could argue that these components of the 'mechanism of war' comprise matters common to all belligerents (except in 'small wars' between regular and irregular forces), and therefore inappropriate for prominent treatment in a general theory. Omission of detailed consideration of these factors helps incline *On War* into a treatise on generalship, after the fashion of Jomini. Whether or not the net effect of Clausewitz's decision not to discuss 'the mechanism of war' extensively in *On War* is tolerable for the integrity of his general theory, the issues implicit in the decision certainly required more explanation and

[127] Archibald Wavell, *Generals and Generalship* (New York, 1943), 10.
[128] Clausewitz, *On War*, 131.
[129] Ibid. 132.
[130] Murray and Grimsley, 'Introduction: On Strategy', 7–9. See the contrasting arguments in Martin van Creveld, *Supplying War: Logistics from Wallenstein to Patton* (Cambridge, 1977), and John A. Lynn, 'The History of Logistics and *Supplying War*', in Lynn (ed.), *Feeding Mars: Logistics in Western Warfare from the Middle Ages to the Present* (Boulder, Colo., 1993), 9–27. Tom Kane, 'Getting It There: The Relationship between Military Logistics and Strategic Performance' (Ph.D. thesis, Hull, 1998), provides powerful support for the Lynn 'camp'.

discussion than they received. Clausewitz focused on the engagement and its consequences; he did not dwell on the military system that enables the engagement to be conducted. The question is whether or not that decision on his part is damaging to his general theory. Clausewitz certainly states clearly why and how logistics matters, but arguably he leaves his judgement understated relative to topics of operational artistry and battlefield command.

Clausewitz's operational and tactical advice to be very strong 'at the decisive point' is unhelpful.[131] Are 'decisive points' objectively determinable, or are they created by the theoretically educated intuition, the *coups d'œil*, of the military genius as commander? There is some ambiguity in *On War* over the exact meaning of 'genius in war', whether it refers mainly to the extraordinary individual or rather to the possibility of extraordinary military performance that lurks in many people.[132] Less ambiguity attaches to the problems that Clausewitz's attraction to the battlefield concept of the *coup d'œil* can pose for rational decisionmaking.[133] True military genius is so rare a quality, and so hard to identify in advance of unambiguous demonstration, that a country is well advised to seek victory through a better system rather than through inspiration. Readers who take Clausewitz too seriously on the subject of genius are likely to undervalue strategic calculation and careful planning.[134] Modern texts on defence planning are not eloquent on the importance of placing certified genius in a position of command in war.[135] Of course, those modern texts have no method for coping with the possibility of genius in command. A cynic, at least a sceptic, could say that the bureaucratic mentality that promotes 'safe', if modest, talent, rather than the maverick who may be idiot or genius—or both—virtually predetermines only an average quality of military performance in command.

It is probably trivial to observe that there is no discussion of naval warfare in *On War*—in fact naval matters are cited only twice and then strictly in passing[136]—while it is even more trivial to point to the necessary absence of discussion of air, space, and nuclear warfare. There is, nonetheless, a serious question hovering here. Would Clausewitz's general theory of war and strategy have been different had it been informed by a mastery of naval warfare, and some grasp of maritime strategy, as well as of combat on land? The answer is probably in the negative, but

[131] Clausewitz, *On War*, 204.
[132] Ibid. bk. i, ch. 3.
[133] Handel, *Masters of War*, 156.
[134] Williamson Murray and Allan R. Millett (eds.), *Calculations: Net Assessment and the Coming of World War II* (New York, 1992), provides some corrective.
[135] E. S. Quade (ed.), *Analysis for Military Decisions* (Chicago, 1964); id. and W. I. Boucher (eds.), *Systems Analysis and Policy Planning: Applications in Defense* (New York, 1968). More recent treatment is Paul K. Davis (ed.), *New Challenges for Defense Planning: Rethinking How Much Is Enough* (Santa Monica, Calif., 1994); Strategy and Force Planning Faculty (Naval War College) (ed.), *Strategy and Force Planning* (Newport, RI, 1995), pt. 1; Zalmay M. Khalilzad and David A. Ochmanek (eds.), *Strategy and Defense Planning for the 21st Century* (Santa Monica, Calif., 1997).
[136] Clausewitz, *On War*, 220, 634.

with a footnote to the effect that his discussion must have been enriched had his understanding encompassed the full panoply of war in his period.[137] Clausewitz strictly did not need an understanding of naval warfare for his general theory to have integrity. Nonetheless, we would repose even more confidence in his writing had he been able to develop it on the basis of military mastery of the terms of combat, the grammar of war and strategy, in more than one geographical environment. Appreciation of the 'enabling' character of naval power, for example, might have encouraged him to modify, at least broaden, his treatment of battle and the centrality of fighting. Similarly, mastery of the grammar of sea warfare might have persuaded him to devote more attention to logistics. Some armies of the Napoleonic era could succeed despite their somewhat cavalier approach to the relationship between supply and movement, but navies, in any period, can succeed only with the benefit of the most careful logistical preparation and management.[138] Although strategy has to be 'done' tactically by armed forces equipped to function in particular geographical environments, any general theory of war and strategy can, and probably should, strive to transcend the particulars of geography: the challenges posed by those particular physical conditions that shape technology which, in turn, shapes tactics. The policy logic of war is above all that. The question is: to what degree can a theorist, even the greatest of theorists, genuinely transcend a military culture rooted in just one geography so as to generalize authoritatively for the strategic effect in war garnered from 'engagements' of all kinds in all geographies? *On War* would have been a stronger book still had its author secured an understanding of, and empathy for, 'joint' warfare involving the cooperative and even integrated operation of land and sea forces. The point is not that most of his larger and more penetrating ideas require evidential augmentation from environments other than the land, but rather that the military behaviour from which ultimately he drew theoretical inspiration was narrower in kind than it need have been.

To theorize about war and strategy *per se*, it should not matter whether one's historical empirical referents include some, or all, of land, sea, air, space, and

[137] I do not find Paret's defence of Clausewitz's omission of maritime matters (*Understanding War*, 117–18) entirely convincing. 'Clausewitz has often been criticized for his inability to transcend his experiences as a soldier of a landlocked monarchy and to recognize the other half of war of his time. But this criticism confuses his theory with the experiences from which it sprang. It is possible to develop and analyze a concept without illustrating it exhaustively. Friction, escalation, the interaction of attack and defense exist in war on and under the sea—and in the air—much as they do on the land. It is fallacious to consider the theoretical structure of *On War* incomplete on the ground that its illustrations are drawn only from the types of conflict that Clausewitz knew best and that interested him the most.' There is merit in Paret's pleading here, but it leaves too many questions unasked.

[138] Daniel A. Baugh, *British Naval Administration in the Age of Walpole* (Princeton, NJ, 1965); John Francis Guilmartin, Jr., *Gunpowder and Galleys: Changing Technology and Mediterranean Warfare at Sea in the Sixteenth Century* (Cambridge, 1974); John H. Pryor, *Geography, Technology, and War: Studies in the Maritime History of the Mediterranean, 649–1571* (Cambridge, 1988); Jeremy Black and Philip Woodfine (eds.), *The British Navy and the Use of Naval Power in the Eighteenth Century* (Leicester, 1988); Lynn, *Feeding Mars*, chs. 5, 6, 10.

cyberspace experience. It is, after all, the master theme of this book that there is an essential unity, a fundamental sameness, to all strategic experience. In principle at least, Clausewitz can draft a theory of war and strategy that rests upon the strategic history either of the land, or the sea, or of both approached 'jointly'. General theory should be unaffected by particular geographically shaped technical and therefore tactical details. In practice, however, even successful general theory, such as that designed by Clausewitz, will show some bias towards concepts and kinds of behaviour especially characteristic of the environment for warfare concerning which the theorist is most knowledgeable. Clausewitz is the greatest theorist of war: he is also, however, a theorist of war whose theory is influenced noticeably by its continentalist empirical base. One reason for writing this book on modern strategy, in a period when no fewer than five geographical environments—land, sea, air, space, and now cyberspace—require 'joint' understanding and exploitation, is to help ensure that environmental bias does not lurk under-recognized in purportedly general theory.

Clausewitz's strategic theory nowhere reveals its fragility more clearly than in his arguments for the relative strength of the defence over the offence. His eloquent and persuasive reasoning on behalf of the relative strength of the defence applies only to warfare on land, and possibly only to large-scale conventional warfare in European conditions.[139] With the same logic that drove him to praise defence as 'the stronger form of waging war' on land (my addition, or clarification), today he might have praised offence as the stronger form of war at sea, in the air, in missile war, in space war in low earth orbit, and in irregular conflict.[140] Geography matters: there is a grammar, a tactical-technical logic, to war specific for each geographical environment. As Clausewitz would be the first to recognize, the rich particularity of each historically specific conflict matters most of all. Tank armies are obsolete today, but they are obsolete only if one is fighting the information-led armed forces of the United States. War is war, and strategy is strategy, across time, geography, and technology, but the terms of engagement between offence and defence are different among the distinctive geographical environments. Clausewitz's theory of war thus, again, shows its limitations when it ventures into generalization for all of combat on the basis of unduly narrow geostrategic referents. The expansion of battlespace from the land and the sea into the air, space, and cyberspace renders the perils to theory of expertise in only a single geography ever more pressing.

Despite noting the contextual efficacy of people's irregular war in Spain, Clausewitz's world was one of regular armies contending on behalf of the gov-

---

[139] Clausewitz, *On War*, 359. By way of sharp contrast, the general strength of the offence for regular forces campaigning against irregulars in 'uncivilized' warfare is emphasized in Charles E. Callwell, *Small Wars: A Tactical Textbook for Imperial Soldiers*, repr. of 1906 edn. (London, 1990), esp. ch. 6.

[140] Colin S. Gray, *Weapons Don't Make War: Policy, Strategy, and Military Technology* (Lawrence, Kan., 1993), 13–15.

ernments of states. Notwithstanding the growing evidence in his period for the military effectiveness of irregular forces, which is to say of the people in arms but not in (much) uniform, Clausewitz offers little of value in explanation of their role or future.[141] This charge has some merit, but it needs to be appraised in light of its authors' contemporary preoccupation with war as a cultural pursuit and with an alleged 'transformation of war' today away from combat between the regular armies of states.[142] Some unhistorical motives appear to have shaped this particular indictment of Clausewitz. Again, what *On War* has to say about war and strategy is not significantly impoverished by the relative brevity of its treatment of irregular warfare. As I argue in a later chapter, irregular conflict is governed no less by strategic reasoning than is regular. It is true that Clausewitz's 'remarkable trinity' looks fragile in the face of conflicts between peoples who have neither recognized governments nor organized armies, but announcement of the demise of regular war is premature. Moreover, in the 'small wars' of regular soldiers against irregular warriors, one belligerent at least certainly still looks distinctly Clausewitzian. As frequently is the case when one examines *On War* closely, one finds that some of Clausewitz's critics have not read his text with sufficient care. Those who see war as a manifestation of culture, rather than as an expression of policy, and those who deem the 'trinity' atavistic as more and more belligerents are security communities other than recognized states, need to reread what Clausewitz wrote. He advises that one cannot 'fix an arbitrary relationship' between 'these three tendencies': violence, hatred, enmity; chance and probability; and rationality and instrumentality. In other words, Clausewitz allows for, though does not dwell upon, the conduct of war wherein the passions of the people, or the behaviour of the army, or the reasoning of the government, plays an unusually preponderant role in the remarkable trinity that is war.

British commentators have long been troubled by Clausewitz. Most recently, John Keegan, following in the tradition accelerated by Basil Liddell Hart,[143] elected to demonize Clausewitz in his book *A History of Warfare*. Some theorists and historians plainly have encountered severe difficulty understanding *On War*. The question remains, however, of how hard they tried. Christopher Bassford exaggerates when he writes: 'And, for those who actually read *On War*, Clausewitz is not all that difficult to fathom. Three minutes thought is usually sufficient to clarify any one of Clausewitz's many interesting propositions.'[144] The critics do have a point, though whether it is a point of significance is less clear. Whether or not particular critics of *On War* have read it with the necessary care and empathy, one suspects that many of Clausewitz's more ardent admirers exaggerate—as did Bassford as

---

[141] Clausewitz, *On War*, Bk. vi, ch. 26; Handel, *Masters of War*, ch. 8.

[142] Van Creveld, *Transformation of War*, 36–7; Keegan, *History of Warfare*, 221.

[143] Liddell Hart, *Strategy*, 224–7, 352–7; id., 'Foreword' to Gerhard Ritter, *The Schlieffen Plan: Critique of a Myth* (London, 1958), 5.

[144] Bassford, 'Keegan', 322.

quoted—the clarity of the great man's message. Long familiarity with what one believes *On War* says promotes some internalization of its argument and a notable lack of objectivity towards the genuine difficulties in the text.

As published in 1832, *On War* was a draft manuscript that had a baffling organization and intellectual trajectory, a ponderous and elaborate style, and at least apparently underreconciled central concepts of absolute and real war because the author added a layer of dialectical reasoning after 1827. To those barriers to accurate comprehension, the eventual English language versions of *On War* treated their readers to questionable translations of key concepts and, overall, to what can appear to the uninitiated as a teutonic confusion of quasi-philosophical ponderings. Such a judgement is unfortunate. The method, language, and style of *On War*, however, do lend themselves to poor understanding. If *On War* were to appear today as an unsolicited manuscript in the office of any major scholarly publisher, there can be no doubt that it would be rejected out of hand on technical grounds, *inter alia*.

THE INESCAPABLE CLAUSEWITZ

Regardless of how readers might wish to 'mark' Clausewitz, according to the test of rival arguments, the consensus remains that *On War* is the gold standard for general strategic theory. So intellectually inescapable is Clausewitz that, in one key sense or another, modern strategic theorists are all either neo-Clausewitzian, like this author, or self-avowedly post-Clausewitzian, like Martin van Creveld. It is fitting to close this chapter of critical celebration of *On War* with the words of a modern military historian who subsequently reversed his judgement. In 1991, van Creveld advised that

contemporary 'strategic' thought about every one of these problems ['some of the most fundamental problems posed by war in all ages: by whom it is fought, what it is all about, how it is fought, what it is fought for, and why it is fought'] is fundamentally flawed; and, in addition, is rooted in a Clausewitzian world picture that is either obsolete or wrong.[145]

Five years earlier, in an article entitled 'The Eternal Clausewitz', van Creveld offered this notable judgement:

among all the better-known writers on military theory within Western civilization it is Clausewitz alone whose work appears able to withstand every kind of political, social, economic, and technological change since it was published, and seems to stand a fair chance of remaining forever of more than purely historical interest.[146]

The discussion now turns to a review of the reasons why the would-be successors to Clausewitz in the twentieth century were none of them truly fit to fill his inkwell.

[145] Van Creveld, *Transformation*, p. ix.
[146] Martin van Creveld, 'The Eternal Clausewitz', in Handel, *Clausewitz and Modern Strategy*, 35.

Chapter 4

THE POVERTY OF MODERN STRATEGIC THOUGHT

The reasons why there were no worthy twentieth-century successors to Clausewitz as theorists of war and strategy are linked directly to themes central to this book. In particular, the issues raised here include such themes as the interplay between theory and practice, the growing complexity of modern war, the validity of general theory for strategy across time, geography, and technology (in other words, the superior merit in the historical rather than the material school of strategic thought), and the essential unity of strategic experience regardless of its shifting tactical forms.

There is a culminating point of victory in argument about the merit of *On War* as compared with possible rivals. Although probably few people would wish to contest my admiration for Clausewitz, there will always be people unconvinced that *On War* is by far the best book on its subject. I do not accept that the achievements of *On War* are definitively unsurpassable. There are reasons, however, why in the twentieth century it was unlikely that Clausewitz would find a peer, let alone a superior, as a general theorist of war and strategy.

This discussion is organized around nine explanations for the relative (to Clausewitz) poverty of modern strategic thought. Numbers 1–3 are unpersuasive, while explanations 4–9, in some uncertain mixture, provide adequate understanding of why there was no great general work on war and strategy written in the twentieth century.

1. The twentieth century has not produced the 'Great Captains' or war leaders likely to inspire great interpretative theory.
2. Warfare in the twentieth century has become too complex for mastery by single theorists working alone.
3. As Clausewitz perceived, everything in strategy, and indeed in war, is simple to explain and understand, but difficult to do. In point of fact Clausewitz tackled a relatively easy subject; much more difficult is the task that has preoccupied so many modern scholars, the problem of explaining the resort to war itself and hence the challenge of understanding how the conditions for a lasting peace might be advanced. Clausewitz took war for granted as a permanent social and political institution. At least since the Armistice on 11 November 1918, scholars have focused on the terrain of war causation that Clausewitz ignored entirely.

4. The twentieth century has failed to produce a theorist, or theorists, with sufficient talent.
5. Even the greatest of classics have to be recognized and promoted as such. Clausewitz's fame was sealed after his work won high praise from the victor in the wars of German unification, Field Marshal Helmuth Graf von Moltke.[1] There may be worthy twentieth-century successors to *On War*, but it is too soon to know. Sometimes a classic matures slowly.
6. The mission has been fulfilled: Clausewitz has done it already.
7. The field of potential strategic theorists is exceedingly small because soldiers tend not to be scholars, civilians tend not to be comfortable theorizing about strategy, and strategy as a vocation falls between the political and military realms.
8. The potential grand theorists of war and strategy in the twentieth century were diverted from truly grand theory by the pressing demands of immediate national security. If Americans continue to be dominant in strategic studies, this diversion is likely to continue to be a general rule. The US defence community is uniquely able to reward scholars who address near-term issues.
9. Many theorists have mistaken partial theories for grand unified theory. Panaceas have attracted scholars and policymakers in search of manageably simple solutions to the complexities of modern war and strategy.

WHY NO SUCCESSORS?

NO GREAT CAPTAINS

The explanation that the absence of great practitioners of strategy deprives potentially great strategic theorists of their muses is unpersuasive, though not without interest. It is difficult to understand why the discovery of 'the modern style of warfare' in 1916–18,[2] and its subsequent refinement as the complexities of twentieth-century war increased, should not have been as inspiring as was the Napoleonic example for Clausewitz. If the prospect of a global nuclear war that could approximate Clausewitz's notion of 'absolute war' failed to concentrate the minds of strategic theorists into the zone wherein masterworks are created, it is hard to conceive of what would. From a statistical population of just one historical

---

[1] Michael Howard, 'The Influence of Clausewitz', in Carl von Clausewitz, *On War*, trans. Howard and Peter Paret (Princeton, NJ, 1976), 29–31; Christopher Bassford, *Clausewitz in English: The Reception of Clausewitz In Britain and America, 1815–1945* (New York, 1994), 3, 19. Even if Clausewitz's fame was sealed by Moltke, Bassford explains persuasively that Clausewitz's writings were discussed in Britain before Prussian arms acquired an aura of invincibility (35–6). See also Daniel J. Hughes (ed.), *Moltke on the Art of War: Selected Writings*, trans. Hughes and Harry Bell (Novato, Calif., 1993).

[2] Jonathan Bailey, *The First World War and the Birth of the Modern Style of Warfare*, Occasional Paper 22 (Camberley, 1996).

nexus, Clausewitz and Napoleon, it is unreasonable to postulate the need for such teamwork if master texts on strategic theory are to emerge. Strategic theory always requires inspiration from the real world of strategic application, which is scarcely surprising given the practical character of strategy. It is not equally true to claim that an Iron Law of Inspiration obliges each strategic theorist to find a Paladin-strategist.

UNDUE COMPLEXITY

The increasing complexity of war, and hence of instruments for strategic effect, in this century might account for the absence of a great strategic theorist. Modern war, and therefore modern strategy, have so expanded in scope and complexity since the 1820s that no individual, regardless of the wattage of his genius, the efficiency of his labour, or the duration of his working life, reasonably could aspire to perform as a Renaissance, let alone Enlightenment, Person for the subject. Because no one or two classic texts on war and strategy stand out among modern writings, it is seductive to conclude that the job could not be done. In his comparative commentary upon Sun Tzu, Clausewitz, and Jomini, Michael Handel is eloquent on this point.

The second factor [explaining the longevity and pre-eminence of *Art of War* and *On War*] is the greatly increased complexity of modern warfare. Sun Tzu and Clausewitz already viewed war as infinitely complex in their own times, but modern technological developments have added an entirely new dimension of uncertainty; and this has so obfuscated the fundamental principles of strategy that constructing the type of relatively simple framework which sufficed in the pre-industrial age is now impossible.[3]

Handel proceeds to note: 'The technological revolution in war that began to accelerate at a geometric pace after the mid-nineteenth century.'
   He suggests that that revolution

created a situation not unlike that facing scholars in the natural sciences: that is, the proliferation of specialized fields of research and the exponential growth in knowledge made it extremely unlikely that a single expert could cultivate an in-depth understanding of all the developments taking place. Just as it would hardly be possible to write one book encompassing the whole of modern science, it would be exceedingly difficult to compress all that is known and relevant about war into a single tome. And although no-one has yet succeeded in writing a new, comprehensive study of war—despite a number of heroic attempts—such an undertaking nevertheless poses a worthy challenge.[4]

These extensive quotations from Handel's *Masters of War* contain a powerful thesis, the claim for complexity as a fatal impediment to a truly grand unified theory of war and strategy; yet their very quality threatens to mislead. First, why should the

---

[3] Michael I. Handel, *Masters of War: Classical Strategic Thought*, 2nd edn. (London, 1996), 2.
[4] Ibid.

growing complexity of war much matter for the would-be grand theorist? The answer is one that is deployed today in the debate over the implications for war and strategy of information technologies, just as it was deployed a century ago concerning the meaning of new naval technologies. To employ the distinction coined by Admiral Sir Reginald Custance in a book in 1907,[5] theorists tend to belong to materialist or historical schools of thought. Whereas strategic materialists are forever discerning technologically driven transformations of war, historical (or 'classical') strategists, in the apt description of Eugenia C. Kiesling, share 'the premise that strategy contains elements independent of contemporary material conditions and common therefore to every time and place'.[6] I should hasten to add that material-minded strategic theorists are not the only prophets of strategic transformation.[7] Clausewitz's deliberate silence on matters narrowly naval, and even broadly maritime, weakened *On War* without inflicting fatal damage. If a latter-day would-be Clausewitz were to ignore air and space, in addition to maritime, conditions (nuclear might be another matter altogether), provided the character and general terms of war and strategy were treated with Clausewitzian rigour and insight, it is not obvious that lethal damage would be inflicted on the resulting grand theory. The larger and more penetrating ideas in *On War* are independent of geographical environment.

The second reason why Handel's persuasive-sounding argument might seduce the unwary is that it could encourage the idea that some modern successor to Clausewitz would have to aspire to emulate the substantive achievement of the master. This need not be so—at least not strictly. Even if Handel is correct in his emphasis upon the significance of the growing complexity of war and strategy for the theorist, to date why has no theorist succeeded in writing an outstanding book of a kind that accepts the constraints imposed by complexity? This author suspects the operation of the self-fulfilling prophecy. Theorists can be intimidated by the wealth of technical information that appears to stand between them and mastery of the nature, function, and working of strategy. Indeed, they can be so overawed by the technical and other sources of complexity of the subject that they fail to notice the possibility that there might be a strategic lore which transcends characteristic terms of tactical engagement in different environments.

WAR: PROBLEM OR CONDITION?

The third candidate in possible explanation of the absence of a Clausewitz in the twentieth century amounts to a claim for opportunity costs. Many of the scholars

---

[5] 'Barfleur' (pseud. for Reginald Custance), *Naval Policy: A Plea for the Study of War* (Edinburgh, 1907), pp. vii–ix.

[6] Eugenia C. Kiesling, 'Introduction' to Raoul Castex, *Strategic Theories*, trans. and ed. Kiesling (Annapolis, Md., 1994), p. xiii.

[7] Martin van Creveld, *The Transformation of War* (New York, 1991); Ralph Peters, 'Constant Conflict', *Parameters*, 27 (1997), 4–14.

who might have devoted their genius to further development of grand and uni-fied theories of war and strategy have instead chosen to define the continuing existence of war as the superordinate problem for scholarship and public policy. While some scholars have tried to find ways to tame the beast of war—witness the growth of the large transnational community of scholars of arms control—other scholars have gone off the map on intellectual safari in quest of the causes of war (or is it the causes of wars?).[8]

There is some merit in this third reason. One cannot deny that among the ranks of scholarly investigators into the causes of war there might be a strategic grand theorist or two *manqués*. Nonetheless, after 1944–5 in particular, variants of the realist paradigm were so massively prevalent in Western scholarship on security topics that it would be faintly ludicrous to claim that scholars were distracted by the siren call of fundamental enquiry into the war-prone condition of human-kind.[9] Some scholars intellectually shellshocked by Verdun, the Somme, and Passchendaele may have succumbed to the hubris of the 'Scholarly Fallacy'—the conviction that knowledge can set us free (from war, crime, injustice, or whatever)—but the hardy veterans of World War II who tackled security problems in the 1950s and after by and large sought safety through strategy, not in funda-mental opposition to it. This is not to deny that many theorists for the nuclear era approached their subject from the perspective of preventing (nuclear) war rather than winning it. Both perspectives, however, require strategic reasoning.

LACK OF TALENT

The fourth explanation for Clausewitz's lonely preeminence is the Shakespearean analogy: no one with sufficient talent has appeared. It is not always the case that the occasion produces the necessary person; that belief is the kind of erroneous thought in which the British Army found false comfort on the eve of World War I, considering such past great captains as the Dukes of Marlborough and Wellington, not to mention the recent great joint captaincy of Lord Roberts and General Kitch-ener in South Africa. In practice in the twentieth century, the British armed forces were to serve under field commanders who typically were good enough—better than merely good enough in the cases of Haig, Montgomery, and Slim[10]—but

[8] Quincy Wright, *A Study of War* (2 vols., Chicago, 1942); Kenneth N. Waltz, *Man, the State and War: A Theoretical Analysis* (New York, 1959); Geoffrey Blainey, *The Causes of War* (London, 1973); Jack S. Levy, 'The Causes of War: A Review of Theories', in Philip E. Tetlock et al. (eds.), *Behavior, Society, and Nuclear War* (New York, 1989), i. 290–333; Hidemi Suganami, *On the Causes of War* (Oxford, 1996).

[9] William C. Olson and A. J. R. Groom, *International Relations Then and Now: Origins and Trends in Interpretation* (London, 1991), ch. 6; Torbjörn L. Knutsen, *A History of International Relations Theory* (Man-chester, 1992), ch. 9; Scott Burchill, 'Realism and Neo-realism', in Burchill, Linklater et al., *Theories of International Relations* (London, 1996), 67–92.

[10] E. K. G. Sixsmith, *British Generalship in the Twentieth Century* (London, 1970); John Keegan (ed.), *Churchill's Generals* (New York, 1991); Brian Bond (ed.), *The First World War and British Military History* (Oxford, 1991); Hugh Cecil and Peter H. Liddle (eds.), *Facing Armageddon: The First World War Experienced* (London, 1996), pt. 2.

certainly were not men from the mould of Marlborough and Wellington. Possibly, the conditions and complexity of modern warfare has denied to generalship the scope for exercise of genius open to the commanders of armies in pre-industrial times. Naval command is another matter entirely, because the time-lines for decision are so much shorter than for war on land, and the combat value of forces is distributed among so few major units. Navies can be ruined much more rapidly than can armies, as Admiral Jellicoe well understood on 31 May 1916 at Jutland, and as Admirals Yamamoto and Nagumo demonstrated on 4–5 June 1942 at Midway.

Readers should consider the possible Shakespearean analogy seriously. If Shakespeare had not existed, no one else would have written those plays. If Clausewitz had not existed, it seems improbable that someone would have stepped up to do the job. Clausewitz, though necessarily a person of his time who could not but help write as a continental-minded Prussian, was also a true original. This explanation may appear crude and obvious, but one should not dismiss out of hand the simple proposition that over the past two centuries only Carl von Clausewitz had the ability to write with the insight shown in the flawed masterpiece that is the unfinished manuscript published after his death by his doting and competent wife, Maria.

NO INSTANT 'CLASSICS'

Explanation no. 5 is the mildly subversive thought that several truly classic works on strategy and war may well have been published in the twentieth century, but as yet it is too soon to be certain of their potential for classic status. Scholars who teach the history of strategic thought are challenged to distinguish modern classics—if that category is not oxymoronic—from among the merely noteworthy and fashionable ephemera of the literature of strategic debate. Studies of war and strategy are rapidly dated and datable by the subjects of their enquiry, as well as by their assumptions about politics, technology, and material conditions in general. However, it would be a fallacy to argue that because modern strategic theorists must cope with a decidedly dynamic material context for their work, that work is condemned to a short professional half-life. What is important is not the subject under professional analysis but the purpose and character of the analysis. The actual terms and conditions—including material conditions—of war must always be important, because strategy has to be done in the tactical world of behaviour. If the historical school of strategic thought is judged persuasive, a strategic study can explore timeless themes by means of illustrative recent, contemporary, or anticipated future, problems. For example, to explore the Clausewitzian omnibus concept of friction, scholars have examined *inter alia* 'the anatomy of error', 'military misfortunes', 'the march of folly', in all historical periods, from the classical age of Greece to the Gulf War of 1991 and beyond.[11] Only if scholars choose to key answers to questions bounded by particular, transient, material and social arrangements must their work similarly be ephemeral. Admittedly, most work in the broad field of strategic, defence, and security studies is ephemeral more because of lack of quality in method and argument than because of topicality.

Therefore, this explanation should be rejected, albeit with the caveat that there could be a diamond or two lurking currently under-appreciated amongst the many modern works on strategic theory. The reason why one should decline to be impressed by the claim that true classics of general strategy cannot be written in times marked by rapid change lies in the sound premise of the historical school of strategic thought. A general theory of war and strategy applies as much to the tactical and operational use of triremes by Periclean Athens as it does to efforts by the US Joint Chiefs of Staff today to craft a 'strategic vision' for future joint warfare.[12]

CLAUSEWITZ IS ALL WE NEED

My sixth explanation for the absence of a new Clausewitz points to the fact that Clausewitz did his job so well. This factual claim, by analogy, might be likened to the assertion that the fundamental theoretical work of Sir Isaac Newton, Adam Smith, and Charles Darwin, though in each case incomplete and flawed, nonetheless could be done only once. If Clausewitz 'discovered' the dependency of war upon policy, or politics, how often could that central principle be rediscovered to the honour of the rediscoverer? One could argue that Clausewitz's great contribution to development of a general theory of war, notwithstanding the limitations which beg for treatment by later scholars, could only be made once. In other words, there may be a sense in which Clausewitz has an intellectual patent on the theory of war and on the nature and function of strategy.

As a working strategic theorist I am troubled by this explanation. If Clausewitz cracked the code on the nature of war and on the relationships among policy, war, strategy, and tactics, no one else can repeat, or emulate, that inherently unique achievement. The principal reason why this explanation fails to satisfy completely is—as outlined in the previous chapter—that Clausewitz leaves untrodden too much terrain that is important to a general theory of war and strategy. Of course, if one is of a materialist, or other transformationist, theoretical persuasion, then one must reject this explanation out of hand. In that case, even if one is inclined to

---

[11] Barry S. Strauss and Josiah Ober, *The Anatomy of Error: Ancient Military Disasters and Their Lessons for Modern Strategists* (New York, 1990); Eliot A. Cohen and John Gooch, *Military Misfortunes: The Anatomy of Failure in War* (New York, 1990); Barbara W. Tuchman, *The March of Folly: From Troy to Vietnam* (New York, 1984).

[12] Joint Chiefs of Staff, 'Joint Vision 2010: America's Military—Preparing for Tomorrow', *Joint Force Quarterly*, 12 (1996), 34–49.

grant that Clausewitz had wise things to say at a high level of abstraction, still one must argue that technological, political, or social change—among the many dimensions of war—either perpetually or irregularly transform war and the challenge to strategy. In the materialist view, Clausewitzian theory, even if true, simply does not reach down far enough into the actual, and changing, material realities of war and strategy to be of much other than historical interest. Indeed, this sceptical view would argue that it is just as well that Clausewitz wrote as an analyst-philosopher in *On War*, as distinct from his voluminous and scholarly historical studies,[13] because otherwise his material and social assumptions would have condemned the work strictly to the status of a period piece.

WHO MINDS THE STORE OF STRATEGY?

Explanation 7 for the loneliness of *On War* in the premier league of general works on war and strategy is sociological. Bernard Brodie notes, 'His is not simply the greatest but the only truly great book on war.'[14] He also then argues, cleverly, though not unchallengeably:

While genius has scarcity value in every field of human endeavour, in the field of strategic writing it has a special rarity. The reason is that soldiers are rarely scholars, and civilians are rarely students of strategy. Clausewitz's genius is indisputable, and also in his field unique.[15]

Strategy is as difficult to perform well in a purposive manner as it is all too rarely performed consciously at all. Probably more polities have been the beneficiaries of uncalculated, though perhaps otherwise deserved, successful strategic effect than have merited such success by virtue of superior strategy. Brodie has identified an important truth. Whereas professional physicists, economists, and biologists logically can strive to expand the bounds of powerful theory in their fields, who, exactly, peoples the profession of strategists? Who professes strategy? Soldiers typically receive no education, let alone training, in strategy, because strategy is 'above their pay grade'; it is not their responsibility. Politicians and senior civil servants likewise receive no education in strategy. Even if some soldiers and civilians attend classes on strategy at a college of higher defence studies, or a national war college, they cannot learn how to threaten or use force as an intended purposeful instrument of policy except by actually doing it. There is wisdom in Napoleon's Maxim 77:

Generals-in-chief must be guided by their own experience or their genius. Tactics, evolutions, the duties and knowledge of an engineer or an artillery officer may be learned in

[13] e.g. Carl von Clausewitz, *The Campaign of 1812 in Russia*, repr. of 1843 edn. (London, 1992); id., *Historical and Political Writings*, trans. and ed. Peter Paret and Daniel Moran (Princeton, NJ, 1992).

[14] Bernard Brodie, 'The Continuing Relevance of *On War*', in Clausewitz, *On War*, 53.

[15] Ibid. 52.

treatises, but the science of strategy is only to be acquired by experience, and by studying the campaigns of all the great captains.[16]

Napoleon should have noted that some education in strategy can be acquired by careful study of the works of a great theorist of strategy. It requires a great theorist, however, to forewarn his readers about the perils of theory. In the words of the master:

Theory cannot equip the mind with formulas for solving problems, nor can it mark the narrow path on which the sole solution is supposed to lie by planting a hedge of principles on either side. But it can give the mind insight into the great mass of phenomena and their relationships, then leave it free to rise into the higher realms of action.[17]

In the process of praising and explaining Clausewitz, Brodie was not above exorcising some of the demons that impeded his own career, but his claim for the importance of history, a claim endorsed by Napoleon and Clausewitz, is as convincing as it is also self-serving:

Our own generation is unique, but sadly so, in producing a school of thinkers who are allegedly experts in military strategy and who are certainly specialists in military studies but who know virtually nothing of military history, including the history of our most recent wars, and who seem not to care about their ignorance . . . the only empirical data we have about how people conduct war and behave under its stresses is our experience with it in the past, however much we have to make adjustments for subsequent changes in conditions.[18]

In this forceful and personal restatement of the viewpoint of the historical school of strategic thought, Brodie is arguing not only that history is 'the only empirical data we have' about war and strategy, but also that many influential modern strategic theorists are historically severely challenged and are content to remain such. This argument by Brodie is probably less true today than it was in the 1950s, 1960s, and 1970s, but it continues to warrant respect.

Those who try to mind the store of strategy by keeping faith with the historical school of thought are always targets for assault by the transformationist theorists who see in each major technological, or social, change the engine for the reordering of ideas. The lure of transformationist explanation has thinned the ranks of would-be grand theorists of strategy. The novel tends to be more attractive than the familiar.

URGENT BUT LESS IMPORTANT

The eighth explanation for the paucity of great general theory on war and strategy points an accusing pen at the commitment by modern strategic theorists to

---

[16] David G. Chandler (ed.), *The Military Maxims of Napoleon*, trans. Lt.-Gen. Sir George C. D'Aguilar, repr. of 1901 edn. (New York, 1988), 81.

[17] Clausewitz, *On War*, 578.

[18] Brodie, 'Continuing Relevance', 53–4.

immediate tasks. Few among those theorists would have the confidence, arrogance perhaps, to admit to Thucydides' ambition: 'I have written my book, not as an essay which is to win the applause of the moment, but as a possession for all time.'[19] By contrast, it would not be unreasonable for a modern theorist to share the aspirations that Clausewitz expressed:

I wanted at all costs to avoid every commonplace, everything obvious that has been stated a hundred times and is generally believed. It was my ambition to write a book that would not be forgotten after two or three years, and that possibly might be picked up more than once by those who are interested in the subject.[20]

Because strategy is a practical subject, and moreover is a practical subject with the most far-reaching of implications for society and individuals, those who would advise about it are obliged to provide answers to the questions posed by pragmatically minded political and military clients. Because of the political ambition to be influential, for economic motives, and because of the call of fame, a kind of Gresham's Law applies to strategic studies. The study of war and strategy is sidelined by the pressing needs of the state for immediate answers to problems of weapons choice and deployment, or arms control negotiating tactics, or the use of airpower in irregular conflicts.

Politicians and military leaders live in a world of short time horizons, and indeed in a world where 'the long term' finds expression in an endless sequence of incremental decisions. The polity, which is to say the principal client for the advice of modern strategic theorists, never confronts challenges over war or strategy *per se*. As with deterrence, war and strategy need concrete references in time, place, and opponent. When those references are missing, as is largely true today for the United States and NATO, then conflict-planning scenarios are invented on the basis of friendly interests at risk, rather than threats directly perceived.[21]

Strategy is an issue area understood by politicians, military leaders, and society at large with regard to specific circumstances of security and insecurity. Strategic theorists typically are concerned citizens, as well as scholars, and they inhabit the same historical space and time as do their 'clients'. As a result, many works of theory have a way of descending into the field of application, or applied strategic study. There is a need for advice on the issues of the day. The practical character of strategy, married to the human dimension of personal rewards, has the effect of creating a magnetic pull towards practicality in strategic studies. Such practicality has the characteristic of immediacy of relevance to official decisions, which is to say of disinterest in solutions that cannot be attempted and completed in the near

[19] Robert B. Strassler (ed.), *The Landmark Thucydides: A Comprehensive Guide to 'The Peloponnesian War'*, trans. Richard Crawley, rev. edn. (New York, 1996), 16.
[20] Clausewitz, *On War*, 63.
[21] Colin S. Gray, 'Defense Planning for the Mystery Tour: Principles for Guidance in a Period of Nonlinear Change', *Airpower Journal*, 5 (1991), 18–26; Emily O. Goldman, 'Thinking about Strategy Absent the Enemy', *Security Studies*, 4 (1994), 40–85.

term. The strategic theorist as strategic adviser to the polity is obliged—if he or she would be useful—to accept the world-view and terms and conditions of those to be advised.[22]

The practical world of policy and strategy-making, and of military execution, is not a perilous distraction for strategic theorists from their real task of producing superior strategic theory; rather, real-world behaviour is the reason for superior strategic theory. After all, the purpose of enquiry into the nature of war and strategy is to develop theory that can help educate the world of practice. This eighth venture in explanation of why the library of great theoretical writings on war and strategy is so thin points to the appeal of the immediate as a guilty party. Nonetheless, it has always been the case that significant advances in theoretical understanding have been spurred by the challenges of the day. The messy world of defence policy and the use of force provides both the permanent reason why strategic theory is important and the specific triggers necessary to fuel scholarship.

The relationship between the theory and the practice of strategy is tense yet creative, albeit always threatening to stultify original thinking. Too close a connection with the world of action deprives theorists of the space to be creative. Too independent a stance by theorists easily translates into a condition of irrelevance—to their time and place, at least—because the questions addressed in theory are not the questions that responsible officials or soldiers are at liberty to ask, or because the answers provided even to policy-relevant questions are genuinely beyond the bounds of practicable policy and strategy. Additionally, scholars unused to communicating their ideas to non-scholars can have difficulty securing access to the attention, or thought processes (even if attention is secured), of politicians and soldiers. Whatever its narrowly professional merits may be, much of contemporary scholarship on the theory of international relations, to take a leading example, is all but impenetrable to those who are not professional initiates.[23]

The better works of strategic studies often comprise a sometimes uneasy blend of practical advice and wisdom on fundamentals; that wisdom can be expressed explicitly in general terms, or it can be hidden in specific recommendations. Superior examples of the genre can readily be identified that were written 1500 years apart, yet which are comparable in purpose and key characteristics. Consider the similarities between the *Epitoma Rei Militaris* (Epitome of Military Science) by Publius Flavius Vegetius Renatus, most probably compiled for Emperor Theodosius I in the early 390s, and *Selection and Use of Strategic Air Bases* and *Protecting U.S. Power to Strike Back in the 1950s and 1960s*, written by Albert Wohlstetter and his

[22] Colin S. Gray, *Strategic Studies and Public Policy: The American Experience* (Lexington, Ky., 1982), ch. 11.

[23] William Wallace, 'Truth and Power, Monks and Technocrats: Theory and Practice in International Relations', *Review of International Studies*, 22 (1996), 301–21; Ken Booth, 'Discussion: A Reply to Wallace', *Review of International Studies*, 23 (1997), 371–7.

colleagues at RAND for the US Air Force in the early and mid-1950s.[24] These texts are applied strategy: they are replete with detailed practical advice, and they all point to a pressing peril to the state (respectively, the barbarization of the Roman army and the vulnerability of the Strategic Air Command (SAC) to a Soviet first strike). Notwithstanding their 'cookbook' practicality, these works transcend immediate military concerns and succeed in registering some timeless strategic wisdom. Vegetius slipped into his somewhat archaic discussion of the Roman legions a chapter 26 on the 'General Rules of War', while Wohlstetter managed to make important statements about surprise, vulnerability, and prudent strategic behaviour in the course of recommending a wholly transoceanic strike capability for SAC from North American bases.

PARTIAL THEORIES AND GENERAL THEORY

The ninth and final reason which helps explain the absence of outstanding general theories of war and strategy since Clausewitz is the development of partial theories masquerading as such general and unified theories. As war has become more complex since the early nineteenth century, more candidates have been endorsed by strategic prophets as offering decisive advantage to their exploiters. The candidates in question range from a particular model of a particular weapon system (e.g. the Soviet T-34 tank, the Spitfire, the P-51 Mustang), a category of weapon (e.g. the tank, artillery, or nuclear weapons), a geographically specific form of military power (e.g. seapower, airpower, or information-power), a style of war (e.g. attrition, manoeuvre, control), or a whole dimension of war (e.g. technology, logistics, the human element).

Many theorists of war and strategy slip almost imperceptibly into the role of general theorist, as the domain and quality of effectiveness they claim for their preferred military instrument and method expands. The problem here is not so much with the intentional exaggeration of the propagandist. Rather, it resides with the honest strategic theorist and defence analyst who confuses a partial approach to war with general theory.

The roots of this phenomenon lie in the nexus between the theory and practice of strategy. Policy and strategy has to be 'done' by people in chariots, ships, aeroplanes, and missile silos. The strategic theorist speculates about the effect of particular military instruments upon the course of history.[25] No matter how abstract and general a theory of strategy may appear to be, that theory has to relate to the actual potential behaviour of Roman legionaries, Napoleonic guardsmen, or

---

[24] Vegetius, *Vegetius: Epitome of Military Science*, trans. N. P. Milner (Liverpool, 1993); A. J. Wohlstetter et al., *Selection and Use of Strategic Air Bases*, R-266 (Santa Monica, Calif., Apr. 1954); id., *Protecting U.S. Ability to Strike Back in the 1950s and 1960s*, R-290 (Santa Monica, Calif., Apr. 1956).

[25] Unusually explicit treatments include Alfred Thayer Mahan, *The Influence of Sea Power upon History, 1660–1783*, repr. of 1890 edn. (London, 1965), and—with gratitude to Mahan—Colin S. Gray, 'The Influence of Space Power upon History', *Comparative Strategy*, 15 (1996), 293–308.

American bomber crews. Fine writing about war and strategy is always about the threat or use of force by one group of variably equipped people against symmetrical or asymmetrical foes. Thought about strategy has to begin with the realms both of politics and of the battlefield. Clausewitz was a dedicated and prolific military historian. His general theory of war and strategy rested upon his empirical knowledge and understanding of actual warfare, a knowledge and understanding learnt both by personal experience and from the study of military history. It was his genius to be able to construct a (more or less) unified general theory from his self-admittedly partial grasp of tactical and operational realities (i.e. the conduct of war on land).

Even the strategic studies that do succeed in elevating their sights from a particular geographical environment or class of weapon to the rarefied heights of war and strategy still tend to fail as general theory. It is genuinely difficult to leap from, say, an excellent discussion of airpower to a discussion of airpower as exemplar of matters strategic. At the level of strategy one is not interested in airpower *per se*, but only in the effect of airpower as an instrument forwarding the interests that lurk behind the goals of policy.

There are two ways in which partial theory fails to clear the jumps to proceed into the zone of general theory. On the one hand, authors may simply allow themselves to be captured by the strategic promise in their preferred kind of military capability—a fact which leads them to mistake, for example, sea-heavy, air-heavy, or generically bombardment-heavy theory for a general theory of war and strategy. On the other hand, no matter how competently theorists tell the airpower, seapower, or whatever, story, and no matter how well they integrate that story into a coherent, all-environments explanation of the subject, that explanation must fail as timeless general theory to the degree that it rests on claims for the relative effectiveness of particular kinds of military power. The character of war changes with technology and social and political conditions, so any attempt at general theory keyed to particular forms of military power must be limited by them. By analogy, efforts to explain the general character of land warfare would be limited in their authority if they were tied to the trinitarian combined-arms capabilities of foot infantry, horse cavalry, and artillery.

Four levels of a general theory of war emerge as valid possibilities.

1. A level that transcends time, environment, political and social conditions, and technology.
2. A level that explains how the geographical and functional complexities of war and strategy interact and complement each other.
3. A level that explains how a particular kind or use of military power strategically affects the course of conflict as a whole.
4. A level that explains the character of war in a particular period, keyed to

explicit assumptions about the capabilities of different kinds of military power and their terms of effective engagement.

If Clausewitz's *On War* and Sun Tzu's *Art of War* fit into level 1, Julian S. Corbett's *Some Principles of Maritime Strategy* and even my own work on *The Leverage of Sea Power* approximate what general theory at level 2 should provide.[26] Corbett's and my book qualify for category 2 because, notwithstanding our maritime focus, we both approached maritime matters explicitly in the context of war as a whole. Corbett suggestively entitled the first chapter of his great study of the Seven Years War, 'The Function of the Fleet in War'.[27] In *Some Principles* he declares: 'by maritime strategy we mean the principles which govern a war in which the sea is a substantial factor'.[28] Raoul Castex noted that Corbett's 'maritime strategy' was an Englishman's label for what he, Castex, called *stratégie générale*. Eugenia C. Kiesling, Castex's English-language editor, notes the congruence in meaning of 'maritime strategy' and *stratégie générale* with the more familiar concepts of grand and national strategy.[29] The writings of the British royal marine George Aston, to take a prominent example, were more balanced in content among the different geographical environments than the naval writings of Corbett,[30] but the higher quality of insight of the latter provided substantial compensation for their lack of 'jointness'.

The third level of general theory is epitomized by the writings of Alfred Thayer Mahan, Giulio Douhet, and possibly even some of the more dazzling writings of Thomas C. Schelling.[31] Each of these theorists offers a broad-gauge theory of war that rests on a narrow base of military power or skill in statecraft. Mahan and Douhet promise strategic success respectively through seapower and airpower, while Schelling, in his brilliant book *Arms and Influence*, appears to promise strategic success by a process of fine-tuned coercion. There is much merit in the writings of all three of these distinguished theorists. Problems arise only if one mistakes their partial theories for whole theories of war and strategy.

Several recent works on airpower illustrate the fourth level of general theory, which explains how a particular kind of military power contributes to strategic effect in a particular era. Whereas, say, Robert A. Pape's study of the value of

[26] Sun Tzu, *The Art of War*, trans. Ralph D. Sawyer (Boulder, Colo., 1994); Julian S. Corbett, *Some Principles of Maritime Strategy*, ed. Eric Grove, repr. of 1911 edn. (Annapolis, Md., 1988); Colin S. Gray, *The Leverage of Sea Power: The Strategic Advantage of Navies in War* (New York, 1992).

[27] Julian S. Corbett, *England in the Seven Years' War: A Study in Combined Strategy*, repr. of 1918 edn. (London, 1973), vol. i, ch. 1.

[28] Corbett, *Some Principles*, 15.

[29] Castex, *Strategic Theories*, 44–5, n. 8.

[30] George Aston, 'Combined Strategy for Fleets and Armies; or "Amphibious Strategy"', *Journal of the Royal United Service Institution*, 51 (1907), 984–1004; id., *Sea, Land, and Air Strategy: A Comparison* (London, 1914).

[31] Mahan, *Influence of Sea Power upon History*; Giulio Douhet, *The Command of the Air*, trans. Dino Ferrari, repr. of 1942 edn. (New York, 1972); Thomas C. Schelling, *The Strategy of Conflict* (Cambridge, Mass., 1960); id., *Arms and Influence* (New Haven, Conn., 1966).

airpower as a coercive tool in war plainly falls within my third level of general theory, the books by Richard P. Hallion and Williamson Murray about airpower in the Gulf War both qualify for category 4.[32]

WHO NEEDS A GENERAL THEORY OF WAR AND STRATEGY?

Modern general strategic theory fails to impress, and that failure matters. The argument advanced in Chapters 3 and 4, though focused upon somewhat abstract general theory, fuels judgement on practical, not aesthetic, matters. The claim that modern general strategic theory falls far short of the standard set by Clausewitz does not amount to an intellectual lament concerning philosophical impoverishment. The impoverishment, rather, is one that pertains to understanding of all aspects of war, and war has been a subject of the utmost practical significance.

Every war is both unique yet also similar to other wars. This was the dilemma with which Clausewitz grappled as he sought to reconcile the particularities of historical knowledge with a general understanding that transcends the historically unique for creation of a theory useful for public behaviour. The dilemma that he faced persists to this day. In modern times it has become ever easier for policymakers and military commanders to be so diverted by the proliferation of different forms of war that they have neglected 'the basics' of strategy.

To approach war as it should be approached, holistically, and to see all the forms of war as potential strategic effect, requires the educational advantage that only general theory can provide. By 'theory', Clausewitz referred to activity and a product that modern social science would call 'pre-theory'. He is concerned that theory should educate and guide, rather than seek to direct. Theory to Clausewitz is little more than clear and suitably nuanced thinking, and the avoidance of pseudo-scientific formulae and 'naive reductionism' to 'principles and rules'.[33] He is so insistent upon the need to avoid 'positive doctrine, a sort of *manual* for action',[34] that he risks erring in the direction of undue modesty. He advises: 'The primary purpose of any theory is to clarify concepts and ideas that have become, as it were, confused and entangled.'[35] Further, he argues:

[32] Robert A. Pape, *Bombing to Win: Air Power and Coercion in War* (Ithaca, NY, 1996); Richard P. Hallion, *Storm over Iraq: Air Power and the Gulf War* (Washington, DC, 1992); Williamson Murray, *Air War in the Persian Gulf* (Baltimore, 1995). In addition to offering a withering critique of Pape (*Bombing to Win*), Barry D. Watts, 'Ignoring Reality: Problems of Theory and Evidence in Security Studies', *Security Studies*, 7 (1997/8), 115–71, is a major contribution to sensible thought on how, and how not, to theorize about strategy.

[33] John Mueller, 'The Impact of Ideas on Grand Strategy', in Richard Rosecrance and Arthur A. Stein (eds.), *The Domestic Bases of Grand Strategy* (Ithaca, NY, 1993), 48.

[34] Clausewitz, *On War*, 141 (emphasis original).

[35] Ibid. 132.

Whenever an activity deals primarily with the same things again and again—with the same ends and the same means, even though there may be minor variations and an infinite diversity of combinations—these things are susceptible of rational study. It is precisely that enquiry which is the most essential part of any *theory*, and which may quite appropriately claim that title. It is an analytical investigation leading to a close *acquaintance* with the subject; applied to experience—in our case, to military history—it leads to thorough *familiarity* with it. The closer it comes to that goal, the more it proceeds from the objective form of a science to the subjective form of a skill, the more effective it will prove in areas where the nature of the case admits no arbiter but talent. Theory will have fulfilled its main task when it is used to analyze the constituent elements of war, to distinguish precisely what at first sight seems fused, to explain in full the properties of the means employed and to show their probable effects, to define clearly the nature of the ends in view, and to illuminate all phases of warfare in a thoroughly critical enquiry.[36]

To shape strategy for a particular war, a high command should understand how war in general, *qua* war, 'works'. General theory, following Clausewitz, educates politicians and commanders broadly as to the nature, structure, and dynamic workings of the instrument to which they might have resort. They will know that operational military objectives must match political goals, but they also will be aware that the very grammar of war, not to mention the unexpected behaviour of the enemy, may require modification of those goals. People educated in a sound theory of war will not permit variants of 'dominant weapon' arguments to preempt strategic choice. Furthermore, such people will not so fail to grip the process of strategy-making and execution that, as with the less-than-truly 'joint' conduct of the Gulf War of 1991, they staple together most of the activities preferred by distinctive military cultures and call the result a plan.[37] As Clausewitz judged: 'So long as no acceptable theory, no intelligent analysis of the conduct of war exists, routine methods will tend to take over even at the highest levels.'[38] The chief utility of a general theory of war and strategy lies in its ability not to point out lessons, but to isolate things that need thinking about. Theory provides insights and questions, not answers.[39] Policymakers and military commanders educated with the ideas in Chapter 3 should be well armed conceptually to investigate the particular details pertaining to *their* wars, no matter how unique those wars may seem to be.

[36] Clausewitz, *On War*, 141 (emphasis original).
[37] Michael R. Gordon and Bernard E. Trainor, *The Generals' War: The Inside Story of the Conflict in the Gulf* (Boston, 1995), 471–3.
[38] Clausewitz, *On War*, 154.
[39] For a similar view of the role of history, see Geoffrey Till, *Maritime Strategy and the Nuclear Age* (London, 1982), 224, 225.

Chapter 5

STRATEGIC CULTURE AS CONTEXT

No one and no institution can operate 'beyond culture'. The discussion here is a detailed illustration and explanation of the master theme of the book, which argues for an essential unity to all strategic experience. It is not the case that the choices and activities of some policymakers and warriors can be explored usefully in culturalist perspective, while others cannot. Not all policymakers and warriors are able to act out their cultural preferences, but that is another matter entirely. In addition to providing vital expression of my claim for the unity of strategic experience, the analysis here also addresses the question of how ideas and practice interact.

This exploration of strategic culture is written in the light of contemporary debate about both the nature and terms of possible significance of its subject. I argue that culture embraces both ideas and behaviour and that it is inescapable: one cannot sensibly contrast culturalist with other approaches to politics or strategy, because all human beings are culturally educated or programmed. So, all strategic behaviour is cultural behaviour. This is inconvenient for scholars who wish to study the distinctive influence of culture. If cultural phenomena cannot be readily identified and isolated, they may well prove too elusive for rigorous examination by social scientists. That caveat duly recorded, it is most useful to approach the idea of strategic culture in terms of context, a term presented here in two senses. On the one hand, culture as context provides meaning for events. On the other hand, the human hosts of strategic culture are inalienably part of their own strategic context. The context weaves together socialized humans and their world 'out there'. They are a part of their strategic context.

Three generations of scholars in rapid succession have addressed the concept of strategic culture.[1] There are sharp differences over what constitutes the proper

---

[1] The postulate of three generations is offered by Alastair Iain Johnston, 'Thinking about Strategic Culture', *International Security*, 19 (1995), 36–43; id., *Cultural Realism: Strategic Culture and Grand Strategy in Chinese History* (Princeton, NJ, 1995), 4–22; id., 'Cultural Realism and Strategy in Maoist China', in Peter J. Katzenstein (ed.), *The Culture of National Security: Norms and Identity in World Politics* (New York, 1996), 221–2, n. 8. Although the generations overlap, the peak of their intellectual activity respectively can be associated primarily with the late 1970s, the 1980s, and the 1990s. It is worth mentioning that all of these 'generations' together would make only for a small party. First-generation scholars by and large were looking for a more Russian, and Soviet, USSR than contemporary policy and strategic theory recognized. Second-generation scholars sought the cunning coded messages behind the language of strategic studies. The third generation appears primarily interested in researchability. The current, or third, wave of cultural theorizing has many elements. In a recent article, Michael C. Desch identifies four strands as dominant: 'organizational, political, strategic, and global': 'Culture Clash: Assessing the Importance of Ideas in Security Studies', *International Security*, 23 (1998), 142.

domain of culture and possibly, though less certainly, over how culture may shape impulses to act. The subject of strategic culture matters deeply because it raises core questions about the roots of, and influences upon, strategic behaviour. Recent scholarship on strategic culture is seriously in error in its endeavour to distinguish culture from behaviour.

So limited is the empirical and theoretical scholarship currently available on strategic culture that we would probably be best advised to look more for complementarities of approach than to try and elect one or another view the methodological winner. Strategic culture should be approached both as a shaping context for behaviour and as itself a constituent of, and therefore as manifested in, that behaviour. The theoretical, let alone empirical, difficulties raised by the latter approach are obviously severe. Readers could do worse than consider this discussion with reference to the distinction drawn by Martin Hollis and Steve Smith between 'explaining and understanding international relations'.[2] One can think of strategic culture as being 'out there' as a rich and distilled source of influence which might cause behaviour. Alternatively, or perhaps in addition, one can regard strategic culture as being in good measure socially constructed by both people and institutions, which proceed to behave to some degree culturally.

The methodologically awesome qualifier 'to some degree' is the nub of the problem. It is not the case, however, that to see all strategic behaviour as culturally influenced is to explain everything and therefore to explain nothing. There is vastly more to strategy and strategic behaviour than culture alone. Nonetheless, the dimensions of strategy are expressed in behaviour by people and institutions that have internalized strategic culture while at the same time constructing, interpreting, and amending that culture. The strategic cultural context for strategic behaviour includes the human strategic actors and their institutions which 'make culture' by interpreting what they discern. Arcane though it may sound, this discussion bears directly upon such matters as whether, why, and how people, polities, and would-be polities fight.

Definitional clarity is usually useful, but one needs to remember that the price of clarity can be clear error. As noted already, there is a key dualism in social scientific definitions of context. Context can be considered as something 'out there', typically in concentric circles, meaning 'that which surrounds'.[3] Alternatively—or, methodologically perilously, as well—one can approach context as 'that which weaves together' (from the Latin *contextere*, 'to weave together'). Strategic culture can be conceived as a context out there that surrounds, and gives meaning to, strategic behaviour, as the total warp and woof of strategic matters that are thoroughly woven together, *or as both*.

---

[2] Martin Hollis and Steve Smith, *Explaining and Understanding International Relations* (Oxford, 1990).
[3] This discussion draws heavily upon the excellent analysis in Michael Cole, *Cultural Psychology: A Once and Future Discipline* (Cambridge, Mass., 1996), 131–7.

IDEAS AND BEHAVIOUR

In the mid-1970s a small number of strategic theorists came to believe that strategic ideas and some strategic behaviour were more the product of an educational process of social construction than the professional literature on defence then recognized. Those scholars were much taken by Bernard Brodie's claim: 'good strategy presumes good anthropology and sociology. Some of the greatest military blunders of all time have resulted from juvenile evaluations in this department.'[4] Brodie's words rank among the wisest of observations in the entire history of strategic thought. The fact that he rediscovered the obvious does not much detract from its luminosity.

The initial, or first-generation, literature on the startlingly familiar yet strangely under-explored notion of strategic culture was more workmanlike than truly scholarly.[5] That point noted, still it seems that the study of strategic culture has advanced boldly into avoidable conceptual, methodological, and practical ambush. The most prominent and influential of the latest generation of theorists is Alastair Iain Johnston. Although almost any scholarly work on strategic culture is granted importance because of its rarity, Johnston's work is especially significant because it contains errors of a kind that, if allowed to pass unchallenged, are apt to send followers into an intellectual wasteland. I will address those errors below.

How should we think about strategic culture, and why does it matter? As Chapter 1 explained, strategy has many dimensions, one of which is the cultural. Culture or cultures comprise the persisting socially transmitted ideas, attitudes, traditions, habits of mind, and preferred methods of operation that are more or less specific to a particular geographically based security community that has had a unique historical experience. A particular community may well contain more than one strategic culture, just as there are military cultures associated with particular missions or geographical environments.[6] Furthermore, strategic culture(s) can change over time, as new experience is absorbed, coded, and culturally translated. Culture, however, changes slowly. Scholars who prefer to look only to

---

[4] Bernard Brodie, *War and Politics* (New York, 1973), 332.

[5] Works from the first generation include: Jack L. Snyder, *The Soviet Strategic Culture: Implications for Limited Nuclear Operations*, R-2154-AF (Santa Monica, Calif., Sept. 1977); Colin S. Gray, 'National Style in Strategy: The American Example', *International Security*, 6 (1981), 21–47; id., *Nuclear Strategy and National Style* (Lanham, Md., 1986); id., *War, Peace and Victory: Strategy and Statecraft for the Next Century* (New York, 1990), esp. ch. 2; Carnes Lord, 'American Strategic Culture', *Comparative Strategy*, 5 (1985), 269–93; Carl G. Jacobsen (ed.), *Strategic Power: USA/USSR* (New York, 1990), pt. 1.

[6] Carl H. Builder, *The Masks of War: American Military Styles in Strategy and Analysis* (Baltimore, 1989); Deborah D. Avant, *Political Institutions and Military Change: Lessons from Peripheral Wars* (Ithaca, NY, 1994); Elizabeth Kier, *Imagining War: French and British Military Doctrine between the Wars* (Princeton, NJ, 1997); Theo Farrell, 'Figuring Out Fighting Organizations: The New Organizational Analysis in Strategic Studies', *Journal of Strategic Studies*, 19 (1996), 122–316; id., 'Culture and Military Power', *Review of International Studies*, 24 (1998), 407–16; Williamson Murray, 'Does Military Culture Matter?', *Orbis*, 43 (1999), 27–42. See also the other articles on military culture in that issue of *Orbis*: Don M. Snider, 'An Uninformed Debate on Military Culture', 11–26, and John Hillen, 'Must U.S. Military Culture Reform?', 43–57.

recent history as the determining influence upon contemporary strategic culture would be well advised to change concepts. If strategic culture is held to be significantly reshapable on a year-by-year, or even on a decade-by-decade, basis, then 'culture' is probably unduly dignified, even pretentious, a term to characterize the phenomena at issue.

The dimensions of strategy interpenetrate. Everything a security community does, if not a manifestation of strategic culture, is at least an example of behaviour effected by culturally shaped, or encultured,[7] people, organizations, procedures, and weapons. A critic would be correct in observing that if strategic culture is everywhere it is, in practicably researchable terms, nowhere. That critic, however, would have missed the point (that, for example, Germans are Germans and, it is postulated, have had certain strategic cultural tendencies). In their strategic behaviour, Germans cannot help but behave except under the constraints of Germanic strategic culture, even when they are unable to adhere strictly to the dominant ideas and preferences of that culture. Hitler sought to draw strength in 1942–5 from the common German belief that theirs was the historic duty of protecting Europe from the barbarians to the East. This belief, or myth, had power over contemporary German imagination.

The most persuasively plausible definition of culture is that offered by the sociologist Raymond Williams. He claims that the definition of culture has three general categories: the 'ideal', the 'documentary', and the 'social'. Respectively, Williams's categories include values pertaining to some 'timeless order' and '"the artefacts" of intellectual and imaginative work in which human thought and experience are variously recorded'; finally he advises that culture 'is a description of a particular way of life which finds expression in institutions and ordinary behaviour'.[8] In other words, culture is ideals, it is the evidence of ideas, and it is behaviour. Both the Oxford and Webster's dictionaries define culture as embracing ideas *and* patterns of behaviour.

Anyone who seeks a falsifiable theory of strategic culture (as does Johnston) commits the same error as a doctor who sees people as having separable bodies and minds. In his writings about Chinese strategic culture, Johnston's apparently methodologically progressive determination to consider culture distinctively from behaviour, for the purpose of studying the influence of the former on the latter, turns out to be a scholarly step backwards. There is an obvious sense in which positivistically he is seeking to explain how the cultural context (as 'that which surrounds') does, or does not, influence the realm of action. From the

---

[7] I apologize for the neologism of 'encultured,' but it would seem to be licensed at least implicitly by the long-recognized words 'accultured' and 'acculturation'. If one can be accultured, as the Oxford and Webster's dictionaries allow, logically initially one must have been *en*cultured. In order to transfer one's culture, first one must have a culture to be transferred.

[8] Raymond Williams, 'The Analysis of Culture', in John Storey (ed.), *Cultural Theory and Popular Culture: A Reader* (Hemel Hempstead, 1994), 56.

perspective of methodological rigour it is hard to fault him. The problem is that one cannot understand strategic behaviour by that method, be it ever so rigorous. Strategic culture is not only 'out there', it is also within us; we, our institutions, and our behaviour are in the context.

Whatever the sins of omission and commission in the first generation of writings about strategic culture, those writings were plausible on the most important matters; moreover, even with hindsight and in the light of fierce criticism, they still look plausible. What did those theorists attempt to say? On the basis of familiarity with strategic history, they hypothesized that different security communities and sub-communities tend to exhibit in their strategic thought *and behaviour* patterns that could be collectively termed cultural, and that strategic culture finds expression in distinctively patterned styles of strategic behaviour. When Johnston criticizes my early work on strategic culture for being deterministic,[9] he misunderstands the nature of the subject in dispute. His real source of unhappiness with my writings lies in dislike of my definition of the concept of strategic culture. I conflate strategic ideas and behaviour, to the effect, according to Johnston, that my theory is tautological and therefore unfalsifiable.[10]

Johnston commits several errors. First, he requires 'a notion of strategic culture that is falsifiable, at least distinguishable from nonstrategic-culture variables'.[11] Reasonable though that requirement should be, he does not understand a point raised by anthropologist Leslie A. White: 'Culture is not basically anything. Culture is a word-concept. It is man-made and may be used arbitrarily to designate anything, we may define the conception we please.'[12] Even scholars can forget that definitions are neither right nor wrong. Second, although definitions are arbitrary, a definition driven by the needs of theory-building rather than by the nature of the subject, is unusually likely to lead scholars astray.

There is something to be said for restricting the concept of culture to the realm of ideas, to the assumptions that lie behind strategic behaviour. But there is sense in Robert B. Bathurst's words when he writes (to adapt), 'Strategic culture, here, refers to those prominent patterns of . . . [strategic] behaviour which are indicative of social ways of seeing and responding to "reality".'[13] Similarly, in an invented conversation, Clyde Kluckhohn and William H. Kelly's 'Second Anthropologist' advises that 'what the anthropologist does is to record the distinctive ways of behaving which he sees and those results of behavior which are also characteristic. These constitute the culture of the group.'[14] Finally, for a variant,

[9] Johnston, *Cultural Realism*, 8.
[10] Johnston, 'Thinking about Strategic Culture', 36–9; id., *Cultural Realism*, 7–10.
[11] Johnston, 'Thinking about Strategic Culture', 45.
[12] Leslie A. White, *The Concept of Cultural Systems: A Key to Understanding Tribes and Nations* (New York, 1975), 4n.
[13] Robert B. Bathurst, *Intelligence and the Mirror: On Creating an Enemy* (London, 1993), 24.
[14] Clyde Kluckhohn and William H. Kelly, 'The Concept of Culture', in Charles C. Hughes (ed.), *Custom-Made: Introductory Readings for Cultural Anthropology*, 2nd edn. (Chicago, 1976), 188.

anthropologist Marvin Harris informs us: 'Culture ... refers to the learned repertory of thoughts and actions exhibited by the members of social groups — repertories transmissible independently of genetic heredity from one generation to the next.'[15]

The traffic between ideas and behaviour in strategic affairs is continuous, hence my preference for the idea that context is more about 'that which weaves together' than about 'that which surrounds'. As the intellectual history of strategy, including its manifestation in national or sub-national strategic and military culture, bears the stamp of particular perceptions and interpretations of strategic experience, so strategic behaviour is shaped by the attitudes and ideas that we know as strategic culture. In the practical world of strategy, strategic ideas apply to experience, while strategic experience constitutes ideas in action, albeit as modified by the constraints of imperfect practice.

Johnston's approach flags important concerns. For example, up to a point he is correct to signal the perils of determinism in sweeping claims for the explanatory value of the concept of strategic culture. Also, his work is useful in reminding us of the probable facts that a security community may have several strategic cultures, that culture evolves over time, and that strategic culture may comprise more a litany of canonical idealized beliefs than a set of attitudes, perspectives, and preferences that are operational as real guides to action. Furthermore, Johnston is partially correct when he alerts scholars to the difficulties posed by a concept of strategic culture that comprises so extensive a portfolio of ingredients, and is so influential upon behaviour, that it can explain nothing because it purports to explain everything.[16] Nonetheless, it would seem that Johnston read the score rather than listened to the music.

We first-generation scholars of strategic culture, albeit with exceptions, were not advancing a culturally distinctive theory of strategy — at least we did not think that we were. At times some of us, myself included, may well have appeared both careless in our all-too-implicit causalities (connecting cultural preference and behaviour) and perilously tautological. It is useful to have those weaknesses signalled clearly, so that scholars speak more plainly. Although the written products of our speculation may have seemed somewhat deterministic, by and large all that we intended was to remind readers and official clients that there was a notably Soviet–Russian dimension to the Cold War foe; we were not competing with some abstract superpower A or B that was beyond culture. Probably we overemphasized the cultural argument, but that is not unusual when arguments are novel.

Johnston does not grasp the nature of strategic culture. He objects to a theory that is effectively untestable because its evidential domain is pervasive. The problem, though, does not lie so much in poor methodology and casual conceptualization — though that charge may have merit — as in his overly simple

---

[15] Marvin Harris, *Cultural Materialism: The Struggle for a Science of Culture* (New York, 1979), 47.
[16] Johnston, *Cultural Realism*, 12–13.

view of strategy. Although each dimension of strategy can be discussed in isolation, all dimensions function synergistically to constitute the whole.

On balance, it may be desirable to fence in the concept of strategic culture with reference to ideas, attitudes, traditions, and preferences for kinds of action, and to consider the actual behaviour of a strategic culture, or cultures, as the realm of 'style'.[17] It is important to understand that even when a security community is performing missions that traditionally it has not much favoured, if not actually alien, it must behave in a culturally shaped manner. Germans cannot help but be Germans, whether they are waging war as they would prefer or as they must. Culture is behaviour, because those responsible for the behaviour are necessarily encultured as Germans, Britons, and so forth.[18]

One should resist the suggestion in some recent scholarship that somehow strategic culture can be sidelined and offset by other influences upon strategic choice.[19] The idea of strategic culture does not imply that there is a simple one-to-one relationship between culturally traceable preferences and actual operational choices.[20] The claim, rather, is that culture shapes the process of strategy-making, and influences the execution of strategy, no matter how close actual choice may be to some abstract or idealized cultural preference. This simple but crucial point, can elude the intellectual grasp even of careful scholars. For example, in a recent major review of 'culturalist' theories of security, Michael Desch draws an invalid distinction between culturalist theories and realist theories of national security.[21] He does not seem to understand that 'realist' analysis and policy is undertaken by particularly encultured people and organizations. Perhaps the point is too obvious to notice.

The unity of cultural influence and policy action denies the existence of the boundaries needed for the study of cause and effect. If there is cause in the effect, how can cause be assessed for its effect? Happily, the problem lies with the question, not the answer. Strategic culture and patterns of strategic behaviour are related integrally much as are strategy, operations, and tactics. Just as all strategy has to be 'done' by operations which consist of tactical behaviour, so all strategic, operational, and tactical behaviour is 'done' by people and organizations that have been encultured supra-nationally, nationally, or sub-nationally. As anthropologist Edward T. Hall has emphasized, culture provides context for events and

---

[17] Gray, *Nuclear Strategy and National Style*, ch. 2.

[18] Dean Peabody, *National Characteristics* (Cambridge, 1985); Edward L. Keenan, 'Muscovite Political Folkways', *Russian Review*, 45 (1986), 115–81; Emilio Willems, *A Way of Life and Death: Three Centuries of Prussian-German Militarism, An Anthropological Approach* (Nashville, Tenn., 1986), are all useful.

[19] This idea helps drive Johnston's methodology in *Cultural Realism*.

[20] Ibid. 8.

[21] Desch, 'Culture Clash', has as its central theme comparison of the utility of culturalist and realist theories of international relations. To draw a distinction between realism and culturalism is to miss the point that strategy and security is always 'done' by people and organizations who must function within the domain of cultural influences.

ideas.[22] Some societies (e.g. Russian) are high-context, some are low-context: some societies take a relatively complex and organic view of events, seeing subtexts and subplots and subtle interconnections, while others (e.g. American) are prone to see simple oppositions (e.g. particular weapons are either stabilizing or destabilizing) and to approach each event on its isolated merits, monochronically.[23] But even a low-context strategic culture is still a strategic culture. This application of the concept of context illustrates a way to apply the notion in both the senses introduced at the beginning of this chapter: context as 'that which surrounds' and context as 'that which weaves together'.

In practice, polities cannot afford to listen to much speculation of the scholarly kind suggested in Johnston's work. The policy interest in strategic culture lies not so much in prediction by scholars of how culture 'out there' might influence behaviour, because behaviour can be triggered by many factors. Instead, the vital contextual question is 'what does the observed behaviour mean?' It is more modest to seek to interpret than to predict, but strategic cultural scholarship is as likely to be useful in the former role as it will be unduly challenged in the latter.

STRATEGY IS UNIVERSAL, BUT CULTURAL

The nature and function of strategy is permanent and universal; it is also, in its particular and dynamic historical form and content, inescapably cultural. Johnston laments that '[m]uch empirical work on strategic culture has also been hampered by a lack of methodological rigor'.[24] Alas, the concept of strategic culture, in common with the idea of paradox,[25] expresses an important pervasive, yet in detail typically elusive, truth about the nature and practice of strategy. It is in the nature of strategy to be subject to a paradoxical logic, just as it is in the nature of strategy to reflect the culture of its particular maker and executor. Strategic culture, like paradox in strategy, is a useful notion provided one does not ask too much of it.

In discussing Sun Tzu, historians Barry S. Strauss and Josiah Ober draw attention to his pithy advice on 'the issue of ideology, by which we mean the matrix of unexamined assumptions, opinions, and prejudices that every human being

---

[22] Edward T. Hall, *Beyond Culture* (Garden City, NY, 1977), chs. 6–8.

[23] Bathurst, *Intelligence and the Mirror*, ch. 3.

[24] Johnston, 'Thinking about Strategic Culture', 63. He is no less severe in 'Cultural Realism and Strategy in Maoist China', 221–2. Interestingly enough, while Desch (in 'Culture Clash', 170) judges 'the Cold War wave of theory to be largely discredited', he argues also that that 'wave of cultural theorizing had the virtue of making clear empirical predictions that made it possible to test its theories against both real-world evidence and alternative theories' (158). Johnston, by contrast, finds us Cold War theorists guilty of purveying untestable theories.

[25] Edward N. Luttwak, *Strategy: The Logic of War and Peace* (Cambridge, Mass., 1987).

brings to the decision-making process'.[26] The authors note 'Sun Tzu reminds us that sense [as in common sense] is usually idiosyncratic and seldom crosses cultural lines'. It is powerfully plausible to postulate that people and the institutions through which they operate are educated by their distinctive contexts to bear more or less particular cultural preconceptions. Just as friction in war cannot be eliminated by technological advance, in part because people must employ the new machines,[27] so 'people, being of the human condition . . . are necessarily enmeshed in a network of preconceptions'.[28] Why should this be so? In her brilliant pioneering study *Politics and Culture in International History*, Adda B. Bozeman advises 'that each society is moved by the circumstances of its existence to develop its own approach to foreign relations. This means that diplomacy, as for that matter every other social institution, is bound to incorporate the traditions and values peculiar to the civilization in which it is practiced.'[29] Similarly, Bathurst argues that people cope with incoming data in files that organize their understanding of the world. Moreover, he suggests,

Cultures teach us to see according to the labels on the files . . . [I]t follows that a nation's wars are congruent with that nation's political and social structures. The way it chooses, defines and perceives its enemies, estimates their intentions and plans to counter them necessarily comes from its unique expression, arising out of its systems and organisations.[30]

Bozeman and Bathurst are persuasive to the degree that one wonders how they could possibly be wrong. To be German, American, Russian at a particular time is to be 'encultured' in particular ways. Those ways will vary modestly among, say, Germans at different times in German history, and there may be noteworthy distinctions among Germans even in the same period. Nonetheless, it is reasonable to postulate the presence of some important cultural features among people who share a common heritage, particularly if they are of a similar age. At least until the mid-1940s, Germans believed that they were the Eastern bulwark of European civilisation. Until perhaps 1968, Americans had great difficulty even conceiving of their country losing a war. In the winter of 1942–3, the Soviet defenders of Stalingrad believed that history was with them, both 'scientifically'—compliments of Marx, Lenin, and Stalin—and essentially morally, because they represented Mother Russia. The alternative to the argument just advanced is close to absurd. How could there be a Strategic Person 'beyond culture'? A noteworthy strain in American defence analysis during the Cold War

---

[26] Barry S. Strauss and Josiah Ober, *The Anatomy of Error: Ancient Military Disasters and Their Lessons for Modern Strategists* (New York, 1990), 6–7.

[27] Barry D. Watts, *Clausewitzian Friction and Future War*, McNair Paper 52 (Washington, DC, Oct. 1996), esp. ch. 8.

[28] Bathurst, *Intelligence and the Mirror*, 121.

[29] Adda B. Bozeman, *Politics and Culture in International History* (Princeton, NJ, 1960), 324. This book is an under-recognized classic.

[30] Bathurst, *Intelligence and the Mirror*, 125.

expressed transcultural confidence that it had unlocked the universal mysteries of, for example, strategic stability in the nuclear age. One need hardly add that such arrogant positivism was itself profoundly cultural.[31] As this text explains in Chapter 12, there was eventually a noteworthy convergence between the super-powers concerning a prudential code of nuclear lore. On some key matters of theory and doctrine, however, fashionable American ideas did not find favour in Soviet strategic culture. For example, the Soviet defence establishment never shared the American belief in the stabilizing merit in mutual vulnerability.

In criticizing theorists of the first generation, Johnston stumbles over reality, though without quite realizing what he has uncovered. In his words:

To date, many of those who have explicitly used the term *strategic culture* have tended to define it in ways that make it unfalsifiable and untestable. Especially egregious in this regard is what could be called the first (and most influential) generation of studies in stra-tegic culture. Definitionally, this literature subsumed both thought and action within the concept of strategic culture, leaving the mechanically deterministic implication that stra-tegic thought led consistently to one type of behavior. The literature also tended to include everything from technology to geography to ideology to past patterns of behavior in an amorphous concept of strategic culture, even though those variables could stand as separ-ate, even conflicting explanations for strategic choice. This left little conceptual space for non-strategic culture explanations of behavior.[32]

Johnston is wrong, but he is wrong for the right reasons. The point is that strategic culture does indeed emerge from the kind of mixed stew of ingredients that John-ston finds so methodologically frustrating in the early literature. To adapt Dennis Kavanagh's definition of political culture, 'we may regard the strategic culture ['political culture', in original] as a shorthand expression to denote the emotional and attitudinal environment within which the defence community ['political sys-tem', in original] operates.'[33] Ideas about war and strategy are influenced by phys-ical and political geography—some strategic cultures plainly have, for example, a maritime or a continentalist tilt—by political or religious ideology, and by famil-iarity with, and preference for, particular military technologies. Strategic culture is the world of mind, feeling, *and habit in behaviour*. Johnston is systemically wrong in two respects in conceiving of culture as clearly distinctive among 'conflicting explanations for strategic choice'. He errs in failing to recognize a cultural dimen-sion to all that human beings think and feel about war and strategy. Culture is the context that 'surrounds' and the context that 'weaves together'. Johnston fails to spot the absurdity of the opposition that he postulates when he complains that

[31] Colin S. Gray, 'Strategy in the Nuclear Age: The United States, 1945–1991', in Williamson Murray, MacGregor Knox, and Alvin Bernstein (eds.), *The Making of Strategy: Rulers, States, and War* (Cambridge, 1994), 589–98. Bruno Colson, *La culture stratégique américaine: l'influence de Jomini* (Paris, 1993), is not without merit.

[32] Johnston, 'Cultural Realism and Strategy in Maoist China', 221–2 (emphasis original).

[33] Dennis Kavanagh, *Political Culture* (London, 1972), 10.

there is little conceptual space remaining for explanations of behaviour beyond strategic culture. Let me state the methodologically appalling truth that there can be no such conceptual space, because all strategic behaviour is effected by human beings who cannot help but be cultural agents.

Occasionally, an overwhelmingly maritime strategic culture, like the British in World War I, is obliged to play an uncharacteristically major continental military role. However, the fact of the huge British continental commitment of 1914–18 did not alter the dominant British strategic culture, notwithstanding the infantry experience of a whole generation of Britons. Indeed, exaggerated claims for a traditional British maritime orientation were pressed in the 1920s and 1930s in ways that overstated the degree to which the rôle and responsibility of the BEF of 1916–18 was extraordinary for British culture.[34] Strategic culture explains why the continental role was, certainly psychologically, so different for Britain, as contrasted with some other great powers; it does not explain why Britain chose to wage war as a continental power in those years. In other words, strategic culture provides context, even where the final choice is all but counter-cultural.

For another example, the United States has joined and, in one case, even led three coalitions in the twentieth century, the third of which (i.e NATO) is now of fifty years' duration. Those impressive facts notwithstanding, isolationism, certainly unilateralism, remains a potent icon and impulse for policy in the United States.[35] There is a decidedly hollow ring to Richard Holbrooke's bold claim that 'the United States has become a European power in a sense that goes beyond traditional assertions of America's "commitment" to Europe'.[36] Even when security communities function strategically in ways contrary to a dominant tradition—Britain in 1916–18, or America's repeated involvement in entangling alliances—those actions do not, certainly may not, produce a seismic shift in strategic culture. Furthermore, when a preponderantly maritime culture commits to continental warfare on the largest of scales, or when an isolationist culture becomes a partner in coalition-style strategic ventures, the stamp of those basic moulds will be seen in the ways behaviour is adapted to the practical needs of the uncharacteristic roles. For example, Hew Strachan has shown how resistant to revolutionary change was the traditional 'British way of war', even under the greatest of pressures of continental military crisis in World War I.[37]

---

[34] The relevant issues are addressed in Basil H. Liddell Hart, *The British Way in Warfare* (London, 1932), ch. 1; Michael Howard, *The Continental Commitment: The Dilemma of British Defence Policy in the Era of the Two World Wars* (London, 1972); Hew Strachan, 'The British Way in Warfare Revisited', *Historical Journal*, 26 (1983), 447–61; id., 'The British Way in Warfare', in David Chandler (ed.), *The Oxford Illustrated History of the British Army* (Oxford, 1994), 417–34.

[35] Arthur Schlesinger, Jr., 'Back to the Womb? Isolationism's Renewed Threat', *Foreign Affairs*, 74 (1995), 2–8.

[36] Richard Holbrooke, 'America, a European Power', *Foreign Affairs*, 74 (1995), 38.

[37] Hew Strachan, 'The Battle of the Somme and British Strategy,' *Journal of Strategic Studies*, 21 (1998), 79–95.

Cultural preconceptions are inescapable, but they are not of some malign necessity pathological. To be encultured as a German or American may be unavoidable, but there is nothing about being German or American that requires one to fail to recognize the cultural distinctiveness of others. I may be British and American, but I do not have to believe that all the world thinks and feels as do Britons and Americans. Cultural reductionism, even stereotyping, and their polar opposite, ethnocentrism, are to a degree unavoidable.[38] In strategy we have to deal with human beings—Germans, Chinese, and so forth—collectively, and we can only interpret incoming information with reference to what we know in our culture of their culture (which is an unavoidable brand of ethnocentrism). Nonetheless, while recognizing ethnocentrism as a cardinal sin against the gods of sound strategy, some cultural reductionism and stereotyping is inescapable and can even yield judgements of tolerable accuracy.

The term 'cultural preconception' has pejorative connotations that may mislead the unwary. Whereas many American soldiers entered World War II with scant respect for a German army which their preconceptions told them was bound to be rigidly teutonic in action, British soldiers—trained by experience in 1914–18 and 1940–1—were apt to hold the accurate preconception that the German army was formidable in its tactical flexibility.[39] The British were correct, as Americans learnt in Tunisia, Italy, and later in France. For another example, during the Napoleonic wars British admirals and generals typically held strategic cultural preconceptions about their French foe at sea and on land that were good enough to provide an accurate frame of reference within which campaigns and battle plans could be prepared with reasonable confidence. When Vice-Admiral Horatio Nelson planned the apparently reckless ploy of attacking the Franco-Spanish line of battle firstly in three, then ultimately in two, columns off Cape Trafalgar in October 1805, he rested his plan upon preconceptions about the enemy that expressed the wisdom of great experience. Nelson knew his enemy well enough.[40]

Even if one elects to restrict the concept of strategic culture to the mind and the emotions, and to treat strategic behaviour as activity that can flow from several motives or influences, including the cultural, where does that culture originate? Strategic culture may be regarded as the zone of ideas, but ideas about strategy have to derive from intellectual and emotional interaction with experience, widely understood and however gathered and processed. Since there may be contending orientations and schools of strategic thought, strategic culture appears existentially as those working 'assumptions underlying everyday life' that provide

[38] Ken Booth, *Strategy and Ethnocentrism* (London, 1979), is essential.

[39] David Fraser, *And We Shall Shock Them: The British Army in the Second World War* (London, 1983); Martin van Creveld, *Fighting Power: German and U.S. Army Performance, 1939–1945* (Westport, Conn., 1982); Michael D. Doubler, *Closing with the Enemy: How GIs Fought the War in Europe, 1944–1945* (Lawrence, Kan., 1994).

[40] Alfred Thayer Mahan, *The Life of Nelson: The Embodiment of the Sea Power of Great Britain*, 2nd edn. (London, 1899), chs. 22 and 23; Julian S. Corbett, *The Campaign of Trafalgar* (London, 1910).

'the emotional and attitudinal environment'.[41] The policymaker, the military pro-fessional, and the concerned citizen cannot approach contemporary challenges in a strategic cultural void. Human beings are encultured as people who live in communities, and because, alas, those communities are communities for security, humans have no choice other than to undergo a process of strategic enculturation. Not only do they behave strategically under cultural influence. In addition, human beings are agents of culture, helping to shape their strategic environment according to such of their cultural preferences as circumstances permit. Thus are cultural agent and cultural influence woven together as total context.

CULTURE IS AS CULTURE DOES

It may appear paradoxical that a chapter drafted to explore the salience of local contexts for the making and execution of strategy is so abstract. But in the absence of scholarly consensus about the meaning and functioning of strategic culture, historical case studies can illustrate nothing much beyond the conceptual appar-atus preferred by theorists. Because strategic culture, no less than culture itself, is a contested concept, no amount of rigorous empirical enquiry will liberate scholars from the perils of arguable definitions. Nonetheless, perhaps against the odds, there is a useful way to understand the nature and behavioural implications of strategic culture.

Because of its nature, function, and content, strategy attracts 'interested' scholarship. In the same way that British scholars, even though they should be culturally self-aware, cannot help but be British, so theorists and other com-mentators of every political affiliation can hardly help but be interested in the strategic choices that must affect the public, and their personal, security. The preponderant interest of scholars may lie in the value of books for their profes-sional résumés as the agent of personal advancement. However, choice of strategic topic, and the character of argument developed, is likely to express more or less overt commitment to the value of national or international security. Scholars, scarcely less than politicians and generals, cannot be decultured, as opposed to accultured, or somehow rendered indifferent to the practical consequences of strategic debate. Strategic theory should be honest, but it can hardly be disinter-ested. Even when strategic theorists seek evidence and inspiration from tempor-ally far distant contexts, the essential unity of all strategic experience guarantees the feasibility of a current policy agenda. Two modern historians of antiquity address directly the issue of an enduring historical unity to strategic matters.

Can modern policymakers really derive lessons from ancient warfare? . . . The advent of modern technology has in no way lessened the strategist's need to adapt his military plan

---

[41] Peter Burke, *Popular Culture in Early Modern Europe*, rev. edn. (Aldershot, 1994), p. xxii.

to social and political realities. The second half of the twentieth century has seen a series of startling defeats handed to great powers by warriors whose strategic insight made up for their inferior weapons. Algeria, Vietnam, and Afghanistan are cases in point. Evidently, technology has not replaced strategy as the determining factor in military success. *We believe it is precisely the technologically low level of ancient warfare that makes it so valuable an object of modern study.*[42]

Whether or not one agrees with Strauss and Ober—plainly something provided adequate compensation for inferior weapons in Algeria, Vietnam, and Afghanistan[43]—their approach is instructive. In *Anatomy of Error*, Strauss and Ober affirm the universality of strategy in time and place, the value of a policy agenda as a focus and guide for scholarship, and the salience of strategic history, even temporally far-distant strategic history, for strategic enlightenment today.

It can be difficult to talk about the ubiquity and importance of strategic culture without appearing reductively to claim that it is the golden key to strategic understanding. For reasons explored already, strategic culture is not, and cannot be, such a key: culture offers context, not reliable causality. A dominant culture need not be associated with a particular national group; some cultural pluralism is possible, even likely. Strategic cultures change over time, albeit probably slowly (otherwise the phenomenon would not merit description as cultural), and occasionally strategic choices are made that contradict the dominant culture.[44]

Six general points serve to help advance understanding of the nature and working of strategic culture.

STRATEGIC BEHAVIOUR CANNOT BE BEYOND CULTURE

Strategic behaviour can be eccentric from some viewpoints, incompetent, unsuccessful, even contrary to cultural norms, but it cannot be acultural, beyond culture. A decultured person, organization, or security community would have to be deprogrammed even of the process of learning about, and from, his or its own past. The proposition of extraculturality is ridiculous. It is not at all ridiculous to postulate a person, organization, or security community which treats a strategic issue in isolation from any context but the one apparent to itself, though even in the case of such strategic autism—which is perhaps a distinctive culture—the agent would need to know enough beyond the issue to recognize a *strategic* matter for what it was. One can claim, for example, that the United States is a pragmatic problem-solving culture. But although such a claim affirms the existence of a socially programmed approach to challenges, it does not imply that all American strategy-makers must agree on the details of the solutions preferred. Overall, culture is context. In the absence of such context, events must lack meaning.

[42] Strauss and Ober, *Anatomy of Error*, 9–10 (emphasis added).

[43] A forthcoming book addresses the pertinent issues superbly: A. J. Bacevich and Brian Sullivan (eds.), *The Limits of Technology in Modern War*.

[44] Gray, *Nuclear Strategy and National Style*, 35.

ADVERSITY CANNOT CANCEL CULTURE

Strategically encultured Americans, or Russians, do not cease to be so encultured just because they are obliged to function under conditions of severe constraint. Plainly, the grimmer the national circumstance, the less the scope for exercising strategic cultural preferences. Nonetheless, even when the enemy has the initiative, one does not lose strategic cultural identity. The USSR was ideologically hollow at the core, with the quaint pseudo-science of Marxism-Leninism contrasting ever more starkly with the unmistakable absurdities of Soviet life. That USSR, however, was notably the product of the distinctive beliefs and rhythm of Russian culture. Central authority in Russia collapsed precipitately three times in the twentieth century (1905, 1917, and 1991). In adversity or in triumph, Russians have to be Russians. Even when Russians behave in an arena not preferred by their dominant strategic culture, for example at sea, they behave in ways, and for purposes, that are still culturally characteristic.[45] In the 1980s, US maritime strategists, unsurprisingly, sought to find and comprehend a Soviet maritime strategy that matched or sought to offset US maritime strategy, much as US theorist-practitioners of arms control sought in vain to find a matching Soviet concept of strategic stability. In neither instance did the leading school among Americans appreciate suitably that Russian strategic culture organized its strategic world differently. As land-minded people, Russians conceived maritime operations very much as adjuncts to continental enterprises.

This is not to succumb to the relativist trap of what has been called 'ethnic chic', with particular reference to an alleged sinological fallacy.[46] Chinese, or Germans, do not necessarily respond to strategic stimuli in noticeably, let alone eccentrically, Chinese or German ways. But, Chinese and Germans are socially educated distinctively in their strategic assumptions and, even when obliged to act under duress, are likely to assess distinctively their options and the consequences of exercising each of them. The greater the pressure upon an individual or organization to act, and the more hastily the decision is taken, the greater the likelihood of behaviour manifesting what Bathurst usefully calls 'cultural instinct'.[47] When there is little time to explore the details of the pressing case, strategists then are obliged to go with what they know already and to act according to what they judge, and feel, to be correct: 'Culture Rules.'

[45] Bathurst, *Intelligence and the Mirror*.

[46] Gerald Segal, 'Strategy and "Ethnic Chic"', *International Affairs*, 60 (1983-4), 15–30. Michael I. Handel, *Masters of War: Classical Strategic Thought*, 2nd edn. (London, 1996), 3. For the opinion that there are contrasting broadly Western and Eastern, or Oriental, strategic cultures, see Victor Davis Hanson, *The Western Way of War: Infantry Battle in Classical Greece* (London, 1989), and John Keegan, *A History of Warfare* (London, 1993).

[47] Bathurst, *Intelligence and the Mirror*, 25–6.

STRATEGIC CULTURE IS A GUIDE TO ACTION

Strategic culture has to be a guide to strategic action, whether or not the kind of action that culture prefers is practicable. Moreover, unlike strategic theory, which, as Clausewitz argues, 'need not be a sort of *manual* for action' that would 'accompany [the future commander] to the battlefield',[48] strategic culture is on the battlefield inalienably because it pervades the combatants and their military organizations. Soldiers carry their culture with them into battle. It may well be the case that one can locate, as did Johnston with Ming dynasty China, a polity that has two or more cultures, at least one of which is more a set of ideal standards than a practical manual for behaviour.[49] However, strategic culture, or cultures, has to be a guide to action as well as comprising, existentially, descriptive reality. That is true regardless of the fact that an adverse strategic necessity can frequently subvert or utterly overthrow culture's influence. The prescriptive character of strategic culture flows inexorably from the nature of strategy. If strategy is about what works in the world to bridge the potential chasm between political ends and military agents, it has to follow that strategic culture is at least contingently prescriptive.

STRATEGIC CULTURE EXPRESSES COMPARATIVE ADVANTAGE

For a particular security community, the same blend of comparative advantages (e.g. easy access to the open sea) and disadvantages (e.g. absence of 'natural' frontiers on land) that yields a dominant strategic culture also yields a distinction between the kind of strategic activities that that community will tend to perform either well or poorly. This is not to deny the possibility of strategic cultural pluralism, or the (generally slow) evolution of culture under the press of new experience. For example, for reasons that one can at least ultimately call cultural, the United States is relatively poor at the conduct of special operations, whereas Israel, Britain, and the former USSR are relatively competent.[50] If technology and technique, which is to say tactical prowess, were all that there were to the effectiveness of special operations forces, then the US Army's Delta Force, Green Berets, and Rangers, and the US Navy's SEALs, would be as good as, or better than, anyone's special units. The problem for US special forces is that the US armed forces as a whole are not friendly to less than wholly regular troops, and that US organizations for strategy-making and execution are not receptive to the strategic and operational promise in special operations. The leading difficulty lies with military cultures and strategic culture. In the 1980s and 1990s times appeared to be changing in the United States in favour of special operations' capabilities, but

---

[48] Clausewitz, *On War*, 141 (emphasis original).
[49] Johnston, *Cultural Realism*.
[50] Colin S. Gray, *Explorations in Strategy* (Westport, Conn., 1996), pt. 3.

cultural resistance to allowing special warriors to wage war in their own kind of way remained powerful.[51]

When dominant security communities are obliged either by adverse circumstances or by eccentric policy and strategy-making to behave in culturally radically atypical ways, success will be unlikely. A security community is unlikely to perform well at unfamiliar tasks—for example the Germans and the Russians in surface naval warfare. After all, the strategic cultures that focus upon land warfare are the cultures pressed by long and painful experience to devote far more resources to continental than to maritime affairs. Also, there are physical reasons why particular communities have evolved their individual dominant strategic cultures. Both Russia and Germany have had strategically chronic problems securing access to the open sea.[52]

A security community can behave in ways massively contrary to the strategic preferences implied by its dominant strategic culture; Britain and the United States did exactly this, respectively in World War I and in Vietnam. Even though the Great War was won, general public and much military expert opinion in the interwar years came to believe that never again should Britain wage mass continental warfare, a form of conflict popularly deemed to be lethally un-British.[53] In Vietnam, the US armed forces waged the American way of war in accordance with a dominant American strategic culture that favoured mechanized combat of all kinds, but they waged a form of war that probably could not succeed.[54] The American offence against its dominant culture, therefore, lay not in the chosen acts of military commission *per se* but rather in their strategically inappropriate application. To resort to Clausewitz, because the United States could not settle upon a plausible military objective to fit a sound and stable political objective,[55] strategy failed. 'Engagements' could not advance 'the object of the war'. American politicians and American soldiers were punished by American society because they

[51] Susan L. Marquis, *Unconventional Warfare: Rebuilding U.S. Special Operations Forces* (Washington, DC, 1997).

[52] Wolfgang Wegener, *The Naval Strategy of the World War*, trans. Holger H. Herwig (Annapolis, Md., 1989), is a powerful German statement of the importance of geography to naval strategy.

[53] Brian Bond, *British Military Policy between the World Wars* (Oxford, 1980).

[54] Harry G. Summers, Jr., *On Strategy: A Critical Analysis of the Vietnam War* (Novato, Calif., 1982); Andrew F. Krepinevich, Jr., *The Army and Vietnam* (Baltimore, 1986); Robert Buzzanco, *Masters of War: Military Dissent and Politics in the Vietnam Era* (Cambridge, 1996); H. R. McMaster, *Dereliction of Duty: Lyndon Johnson, Robert McNamara, the Joint Chiefs of Staff, and the Lies That Led to Vietnam* (New York, 1997); Michael A. Hennessy, *Strategy in Vietnam: The Marines and Revolutionary Warfare in I Corps, 1965-1972* (Westport, Conn., 1997); Jeffrey Record, 'Vietnam in Retrospect: Could We Have Won?', *Parameters*, 26 (1996–7), 51–65. Although US defeat in Vietnam appears to have been foreordained, some powerful arguments suggesting, and evidence for, US success in Vietnam have yet to receive a decent hearing. If a line in the jungle *had* to be drawn—which is a different and more fundamental matter—it should have been drawn in defence of Laos in 1961, not South Vietnam in 1965. C. Dale Walton, 'Victory Denied: The Myth of Inevitable American Defeat in Vietnam' (Ph.D. thesis, Hull, 1999), is a bold and valuable corrective to unduly orthodox beliefs.

[55] Clausewitz, *On War*, 579.

waged an American-preferred way of war in conditions where that way could not deliver victory, in a cause deemed by many people to be un-American. It is common for strategic failure to be punished politically, at home as well as abroad. When that failure is delivered by armed forces directed to conduct forms of war that offend dominant cultural preferences, however, the domestic political backlash is apt to be severe and protracted.

In addition to countries having one or more strategic cultures, they also have several military cultures. Military cultures can be specific to armed service, branch of service, or trans-service function or weapons focus (e.g. 'special' warriors, aviators, and nuclear missileers). There is an emerging literature on military culture which, though scholarly, is in the great tradition of strategic studies in that it has been triggered by perceptions of the problems of the day. Military culture(s) cannot be studied apart from their broader context, but to date scholarship has little to offer on the subject of how that kind of culture relates to the character of strategic culture discussed here. Obviously, it would be absurd to claim that sailors are sailors regardless of national affiliation. But how much, and exactly why and how, does it matter that a sailor is German, rather than British? After all, they must to some degree share the seaman's world-view. At present, the literatures on strategic and on military culture have yet to effect a productive discourse. Suffice it to say, given the focus upon broad strategic culture in this chapter, that at least an awareness of military cultures should alert us to the possible perils of generalization. Williamson Murray provides an admirable cautionary note:

The German military style reflected a national attitude that took war very seriously—a predeliction inspired by the numerous invasions that German states had suffered over the course of centuries. The German navy, however, proved in two world wars that there was nothing innately competent about German military organizations; as a result, one should hesitate before ascribing undue influence to national culture in how service cultures develop.[56]

Murray's persuasive point does not threaten to invalidate strategic cultural analysis at the national level. It does, however, serve as a timely warning against the kind of undue reductionism into which social scientific theory-building is wont to fall in its pursuit of an elegant parsimony.

STRATEGIC CULTURE CAN BE DYSFUNCTIONAL

Strategic cultures can contain strongly dysfunctional elements. It is possible for scholars to be so fearful of the accusation of ethnocentrism that they embrace a cultural relativism that blinds them to evidence of functionally irrational (as contrasted with unreasonable) ideas and behaviour. Societies are prone to high risks of strategic failure when it appears that the broad precepts of a dominant strategic

[56] Murray, 'Does Military Culture Matter?', 30.

culture have knowingly been flouted. Security communities, however, can have such notably dysfunctional elements in their strategic cultures that, even when polities act congruently with their culture, they are likely to fail badly. In my early writings on strategic culture I believed that strategic culture evolved as an expression of generally successful adaptation to challenge. In other words, the dominant strategic culture of Germany should comprise ideas, attitudes, and habits that worked well for Germans. That logic seemed compelling because, given the long time-frame implied by the quality or dimension deemed cultural, it ought to be the case that maladaptive cultures would vanish in more or less bloody fashion.

On further reflection, the issue of the dysfunctional element in strategic culture appears more complex. To identify the characteristics of, say, a dominant Russian strategic culture is not necessarily to identify a culture that maximizes the prospects for Russian strategic success. It is probably more accurate to claim that Russian strategic culture has contributed massively to the three wholesale Russian/Soviet collapses of the twentieth century, and might have yielded an utterly irretrievable collapse in 1941-2. It is possible to argue that Russia's historical survival, notwithstanding periodic catastrophic or near-catastrophic shocks, demonstrates that its dominant strategic culture has been strong enough to meet the traffic of historical challenges. But one could also argue that the constituents of Russia have been sufficiently robust to survive the behavioural consequences of a somewhat self-destructive culture.

The qualities functional and dysfunctional, like concepts of offensive and defensive or stabilizing and destabilizing, can have no meaning out of historical context. The machine-mindedess that is so prominent in the dominant American 'way of war' is inherently neither functional nor dysfunctional. When it inclines Americans to seek what amounts to a technological, rather than a political, peace, and when it is permitted to dictate tactics regardless of the political context, then on balance it is dysfunctional. Having said that, however, prudent and innovative exploitation of the technological dimension to strategy and war can be a vital asset. At the very least it is important for a security community to avoid being caught on the wrong end of a true technical deficiency, because then it is obliged to find operational, tactical, human, or other compensation on a heroic scale. For example, if enemy tanks are immune to our anti-tank artillery, and if friendly airpower cannot provide reliable protection, then we leave our infantry to their courage, skill, and terrifyingly personally deliverable devices, when confronted by hostile armour.

Strategic cultures obviously pass at least minimal tests of consistency with community survival. Strategic culture, including the assumptions that underlie, but do not dictate, strategic behaviour, has to make sense to its human agents and client organizations. It is tempting to argue that security communities acquire and have their histories shaped by strategic and military cultures that have obviously worked for them. The proof is existential, if perilously circular. The community endures over decades, even centuries, so, self-evidently, the dominant strategic culture has to have been of net positive functional value—in the past, at least. After all, strategic culture in part is a celebration of community beliefs about historical strategic experience, and no community is knowingly going to enshrine advice for failure. Even when communities celebrate apparent failures, those failures are apt to be tactical (e.g. the Alamo), at most operational (e.g. Dunkirk, Stalingrad), and are rendered into heroic fable for purpose of public inspiration. Strategic attitudes and beliefs can be simultaneously functional and dysfunctional (e.g. Nazi Germany's racial doctrine), and objectively dysfunctional and irrational, yet culturally inescapable in the short term (e.g. extreme Russian centralization of political and military authority).

STRATEGIC CULTURES CAN BE VARIOUSLY CATEGORIZED

The study of modern strategy has yet to yield careful classification of strategic cultural orientations. Recent theoretical writing on strategic culture leaves much work to be done. Instead of focusing on the question of whether ideas and behaviour are separable, with only the former being the zone of (strategic) culture, the beliefs and behaviour of the human and organizational agents of culture(s) can best be understood with respect to seven non-exclusive categories of strategic cultural discrimination.

Nationality (the Security Community as a Whole)

Distinctive historical experience encultures peoples more or less differently. Information is received and coded culturally, and strategic choices are made and exercised by people and organizations equipped with dominant national (or sub-national) strategic cultural lenses—bearing in mind that those lenses have been ground by historically distinctive experience.

Geography

The physical characteristics of each distinctive geographical environment, notwithstanding technological change, yield noticeably distinctive strategic, certainly military, cultural attitudes and beliefs. In the insightful words of J. C. Wylie:

[T]he connotation of the word 'strategy' is not the same to the soldier as to the sailor or airman. The reason for this is elusive but very real. It has to do with the environment in which the conception is set. Where the sailor or airman think in terms of an entire world, the soldier at work thinks in terms of theaters, in terms of campaigns, or in terms of battles. And the three concepts are not too markedly different from each other. This state of mind in which the soldier derives his conception of the strategic scene is brought about primarily by the matter of geography.[57]

---

[57] J. C. Wylie, *Military Strategy: A General Theory of Power Control*, ed. John B. Hattendorf, repr. of 1967 edn. (Annapolis, Md., 1989), 42.

Service, Branch, Weapons, and Functions

In addition to being, for example, an American sailor, a person may be a naval aviator, submariner, or intelligence specialist, each professional orientation yielding what can fairly be called a cultural influence all its own. Special operations forces provide distinctive functions which should often work synergistically with and be complementary to the entire 'joint' effort of military power. Nonetheless, there is an unconventional mindset for the special warrior that has a cultural quality.[58]

Simplicity–Complexity

Following the suggestion of anthropologist Edward T. Hall, and political scientist and naval intelligence professional Robert B. Bathurst, one can broadly categorize strategic cultures with reference to their attitude to simplicity and complexity of context. One can classify monochronic, one-thing-at-a-time cultures, and polychronic, everything-is-interconnected cultures. Bathurst argues persuasively that the United States adheres to the former tendency, while Russia/the USSR is an exemplar of the latter.[59] Rephrased, some strategic cultures favour holistic analysis, others are wont to be more Cartesian, dissecting strategic problems for discrete, sequential treatment. There is an empirical difficulty with this discriminator in that most of the strategic-cultural speculation that is sensitive to this test of complexity has focused on American and Soviet/Russian phenomena. We need case studies of other cultures.

Generation

Individuals and age cohorts have their strategic world-view shaped by particular historical experience. In addition to being, say, an American sailor who is a career submariner inclined to monochronic decisionmaking, a person will also have his strategic culture influenced by the events that touched his life and imagination with special impact. Such events can be truly personal, or they can be historical-contextual (in the sense, for example, that all contemporary Americans shared a virtual, if not actual, presence at the Berlin and Cuban crises of the early 1960s). Different generations will have their attitudes shaped by some different strategic-historical cultural influences. When looking back from today to World War II, for instance, it is easy to forget that the policymakers and leading military commanders of the 1939–41 period were nearly all survivors of combat in the Great War of 1914–18, and that they had learnt about modern war from that experience. All people have some strategic cultural equivalent(s) to the example just given, even if it is not as traumatic. This is not to say that matters of age cohort affiliation overwhelm or negate strategic culture. It is to say, however, that a dominant strategic culture will be reintegrated by each generation in the light of its own distinctive experience. Culture evolves.

[58] Gray, *Explorations In Strategy*, 156.
[59] Bathurst, *Intelligence and the Mirror*, ch. 3; Hall, *Beyond Culture*, chs. 6–8.

Grand Strategy

For reasons that warrant classification as cultural, strategic cultures and sub-cultures can be categorized according to grand strategic preference. A pattern of reliance upon one or several of the range of instruments of grand strategy (overt military power, diplomacy, espionage and covert action, positive and negative economic sanctions, and so forth) tends to characterize particular cultures. In practice, it is not usually a question of a polity neatly picking the winner from among its array of instruments; rather is it a matter of selecting the appropriately weighted mixture of instruments. Particular national-level strategic cultures can be approximately categorized according to their pattern of preference when choosing among policy instruments.

ALL DIMENSIONS OF STRATEGY ARE CULTURAL

The distinctive experience of a security community finds social expression in a more or less distinctive pattern of enduring assumptions about strategic matters, and those patterns warrant description as cultural. Strategically encultured people will behave in ways influenced by their pattern of assumptions. Strategic culture need not dictate a particular course of action; indeed, domestic and external constraints frequently prohibit such behaviour. But the effects of strategic culture will be more or less strongly stamped upon strategic behaviour of all kinds. Maritime Britain functioned as a major continental power from 1916 until 1918, but that brief continental performance did not cancel or deny the contrary character of Britain's dominant strategic culture. Actions taken apparently out of strategic cultural character are likely eventually to confirm the rule rather than change it.

Rarely can conceptual and empirical problems have posed such synergistic difficulties as with strategic culture. If culture is everywhere, then, inescapably, culture is nowhere. Plainly, cultural enquiry in the field of strategic and security studies is in urgent need of a few working rules. Above all else, strategic culture should be approached as the context that provides understanding of what behaviour means. Unfortunately, though, context means both 'that which surrounds' and 'that which weaves together'. It is as certain as anything can be in the social sciences that it is wrong to try to separate ideas from behaviour. Culture is as culture does: we are culture, we are part of our context. However, recent scholarship is certainly correct when it points to the real or apparent confusion of cause and effect of culture and policy, and when it complains about tautologies between cultural influences and culture *in behaviour*. Particularly strategically encultured polities will not be allowed by objective or subjective circumstance always to indulge their culturally preferred policy choices.

The scholastically effective solution to these dilemmas is simply to decree that strategic culture is the realm of ideas and attitudes, which leaves the zone of strategic behaviour amenable to assay for strategic-cultural influence. Aside from the minor fact that this convenient distinction contradicts common linguistic usage, not to mention persuasive anthropological theory, it offends against the evidence of experience. Theory should not rule when method fails to fit the evidence.

Chapter 6

WINDOWS ON WAR

Modern strategy and strategic theory must accommodate strategic experiences that are apt to burst the confines of favoured plans and concepts. The strategic history important to this book includes the great wars that occurred—1914-18, 1939-45, and the Cold War of 1947-89—as well as a great war that was feared, but did not occur—a nuclear World War III.[1] In addition, there is instructive strategic behaviour in diplomatic incidents of coercive diplomacy, in raids and *coups de main*, in protracted insurgencies, and in the regular limited wars that marred every decade of the twentieth century. This chapter brings order to the chaotic and all too prolific evidence of modern strategic behaviour and misbehaviour. The discussion develops complementary 'windows on war' and strategy through which different features of modern strategic experience can be examined.

This analysis provides another exercise in expression of the overall theme of the book, the essential unity of all strategic experience. Each of the many 'windows' opened here provides a different view of the whole complex phenomenon that is war. This approach allows appreciation of the growing complexity in the character of modern strategic experience, while not losing sight of the whole nature of the subject. Just as this discussion easily accommodates complexity, so also it helps provide answers to another of the questions that weave through this text: what changes and what does not in the strategic realm?

Unsurprisingly, Chapter 6 argues that strategic history matters deeply; the consequences of the threat and actual use of force for political goals—the touchstone for 'strategic' content—represents a huge engine for change in modern history. Modern strategic history can be regarded from many different perspectives. Thirteen such 'windows on war' are opened here, including political commitment, scale of combat, style of war, environments for conflict, historical period, and duration. Each window sheds additional light. The chapter closes with reflection on Clausewitz's metaphor that war resembles a chameleon: it seems able to assume an almost infinite variety of forms as conditions alter.

---

[1] 'Strategic history' is not a concept or category of scholarship in widespread use. Because I have come to find it indispensable, and because its meaning is self evident—the history of things strategic—I employ it here without apology or further comment. See Clark G. Reynolds, *Command of the Sea: The History and Strategy of Maritime Empires*, 2nd edn. (2 vols., Malabar, Fla., 1983), i. 9-12.

STRATEGIC HISTORY

The evidence of modern strategy consists of an uneasy marriage between strategic history and strategic fiction, which is to say the strategic prediction of imagined futures. One cannot exclude consideration of potentially enlightening counterfactual possible 'events' (e.g. success for the German Invasion plan in August–September 1914, or a German denunciation of Japan's 'day of infamy' at Pearl Harbor).[2] The social scientist as strategist is more comfortable than is the historian with invented strategic 'action chains'.[3] The strategic theorist confronts the challenge of uncertainty, as do the human agents in dramatic reconstructions by historians. It can be difficult for historians to escape comprehensively the perils of hindsight. Policy-oriented strategists today have no such problems. They do not know, for example, what new information-led weaponry will mean for future crises and wars. This condition of inescapable ignorance breeds easy empathy for the past makers and executors of strategy who, in their time, necessarily shared our condition of ignorance about the future. Unfortunately, social scientists have a limited education which can more than offset the likelihood that they will be both more understanding of past dilemmas of strategic choice and more willing to consider historically counterfactual strategic possibilities than will historians. As Bernard Brodie pointed out bluntly, the most characteristic weakness of the social scientist as strategic theorist is a failure to grasp strategic history.[4] Brian Holden Reid is self-serving as a professional historian, but still correct, when he writes: 'History might not offer clear-cut "lessons" to decision makers, but experience shows how unwise it is to base opinions on operations and strategy if you misunderstand their historical setting.'[5]

Strategic knowledge cannot be entirely historical knowledge, because 'history' is replete with rumours of wars that never occurred. The conceptual jewel in the crown of nuclear-age strategy, stable deterrence, has a historical record of apparent behavioural success that is entirely beyond demonstration, though not beyond plausible inference. Nonetheless, the strategic historical record of both events and persuasively possible non-events (e.g. a nuclear war between East and West to conclude the Cold War) has to be our evidential base. There is at least a quasi-historicity to, say, German General Staff views in 1911–12 of the prospects for success in a general war in 1916–17 and after,[6] the British official view in 1938–9 of

---

[2] On counterfactuals, see Niall Ferguson (ed.), *Virtual History: Alternatives and Counterfactuals* (London, 1997); Kenneth Macksey, *Invasion: The German Invasion of England, July 1940* (London, 1981).

[3] Edward T. Hall, *Beyond Culture* (Garden City, NY, 1976), ch. 10.

[4] Bernard Brodie, *War and Politics* (New York, 1973), 474–5.

[5] Brian Holden Reid, 'Introduction' to 'Military Power: Land Warfare in Theory and Practice', *Journal of Strategic Studies*, 19, special issue (1996), 9.

[6] Arden Bucholz, *Moltke, Schlieffen, and Prussian War Planning* (New York, 1991), ch. 5; Holger Herwig, *The First World War: Germany and Austria-Hungary, 1914–1918* (London, 1997), 18–23.

the probable course and outcome of immediate war with Nazi Germany,[7] and US and Soviet official opinions on general nuclear war.[8] None of those wars actually happened, but contemporary judgements on each of those fictitious 'events' tell us a great deal about the historical contexts whence they derived. Wars, or lesser events of force, that are imagined and can play some significant role in the shaping of behaviour, constitute a kind of 'virtual' strategic history.

This book risks seeking to explain modern strategy without first chronicling the story of that strategy. A historian would probably approach this task by means of a solid body of fairly narrative strategic history suitably adorned with interpretive commentary. As a social scientist I am more comfortable with a theoretical and analytical discussion, supported by illustrative examples. Rather than offer an abbreviated account of modern strategic history, I prefer to direct readers to the scholarly chronicles that are readily accessible. For example, interpretations of modern strategy in the complex case of World War II can rest with some confidence upon the all but official German histories being produced by the Research Institute for Military History at Freiburg-im-Breisgau, upon the writings of Gerhard Weinberg, and—for the war in Eastern Europe—upon the scholarship of David Glantz and the somewhat older, but still generally reliable, work of John Erickson.[9]

Even though there is a vital unity to all strategic experience which can abolish the significance of time, place, and technology, there is still a historical trajectory of causes and effects that helps explain strategic experience. Strategists of different eras may confront categorically similar challenges of, for example, imperial policing or threat assessment, but each performs in historical real time. Strategic history is acted out by particularly strategically encultured people and institutions. Strategy *per se* may be generically beyond culture, time, place, and technology, but particular strategists and their strategies are not.

Wars of different kinds both punctuate modern strategic history and, as anticipated events, shape strategic behaviour in time of peace. To repeat the Clausewitzian aphorism: 'The decision by arms is for all major and minor operations in war

---

[7] N. H. Gibbs, *History of the Second World War, Grand Strategy, i: Rearmament Policy* (London, 1976), chs. 26 and 27; Wesley K. Wark, *The Ultimate Enemy: British Intelligence and Nazi Germany, 1933–1939* (Ithaca, NY, 1985), ch. 8. Williamson Murray and Allan R. Millett (eds.), *Calculations: Net Assessment and the Coming of World War II* (New York, 1992), as so often with this dynamic pair of editors, hits the spot precisely.

[8] Richard K. Betts, *Nuclear Blackmail and Nuclear Balance* (Washington, DC, 1987); Director of Central Intelligence, *Soviet Capabilities for Strategic Nuclear Conflict, 1982–92*, National Intelligence Estimate, i: *Key Judgments and Summary*, NIE 11-3/8-82 (Top Secret), decl. 19/2/93 (Washington, DC, 15 Feb. 1983); John G. Hines, Ellis M. Mishulovich, and John F. Shull, *Soviet Intentions, 1965–1985* (2 vols., McLean, Va., 22 Sept. 1995).

[9] Gerhard Weinberg, *A World at Arms: A Global History of World War II* (Cambridge, 1994); id., *Germany, Hitler, and World War II* (Cambridge, 1995); David Glantz and Jonathan House, *When Titans Clashed: How the Red Army Stopped Hitler* (Lawrence, Kan., 1995); John Erickson, *The Road to Stalingrad: Stalin's War with Germany* (London, 1975); id., *The Road to Berlin: Continuing the History of Stalin's War with Germany* (Boulder, Colo., 1983).

what cash payment is in commerce.'[10] War is not what strategy is about, any more than is battle. Strategy is about achieving the policy goals that translate as peace with security, whatever those two contestable concepts may mean to particular communities (and they might mean a global dominion for the home side). Notwithstanding the abominably bloody strategic history of the twentieth century, the making and the execution of strategy by every security community over the past hundred years has overwhelmingly been a peacetime exercise. Polities, and would-be polities, make and execute strategy through continuous organized processes in peace and war. Indeed, given that war fortunately is rarely valued for its own sake as a bracing, glorious, or healthful, social experience, its prevention on terms of tolerable security is a widespread object of policy sought necessarily via strategy. When seeking to identify the evidence for modern strategy, it is essential to bear in mind the important, if over-quoted and frequently misunderstood, idealized judgement of Sun Tzu: 'Subjugating the enemy's army without fighting is the true pinnacle of excellence.'[11]

The strategic history of the twentieth century is all but indistinguishable from general history. Recall the argument quoted from Reid about the significance of the historical setting. Strategic attitudes, habits of mind, and preferences among behavioural patterns in coping with challenges can have sources deep in a community's historical experience.[12] Moreover, strategic culture is nourished by the totality of a security community's ethical, economic, social, political, and broadly geographically anchored experience. Although modern strategic history must focus upon preparation of the means, the threat to use, and the actual resort to force, strategic history cannot possibly have scholarly integrity in and of itself. Just as one can follow Clausewitz's lead and distinguish 'war proper' from the activities 'that are merely preparations for war',[13] so it is practicable and necessary to distinguish strategic history from its broader meaning. War is a social institution, and the aspects of preparation for its conduct, albeit often in hope of its avoidance, that we term 'strategy', must have a social context. Nonetheless, when polities wage 'total war' and 'people's war', can there be a boundary to strategic history?

Strategic history is woven into general history, with no strict fixed boundaries separating the strategic from the non-strategic. For example, the historically systemic anti-Semitism that Daniel Jonah Goldhagen alleges in his controversial book *Hitler's Willing Executioners*[14] had the most profound implications for the

[10] Carl von Clausewitz, *On War*, trans. Michael Howard and Peter Paret (Princeton, NJ, 1976), 97.

[11] Sun Tzu, *The Art of War*, trans. Ralph D. Sawyer (Boulder, Colo., 1994), 177.

[12] Not all theorists agree upon the proposition that there needs to be historical depth to strategic culture. See e.g. Jack L. Snyder, *The Soviet Strategic Culture: Implications for Limited Nuclear Operations*, R-2154-AF (Santa Monica, Calif., Sept. 1977).

[13] Clausewitz, *On War*, 131.

[14] Daniel Jonah Goldhagen, *Hitler's Willing Executioners: Ordinary Germans and the Holocaust* (London, 1996), risks ruining a good case by overstatement.

strategic history of the mid-twentieth century. In an important sense Hitler's Germany, like militant Islam in the seventh century, was an imperial explosion fuelled by ideology. To take another example, to understand why the US armed forces fought as they did in Vietnam in the 1960s and early 1970s, and why the absence of easily demonstrable success in the field helped trigger political crisis at home, one has to delve deeply into the roots of an American strategic culture that has a notably moral, or moralistic, dimension. Many Americans have believed that their polity is a 'city on a hill', uniquely blessed by the Almighty. Failure, or pro-tracted absence of success, in battle could be interpreted as the result of a fall from grace occasioned not so much by strategic incompetence as by the unworthiness of the particular mission. War and strategy as social activities can produce a moral, and hence a political, crisis out of military failure.

APPROACHES TO STRATEGIC EXPERIENCE

Modern strategy lends itself to analytical treatment according to the inspiration variably provided by at least thirteen different, but complementary, organizing principles. Any conflict can be studied in the light of this typology. These categories identify real and important differences, even though these are differences within the essential unity of war and strategy. The nature, function, and way of working of strategy and strategic effect are permanent and ubiquitous. Nonetheless, the content of strategy must differ markedly within these categories. For example, Jomini's 'one great principle underlying all the operations of war. . . . To throw by strategic movements the mass of an army successively upon the decisive points of a theater of war, and also upon the communications of the enemy as much as pos-sible without compromising one's own'[15] is an absurd irrelevance in the strategic context of 'small wars' against irregulars who decline to stand and fight *en masse*, and who have no obvious lines of communication. Similarly, strategy is one subject with one structure, but when Clausewitz advises, as a rule correctly, that 'defense is the stronger form of waging war',[16] one needs to editorialize and add 'on land'.

Any war, conflict, or other episode involving strategic behaviour can be analysed according to the following discriminators:

COMMITMENT, SCOPE, AIM

War can be general or 'total' (a concept that has been used only rarely since the late 1940s[17]), limited, or—a concept now mercifully defunct—sub-limited. In

---

[15] Antoine Henri de Jomini, *The Art of War*, repr. of 1862 edn. (London, 1992), 70.

[16] Clausewitz, *On War*, 359.

[17] Hans Speier, 'Ludendorff: The German Concept of Total War', in Edward Mead Earle (ed.), *Makers of Modern Strategy: From Machiavelli to Hitler* (Princeton, NJ, 1941), 306–21; Ian F. W. Beckett, 'Total War', in Colin McInnes and G. D. Sheffield (eds.), *Warfare in the Twentieth Century: Theory and Practice* (London, 1988), 1–23; Herwig, *First World War*, 254–66.

Anglo-American strategic discourse since the mid-1950s, general war has meant general nuclear war up to and including 'a full SIOP' response.[18] After a brief flurry of Western scholarly enthusiasm for limited nuclear war, limited war largely denoted non-nuclear, typically conventional or regular, war.[19] From the early 1960s until the present day, official US and NATO strategy has been to employ nuclear weapons, when deemed necessary for escalation control and intra-war deterrence, in more or less limited ways.[20] Wars tend to become 'total' as the price of victory rises and the quest for decision remains unsatisfied. In World War I, for example, Britain did not embark purposefully upon a total war in 1914, and it did not insist upon a truly total victory and peace in 1918–19 (witness the contrast with 1945, which is an exemplar of total defeat, albeit still low on the strategic Richter scale of catastrophe compared with the fate of Carthage after the Third Punic War), even though the British war effort was by 1916–18 as practicably total as one could imagine.[21]

SCALE

As an enriching variant upon the commitment discriminator, one can classify conflicts according to their scale. Conflicts graduate down from some contemporary approximation to Clausewitz's concept of 'absolute war',[22] which most usually these days is termed 'world war', to major regional conflict (or major theatre war), to minor regional conflict, to civil war, and finally to problems of internal security (which can be variously labelled—'the troubles', for one example). In 1939, Adolf Hitler launched what he intended initially to be only a minor, bilateral German–Polish war, and was led by events that he could not control into the total, and fatal, peril of a world war.[23] Hitler's ambitions for his intended Thousand-Year Reich were certainly at least pan-Eurasian in scope, but assuredly he did not 'plan' to

[18] SIOP, Single Integrated Operational Plan, or the US nuclear war plan writ large. Desmond Ball, 'The Development of the SIOP, 1960–1983', in id. and Jeffrey Richelson (eds.), *Strategic Nuclear Targeting* (Ithaca, NY, 1986), 57–83.

[19] William W. Kaufmann, 'Limited Warfare', in Kaufmann (ed.), *Military Policy and National Security* (Princeton, NJ, 1956), 102–36; Robert E. Osgood, *Limited War: The Challenge to American Strategy* (Chicago, 1957); Bernard Brodie, *Strategy in the Missile Age* (Princeton, NJ, 1959), ch. 9; Morton H. Halperin, *Limited War in the Nuclear Age* (New York, 1963).

[20] J. Michael Legge, *Theater Nuclear Weapons and the NATO Strategy of Flexible Response*, R-2964-FF (Santa Monica, Calif., Apr. 1983); David N. Schwartz, *NATO's Nuclear Dilemmas* (Washington, DC, 1983); Jane Stromseth, *The Origins of Flexible Response: NATO's Debate over Strategy in the 1960s* (London, 1988); Helga Haftendorn, *NATO and the Nuclear Revolution: A Crisis of Credibility, 1966–1967* (Oxford, 1996). The best guide to nuclear issues in the Cold War remains Lawrence Freedman, *The Evolution of Nuclear Strategy*, 2nd edn. (New York, 1989).

[21] John Gooch, 'Soldiers, Strategy and War Aims in Britain, 1914–18', in Barry Hunt and Adrian Preston (eds.), *War Aims and Strategic Policy in the Great War, 1914–1918* (London, 1977), 21–40; Erik Goldstein, *Winning the Peace: British Diplomatic Strategy, Peace Planning, and the Paris Peace Conference, 1916–1920* (Oxford, 1991); David French, *The Strategy of the Lloyd George Coalition, 1916–1918* (Oxford, 1995).

[22] Clausewitz, *On War*, 579–81.

[23] Weinberg, *World at Arms*, ch. 2; id., *Germany, Hitler, and World War II*, ch. 11.

wage war simultaneously against most of the world. One should not be misled by Clausewitz's wise but simple-sounding advice on the necessity for understanding the kind of war upon which one embarks.[24] Many conflicts, probably most, do not have some 'essential' character or 'natural' place on the scale of violence; rather, their scales and characters are subject to a process of resolution by the 'diplomacy of violence'.[25] The civil wars and inter-'state' wars in the former Yugoslavia in the 1990s had the potential to escalate to a major regional conflict.

INTENSITY

Strategy purportedly can be made and exercised for contexts of low-, medium-, and high-intensity warfare or conflict. The challenges for government include the problem of identifying what is common and what is not across the boundaries among these three amorphous categories. Governments also have the enduring problem of deciding whether, with ever-scarce resources to devote to security functions, they can choose to build armed forces excellent only in, say, one of these three categories. Could Britain afford politically and strategically to maintain an army suitable in structure and equipment only for colonial occupation and campaigning in low-intensity conflict; or did Britain require, in addition, a multi-role field army able to make a difference in a continental war in Europe? In differing forms, that particular question has faced the British from the early 1900s until today.[26] Polities that elect to develop competent armed forces for the prospectively decisive conduct of large-scale regional warfare, such as Iraq in the 1980s, are apt to lack the 'top cover' for counter-deterrence that may be needed to discourage intervention by a superpower equipped to fight with high intensity.[27] Similarly, if a regional power chooses to specialize in military and police prowess *vis-à-vis* low-intensity threats (terrorism, rural or urban insurgency, or violent criminal activities), it could be severely embarrassed were it to face threats of medium intensity at short notice. It is usually the case that, while large-scale conventional forces can have some prospect of success in dealing with low-intensity conflict, lightly armed forces optimized to wage such conflict would be hopelessly outgunned if a large conventional military problem arises suddenly. I am uncomfortable with combat intensity as a rule of discrimination. Whereas combat will vary in scale, it is always going to be maximally intense, which is to say lethal, on the battlefield for those who have to 'do' strategy tactically.

[24] Clausewitz, *On War*, 88.

[25] With thanks to Thomas C. Schelling, *Arms and Influence* (New Haven, Conn., 1966), ch. 1.

[26] Correlli Barnett, *Britain and Her Army, 1509–1970: A Military, Political and Social Survey* (London, 1970), pts. 4 and 5; John Gooch, *The Plans of War: the General Staff and British Military Strategy, c.1900–1916* (London, 1974); Brian Bond, *British Military Policy between the Two World Wars* (Oxford, 1980); Colin McInnes, *Hot War, Cold War: The British Army's Way in Warfare, 1945–95* (London, 1996).

[27] Iraq certainly has tried to acquire a nuclear, biological, and chemical (NBC) 'counter-deterrent'. See Office of Technology Assessment, US Congress, *Technologies Underlying Weapons of Mass Destruction*, OTA-BP-ISC-115 (Washington, DC, Dec. 1993), 150–1, 168–9.

STYLE I: REGULAR OR IRREGULAR

An important distinction among conflicts is between the conventional and the unconventional, or, in an alternative formula, between the regular and the irregular. Wars can be waged between conventional regular armies, between regulars and irregulars, and between irregular opponents. This fourth discriminator does not suggest that conventional/unconventional means conventional as contrasted with nuclear, and neither does it carry the meanings of *cheng* (regular, expected) and *ch'i* (irregular, unexpected) found in classical Chinese military thought.[28] The *cheng/ch'i* distinction, as with Liddell Hart's direct/indirect approaches,[29] applies to all kinds of forces in all kinds of conflicts. Scholars of the Vietnam War are still debating to what degree that war was a conventional as opposed to an unconventional struggle. Debate on this issue is related to how armed forces are directed to define their mission, train and equip themselves, and conduct operations in the field. For example, the writings of Harry G. Summers and Andrew Krepinevich represent opposite positions on whether the dominant style in the conduct of war needed to achieve victory in Vietnam should have been conventional or unconventional.[30] The truth may lie not so much in the middle on this particular historical controversy, as in a framework that embraces both poles. The American military problem in Vietnam was that several styles of war were required simultaneously to subdue the North Vietnamese and their Vietcong allies.

STYLE II: ATTRITION, MANOEUVRE, CONTROL

A discriminator is also needed to accommodate a spectrum of combat style that interrelates attritional, manoeuvre, and control modes. In historical practice, the strategic effect generated by a belligerent from his military effectiveness flows from a synergistic combination of attrition and manoeuvre. As with defence and offence, and tactically with fire and movement, so the relationship between attrition and manoeuvre is one of interdependence. The mobile German campaign of August–September 1914, for example, constituted a grand manoeuvre that even in failure placed the French and British in an operational condition where they had no politically or logistically practicable alternative to waging a war of attrition under disadvantageous terms of tactical engagement. The proposition behind this discriminator is that military styles may emphasize: the wearing out of the enemy; the outmanoeuvring of the enemy in quest of a Napoleonic or Moltkeian decision; or, following the examples set by the Mongols and,[31] rather more

---

[28] Sun Tzu, *Art of War*, 147–50.

[29] B. H. Liddell Hart, *Strategy: The Indirect Approach* (London, 1967).

[30] Harry G. Summers, Jr., *On Strategy: A Critical Analysis of the Vietnam War* (Novato, Calif., 1982); Andrew F. Krepinevich, Jr., *The Army and Vietnam* (Baltimore, 1986).

[31] David Morgan, *The Mongols* (Oxford, 1986); Archer Jones, *The Art of War in the Western World* (Urbana, Ill., 1987), 142–3; John Keegan, *A History of Warfare* (London, 1993), 200–7.

recently, by the coalition that won the Gulf War of 1991, the functionally fatal disruption of the enemy's ability to control his war effort. The three styles of strategic behaviour intend to exhaust (attrition), to annihilate (manoeuvre), or to paralyse (control).[32]

Attrition tends to receive low marks from scholars because it appears unimaginative, it is certain to be expensive (relative to *successful* decisive manoeuvre), and it makes for longer wars. More often than not, though, an attritional emphasis in combat style is required if decisive manoeuvre is to be possible.[33] In World War I, after a siege condition was established from the Belgian coast to Switzerland, the only form of decisive manoeuvre feasible would be operational exploitation of a breakthrough out of a tactical break-in to the continuously fortified zone. By early 1917 both sides had discovered, actually calculated, a reliable solution to the tactical problem of the break-in,[34] but neither had a practicable answer to the challenge of the breakthrough and subsequent exploitation (the pursuit). In combat between peer belligerents, it is rare indeed that operational manoeuvre according to cunning plans is well enough executed to deliver such decisive success that hard fighting is not required. The Manstein Plan executed in May 1940 against France and Britain was one such exception.[35]

No matter how much movement there has to be by forces of all kinds in all geographical environments, mere mobility rarely wins campaigns and wars. The Pacific War of 1941–5 is a story of great mobility, indeed of a truly vast scale of movement of forces in a huge maritime theatre. Nonetheless, manoeuvre and attrition worked synergistically to yield the necessary strategic effect for victory and defeat. The United States manoeuvred extensively to oblige the Empire of Japan to fight under disadvantageous conditions. The land–sea–air campaign in the Southern Solomon Islands in 1942, for example, was an attritional struggle that helped to reduce Japanese military assets so that further US manoeuvre was practicable.[36]

Germany and its continental allies, holding a central position in the European peninsula, could not be manoeuvred into defeat in either of the world wars. Operational disaster could, and did, threaten: for example, on the Marne in the first

---

[32] John Arquilla, 'The Strategic Implications of Information Dominance', *Strategic Review*, 22 (1994), 26; David S. Fadok, 'John Boyd and John Warden: Airpower's Quest for Strategic Paralysis', in Phillip S. Meilinger (ed.), *The Paths of Heaven: The Evolution of Airpower Theory* (Maxwell AFB, Ala., 1997), 357–98.

[33] David French, 'The Meaning of Attrition, 1914–1916', *English Historical Review*, 103 (1988), 385–405.

[34] 'Trial and error showed that there should be less than ten yards of friendly frontage for every gun, and 400 pounds of shell—or more—for every yard of enemy trench within the area to be attacked': Paddy Griffith, *Battle Tactics of the Western Front: The British Army's Art of Attack, 1916–18* (New Haven, Conn., 1994), 149.

[35] Robert Allan Doughty, *The Breaking Point: Sedan and the Fall of France* (Hamden, Conn., 1990); Telford Taylor, *The March of Conquest: The German Victories in Western Europe, 1940* (Baltimore, 1991).

[36] Richard B. Frank, *Guadalcanal: The Definitive Account of the Landmark Battle* (New York, 1992), esp. ch. 24. For the context: John Costello, *The Pacific War* (New York, 1982); Ronald H. Spector, *Eagle Against the Sun: The American War with Japan* (New York, 1985); Dan van der Vat, *The Pacific Campaign: World War II, The U.S.–Japanese Naval War, 1941–1945* (New York, 1991).

week of September 1914, in front of Moscow early in December 1941, on the Volga and the Don in November 1942, and in Normandy in mid-August 1944. Battles might be won or lost by a mobile style of warfare in execution of decisive manoeuvre, but neither campaigns (with the exception of May 1940) nor certainly wars could be won that way. Germany (and Japan) could be beaten only by means of what Sir Douglas Haig, harking back to his staff college education on the structure of battle, referred to as the 'wearing-out' fight.[37]

Decisive manoeuvre is possible, as Germany showed in 1940, as General Douglas MacArthur illustrated at Inchon in September 1950 in the Korean War, and as General Schwartzkopf demonstrated in Desert Storm in 1991. Conditions for terms of engagement, however, have to be exceptionally permissive to avoid painful attritional combat. In 1940 the Anglo-French armies were misled as to the axis of the German Schwerpunkt and committed on their left wing virtually the same kind of operationally erroneous advance that the French army had attempted on its centre-right in August 1914 with its Plan XVII.[38] But whereas in 1914 the French disasters in the Battles of the Frontiers (14–25 August) did not result in definitive defeat because the German right wing lacked the necessary tempo in (walking) pace of operational manoeuvre, in May 1940 General Paul von Kleist's Panzer group (and General Hermann Hoth's Panzer corps) achieved a tempo of advance on an unexpected axis which precluded Anglo-French recovery. On 15 September 1950 at Inchon, General MacArthur succeeded brilliantly with an operational manoeuvre from a totally commanded sea that threatened with annihilation the North Korean forces who were far south in South Korea. Similarly, on 23 February 1991 General Norman Schwartzkopf executed a classic operational-level envelopment of Iraqi forces deployed in Kuwait and in southern Iraq that should have achieved the annihilation of the foe, had coalition ground forces acted with greater expedition and had more time been allowed.[39]

Although each of these three historical cases demonstrates the potential for campaign success by decisive operational manoeuvre, each has an important complementary attritional element. In 1940, while General Heinz Guderian's Panzers approached the Meuse at Sedan with the real thrust, Allied attention was

[37] J. H. Boraston (ed.), *Sir Douglas Haig's Despatches (December 1915–April 1919)*, repr. of 1919 edn. (London, 1979), esp. 320. See also Brian Bond, *The Victorian Army and the Staff College, 1854–1914* (London, 1972); Tim Travers, *The Killing Ground: The British Army, the Western Front and the Emergence of Modern Warfare* (London, 1987), ch. 4. Even in long retrospect, the concept of the 'wearing-out' fight looks sensible. The trouble is that Haig was self-serving in his reliance on this idea as retrospective authority for his 'art of war'. Poorly conducted, as by the British in 1917, 'the wearing-out' fight can wear you out more than it does the enemy.

[38] S. R. Williamson, 'Joffre Reshapes French Strategy, 1911–1913', in Paul M. Kennedy (ed.), *The War Plans of the Great Powers, 1880–1914* (London, 1979), 133–54.

[39] Jeffrey McCausland, *The Gulf Conflict: A Military Analysis*, Adelphi Paper 282 (London, Nov. 1993); Michael R. Gordon and Bernard E. Trainor, *The Generals' War: The Inside Story of the Conflict in the Gulf* (Boston, 1995), pt. 2; John Mueller, 'The Perfect Enemy: Assessing the Gulf War', *Security Studies*, 5 (1995), 77–117.

focused upon the ponderous advance across Belgium by General Fedor von Bock's Army Group B. MacArthur's amphibious left hook to Inchon was feasible because North Korean eyes were fixed upon the hard attritional combat around the southern port of Pusan. In the case of Desert Storm, the operational manoeuvre to achieve the wide envelopment of Iraqi forces required *inter alia* nearly five weeks of preparatory attritional bombardment from the air as well as the focusing of Iraqi attention upon a threat of direct land and amphibious assault upon occupied Kuwait. In other words, if manoeuvre and attrition are hammer and anvil, even in these three classic examples of successful manoeuvre the anvil was still significant.

GRAND STRATEGIC INSTRUMENT

Because strategy works in peacetime and wartime, and because it can refer to direction of virtually all the resources of a security community (e.g. the realm of grand strategy, national strategy, or *stratégie générale*),[40] it is necessary to accommodate a discriminator at the level of choice among grand strategic instruments. Instead of the threat or use of force, the grand strategist may be tempted to wage political, psychological, subversive, diplomatic, economic, or cultural war. Of course, the military instrument is wielded to psychological and political effect, and subversive war naturally must have psychological and political purposes. Strategic effect is generic. If, as Clausewitz insists rightly, it has to be the broad purpose in war 'to impose our will on the enemy',[41] it does not follow strictly that force has to be either the immediate instrument of strategy or, as the enemy's latent capability, the direct object of that strategy. Diplomacy, propaganda, cultural subversion and demoralization, trade embargoes, espionage and sabotage can all have strategic effect and may merit some roles in a theory of victory over a particular foe. Within the conduct of great wars, there is likely to be a strategic theme of action taken for economic impact upon the strength and will of the foe. For example, the *Entente* powers waged economic warfare, far beyond the mere imposition of maritime blockade, upon the Central powers in World War I.[42] Britain and France campaigned economically against each other energetically, if selectively, during the Napoleonic wars.[43] One can also recall the intense debate in late 1990 over the measure of reliance that should be placed upon economic sanctions to make Saddam Hussein disgorge Kuwait.[44]

[40] Raoul Castex, *Strategic Theories*, trans., abridged, and ed. Eugenia C. Kiesling (Annapolis, Md., 1994), 44–5, n. 8.

[41] Clausewitz, *On War*, 75.

[42] A. C. Bell, *A History of the Blockade of Germany and of the Countries Associated with Her in the Great War, Austria-Hungary, Bulgaria, and Turkey, 1914–1918* (London, 1937).

[43] Eli F. Heckscher, *The Continental System: An Economic Interpretation*, repr. of 1922 edn. (Gloucester, Mass., 1964); Paul M. Kennedy, *The Rise and Fall of British Naval Mastery* (New York, 1976), ch. 5.

[44] Lawrence Freedman and Efraim Karsh, *The Gulf Conflict, 1990–1991: Diplomacy and War in the New World Order* (Princeton, NJ, 1993), pts. 3–4.

Just as there are wars wherein, for example, the maritime or the air element is dominant, so there are conflicts wherein economic, political, or subversive instruments of grand strategy are accorded the status of leading edge. The omnipresent possibility of the use of force, even when the other instruments of strategy are leading the charge, shapes the impact of specific non-military initiatives. Plainly, trade 'wars', or intense competitions for political influence that find expression in political tools, could become explicitly violent. As a general rule in any conflict, whether actively military or wherein military power has yet to be exercised, every instrument of grand strategy will have some role to play in the strategy team for policy.

ENVIRONMENT

Modern strategy and war has increasingly become a 'joint' endeavour, because operations in each geographical environment require the active cooperation of forces that function in other environments.[45] There is a growing complexity to modern war, notwithstanding the partially offsetting fact of a growing cooperation among environmentally specialized military elements. At the beginning of the century war could be conducted on land, at sea, or amphibiously. By 1914, as J. F. C. Fuller explains, the marriage of the invention of the internal combustion engine to a flying machine, and the invention and rapid development of wireless telegraphy

introduced warlike possibilities which went far beyond anything as yet accomplished by either gunpowder or steam power. The former [internal combustion engine] not only led to a revolution in road transport, and consequently in land warfare, but as it solved the problem of flight it raised war into the third dimension. The latter [wireless telegraphy] virtually raised it into the fourth dimension; for to all intents and purposes the wireless transmission of energy annihilated time as well as space. Thus two new battlefields were created—the sky and the ether.[46]

By 1914, virtually every geographical dimension to war and strategy was militarily in play. In World War I, war was conducted on land, on the surface and from beneath the sea, in the air, and, with early radio, on at least a narrow band along the electromagnetic spectrum. All that remained to be added was use of the space environment, a development which can be dated conveniently as beginning in

---

[45] 'Joint' operations refer to operations conducted by the different, geographically specialized, armed services. See UK Ministry of Defence, *British Defence Doctrine*, Joint Warfare Publication (JWP) 0–01 (London, 1996). Britain has surrendered on terminology to the United States, in that 'joint' means what the British used to refer to as 'combined'. Today, 'combined' means 'multinational'. Michael D. Hobkirk, *Land, Sea or Air? Military Priorities, Historical Choices* (London, 1992), is a useful historical ramble with an appropriate analytical focus.

[46] J. F. C. Fuller, *A Military History of the Western World, iii: From the American Civil War to the End of World War II* (New York, 1957), 185.

1942 with the first test of Germany's A-4 (V-2) rocket,[47] and full exploitation of the electromagnetic spectrum (from extremely low frequency (ELF) radio transmissions at a frequency of approximately 1 kHz, all the way to inducing gamma radiation at 10^{20}Hz–10^9K). Every war, every collective case of strategic behaviour which generates strategic effect upon the course of events, can be analysed according to its more or less complex geographical dimensionality.

Whereas some of the principles of discrimination deployed in this chapter are no more than mental constructs for the filing and coding of data (e.g. total, as contrasted with limited, war), the geographical discriminator is preeminently, though not exclusively, material and geophysical.[48] War is waged on land, at sea, in the air, with space systems, if not yet in space, and in what used to be called, inaccurately, 'the ether'. One can distinguish among (to take a key example) war at sea, sea warfare, and sea war. War at sea and sea warfare—or, if preferred, substitute land, air, space, and perhaps even the ether—imply a maritime dimension to a wider conflict. 'Sea war', however, carries the unhelpful connotation of war waged wholly at sea (similar connotations would accompany 'land war', 'air war', or 'space war'—and perhaps, one day, 'cyberwar').

Polities do not wage land, sea, or air war: instead, they wage war. The wars that communities waged in the twentieth century had as their cutting edge the quantities of *net* strategic effect, or effect upon the will or ability of the enemy to fight on. Every war, every whole passage of strategic behaviour, must have a distinctive blend of threat and action as among these environments. It is quite often also practicable and advisable to distinguish between rural and urban environments, among different kinds of terrain (e.g. mountain, desert, forest), and the different climatic conditions to which strategic behaviour can be subject.[49]

Because humans are land animals whose security communities are territorially defined, strategy ultimately has a landward focus, even if land warfare—more narrowly still, ground warfare[50]—constitutes but a modest share of the action. A particular form of military power may have, or appear to have, the status of 'key force',[51] as, for example, with naval forces in the Falklands War of 1982, or air forces in the Gulf War of 1991. But even when land, sea, or air forces play the leading role and seem to generate the quantity and quality of strategic effect that decides who wins, war still remains a team game. The other, adjunct forms of

---

[47] Michael J. Neufeld, *The Rocket and the Reich: Peenemünde and the Coming of the Ballistic Missile Era* (Cambridge, Mass., 1995).

[48] In addition to physical geography there is the geography of the imagination. To Anglo-American minds at least, 'the Orient' or 'the Balkans' are almost as much concepts as they are geographical designations. See Colin S. Gray, 'Inescapable Geography', *Journal of Strategic Studies*, 22, special issue on 'Geopolitics, Geography, and Strategy' (1999).

[49] John M. Collins, *Military Geography for Professionals and the Public* (Washington, DC, 1998); Harold A. Winters, *Battling the Elements: Weather and Terrain in the Conduct of War* (Baltimore, 1998).

[50] Martin Edmonds, 'Land Warfare', in Roger Carey and Trevor C. Salmon (eds.), *International Security in the Modern World* (London, 1996), 185–6.

[51] John A. Warden III, *The Air Campaign: Planning for Combat* (Washington, DC, 1989), 123–7.

military power, not to mention action in areas of grand strategy apart from the military (e.g. the diplomatic and subversive), can all play essential enabling roles.

Every war, and every belligerent in every war, manifests a distinctive pattern of strategic behaviour among an expanding list of geographical environments. It is true that modern strategy and war registers trends towards ever greater complexity, ever greater 'jointness' to offset and exploit that complexity, and in the maturing potency of new modes of combat (i.e. in the air, in space, along the EMS). It is no less true, however, that land, even ground, warfare has yet to be demoted to an adjunct, auxiliary, or administrative, role vis-à-vis superficially more modern modes and foci of fighting.

BATTLESPACE, POLITICAL GEOGRAPHY, AND GEOPOLITICS

In addition to the discriminator of physical geography, one can classify wars and strategies according to their geopolitical focus. Land warfare can differ mightily in its specific character and terms of engagement according to its precise political geographical locus. The German Army was wonderfully competent in the conduct of fast-moving operations in the restricted but still hugely accessible terrain of Western, Central, and much of East-Central Europe. That same army, however, suffered unexpected physical and psychological attrition when it was committed to the conduct of continental warfare on the widest scale against the USSR.[52] The options for registering superior strategic effect vary in weight and availability among different geopolitical contexts. In World Wars I and II, for example, it was necessary, though not sufficient, that Germany should be defeated in land warfare. In the Pacific War of 1941–5, the strategic effect of cumulative failure at sea—more accurately, in the air over the sea—determined the certainty of Japanese defeat.

The particular geographical conditions in each region, and the geopolitical characteristics of the leading security communities in each region, provide a workable basis for categorizing war and strategy according to its political geography. It makes some sense, and can be useful, to think of conflicts in Europe, Asia, the Middle East, Africa, and—of course—in political geographical subregions of those grander identities.

Each of the three greatest conflicts of the twentieth century were waged preponderantly in, and concerned the strategic fate of, peninsular Europe. The 'world war' of 1914–18 was conducted overwhelmingly in continental Europe, by European states, for European motives. For geopolitical and logistical reasons, combat on land beyond Europe was relatively minor in scale. The Great War in colonial

---

[52] The sheer geographical extent of Russia, married to the brutal extremes of its climate, had a dire effect upon the German army. James Lucas, *War on the Eastern Front, 1941–1945: The German Soldier in Russia* (London, 1979), esp. 33; Omer Bartov, *Hitler's Army: Soldiers, Nazis, and War in the Third Reich* (New York, 1991), ch. 1; Stephen G. Fritz, *'Frontsoldaten': The German Soldier in World War II* (Lexington, Ky., 1995), ch. 5.

Africa, for example, though fitfully persistent, was anything but great in its scale or general significance.[53] World War II comprised many wars within a truly global framework of conflict:[54] nonetheless, the larger of those separable wars never really escaped the regional bounds of a war for Europe. Even the Cold War of 1947–89, notwithstanding its central structure of competition between two polities that were either not European or not entirely so (in the Soviet case), was the product largely of strategic concerns about the fate of continental Europe.

No inhabited continent, let alone subcontinental region, was an isolated island in the twentieth century; advances in communication technologies eliminated this possibility. Nonetheless, it is instructive to classify modern strategy with reference to distinctive political geographies. It is not merely a matter of professional expediency for much of strategic scholarship to be organized according to boundaries that delineate regional expertise.[55] There is some strategic historical coherence to a focus upon, say, problems of European, East Asian, Pacific, or sub-Saharan African security.

Geopolitics is not a body of theory that provides a golden key to unlock what otherwise would be the mysteries of statecraft, but it serves the valuable function of reminding people, about 'the relation of international political power to the geographical setting'.[56] The United States has one army, but the wars that that army might wage in, for example, East-Central Europe, South-East Asia, South Asia, and Central America would, for geopolitical reasons, be very different.

IDENTITY OF BELLIGERENTS

War and strategy are frequently approached as behaviour in the historical experience of particular polities or sets of polities. The literature on modern strategy is heavy with contributions on different aspects to the strategic history of the principal belligerents, or potential belligerents. In some periods, persisting traditional rivalries dominate strategic historiography: such opposed pairs as Athens and Sparta, Rome and Carthage, Rome and Persia, Byzantium and the Caliphate, or Britain and France were regionally strategically prominent in their time.

In the historical experience of modern strategy, there is much to be gleaned from culturally empathetic study of particular polities.[57] No matter how one elects to theorize in pursuit of strategic understanding, modern strategy comprises a continuous stream of historical action by strategic agents. Indeed, modern strategy is the strategic behaviour of the strategic players of the twentieth century.

[53] Charles Miller, *Battle for the Bundu: The First World War in East Africa* (London, 1974), is outstanding.

[54] Gerhard Weinberg's book, *World at Arms*, is unlikely to be surpassed as the leading effort by a single author to capture the whole complexity of the Second World War in a single volume.

[55] Ken Booth has written: 'Strategic studies divorced from area studies is largely thinking in a void': *Strategy and Ethnocentrism* (London, 1979), 147.

[56] Saul B. Cohen, *Geography and Politics in a Divided World* (London, 1964), 24. Geoffrey Parker, *Geopolitics: Past, Present, and Future* (London: Pinter, 1998), is an excellent survey.

[57] Booth, *Strategy and Ethnocentrism*, reinforces the common sense of the point.

Although it is legitimate to proceed, as here, with the analysis of strategic ideas and functions, nonetheless strategy is made and executed by Germany, Britain, the United States, NATO, the Provisional wing of the Irish Republican Army, and so forth. There is a multidimensional context to strategy which can be captured in classification by particular belligerent and by particular 'event' (e.g. crisis or war). Strategy can be viewed as from Mount Olympus, but in practice it is always an expression of agency on behalf of the will of a security community. Virtually all of the world's strategic theorists and strategic practitioners are obliged to focus upon the strategic performance of specific agents. For example, war in the air has to be conducted by, and on behalf of, a distinctive political actor.

CHARACTER OF BELLIGERENTS

The character of a particular war, and the decisions on strategy that shape its course and outcome, are both much influenced by the character of the belligerents. Wars and other passages of strategic engagement lend themselves to classification according to whether they were waged: (1) as an exercise in the enforcement of collective security by what amounts to the entire world community; (2) by a great coalition; (3) by an alliance; (4) by a single country; or (5) by some sub-state entity, be it nation, group, or faction. The fact or anticipation of alliance is always important for all parties, even when the disproportion in strength between allies is very marked. Indeed, modern strategic history, for all the diversity that these categories discussed here illustrate, is thoroughly permeated with alliance politics. Those politics include passages of pre-alliance courtship and efforts at seduction—think of France and Britain from 1905 to 1914, and again in the 1930s, or of Britain and the United States in 1940-1[58]—as well as periods of formal or tacit partnership in eras of crisis, war, and postwar reconstruction.

Statecraft and strategy are enterprises that any number can pursue in concert. A belligerent 'side' can consist of a single player, say Argentina or Britain in the Falklands War of 1982; a team essentially of two, say the United States and South Vietnam (with modest or token assistance from regional allies) in the 1960s; a team of several that grows with strategic success into a team of dozens, as in the Grand Alliance against Nazi Germany that began with Britain and her Empire all but alone after the surrender of France on 22 June 1940; and a crowd for collective security in a great coalition, as was assembled in 1990-1 to teach Saddam Hussein the error of his ways.

The alliance dimension has been either decisively significant or at least important to the making and execution of strategy in the two world wars, in the Cold

[58] Samuel R. Williamson, Jr., *The Politics of Grand Strategy: Britain and France Prepare for War, 1904-1914* (Cambridge, Mass., 1969); Barry R. Posen, *The Sources of Military Doctrine: France, Britain, and Germany between the World Wars* (Ithaca, NY, 1984); Steve Weiss, *Allies in Conflict: Anglo-American Strategic Negotiations, 1938-44* (London, 1996).

War, and in Vietnam. Not for nothing did Sun Tzu identify the political cohesion of an opposing alliance as a desirable target for attack second only to the enemy's plans.[59] Given that alliances and coalitions in international politics are temporary arrangements of convenience and expediency, the wise statesman aspires to weaken the enemy team while strengthening his own. Frederick the Great was saved from disaster 'at the eleventh hour' by the death of the Tsarina Elizabeth on 5 January 1762 and the consequent Russian defection from a hostile coalition. Napoleon at his peak, in contrast, was a master of coalition dismemberment.

The strategic history of the twentieth century shows how the garnering of allies need not augment strength overall. If it could be said with justice that Germany's Great War alliance with the dual monarchy was akin to being shackled to a corpse, a similar opinion could be applied to Germany's alliance with Italy in World War II, and later for the United States' alliance with South Vietnam.[60] In each of these cases, the unquestionably senior partner, respectively Germany and the United States, was hampered in its endeavour to generate the strategic effect necessary for success by the folly and weakness of the junior ally (client). One must add that the deeply unenviable condition of security dependency upon an overbearing ally did little to discourage folly and weakness, in those cases at least.

Defence analysis favours methods that express a determined quest for rational and calculable choices. Allies can certainly function synergistically, with the consequence that their total strategic performance is stronger than is the sum of their several alliance parts. Furthermore, allies are sometimes acquired by accident rather than careful selection (e.g. Poland for Britain and France in 1939, and South Vietnam for the United States in the early 1960s). As with relatives, historical context rather than rational choice is wont to pick your partners for you. In the Cold War, what became NATO-Europe was very much the proximate 'stake' in the contest, as well as a regional contributor, positive or negative, to the 'public good' of security that the US-led NATO alliance generated as a whole.[61] The history of US nuclear strategy in the Cold War was nothing if not a saga of attempts to mesh contingent strategic promises that should both deter the Soviet Union—should it need to be deterred—and reassure NATO allies in Europe. US strategic nuclear capabilities, and the public doctrine governing their employment, was dominated by the presumed demands of extended deterrence and reassurance.[62]

---

[59] Sun Tzu, Art of War, 177.

[60] Erich Ludendorff, My War Memories, 1914–1918, 2nd edn. (London, n.d.), 241; Herwig, First World War; Gerhard Schreiber, Bernd Stegemann, and Detlef Vogel, Germany and the Second World War, iii: The Mediterranean, South-East Europe, and North Africa, 1939–1941 (Oxford, 1995); Robert D. Schulzinger, A Time for War: The United States and Vietnam, 1941–1975 (New York, 1997).

[61] Mark A. Boyer, International Cooperation and Public Goods: Opportunities for the Western Alliance (Baltimore, 1993).

[62] Edward Luttwak, 'The Problems of Extending Deterrence', in The Future of Strategic Deterrence, pt. 1, Adelphi Paper 160 (London, autumn 1980), 31–7; Michael Howard, 'Reassurance and Deterrence: Western Defense in the 1980s', Foreign Affairs, 61 (1982/3), 309–24; Freedman, Evolution of Nuclear Strategy, esp. 424–6.

Allies are both a curse and a blessing. They can share the strategic load, but they can also increase it. They can provide wise counsel and valuable knowledge; but alternatively they can pursue an independent path to glory—as for example did Mussolini's Italy in the Balkans and Africa in 1940-1,[63]—which obliges the senior partner to direct scarce assets, invest fragile prestige, and expend irrecoverable time upon projects that are not its own. The irony is important in the title of a book about Anglo-American relations: *Fighting with Allies*.[64]

WEAPONS

I confess to a prejudice in favour of holistic analysis, which encourages the intimidating thought that it is hard to understand anything unless one at least attains some minimal understanding of everything. For that reason I was always troubled by the title and conceptual premise of John Mearsheimer's book on *Conventional Deterrence*.[65] How can conventional deterrence have intellectual, political, strategic, or operational integrity in a nuclear age? In contrast, the roles and contributions of non-nuclear forces in a nuclear context can be studied. The problem with 'conventional deterrence' is that the noun requires, or invites, judgement about strategic effect from a source that cannot be isolated for such judgement. The subject is deterrence; it cannot sensibly be treated as either conventional or nuclear.

Modern strategy and modern wars can be analysed in terms of the roles and contributions of particular kinds of weapon systems or weapon effects, and even in specific regard to a particular model of weapon. However, if one writes about 'tanks in war', there is always the peril that one might slide all but unknowingly from the mission of discerning 'the tanks with which the war was won (or lost)' into the journalistic dominant weapon fallacy of discussing 'the tanks that won (or lost) the war'. To understand the whole of strategy and war, the several parts of the subject must be mastered both in detail and in joint and combined arms contexts. If scholars would study, say, 'the great war at sea',[66] strictly speaking they need know only sufficient about other, non-maritime, dimensions of the great war to make sense of the war at sea. If, however, they proceed to theorize about the significance of war at sea relative to war on land, in the air, and in the 'ether', for its overall strategic contribution to the course and outcome of the conflict, then they must comprehend how the war 'worked' as a whole. A failure to demonstrate such overall mastery of the relevant strategic history is especially marked in, and damaging to the credibility of, Alfred Thayer Mahan's study of the

---

[63] MacGregor Knox, *Mussolini Unleashed, 1939–1941: Politics and Strategy in Fascist Italy's Last War* (Cambridge, 1982); Weinberg, *World at Arms*, 205–34; Schreiber et al., *Germany and the Second World War, iii*.

[64] Robin Renwick, *Fighting with Allies: America and Britain in Peace and at War* (New York, 1996).

[65] John J. Mearsheimer, *Conventional Deterrence* (Ithaca, NY, 1983).

[66] My example is random; no criticism is intended of Richard Hough, *The Great War at Sea, 1914–1918* (Oxford, 1983).

wars of the French Revolution and Empire.[67] His impressive concluding chapters on the strategic value of seapower beg for complementary comparative analysis of the extra-maritime dimensions to the wars in question.

Writing in 1905, Charles E. Callwell emphasized the mutual dependence of 'military operations and maritime preponderance'. In his day, even for a nominally amphibious power like Britain, appreciation of the tactical, operational, and strategic relations between the army and the navy was neither deep nor widespread. Callwell observed: 'In the present day the land-service and the sea-service are alike in this, that both know their own particular business, and know it well.' He proceeded to pose the following question: 'But do they know enough about each other's business?'[68] Whether or not the British Army and Navy understood each other's business, the fact was that at least until the autumn of 1911 the two services were planning to wage very different wars against Germany. The rival, service-specific theories of victory were exposed in a dramatic head-to-head exposition at the crucial 114th meeting of the Committee of Imperial Defence on 23 August 1911.[69] The Royal Navy hoped to be allowed to harass the coasts of Germany, while the Army expected to be licensed to dispatch its recently organized expeditionary force to fight in concert with the French.[70]

One should not assume that single-service, even dominant-weapon, theories of war passed into history with the horse cavalry and the super dreadnought. As recently as the 1980s, the US Navy endorsed as its official strategic vision what it called 'the maritime strategy', a notional strategy that did not explain very convincingly why its strategic assumptions were sound or just how it would relate to the non-maritime dimensions of the war in prospect.[71] In the 1990s the character of the Gulf War encouraged a fresh burst of theory on the subject of 'the air weapon'.[72]

---

[67] Alfred Thayer Mahan, *The Influence of Sea Power upon the French Revolution and Empire, 1793–1812* (2 vols., Boston, 1892).

[68] Charles E. Callwell, *Military Operations and Maritime Preponderance: Their Relations and Interdependence*, ed. Colin S. Gray, repr. of 1905 edn. (Annapolis, Md., 1996), 22.

[69] C. J. Lowe and M. L. Dockrill (eds.), *The Mirage of Power: British Foreign Policy, 1902–22, iii: The Documents* (London, 1972), 445–8; Gooch, *Plans of War*, 285–92.

[70] For the important background of army–navy debate in 1905, see Callwell, *Military Operations*, 445–56.

[71] James D. Watkins et al., *The Maritime Strategy* (Annapolis, Md., Jan. 1986); George W. Baer, *One Hundred Years of Sea Power: The U.S. Navy, 1890–1990* (Stanford, Calif., 1994), ch. 17. On reflection, I suspect that I was unduly generous in my appraisal, 'Sea Power for Containment: The U.S. Navy in the Cold War', in Keith Neilson and Elizabeth Jane Errington (eds.), *Navies and Global Defense: Theories and Strategy* (Westport, Conn., 1995), esp. 202–3. Also on reflection, and with the advantage of better knowledge of Soviet strategic thinking at the time, I still believe that the authors of 'the maritime strategy' were more correct than were their leading contemporary critics. Nonetheless, the more heroic assumptions upon which the strategy rested—a protracted, non-nuclear, global war—were not sufficiently justified (if, indeed, they were justifiable). Norman Friedman, *The US Maritime Strategy* (London, 1988), offered a forceful defence.

[72] Andrew G. B. Vallance, *The Air Weapon: Doctrines of Air Power Strategy and Operational Art* (London, 1996). See also Eliot A. Cohen, 'The Meaning and Future of Air Power', *Orbis*, 39 (1995), 189–200; Benjamin S. Lambeth, 'The Technology Revolution in Air Warfare', *Survival*, 39 (1997), 65–83; Richard P. Hallion (ed.), *Air Power Confronts an Unstable World* (London, 1997).

Modern strategic history can be approached from the perspective of the weapons that have been used or threatened, and that history can descend into fine-grained tactical, technical, logistic, and organizational analysis. Moreover, just as every war, and every period of crisis, must differ in the particular weighting and interactions among the many dimensions of war, so must the mix of weapons for tactical and operational effectiveness vary both within each historical case and from case to case. For example, unless one is writing strictly for the 'boy's toys' market, for which technical detail is all, analysis of the military significance even of so prominent a weapon as the Soviet T-34 tank has to consider that tank in relation to other Soviet tanks, the importance of armour in the evolving Soviet way of ground warfare from 1941 to 1945, and ground combat in the context of Soviet military effort in other environments.[73] In addition, one might wish to complicate matters by introducing both a dynamic foe and distant allies who also contributed strategic effect towards the defeat of Nazi Germany. Consideration of, say, artillery in general in World War I, or, specifically of the P-51 Mustang in World War II, the Bell UH-1 'Huey' helicopter in Vietnam, or the Lockheed F-117A 'stealth' fighter in the Gulf War must relate the weapon in question to the unique conditions of the particular war under discussion.

PERIOD

It is easy to sympathize with John Terraine when he proclaims, with particular reference to World War I, 'It has long been my belief that chronology is the spinal cord of history, and that every step away from chronological sequence is highly dangerous.'[74] Although my purpose is not historical, and hence Terraine's admonition does not strictly apply here, I understand that my subject, modern strategy, happened historically: it happened in a particular period; it occurred as a constant consequential flow of experience; and its human agents were all, necessarily, historical figures. Every illustrative case for every discriminating category of classification suggested here, is historically specific.

Periodization into 'eras', 'ages', and the like is a matter of judgement. Moreover, judgements on how, for example, the twentieth century should be dissected for its better explanation, draw upon beliefs and assumptions that are pregnant with implications for understanding. To cite but a few examples: did 'the modern style of warfare' begin in 1917–18? If one talks of 'the era of the two world wars' is one conflating two radically different 'events' in that one is suggesting that World War II was 'Round 2'? Is it useful to define the period 1945–89 as 'the first nuclear

---

[73] On the impact of the T-34, see Rudolf Steiger, *Armour Tactics in the Second World War: Panzer Army Campaigns of 1939–41 in German War Diaries* (New York, 1991), 78–86.

[74] John Terraine, 'The Substance of the War', in Hugh Cecil and Peter H. Liddle (eds.), *Facing Armageddon: The First World War Experienced* (London, 1996), 12.

age', a designation that plainly implies notable difference from a 'second nuclear age'?[75]

Just as punctuation alters meaning in literature, so does periodization by historians. To illustrate: the twentieth century can be subdivided to show the rise and rise of the United States as a great and then a superpower; the rise and fall of 'total war' as a mega-doctrine; or the strategic experience of the century can be approached so as to demonstrate the birth, adolescence, and practically full maturity of airpower. Function drives form.

DURATION

The importance of time and timing is stamped on every page of modern strategy. But time is a dimension of strategy that is often neglected in works on theory. The military profession, though frequently deficient in practice, is culturally so deeply imbued with the significance of timing and tempo that it celebrates this dimension of its behaviour less than it should. The civilian theorist of strategy knows the significance of time as typically elastic deadlines, rather than as a matter of life or death. In other words, it is not difficult to find plausible reasons why the literature of strategic theory under-recognizes the importance of the temporal dimension. Of the modern strategic theorists selected for special notice in Chapter 3, only one, Colonel John Boyd with his 'OODA loop', allowed central significance to the temporal dimension of strategy.[76] There are important temporal implications both to Basil Liddell Hart's theory, and doctrine, of the indirect approach in strategy and to Edward N. Luttwak's paradoxical logic.[77] The former can reduce to the claim that an indirect axis or form of attack will deny an enemy the time to respond effectively; while the latter amounts to the claim that in time every strategically effective approach, tactic, and tool will, by virtue of its demonstrated success, motivate foes to locate and apply countermeasures. Boyd's theory alone, however, has time at its very core.[78]

Aside from time, timing, and tempo in the essential logic of competitive

[75] Jonathan Bailey, *The First World War and the Birth of the Modern Style of Warfare*, Occasional Paper 22 (Camberley, 1996); Michael Howard, *The Continental Commitment: The Dilemma of British Defence Policy in the Era of the Two World Wars* (London, 1972); T. V. Paul, Richard K. Harknett, and James Wirtz (eds.), *The Absolute Weapon Revisited: Nuclear Arms and the Emerging International Order* (Ann Arbor, Mich., 1998); Colin S. Gray, *The Second Nuclear Age* (Boulder, Colo., 1999).

[76] John R. Boyd, *A Discourse on Winning and Losing* (MS, Aug. 1987).

[77] Liddell Hart, *Strategy*; Edward N. Luttwak, *Strategy: The Logic of War and Peace* (Cambridge, Mass., 1987).

[78] In the historical case that led to Boyd's theory, aerial combat between MiGs and Sabres, the critical US combat advantage lay in the bubble canopies of American planes which afforded decisively superior observation and orientation, not in superior speed. Charles Grant, 'The Use of History in the Development of Contemporary Doctrine', in John Gooch (ed.), *The Origins of Contemporary Doctrine*, Occasional Paper 30 (Camberley, Sept. 1997), 11.

behaviour, the temporal dimension of war and strategy resides in war duration.[79] The strategic history of the twentieth century yielded wars or quasi-war 'engagements' on a scale of longevity ranging from forty-two years (the East–West Cold War of 1947–89) to a few hours (the US air raid on Libya on 16 April 1986). One can distinguish among conflicts that are: (1) all but perennial (e.g. the Irish 'troubles', and Arabs and Israelis over Palestine); (2) protracted, virtual, and strategic culturally systemic (e.g. the Bolshevik Republic and then the USSR was politically, though not militarily, permanently at 'war' with encircling capitalist polities, and Nazi Germany was effectively at war in time of 'peace'); (3) protracted, virtual, but specifically focused (e.g. the East–West Cold War of 1947–89); (4) long wars (e.g. World War I, World War II, and Vietnam (US phase, 1965–73), Gulf War I (Iraq–Iran, 1980–8)); (5) short wars, i.e. wars comprising no more than one or two campaigns (e.g. Russo-Japanese War, 1904–5, Germany and Poland in September 1939, Germany and France in May–June 1940, the October War in the Middle East in 1973, the Falklands in April–June 1982, and Gulf War II in January–February 1991); (6) a single small operation (e.g. the US invasion of Grenada in October 1983); (7) and 'incidents' (e.g. commando raids and other brief special operations that depend upon surprise and speed of execution, such as the abortive US mission in April 1980 to rescue hostages taken by Iran or the NATO air strikes against the Bosnian Serbs in August–September 1995).

This temporal 'window on war', therefore, says that our subject includes passages of actual or threatened violence that include perennial conditions of conflict lasting for decades; wars of many years' duration; wars of only several years' duration; wars that are coterminous with one or two campaigns; wars that are single operations; and 'engagements' that are brief raids or incidents.

The longer the war the more likely that the impact of all of the dimensions of strategy will be apparent. If war amounts to a single great battle of annihilation that caps a grand manoeuvre, as legend has it (incorrectly) Germany attempted in France in 1914, then prewar planning and preparation, and the condition of the armies at the starting-gate, must be at a premium. If, however, the grand manoeuvre falters, then each side will need to draw upon more and different sources of strength. It is paradoxical, perhaps, that Chinese strategic history has yielded, in Sun Tzu's writings, both the clearest advice against the conduct of protracted war and, in the theory and practice of Mao Tse-tung, the exemplar of just such a mode of warfare.[80] Long wars are feared because they imply high costs—casualties tend to be correlated with duration of exposure to danger—and because they

---

[79] Colin S. Gray, 'Defense Planning and the Duration of War', *Defense Analysis*, 1 (1985), 21–36; Karl P. Magyar and Constantine P. Danopoulos (eds.), *Prolonged Wars: A Post-Nuclear Challenge* (Maxwell AFB, Ala., 1994).

[80] Sun Tzu, *Art of War*, 173; Mao Tse-tung, *Selected Military Writings* (Peking, 1966), 187–267. The proposition that different cultures may approach time with different attitudes is explored in Robert B. Bathurst, *Intelligence and the Mirror: On Creating an Enemy* (London, 1993), 31–6. I am grateful to James Kiras of Hull University's Centre for Security Studies for emphasizing this point to me.

carry the possibility of an enemy learning the modern trade of war. Defeat is a potent educator, and battlefield experience tends to concentrate the mind on essentials. It follows that the experience of partial defeat provides optimum conditions wherein an enemy who is down but not out is likely to find the inspiration for improved performance. All belligerents make mistakes in war, but in short wars the disadvantaged enemy lacks the time to take self-corrective measures. For example, in World War II the French lacked the space, and hence the time, to learn how to wage modern war; the British and the Russians, notwithstanding a succession of clear defeats, had the space, and hence the time, to improve their strategic performance.

CLAUSEWITZ'S CHAMELEON

The many 'windows on war' opened in this chapter constitute complementary, non-competitive perspectives upon the single stream of phenomena that is modern strategic history. Every war, quasi-war, or other reasonably discrete passage of competitive strategies can be examined according to these categories. Although the strategic theorist is challenged to identify the factors, or categories, that most powerfully shape the character of a particular conflict, there is a parallel, indeed superordinate, challenge not to succumb to an unduly essentialist urge. In addition, much as Clausewitz advised as to the unstable relations among passion, chance, and reason in his trinitarian view of war,[81] so it is prudent to recognize that the windows on war suggested here are anything but settled for each passage of strategy. Unlike chess, for example, the game of strategy in a particular conflict does not use a finite number of pieces of set value whose moves are prescribed by absolute rules. On the contrary, a great war typically comprises several smaller wars wherein local conditions and motives promote resort to distinctive styles of combat. Moreover, within the bowels of many irregular conflicts there will be conventionally regular struggles waiting to emerge: indeed, this idea is built into the very structure of Mao Tse-tung's three-stage theory of protracted war.

Modern strategic theory has all but abandoned the quest for the universal in its pursuit of what amounts to partial views of the subject. Modern strategic history can be interpreted in the light of distinctive theories that lean upon one or other of the categories deployed above. For example, strategic histories can tell the story of airpower, of limited war, of irregular conflict, of psychological warfare, of warfare on land, or in the desert, or in the Middle East. These complementary windows on war and strategy, though sometimes abstract and notional, are empirically grounded.

---

[81] Clausewitz writes: 'War is more than a true chameleon that slightly adapts its characteristics to the given case': *On War*, 89.

Chapter 7
PATTERNS IN STRATEGIC EXPERIENCE

The determined scholar armed with a favourite theory is certain to find evidence in its support. My purpose here is to suggest, hopefully to demonstrate, that truth in the interpretation of strategic experience can speak with several different voices. This polyphonic exercise is conducted by means of subjecting the broad sweep of modern strategic history to a series of distinctive, but largely complementary, interpretations, each of which yields a unique strategic chronology. Each chronology is true, but none contains the whole truth. The spirit of this enquiry is reverence for the richness and variety of the pieces of the strategic puzzle.

As there are complementary 'windows' to open upon wars and other passages of strategic experience, so complementary patterns can be suggested for the understanding of modern strategic history. This chapter examines the course of the whole of modern strategy both in order to deepen appreciation of the unity of that whole, and also to explore the question of what has changed and what has not over the past century.

The exercise of distinctive organizing principles upon the strategic history of the twentieth century yields different, though not necessarily competing, histories. Six such organizing principles are found to be quite useful as an aid to understanding, while a further two are not. The chapter begins by arguing that the popular distinctions between offence and defence, and attrition and manoeuvre, cannot serve to suggest historical patterns in strategic experience. In contrast: (1) the irregular succession of major wars; (2) industrial revolutions; (3) the rise and fall of a 'total' approach to war; (4) the legitimacy of force; (5) the military effectiveness of conventional conflict; and (6) revolutions in military affairs (RMAs), though of decidedly mixed merit, nonetheless are all ideas well worth considering.

A HOLISTIC PERSPECTIVE

The general explanations of the trajectory of modern strategic history discussed below have been chosen with the interdependencies among different levels of behaviour (e.g. political, strategic, operational, tactical), and different geographical environments, very much in mind. In order to maintain a potentially powerful domain to theory, however, each approach adopted here applies to the levels of policy, grand strategy, and military strategy. I recognize, of course, the vital significance of the military operational dimension of strategy for those higher levels of focus. No matter how elevated the explanation of the course of strategic history, one must endorse Cyril Falls's advice that 'we must never forget that it is the unknown fighting man who garners the fruits of strategy. Dogmatism which leaves out of account the human factor is worthless.'[1] Falls is not sound when he writes, 'I regard tactics as if anything more important than strategy.'[2] He is entirely correct, though, when he notes that, when strategy has played its role, what remains is for 'the decision to be gained by tactics'.[3] If tactics fail in the field, so does strategy also. In the Hundred Days Campaign of 1815, for example, Napoleon's strategy, operational art perhaps, was brilliant, but the tactical handling of his army was formulaic at best and incompetent at worst— neither of which was good enough against the Iron Duke at the top of his tactical (though not operational) form (notwithstanding the distinctly mixed quality of his multinational forces and the absence of unity of command among the Allies).[4]

PERSISTING DIALECTICS, (1): ATTRITION AND MANOEUVRE

The two principles rejected for inclusion among the interpretations below are those which postulate that the course of modern strategy can be explained in terms of the dynamic relationships between offence and defence and attrition and manoeuvre. Neither of these simple axes provides a conceptual road sufficient to bear the traffic of strategic history. Consider the situation in the summer and autumn of 1918. In the closing months of World War I tactical offence was ascendant over tactical defence—any defence line or zone could be breached, including the abundantly fortified Hindenburg Line—but operational-level defence remained superior over operational-level offence.[5] Nonetheless, the cumulative physical and moral attritional damage suffered by a succession of tactical defeats, albeit without a clear operational-level defeat, produced a strategic failure of German arms. If one understands 'manoeuvre' in the French

[1] Cyril Falls, *The Nature of Modern Warfare* (London, 1941), 101.

[2] Ibid. 80.

[3] Ibid.

[4] David Chandler, *The Campaigns of Napoleon* (London, 1967), pt. 17; Gunther E. Rothenberg, *The Art of Warfare in the Age of Napoleon* (Bloomington, Ind., 1980); Peter Paret, 'Napoleon and the Revolution in War', in Paret (ed.), *Makers of Modern Strategy: From Machiavelli to the Nuclear Age* (Princeton, NJ, 1986), 123–42; Rory Muir, *Tactics and the Experience of Battle in the Age of Napoleon* (New Haven, Conn., 1998).

[5] John Terraine, *To Win a War: 1918, The Year of Victory* (New York, 1981); Tim Travers, *How the War Was Won: Command and Technology in the British Army on the Western Front, 1917–1918* (London, 1992); Paddy Griffith, *Battle Tactics of the Western Front: The British Army's Art of Attack, 1916–18* (New Haven, Conn., 1994); Griffith (ed.), *British Fighting Methods in the Great War* (London, 1996); Martin Samuels, *Command or Control? Command, Training and Tactics in the British and German Armies, 1888–1918* (London, 1995).

sense of positioning, or repositioning, to achieve an advantage, as opposed to its common English meaning of movement or mobility, one can see that in 1918 the Allied armies on the Western Front did indeed win the war in the field by decisive manoeuvre, even though that victory was achieved by a broadly linear advance secured by attrition.

There is no doubt that mechanization made tactical and operational mobility possible by the late 1930s. If over-impressed by the distances traversed by the belligerents' armies from 1939 to 1945, one might look to the attrition–manoeuvre axis, melded with assumed implications for defence–offence, to bear a heavy burden of historical interpretation. Can the strategic history of the period from 1914 until 1945 be explained by the initially slow and then galloping pace of technical feasibility of military movement at the tactical and operational levels of war? Does the rise of oil power in war mean that militarization of the internal combustion engine allowed combatants to eschew the attritional stalemate of trench warfare and instead seek decision through manoeuvre by mobile forces?[6] The answer is no.

Battles, campaigns, and even wars can be won by decisive manoeuvre of the kind demonstrated repeatedly by Napoleon prior to 1809, and as over-celebrated in the writings of Clausewitz and especially Jomini. Germany may have approached victory by decisive manoeuvre in August–September 1914. Unarguably, Germany achieved great operational-level success with her Gorlice–Tarnow breakthrough on the Eastern Front in May–June 1915, Russia came close to dispatching Austria-Hungary strategically with the campaign success of summer 1916 known to history as the Brusilov Offensive, while later in that same year the hapless Romanians were to function as cooperative victims of an unusually adept example of German operational art.[7] Examples are not hard to find of superior operational art delivering campaign success in tactically (and operationally) permissive conditions.

Just as one can cite cases of a manoeuvrist style of warfare in World War I, so also one can locate examples of grim attritional struggles in World War II and after. As a general rule, powerful countries, or 'causes-in-arms' that would like to be countries, cannot be manoeuvred into defeat. There is a perpetual dialectic or dialogue between attrition and manoeuvre, defence and offence, and fire and movement. Abysmal policy, inept generalship, unforgiving geography, low morale—any, let alone several, of these factors, *inter alia*, can leave a polity open to

[6] Field Marshal Lord Carver, *The Apostles of Mobility: The Theory and Practice of Armoured Warfare* (London, 1979); Richard Simpkin, *Race to the Swift: Thoughts on Twenty-First Century Warfare* (London, 1985), pt. 1; Robert Leonard, *The Art of Maneuver: Maneuver-Warfare Theory and AirLand Battle* (Novato, Calif., 1991), pt. 1; Richard D. Hooker, Jr. (ed.), *Maneuver Warfare: An Anthology* (Novato, Calif., 1993); Martin van Creveld, with Steven L. Canby and Kenneth S. Brower, *Air Power and Maneuver Warfare* (Maxwell AFB, Ala., July 1994); Shimon Naveh, *In Pursuit of Military Excellence: The Evolution of Operational Theory* (London, 1997); Azar Gat, *Fascist and Liberal Visions of War: Fuller, Liddell Hart, Douhet, and Other Modernists* (Oxford, 1998).

[7] Norman Stone, *The Eastern Front, 1914–1917* (London, 1975); Holger Herwig, *The First World War: Germany and Austria-Hungary, 1914–1918* (London, 1997); John Keegan, *The First World War* (London, 1998).

swift military overthrow. It is equally clear, however, that the strategic history of the twentieth century does not demonstrate simple trends in the relationships between so-called attritional and manoeuvre warfare,[8] or between the power of defence and the power of offence.

Germany was not defeated in either of the hot world wars by decisive manoeuvre, in the sense of particular cunning movement by Allied forces. The wars at sea and in the air, though conducted by inherently 'manoeuvre' forces, which is to say by vehicles whose very nature is to move, were bloody struggles of attrition, waged ship by ship and plane by plane.[9] The continental scope of the great land campaigns of World War II—the war on the Eastern Front from 1941 to 1945, and the Allied campaigns in Italy from 1943 to 1945 and in the West from 1944 to 1945—demonstrated that sweeping operational manoeuvre was feasible only because of prior or simultaneous attritional effort.

For every case of decisive manoeuvre after 1945, there is ample offsetting evidence for the persistence, even the prevalence, of an attritional style of combat. The Arab–Israeli wars (1948, 1956, 1967, 1973, 1982) have tended to favour a manoeuvrist style because Israel's geopolitical condition, and small population, offered her no prudent alternative. It would be a mistake, however, to believe that even Israel's more adept tactical and operational 'arabesques' were achieved without hard fighting.[10]

When one considers the principal American shooting wars since 1945, in no cases can manoeuvre be judged either plausibly to have been decisive or even to have dominated attritional behaviour in relative contribution to overall strategic effect. For example, although Douglas MacArthur's amphibious outflanking of the North Korean Army by means of the Inchon landing was substantially successful, that manoeuvre seduced the general into an advance to the River Yalu that exceeded by far his 'culminating point of victory'.[11] The net result of the immediate consequences of the Inchon manoeuvre was a war of attrition. To take another example, in the Gulf War of 1991 General Schwartzkopf's somewhat obvious great 'left hook' through the desert was launched only following five weeks of attritional bombardment of the enemy from the air.[12] Iraq was defeated more by the physical and moral attrition of her forces in the field than she was either by attempts at decisive manoeuvre in the form of a strategic air campaign or by the

[8]   But see Edward N. Luttwak, *Strategy: The Logic of War and Peace* (Cambridge, Mass., 1987), ch. 7.

[9]   A point well made in B.H. Liddell Hart, *The Revolution in Warfare* (London, 1946), 25.

[10]   Anthony H. Cordesman and Abraham R. Wagner, *The Lessons of Modern War, i: The Arab Israeli Conflicts, 1973–1989* (Boulder, Colo., 1990); Michael I. Handel, 'The Evolution of Israeli Strategy: The Psychology of Insecurity and the Quest for Absolute Security', in Williamson Murray, MacGregor Knox, and Alvin Bernstein (eds.), *The Making of Strategy: Rulers, States, and War* (Cambridge, 1994), 534–78.

[11]   Robert Debs Heinl, *Victory at High Tide: The Inchon–Seoul Campaign* (London, 1972); D. Clayton James, *Refighting the Last War: Command and Crisis in Korea, 1950–1953* (New York, 1993), pt. 2; Carl von Clausewitz, *On War*, trans. Michael Howard and Peter Paret (Princeton, NJ, 1976), bk. vii, ch. 22.

[12]   Eliot A. Cohen (director), *Gulf War Air Power Survey* (5 vols. and summary, Washington, DC, 1993); Williamson Murray, *Air War in the Persian Gulf* (Baltimore, 1995).

attempt at envelopment on the ground. In practice, Schwartzkopf's grand manoeuvre was not executed with sufficient energy to achieve its main objective of
trapping the bulk of Iraq's élite republican guard in or very close to the Kuwaiti
theatre of operations.

The mere existence of mechanized vehicles does not translate automatically
into a new form of warfare that favours manoeuvre over attrition. Any such assertion would meet with a very rude response from the German and Russian tank
crews who survived the Kursk salient battle of July 1943,[13] or the British crews who
survived the battles in front of Caen in July 1944.[14] Mechanization in all its forms
has certainly altered the character of modern warfare, but it should not be
equated normatively with some notion of 'progress' in the strategic feasibility of
success by decisive manoeuvre. The most prevalent kind of conflict in the twentieth century—as also in the nineteenth—was at the low end of the spectrum of
violence, embracing anticolonial and other forms of insurgency and small wars.
Theorists attracted to the proposition that the rapidly evolving technologies useful in war have diminished the salience of an attritional style of combat, need to
confront the fact that irregular warfare almost invariably is inescapably an exercise in attrition.[15] Virtually by definition, typically dispersed irregular soldiers can
neither be defeated decisively nor win, by manoeuvre. Although one can conceive
of options for decisive manoeuvre that the United States might have attempted in
Vietnam, the fact is that the American war in Vietnam was a long war of
attrition.[16]

PERSISTING DIALECTICS, II: OFFENCE AND DEFENCE

Offence and defence are matters of such subjective judgement at the level of
policy, and are so closely interwoven and interdependent in tactics, operations,
and military strategy, that they have limited merit as the base of a theory to
understand strategic history.[17] For example, static garrison artillery, minefields,
and associated fortifications would seem to be defensive by any definition.

[13] John Erickson, *The Road to Berlin: Continuing the History of Stalin's War with Germany* (Boulder, Colo.,
1983), ch. 3; David M. Glantz and Jonathan M. House, *When Titans Clashed: How the Red Army Stopped Hitler*
(Lawrence, Kan., 1995), ch. 11.

[14] John Keegan, *Six Armies in Normandy: From D-Day to the Liberation of Paris, June 6th–August 25th, 1944*
(New York, 1982), chs. 4 and 5; John Ellis, *Brute Force: Allied Strategy and Tactics in the Second World War*
(New York, 1990), ch. 7.

[15] John J. Weltman advances the interesting contrary argument that 'we are likely to see a continuation of this trend toward attrition in warfare': *World Politics and the Evolution of War* (Baltimore, 1995),
p. xi.

[16] In principle, the US had options for operational manoeuvre against North Vietnam—though not,
of course, against the Vietcong—either directly, or indirectly via raids or invasions into Laos and
Cambodia. See Norman B. Hannah, *The Key to Failure: Laos and the Vietnam War* (Lanham, Md., 1987).

[17] A view similarly sceptical of the analytical value of the offence/defence distinction is Lawrence
Freedman, *The Revolution in Strategic Affairs*, Adelphi Paper 318 (London, Apr. 1998), 44.

Regarded tactically, a barrier defence made of concrete and steel is a barrier defence made of concrete and steel. Regarded operationally, strategically, and politically, however, in 1939 Nazi Germany's Siegfried Line was a defensive shield that helped provide Germany freedom of offensive action in the East against Poland.[18] Also in 1939, France's Maginot Line, though tactically generically identical with the Siegfried Line—in military fact the Maginot Line was much the more formidable of the two—expressed a profoundly defensive intention operationally, strategically, and politically.[19] There are no inherently defensive, or inherently offensive, weapons.

From time to time, strategic theorists attempt to elevate the dynamic relationship between offence and defence to the status of master tool of explanation.[20] Allegedly, when the terms of military engagement either favour, or are believed to favour, offence over defence, aggression is encouraged and wars of conquest are more likely. Viewed out of strategic historical context, offence and defence are abstractions. Even though tactically a tank is a tank, its historical meaning is always specific and provided by the operational, strategic, and political levels of command. The two world wars were not initiated because the power of the military offence was believed to be greater than the power of the military defence, though obviously the statesmen who chose to fight believed that their military instruments were capable of delivering victory, an outcome that eventually would require successful offensive action. Nonetheless, one should not confuse a necessary with a sufficient condition. Although it is necessary for the polities that begin wars to believe that victory is either certain or probable, such belief is not sufficient to explain the outbreak of wars.

The meaning of military trends at the tactical level of engagement lies in the political, social, and cultural character of particular polities. For example, the long range nuclear-armed, so-called 'strategic offensive' forces of the superpowers in the Cold War were defensive measures and did not license or notably encourage aggression. Even before the 'balance of terror' became fairly reliably mutual, with the maturing in the 1960s of US belief in Soviet ability to ride out a surprise attack and then retaliate to inflict an unacceptable level of damage, the tactical suprem-

---

[18] Klaus A. Maier et al., *Germany and the Second World War, ii: Germany's Initial Conquests in Europe* (Oxford, 1991), 230–1.

[19] Anthony Kemp, *The Maginot Line: Myth and Reality* (New York, 1982); Robert Allan Doughty, *The Seeds of Disaster: The Development of French Army Doctrine, 1919–1939* (Hamden, Conn., 1985), ch. 3; Elizabeth Kier, *Imagining War: French and British Military Doctrine Between the Wars* (Princeton, NJ, 1997), chs. 3 and 4.

[20] George H. Quester, *Offense and Defense in the International System* (New York, 1977); Stephen Van Evera, 'Offense, Defense, and the Causes of War', *International Security*, 22 (1998), 5–43; Charles L. Glaser and Chaim Kaufmann, 'What Is the Offense–Defense Balance and Can We Measure It?', *International Security*, 22 (1998), 44–82. Jack S. Levy, 'The Offensive/Defensive Balance of Military Technology: Theoretical and Historical Analysis', *International Studies Quarterly*, 28 (1984), 219–38, and Sean M. Lynn-Jones, 'Offense–Defense Theory and Its Critics', *Security Studies*, 4 (1995), 660–91, offer friendly surveys of the relevant theory. By contrast, Colin S. Gray, *Weapons Don't Make War: Policy, Strategy, and Military Technology* (Lawrence, Kan., 1993), chs. 1 and 2, is unfriendly to the theory.

acy of the offence did not lead American policy into perilous adventures. The tactically unstoppable strategic offensive forces of the 1960s, 1970s, and 1980s were neutered strategically and politically by the mutuality of the nuclear hostage relationship.[21] The whole military context, let alone the political—which raises other questions, for example of intent[22]—thus renders moot any narrow judgement about the meaning of superiority of 'offensive' forces in a strictly tactical perspective. The nuclear-armed long-range missile would always get through. Viewed in some retrospect, it is very far from certain that the 'strategic offensive' forces of either superpower could have ridden out a surprise attack in the 1960s, 1970s, or 1980s. It is vastly less certain still that either side's strategic command system could have functioned after such an attack. However, neither side would dare to roll the dice on the basis of strictly peacetime calculation of enemy vulnerabilities. This topic is pursued in Chapters 11 and 12.

Military forces of like technical and tactical character—ICBMs, for example, or armoured units—may have different strategic meaning according to the geopolitical position and strategic culture of their owners. The power that accepts responsibility for the stability of a particular regional or more general international order needs offensive striking power to deter, actively to coerce, and if need be to defeat, polities who would disturb the peace. Superior offensive maritime striking power in the South China Sea has quite different strategic and political meaning according to whether its owner is American or Chinese (People's Republic of China). Offence and defence therefore lie in judgements that include attitudes towards the legitimacy of policy goals.[23] These qualities are socially constructed. They do not lurk inherently and exclusively in particular weapons.

INTERPRETING STRATEGIC EXPERIENCE: COMPLEMENTARY CHRONOLOGIES

Modern strategic history has unfolded as a single stream of continuous experience, but it does not yield a single dominant meaning. To understand the experience of modern strategy, we must turn to theory. 'De quoi s'agit-il?' ('What is it all

[21] Wolfgang K. H. Panofsky, 'The Mutual Hostage Relationship between America and Russia', *Foreign Affairs*, 52 (Oct. 1973), 109–18; Robert Jervis, 'Why Nuclear Superiority Doesn't Matter', *Political Science Quarterly*, 94 (1979), 617–33; Kenneth N. Waltz, 'Nuclear Myths and Political Realities', *American Political Science Review*, 84 (1990), 732–45.

[22] John Mueller, *Retreat from Doomsday: The Obsolescence of Major War* (New York, 1989), was a bold venture into underexplored country.

[23] Marion William Boggs, *Attempts to Define and Limit 'Aggressive' Armament in Diplomacy and Strategy*, University of Missouri Studies 16 (Columbia, Mo., 1941), provides historical perspective, as does the cautionary tale in B. J. C. McKercher, 'Of Horns and Teeth: The Preparatory Commission and the World Disarmament Conference, 1926–1934', in McKercher (ed.), *Arms Limitation and Disarmament: Restraints on War, 1899–1939* (Westport, Conn., 1992), 173–201.

about?'), to quote Marshal Foch.[24] Thus far I have eschewed chronological approaches to modern strategy. By contrast, this chapter is keyed to understanding events chronologically. The challenge is to find the principle, or principles, to organize the historical chronology to make sense of a multidimensional strategic experience. Although this text does not 'tell the story' of modern strategy in detailed narrative, it does tell the story by way of complementary explanatory principles. No one, or even several, of these principles of organization and explanation can tell the whole truth: they simply shed light upon the subject. Each complementary principle, with its distinctive associated chronology and even periodization, is valid in the same way that each book in Laurence Durrell's *Alexandria Quartet* is true: each narrative provides a unique perspective and helps advance understanding. There are some actual, or at least implicit, clashes of interpretation among the principles of organization. What follows, therefore, are complementary, yet distinctive, interpretations of the course of modern strategy.

THE ARRHYTHMIC PULSE OF MAJOR CONFLICT

Most of the history that serves as the evidence for this study of modern strategy is captured by the irregular pulse of major conflict. The twentieth century registered three great conflicts (1914–18, 1939–45, 1947–89), divided by inter-war periods of twenty-one and of two years. The seventy-five-year span of the era of those three world conflicts (the 'short twentieth century')[25] is framed by interwar periods of, arguably, ninety-nine (1815–1914), fifty-nine (1855–1914), or forty-three years (1871–1914), and the contemporary open-ended count from 1989.[26]

Notwithstanding the obvious differences between the actual global wars of 1914–18 and 1939–45 and the global virtual war of 1947–89, it is sensible to treat the East–West Cold War as a surrogate for hot war. The Cold War was the inevitable product of the success achieved in the anti-hegemonic war to defeat Nazi Germany. Moreover, far from being a severe problem of international conflict, the condition of cold war between East and West should probably be viewed with comfortable hindsight as a solution to an acute set of difficulties of international

[24] Marshal Ferdinand Foch, quoted in Bernard Brodie, *War and Politics* (New York, 1973), 1.

[25] 'Historical' time and the calendar for strictly chronological time do not coincide. I am grateful for the inspiration provided by David Blackbourn, *Fontana History of Germany, 1780–1918: The Long Nineteenth Century* (London, 1997).

[26] Perhaps prudently, many scholars today are unwilling to commit to the proposition that this is yet another 'inter-war' period. For example, a special issue of the *Review of International Studies*, 25 (1999), is titled 'The Interregnum: Controversies in World Politics, 1989–1999'. Most scholars today recognize the essential vacuity of reference to the 'post-Cold War world', but few are comfortable with the idea implicit in the subtitle of Colin S. Gray, *Villains, Victims and Sheriffs: Strategic Studies and Security for an Inter-War Period* (Hull, 1994).

order.[27] Be that as it may, the lion's share of the phenomena of modern strategy is readily accommodated by this arrhythmic pulse of major conflict.

Each of the three great conflicts can be viewed usefully as crisis-solving mechanisms, or as attempts at crisis resolution. The history of modern strategy is a record of 'crisis slides' into protracted episodes of efforts at military resolution of the issues that had gathered potency in the previous post-, inter-, and then prewar periods.[28] The outcome to the great war of 1914–18 decided for two decades, at least, that the recently unified German Reich could not reorganize and direct the European states system in its favour.[29] That war also decided the question of which polities would count the most in the next round of great conflict. French human exhaustion, Russian political exhaustion, British financial exhaustion, and arguably Allied moral exhaustion, revealed by 1916–17 that serious extra-European assistance was needed if Germany was to be defeated. The global strategic necessity for 'the American century' was born of imminent British bankruptcy in the winter of 1916.[30]

In much the same way that the American Civil War cannot be understood without reference to slavery, even though the war was not directly 'about' slavery, so the occurrence of World War II evades comprehension except as a consequence of World War I.[31] Had World War I not occurred, it is unimaginable, no matter how attractive one finds historically counterfactual speculation, that Adolf Hitler, or anybody remotely like him, could have captured the commanding political heights of Germany.[32] Similar logic applies to the onset of the Cold War. The Soviet Union, certainly Joseph Stalin's Soviet Union of the late 1930s and early 1940s, was ideologically obliged to be in a condition of permanent, if happily largely only 'virtual', war with the capitalist world. Nonetheless, the historical Cold War of 1947–89 was very much the immediate geopolitical, not ideological, result of the political-military erasure of Germany in 1945.

Even had the twentieth century been spared the conquest of Russia by what became the state religion of Marxism-Leninism, it is more likely than not that a Russia victorious in a great and preeminently necessarily land war in 1945 over

[27] The political rigidity of a bipolar order imposed upon Europe by largely extra-European, and eventually heavily nuclear-armed, superpowers, provided a respite for the continent after the uncertainties and exhausting hyperactivity of the previous century and a half.

[28] The concept of a 'crisis slide' is borrowed gratefully from Coral Bell, *The Conventions of Crisis: A Study in Diplomatic Management* (London, 1971).

[29] A view also offered in Michael Howard, 'Out of the Trenches', *Times Literary Supplement*, 13 Nov. 1998, 3–4, *contra* the argument of Niall Ferguson, *The Pity of War* (London, 1998).

[30] Ferguson, *Pity of War*; Hew Strachan, 'Economic Mobilization: Money, Munitions, and Machines', in Strachan (ed.), *The Oxford Illustrated History of the First World War* (Oxford, 1998), 134–48.

[31] Gerhard Weinberg, *A World at Arms: A Global History of World War II* (Cambridge, 1994), introduction and ch. 1, most usefully corrects any fallacious assumption that World War II was simply 'round two', but at the price of undue encouragement of perception of historical discontinuity.

[32] Ian Kershaw is persuasive when he writes: 'Without the changed conditions, the product of a lost war, revolution, and a pervasive sense of national humiliation, Hitler would have remained a nobody': *Hitler, 1889–1936: Hubris* (London, 1998), 132.

Germany would have sought the kind of hegemony over East-Central Europe that its erstwhile Allies would have judged troubling, at best. Strategic history is played out in a continuous if often baffling process of multiple causes and many effects. These effects include the apparent discontinuities that occur when nonlinear outcomes emerge, as when water becomes steam or a snowfield becomes an avalanche. Strategic history records an uneven pulse of major conflict, a repeated pulse that invites the theorist to regard the varying intervals between pulses as inter- and prewar periods. The recurrence, albeit arrhythmic recurrence, of major conflict is simply a historical fact.

Theorists of modern strategy cannot fail to notice that the subject is dominated historically by a chronology of crisis slides into periods of functionally attempted crisis resolution, or wars (hot and cold). Furthermore, it is not parochial to note that modern strategic history is very much Western strategic history. The European states system of the 1900s could not cope strategically in World War I with its internal problem of an overly potent Germany. The result was the recruitment of American participation in the effort to restore security in Europe. By 1945, the process of strategic enlargement of the Western world had matured to the point where the principal arbiters of European security, and the security of virtually everywhere else, consisted of one wholly extra-European power (the United States) and one partially extra-European (the USSR). The military preeminence of Europe, and the 'West' more generally, over everywhere else that was first demonstrated by Portugal and Spain in the sixteenth century continues today.[33] The 'American revolution in military affairs' that has been over-trumpeted of recent years is a story of, and really a claim for, continuing American—and Western—military hegemony.[34]

The pulse of major conflict cannot explain the whole of modern strategic history. But when one tracks the strategic historical narrative of wars for colonial empire, wars to contest colonial empire, and conflicts fuelled largely by the circumstances of the three great wars that constitute that pulse of major conflict, then the pervasive salience of the spinal cord of *grande guerre* becomes all too apparent. Most of the wars in the Middle East after 1945, for example, stem from the way in which the Turkish Empire was defeated in, and dismembered after, World War I, by the impetus to Jewish immigration given by Britain in World War I, and by the events in Germany after 1933.

Although every locality and region brings its own parochial fuel to what might become a local or regional conflagration, the pulse of major conflict affects those local belligerents. Examples abound. Japanese ambitions in China and elsewhere in East Asia in the 1930s and early 1940s stood entirely apart from the motives

---

[33] Geoffrey Parker, *The Military Revolution: Military Innovation and the Rise of the West, 1500–1800* (Cambridge, 1988).

[34] John Arquilla and David Ronfeldt (eds.), *In Athena's Camp: Preparing for Conflict in the Information Age* (Santa Monica, Calif., 1997).

behind German high policy. It was the opportunity apparently created by the German victories of 1939–41, however, that appeared to make feasible Japan's attempt at a military solution to the economic warfare to which she was subjected by the United States in 1940–1.[35] Japan's second war of conquest, launched in 1941– 2—which is to say in addition to her extant and longstanding war of conquest against China—was thus an opportunist venture, 'piggy-backed' on the German war effort. The anti-colonial campaigns launched in (French) Indochina, the (Dutch) East Indies, (British) Malaya, and the (American) Philippines were all enabled by the condition of temporary colonial military expulsion effected by the Japanese.

For a more recent case, consider the history of the former Yugoslavia. Although fuel for the inter-state and uncivil civil wars of the 1990s can be traced in part back to medieval times,[36] the bloodletting is the immediate product of the removal of the external threat of Soviet power and influence. Modern Yugoslavia only cohered as a polity when it was under pressure from outside. To take a contrast-ing example of the connection between regional and global conflict, President Anwar Sadat could begin a war against Israel in October 1973 which he knew he could not win because he was confident that the cold war condition of Soviet–American relations would produce a superpower exercise in war termination, or rescue.

Modern strategic history is dominated by irregularly spaced major conflicts among great and super states which have had pervasive ramifications for conflict worldwide. The strategic history of the twentieth century suggests that the seeds of great conflicts are sown in the past, and that every new condition of order created out of resolution by war will decay in a crisis slide to a situation that, yet again, requires resolution by actual or virtual conflict. This is not necessarily the way that history has to proceed, but it is the way that modern history has happened.

THREE INDUSTRIAL REVOLUTIONS

The second chronology of modern strategy that yields understanding from mere historical narrative is that suggested by John Terraine's hypothesis of three suc-cessive but overlapping industrial revolutions.[37] The wars, arms competitions, and other preparations for war of the twentieth century have all expressed the polit-ical, social, general economic, industrial, and especially technological conditions promoted by a particular source of power. In this view, the course of modern

[35] Nobutaka Ike (ed.), *Japan's Decision for War: Records of the 1941 Policy Conferences* (Stanford, Calif., 1967); Jonathan G. Utley, *Going to War with Japan, 1937–1941* (Knoxville, Tenn., 1985); Michael A. Barnhart, *Japan Prepares for Total War: The Search for Economic Security, 1919–1941* (Ithaca, NY, 1987).

[36] Carnegie Endowment for International Peace, *Report of the International Commission to Inquire into the Causes and Conduct of the Balkan Wars* (Washington, DC, 1914); Robert D. Kaplan, *Balkan Ghosts: A Journey through History* (New York, 1993).

[37] John Terraine, 'The Substance of the War', in Hugh Cecil and Peter H. Liddle (eds.), *Facing Armaged-don: The First World War Experienced* (London, 1996), 3–15.

strategic history has been shaped successively by steampower, oilpower, and the power of the atom (as an energy source, as a weapon through fission and fusion, and as electronics).

It should come as no surprise that security communities prepare and wage war according to their evolving multidimensional character, always allowing for the pervasive role of culture and for the pressure of necessity. As Lord Kitchener put it: 'We cannot make war as we ought, we can only make it as we can.'[38] The great wars of the twentieth century were stamped with the mark of their economic, social, and technological context. World War I was a war of the industrial age and of nationalized masses, notwithstanding the socialist challenge to workers' national identities. The age of coal and steel yielded a strategic experience wherein artillery in unprecedented numbers and prowess was the monarch of the battlefield.[39] The armies of 1914–18 were mobilized for war, redeployed across the battlefronts, and logistically sustained by the steampower of the mature railway systems of industrial Europe. Tactical and operational movement (in the battle zone, at least) remained a matter of animal power. The internal combustion engine was increasingly important as motorization supplemented railway logistics close to the action, and as the aeroplane advanced from the status of a curiosity. World War I was a conflict of the first industrial age, and the key military reasons for the character of that war—especially the lack of reliable operational mobility and the absence of robust tactical communications—can be traced to the contemporary industrial-technological context.[40]

World War II was a conflict shaped by a second industrial revolution. The war was a great conflict whose tactics and operations were dominated by the maturing of the technological promise that many people discerned in the latter part of World War I. World War II was the first massively mechanized war, even though most soldiers in the German army, the most potent army in the conflict, still marched into action and relied upon horse-drawn logistics.[41] Systematic exploitation of the internal combustion engine and of the possibilities of electronics stamped the years 1939–45 just as firmly as coal-fired industries had stamped 1914–18. The arrival of airpower and of mechanized ground forces as essential strategic players did not effect a miraculous shift in the most successful way in style of war from attrition to manoeuvre. In World War II, the attrition of

---

[38] John Terraine, 'The Substance of the War', in Hugh Cecil and Peter H. Liddle (eds.), *Facing Armageddon: The First World War Experienced* (London, 1996), 14.

[39] John Terraine, 'Indirect Fire as a Battle Winner/Loser', in Correlli Barnett et al., *Old Battles and New Defences: Can We Learn from Military History?* (London, 1986), 7–31; J. B. A. Bailey, *Field Artillery and Firepower* (Oxford, 1989), ch. 14; id., 'British Artillery in the Great War', in Griffith (ed.), *British Fighting Methods*, 23–49; Bruce I. Gudmundsson, *On Artillery* (Westport, Conn., 1993), chs. 3–6.

[40] John Terraine, *White Heat: The New Warfare, 1914–18* (London, 1982); Guy Hartcup, *The War of Invention: Scientific Developments, 1914–18* (London, 1988).

[41] Albert Seaton, *The Russo-German War, 1941–45* (New York, 1971), esp. ch. 24; Martin van Creveld, *Supplying War: Logistics from Wallenstein to Patton* (Cambridge, 1977), ch. 5; Omer Bartov, *Hitler's Army: Soldiers, Nazis and War in the Third Reich* (New York, 1991), ch. 1.

mechanized vehicles on land and in the air was simply added to the traditional need to attrit the infantry. The two great wars at sea, albeit increasingly oil-fired and, in the Pacific in 1941–5, air-dominated, remained quintessentially attritional conflicts. Nothing could be more attritional than the 'tonnage wars' waged by German U-boats in both wars, and by the US Navy against the Japanese mercantile marine in the Pacific in World War II. The growing significance of the electronic war is illustrated by the victory of the world's first integrated air defence system in the Battle of Britain in August–September 1940, in the subsequent tactically defensive and offensive uses of new radar technologies, in the 'strategic' air wars, and in the intelligence and counterintelligence conflicts waged by the interception and exploitation of radio traffic.[42]

The third industrial age, or revolution, of interest here is that associated with the several uses to which the power of the atom and its (subatomic) particles can be put. The now long-trumpeted 'nuclear revolution' is urgently in need of reconsideration in the light shed by the passage of time and the termination of the Cold War.[43] In the understandably fearful imagination of prudent Cold War strategists, it is unremarkable that nuclear energy should have been judged the factor that defined a whole age. When the best and the brightest among America's and Britain's strategic thinkers in 1946 could write books about atomic weapons with such titles as *The Absolute Weapon: Atomic Power and World Order*, *There Will Be No Time: The Revolution in Strategy*, and *The Revolution in Warfare*, the technological context for strategic policy and theory was deemed to have undergone a paradigm shift.[44]

In retrospect, even though the 'absolute weapon' was to prove too absolute for obvious operational utility once its possession ceased to be an American monopoly, every conflict and crisis conducted within, or even just associated with, the political framework of the Cold War was a nuclear conflict and a nuclear crisis. Notwithstanding the genuine and deep ideological and geopolitical bases for Soviet–American antagonism, there was increasingly a sense in which the nuclear peril that both alliance leaders and their clients shared became central to what the conflict was all about. The horse of nuclear armament, and its associated process of arms control, came to lead the cart of political purpose. Not only was this true, at least plausible, politically, but it was also the case in the realm of war planning. In

---

[42] R. V. Jones, *Most Secret War: British Scientific Intelligence, 1939–1945* (London, 1978); Tony Devereux, *Messenger Gods of Battle, Radio, Radar, Sonar: The Story of Electronics in War* (London, 1991); Ralph Bennett, *Behind the Battle: Intelligence in the War with Germany, 1939–45* (London, 1994); Robert Buderi, *The Invention That Changed the World: The Story of Radar from War to Peace* (New York, 1996).

[43] Reconsideration is under way. Richard Ned Lebow and Janice Gross Stein, *We All Lost the Cold War* (Princeton, NJ, 1994); Keith B. Payne, *Deterrence in the Second Nuclear Age* (Lexington, Ky., 1996); T. V. Paul, Richard K. Harknett, and James J. Wirtz (eds.), *The Absolute Weapon Revisited: Nuclear Arms and the Emerging International Order* (Ann Arbor, Mich., 1998); Colin S. Gray, *The Second Nuclear Age* (Boulder, Colo., 1999).

[44] Bernard Brodie (ed.), *The Absolute Weapon: Atomic Power and World Order* (New York, 1946); William Liscum Borden, *There Will Be No Time: The Revolution in Strategy* (New York, 1946); Liddell Hart, *Revolution in Warfare*.

rational and prudent, if not always reasonable, pursuit of advantage, both super-powers constructed global death machines.

Terraine's three industrial revolutions, their distinctive eras and most characteristic styles of warfare, have overlapped, so the electronic age that began scientifically in the 1890s, and found ever more significant military uses in World War I, World War II, and then the Cold War, today is supposedly blossoming into the status of military-technological Schwerpunkt. From the weapon that defined the nuclear age of the Cold War, the atomic structure and its exploitation on the electromagnetic spectrum is now heralded as introducing a new information age. The industrial revolution that is advanced electronics is allegedly introducing a new dominant style in warfare. Information war, and information-led war, is at the heart of a new revolution in military affairs—or so some contemporary strategic theorists believe.[45]

THE RISE AND FALL OF 'TOTAL WAR'

With two notable caveats, one can interpret modern strategic history by referring to the rise and fall of the theory and practice of total war. What is total war? In the words of its leading exponent, General Erich Ludendorff, written late in 1918:

The armies and fleets fought as they had fought in days past, even though numbers and equipment were mightier than ever before. What made this war different from all others was the manner in which the home populations supported and reinforced their armed forces with all the resources at their disposal. Only in France, in 1870–71, had anything of the kind been seen before.

In this war it was impossible to distinguish where the sphere of the Army and Navy began and that of the people ended. Army and people were one. The world witnessed the War of Nations in the most literal sense of the word.[46]

The war that was launched on 1 August 1914 was not, in the minds of its authors, the war that Ludendorff described four years later. What had happened was that 'total war' was invented and pursued with varying severity and efficiency by each of the belligerents as the demands of modern industrial age mass warfare became undeniable. The most dramatic and traumatic reorganization for 'total war' occurred in Germany, with the Hindenburg Programme of 1916–17. Recent research conducted in the long-inaccessible Soviet and East German archives reveals that Germany's midwar reorganization may have been 'largely smoke and mirrors'.[47] Nonetheless, the formal intention was to achieve the total direction of the nation's resources for the conduct of war.

[45] Martin C. Libicki, *The Mesh and the Net: Speculations on Armed Conflict in a Time of Free Silicon* (Washington, DC, Aug. 1995); Arquilla and Ronfeldt, *In Athena's Camp*.

[46] General [Erich] Ludendorff, *My War Memories, 1914–1918* (2 vols., London, n.d.), i. 1–2.

[47] Herwig, *First World War*, 263.

'Total war' was thus invented in 1916–17, was apparently vindicated by the strategic history of 1916–18, contended with mixed fortunes in the 1920s and 1930s with the more exciting theories of swift victory through airpower and élite, fast-moving armoured or mechanized forces, was vindicated yet again in the years 1942–5, but then as a strategically rational concept was buried by the fortuitous invention and the exploitation of atomic weaponry since 1945.[48] The age of total war thus appears to be framed precisely by the years 1916 and 1945, which correspond to the battles of Verdun and Berlin (and Hiroshima). However, because of the two caveats or addenda to which reference was made, the 'total war chronology' of modern strategy is not quite that neat.

The caveats are to the effect, first, that guerrilla, or 'people's', war, in theoretical aspiration at least, is total war, and second that nuclear war offers a credible promise of totality. Indeed, it was the very totality inherent in the awesome prospect of nuclear war that drove Cold War strategists to rediscover the theory and practice of war limitation, in fact to do so while under fire in real time in Korea in 1950–1.[49] The military objectives of the superpowers typically were holistically framed for maximum deterrent effect, as well as for reasons of elementary strategic prudence, albeit within the framework of a logic of general, which is to say total, war.[50] An East–West World War III in, say, 1980 would not have been total in the sense of Ludendorff's words when he reported:

The war called on us to gather together and throw into the scale the last ounce of our strengths, either in the fighting line or behind the lines in our war industries or other work at home, or in government service. Each citizen could only serve his country in one post, but in some way his strengths should be used to that end. Service to the State was the important thing.[51]

Most American citizens in 1980 served their state passively as uncomplaining hostages to the possibility of a total nuclear conflict. The chronology of total war that extended from 1916 to 1945 was a chronology of total 'regular' conflict among modern societies using the military tools of the first and second industrial revolutions. The modern origins of that all but total commitment of society to the political purposes of the state in war can be traced directly to the consequences of the American and French revolutions, and to the nationalizing influence of French conquests upon many of France's victims. Total war did not expire in the rubble of Hiroshima and Nagasaki in August 1945. Instead, it changed its focus, first, as

[48] Ian F. W. Beckett, 'Total War', in Colin McInnes and G. D. Sheffield (eds.), *Warfare in the Twentieth Century: Theory and Practice* (London, 1988), 1–23.
[49] William W. Kaufmann, 'Limited Warfare', in Kaufmann (ed.), *Military Policy and National Security* (Princeton, NJ, 1956), 102–36; Robert E. Osgood, *Limited War: The Challenge to American Strategy* (Chicago, 1957); Bernard Brodie, *Strategy in the Missile Age* (Princeton, NJ, 1959), ch. 9.
[50] Desmond Ball and Jeffrey Richelson (eds.), *Strategic Nuclear Targeting* (Ithaca, NY, 1986); John G. Hines, Ellis M. Mishulovich, and John F. Shull, *Soviet Intentions, 1965–1985* (2 vols., McLean, Va., 22 Sept. 1995); Andrei A. Kokoshin, *Soviet Strategic Thought, 1917–91* (Cambridge, Mass., 1998).
[51] Ludendorff, *War Memories*, i. 328.

military technology allowed a professional military élite to impose total destruction in a matter of hours (as contrasted with the years required by the Allied Combined Bomber Offensive of 1943–5),[52] and second as political-military 'underdogs' discovered and practised methods of asymmetrical, though still total, warfare. The spirit behind the words of Erich Ludendorff quoted above is synonymous with the spirit of 'people's war' as conducted by Mao Tse-tung and Vo Nguyen Giap.[53]

From the turn of the century until mid- to late 1916, *grande guerre* was approached after the fashion of Napoleon, Robert E. Lee, Moltke the Elder, and as envisaged by Alfred von Schlieffen. This conflatably Clausewitzian–Jominian world-view anticipated the rapidly decisive conduct of war. War would be waged on a large, rather than total, scale, and its consequences would be politically very significant but not revolutionary. Moving on, from 1916 until 1945 total war was the practice required to be competitive in the great wars of the era, though theories of political, air, and manoeuvrist (mechanized) land warfare did challenge the dominant vision of industrial-age attritional brute force. After 1945, and especially after 1952 (with the first test of a hydrogen fusion device),[54] total war appeared so appalling that its very prospect became the basis of a policy, and an increasingly elaborate theory, of deterrence. Limited and irregular warfare characterized the strategic practice of the protagonists in the Cold War, because total war in its nuclear guise was judged to be too total in the violence it would unleash.

The post–Cold War period ushered in by the fall of the Berlin Wall in November 1989 and the subsequent collapse first of the Soviet imperium in East-Central Europe and then of the Soviet Union itself in 1991, has produced yet another phase in the chronology of modern strategy. The leading state players envisage in the near term no salience to total war in any form; indeed, now they have difficulty even envisaging 'major' war.[55] The contemporary trend among super- and great powers is more toward a variant of eighteenth-century-style limited warfare than towards the kind of limited war that occupied fertile strategic brains in the 1950s and 1960s.[56] In an allegedly post-heroic age, wherein vital, let alone survival, interests are rarely at serious risk, only post-heroic military performance is required or expected—at least for super- and great powers.[57] That performance is highly demanding of military professional competence. Soldiers today are

---

[52] David A. Rosenberg, 'A Smoking Radiating Ruin at the End of Two Hours: Documents on American Plans for Nuclear War with the Soviet Union, 1945–1955', *International Security*, 6 (1981–2), 3–38.

[53] Mao Tse-tung, *Selected Military Writings* (Peking, 1963); Vo Nguyen Giap, *People's War, People's Army* (New York, 1962).

[54] Lawrence Freedman, *The Evolution of Nuclear Strategy*, 2nd edn. (New York, 1989), 65–8; David Holloway, *Stalin and the Bomb: The Soviet Union and Atomic Energy, 1939–1956* (New Haven, Conn., 1994), ch. 14; Richard Rhodes, *Dark Sun: The Making of the Hydrogen Bomb* (New York, 1995).

[55] John J. Weltman, *World Politics and the Evolution of War* (Baltimore, 1995), ch. 13; Michael Mandelbaum, 'Is Major War Obsolete?', *Survival*, 40 (1998–9), 20.

[56] Morton H. Halperin, *Limited War in the Nuclear Age* (New York, 1963).

[57] Edward N. Luttwak, 'Toward Post-Heroic Warfare', *Foreign Affairs*, 74 (1995), 109–22.

expected to keep, enforce, or restore peace with security, both swiftly and with only slight casualties on both sides. Snake-bitten by the 'CNN effect', modern militaries are being tempted, if not actually seduced, by the prospect of moving from an era of very limited war into a temporal zone of truly virtual conflict. If enemies tomorrow are heavily cyberdependent, then Western cyberwarriors may be able to succeed in strategic coercion by the conduct of bloodless information warfare in cyberspace.

The era of total war encompassed by the years 1916 to 1945, and then in different guise by the years of the Cold War, was stamped not only with the heavy imprint of the technological products of the industrial ages of coal, steam, and steel, and then of petroleum and—increasingly—electronics, but also with the hallmark of powerful ideology. The great wars of the twentieth century were about the balance of power in Europe and Asia. They were also about competing ideas on man, society, and the state.

THE UTILITY, LEGITIMACY, AND CONTROL OF FORCE

It may be useful to suggest a modern strategic chronology that reflects both a declining political utility and an associated declining legitimacy for the use of force on a large scale. Some readers will want to challenge my qualification of this argument with reference to scale. The hypothesis is that, from a high point of nationally focused enthusiasm in 1914–15, the strategic history of the century shows a cumulatively radical, if erratically punctuated, decline in the willingness of Western societies to resort to force. The pace of development of what amounts to a conditional taboo against war has varied from society to society, as cultural analysis leads us to expect, but nonetheless the trend has been global and progressive, if unsteady.[58]

In 1899, imperial Britain was not overly displeased to find that an imprudent Paul Kruger had licensed the teaching of a lesson in the reality of manifest destiny in Southern Africa. British jingoism came to be tempered with respect for the Boer as an irregular warrior, empathy for him as a fellow white man in the dark continent, shame at the brutal treatment inadvertently accorded Boer civilians, and some disquiet at the evidence of British military incompetence. But, overall, British society entered the twentieth century content to wage at least 'small wars' of empire as strategic conditions required.[59] In addition, from 1900 until 1914, both semi-officially and at the popular level, Britons were encultured to be ready to play whatever role might be required, including continental intervention, to help

---

[58] Michael Howard (ed.), *Restraints on War: Studies in the Limitation of Armed Conflict* (Oxford, 1979); Geoffrey Best, *War and Law since 1945* (Oxford, 1994); Michael Howard, George J. Andreopoulos, and Mark R. Shulman (eds.), *The Laws of War: Constraints on Warfare in the Western World* (New Haven, Conn., 1994).

[59] Charles E. Callwell, *Small Wars: A Tactical Textbook for Imperial Soldiers*, repr. of 1906 edn. (London, 1990).

keep or restore a tolerable balance of power in Europe.[60] Early symptoms of what a later period would come to know as the 'CNN effect' had emerged from journalists' endeavours in the Crimean War (1853–6) and in South Africa (1899–1902), but war to the generation of 1914, in the event, albeit only briefly, still could appear as a heady mixture of great adventure, sacred national duty, and moral crusade.[61] For British society, the Somme in 1916 was the watershed.

I select Britain for particular notice here only to illustrate a general strategic argument. For Britain, as for some other countries, the twentieth century delivered a cumulative series of hammer blows against public willingness to tolerate the use of force, except when the country is in the grip of dire necessity. First, 1914–18 taught a lesson in the multidimensional cost of modern war that Britons took deeply to their hearts. Second, that appalling 'butcher's bill', which lost nothing in the mythology of a 'lost generation' that was propagated by the early 1930s,[62] unsurprisingly lent great force to a moral revulsion both against a system of statecraft that could wield war as an instrument of high policy and against the institution of war itself. This revulsion found some expression in hostility to arms manufacturers (the so-called 'merchants of death'), and in hopes for disarmament.

World War II was waged with grim determination by most belligerents, but with little of the public enthusiasm of 1914–15. The experience of this second catastrophe so soon after the first, however, did reinforce the currents working for broad debellicization. In Britain, for example, the war had been a necessity, but it was a regrettable necessity. There was much about the national performance in which pride could be taken, but the winning of the war was preferable only to the losing of the war, not to war avoidance. Understanding of the dreadful cost of war as an institution that could not pay its way, let alone show a profit,[63] was

[60] I use the curious term 'semi-officially' because Britain's commitments towards the European continent remained ambiguous until Aug. 1914: Samuel R. Williamson, *The Politics of Grand Strategy: Britain and France Prepare for War, 1904–1914* (Cambridge, Mass., 1969). A trouble with inescapable historians' hindsight is that a mixture of contemporary motives and aspirations tends to be reduced to a narrative dominated by its consequences. Although, strictly, Britain did prepare for war before 1914—bear in mind that there is a sense in which all militaries prepare for war—it would be more just, historically, had Williamson subtitled his excellent book 'Britain and France prepare for peace with security, 1904–1914, but are disappointed'. Michael Howard, 'Empire, Race and War in pre-1914 Britain', in *The Lessons of History* (New Haven, Conn., 1991), is particularly finely nuanced.

[61] Paul Fussell, *The Great War and Modern Memory* (New York, 1975); Robert Wohl, *The Generation of 1914* (London, 1980).

[62] 'The myth is, briefly, the fixed belief that the First World War was the deadliest experience in human history': John Terraine, *The Smoke and the Fire: Myths and Anti-Myths of War, 1861–1945* (London, 1980), 35. Chs. 3–5 of Terraine's book are dedicated to expose what he calls 'the great casualty myth'. His argument is more reasonable than the forcefulness of his style might mislead readers to believe.

[63] Even Napoleon could not reliably show a profit from the conduct of war. 'Thus, like his predecessors, he [Napoleon] ultimately found the solution to his financial problems in conquest. War, not loans or taxes, provided the means with which Napoleon balanced his budget': David Kaiser, *Politics and War: European Conflict from Philip II to Hitler* (Cambridge, Mass., 1990), 247. Brian Bond writes: 'in effect Napoleon wittingly placed himself on a treadmill of perpetual war in order to maintain his armies and

reinforced yet again in the decades of Cold War when Britons harboured no illusions about national survival in the event of a general nuclear conflict.

In British perspective, a perspective shared with other societies, the twentieth century thus recorded a series of blows to the utility and legitimacy of the use of force on a large scale. The casualty lists were unprecedented, unexpected, and tolerable only with the most serious of policy, and moral, justification. Even when great wars were won, the rewards of victory appeared either notional or non-existent. With the dawn of nuclear peril, for Britain great war assumed the prospective character more of a malign act of God than of an instrument of policy. At century's end, although 'war' is still recognized in principle as a necessary regulatory mechanism for international order, it appears massively atavistic in international affairs. No Western audience today would be relaxed about a claim by a political leader that '[t]he function of war is to settle disputes'.[64] In a world where wealth is not associated primarily with control of geography, let alone with control of potentially hostile people, the idea of fighting for gain is widely considered absurd. Unfortunately, this analysis is dangerously parochial: it would take the behaviour of only one or two 'rogue', or just plain old-fashioned dissatisfied or desperately ambitious, polities to negate the otherwise happy message delivered here.

As a special case in the control of force, it is necessary to offer a brief commentary on the experience of modern strategy with arms control. Little is said in this text about arms control as the topic generally is understood. Similarly, few thoughts and little commentary is offered here directly on the subject of war causation. The principal reason for this apparent neglect is that the substance of both issues coincides with the theory and analysis of modern strategy. This whole book is about the control of arms by strategy. For a parallel claim, many strategic theorists, who seek honestly to tell truth to power, believe that they contribute to the conditions that encourage peace with security. If modern strategic theory, especially the ideas developed under the rubric of deterrence, has not been addressing at least the immediate precipitating causes of war, what can it have been about? In an overview of arms control after the Cold War, a recent author may be more correct than he knows when he claims that arms control 'is about setting political limits on military policy'.[65] Strategy controls the threat and use of military force according to the political limits of policy.

The literature on arms control needs reclassification within the broader

imperial commitments ... Quite apart from maintaining the bulk of his armies at his opponents' expense, Napoleon's conquests provided the French treasury with 10 to 15 per cent of its annual revenue from 1805 onwards.' *The Pursuit of Victory: From Napoleon to Saddam Hussein* (Oxford, 1996), 36–7. The trouble was that military effort produced deficits, which required financial alleviation by loot from further conquests. John Brewer, *The Sinews of Power: War, Money and the English State, 1688–1783* (New York, 1989), is a classic treatment of the political economy of (sometimes) profitable war.

[64] Liddell Hart, *Revolution in Warfare*, 42. His 1946 statement is today more unfashionable than untrue.

[65] Stuart Croft, *Strategies of Arms Control: A History and Typology* (Manchester, 1996), 15.

framework of the concept of the control of arms. Even attempts to broaden understanding of the scope and value of arms control as traditionally understood, alas typically fail to grip their subject persuasively.[66] The core dilemma for traditional notions of arms control—which is to say, for arms control defined as formal or tacit collaboration in military restraint between potential enemies[67]—is that it has always foundered, indeed must founder, on the rocks of a central paradox. As I have explained elsewhere in a somewhat polemical tract, the arms control paradox holds that the polities most in need of the purported benefits of arms control are the very polities least able to achieve it.[68] The greater the political need for arms control, the less probable is the supply. The very suspicion and antagonism that makes arms control relevant is precisely the cause of its infeasibility.

My apparently blasphemous assault upon the arms control canon was intended to dethrone a seriously erroneous, at least eminently contestable, organizing assumption. The error is to believe that an arms control process can contribute usefully to the prevention of war. My choice of intellectual and policy target was not a random one. The canon of theoretical writings upon arms control, a generation of politicians' rhetoric, and apparent common sense all claimed that the prevention of war was the uniquely significant legitimizing objective for arms control effort. Once one begins to question the merit in arms control processes for the prevention of war, it is but a short step to the posing of fundamental questions about war causation. If both historically specific and general theory on the causes of war(s) is prodigiously contestable, what sense can there be advocating this or that measure of arms control as a contributor to peace (with security)? These are unsettling thoughts for tidy minds that had learnt that armaments, or certain kinds of armaments, promoted the dreaded pestilence of instability (a kind of strategic cholera). Many Anglo-American theorists of modern strategy were persuaded that weapons that menaced other weapons were destabilizing, or bad, while weapons that menaced only people and property were stabilizing, or good.[69]

Mental deprogramming from the orthodox strategic thought of the 1960s and 1970s clears the way for useful reconceptualization of the problem. Arms control should not be the focus of attention. Instead, the issue is the control of arms.[70] Arms control has an intellectually contestable, politically controversial, and lethally limited domain. But reconceptualized, arms control easily lends itself to

---

[66] Croft, *Strategies of Arms Control*, 15.

[67] Thomas C. Schelling and Morton H. Halperin, *Strategy and Arms Control* (New York, 1961), 2, is the classic definition. Jennifer E. Sims, *Icarus Restrained: An Intellectual History of Nuclear Arms Control, 1945–1960* (Boulder, Colo., 1990), is useful, though I do not find her argument wholly persuasive.

[68] Colin S. Gray, *House of Cards: Why Arms Control Must Fail* (Ithaca, NY, 1992), esp. ch. 1.

[69] Ian Smart, *Advanced Strategic Missiles: A Short Guide*, Adelphi Paper 63 (London, Dec. 1969); Jerome Kahan, *Security in the Nuclear Age: Developing U.S. Strategic Arms Policy* (Washington, DC, 1975), both propagate this thesis.

[70] Bruce D. Berkowitz, *Calculated Risks: A Century of Arms Control, Why It Has Failed, and How It Can Be Made to Work* (New York, 1987), ch. 2, 'Does Arms Control Control Arms?'; Colin S. Gray, 'Arms Control Does Not Control Arms', *Orbis*, 37 (1993), 333–48.

recycling within the broad family of activities that are captured by the idea of the control of arms. This entire work on modern strategy is about ideas for, or achievement of, the control of arms by strategy for political ends. Arms are controlled by politics, ethics, economics, culture, doctrine, strategic ideas, the enemy, *and by strategy.*

Chronologies for the twentieth century focused upon arms control, as contrasted with the control of arms, or force, tell rather different stories. The arms control history of modern strategy is a story wherein essentially repeated conditions unsurprisingly generate repetition of outcome.[71] From the 1920s to the 1990s, a detailed chronology of arms control activity demonstrates that when political contexts are benign states can agree to collaborate in limited ways in the mutual exercise of military restraint. When political contexts cease to be benign— the 1930s as contrasted with the 1920s, and the decades of the Cold War—then arms control either is impracticable or itself becomes on balance a source of tension. Modern strategy shows no obvious learning curve on arms control.[72] The temporary feasibility of arms control in the late 1980s and early 1990s illustrates exactly the same principle—just enunciated—as did its temporary feasibility in the 1920s.[73] The chronology of the control of arms in the twentieth century does show, albeit unevenly and erratically, a trajectory among Western powers towards ever greater doubts about the legitimacy of the resort to force. The growth of an arguable taboo against the conduct of war, a taboo that works synergistically with an international law that is distinctly restrictive with reference to *jus ad bellum*, may prove a trend of lasting significance: then again, it may not.

What can strategic experience tell us about the reasons why wars happen? There is great value to be derived from the study of the motives behind particular conflicts. Furthermore, there are probably both 'family resemblances amongst war origins' and similarities in causes among wars in the same periods.[74] Overall, however, the scholarship on the causes of war that has accumulated since the 1920s remains convincingly inconclusive. The literature on the subject yields nothing very useful, let alone near-conclusive, obviously superior to the common lore of statecraft and strategy. Scholarship advises that

actual instances of war appear varied, and a single scientific theory pointing to a necessary condition of all instances of war is unlikely to be found. War is a multi-causal phenomenon

[71] Gray, *House of Cards*.

[72] My *House of Cards* is not especially controversial when its argument is compared with that to be found in the sceptical literature of an earlier generation. The arms-control theorists of the 1950s, 1960s, and 1970s offered scant evidence of familiarity with such prescient works as Salvador de Madariaga, *Disarmament* (New York, 1929); John W. Wheeler-Bennett, *The Disarmament Deadlock* (London, 1934); Merze Tate, *The United States and Armaments* (Cambridge, Mass., 1948).

[73] Robert Gordon Kaufman, *Arms Control During the Pre-Nuclear Era: The United States and Naval Limitations between the Two World Wars* (New York, 1990); Emily O. Goldman, *Sunken Treaties: Naval Arms Control between the Wars* (University Park, Pa., 1994).

[74] Hidemi Suganami, *On the Causes of War* (Oxford, 1996), 206; Kaiser, *Politics and War*, 1–5.

not only in the oft-noted sense that a variety of factors contribute to the making of a war, but also the less obvious sense that there are multifarious causal paths to the outbreak of war.[75]

The author of these wise, if unhelpful, words, Hidemi Suganami, finds 'government actions' 'to be the key constituent of the story of war origins'. He analyses these government actions 'in the light of the six categories: (1) resistance; (2) acts with belligerent intent; (3) contributory negligence; (4) insensitive acts; (5) thoughtless acts; and (6) reckless acts'.[76] This is plausible, but given the gravity and sometimes the urgency of the problem or condition of war, it does not advance understanding. Readers of Suganami's intellectually rigorous and sophisticated study of war causation learn at the conclusion of their journey that the author does not know why wars happen. Moreover, fair reading of his book encourages judgement that scholarly assault on the causes of war is a forlorn hope. If major war truly was out of style at the end of the twentieth century, credit for that happy condition did not attach to the scholars who have studied its causes.[77] When eighty-plus years of modern scholarship can produce no better insight for a general theory of the causes of war than was suggested 2400 years ago by Thucydides — 'fear, honor, and interest'[78] — probably the time is overdue to revisit basic assumptions. This is a book only about modern strategy, but my master theme, that the nature and function of war and strategy are as permanent as their character and conduct are ever in flux, indicates a similar division over war causation. The origins, causes, and precipitating or triggering events must be distinctive for every war. The distinctiveness of those details can be organized for better understanding quite plausibly in the larger test of the Thucydidean formula.

Strategic commentators are wont to be unheroic when confronted by well-meaning, hugely politically correct, and even methodologically sophisticated scholarship on the causes of war or the conditions of peace. Aside from the non-trivial problems of social-science jargon, theoretical assault in pursuit of the conditions of peace has a way of descending into unrecognized circularity of argument. For example, Emanuel Adler tells us that 'peace is, first and foremost, itself a *practice*'. He proceeds to explain:

---

[75] Suganami, *Causes of War*, 202.

[76] Ibid. 205.

[77] Quincy Wright, *A Study of War* (2 vols., Chicago, 1942); Geoffrey Blainey, *The Causes of War* (London, 1973); Michael Howard, *The Causes of Wars and Other Essays* (London, 1983), 7–22; Robert I. Rotberg and Theodore K. Rabb (eds.), *The Origins and Prevention of Major Wars* (Cambridge, 1989); Jack S. Levy, 'The Causes of War: A Review of Theories and Evidence', in Philip E. Tetlock et al. (eds.), *Behavior, Society, and Nuclear War* (New York, 1989), i. 209–333; Suganami, *Causes of War*; Daniel Byman and Stephen Van Evera, 'Why They Fight: Hypotheses on the Causes of Contemporary Deadly Conflict', *Security Studies*, 7 (1998), 1–50; Jeremy Black, *Why Wars Happen* (London, 1998). Black offers the judgement that bellicose societies are more likely to go to war than are non-bellicose societies.

[78] Robert B. Strassler (ed.), *The Landmark Thucydides: A Comprehensive Guide to 'The Peloponnesian War'*, trans. Richard Crawley, rev. edn. (New York, 1996), 43.

Practices are real, not only because their physical and material manifestations can be empirically described, but also in the socio-ontological sense that they embody the collective meaning that people give to material reality. In other words, peace as it exists today can be traced back to the cognitive structures or collective understandings — mainly collective identities — that constitute the practices of security communities.[79]

Adler's punch-line is 'the equation of peace with the security community', a contestable notion which licenses the reasonable claim that 'like all practices it [peace] can be arrived at through *learning* ... In other words, peace is socially constructed.'[80] All or some of which, and much more in similar vein, is probably true. The difficulty is that the so-called 'security community approach' to peace,[81] though attractive, in fact simply constitutes a sophisticated reformulation of the initial problem. It is really neither clever nor especially useful to argue that creation of a true security community equates to the coterminous practice, or making, of peace. A 'security community approach' cannot be a magical elixir to purge the human condition of the scourge of war, because competition among security communities appears to be endemic to that condition. Of course, people should learn the ways of peace through the practice of peaceful arts. The problem is not that people cannot so learn, rather it is that at least a significant minority of them seem unable or unwilling to do so.

THE MILITARY EFFECTIVENESS OF CONVENTIONAL WARFARE

Can the strategic history of the twentieth century be understood in terms of the varying military effectiveness of large-scale 'conventional' war? I am not comfortable with the concept of 'conventional' warfare. Categorically, if by conventional warfare one means nothing more taxing intellectually than warfare that is non-nuclear and is waged between regular-looking and behaving forces, then by definition, and none too helpfully, it was the only kind of large-scale warfare that could be waged before 1945. Moreover, the record of conditions for success in large-scale conventional warfare is much the same for 1916–18 as it was to prove for 1942–5. Victory in the conduct of large-scale (conventional) warfare against a great opponent required the commitment of all but total effort, the help of strong allies, and the acquisition by one's armed forces of the necessary skills in the waging of modern combat. There were no short cuts to victory in 1916–18 or 1942–5.

Despite the general consensus that a nuclear era was heralded by the attacks on Hiroshima and Nagasaki in August 1945, subsequent strategic history has witnessed combat of every kind except the nuclear. Though modest by the heroic standards set by the world wars, conventional warfare in the nuclear age has been

[79] Emanuel Adler, 'Condition(s) of Peace', *Review of International Studies*, 24, special issue (1998), 167 (emphasis original).

[80] Ibid. 168 (emphasis original).

[81] Ibid. 179.

extensive and intensive. One or other superpower waged a conventional style of war on a large scale in Korea (1950–3), Vietnam (1965–73), Afghanistan (1979–88), and the Gulf (1991). It is true that Vietnam and Afghanistan were both 'small' unconventional wars, but it is also true to claim that the superpower in question in both cases sought to conduct as conventional and regular a style of war as it could.[82]

Notwithstanding the recurring reality of conventional warfare in the nuclear era conducted in regions geopolitically distant from the old line of East–West demarcation in Europe, the strategic chronology of expectations about modern conventional war shows notable shifts in attitude over time. Although conventional warfare has been a feature of strategic history after 1945, most probably there has been less of it than there might have been because of the global structure and ramifications of Cold War alliance systems. Even when the Cold War principals were not involved directly, the conduct of conventional wars in South Asia (between China and India and India and Pakistan) and the Middle East was subject to some discipline imposed by outside powers who had nuclear fears in mind. The superpowers sought clients in the Cold War, but they were nervous about the dangers that lurked in the protection business. Imperfectly controlled security clients, such as Cuba in 1962 for the Soviet Union and Israel in 1973 for the United States, had the potential to light a powder trail that could lead to nuclear war.[83]

In the years of the Cold War, the United States moved from (1) an expectation in the late 1940s of possibly 'total war', after the style of World War II but with the addition of an inconclusive campaign of atomic bombardment,[84] (2) through a decade-long (early 1950s to early 1960s) effective demotion of non-nuclear military forces, (3) through a brief official embrace of large-scale conventional war under the guise of 'flexible response' (early to mid-1960s, terminated by Allied rejection for NATO strategy and by the cost of the war in Vietnam), (4) through a long period of uncertainty after Vietnam and de facto acceptance of the primacy of nuclear escalation for deterrence (in the 1970s), (5) to flirtation (in the 1980s) yet again with the exciting idea of an all-conventional defence for NATO in Europe, albeit in the context of modernization of short- and intermediate-range nuclear weapons.[85] In the post-Cold War period, the radical changes in political context—

---

[82] Though the US was not regular enough in Vietnam to satisfy Harry G. Summers, Jr., in his influential study, *On Strategy: A Critical Analysis of the Vietnam War* (Novato, Calif., 1982). Jeffrey Record, *The Wrong War: Why We Lost in Vietnam* (Annapolis, Md., 1998), is not sympathetic to Summers' thesis that the real war was with the distinctly regular People's Army of Vietnam (PAVN).

[83] Aleksandr Fursenko and Timothy Naftali, *'One Hell of a Gamble': Khrushchev, Castro, Kennedy, and the Cuban Missile Crisis, 1958–1964* (London, 1997); Lebow and Stein, *We All Lost the Cold War*.

[84] David Alan Rosenberg, 'U.S. Nuclear War Planning, 1945–1960', in Ball and Richelson, *Strategic Nuclear Targeting*, 35–56; Steven T. Ross, *American War Plans, 1945–1950* (London, 1996).

[85] David N. Schwartz, *NATO's Nuclear Dilemmas* (Washington, DC, 1983); J. Michael Legge, *Theater Nuclear Weapons and the NATO Strategy of Flexible Response*, R-2964-FF (Santa Monica, Calif., Apr. 1983); Freedman, *Evolution of Nuclear Strategy*; John S. Duffield, *Power Rules: The Evolution of NATO's Conventional Force Posture* (Stanford, Calif., 1995); Helga Haftendorn, *NATO and the Nuclear Revolution: A Crisis of Credibility, 1966–1967* (Oxford, 1996); Beatrice Heuser, *NATO, Britain, France and the FRG: Nuclear Strategies and*

no superpower, which is to say peer, competitor—and the apparent promise of what may amount to a revolution in military affairs keyed to the exploitation of information technologies, combine to make conventional warfare the flavour of the era for the United States.[86]

Although the United States waged conventional warfare in Korea and generally in Vietnam also, the probability of nuclear escalation in any direct military clash between the superpowers was always sufficiently high to cast severe doubts upon the integrity of the concept, or likely viability of the practice, of conventional war. In the early years after 1945, large-scale conventional war was officially judged necessary in military planning, because of the anticipated strategic shortfall in the military effectiveness of the small atomic arsenal of the period. As the nuclear arsenal grew by leaps and bounds in the 1950s, so it became increasingly plain that the military effectiveness of conventional forces could be trumped strategically by nuclear threat or nuclear use. This discouraged interest in conventional warfare. Nuclear weapons were 'modern', were therefore apparently strategically inevitable, and could offset and negate whatever strategic outcome conventional operations might secure. So at least it seemed to most strategists in the mid-1950s.[87]

The United States today, strategically liberated from military menace by a continental superstate whose long suit was in the tools of land warfare, has transformed its Cold War dependence upon nuclear weapons into a condition of almost total non-dependence. But, today, as in the Cold War, American attitudes towards conventional warfare could be rendered irrelevant because of the asymmetries of conflict.[88] US aspirations in the early 1960s for an all-conventional variant of flexible response, even if acceptable to NATO allies (which they were not and could not be),[89] were always hostage to Soviet strategic cooperation. Whether or not the US armed forces can demonstrate a unique competence in information-led conventional combat will be affected by the willingness of America's opponents to wage a style of war that allows the United States to obtain the most from its comparative advantages in high technology, organization, and training. Weapons of mass destruction, or unconventional warfare, could prove to be great strategic levellers.

Forces for Europe, 1949–2000 (London, 1997). Because of the synergisms, intended and otherwise, between prospective conventional and nuclear operations in Europe, the story of conventional strategy for NATO (and the USSR) in the Cold War decades also is the story of nuclear strategy.

[86] Frank Barnaby, *The Automated Battlefield* (London, 1986); Guy Hartcup, *The Silent Revolution: The Development of Conventional Weapons, 1945–85* (London, 1993); Robert H. Scales, Jr., *Firepower in Limited War*, rev. edn. (Novato, Calif., 1995); Arquilla and Ronfeldt, *In Athena's Camp*; Freedman, *Revolution in Strategic Affairs*.

[87] Colin S. Gray, *Strategic Studies and Public Policy: The American Experience* (Lexington, Ky., 1982), ch. 3; Mark Trachtenburg, *History and Strategy* (Princeton, NJ, 1991), ch. 3; Saki Dockrill, *Eisenhower's New-Look National Security Policy, 1953–61* (London, 1996), ch. 4.

[88] Lloyd J. Matthews (ed.), *Challenging the United States Symmetrically and Asymmetrically: Can America Be Defeated?* (Carlisle Barracks, Pa., July 1998).

[89] Haftendorn, *NATO and the Nuclear Revolution*.

REVOLUTIONS IN MILITARY AFFAIRS (RMA)

The final strategic chronology I will introduce is the eminently contestable concept of a revolution in military affairs (RMA). There is no single RMA chronology for the twentieth century.[90] As one would expect of such a grand concept which seeks to impose order for understanding upon a rich historical record, many RMA chronologies vie for attention and authoritative coronation as the one that identifies the 'correct' pattern in strategic experience. Strategic theorists and military historians will never attain consensus on whether this or that complex phenomenon constitutes a true RMA, or something else. Scholars suggest that strategic history can be interpreted usefully with reference to chronologies keyed to military revolutions (MRs), RMAs, and military technical revolutions (MTRs).[91] MRs produce broad and deep changes in the character of war, with those changes effected by more or less distinctive RMAs, some of which are propelled by technological innovations and hence warrant description as MTRs. Of these three concepts, the first (MR) is by far the rarer and more fundamental, while the second and third (RMA and MTR) tend to be more immediately visible and hence provide the principal focus for contemporary attention. Williamson Murray writes:

We might compare them [MRs] in geological terms to earthquakes ... Such 'military revolutions' [as examples Murray cites the creation of disciplined military power in service of newly developed nation-states in the seventeenth century, the French and Industrial Revolutions, and World War I] recast the nature of society and the state as well as of military organization.[92]

Still, the notion simply of RMAs is on balance helpful for strategic understanding. The core idea is that from time to time there is a radical change in the character of warfare, a change that may or may not be sparked by technological developments. To endorse that unremarkable claim, one needs to believe neither that everything about warfare changes nor that the nature of war is transformed.[93]

Definitions of RMA risk fuelling academic squabbles. Nonetheless, this offering by Andrew F. Krepinevich is as good as any and better than most:

What is a military revolution? It is what occurs when the application of new technologies into a significant number of military systems combines with innovative operational

---

[90] See the discussion in Ch. 9 below.

[91] By far the best brief analysis of these distinctions is Williamson Murray, 'Thinking about Revolutions in Military Affairs', *Joint Force Quarterly*, 16 (1997), 69–76.

[92] Ibid. 71.

[93] The nature, unlike the character, of war cannot be transformed. If the nature of war is transformed then war ceases to be war, not merely 'war as we know it', and instead becomes something entirely different. Martin van Creveld is brilliantly wrong in his *The Transformation of War* (New York, 1991), in part because he elects to understand 'war' in a narrowly Westphalian way. Also in part he is wrong, at least unwise, to be so dismissive of the future of inter-state 'war'.

concepts and organizational adaptations in a way that fundamentally alters the character and conduct of conflict.[94]

The following offering by Secretary of Defense William S. Cohen is rather less satisfactory:

A Revolution in Military Affairs (RMA) occurs when a nation's military seizes an opportunity to transform its strategy, military doctrine, training, education, organization, equipment, operations, or tactics to achieve decisive results in fundamentally new ways.[95]

Cohen proceeds to illustrate:

History offers several such examples: the revolutionary French Republic's levee en masse; the development of blitzkrieg by the German Air Force and Army; and extensive, sustained, open ocean maritime operations developed by the U.S. Navy. In all of these examples, the underlying technologies which made these revolutions possible were readily available to many countries. But in each case, only one country transformed the essential elements of its armed forces in such a manner as to achieve a dominant and decisive advantage in warfare.

Apart from being unduly encyclopedic, Cohen's definition betrays a distinctly challengeable faith in the ability of RMAs to secure 'decisive results'. Contrary to Cohen's claim, there is no inherent reason why exploitation of an RMA has to promote the likelihood of military decision. Indeed, the RMA of the Industrial Revolution in the nineteenth century, married to a huge expansion in nationalized army numbers, led directly to the stalemate of 1914–17. For another case, the RMA that won 'the nuclear revolution' promoted anything but the possibility of 'decisive results'! Another element of poor history that impairs Secretary Cohen's over-elaborate definition and examples is the absence of appreciation of the strictly temporary character of the military and strategic advantages that an RMA can bequeath. He does not inform readers that of his three cited historical RMA cases, two—the French and the German—contributed to a course of events that led to the comprehensive defeat of the RMA leader. In my opinion, poor history is probably more dangerous to sound policy than is no history. RMA chronologies of this century, though linked closely with the stimuli of anticipated, or actual, historical strategic experience, are not at all what strategic history tells us are the leading markers on the calendar.

Whereas the narrative history of great events is anchored to discrete dates, RMAs, in anyone's theory, occur over time and often with obscure beginnings, milestones, and consequences.[96] One theorist, for example, offers an interpretation

[94] Andrew F. Krepinevich, 'Cavalry to Computer: The Pattern of Military Revolutions', *The National Interest*, 37 (1994), 30.

[95] William S. Cohen (Secretary of Defense), *Annual Report to the President and the Congress* (Washington, DC, 1999), 122.

[96] Peter Paret, 'Revolutions in Warfare: An Earlier Generation of Interpreters', in Bernard Brodie, Michael D. Intriligator, and Roman Kolkowicz (eds.), *National Security and International Stability* (Cambridge, Mass., 1983), 157–69.

of modern strategic history within the framework of a single, master RMA. Jonathan Bailey's twentieth century is dominated by the following claim:

Between 1917 and 1918, a Revolution in Military affairs took place which, it is contended, was more than merely that; rather it amounted to a Military Revolution which was the most significant development in the history of warfare to date, and remains so. It amounted to the birth of what will be termed the Modern Style of Warfare with the advent of 'three dimensional' [depth, breadth, and height], artillery indirect fire as the foundation of planning at the tactical, operational and strategic levels of war. This was indeed so revolutionary that the burgeoning of armour, airpower and the arrival of the Information Age since then amount to no more than complements to it—incremental technical improvements to the efficiency of the conceptual model of the Modern Style of Warfare—and they are themselves rather its products than its peers.[97]

It is difficult to view nuclear weapons as only 'incremental technical improvements', but still Bailey advances a powerful and generally plausible argument. Land warfare in 1914–15 by and large remained a loosely coordinated matter of foot, guns, and horse that in its essentials would have been familiar to a soldier of 1871, 1865, or even 1815. By 1918, however, land warfare at its most modern was a joint enterprise of tightly coordinated combined-arms action by suppressive artillery, combat teams of infantry infiltrators, supporting armour, and 'tactical' airpower providing close support.[98] The elements of the Allies' Hundred Days' campaign in autumn 1918 would have been entirely familiar to soldiers of 1991, or 1945, had they travelled backwards in time.

If Bailey's metatheory of modern strategic history appears unduly economical in number of great 'events', how might one thicken the brew? It is possible to identify at least six principal phases in modern strategic history:

1. *Late nineteenth century to 1915–16.* The industrial, technical, and agricultural muscle was ready for mass warfare, but military professionals had yet to learn how to fight a modern war. Quick-firing artillery, high explosives, heavy machine guns, magazine-fed rifles using ammunition propelled by smokeless powder, and barbed wire yielded a temporary advantage to the tactical defensive in 1914–16.

2. *1916–18.* The major belligerents applied the lessons of two years of war and found reliable solutions to the tactical problem of how to conduct 'bite and hold' operations to break in to the enemy's fortified zone.[99] The 'modern style

---

[97] Jonathan Bailey, *The First World War and the Birth of the Modern Style of Warfare*, Occasional Paper 22 (Camberley, 1996), 3 (emphasis original).

[98] Shelford Bidwell and Dominick Graham, *Fire–Power: British Army Weapons and Theories of War, 1904–1945* (London, 1982), bk. ii, and Terraine, 'Substance of the War', both argue along lines strongly supportive of the Bailey thesis.

[99] Robin Prior and Trevor Wilson, *Command on the Western Front: The Military Career of Sir Henry Rawlinson, 1914–18* (Oxford, 1992); id., *Passchendaele: The Untold Story* (New Haven, Conn., 1996). It is possible, however, to be overimpressed with the idea that the BEF had devised a 'winning formula' by 1918. The argument in the outstanding studies by Prior and Wilson, just cited, needs to be augmented by

of warfare' lacked operational dexterity to exploit the break-in, but when applied competently it was tactically all but unstoppable by mid- to late 1918. Paul Kennedy wrote that 'the problem [of effectiveness in World War I] was not about strategy so much as the *practical application* of that strategy; that is, tactics and operations'.[100] By 1918, the tactical problem of how to generate effective fighting power had been solved, but not the operational one of how to exploit tactical success so as to score a wider scale of victory.

3. *1935–43*. What journalists and others were to call the Blitzkrieg concept was born in October 1935 with Germany's organization of her first three Panzer divisions.[101] An inter-war revolution in mechanization, aviation, and communications yielded the apparently unstoppable power of the Wehrmacht from 1939 until the late Autumn of 1942. The Panzer divisions added speed and weight to the innovative combined-arms stormtroop tactics of 1918 — as reviewed and revised by General Hans von Seeckt's élite Reichswehr early in the 1920s — and were complemented vitally in their mobility by the firepower available flexibly from altitude courtesy of the Luftwaffe.[102]

4. *1943–5*. In these years the Allies, East and West, showed that they could learn the trade of modern war well enough. They won both by copying what their strategic and military cultures permitted them to copy, adopt, and adapt and by applying the classical rules of war (e.g. a strategic matching of means to ends, determination to achieve superiority in military mass, taking infinite pains to deceive and thereby achieve exploitable surprise). Germany was beaten by an attritional style in warfare waged in all geographical environments. Allied forces covered great distances by land, sea, and air, but they did not win by decisive manoeuvre.[103]

5. *1945–91*. The (first) nuclear age has no direct strategic history involving the actual employment of its most characteristic weapon. There is general

J. P. Harris, with Niall Barr, *Amiens to the Armistice: The BEF in the Hundred Days' Campaign, 8 August–11 November 1918* (london, 1998), esp. 297–300. The superiority in artillery which was key to the BEF's tactical effectiveness in 1918, as earlier, could be negated by bad weather which prevented aerial observation, and by a style of open warfare wherein unplanned encounter battles rather than set-piece assaults were the norm.

[100] Paul Kennedy, 'Military Effectiveness in the First World War', in Allan R. Millett and Williamson Murray (eds.), *Military Effectiveness, i: The First World War* (Boston, 1988), 345 (emphasis original).

[101] On the myth of the Blitzkrieg concept, see S. J. Lewis, *Forgotten Legions: German Army Infantry Policy, 1918–1941* (New York, 1985), 45–6, n. 1.

[102] Norman L. Kincaide, '"Sturmabteilung" to Freikorps: German Army Tactical and Operational Development, 1914–1918' (Ph.D. thesis, Tempe, Ariz., 1989); Bruce I. Gudmundsson, *Stormtroop Tactics: Innovation in the German Army, 1914–1918* (New York, 1989); James R. Corum, *The Roots of Blitzkrieg: Hans von Seeckt and German Military Reform* (Lawrence, Kan., 1992); id., *The Luftwaffe: Creating the Operational Air War, 1918–1940* (Lawrence, Kan., 1997). Williamson Murray and Allan R. Millett (eds.), *Military Innovation in the Interwar Period* (Cambridge, 1996), is a set of case studies of exceptional merit.

[103] Millett and Murray, *Military Effectiveness, iii: The Second World War*; John Ellis, *Brute Force: Allied Strategy and Tactics in the Second World War* (New York, 1990); Glantz and House, *When Titans Clashed*; Richard Overy, *Why the Allies Won* (London, 1995).

agreement among strategic theorists, policymakers, and publics, that there was a phenomenon worth calling the 'nuclear revolution'.[104] This revolution cast a shadow over all statecraft and strategy.

6. *1991–*. An information age of warfare allegedly dawned in the Gulf War of 1991.[105] Whereas one could regard that war as the last to be waged with old-fashioned massed armour and tactical airpower, alternatively one might discern the light of revolution in its 'smarter' aspects. To debate whether the Gulf War was the first modern war, or the last old one, is about as useful as debating the same issue over interpretation of the American Civil War. Alas for neatness in chronology, the purported dawning of the information age of warfare is accompanied by possibly competing claims for a new strategic era stamped indelibly with the strategic consequences of (1) fully mature air-power,[106] (2) emerging spacepower,[107] (3) or the all but global erosion in the authority and power of the state and the prevalence of sundry forms of irregular conflict.[108]

The strategic chronology presented above theorizes with such broad-brush strokes that much detail is obscured. That story can be supplemented by chronologies which tell the history of modern strategy at the level of specific military technologies. The course of modern strategy can be approached not only via chronologies of important developments in land (and ground), sea, air, space, electronic, and nuclear warfare, but also with reference to categories of weapon systems within those environmental or technical-functional baskets (e.g. submarine warfare, armoured warfare, 'strategic' air and missile defence and attack). But one must never forget that polities wage war, they do not just wage land, ground, mechanized, armoured, or tank warfare.

Military-technical enthusiasm is most appropriate when it is tied to some dominant weapon, or 'leading-edge' theory of strategy. One might theorize that there is a pattern in modern strategic experience wherein first one, then another, category of weapon successively is queen of the relevant battlespace. A strategic chronology slaved to this proposition most probably would claim leading-edge status for the infantry in the period 1900–15, the artillery in 1917–18, and the tank, at least in its Panzer division format (of combined arms), in 1935–43. Probably there would be no single nominee for 1943–5. The period 1945–91 would have to be claimed generically for nuclear weapons, though with a bow in the direction of

[104] Robert Jervis, *The Meaning of the Nuclear Revolution: Statecraft and the Prospect of Armageddon* (Ithaca, NY, 1989).

[105] Thomas A. Keaney and Eliot A. Cohen, *Gulf War Air Power Survey: Summary Report* (Washington, DC, 1993), ch. 10; Eliot A. Cohen, 'A Revolution in Warfare', *Foreign Affairs*, 75 (1996), 37–54.

[106] Benjamin S. Lambeth, 'The Technology Revolution in Air Warfare', *Survival*, 39 (1997), 65–83.

[107] James Oberg, *Space Power Theory*, (Washington, DC, 1999).

[108] Van Creveld, *Transformation of War*; id., 'The Fate of the State', *Parameters*, 26 (1996), 4–18.

ballistic missilery.[109] The period from 1991 onwards is variously claimed for airpower, the computer, spacepower, and biological, toxin, and chemical arms (possibly in the hands of terrorists).

THE WIDENING GYRE

Each of the strategic chronologies developed here has some merit. Modern strategy has become ever more polychronic. The different phases in strategic history discussed above did not occur only seriatim; each of them has continued to play a role in the ever larger team that can figure in modern conflict. The twentieth century did not witness the strategic demise of any of the variably contestably 'dominant' weapons of the RMAs suggested here. Infantry, artillery, armoured forces, nuclear weapons, ballistic missiles, aeroplanes, and submarines, once added to the team, have remained on it.

The most compelling pattern visible in modern strategic experience is thus the widening gyre, the expanding vortex, of war and all its works. There has been a growing complexity in the trade of war and in the subjects requiring mastery for exploitation by the art of strategy. As this complexity has increased, so warfare is recognized as requiring an approach that is more coherent than mere coordination or synchronization, and that instead proceeds beyond even the 'joint' into the military-culturally perilous realm of true functional interdependence. Strategic history can be told as a tale of pathologies of separate efforts by elements that should operate as one in pursuit of common military objectives. Alternatively, that history can be presented as the story of the slow but inexorable triumph of a genuinely 'joint' military culture and strategic practice by institutions whose changing patterns of behaviour must express the widening gyre that is the content of modern strategy.

The twentieth century experienced a growing complexity in the character of war, as the depths of the sea, air, space, and 'the ether' (electronic warfare), have been added as military environments to the land and the surface of the sea. Military success for strategic effect also has come to depend as never before upon cooperation among the several environmentally specialized fighting forces. Nonetheless, operational, tactical, or technical harmony among the players on the whole military team does not serve as the contemporary equivalent of Jomini's 'one great principle', adherence to which allegedly guarantees strategic success.[110] Wonderfully joint, even truly interdependent, military forces may well be unleashed to wage the wrong war in the wrong way.

---

[109] Note that the greatest American theorist of the Cold War decades, Bernard Brodie, titled his masterful 1959 book *Strategy in the Missile Age*, not 'in the nuclear age'.

[110] Antoine Henri de Jomini, *The Art of War*, repr. of 1862 edn. (London, 1992), 70.

Chapter 8

THE GRAMMAR OF STRATEGY, I: TERRESTRIAL ACTION

This chapter and the next consider in turn the grammar of strategy in its evolving forms as landpower, seapower, airpower, spacepower, and now cyberpower, as environmentally focused instruments. Each military instrument is subjected to the same four questions: (1) what is its distinctive character? (2) What are its operational strengths and limitations? (3) What are the conditions that enhance, or detract from, its operational effectiveness? And (4) how has it evolved over the course of modern strategic history? This chapter begins by supplying some guiding arguments about strategy, terms of combat for effectiveness, and geography, which serve as general intellectual architecture for what follows. Then it proceeds to explore the traditional terrestrial realms of land and sea.

This analysis shows how modern landpower and seapower have adapted to a succession of tactical transformations which, nonetheless, have left armies and navies recognizable as such. Landpower and seapower, though increasingly 'joint' in action, have retained their geographical foci, and the former its overriding priority, of course, for land-bound humans, but each has coopted and exploited new military forms. 'Revolutions' in electronics, aviation, materials, fuels, and many other areas have radically altered the character of land and naval combat, but not their strategic meaning and certainly not the authority of the classical rule which requires a contest for each geographical medium that is to be used.

Landpower and seapower here, airpower, spacepower, and cyberpower in the next chapter, are all manifestations of strategy being 'done'. The changes in tactical forms and operational possibilities enabled by the new technologies that drive military behaviour do not transform strategy and war. The story here, and in the next several chapters, is one of growing complexity, but not of the need for the subject of strategy to be rewritten.

CLASSICAL STRATEGY AND NEW GEOGRAPHY

Whereas Chapter 6 suggested theoretical tools for modern wars, and Chapter 7 identified complementary patterns in modern strategic experience, Chapters 8 and 9 look at how modern wars have been fought. The twin starting-points for this analysis are, first, Clausewitz's thought that war's 'grammar, indeed, may be its own, but not its logic',[1] and second, the aphorism that strategy proposes, but tactics disposes. This chapter is about the doing of strategy by those organized man–machine tools of war which actually wage the 'engagements' that strategy must use 'for the object of the war'.[2] Military organizations do not simply fight, and neither do they wage war in some general manner. Instead, combat occurs in particular geographies, just as it always occurs at a particular time, and against a particular foe. War, preparation for war, and therefore strategy also, can no more occur beyond space and time than they can function innocent of influence by culture.

Six interconnected arguments shape the discussion. First, the land matters most. Whether or not land constitutes the principal geographical medium on which combat is waged, strategic effect ultimately must have its way in a territorial context. Most wars entail some fighting on the geography where the belligerents live, the land. Even if a war is dominated by the ebb and flow of combat at sea and in the air, still the whole object of the exercise is to influence the behaviour of an enemy who needs to be controlled where he lives, on land.[3] Against the territorially defined security communities of modern times, the *coup de grâce*, at least, typically has had to be delivered on land by ground forces. The political centre of a belligerent's gravity is almost bound to have discrete territorial definition.[4] This point remains important whether force is applied as coercive diplomacy, as limited war, or in a war of annihilation. Spiritual values and cultural identity may be beyond the reach and grasp of an enemy's force, but most human values have either tangible physical reality or specific geographical association. The modern state is legally a territorial entity, and nearly everything that we care about deeply exists on land. References to the Spanish seaborne empire, more broadly to European maritime empires, and today to virtual communities are none of them incorrect, but each can mislead the unwary.[5] Human beings do not live at sea, or in cyberspace.

Second, an identical strategic logic governs the development of every geographically distinctive form of military power, even though the terms of tactical engagement and the scope for operational ambition vary from environment to

[1] Carl von Clausewitz, *On War*, trans. Michael Howard and Peter Paret (Princeton, NJ, 1976), 605.

[2] Ibid. 128.

[3] 'Since men live upon the land and not upon the sea, great issues between nations at war have always been decided—except in the rarest cases—either by what your army can do against your enemy's territory and national life, or else by the fear of what the fleet makes it possible for your army to do': Julian S. Corbett, *Some Principles of Maritime Strategy*, ed. Eric J. Grove, repr. of 1911 edn. (Annapolis, Md., 1988), 16. Control is the instrumental ability central to J. C. Wylie, *Military Strategy: A General Theory of Power Control*, ed. John B. Hattendorf, repr. of 1967 edn. (Annapolis, Md., 1989).

[4] Jeffrey A. Harley, 'Information, Technology, and the Center of Gravity', *Naval War College Review*, 50 (1997), 66–87.

[5] J. H. Parry, *The Spanish Seaborne Empire*, 2nd edn. (London, 1967); G. V. Scammell, *The World Encompassed: The First European Maritime Empires, c.800–1650* (London, 1981); Howard Rheingold, *The Virtual Community* (New York, 1993).

environment. As each new geography in addition to the land (and coastal and inland waters)—the open ocean ('blue water'), the air, space (earth orbit or the Earth-Moon system, at least), and cyberspace ('the global information infrastructure')—acquires military significance, so its exploitation becomes a matter for contention by force or its 'virtual' equivalent. This argument was advanced speculatively with reference to airpower as early as 1914. Sir George Aston suggested:

if our deductions are correct, then combats between aircraft will be the exception rather than the rule. Still we must realise that they will sometimes take place, and some day perhaps, when aircraft have developed further, and have been specialised in design to perform various functions in time of war, the local command of the air will be fought for, even as we have battles to establish, for some purpose, the local command of the sea.[6]

On 5 October 1914, five months after those words were written, a French Voisin shot down a German Aviatik in the first victory recorded in aerial combat.[7] Scarcely less prophetic was the following view delivered by F. W. Lanchester on 4 September 1914:

if to-day we had a perfect organisation [for airpower] based on existing conditions [of war], the first great Power to be similarly equipped would require to be answered in the form of a further equipment especially directed to his destruction, and so (as in the evolution of the Navy) we may in due time have aerial destroyers and 'super' destroyers, and again still faster and more heavily-armed machines for the destruction of these.[8]

Although World War I revealed that the right to exploit the air medium was subject to the dynamic verdict delivered by trial by combat, 'bomber barons' in Britain and the United States in the 1930s and early 1940s chose to deny the force of that revelation. Both RAF Bomber Command and the USAAF's Eighth Air Force sought to defeat Germany by bombardment from the air prior to the defeat of the Luftwaffe. This proved a costly error. In the restrained words of a British official historian, Noble Frankland, who had been present over Germany during the air war:

The cardinal mistake was to prepare and launch a campaign which made scarcely any provision for the destruction and neutralization of the opposing air force in being. The theory of the self-defending bomber proved to be illusory. The theory of penetration by evasion proved to be self-defeating. *The whole belief that the bomber was revolutionary in the sense that it was not subject to the classical doctrines of war was misguided.* In a sentence, the preference, whether conscious or otherwise, for the teachings of Douhet over those of Mahan was disastrous.[9]

---

[6] George Aston, *Sea, Land, and Air Strategy: A Comparison* (London, 1914), 268.

[7] John H. Morrow, Jr., *The Great War in the Air: Military Aviation from 1909 to 1921* (Washington, DC, 1993), 64.

[8] F. W. Lanchester, *Aircraft in Warfare: The Dawn of the Fourth Arm* (London, 1916), 2.

[9] Noble Frankland, *The Bombing Offensive Against Germany: Outlines and Perspectives* (London, 1965), 105–6 (emphasis added).

One of the most prophetic in style of the revolutionary theorists of 'information warfare' advances the same sound genus of argument as did Aston, Lanchester, and Frankland. The would-be cyberwarrior, Winn Schwartau, insists: 'Cyberspace is indeed a fourth dimension [after land, sea, and air], and conflict there operates with different rules. Yet the fundamentals of military doctrine and policy must hold for it to become a viable battlefield.'[10] To make advantageous use of an army, navy, air force, space force, and information force, it is necessary as a prerequisite to seek out and defeat the geographically similar forces of the enemy. If use of the sea is vital to us, in consequence it is vital to an enemy that he should be able to contest our ability to use the sea. The same strategic logic applies to the air, to orbital space, and to cyberspace. The technologies, tactics, and operational aims must vary with what is feasible in each unique geographical environment: the strategic logic, however, is uniform.

Third, each geographically tailored form of military power contributes to the course and outcome of the war in the super-currency of *strategic effect*. This idea shapes the treatment of 'the grammar of strategy' across all distinctive geographical environments of conflict. To draw an analogy with soccer, or American football, although typically it is only the players in two or three of the so-called 'skill positions' who actually score the goals or touch-downs, it is the controlling (strategic) effect generated by the total effort of all the players that really produces the points. Landpower was the 'leading edge' of military effectiveness in World War I, and artillery was the leading edge of that leading edge. But, the victory of that continentalist leading edge for the Allies was enabled by superior seapower, and behind that superior seapower lay a superior array of economic resources.

Speaking in 1947, Marshal of the Royal Air Force Lord Tedder, an observer-practitioner of modern strategy at the highest level, reflected sadly:

I feel we must frankly admit that after World War I we as a nation [Britain] completely failed to see war as a single problem in which the strategy, the tactics, and the technique of sea, land, and air warfare respectively are inevitably and closely interlocked. There were a few voices crying in the wilderness, but generally speaking the unities of land, sea, and air of which I have spoken were maintained in the narrowest and most exclusive sense and not—as I feel they should—as parts of a greater and comprehensive unified/national defence.[11]

For a country whose geography literally mandated that its strategy should be joint in character—initially amphibious, later triphibious—Tedder's charge was a serious one indeed. It is interesting to note that another great power with a strategic geography not entirely dissimilar from the British, imperial Japan, performed

[10] Winn Schwartau, 'The Fourth Force', in Schwartau (ed.), *Information Warfare, Cyberterrorism: Protecting Your Personal Security in the Electronic Age*, 2nd edn. (New York, 1996), 470.

[11] Lord Tedder, *Air Power in War* (London, 1947), 24. Michael D. Hobkirk, *Land, Sea or Air? Military Priorities, Historical Choices* (London, 1992), explains and illustrates the difficulty in selecting the right balance among land, sea, and air forces.

even less jointly in coherent pursuit of military effectiveness.[12] Had the Japanese Army been willing to provide a proper level of support for the navy's expeditions and raids into the Indian Ocean and the South-West Pacific, the course, if not the final outcome, of World War II might well have tended even more favourably in 1942 towards the Axis powers.

The purpose of strategy is to achieve physical or psychological control over an enemy.[13] Such control can be secured by the threat or use of any of the instruments of grand, or military, strategy. This strategic effect is akin to the calories that items from different food groups contribute as energy for an individual. From bayonets to NAVSTAR GPS satellites, each ingredient in the military team ultimately finds strategic expression as influence over the will or physical capability of an enemy to resist.

Fourth, recognition of the necessary unity of national or alliance strategic effort has to be balanced by an appreciation for the distinctive character of military contributions made by geographically specialized armed forces. All of those armed forces can help deter, and they can all wage war, but the war they wage will embrace a host of geographically shaped different activities. The relations of interdependence among land, sea, air, space, and cyberspace forces must alter both as technologies evolve and as the multidimensional context varies from one conflict to another. Nonetheless, there remains a ubiquitous, enduring, and geographically focused 'grammar of strategy' comprising the general terms of engagement and generic strengths and limitations of each of the armed forces. Of course, a theatre commander will ask, 'What can *my* airpower effect against *my* enemy *today*?' He will not ask the general question, 'What can airpower contribute?' Nonetheless, the soldier or sailor as theatre commander—not to mention the policymaker, who is likely to be held ultimately responsible for disaster in the theatre of war—should be sufficiently educated in the grammar of strategy with reference to the general strengths and weaknesses of airpower to be able to identify impracticable proposals for the exploitation of airpower.[14] The policymaker and the unified, or joint, force commander has to understand how the promise of military effectiveness from each geographically specialized element is predicated upon each element, with assistance from the others, winning its geographically specialized campaign (on land, at sea, in the air, in space, in cyberspace).

Military fungibility, the 'substitution doctrine',[15] is always possible at the

[12] Alvin D. Coox, 'The Effectiveness of the Japanese Military Establishment in the Second World War', in Allan R. Millett and Williamson Murray (eds.), *Military Effectiveness, iii: The Second World War* (Boston, 1988), 1–44, is outstanding.

[13] Wylie, *Military Strategy.*

[14] '[A] certain grasp of military affairs is vital for those in charge of general policy': Clausewitz, *On War*, 608.

[15] For example: 'The air-power substitution doctrine is based on the proposition that the capabilities of aviation forces can provide more cost-effective substitute for those of land and sea forces in many operational or even strategic situations': Andrew G. B. Vallance, *The Air Weapon: Doctrines of Air Power Strategy and Operational Art* (London, 1996), 38.

margin of military effectiveness, and is occasionally feasible on a grander scale, but still there are powerful limits to its practicability and efficiency. These limits are expressed in the grammar of strategy. This grammar explains why the concept of 'balanced forces' retains its appeal.[16]

For example, Britain has regarded naval power as the final military guarantor of its security and prosperity for five centuries, yet has never chosen to lay all functions of national security upon the navy alone.[17] Military competence is rarely omnicompetence. Even as a particular element among the armed forces appears to mature to leading-edge status, as is claimed for American airpower today,[18] still there are physical laws and geopolitical constraints that limit military effectiveness. Airpower can take and even hold ground, but it cannot occupy it. For reasons of physical, political, and economic geography, the economics of sea transportation for heavy and bulky cargo remain superior to the economics of transportation by land or air. A military logistician in 1900 who appreciated the physics, economics, and politics of land versus sea transportation would have been well equipped to understand that same relationship a century later.

Fifth, the grammar of strategy is evolving because '[t]he technique of warfare is always changing, sometimes drastically',[19] but it is not evolving towards some extra-geographical, homogenized combat capability. One should reject an approach to modern strategy which interprets the strategic experience of the past hundred years as an irregularly cadenced march towards a unified armed force that transcends geographical specialization. As weapons and support services with ever longer reach are developed, and as military (and civil) exploitation of the overhead flanks of air, space, and cyberspace have matured, so there has been less physical exclusivity among geographies. The air, space, and cyberspace environments that transcend the terrestrial land–sea divide do not carry a serious promise of providing other than a leading edge to military power in some strategic contexts. The strategic interdependence of geographically specialized armed forces is necessary. Operational-level interdependence is less ubiquitous, but is still stamped indelibly upon the pages of every era of strategic history (consider the relations between seapower and landpower in ancient Greece, for Rome, or for the crusaders),[20] while the tactical interdependence of forces geared

[16] Colin S. Gray, *Explorations in Strategy* (Westport, Conn., 1998), 20–3.

[17] Prior to the Act of Union with Scotland of 1707, the polity was England, not Britain.

[18] Benjamin S. Lambeth, 'The Technology Revolution in Air Warfare', *Survival*, 39 (1997), 65–83; Richard P. Hallion, 'Introduction: Air Power Past, Present and Future', in Hallion (ed.), *Air Power Confronts an Unstable World* (London, 1997), 1–11. A somewhat more sceptical view pervades Eliot A. Cohen, 'The Mystique of U.S. Air Power', *Foreign Affairs*, 73 (1994), 109–24; Carl H. Builder, *The Icarus Syndrome: The Role of Air Power Theory in the Evolution and Fate of the U.S. Air Force* (New Brunswick, NJ, 1994).

[19] Tedder, *Air Power in War*, 18.

[20] Colin S. Gray, *The Leverage of Sea Power: The Strategic Advantage of Navies in War* (New York, 1992), ch. 4; John H. Pryor, *Geography, Technology, and War: Studies in the Maritime History of the Mediterranean, 649–1571* (Cambridge, 1988), ch. 5. John France argues that 'naval aid [from 'the fleets of Genoa, Pisa and the "English"'] was essential for the success of the expedition [of the First Crusade]': *Victory in the East: A Military History of the First Crusade* (Cambridge, 1994), 98.

to operate in different environments has grown exponentially in the twentieth century.

The teleological fallacy must be avoided. Tactically, and to an important degree operationally, the grammar of modern strategy can appear to demonstrate a march from coordination, through 'jointness', to true interdependence, to actual unification. Similarly, the grammar of modern strategy must speak to an evolving strategic context wherein land, sea, air, space, and cyber warfare is not waged by distinctively uniformed land, sea, air, space, and cyber forces. By 1943-5, for example, airpower—albeit airpower 'owned' by navies—had become the leading edge in the struggle for sea control.[21] *E pluribus unum*, therefore, expresses a strategic truth, since polities wage war, not war on land or war at sea. But combat in cities, beneath the sea, in the air, in orbit, and in cyberspace shows no clear and credible evidence of yielding to a generic tactical prowess independent of geographical particulars. This is not to deny that the official American 'joint vision' of warfare in the twenty-first century does indeed begin to approach a conception of military operations that transcends geographical specificity.[22]

Sixth, discussion of a grammar of strategy that, though different across geographical environments, still speaks to a common framework for strategic understanding sits uneasily beside the geographically non-specific subjects of nuclear warfare and low-intensity conflict. There is a grammar of strategy for nuclear, and for irregular, conflicts. However, that grammar is different from the general rules and principles that govern modern war among regular (and non-nuclear) forces on land, at sea, in the air, in space, and in cyberspace. Neither nuclear nor irregular warfare, however, are beyond strategy, any more than modern conventional warfare can be conducted beyond geography.

THE LAND MATTERS MOST

Modern land warfare is the most conclusive, yet also the least exclusive, of the geographically focused branches of conflict. Because the belligerents in modern strategic history, with only minor and partial exceptions,[23] have been territorially defined, victory or defeat on land has been all but equivalent to victory or defeat in war. Most wars have either territorial stakes or well-recognized territorial

---

[21] Clark G. Reynolds, *The Fast Carriers: The Forging of an Air Navy* (New York, 1968); Correlli Barnett, *Engage the Enemy More Closely: The Royal Navy in the Second World War* (New York, 1991), ch. 15.

[22] US Joint Chiefs of Staff, 'Joint Vision 2010: America's Military—Preparing for Tomorrow', *Joint Force Quarterly*, 12 (1996), 34-49; Stuart E. Johnson and Martin C. Libicki (eds.), *Dominant Battlespace Knowledge*, rev. edn. (Washington, DC, Apr. 1996).

[23] There are 'irregular' belligerent actors, in the form of terrorists, who at least in motivation are 'beyond geography'. They conduct expressive acts of violence for, or more usually against, some great principle. Walter Laqueur, 'Postmodern Terrorism', *Foreign Affairs*, 75 (1996), 24-36; Bruce Hoffman, *Inside Terrorism* (London, 1998), esp. ch. 7. Even irregular warriors who are soldiers for some vague cause have addresses, albeit often only temporary ones, with targetable geographical coordinates.

referents for the real stakes (which may be honour, reputation, and so forth). Whatever the motives (policy objectives, war aims) may be that are not narrowly territorial in kind, war has to be waged in geography and for geography.[24] The only geography that can really be controlled is the only geography that lends itself physically to human occupation, the land. Moreover, there is land that has the highest possible intrinsic and symbolic value to belligerents, their homelands.

Modern strategy provides ample evidence of geostrategically symmetrical conflicts (Germany versus France, 1914–18, or Germany versus the USSR, 1941–5), as well as asymmetrical (Germany versus Britain in both world wars, America versus the Soviet Union, 1947–89, America (for the UN) versus North Korea and China, 1950–3, America (for the UN) versus Iraq, 1991). Even when neither belligerent fears conquest and occupation of its homeland (as in the Anglo-Argentinian war over the Falklands in 1982), still there will be a territorial playing-field with the equivalent of goalposts or end-zones. Continental powers (Sparta, Rome, France, Germany, Russia) can only be beaten conclusively on land, and maritime powers (Athens, Carthage, arguably Byzantium, Venice, Britain) can only be beaten at sea, to set aside nuclear complications for the moment. But land warfare must play a critical synergistic role with sea warfare even for the most insular of polities. For five centuries the English waged land warfare in Europe, and helped finance continental allies to wage such warfare, for the primary strategic purpose of diverting the would-be hegemonic menace of the period from concentration upon mounting a maritime threat.[25] The posing of an unanswerable threat to Britain at sea would translate as the credible threat of invasion, or land warfare at home.[26]

Although every war must differ, it is in the very character of land warfare to hold at risk the highest values of a security community, which are territorially defined and located. Such warfare is also the most involving for civil society, since (unlike sea, air, space, or cyber warfare) it is waged where people live. Warfare on land is people—rather than technology—intensive (we equip soldiers, whereas air and naval personnel 'man' equipment).[27] Also, land warfare is politically entangling, in that soldiers are 'in country' in a way in which sailors and air personnel are not. Finally, this kind of war is shaped by the physical and other dimensions (political, economic, cultural) of geography.

The inherent strength of land combat is that it carries the promise of achieving

[24] Colin S. Gray, 'The Continued Primacy of Geography', *Orbis*, 40 (1996), 247–59.

[25] John M. Sherwig, *Guineas and Gunpowder: British Foreign Aid in the Wars with France, 1793–1815* (Cambridge, Mass., 1969); David French, *The British Way in Warfare, 1688–2000* (London, 1990).

[26] 'If we [British] have gained complete command [of the sea], no invasion can take place, nor will it be attempted. If we have lost it completely no invasion will be necessary, since, quite apart from the threat of invasion, we must make peace on the best terms we can get': Corbett, *Some Principles of Maritime Strategy*, 239.

[27] A point well made in Vallance, *Air Weapon*, 31. See also Martin van Creveld, *Technology and War: From 2000 B.C. to the Present* (New York, 1989), esp. 272.

decision. Whereas dominance at sea, in the air, or in space might enable a war to be won, dominance on land should translate as victory in war as a whole. There is an obvious military operational sense in which belligerents seek to win at sea, in the air, in space, and now in cyberspace, *in order to win on land*. Success at sea, or in the air, may well mean nothing much for a long time: witness the British victory in battle at Trafalgar on 21 October 1805, or the British campaign success in the Battle of Britain of August–September 1940. Both of those famous victories were real enough. Each of them secured irreversible advantages for Britain in a particular combat environment, but neither decided that the defeated party would lose the war. Superiority in fighting prowess on land itself can win wars, whereas such superiority in every other geographical medium of conflict can only enable wars to be won. Moreover, victory in most wars eventually requires demonstration of superiority in land combat.

If the strength of land warfare lies in its ability to achieve decision, such a favourable conclusion typically cannot be secured in the absence of air superiority, and frequently of sea control. At least since the opening of the Battle of Amiens on 8 August 1918, air–land battle, as it has come to be called, has been the tactical, operational, and strategic reality of land (as opposed to ground) warfare.[28] Although some terrain has been more flattering to the combat prowess of the airpower of the day than has others—desert and other open terrain, as opposed to urban, mountainous, or heavily wooded country—since the 1930s success in regular forms of land warfare has been improbable in the absence of superior airpower.

General theorists of modern strategy can hardly fail to notice that the country with the finest army of the era—respectively Germany twice, and the Soviet Union once—lost each of the three great conflicts of the twentieth century. The strategic point is not so much that seapower, or even maritime coalitions, defeated landpower or continental coalitions, but rather that belligerents preponderant at sea have demonstrated a systemic advantage in generating competitive strategic effect. The maritime-oriented belligerent repeatedly showed the ability to translate maritime (and later aerial) advantage into superior power on land.[29] The ancient and medieval strategic history of the Mediterranean showed exactly the reverse. Writing about the last two decades of the Peloponnesian War, Donald Kagan writes:

To win, each [Athens and Sparta] had to acquire the capacity to fight and succeed on the other's favorite domain. The Athenian defeat in Sicily [415–413 BC] gave the Spartans the opportunity to succeed by making an alliance with Persia. After many failures, they won the war by defeating the Athenian fleet [Aegospotami, 405 BC]. There was no other way to

---

[28] Gregory Blaxland, *Amiens: 1918* (London, 1968); Paddy Griffith, *Battle Tactics of the Western Front: The British Army's Art of Attack, 1916–18* (New Haven, Conn., 1994).
[29] The thesis of Gray, *Leverage of Sea Power*. See also Raja Menon, *Maritime Strategy and Continental Wars* (London, 1998).

win. To win a true victory rather than a Periclean stand-off, the Athenians would have had to find a way to defeat the Spartans on land![30]

It is important to distinguish between success in land warfare and success in war. Victory on land is ever likely to translate into victory writ large, provided the enemy's homeland, or other lands of high value to him, is accessible to the preponderant landpower. If such access is denied by a defended moat—the English Channel in 1940, for example—or by a politico-military context that denies that preponderant landpower the ability to wage regular warfare for a 'regular' decision—the American dilemma in Vietnam—then even magnificent landpower will be thwarted.

The grammar of modern strategy in the form of land warfare has shown continuous tactical, operational, organizational, and technological evolution, but remarkably little of substance has changed at the strategic level of war.[31] Land warfare has been all but revolutionized several times at the tactical level, especially with reference to the advent of reliable radio communications, the introduction and proliferation of mechanized (for combat and transport) vehicles, the perfection of 'predicted' artillery fire, and the arrival of close air support. However, once the 'trenchlock' of 1914–16 had demonstrated the problems in symmetrical land warfare, and once a workable tactical solution had been evolved in 1916–18, the succeeding modern operational and strategic history of war on land was unremarkable. The so-called Blitzkrieg victories by Germany in the period 1939–41 were the product of a new technique of war which was multiplied severalfold in its effect by the rank incompetence of Germany's enemies. In retrospect, what stands out from the events of 1939–45 are the facts that Nazi Germany neither won nor was defeated by virtue of radical new departures in the ways of combat. Germany may have waged land warfare with an army that included the innovative all-arms Panzer division, and with the assistance of a Luftwaffe optimized for support of ground forces. Nonetheless, Germany was finally beaten in 1945 in a land war characterized by an attritional combat style.[32] That same style had been characteristic in 1915–18. This is not to suggest that Germany's foes repeatedly were unskilled in the trade of war, but simply were better endowed with resources. The Allies in both world wars had to learn how to achieve attrition

[30] Donald Kagan, *The Fall of the Athenian Empire* (Ithaca, NY, 1987), 423.

[31] John A. English, *A Perspective on Infantry* (New York, 1981); Richard Simpkin, *Race to the Swift: Thoughts on Twenty-First Century Warfare* (London, 1985); Chris Bellamy, *The Future of Land Warfare* (New York, 1987); id., *The Evolution of Modern Land Warfare: Theory and Practice* (London, 1990); Martin Edmonds, 'Land Warfare', in Roger Carey and Trevor C. Salmon (eds.), *International Security in the Modern World* (London, 1992); 'Military Power: Land Warfare in Theory and Practice', *Journal of Strategic Studies*, 19, special issue, ed. Brian Holden Reid (1996); William T. Johnsen, *Redefining Land Power for the 21st Century* (Carlisle Barracks, Pa., 7 May 1998).

[32] Griffith, *Battle Tactics*; Millett and Murray, *Military Effectiveness*, i: *The First World War*, and iii: *The Second World War*; David M. Glantz and Jonathan House, *When Titans Clashed: How the Red Army Stopped Hitler* (Lawrence, Kan., 1995); Richard Overy, *Why the Allies Won* (London, 1995).

effectively, though, unarguably, 'bigger battalions' were a necessary condition for victory when fighting Germans.

The style of land warfare was transformed in the years 1916–18, as compared with 1914–15. At least, armies in the later years understood how, and were equipped, to fight in prevailing tactical conditions. With the exception of the changes wrought in the middle years of World War I, however, changes keyed to the perfection of indirect artillery fire,[33] the great transformations heralded for modern land warfare have tended to disappoint. Although the face of regular and fairly symmetrical land warfare was altered by the arrival of mechanization *en masse* in World War II, *potentially* fast-moving forces for operational exploitation depended upon both the prior attrition of the enemy and the availability of logistic support (particularly fuel, ammunition, and spare parts). Air-supported armies in 1944–5 had the mechanized and (less reliably) airborne-adjunct means to turn tactical success into operational success, but the reality of combat did not show revolutionary changes. In other words, the vital difference for the performance of the German Army as between 1918 and 1945 did not lie merely in the operational mobility of Germany's foes in the latter year.

Land warfare could have been paralysed in the second half of the twentieth century, if not strategically sidelined almost altogether, by the nuclear revolution. Nonetheless, nuclearized land combat did not occur, and it is viewed with deep disfavour today in America and the other NATO powers. If there is a revolution pending in land warfare, it is likely to be a revolution triggered by the recent prowess demonstrated by the information-led armed forces of the United States in particular.[34] The US Army today may nurture the aspiration to conduct swift campaigns of decisive manoeuvre against hapless foes paralysed by systemic disadvantage on their OODA loops,[35] but strategic history suggests that that understandable aspiration is likely to be disappointed. The Gulf War in 1991 did not show us the future of land warfare. Instead, it showed yet again what every decade of the century had already demonstrated. When war is waged between two sides grossly mismatched in military prowess, the outcome will be a swift victory for the markedly superior party. Against wilier foes, Western armies, no matter how well endowed technologically, could find the playing-field of combat somewhat levelled by such inconveniences as nuclear weapons, by rapid attrition of the information assets most critical to the Western conventional advantage, or by the enemy's strategic denial of provision of accessible centres of gravity. The knights of information-led warfare are no more likely to achieve swift and cheap decision

---

[33] Correlli Barnett et al., *Old Battles and New Defences: Can We Learn from Military History?* (London, 1986), essays by John Terraine (7–31) and Shelford Bidwell (115–40); Jonathan Bailey, *The First World War and the Birth of the Modern Style of Warfare*, Occasional Paper 22 (Camberley, 1996).

[34] Brian Nichiporok and Carl H. Builder, *Information Technologies and the Future of Land Warfare* (Santa Monica, Calif., 1995).

[35] John R. Boyd, *A Discourse on Winning and Losing*, (MS, Aug. 1987).

in land warfare than were the knights of mechanized warfare in the land campaigns of the early 1940s.

MAHAN WAS (MAINLY) RIGHT

The strategic experience of the twentieth century has demonstrated that Rear Admiral Alfred Thayer Mahan (USN) was wiser than his critics. Indeed, Mahan is a serious candidate for nomination as the most underrated theorist of modern strategy. No less a historian than Paul M. Kennedy, in a book chapter unwisely titled 'Mahan versus Mackinder', succeeds in misrepresenting Mahan, misunderstanding the common and uncommon elements in the strategic ideas of the two theorists, and misreading the strategic history of this century—no small achievement by a prominent contemporary historian of seapower.[36] Contrary to Kennedy's argument, as geopolitical and geostrategic thinkers both Sir Halford Mackinder and Mahan are more correct than in error, and their strategic theories generally are complementary. Mahan was right to emphasize the strength of the influence of seapower upon history.[37] But Mackinder was right to predict that the pecking order in world power among polities was shifting in favour of great continental states as a consequence of the revolution in convenience of ground transportation effected first by the railway and then by the internal combustion engine.[38] Far from eclipsing seapower, however, the rise of great unified and cohesive continental powers, especially the United States, has resulted in Mackinder's 'Columbian Era' (c.1500–c.1900) being extended indefinitely.[39] A small insular power such as Britain (notwithstanding its empire upon which the sun never set) could not compete alone against a very large continental power with mature land communications. But, except from 20 June 1940 until 22 June 1941, Britain was not obliged to stand alone in a stark confrontation between dominant landpower and dominant seapower.

The careful reader of a substantial fraction of Mahan's writings, particularly if that reading is augmented by acquaintance with the histories and theoretical texts of Sir Julian Corbett, would be well equipped to understand both seapower in strategic history in general and the prospective advantages and limitations of seapower in the twenty-first century.[40] Seapower, especially naval power,

[36] Paul M. Kennedy, *The Rise and Fall of British Naval Mastery* (New York, 1976), ch. 7.

[37] Alfred Thayer Mahan, *The Influence of Sea Power upon History, 1660–1783*, repr. of 1890 edn. (London, 1965), 'Introductory' and ch. 1.

[38] Halford J. Mackinder, *Democratic Ideals and Reality* (New York, 1962).

[39] The period of maritime supremacy which in 1904 Mackinder dated approximately to the span of years beween 1500 and 'soon after the year 1900': ibid. 241.

[40] John B. Hattendorf (ed.), *The Influence of History on Mahan: The Proceedings of a Conference Marking the Centenary of Alfred Thayer Mahan's 'The Influence of Sea Power upon History, 1660–1783'* (Newport, RI, 1991), and James Goldrick and John B. Hattendorf (eds.), *Mahan Is Not Enough: The Proceedings of a Conference on the Works of Sir Julian Corbett and Admiral Sir Herbert Richmond* (Newport, RI, 1993), provide empathetic, yet

certainly does not enjoy today the kind of unique prominence in public strategic and political symbolic regard that it did a century ago. Nonetheless, even though the growing complexity of the grammar of strategy requires modern seapower to compete for attention with weapons of mass destruction, with very smart weapons deliverable by airpower, and with information warfare, it has proved more than equal to the challenge. If great navies, in particular the greatest of navies, lost strategic significance relative to the other services as the twentieth century advanced—a debatable proposition, at best—still they reached century's end with the stamp of strategic indispensability upon them. The predictions of a century ago that seapowers would be overwhelmed by landpowers have been shown to be as unfounded as were the predictions in mid-century to the effect that airpower in general, and atomic-armed air (and missile) power in particular, must consign military seapower to the column of yesterday's instrument of war.

It is of the essence of seapower to function as a great enabling instrument of strategy, to be adaptable to evolving technological and tactical conditions, and to function at all levels of conflict with enormous flexibility.[41] Seapower is no longer *the* enabling instrument that once it was prior to the development of airpower; indeed, modern seapower both incorporates, and itself is enabled to operate by, airpower. Nonetheless, the significance of seapower for modern strategy is well captured in parallel claims made by Admiral Sir Herbert Richmond and by historian Correlli Barnett. Richmond writes of World War II that although '[s]ea power did not win the war itself: it enabled the war to be won'.[42] Barnett offers the judgement that '[f]or the Western Allies, therefore, seapower remained as ever the midwife of victory on land'.[43] Generically similar, if weaker, claims can be advanced for the strategic enabling contributions of seapower towards the Western victories of 1918 and 1989. In the two world wars and the Cold War the Western Allies functioned as a maritime alliance, which is to say that the principal lines of communication among allies were maritime rather than continental.

Seapower in all its forms, military and civilian, played critical strategic enabling roles in the years 1914–18, 1939–45, and, for NATO and the defence of Japan and other East Asian friends and allies of the West, from 1949 until 1989.[44] From 1940 until 1944 for war in Europe, and necessarily for the whole of the Pacific War, the

---

not uncritical, commentaries. Donald M. Schurman, *Julian S. Corbett, 1854–1922: Historian of British Maritime Policy from Drake to Jellicoe* (London, 1981), and Barry D. Hunt, *Sailor-Scholar: Admiral Sir Herbert Richmond, 1871–1946* (Waterloo, Ont., 1982), are the standard biographies.

[41] Herbert Richmond, *Statesmen and Sea Power* (Oxford, 1946); S. W. Roskill, *The Strategy of Sea Power* (London, 1962); Gray, *Leverage of Sea Power*.

[42] Richmond, *Statesmen and Sea Power*, 336.

[43] Barnett, *Engage the Enemy More Closely*, 838.

[44] The maritime contribution to the successive defeats of Germany is well documented and relatively uncontentious. Not so the maritime contribution to the defeat of the USSR in the Cold War. A strategic appraisal of the US Navy in the Cold War is Colin S. Gray, 'Sea Power for Containment: The U.S. Navy In The Cold War', in Keith Neilson and Elizabeth Jane Errington (eds.), *Navies and Global Defense: Theories And Strategy* (Westport, Conn., 1995), 181–207.

Western Allies were obliged by geostrategic circumstances to adopt a maritime strategy in the strictest of the senses conveyed by Corbett. He wrote: 'By maritime strategy we mean the principles which govern a war in which the sea is a substantial factor.'[45] The expulsion of the BEF from the Continent in May–June 1940 meant that the eventual Allied return to the European land war could be achieved only by amphibious operations on the grandest of scales. The years 1943 and 1944 witnessed the exercise of an amphibious maritime strategy with a vengeance indeed.[46]

The operational and strategic contexts of World War I and the Cold War were radically different for the Western Allies from the circumstances of 1940–4. In both 1914–18 and 1947–89, Western-Allied seapower sustained, enabled perhaps, respectively an extant or a potential fighting front on land. Neither in World War I nor in the Cold War was amphibious strategy ever a major enterprise, let alone the main event. Military planners during the Cold War were generally unimpressed by the operational practicability of amphibious action in the face of nuclear threat. In addition, deep generic uncertainties pervaded maritime operations in the context of a World War III. Had Soviet forces well on the road to Calais after only three or four days of fighting triggered a nuclear response by NATO, and had that nuclear response tripped the switches for a general nuclear 'exchange', it is difficult to understand how seapower could have played its traditional strategic enabling role.

The adaptability characteristic at least of a well-funded navy helps explain why seapower broadly, and navies narrowly, have not been eclipsed in tactical, operational, strategic, or political relevance by the 'widening gyre' that is the grammar of modern strategy. Navies responded to each of the more significant military developments of the twentieth century with a strategy of cooption. Far from threatening the strategic integrity of seapower, or navies, the emergence of airpower, the maturing of the nuclear revolution, the arrival of spacepower, and most recently the proclaimed dawning of the Tofflers' 'third wave' of warfare (information war and information-led war)[47] have been exploited so that powerful navies can become still more powerful. In modern strategy thus far, at least, the ever-changing grammar of war has yet to sound the death knell either for navies writ large or for surface naval vessels as major combatants. Small, or technically or tactically inferior, fleets find it more and more difficult to operate at sea in the face of the instruments for oceanic surveillance and transparency owned by the

---

[45] Corbett, *Some Principles of Maritime Strategy*, 15.

[46] Amphibious operations today are just one category of power projection from the sea. See Merrill L. Bartlett (ed.), *Assault from the Sea: Essays on the History of Amphibious Warfare* (Annapolis, Md., 1983); M. H. H. Evans, *Amphibious Operations: The Projection of Sea Power Ashore* (London, 1990); Geoffrey Till, Theo Farrell, and M. J. Grove, *Amphibious Operations*, Occasional Paper 31 (Camberley, 1997); Colin S. Gray, 'Amphibious Operations', in Richard Holmes (ed.), *The Oxford Companion to Military History*, forthcoming.

[47] Alvin Toffler, *The Third Wave* (New York, 1980); id. and Heidi Toffler, *War and Anti-War: Survival at the Dawn of the 21st Century* (Boston, 1993).

leading navies. That condition of operational disadvantage, however, in principle is long familiar.

The flexibility of seapower derives from the facts that the world's land area is essentially insular in geostrategic character (and much of that land area is penetrated by navigable rivers), 71 per cent of the surface of the earth is water, a significant percentage of the world's population lives within 200 kilometres of the sea, and naval power can loiter with variable menace for long periods without intruding into geography owned by friends or potential foes.[48] For the swift obliteration of a roguish foe and its neighbourhood, it would be difficult to improve upon employment of nuclear-armed ICBMs. For the precise and rapid bombardment of an enemy there is no plausible alternative to air, or air-breathing missile, strikes. But for evidence of resolve that translates into the operational ability to loiter for a long time in the region of interest without leaving one's sovereign bases, and to project power of all kinds across the shore (from raiding parties to nuclear strikes), balanced naval power is the military instrument of first choice. A navy can provide the presence that expresses national concern without necessarily threatening a potential adversary. The reason why naval power is so preferred is because it offers prudent policymakers optimum flexibility.

Some of the advantages of seapower also can be viewed as limitations, or indeed are strictly chimerical for many second-class navies. Notwithstanding the occasional feasibility of cunning stratagems and devilish devices that can offset brute superiority, the sea, in common with the air and earth orbit, is unforgiving of weakness. The substantially uniform aspects to those geographical environments deny the second-class navy, air force, or space force anywhere in which to hide with confidence. There can be no fortifiable refuges at sea (though the undersea realm is something of a sanctuary), in the air, or in space which are at all analogous to the defensibility of city rubble, triple-cover jungle, or mountains. The tactical value of humanly altered and natural terrain varies with technology and political context, but overall it continues to offer assistance to those who are at a disadvantage in open and regular land warfare.

Clausewitz insisted plausibly that 'defence is the stronger form of waging war' *on land*.[49] At sea, as Mahan noted in contrast, the offence has a systemic advantage.[50] On land, the side on the tactical offensive has to expose itself as it moves, while the tactical defensive can prepare the ground and remain more or less under cover. At sea, in the air, and in space, the reality of strategy's grammar is that both tactical offence and defence must expose themselves.

[48] Edward N. Luttwak, *The Political Uses of Sea Power*, Studies in International Affairs 23 (Washington, DC, 1974); Ken Booth, *Navies and Foreign Policy* (London, 1977); James Cable, *Gunboat Diplomacy, 1919–1991* (London, 1994); id., *The Political Influence of Naval Force in History* (London, 1998).

[49] Clausewitz, *On War*, 359.

[50] Alfred Thayer Mahan, *Retrospect and Prospect: Studies in International Relations, Naval and Political* (London, 1902), 151–69; id., *Naval Strategy, Compared and Contrasted with the Principles and Practice of Military Operations on Land*, repr. of 1911 edn. (Boston, 1919), 150, 153, 433.

Seapower offers the inherent advantages of adaptability, flexibility, and mobility on, under, and over the environment that covers most of the surface of the earth and which surrounds the continental islands. If seapower characteristically continues to be a (though no longer *the*) great strategic enabler, that quality is a limitation as well as a source of advantage. Except for those rare strategic contexts wherein war at sea, relatively small-scale power projection across the shore, or coercive diplomacy by naval means alone can generate adequate strategic effect for war termination, seapower can be only an enabler.[51] It is a limitation of seapower that it cannot come to grips with great continental power with a realistic prospect of success. Strategic history has registered several notable contexts of stalemate between 'the whale and the elephant' (or 'the tiger and the shark').[52] Superior seapower enables some other kind of (military) power to win a war. Britain's Royal Navy alone could not defeat Napoleonic France or Wilhelmine or Nazi Germany. Furthermore, that Royal Navy could not even compel the navies of France and Germany to put to sea so that they could be sunk.

In addition to the limitation that seapower, even at its most competent, can usually only enable other military instruments to win wars, it is important to recognize just how slowly seapower generates its strategic effect. It is paradoxical that, although naval battles in modern history have lasted only for hours, the benefits (or the disadvantages) of victory (or defeat) can require years to yield their full crop of strategic consequences. The prudent grammar of strategy for war at sea can oblige both sides to conduct a long campaign; witness the two 'Battles' of the Atlantic waged in this century. However, the mighty significance of the technical vehicle for navies—even though, tactically speaking, the human dimension remains critical[53]—translates as a sovereignty of costs that confines fighting fleets to modest numbers of 'capital' ships.[54] A handful of combat events can thus transform the condition of naval balance. So, although maritime geography is merciless on numerically disadvantaged navies, it also is the case that naval superiority for control of the sea is ever likely to be fragile.[55] After all, in modern times the

[51] Gray, *Leverage of Sea Power*; Cable, *Political Influence of Naval Force in History*.

[52] I explore the challenges of asymmetrical strategies between maritime and continental powers in my *War, Peace, and Victory: Strategy and Statecraft for the Next Century* (New York, 1990), ch. 2; id., *Leverage of Sea Power*, chs. 2 and 3; id., *The Navy in the Post-Cold War World: The Uses and Value of Strategic Sea Power* (University Park, Pa., 1994), chs. 4–6.

[53] Arthur J. Marder, *From the Dreadnought to Scapa Flow: The Royal Navy in the Fisher Era, 1904–1919, v: Victory and Aftermath (January 1918–June 1919)* (London, 1970), 332–3; Wayne P. Hughes, Jr., *Fleet Tactics: Theory and Practice* (Annapolis, Md., 1986), 26–8.

[54] Michael Vlahos, 'A Crack in the Shield: The Capital Ship Concept Under Attack', *Journal of Strategic Studies*, 2 (1979), 47–82. Robert L. O'Connell, *Sacred Vessels The Cult of the Battleship and the Rise of the U.S. Navy* (New York, 1991), is relevant.

[55] The Lanchester 'n-square law' purports to explain mathematically why quantity, rather than quality—within reason, at least—is the key to success in naval combat: F. W. Lanchester, *Aircraft in Warfare: The Dawn of the Fourth Arm* (London, 1916), chs. 5 and 6. Of recent decades the Lanchester principle, which argues for a maximum concentration of quantity of force, has been shown by Americans, and especially Israelis, not to apply to modern airpower: Vallance, *Air Weapon*, 31. A

cutting edge of the combat prowess of the US Navy has resided in no more than ten to fifteen discrete vehicles, the fleet aircraft carriers.

It is not a sensible criticism of seapower to note that it functions strategically only slowly; such, simply, is its strategic nature. Understanding of the grammar of strategy has to include recognition that, for all its advantages in flexibility, adaptability, global mobility, and as a great enabler, seapower is constrained systemically by its dominant need to operate successfully in the maritime environment. In other words, seapower has to earn the right through combat at sea before it can work as a strategic instrument to help decide whether a war will be won. The issue, therefore, has to be allowed to descend from the abstractions of seapower and sea lines of communication, down to the historical specificity of actual navies with ships, aircraft, and other weapon systems (e.g. mines and coastal artillery).[56] As Mahan observed on the fundamentals, 'the sea . . . is the great highway', or 'a wide common', and 'both travel and traffic by water have always been easier and cheaper than by land'.[57] These fundamentals, which remained valid throughout the twentieth century, help explain the strategic advantages of seapower as a flexible, adaptive, and mobile 'enabler'. But is the grammar of strategy for seapower the same for maritime as for continental powers? Do second- and third-class navies sail in the same waters of theory and military practice as do the navies of the first rank in combat prowess? Few are the Anglo-American theorists who have recognized this question as referring to a potentially serious strategic challenge. Two exceptions, writing ninety years apart, are Charles E. Callwell and N. A. M. Rodger. In 1905, Callwell observed:

We [British] with our vast naval resources and noble traditions of the sea, are inclined to regard the noble art of maritime war solely from the point of view of the stronger side. We are prone to forget that when in any set of operations the conditions dictate the adoption of an aggressive attitude to one belligerent, those conditions may dictate the adoption of a Fabian policy [i.e. a policy of evasion and delay] to the other belligerent. It is often forgotten that the destruction of a hostile navy cannot easily be accomplished, even when that navy represents only a relatively speaking feeble fighting force, unless it accepts battle in the open sea.[58]

The difficulty the Royal Navy was to find in bringing German major fleet units to battle in 1914–18, and again in 1939–45, attests to the wisdom in Callwell's

---

commentator has simplified matters thus: 'Crudely put, the n-square law states that the measure of combat power is a force's effectiveness times the square of its numerical size': John W. R. Lepingwell, 'The Laws of Combat? Lanchester Reexamined', *International Security*, 12 (1987), 92. With its elevation in significance of force size over effectiveness, the n-square law is a delight to those who approach combat, indeed war, as an exercise in the exchange of firepower and attritional subtraction of military 'units'. It can be hard to find room for the art of war, or for real strategic experience, in the pure world of the mathematical modelling of conflict.

[56]   Eric J. Grove, *The Future of Sea Power* (Annapolis, Md., 1990), 22.

[57]   Mahan, *Influence of Sea Power upon History, 1660–1783*, 25.

[58]   Charles E. Callwell, *Military Operations and Maritime Preponderance: Their Relations and Interdependence*, ed. Colin S. Gray, repr. of 1905 edn. (Annapolis, Md., 1996), 52–3.

cautionary judgement. A much more general variant upon Callwell's theme is recorded by Rodger when he offers the following conclusion upon the naval writings of the twentieth century:

The experience of a century of naval war has taught us many ways in which Mahan's ideas were inadequate and superficial, but it cannot be said that we have today any general explanation of how naval power works and why it is important which can credibly be applied to many different nations and navies (not just the British and the Americans) in the circumstances of the past and the present.[59]

Mahan's ideas (which ideas?) were far from 'superficial' and were to prove no more 'inadequate' than one could reasonably expect of a single theorist. Rodger is right in flagging the absence of a truly general theory of 'naval power . . . which can credibly be applied to many different nations and navies', but it is distinctly possible that he has misunderstood the real problem. It is, after all, in the nature of seapower—let alone naval power, more narrowly—that explanation of its working and strategic effect can constitute only a partial theory of strategy and war. When Corbett advised, 'By maritime strategy we mean the principles which govern a war in which the sea is a substantial factor', he all but invited misunderstanding by his readers. The fact is that great continental powers such as Germany and Russia, notwithstanding the traditional primacy of landpower in their dominant theories of war, have been obliged to find a maritime strategy, even in Corbett's British sense of the concept. From the 1850s until the end of the 1980s, both Russia and Germany waged conflicts in which 'the sea is a substantial factor'. Specifically, Russia's foes in 1854–6, 1904–5, and 1947–89, and Germany's foes in 1914–18 and 1939–45, were countries or coalitions strategically dependent upon the exercise of seapower. Russia and Germany had no strategic need to use the seas as did their essentially maritime opponents, but that is not the point. The point is that Russia and Germany repeatedly had the most pressing need to deny their foes the ability to use the seas at will.

The quest for a theory of naval power that, following Rodger, accommodates the different circumstances among navies of varying purpose, scale, and competence still should probably look no further than to Mahan, Corbett, and the Anglo-American tradition of theory of dominant seapower. Three theoretical points are central. First, 'the function of the fleet in war', to deploy Corbett's famous formula,[60] must always depend upon the general strategy pursued: to repeat, belligerents wage war, not sea war. Second, the significance of the strategic effect of a belligerent's seapower relative to its land, air, space, or cyber power must vary with the details of particular conflicts. Third, war at, and from, the sea is a unity; navies of different levels of military effectiveness are not at liberty to pick the

[59] N. A. M. Rodger, 'Introduction' to Rodger (ed.), *Naval Power in the Twentieth Century* (Annapolis, Md., 1996), p. xx.

[60] Julian S. Corbett, *England in the Seven Years' War: A Study in Combined Strategy*, repr. of 1918 edn. (2 vols., London, 1973), i. 1.

rules of engagement that suit them best while remaining competitive in the maritime sphere. A second-class navy can choose not to risk surface battle, but it cannot so choose and expect to be able to use the seas for positive purposes. Mahan was right. Small, perhaps smaller, navies are of course not only at liberty, they are maximally motivated, to discover and exploit operational, tactical, and technical terms of engagement for the advantageous conduct of asymmetrical war at sea. For example, if the Royal Navy's battlefleet cannot be challenged to trial by combat by the like French or German battlefleets, then the French or German naval authorities will endeavour to defeat the Royal Navy's battlefleet in detail by maritime 'ambush', or will seek to evade its military authority by striking at British trade with the waging of *guerre de course*.[61]

To date, with the interesting and arguable sole exception of the US submarine campaign against the sea lines of communication of imperial Japan,[62] the hunt for ways to evade the Mahanian logic of success in war at sea have not been well rewarded. That logic emphasized the role of the battlefleet to fight for command. If seapower is a great strategically enabling agent for maritime oriented coalitions, then it must follow that the rivals of those coalitions, be they similarly maritime or be they continental in primary focus, have to find ways to disable that otherwise enabling hostile seapower. The efforts at disablement do not have to take maritime form. In common with Alexander the Great, one might disable, indeed annihilate, an enemy's superior seapower by taking its naval bases from the landward side.[63] Alternatively, one might seek to defeat superior seapower politically and strategically. For example, Hitler's Germany sought to defeat superior Anglo(-American) seapower primarily by achieving so extensive and conclusive a range of continental conquest in the East that Britain would judge further conduct of hostilities futile. In addition, Hitler calculated that the defeat of the USSR would so liberate Japan to expand in the Asia-Pacific region that the United States would be distracted from Europe for years to come by that challenge. Bearing in mind the enabling character of seapower, there was indeed strategic reason behind Hitler's move to deprive Britain of a (Soviet) continental sword. Napoleon had entertained the same thought, had let theory be his guide, and had made the same mistake with his crossing of the Niemen and drive on Moscow. In the expansive and over-ambitious words of the Emperor: 'Je veux conquérir la mer par la puissance de terre.'[64]

[61] Gray, *Leverage of Sea Power*, ch. 3.

[62] Clay Blair, Jr., *Silent Victory: The U.S. Submarine War Against Japan* (New York, 1976); Dan van der Vat, *Stealth at Sea: The History of the Submarine* (Boston, 1995). A problem with citing the very successful US submarine campaign against Japan is that this historical case may be held to demonstrate either that the *guerre de course* can succeed against a first-class maritime power or that even such a power can lose a campaign for trade protection if it behaves, as did imperial Japan, with sufficient incompetence.

[63] Richard A. Gabriel and Donald W. Boose, Jr., *The Great Battles of Antiquity: A Strategic and Tactical Guide to Great Battles That Shaped the Development of War* (Westport, Conn., 1994), 256–7.

[64] 'I shall conquer the sea by the power of the land': Napoleon on 6 Dec. 1806, quoted in J. Holland Rose, *Man and the Sea: Stages in Maritime and Human Progress* (Cambridge, 1935), 219.

Mahan advised that seapower was critical to world power, that the core of seapower was the battlefleet, and that offence was the best defence at sea.[65] Modern strategic history has shown that belligerents dominant at sea have consistently been successful in regular forms of major war, and that attempts by disadvantaged navies to evade the problems posed by a superior enemy battlefleet have not succeeded. Mahan's reputation as a theorist was long overdue for the kind of favourable reappraisal effected recently by Jon Sumida. Unlike Corbett, Mahan did not exaggerate the strategic merit in an amphibiously British way in warfare; also unlike Corbett, wisely he saw continuing value in the practice of convoy.[66] Above all else, perhaps, Mahan grasped the point that a belligerent who must control the sea in order to use it — as contrasted with a belligerent who must seek only to deny such control — has to be willing and able to give battle on demand.

Because seapower is only an enabling instrument of strategy, prominent among the conditions for success in its exercise is a conflict of sufficient duration for its working to be strategically effective. There is nothing magically effective about superior seapower for war as a whole, even for a war of long duration. The United States was unchallenged at sea during the war in Vietnam, but the dominance of the US Navy — a navy that truly fused the capabilities of seapower and airpower — did not enable victory to be won. The American war effort on land in Vietnam proved to be beyond help from the sea, no matter how magnificently the sea was commanded. An enemy such as North Vietnam, with a long coastline in a long war, should be notably vulnerable to the strategic effect that seapower can generate. In practice, though, the vital qualification, *ceteris paribus*, intrudes to upset the apparent logic of maritime-friendly geostrategy. For political as well as military reasons, the world's premier navy and marine corps was unable credibly so to menace action across the foe's homeland shore as to oblige North Vietnam to retain its army entirely north of the seventeenth parallel. Countries with long coastlines are not always vulnerable to power projection from the sea, because the details of particular conflicts yield exceptions to general rules. For another example, one to which reference already has been made, Mahan was right, in general, with his claim that the *guerre de course* does not work as an alternative to a quest after sea control via decisive battle.[67] But no general rule can be entirely proof against operational and tactical folly. The imperial Japanese Navy

[65] But Mahan's views, unlike many of the reports of his views, were nuanced and, indeed, not always consistent over a long professional lifetime. The modern defence counsel is Jon Tetsuro Sumida in his *Inventing Grand Strategy and Teaching Command: The Classic Works of Alfred Thayer Mahan Reconsidered* (Washington, DC, 1997).

[66] Grove, 'Introduction', to Corbett, *Some Principles of Maritime Strategy*, p. xxxiv. The 1910s are much more reliably viewed from the strategic perspective of today than they were from the time when Corbett's book went to press in 1911.

[67] But see the discussion of Mahan's view of commerce-raiding in Sumida, *Inventing Grand Strategy*, 45–8, and 149 for references to commerce-raiding in an 'analytical index' of Mahan's writings.

inadvertently did all that it could to ensure the success of the US submarine campaign against its always overstretched merchant marine.

The technical and tactical conditions for war at sea have changed in modern times, but it is less obvious that revolution has attended the course of modern seapower operationally or strategically. That judgement may appear unduly conservative. After all, a century ago navies anticipated the conduct of war at sea with terms of engagement, or the declining of such by the weaker fleet, not radically dissimilar from those of the great war against France. 'Ships of the line', reclassified as battleships or capital ships, would deploy with careful choreography in line ahead to contend for the decision by means of gunnery.[68] This one-dimensional tactical context was increasingly complicated first by the menace of surface torpedo boats, temporally next by the threat of submarine mines, and then by the peril posed by submarines. If there is little surprise that the Battle of Jutland on 31 May 1916 was primarily a brief passage of arms between the great guns of two lines of battleships, with hindsight it is perhaps strange to recollect that as late as 4 June 1942 Admiral Yamamoto intended to use the gunpower of his nine battleships to conclude business with the US Pacific Fleet at Midway.[69]

The detail of sea warfare, the grammar of strategy for war at sea, has manifestly been transformed by the maturing of mine, torpedo, and submarine technologies, by the appearance and development of radio communications, radar, and electronic and counterelectronic warfare, by the development of airpower, by the appearance of missiles for offence and defence, by the arrival, and now apparent departure (for the US if not the Russian fleet) of nuclear armament, by the systematic availability (in times of peace and crisis, at least) of assistance to communicate, navigate, target, and predict the weather from space systems, and, finally, by the exploitation of cyberspace for the conduct of information-led, network-centred warfare at and from the sea. What do those changes mean for the strategic significance of seapower and navies?

The grammar of strategy for sea warfare matters critically, because tactical, technical, or operational misunderstanding of the true terms of contemporary military engagement can be strategically fatal. No matter what the theoretical benefits of superior seapower may be, if that seapower is expended witlessly in tactically hopeless operations of war its strategic leverage will be strictly moot. Having granted the vital importance of military competence in the tactical conditions that obtain, still it must be said that the evolution in those conditions has not translated into a strategic revolution. With the sole exception of nuclear peril, the myriad and synergistic changes in the grammar of strategy as it bears upon seapower have left navies today strategically very much where they were fifty or

---

[68] Andrew Gordon, *The Rules of the Game: Jutland and British Naval Command* (London, 1996).

[69] Paul S. Dull, *A Battle History of the Imperial Japanese Navy (1941–1945)* (Annapolis, Md., 1978), chs. 9–11; H. P. Willmott, *The Barrier and the Javelin: Japanese and Allied Pacific Strategies, February to June 1943* (Annapolis, Md., 1983), pt. 4.

even a hundred years ago. A powerful navy at the beginning of the twenty-first century functions as an enabling instrument of national or coalition strategy. It knits together globally, by means of cost-effectively maritime 'lines' of communication, the resources of allies. It can project military power against and across the shore; and it provides these services flexibly and adaptably.[70] Today, such seapower includes airpower, amphibious striking power, some spacepower, and awesome capability in electronic and counterelectronic warfare. The grammar of strategy for modern seapower, however, for all its often frenetic pace of technical and tactical change, continues to be broadly compatible with ideas on its leverage that require scant amendment for changing eras.

From the ancient strategic geographies of land and sea, the discussion now must expand in scope, with modern war, into the air, space, and cyberspace. The logic of policy and the dimensions of strategy apply equally everywhere. The grammar of that strategy, in all its growing complexity, must not obscure the enduring realities of strategic effect.

[70] Gray, *Leverage of Sea Power*, ch. 10.

Chapter 9

THE GRAMMAR OF STRATEGY, II: ALTITUDE AND ELECTRONS

This text emphasizes the unity of war, defence preparation, and statecraft. None-theless, the grammar of strategy—its doing, that is—occurs on land, at sea, in the air, in outer space, and—an apparent oxymoron—in the placelessness of cyber-space. This chapter elevates the analysis from the surface of the earth into the environments exploited only in this century: air, space, and the electromagnetic spectrum (EMS). Adaptation and cooption yield a significant combined motif for these chapters on the grammar of strategy. The twentieth century registered the addition of the air, space, and EMS mediums to the long traditional mediums of land and sea as venues for man's unpleasantness to man. No environment has been retired militarily on grounds of general obsolescence or irrelevance. Layers of com-plexity and complementarity have been added, but none, to date, has been deleted. If anything, the exploitation of the air, space, and electronic environments have tended to make already powerful armies and navies more potent yet. This chapter explores the military implications of airpower and then proceeds to consider the emergence of spacepower and the contemporary military exploitation of cyber-space within the context of arguments over possible revolutions in military affairs.

This discussion develops the argument that airpower has been cursed by a need felt by air warriors to justify the organizational independence of air forces with reference to a claimed ability to win wars unaided. R. J. Overy may be correct when he suggests about World War II, 'Airpower did not win the war on its own, but it proved to be the critical weakness on the Axis side and the greatest single advan-tage enjoyed by the Allies',[1] but modern strategy and war is inalienably 'joint'. The rise, and further rise, of airpower does not itself represent the story of modern strategy, important though it is. The argument proceeds from an only modest celebration of the strategic effect achievable by airpower, to present an even more modest scale of critical celebration of the trends in strategy's grammar that today, loosely, are identified as the RMA, or RMAs. Several RMAs appear to be under way, one of which is the maturing of airpower. Lawrence Freedman writes eloquently about *The Revolution in Strategic Affairs*, but it is not certain that such a revolution either has been achieved, or even is achievable.[2] This chapter, indeed the whole of

---

[1] R. J. Overy, *Why the Allies Won* (London, 1995), 322–3

[2] Lawrence Freedman, *The Revolution in Strategic Affairs*, Adelphi Paper 318 (London, Apr. 1998), esp. 6–10, 73–8.

this book, does not support the proposition that strategy—or possibly even 'strategic affairs', which is a rather opaque term of art—can be revolutionized. The coming of nuclear weapons warrants description as a revolution in military affairs, certainly a military-technical revolution, but did it rewrite the canon on the nature and function of strategy? I think not.

The analysis below recognizes the permanent significance of information for strategy and war, but the concepts of 'cyberpower' and pure information warfare—as contrasted with information-led warfare with a traditional character of firepower—are judged interesting but overblown as subjects for contemporary ambition and alarm. In contrast, the exploitation of outer space as an environment for the generation of strategic effect is estimated here to have attracted too little ambition and alarm. If an RMA is in the offing today, most probably it lies in the development of space systems and with the early forays into spacepower theory and doctrine.[3]

The argument here exploring airpower, spacepower, and cyberpower addresses all the themes that bind this book together. Under the umbrella of a unified vision of strategic experience, the discussion shows the interplay of ideas with practice, the growing complexity of strategy's grammar, the difficulty of orchestrating a widening gyre of diverse activities, the seductive appeal for dominant-weapon status by airpower—and, one day, spacepower—and a strategic historical narrative that chronicles technical, but not strategic, progress.

WINGS: THE CURSE OF SMUTS

Airpower historian David MacIsaac flew straight and true when he wrote: 'Air power ... has nonetheless [despite its then seventy-five year history of military exploitation: 1911–86] yet to find a clearly defined or unchallenged place in the history of military or strategic theory.' His engine faltered, however, when he proceeded to explain: 'There has been no lack of theorists, but they have had only limited influence in a field where the effects of technology and the deeds of practitioners have from the beginning played greater roles than have ideas.'[4] It is ironic that MacIsaac's judgement as to the leading role of technical development and tactical practice in the grammar of strategy is sound for every geography other than the air. Practice led theories of militarily effective landpower, massively pre-dated Mahan and Corbett's 'discovery' of seapower and maritime strategy, created a lengthy crisis for the theorists of nuclear issues, has yet to catalyse an intellectually compelling theory of spacepower, and has would-be theorists of information warfare scampering to catch up with an ever more networked

---

[3] James E. Oberg, *Space Power Theory* (Washington, DC, 1999) is a signal advance.

[4] David MacIsaac, 'Voices from the Central Blue: The Air Power Theorists', in Peter Paret (ed.), *Makers of Modern Strategy: From Machiavelli to the Nuclear Age* (Princeton, NJ, 1986), 624.

commercial and military environment. The one environment for war for which theorists have been, if anything, well or even overprepared has been the air. Predictions, or visions and prophecy, of aerial warfare appeared at least as early as 1859, with Herman Lang's novel *The Air Battle*. As Michael Paris has demonstrated in a detailed study of the pre-1914 speculative literature, the practice of airpower in World War I was conducted against a historical backcloth rich in theory.[5]

Although it is commonplace to assign shared paternity for the theory of airpower to Marshal of the Royal Air Force Viscount Hugh M. Trenchard, Brigadier General William ('Billy') Mitchell, and General Giulio Douhet—with honourable mentions to F. W. Lanchester and Major Alexander P. de Seversky (and H. G. Wells)[6]—former Boer general, later British imperial statesman, Field Marshal Jan Christian Smuts has proved more influential than any of them. In a report dated 17 August 1917, Smuts expressed a particular vision of airpower that had ramifications which are still important for military strategy today. In his *Second Report of the Prime Minister's Committee on Air Organisation and Home Defence Against Air Raids*, Smuts identified what became the organizational ambition of military aviators everywhere: an independent air service bureaucratically equal to the army and navy. Smuts also offered powerful strategic argument, and a bold strategic vision, in justification of his recommendation for the establishment of an independent air service. He explained why 'the position of an air service is quite different from that of the artillery arm'.[7] Unlike Lanchester, Smuts did not envisage an air service developing as the Army's 'fourth arm', in company with infantry, cavalry, and artillery. He argued instead that an

Air Service . . . can be used as an independent means of war operations . . . Unlike artillery, an air fleet can conduct extensive operations far from, and independently of, both Army and Navy. As far as can at present be foreseen there is absolutely no limit to the scale of its future independent war use. And the day may not be far off when aerial operations with their devastation of enemy lands and destruction of industrial and populous centers on a vast scale may become the principal operations of war to which the older forms of military and naval operations may become secondary and subordinate.[8]

---

[5] Michael Paris, *Winged Warfare: The Literature and Theory of Aerial Warfare in Britain, 1859–1917* (Manchester, 1992).

[6] Eugene M. Emme (ed.), *The Impact of Air Power: National Security and World Politics* (Princeton, NJ, 1959), remains a convenient source of 'classic' writings and speeches on airpower. For principal works by the leading theorists, see Hugh M. Trenchard, *Air Power* (London, Dec. 1946); William Mitchell, *Winged Defense: The Development and Possibilities of Modern Air Power, Economic and Military*, repr. of 1925 edn. (New York, 1988); Giulio Douhet, *The Command of the Air*, trans. Dino Ferrari, repr. of 1942 edn. (New York, 1972); F. W. Lanchester, *Aircraft in Warfare: The Dawn of the Fourth Arm* (London, 1916); Alexander P. de Seversky, *Victory through Air Power* (New York, 1942); H. G. Wells, *The War in the Air* (London, 1908). The history of airpower theory (and some practice) is well surveyed in two essay collections: Alfred H. Hurley and Robert C. Ehrhart (eds.), *Air Power and Warfare* (Washington, DC, 1979), and Phillip S. Meilinger (ed.), *The Paths of Heaven: The Evolution of Airpower Theory* (Maxwell AFB, Ala., 1997).

[7] Jan Christian Smuts, '"Magna Carta" of British Air Power', in Emme, *Impact of Air Power*, 35.

[8] Ibid.

Thus it can be seen that the Second Smuts Report, on 1 April 1918, which led directly to the founding of the world's first independent air force, Britain's Royal Air Force (RAF), keyed its strategic case for organizational independence to the promise of independent, which is to say 'strategic', airpower. The logic in Smuts's analysis was apparently coherent in that his assignment was a political response by Lloyd George's coalition government to the public pressure generated by the German bombing of London.[9] The erstwhile Boer general may have had a politically safe pair of hands, but in this case he produced a truly radical solution to an immature set of problems.

This brief historical foray suggests why the independence of air services from armies and navies has rested upon the strategically foolish aspiration for a stand-alone, perhaps fly-alone, ability to win wars. The established authority of armies and navies explains readily enough why a new form of combat, for a hitherto underexploited geography, should require an extraordinary strategic rationale if it is to escape operational confinement to tasks immediately supportive of war by land and sea forces. Nonetheless, readily understandable or not, the legacy of the Second Smuts Report is the notion that the evolving grammar of strategy for air warfare must record progress towards realization of Smuts's vision of airpower as the decisive weapon. Endorsement of this vision has wrought major, and quite gratuitous, political damage upon air services.[10] The vision has had the practical effect of disturbing the total air effort of particular countries, especially Britain and the United States, in favour of the capabilities that attempt independent missions in war according to a service-exclusive theory of victory.

Serendipity works in mysterious ways. It so happened that the independent air service, the RAF, which General Smuts advocated primarily because he saw in offensive air operations an all but independent promise of strategic victory, was to achieve a decisive defensive success in 1940. Counterfactuality can be perilous, but had the British Army entered World War II with a subordinate Royal Flying Corps (RFC), rather than with the RAF as a distinctly uneasy partner, that RFC most probably would have been committed to, and destroyed in, the Flanders campaign of May 1940 to a degree that would have precluded any subsequent air Battle of Britain.[11] The independence of the RAF after 1 April 1918 had less than completely happy consequences for naval aviation, for the development of airpower geared to cooperation with the army, and even for its anticipated potency as a 'strategic'

[9] Barry D. Powers, *Strategy Without Slide-Rule: British Air Strategy, 1914–1939* (London, 1976); C. M. White, *The Gotha Summer: The German Daytime Air Raids on England, May–August 1917* (London, 1986).

[10] Carl H. Builder, *The Icarus Syndrome: The Role of Air Power Theory in the Evolution and Fate of the U.S. Air Force* (New Brunswick, NJ, 1994); Colin S. Gray, *Explorations in Strategy* (Westport, Conn., 1996), ch. 4.

[11] I am indebted for this counterfactual thought to Richard P. Hallion, 'Air Power Past, Present and Future', in Hallion (ed.), *Air Power Confronts an Unstable World* (London, 1997), 7. A dedicated counterfactualist could try to argue that an RFC, as contrasted with RAF, of 1940 would have provided the kind of land war-oriented airpower that might have enabled the Anglo-French armies to defeat the German offensive. It would be hard to convince with such an argument.

deterrent and war-winner with its favoured bomber arm.[12] Nonetheless, it is hard to imagine how a less than fully independent RAF could have been ready enough for the challenge of summer 1940. Just as Britain was fortunate only to lose most of her army's heavy equipment, rather than the army itself, in France, so also it was fortunate only to lose most of the BEF's Air Component and the Advanced Air Striking Force (AASF), and to suffer painful attrition to Fighter Command in the sorties flown from across the Channel. Britain might, instead, have lost the RAF, and especially Fighter Command, itself. As it was, the RAF lost 900 valuable aircraft in six weeks of continental warfare in May–June 1940, and—of much greater moment—it lost 534 pilots (killed, taken prisoner, and wounded). Technically speaking, logistically and operationally, 'it was impossible to operate the bulk of RAF Fighter Command from France' in May 1940;[13] still, it might have been so ordered in desperation. The eventual result could have been a German-dominated Eurasia for decades to come.

The theory of independent, or 'strategic', airpower is not so much wrong as incomplete. There are conflicts wherein action from the air decides the outcome. It is entirely sensible for air services to strive to attain the prowess to generate as much strategic effect as possible and even to warrant ascription as the 'leading edge' of the military machine.[14] 'Leading edge' has two meanings. First it can refer to the military capability that most effectively takes the war to the enemy. Airpower in Desert Storm is a classic example of 'leading edge', or 'key force', military capability. Second, 'leading edge' can refer to the capability that decides the outcome of a conflict, even if that capability is not itself of a combat kind (e.g. ultra intelligence) or is not itself more than a combat adjunct to other combat forces (e.g. typically naval forces enabling land forces to conclude a war on land). Airpower—in common with land-, sea-, space-, and cyberpower—has enduring, and in some respects inherent, limitations upon its effectiveness which new technology cannot offset. Furthermore, no matter how tactically immaculate a condition advanced airpower may attain, the political contexts of some conflicts will assuredly prove deeply resistant to military surgery from the air.

What is the essential character of airpower? The technical story has evolved in detail almost beyond recognition since 17 December 1903, and that detail mat-

[12] Arthur Hezlet, *Aircraft and Sea Power* (New York, 1970); Geoffrey Till, 'Airpower and the Battleship in the 1920's', in Bryan Ranft (ed.), *Technical Change and British Naval Policy, 1860–1939* (London, 1977), 108–22; id., 'Adopting the Aircraft Carrier: The British, American and Japanese Case Studies', in Williamson Murray and Allan R. Millett (eds.), *Military Innovation in the Interwar Period* (Cambridge, 1996), 191–226; R. J. Overy, *The Air War, 1939–1945* (New York, 1981), ch. 1; Malcolm Smith, *British Air Strategy between the Wars* (Oxford, 1985); John Terraine, *A Time for Courage: The Royal Air Force in the European War, 1939–1945* (New York, 1985), pt. 1; Williamson Murray, 'The Influence of Pre-War Anglo-American Doctrine on the Air Campaigns of the Second World War', in Horst Boog (ed.), *The Conduct of the Air War in the Second World War* (New York, 1992), 235–53.

[13] Terraine, *Time for Courage*, 162.

[14] For an antipodean example, see P. J. Criss and D. J. Schubert, *The Leading Edge: Air Power in Australia's Unique Environment*, Canberra Papers on Strategy and Defence 62 (Canberra, 1990).

tered for the grammar of strategy in almost every twentieth-century conflict.[15] Theorists of airpower have been apt to make the same error as do theorists of arms control: while under the influence of an intellectually intoxicating doctrine they confuse aspiration with achievement. When contrasted with the constraining conditions imposed upon land and naval forces by the multidimensional friction characteristic of their geographies, the promise in airpower can seem exciting, not to say limitless. Even when special pleading by air forces for airpower is not the problem, there are systemic reasons why fair-minded people can easily misunderstand the subject. Because aircraft overfly land and sea, airpower can seem to transcend, and bear the promise to replace, both landpower and seapower. Moreover, the ubiquity of the overhead flank that is the air environment means that airpower, unlike seapower, cannot justly be regarded as having necessarily only an 'enabling' character and role *vis-à-vis* landpower. Seapower cannot grip an enemy in his homeland to effect the final overthrow. Airpower, however, can strike home, and would appear to compete strategically with landpower for the mission of war termination.

It is of the essence of airpower to offer elevation or altitude for superior observation, global domain for unlimited range and reach, high speed in mission performance, physically unrestricted routing, and extraordinary flexibility in operation.[16] Airpower generates strategic effect primarily by bombardment, which is to say by applying firepower against targets on land and at sea. Airpower writ large is synonymous neither with air forces nor with combat aircraft,[17] but as an instrument of war its tactical promise finds expression in the exercise of choice in targeting. No less a figure than Douhet equated targeting with aerial strategy. He argued with exemplary clarity:

the selection of objectives, the grouping of zones, and determining the order in which they are to be destroyed is the most difficult and delicate task in aerial warfare, constituting what may be defined as aerial strategy. Objectives vary considerably in war, and the choice of them depends chiefly upon the aim sought, whether the command of the air, paralyzing the enemy's army and navy, or shattering the morale of civilians behind the lines. The choice may therefore be guided by a great many considerations—military, political, social, and psychological, depending upon the conditions of the moment.[18]

[15] Alfred Gollin, *No Longer an Island: Britain and the Wright Brothers, 1902–1909* (London, 1984). Although there are first-class studies of particular generic applications of airpower (e.g. Philip Anthony Towle, *Pilots and Rebels: The Use of Aircraft in Unconventional Warfare, 1918–1988*, London, 1989), authoritative holistic treatment of the strategic impact of airpower remains noticeably absent.

[16] Andrew G. B. Vallance, *The Air Weapon: Doctrines of Air Power Strategy and Operational Art* (London, 1996), ch. 3; Philip Towle, 'The Distinctive Characteristic of Air Power', in Andrew Lambert and Arthur C. Williamson (eds.), *The Dynamics of Air Power* (Bracknell, 1996), 3–17; Gray, *Explorations in Strategy*, ch. 4.

[17] Definitions do not necessarily improve with time. In *Winged Defense* (1925), Mitchell writes that '[a]ir power may be defined as the ability to do something in the air' (p. xii). In 1990, Criss and Schubert offer the notably less satisfactory claim that '[a]ir power is the extension of war to the third dimension': *Leading Edge*, 1.

[18] Douhet, *Command of the Air*, 50.

'The choice of enemy targets . . . is the most delicate operation of aerial war-fare',[19] not only for the reasons that Douhet summarized so ably, but also because there is not much else that combat airpower can do. Airpower works offensively by destroying, damaging, or otherwise harassing enemy assets. The immediate and instrumental purposes of a campaign to secure air superiority—let alone air supremacy, or 'command of the air'[20]—are to deny reliable use of the air environment to the enemy, and to earn the right oneself to fly at will. The real purpose of such a campaign is, of course, to use the right to fly that has been earnt by aerial combat in order to affect the whole course of a war. Airpower has many forms, and functions in many roles, but most typically the principal character of its intervention in war is as the messenger of destruction from above. When air forces plan for what they anticipate to be their most strategic of contributions to the total war effort, they approach their task as an exercise in bombardment.[21] This prevalent fact is perhaps less grievous a limitation than is the proneness of powerful navies to view success in war at sea as an end in itself. Unwise simplification of war's dynamics though it may be, at least bombardment from altitude in principle can reach the physical sources of an opponent's strength, whereas naval power usually requires some non-maritime transmission to carry its influence into the realm of strategic consequences.

This description of airpower should not be interpreted as criticism. In common with landpower, seapower, spacepower, and cyberpower, airpower has both strengths and limitations that derive from its geographically shaped form. But just as airpower's capabilities are influenced by geography, so also must it always have the detailed strengths and limitations specific to the context of each conflict. French airpower could not sustain the *base aero-terrestre* at Dien Bien Phu in 1954, but US airpower could sustain the isolated Marine Corps base at Khe Sahn in 1968.[22]

Airpower in flight necessarily is geographically impermanent. Aircraft can carry relatively modest payloads of ordnance, are comparatively fragile (when contrasted with fighting platforms on land or at sea, though not when contrasted with space satellites), and are, lethally, hostage to the quality of applied technology and to the skill of air and ground crews. In air as well as sea warfare, enthusiastic amateurs die in short order. The importance of airpower in the total grammar of strategy as it applies to a particular conflict is governed by the details of the specific context. If the war is waged in open desert terrain by regular armed

---

[19] Douhet, *Command of the Air*, 59.

[20] Hallion, 'Air Power Past, Present and Future', 4–5.

[21] Hayward S. Hansell, Jr., *The Air Plan That Defeated Hitler* (New York, 1980); John R. Glock, 'The Evolution of Air Force Targeting', *Airpower Journal*, 8 (1994), 14–28.

[22] Bernard B. Fall, *Hell in a Very Small Place: The Siege of Dien Bien Phu* (New York, 1985), esp. ch. 2; Howard R. Simpson, *Dien Bien Phu: The Epic Battle America Forgot* (Washington, DC, 1994); John Prados and Ray W. Stubbe, *Valley of Decision: The Siege of Khe Sanh* (New York, 1993).

forces, then the side which secures superiority in the air is likely to achieve so significant a military advantage that the enemy will be unable to find offsetting compensation from other military sources. Writing in the context of the Gulf War of 1991, Lawrence Freedman and Efraim Karsh advance the persuasive claim: 'What is beyond doubt is that chronic inferiority in airpower is a strategic liability for which it is almost impossible to compensate *in regular conventional warfare*.'[23]

If seapower has enabled insular landpower to secure the final victory in modern war, then airpower ever more conclusively after the attack on Pearl Harbor on 7 December 1941 has been the most vital enabler for seapower. When the leading navy of the last decade of the twentieth century talked about sea control and projecting power 'from the sea',[24] the 'grammar' of the relevant naval and maritime strategies was a grammar dominated by the menace posed credibly by fixed and rotary wing aviation and cruise missiles. Guns and torpedoes are useful, but the most potent threat posed by the US Navy and Marine Corps resides in their ability to strike from the sky with manned and unmanned aerial vehicles. Airpower and seapower have fused.[25] The tactical, operational, and even strategic relationship between seapower and airpower is so close that to talk of *joint* air–sea, or sea–air, warfare is misleading. Seapower and airpower have become interdependent. This point is clear today, but even in the inherently maritime region of Asia-Pacific in 1944–5 the same point held sway. The US Navy and Marine Corps assaulted the Mariana Islands to acquire bases from which B-29s could bomb the Japanese home islands. What became the symbolically defining battle for the US Marine Corps, the assault on Iwo Jima (and the raising of Old Glory atop Mt Surabachi), was waged strictly for the adjunct purpose of acquiring an emergency recovery base for aircraft returning damaged from the bombardment of Japan.[26]

Airpower, identified ecumenically as anything that flies, can participate in all kinds of conflicts conducted in all kinds of terrains and conditions. Both generic defence and generic criticism of airpower need to be careful that they answer bounded questions in bounded ways. For example, US airpower in its several manifestations did not deliver victory in Vietnam, but it is not true to claim that US airpower failed there. The rules of engagement for US military power, and particularly US airpower, in Vietnam, in the context of the technical conditions

[23] Lawrence Freedman and Efraim Karsh, *The Gulf Conflict, 1990–1991: Diplomacy and War in the New World Order* (Princeton, NJ, 1993), 437 (emphasis added). This claim is as valid for war in the Pacific and in Europe in 1944–5 as it is for the Gulf in 1991.

[24] US Navy and US Marine Corps, . . . *From the Sea: Preparing the Naval Service for the 21st Century* (Washington, DC, 1992).

[25] Hezlet, *Aircraft and Sea Power*; Eric Grove, *The Future of Sea Power* (Annapolis, Md., 1990), 138–45; Tim Benbow, 'Naval Aviation', in Eric Grove and Peter Hore (eds.), *Dimensions of Sea Power: Strategic Choice in the Modern World* (Hull, 1998), 70–86.

[26] Ronald H. Spector, *Eagle Against the Sun: The American War with Japan* (New York, 1985), 493–4; Jeter A. Isely and Philip A. Crowl, *The U.S. Marines and Amphibious War: Its Theory, and Its Practice in the Pacific* (Princeton, NJ, 1951), 432–4.

then obtaining, limited the prospective strategic effectiveness of that airpower.[27] For example, tactically and technically, US airpower lacked the ability to destroy the two extremely well-constructed bridges that funnelled material to the North Vietnamese Army, the Paul Doumer and Thanh Hoa.[28] There was much, much more to the outcome of the war in Vietnam than the US inability to drop those bridges, but this fact of protracted military incapacity had tactical consequences of operational significance.

If we elevate the discussion to the total strategic effect that airpower can achieve, the question arises: when and where can airpower play as a, or the, potentially decisive military instrument? There is merit in George and Meredith Friedmans' argument that there are very few contexts wherein the logic of policy is permissive of a grammar for strategy that includes a strategic air campaign:

Strategic bombardment is viable in a condition of total war, or where the enemy is so weak and isolated that it has no suitable response, as in Iraq. But in a case where the target is neither weak nor isolated, and where total war is something to be avoided, strategic bombardment is not a rational choice. The weakness of strategic bombardment is that, unless it rapidly eliminates the ability of the enemy to respond, it frequently inflicts costs on the bomber greater than the benefits being reaped. It is, therefore, rare to find a case in which the strategic goal is worth the effort of a strategic bombing campaign, or in which a suitably weak and isolated victim can be found. World War II was a case of the former, the Persian Gulf of the latter.[29]

To some degree, certainly, the unprecedented precision with which contemporary airpower can be applied against land and sea targets should draw some of the sting from the Friedmans' strategic contextual caveats. Nonetheless, their argument that it is rare to find a foe both sufficiently weak and isolated and sufficiently demoniacal as to be fit for defeat from the air is important. Indeed, their suggestion that strategic air bombardment enjoys only a narrow domain of political-military relevance is reminiscent of the generically similar thesis advanced by Martin van Creveld with reference to information-led, large-scale

[27] William W. Momyer, *Air Power in Three Wars* (Washington, DC, 1983); Mark Clodfelter, *The Limits of Air Power: The American Bombing of North Vietnam* (New York, 1989); John T. Smith, *Rolling Thunder: The American Strategic Bombing Campaign against North Vietnam, 1964–68* (Walton on Thames, 1994); Robert A. Pape, *Bombing to Win: Air Power and Coercion in War* (Ithaca, NY, 1996); A. J. Bacevich and Brian R. Sullivan (eds.), *The Limits of Technology in Modern War*, forthcoming, chapters on the 1st Air Cavalry Division in the Battle of the Ia Drang Valley (Nov. 1965) and on the air war.

[28] Momyer, *Air Power in Three Wars* 183–8 (esp. the map on 187); A. J. C. Lavelle (ed.), *The Tale of Two Bridges and the Battle for the Skies over North Vietnam* (Maxwell AFB, Ala., 1976). George Friedman and Meredith Friedman, *The Future of War: Power, Technology, and American World Dominance in the 21st Century* (New York, 1996), hold a good argument at risk when they write: 'The entire logistical structure of the North Vietnamese Army and the Viet Cong could have been shattered by destroying two key bridges — the Paul Doumer and the Thanh Hoa — and keeping them from being repaired . . . It was a perfect mission for airpower. It would not be an exaggeration to say that the entire war turned on success of this mission' (233). The Friedmans exaggerate. Nonetheless, these particular bridges were 'bottleneck targets' with an operational level of importance.

[29] Friedman and Friedman, *Future of War*, 232–3.

inter-state conventional combat in the future. On the one hand, van Creveld argues that such combat is becoming so rare as to warrant classification as an endangered species of conflict. On the other, he claims that any country strong enough to risk large-scale war with the information-rich armed forces of the United States would be a country capable of acquiring a nuclear arsenal that would have the effect of politically paralysing all manner of late-model US weaponry.[30] Neither the Friedmans nor van Creveld are entirely persuasive with their somewhat parallel propositions on how particular grammars of strategy are squeezed out of live policy contention, but they both have the great merit of obliging us to consider the strategic relevance of powerful tactical instruments.

Beyond rhapsodies on the themes of global reach, elevation for observation, speed, and flexibility, the strategic world-view of the airperson (or 'air-going people')[31] is very much that of the earth as a dartboard.[32] 'Aerial strategy' reduces to choices in targeting. In worst Jominian fashion, the dartboard of the enemy is assessed by the air strategist as having target sets of definite relative value, a positivistic belief which allows a 'correct' targeting plan 'scientifically' to allocate overwhelming firepower at the 'decisive points'.[33] Moreover, the ghost of the *bête noire* of Sir Arthur Harris, 'panacea targeting', continues to stalk the corridors of the planning cells of air strategists.[34] As Eliot A. Cohen noted:

Air forces normally think of the offensive use of air power in terms of target sets suitable for attack. The history of the offensive use of air power is the history of the quest for key vulnerabilities, for the equivalent of the 'decisive point' in nineteenth-century infantry combat.[35]

This has to mean that intelligence is king. By way of illustration, the effectiveness of the 'strategic' element to the air campaign against Iraq in 1991 was weakened

---

[30] Martin van Creveld, 'New Wars for Old', in *The Economist, The World in 1997* (London, 1996), 91. I admit to some modest, I believe fair, expansion of van Creveld's published argument, based on my interpretation of several of his writings and on views I have heard him express.

[31] Mitchell, *Winged Defense*, 6.

[32] John A. Warden III, 'Employing Air Power in the Twenty-first Century', in Richard H. Shultz, Jr., and Robert L. Pfaltzgraff, Jr. (eds.), *The Future of Air Power in the Aftermath of the Gulf War* (Maxwell AFB, Ala., July 1992), 64–5. Warden argues that the 'centers of gravity—or vulnerabilities' of '[e]very state' 'can be laid out in the form of five concentric circles'. The 'circles', from the bull's-eye ('center circle') outwards, comprise: (1) command; (2) essential production; (3) transportation network; (4) population; (5) fielded military forces. In an article published five years later, Warden refers to the 'Five rings' system, identified as (1) leadership; (2) key production; (3) infrastructure; (4) population; (5) fielded forces: 'Success in Modern War: A Response to Robert Pape's *Bombing to Win*', *Security Studies*, 7 (1997/8), esp. 174–85. See also Glock, 'Evolution of Air Force Targeting'.

[33] David S. Fadok plausibly claims that 'Warden's thoughts are predominantly Jominian': 'John Boyd and John Warden: Airpower's Quest for Strategic Paralysis', in Meilinger, *Paths of Heaven*, 381.

[34] Sir Arthur Harris, commander-in-chief of RAF Bomber Command 1942–5, had no faith in selective targeting, an approach that he ascribed to 'panacea mongers'. Quoted in Charles Webster and Noble Frankland, *The Strategic Air Offensive against Germany, 1939–1945* (4 vols., London, 1961).

[35] Eliot A. Cohen, 'The Meaning and Future of Air Power', *Orbis*, 39 (1995), 195.

by the failure of the campaign's planners and directors to understand how Iraq's state and society actually functioned. The classic example of the central significance of the intelligence dimension to 'aerial strategy' is the frightening level of misunderstanding by Allied planners of the bomber offensive against Nazi Germany. In an outstanding study, Alfred C. Mierzejewski has demonstrated how 'lack of preliminary study [by Britain's Ministry of Economic Warfare] and, in the case of the Americans during the war, due to intellectual conformity, hasty analysis under deadlines set by command authorities, and mirror imaging' successively resulted in gross overestimation, then in gross underestimation, of the German 'potential for economic collapse'.[36] Allied planners did not understand the scope and dynamic functioning of the German problem to which they applied their bombing solutions. Strategic genius should not have been required to appreciate that the German economy ran on coal, not oil, and that that coal fuelled the economy courtesy of its transportation by the Deutsche Reichsbahn, key to which were the rail marshalling yards.[37]

Notwithstanding the 'curse of Smuts' that persists in enticing air people with the vision of, or ambition for, victories to be achieved by independent air action, the strategic history of airpower has been a history of success in the conduct of 'tactical' and 'asymmetric' warfare. In contrast to the Trenchardian and Douhetian vision of victory through bombardment by 'strategic airpower', a vision which today finds doctrinal expression as 'parallel operations' (the 'strike at an enemy state's ability to wage war'),[38] asymmetric operations pit air forces against armies and navies. From the foundations laid in the grand rehearsal of 1914–18, particularly in the offensives and counteroffensives of 1918,[39] the strategic history of the middle decades of the century showed that armies and navies at best could operate only defensively, and then only in permissive geographical conditions, if

---

[36] Alfred C. Mierzejewski, *The Collapse of the German War Economy, 1944–1945: Allied Air Power and the German National Railway* (Chapel Hill, NC, 1988), 180.

[37] The US Strategic Bombing Survey states unequivocally that '[i]n a strictly literal sense it may be said that coal was the basis for the Nazi war economy. Lacking in virtually all other basic raw materials, Germany was much more dependent upon coal than most other industrial countries': *The Effects of Strategic Bombing on the German War Economy* (Washington, DC, 31 Oct. 1945), 90. See also id., *The Effects of Strategic Bombing on German Transportation*, 2nd edn. (Washington, DC, Jan. 1947), esp. chs. 6 and 7.

[38] Jeffery R. Barnett, *Future War: An Assessment of Aerospace Campaigns in 2010* (Maxwell AFB, Ala., Jan. 1996), 8–13; Andrew G. B. Vallance, 'The Changing Nature of Air Warfare', in Hallion, *Air Power Confronts an Unstable World*, p. xix. 'Parallel operations', or the concept of attacking different key target sets in parallel, all but simultaneously, owes much to John Warden's idea of 'hyperwar'. 'The Gulf conflict was also the first example of "hyperwar"—one that capitalizes on high technology, unprecedented accuracy, operational and strategic surprise through stealth, and *the ability to bring all of an enemy's key operational and strategic nodes under near-simultaneous attack*': Warden, 'Employing Air Power in the Twenty-first Century', 79 (emphasis added). Coalition airpower did not and could not enjoy the benefits of 'strategic' surprise in January 1991. Iraq knew that the assault was imminent.

[39] Lee Kennett, *The First Air War, 1914–1918* (New York, 1991), chs. 12 and 13; John H. Morrow, Jr., *The Great War in the Air: Military Aviation from 1919 to 1921* (Washington, DC, 1993), ch. 6.

the enemy enjoyed air superiority or air supremacy.[40] Unsurprisingly, the higher the intensity of the combat, the greater the probable effectiveness of airpower. The enemy who stands and fights is the enemy who can be found and bombarded.

In part because politics is more complex than combat, and in part because there is much more to war than mere bombardment, airpower has been more efficient in breaking or assisting armies and navies than in breaking states and societies. The direct assistance by friendly airpower to armies and navies is as relatively uncontroversial as the strategic value of assault from the air upon the vitals of state and society remains a contested theory.

It is unlikely that technical developments in airpower alone carry the potential to reverse the imbalance in demonstrated effectiveness in 'strategic' and 'asymmetric' warfare. There may or may not be a revolution under way now in the relationship between airpower and land- and seapower. Benjamin S. Lambeth notes correctly in an important article:

Air-power proponents . . . have grown more and more inclined to argue that the ability of modern air-power to affect land warfare has crossed a threshold in which its effects are fundamentally greater than ever before. This development, in their view, has given rise to a paradigm shift in the relationship between air and surface forces which is being resisted by sister services with now—threatened interests to protect.[41]

If one is careful imperially to include space as a component of airpower,[42] to embrace unmanned as well as manned vehicles, and to welcome ballistic as well as air-breathing platforms, then the trend to which Lambeth alludes does indeed appear authoritative. Fairly enough, he refers to airpower's

proven ability to fulfil tasks traditionally performed by other force elements. Most notable among these are its demonstrated capacity to destroy an enemy's fielded army and to achieve declared strategic goals from the outset of fighting. As a result of these new capabilities, air-power now offers the promise of being the determinant factor in an ever-widening variety of circumstances if its future development and evolution are properly planned and underwritten.[43]

This judgement is plausible, but less exciting than it may seem. Certainly, the following purple prose from the pen of an airpower advocate should be read with great caution: 'Rapid developments in aerospace technology now offer a range of options truly vast in their scale and scope. A glittering jeweller's tray of possibilities

---

[40] Richard P. Hallion, *Strike from the Sky: The History of Battlefield Air Attack, 1911–1945* (Washington, DC, 1989); Benjamin Franklin Cooling (ed.), *Case Studies in the Development of Close Air Support* (Washington, DC, 1990); Martin van Creveld, *Air Power and Maneuver Warfare* (Maxwell AFB, Ala., 1994); Thomas Alexander Hughes, *Over Lord: General Pete Quesada and the Triumph of Tactical Air Power in World War II* (New York, 1995); Ian Gooderson, *Air Power at the Battlefront: Allied Close Air Support in Europe, 1943–45* (London, 1998).

[41] Benjamin S. Lambeth, 'The Technology Revolution in Air Warfare', *Survival*, 39 (1997), 65–6.

[42] Benjamin S. Lambeth, 'The Synergy of Air and Space', *Airpower Journal*, 12 (1998), 4–14.

[43] Lambeth, 'Technology Revolution in Air Warfare', 81–2.

lies before airpower planners . . .'[44] So, what is new? For the grammar of strategy it matters that in some kinds of conflicts airpower is becoming so potent relative to land and sea forces that it assumes dominant responsibility for generating the strategic effectiveness required by policy for victory. But the potency of airpower in asymmetrical combat requires both establishment of functional air superiority—including superiority over missile threats—and an enemy on the ground or at sea willing to be located, or at least unable to hide, so that it can be broken from the air. These are not trivial caveats.

Airpower has entered a category of such high potency as a contributor of strategic effectiveness that its negation by those who are air-challenged has to be a consideration of strategically overriding importance. If defeat in the air means defeat in the war, the implications could scarcely be starker for potential foes. However, several asymmetrical answers may solve the problem of air inferiority. Leading candidates include the development of missile-based air defences— missiles are inherently cheaper and more agile than manned aircraft—and to conduct war so that superior enemy airpower is denied the targets that would allow it to play a leading-edge, decisive role. Great armoured offensives in open country definitively have been retired from strategic history, except in conditions of a benign air environment.

It is possible to examine the Instant Thunder air-campaign component of Desert Storm 1991 and draw contrasting conclusions. On the one hand, there is no question that coalition airpower was the leading-edge force among the military instruments employed.[45] Certainly the effective defeat of the Iraqi field army by coalition airpower was a strategic event of some historic significance. On the other hand, it is reasonable to be less impressed with the achievements of coalition airpower, and rather more impressed with the effort and special conditions that shaped, even predetermined, that success. To be successful, coalition airpower first had to defeat Iraq's modern air defence system. That defeat required the employment of special forces and army attack helicopters, the extensive conduct of electronic warfare, the use of Tomahawk cruise missiles and F-117 Nighthawk stealth bombers, and retention of the initiative throughout. The outcome was, as the saying goes, a 'famous victory', but that outcome flattered the potency of airpower and probably obscured the degree to which decision from the sky was enabled by joint and 'combined' partners and by an inadvertently cooperative enemy.[46]

[44] Vallance, 'Changing Nature of Air Warfare', p. xviii.

[45] Richard P. Hallion, *Storm over Iraq: Air Power and the Gulf War* (Washington, DC, 1992); Eliot A. Cohen (director), *Gulf War Air Power Survey* (5 vols., Washington, DC, 1993); Edward Luttwak, 'The Air War', in Alex Danchev and Dan Keohane (eds.), *International Perspectives on the Gulf Conflict, 1990–91* (London, 1994), 224–58; Williamson Murray, *Air War in the Persian Gulf* (Baltimore, 1995).

[46] Anglo-American usage now agrees that 'joint' operations are those conducted by the forces of more than one armed service, while 'combined' operations are those conducted by more than one country. Until quite recently, 'combined' operations in British usage referred to what now are meant

As a new geographically specialized instrument of war, airpower has evolved since 1914 from marginal significance, through periods as important and then indispensable adjuncts (to land and sea forces), into its contemporary zone of leading force *in some wars*.[47] As expressed here, it has been the 'curse of Smuts' for airpower to be saddled with the ambition of functioning as a strategically independent war-winner. It would be a serious misreading of modern strategic history to confuse the maturing of the military exploitation of a new geography for war—in this case, the air—with some inexorable march of the new military instrument from tactical, through operational, to true strategic significance. In short, the story of modern strategy is not usefully to be viewed as the story of the birth, rise, and then triumph of airpower.[48] The tactical and operational grammar of strategy is always changing, and that grammar will differ from conflict to conflict even in the same period.

The discussion of airpower and seapower illustrates the persisting force of the general arguments introduced in Chapter 8 at the beginning of this review of strategy's grammar. Nothing in modern, or prospectively in future, strategy contradicts the aphorism that 'the land matters most'. As a stake of inherent value, or as symbol of status, territory is what human conflict tends to be about. That is not a universal and eternal truth, but it is true enough to warrant respect by theorists of seapower, airpower, spacepower, and cyberpower. The brief but bloody history of airpower illustrates the wisdom in the classical rule that a polity has to earn the right to use a particular geography. Wherever we turn we find that war is a team effort and that, ultimately, polities do not wage war at sea or in the air; rather do they wage *war* writ large. Each geographically specialized military instrument contributes some strategic effect to the ability or will of the enemy to fight on. The concept of strategic effectiveness helps protect strategy against imperial seizure by those who would equate victory at sea, or in the air, or in space, or cyberspace, with victory in war overall.[49] The analysis of airpower is presented here in the context of a grammar of strategy to make the point that, although each military instrument contributes strategic effectiveness according to its strengths and limitations, it should be applied along with the other geographically specialized instruments toward a common goal. Aircraft can be flown from ships, tanks

by 'joint' operations, e.g. Bernard Fergusson, *The Watery Maze: The Story of Combined Operations* (London, 1961). All references in this book to 'joint' or 'combined' operations on warfare have the contemporary agreed Anglo-American meaning. To risk confusion, references to 'combined arms' carry no multinational connotation.

[47] Gray, *Explorations in Strategy*, 102, fig. 5.1.

[48] Beware of such reductionist thoughts as the following: 'As dominant land power characterized a *Pax Romana*, and dominant sea power a *Pax Britannica*, dominant air power is the characteristic of modern America': Hallion, *Storm over Iraq*, 267.

[49] The trouble with such books as de Seversky, *Victory through Air Power*, or James T. Stewart (ed.), *Airpower: The Decisive Force in Korea* (Princeton, NJ, 1957), is that they open the door for the working of Gresham's Law. The hyperbole discredits all arguments advanced in strategic praise of airpower, the reasonable ones included.

and armoured personnel carriers can 'swim', and aerospace planes can enter and leave earth's orbit. Nonetheless, there are limits to our ability to transcend the distinctive geophysics of individual geographical environments. Land, sea, air, space, and—arguably—cyberspace: each sets distinctive conditions, terms of geographical reference (or a stable absence of such, with reference to cyberspace), for the tactical and operational grammar of strategy.

Notwithstanding its inherent ability to outflank from above military operations on land and at sea, airpower is only a team player in the prevention and conduct of war. A general theory of airpower can explain the essential character of aerial vehicles as a military instrument, and that theory must accommodate technical advance. But no general theory of airpower can possibly describe, or reliably prescribe for, the relative significance of airpower in a particular war at a particular time and place. The air revolution, if such it be judged, has permeated and affected all aspects of modern war and strategy. Airpower is organic to armies and navies; it functions in roles more or less directly supportive of soldiers and seamen at the tactical and operational levels of conflict as well as in so-called strategic, or independent, missions.

The air is a distinctive environment in which to fight, though airpower depends heavily upon what we understand, by commonsense definition at least, as landpower, seapower, and spacepower. When an F-15E Strike Eagle teaches some regional 'rogue' the error of its ways, to what degree is the disciplinary violence an expression of airpower? The F-15 will fly from land bases secured by friendly landpower, its fuel and ordnance will have been transported by sea, and the location of its targets and aircraft navigation and weapons guidance could be provided largely by space systems. The air environment is unique, and it imposes its own grammar upon tactical performance, but war has become an interdependent enterprise which the idea of 'jointness' understates noticeably.

It is easy to be dazzled by the technical and military-operational achievements of an airpower that is still in its first century of development. The challenge is to identify what has changed and what has not. With the arguable exceptions of its application in nuclear war and irregular conflict, airpower has transformed the grammar of strategy and war, but it has not transformed those activities in significant ways. This is not to deny that strategy in all its varied forms is 'done' differently as a result of the 'air revolution' of the twentieth century. But strategy remains unchanged in its purpose and function, no matter how many layers of new kinds of military capabilities are added to its grammatical repertoire.

INTO ORBIT: REVOLUTIONS IN MILITARY AFFAIRS (RMAS), SPACE, AND CYBERSPACE

Wisely it is written: 'Nothing becomes so dated as yesterday's tomorrow.'[50] It is difficult to discuss the more contemporary aspects to modern strategy without straying into the zone of prediction. Paradoxically, an author knows more about contemporary than historically distant strategic experience, yet understands it less. The topics raised in this section are all perilously contemporary: RMAs, spacepower, and cyberpower. Neither author nor reader dares trust their understanding of these current matters except within the kind of intellectual framework set for this book. The fact that the issues cited here are those to which we happen to relate most readily does not mean that they are of exceptional strategic significance. Analysis of today's issues must lack depth perception.

WHAT IS GOING ON? RMAS AND ALL THAT

A reviewer of a major post-post-revisionist history of the Cold War observes engagingly, 'Obviously, historians who lack detailed information can still get many of the big issues right, even if they get the small ones wrong.'[51] One should add that even historians and theorists who have access to a mass of detailed information can get many big issues wrong, even if they get a host of the small ones right. For example, historians of the British performance in the First World War, and of US performance in the Cold War, are inclined to get the bigger issues wrong. For Britain, the First World War was a conflict necessary for the prevention of German hegemony in Europe.[52] It was a conflict conducted innovatively at every level, and it was a conflict that was won. Do not take my word for it; the verdict of history was delivered on 11 November 1918. Similarly, the Cold War was a conflict that the United States had to wage if the Soviet Union was to be denied hegemony in Eurasia. Whatever the US errors of omission and commission, its grand strategic performance self-evidently was good enough to be compatible with the comprehensive political rout of the foe in 1989–91.[53] Many, probably most,

[50] Philip E. Agre, 'Yesterday's Tomorrow: The Advance of Law and Order into the Utopian Wilderness of Cyberspace', *Times Literary Supplement*, 3 July 1998, 3.

[51] Timothy Naftali, 'A New Cold War History' (review of John Lewis Gaddis, *We Now Know: Rethinking Cold War History*, 1997), *Survival*, 39 (1997), 155.

[52] I share the opinion expressed in Correlli Barnett, 'The Consequences of the Great War', *RUSI Journal*, 143 (1998), 70–1, that 1918 witnessed 'a victory that was "[h]ard fought and in a just cause"'. See also Brian Bond (ed.), *The First World War and British Military History* (Oxford, 1991); Paddy Griffith (ed.), *British Fighting Methods in the Great War* (London, 1996).

[53] In the opinion of this author, it is much too soon to look for reliable histories of the Soviet-American Cold War. That said, there appears to be some limited merit in the collection of scholarly 'think-piece' essays, Michael Hogan (ed.), *The End of the Cold War: Its Meaning and Implications* (Cambridge, 1992), though I do wonder how in good professional conscience a professor of history (Hogan) could choose such a subtitle, while Peter Schweizer, *Victory: The Reagan Administration's Secret Strategy That Hastened the Collapse of the Soviet Union* (New York, 1994), reads plausibly, and Henry Kissinger, *Diplomacy* (New York, 1994), ch. 30, may well prove quite durable.

theorists and observers of modern strategy are in peril of misunderstanding the significance of spacepower at least on the scale of error on which the First World War and the Cold War are misassessed. The British Army in 1914–18 was not led by 'butchers and bunglers';[54] the Cold War was not a gratuitous exercise in US ideological or commercial hegemonism; and spacepower is neither a lesser, but included, aspect to an alleged information revolution nor an enabling adjunct to airpower.

Spacepower refers to the ability to use space and to deny such use to a foe. In addition, the concept of spacepower, in common with landpower, seapower, and airpower, can be employed simply to refer to space (land, sea, air) capabilities, with no relational implications. Given Clausewitz's wise insistence upon the precept, 'War is thus an act of force to compel our enemy to do our will',[55] and his instrumental approach to strategy, an understanding that spacepower is synonymous with space control is to be preferred.[56] Moreover, because space has been a sanctuary for military activities of many kinds, it is especially appropriate to approach spacepower in a way that reflects the rule of classical strategy that the exploitation of militarily useful geographies is eventually always contested.[57]

RMA, space, and cyberspace are treated together here because spacepower and cyberpower are linked inextricably and rather confusingly in a debate over the grammar of strategy today and for tomorrow. Benjamin S. Lambeth hits the target squarely when he advises: 'Rather than wasting further energy in quarrelling over whether or not a "revolution in military affairs" is upon us, there may be merit in simply acknowledging the appearance of what used to be called, in a different context, strategic superiority.' He does not mince words: 'at bottom, a case can be made that the US has now achieved "strategic superiority" over future opponents without this even having been a conscious policy goal.'[58] Lambeth's near-triumphalism should not be allowed to detract from the plausibility of the claim that the United States has achieved, or simply discovered that it enjoys, a decisive military advantage over most potential enemies in most forms of warfare, symmetrical and asymmetrical. The question of interest, however, is: what is really going on? Among the 'big issues', which truly are the biggest?

[54] John Laffin, *British Butchers and Bunglers of World War One* (Gloucester, 1988).

[55] Carl von Clausewitz, *On War*, trans. Michael Howard and Peter Paret (Princeton, NJ, 1976), 75.

[56] US Space Command, *Long Range Plan* (Peterson AFB, Colo., March 1998), ch. 5; David E. Lupton, *On Space Warfare: A Space Power Doctrine* (Maxwell AFB, Ala., June 1998), ch. 7.

[57] Colin S. Gray, 'Space Is Not a Sanctuary', *Survival*, 25 (1983), 194–204. A contrary view drives Bruce M. DeBlois, 'Space Sanctuary: A Viable National Strategy', *Airpower Journal*, 12 (1998), 41–57. It should be needless to comment that Col. DeBlois's thesis, though well argued and attractice to Americans, contains the small flaw that it denies the authority of strategic experience.

[58] Lambeth, 'Technology Revolution in Air Warfare', 76. Lambeth has a gift for plain speaking. It would be difficult to improve on this: 'Air power is a blunt instrument. It is designed, at bottom, to break things and kill people in the pursuit of clear and realistic policy goals on the ground. If you want to send a message, use Western Union': 'The Uses and Abuses of Air Power', *Wall Street Journal*, 27 July 1995.

The strategic theorist today can identify approximately six choices in broad explanation of what is happening in the prevalent character of conflict. As this discussion makes plain, there is no debate about the meaning and implications of spacepower.[59] Such debate as there might have been was overwhelmed first by a politically more pressing debate over ballistic missile defence,[60] and second by a post-Gulf War syndrome which catalysed debate over the wonders of information, even a reified Information, rather than over the spacepower that collected and communicated much of it. By way of historical analogy, spacepower was sidelined for a focused debate by SDI in the 1980s, and then in the 1990s by an alleged information-led RMA, for many of the same reasons that debate about the performance and promise of airpower in the mid- to late 1940s was overtaken, for a while, by the arrival of the nuclear revolution.[61]

Six alternative schools of thought are shaping the landscape of strategic debate that includes spacepower and cyberpower. The discussion here of RMA is broader than was offered in Chapter 7. The purpose of the previous commentary was to consider the RMA concept for its value as an aid to understanding the course of modern strategic history. The purpose here is to understand what is changing in the grammar of strategy with particular, though not exclusive, reference to space and cyberspace.

The schools of thought analysed below comprise four broad claims for RMAs (Schools 1, 2, 4, and 5), one claim for a significant but not revolutionary advance in military affairs (School 3), and one suggestion that what is under way is really a military revolution (MR), and not just a RMA (School 6).[62] There is, in addition, a noteworthy school of sceptics. Before presenting the six more or less positive schools of thought, it is healthy to display the sceptics' wares.

There is a noisy and growing band of articulate sceptics about the alleged

---

[59] So barren was—indeed, is—the conceptual literature on spacepower that in 1997 US Space Command commissioned a major study to help fill the gap. The product of that study effort is Oberg, *Space Power Theory*.

[60] In the 1980s, military space issues almost invariably were approached with reference to weapons, or support systems, in space for the purpose of BMD. With BMD, and especially the contested and highly controversial SDI, as the inescapable context for military-space debate, it is scarcely surprising that the 1980s was a waste of a decade with regard to theoretical advance for improved understanding of space as an environment for strategic concern. See Ashton B. Carter and David N. Schwartz (eds.), *Ballistic Missile Defense* (Washington, DC, 1984); Keith B. Payne, *Strategic Defense: 'Star Wars' in Perspective* (Lanham, Md., 1986); Edward Reiss, *The Strategic Defense Initiative* (Cambridge, 1992). The political fact that President Ronald Reagan's idealistic vision of an SDI came to be known pejoratively as 'Star Wars' (courtesy of Senator Edward Kennedy) makes plain the popularity of the BMD–space connection. To be fair to some of the critics, it is true that Reagan's vision of missile defence rested initially upon hopes for the feasibility of a space-based, or rapidly space-deployable, X-ray laser BMD weapon that would be fuelled—literally 'pumped'—by a nuclear explosion.

[61] Carl H. Builder, 'Keeping the Strategic Flame', *Joint Force Quarterly*, 14 (1996–7), 79.

[62] Williamson Murray, 'Thinking about Revolutions in Military Affairs', *Joint Force Quarterly*, 16 (1997), 69–76.

information-led RMA.[63] Such scepticism can have both analytical and emotional origins. Even when the reaction to the proposition of a technologically keyed RMA is rooted in personality, at least in personal experience, the acceptable language of dissent is, of course, analytical. One's true position may be to the effect: 'This is not war as I knew it, and know it, and I do not like the idea of an airpower that is increasingly pilotless or of a seapower that leans heavily in favour of arsenal ships that are just floating missile platforms.' As always, there are more and less legitimate forms of dissent. The most acceptable face of scepticism about pure information (I) war and information (I)-led war RMA hypotheses—see the discussion below of Schools 1–3—is an assertion of the complexity of war and defence planning. The broadly sceptical school of thought says that better information is always nice to have, but it cannot translate into a magical military sword. Why not? Because war, or defence, has many dimensions—human, political, economic, ethical, geographical, military operational, and so forth (recall the extensive commentary in Chapter 1)—and an RMA offers improvement, even dramatic improvement, only on one or two of them.[64] As Barry Watts explains in a brilliant reconsideration of Clausewitz's complex concept of friction, the enduring human dimension of war ensures that this RMA will not abolish the fog of war or crisis. 'Human limitations, informational uncertainties, and nonlinearity are not pesky difficulties better technology and engineering can eliminate, but *built-in* or *structural* features of the violent interaction between opposing groups we call war.'[65]

The candidate RMAs, MTRs, and perhaps even an MR, debated of recent years and outlined below, demonstrate in their several ways how different foci direct attention to different dimensions of modern strategy and war. Note also that the contemporary RMA debate has had 'outriders' in prior decades.[66]

This debate can be viewed with advantage in historical-sociological context.[67] A significantly astrategic US defence community does not suddenly reason strategically just because the Soviet Union vanishes and threat analysis requires

---

[63] Unsurprisingly, many of these articulate sceptics are professional historians. A 'flagship' collection of essays sceptical of the *relative* significance of technology in war is Bacevich and Sullivan, *Limits of Technology in Modern War*. The commentators most sceptical of the strategic promise in an information-led RMA typically are not so much distrustful of the RMA concept, as unpersuaded of the potential of technological change *per se*.

[64] Colin S. Gray, 'Fuller's Folly: Technology, Strategic Effectiveness, and the Quest for Dominant Weapons', ibid.

[65] Barry D. Watts, *Clausewitzian Friction and Future War*, McNair Paper 52 (Washington, DC, Oct. 1996), 122 (emphasis original).

[66] John Erickson (ed.), *The Military-Technical Revolution: Its Impact on Strategy and Foreign Policy* (London, 1966); Commission on Integrated Long-Term Strategy, *Discriminate Deterrence* (Washington, DC, 11 Jan. 1988); Eliot A. Cohen, 'A Revolution in Warfare', *Foreign Affairs*, 75 (1996), 39; Freedman, *Revolution in Strategic Affairs*, 19, 22–3.

[67] Colin S. Gray, *The American Revolution in Military Affairs: An Interim Assessment*, Occasional Paper 28 (Camberley, 1997), esp. 5–14; Freedman, *Revolution in Strategic Affairs*, ch. 2.

fundamental thought for the first time in forty years.[68] The people and institutions who in the Cold War were attracted to technological solutions to defence problems have, understandably enough, reappeared in the RMA debate. An American defence community long habituated to seek security through technology naturally enough continues to do so.[69] This weakness is functionally analogous to the proneness of the German General Staff a century ago to pursue security through dexterity at the operational level of war. Germans then, and Americans today, agree in their practical disdain for the messy details of political context.[70]

The RMA debate of the 1900s allowed different factions in the public international debate about security to showcase some of their least attractive features. American devotees of information-led warfare appeared smug and arrogant,[71] while sceptics appeared scarcely more balanced in their dismissal of maximalist claims for the MTR-RMA that was allegedly under way.[72] This is a case when everyone is both right and wrong. On the one hand, the enthusiasts for contemporary RMAs—as pure I-war, as I-led war, as airpower, or as spacepower—are correct, in that many of their technical and tactical claims seem, to this author, broadly sustainable.[73] On the other hand, the sceptics are correct when they point to the limited positive, or even negative, strategic effect of new technologies.[74] The

[68] Carl H. Builder and James A. Dewar, 'A Time for Planning? If Not Now When?', *Parameters*, 24 (1994), 4–15, is very much to the point on the need for transition from the habits of mind and official procedures of an era (of the Cold War) wherein defence 'programming', rather than genuine defence 'planning', was all that was required from year to year, even decade to decade. Planners have to answer the question 'what?'. Programmers only address the question 'how?'.

[69] Colin S. Gray, 'Strategy in the Nuclear Age: The United States, 1945–1991', in Williamson Murray, MacGregor Knox, and Alvin Bernstein (eds.), *The Making of Strategy: Rulers, States, and War* (Cambridge, 1994), 579–613.

[70] I gratefully acknowledge inspiration from Brian Bond, *The Pursuit of Victory: From Napoleon to Saddam Hussein* (Oxford, 1996), esp. 24.

[71] Joseph S. Nye, Jr., and William A. Owens, 'America's Information Edge', *Foreign Affairs*, 75 (1996), 20–36; William J. Perry, 'Defense in an Age of Hope', *Foreign Affairs*, 75 (1996), 64–79.

[72] Because the RMA concept is an essentially contested one, it was easy for critics to pick the RMA-of-choice for massive assault. A characteristically revolutionary version of the RMA, amounting in effect to an information-led MTR, has been advanced by William A. Owens: 'The Emerging System of Systems', US Naval Institute *Proceedings*, 121 (1995), 35–9; id., 'The American Revolution in Military Affairs', *Joint Force Quarterly*, 10 (1995–6), 37–8; id., 'Introduction', to Stuart E. Johnson and Martin C. Libicki (eds.), *Dominant Battlespace Knowledge*, 2nd edn. (Washington, DC, Apr. 1996), 1–14. Strongly worded criticism of the 'Owens variant' of the RMA include A. J. Bacevich, 'Preserving the Well-Bred Horse', *National Interest*, 37 (1994), 43–9; Warren Caldwell, Jr., 'Promises, Promises', US Naval Institute *Proceedings*, 122 (1996), 54–7; Peter Emmett, 'Information Mania: A New Manifestation of Gulf War Syndrome', *RUSI Journal*, 141 (1996), 19–26; Williamson Murray, 'Does Military Culture Matter?', *Orbis*, 43 (1999), esp. 37–40; id., 'Clausewitz Out, Computers In: Military Culture and Technological Hubris', *National Interest*, 48 (1997), 57–64; Brian R. Sullivan, 'The Future Nature of Conflict: A Critique of "The American Revolution in Military Affairs" in the Era of Jointery', *Defense Analysis*, 14 (1998), 91–100; Michael O'Hanlon, 'Can High Technology Bring U.S. Troops Home?', *Foreign Policy*, 113 (1998–9), 72–86; Paul K. Van Riper and F. G. Hoffman, 'Pursuing the Real Revolution in Military Affairs: Exploiting Knowledge-Based Warfare', *National Security Studies Quarterly*, 4 (1998), 1–19.

[73] A point developed in Gray, *American Revolution in Military Affairs*.

[74] Freedman, *Revolution in Strategic Affairs*.

problem, and the answer, lies in the thesis developed in Chapter 1. Strategy has many dimensions. Possible 'revolutions' focused on particular technologies and geographical environments will certainly make a strategic difference. But strategy and war are composed of sufficient different dimensions as to render improbable claims for reliable strategic advantage keyed to just one or even several of them. A contemporary illustration makes the point.

American policymakers and strategic theorists today are advancing the historically extraordinary claim to the effect that the United States can defeat any adversary—or coalition of adversaries—in any geographical environment. In the words of the US Secretary of Defense:

The security environment between now and 2015 will also likely be marked by the absence of a global peer competitor able to challenge the United States militarily around the world as the Soviet Union did during the Cold War. Furthermore, it is likely that no regional power or coalition will amass sufficient conventional military strength in the next 10 to 15 years to defeat U.S. and allied forces, once the full military potential of the United States and its coalition partners are mobilized and deployed to the region of conflict. The United States is the world's only superpower today, and it is expected to remain so through at least 2015.[75]

To find a plausible precedent for official US confidence in its all-environments strategic superiority, one would need to look back to the Roman Empire of the second century AD.[76] The principal strategic problem for the hegemonic United States of today is not that its information-led military capabilities cannot dominate any foe in any kind of battlespace. The problem, rather, is that the political, social, ethical, and cultural dimensions of strategy are wont to attenuate the desired strategic effect. As an instrument of strategic coercion, the contemporary US armed forces are hostage not so much to their own technical-tactical limitations as to political, social, ethical, and cultural contexts that are not very permissive of the exercise of strategic coercion by the superpower.[77]

School 1: Cyberwar, or Strategic Information Warfare

Without condemning bombs and bullets to the dustbin of history, there is a growing, dedicated band of cyberwarriors who predict that we will have to fight for the control of cyberspace: with cyberspace defined as 'the global information infrastructure', or, if one prefers, as 'the sum of the globe's communication links and

---

[75] William S. Cohen (Secretary of Defense), *Annual Report to the President and the Congress* (Washington, DC, 1998), 3.

[76] Edward N. Luttwak, *The Grand Strategy of the Roman Empire: From the First Century A.D. to the Third* (Baltimore, 1976); Yann Le Bohec, *The Imperial Roman Army* (New York, 1994).

[77] Lawrence Freedman (ed.), *Strategic Coercion: Concepts and Cases* (Oxford, 1998). See also Thomas C. Schelling, *Arms and Influence* (New Haven, Conn., 1966); Alexander L. George and William E. Simons (eds.), *The Limits of Coercive Diplomacy* (Boulder, Colo., 1994); Stephen J. Cimbala, *Coercive Military Strategy* (College Station, Tex., 1998).

computational nodes'.[78] Although the conduct of non-violent political warfare is as old as strategy itself, the idea of waging non-violent cyberwar against the information infrastructure of an enemy's state and society is certainly novel.[79] It should be needless to add that the principal citizens in 'byte city' are going to be G-8 people, and that the bad news aspect to the good news of our cyberpower is that we are the ones who are most cyber-vulnerable.[80] It is as well to ponder the implications of the following caveat suggested by Lawrence Freedman: 'Even if a successful strategic information campaign could be designed and mounted, there could be no guarantee that a victim would respond in kind, rather than with whatever means happened to be available.'[81] Such caveats aside, the growing importance of computers for almost all military activities guarantees that cyber-space must be a field for (electronic) warfare, while the machines and operations for information warfare are also bound to attract some crude, old-fashioned physical assaults.

School 2: Information-Led Warfare: The Radical Vision

Complementary to the true cyberwarriors who would wage bloodless electronic combat are those who favour the eventual comprehensive restructuring of the armed forces to reflect the (allegedly) new centrality of high-quality information.[82] The 'bombs and bullets' version of I-war does not ask: 'What can better informa-tion do for the armed forces?' Instead, the question takes the form: 'What char-acter of armed forces best fits the mould of a country that can enjoy the benefits of dominant battlespace knowledge?' This can be a difficult leap of the imagin-ation to effect, even a dangerous one, but if the centre of one's military universe is not the army, navy, or air force of today, but is instead a reliable supply of informa-tion about friendly and enemy forces, and, as targets, the enemy's 'networks', the question then focuses upon how best to exploit a condition of information dom-inance.[83] The radical vision of information-led warfare could have traumatic impact upon patterns in defence expenditure. Investment strategy to implement a radical vision of this RMA would emphasize advanced conventional munitions, multi-spectral active and passive sensors—especially on space systems and on unmanned aerial vehicles (UAVs)—long-range, and preferably low-observable, delivery platforms, internetted digital communications, data management and

---

[78] Roger C. Molander, Andrew S. Riddile and Peter A. Wilson, *Strategic Information Warfare: A New Face of War*, MR-661-OSD (Santa Monica, Calif., 1996), 1; Martin C. Libicki, 'The Emerging Primacy of Infor-mation', *Orbis*, 40 (1996), 261.

[79] Paul A. Smith, Jr., *On Political War* (Washington, DC, 1989).

[80] Michael Vlahos, 'The War after Byte City', *Washington Quarterly*, 20 (1997), 41–72.

[81] Freedman, *Revolution in Strategic Affairs*, 57.

[82] Owens, 'Emerging System of Systems'; Martin C. Libicki, *The Mesh and the Net: Speculations on Armed Conflict in a Time of Free Silicon* (Washington, DC, Aug. 1995); Johnson and Libicki, *Dominant Battlespace Knowledge*.

[83] John Arquilla and David Ronfeldt, 'Cyberwar Is Coming!', *Comparative Strategy*, 12 (1993), 141–65; id., *The Advent of Netwar*, MR-789-OSD (Santa Monica, Calif., 1996). See also Arquilla, 'The Strategic Implications of Information Dominance', *Strategic Review*, 22 (1994), 24–30.

visual display systems, and just-in-time (JIT) 'on-call' logistics.[84] Needless to add, perhaps, the bolder the investment strategy, the greater the risks run. Obviously, there could be much regret should the strategic experience of the next few decades demonstrate that the radical vision of the RMA was flawed. Every military revolution comes with costs as well as benefits, with new vulnerabilities as well as new sources of leverage.

School 3: Information-Led Warfare: The Digital Overlay

It is probably the majority position today to endorse the vision of a future that is much like today, only more so. The sunk costs in existing systems and approaches, in the context of recognition of the technical and political uncertainties about future conflict, not to mention conservative habits of mind and some emotional attachments, all argue for making haste slowly.[85] Military history shows that several RMAs may coexist, albeit uneasily, that armed forces are likely to have to wage different kinds of conflicts in the same period, and that large mistakes in the design and equipment of forces can prove exceedingly expensive. Unfortunately, perhaps, this approach—which amounts to the position that the truth lies somewhere in the middle—may not be as safe as it appears. It is not that difficult to sound responsible and wise when one adheres to what might be called a measured scepticism, but sometimes the truth lies at one or the other end of the spectrum. For example, in the late 1940s it was not unreasonable to predict that the next great war would resemble World War II, only with an atomic overlay that would not yield decisive results.[86] That vision, though probably accurate at the time, and despite its apparent reasonableness, had the flaw that before long it was wrong. You may decline to buy the military power that you might have bought were it not for the fear that it was the wrong choice to make. The problem is that you risk being on the embarrassing end of a true military-technical shortfall if someone else buys that military power and that power works. The first polity to innovate with new military capabilities risks committing serious errors. But a rival intending to innovate with more caution risks military defeat.[87]

School 4: Airpower Is the Real Revolution

There is a view which holds that the real revolution lies in the full maturity of

[84] Owens, 'System of Systems'; James R. Blaker, Understanding The Revolution in Military Affairs: A Guide to America's 21st Century Defense, Progressive Policy Institute Defense Working Paper 3 (Washington, DC, 1997).

[85] Bacevich, 'Preserving the Well-Bred Horse'.

[86] Marc Trachtenberg, History and Strategy (Princeton, NJ, 1991), ch. 3; Steven T. Ross, American War Plans, 1945–1950 (London, 1996); Samuel R. Williamson, Jr., and Steven L. Rearden, The Origins of U.S. Nuclear Strategy, 1945–1953 (New York, 1993).

[87] Matthew Evangelista, Innovation and the Arms Race: How the United States and the Soviet Union Develop New Military Technologies (Ithaca, NY, 1988); Steven Peter Rosen, Winning the Next War: Innovation and the Modern Military (Ithaca, NY, 1991); Murray and Millett, Military Innovation in the Interwar Period.

airpower. In other words, 'Douhet was right', as discussed earlier.[88] The airpower that this school celebrates tends to be the airpower that has pilots, rather than the distant promise of hypersonic long-range cruise missiles that dispense smart submunitions. Whether or not one chooses to judge the military effectiveness of (US) airpower today so great an improvement over past performance—in World War II, Korea, and Vietnam, for example—as to warrant the label of 'revolution' is a matter of taste. Certainly airpower has demonstrated the all-but-independent ability to decide which side will win conflicts waged in open terrain and in permissively 'regular' ways. Nonetheless, impressive though (US) airpower has become since the days of Linebacker I and II (1972), let alone Rolling Thunder (1965–8),[89] airpower is a candidate RMA that has been 'coming' at least since 1918. This is not to demean airpower's potency in some contexts, but its maturing is a story that has been running for so long that it cannot compete for attention as novelty with other candidate RMAs.

School 5: *Spacepower Is the Real Revolution*
A small but growing body of commentators asserts that the real revolution lies with space systems. Most of the information that fuels the alleged information-led RMA is collected by, or is transmitted via, space vehicles. Of course there are alternative platforms on which sensors can be deployed, but the highest of high 'ground', which is to say outer space, offers dramatically superior performance over rival geographies for most intelligence-gathering missions. If space control is lost, an information-oriented RMA will not work. In the view of this school, even if space systems themselves are not the real revolution, at the very least they constitute the key contributing element. If one loses the war for space, or in space, one loses the war (on land, at sea, and in the air) as a whole.

The arrival of spacepower in strategic history is revolutionary in rather commonsense ways in which some other contemporary trends are not. Although it is important to emphasize the broad complementarity among all the ideas itemized here, one performs a disservice if one understates the innovation that is spacepower. Freedman is persuasive when he writes:

There is a danger in exaggerating both the novelty of the information revolution in military affairs, and in particular the difference that information can make on its own. By itself, it does not energize, destroy, shelter or move forces, though it can provide vital support to all these functions.[90]

Information always has been more or less available, and more or less important in warfare. Armies can fight in ignorance, but they tend to perform better when reliable information is at hand. The emphasis in the US Joint Chiefs of Staff

---

[88] John F. Jones, Jr., 'General Douhet Vindicated: Desert Storm 1991', *Naval War College Review*, 45 (1992), 97–101.
[89] Clodfelter, *Limits of Air Power*; Smith, *Rolling Thunder*.
[90] Freedman, *Revolution in Strategic Affairs*, 50.

document, *Joint Vision 2010*, on 'dominant battlespace awareness' would have appealed strongly to Sun Tzu.[91] The great Chinese military philosopher and the US military establishment today have in common an unwise faith in the attainments and value of 'intelligence' in all its forms. However, unlike the systematic exploitation of space, information is a permanent dimension of war. Decisively effective airpower is also strategically new; but it is nowhere near as new as spacepower. Of the technologically focused RMAs discussed here, spacepower is the most revolutionary. Perhaps too much cyber-excitement, too many debates about BMD, over-interpretation of 'magic-bullet' airpower against Iraq, and an overload of fanciful tomorrows from the realm of science fiction have combined to dull strategic senses. Certainly, in 1971, one visionary commentator had already recognized spacepower as an enabler of an information-led warfare RMA. Francis X. Kane saw that space systems could provide

[r]esponsiveness to decisions based on real-time data from sensors located in space; integrated operation of theater forces using a common grid; intimate awareness of changes in the physical environment; direct access to events occuring around the globe on a real-time basis; and improved effectiveness in weapons delivery resulting from our increased geodetic knowledge.[92]

Spacepower, in common with airpower and information-keyed RMA options, has the characteristics of an MTR. However, following willingly in the steps of those who emphasize how limited can be the efficacy of technological change *per se*, one must note that technology is not itself an effective weapon.[93] For the relevant technologies to fuel a capability worth calling spacepower, there have to be military-cultural, institutional, and doctrinal changes.[94] Spacepower does not equate simply with technical developments, any more than seapower or airpower are the products of technology alone.

School 6: A Revolution in Security, Political, or Strategic Affairs

Finally, a small but influential body of opinion advances the view that a revolution in security affairs is well under way and dwarfs in significance whatever may be the merit in an alleged information-led RMA. This revolution in security affairs is about the authors, sources, and roles of conflict, not merely about the military instrument that is the subject of RMA speculation. The real revolution is in political loyalty and pertains to a crisis of the nation-state, and especially to a crisis in

---

[91] US Joint Chiefs of Staff, 'Joint Vision 2010: America's Military—Preparing for Tomorrow', *Joint Force Quarterly*, 12 (1996), 34–49; Sun Tzu, *The Art of War*, trans. Ralph D. Sawyer (Boulder, Colo., 1994).

[92] Francis X. Kane, 'Space Age Geopolitics', *Orbis*, 14 (1971), 913. I am grateful to John Sheldon of the University of Hull's Centre for Security Studies for bringing this article to my attention.

[93] Bacevich and Sullivan, *Limits of Technology in Modern War*.

[94] Andrew F. Krepinevich, 'Cavalry to Computer: The Pattern of Military Revolution', *National Interest*, 37 (1994), 30–42; Cohen, 'Revolution in Warfare'.

the ability or inability of the state to deliver security.[95] Supposedly, states are failing, or failing to provide the non-military forms of security that increasingly matter to people, world-wide. The wonderful military capabilities that the several technologically focused RMAs might produce will matter little for the problems of economic, environmental, or cultural insecurity.

A variant upon the notion that a revolution in security affairs is under way is the proposition that in their enthusiasm for the military value of electronics, excitement about the apparent operational triumph of the heirs of General 'Billy' Mitchell, and conviction that spacepower is the trend that really sets these years apart, theorists may be missing the trends that matter most. The demise of the USSR, and as a consequence the temporary absence of a great balance-of-power, or an ideological, struggle, do put pentium processors, 'stealthy' materials, and satellites in the strategic shade. Notwithstanding its peril, the somewhat imperial concept of a revolution in strategic affairs, advanced by Lawrence Freedman,[96] may yet achieve leading-edge status as the concept of choice among commentators. The idea has the obvious virtue of reminding people that armed force and war are about much more than technology alone. Indeed, Freedman advises that 'the revolution in strategic affairs is driven less by the pace of technological change than by uncertainties in political conditions'.[97] Strategy is the bridge that should cement military power of all kinds to political purpose. The peril lies in the possibility that the valid idea that the particular sources of strategic effect can be revolutionized may be confused with the invalid suggestion that strategy itself might be altered radically in its function, nature, and relevance.

The still somewhat unfashionable view that space, or spacepower, is the real revolution warrants special respect. Discovery of the linked ideas of RMA, information warfare, and information-led warfare is not a stunning intellectual achievement. After all, regardless of labelling, the character and the conduct of war have been transformed several, probably many, times, even in modern history.[98] It is scarcely a brilliant insight to appreciate the importance of information for statecraft, defence planning, and war itself. Writing nearly 2500 years ago, Sun Tzu was as enthusiastic about the strategic value of information superiority and 'dominant battlespace knowledge' as is the most starry-eyed would-be information-warrior of

---

[95] Martin van Creveld, *The Transformation of War* (New York, 1991); id., 'The Fate of the State', *Parameters*, 26 (1996), 4–18; John Baylis and Steve Smith (eds.), *The Globalization of World Politics: An Introduction to International Relations* (Oxford, 1997); David A. Baldwin, 'The Concept of Security', *Review of International Studies*, 23 (1997), 5–26; Barry Buzan, Ole Waever, and Jaap de Wilde, *Security: A New Framework for Analysis* (Boulder, Colo., 1998).

[96] Freedman, *Revolution in Strategic Affairs*.

[97] Ibid. 76.

[98] Krepinevich, 'Cavalry to Computer'; Murray, 'Thinking about Revolutions in Military Affairs'. See also Clifford J. Rogers (ed.), *The Military Revolution Debate: Readings on the Military Transformation of Early Modern Europe* (Boulder, Colo., 1995).

today.[99] Information has not just become important in war, nor has its importance suddenly been recognized. Similarly, the claims for a revolution in security affairs keyed to challenges to the dominant political form of security community, the state, are less than persuasive. The argument for a revolution in political affairs points simply to yet another shift in geopolitical context, while the case for a revolution in strategic affairs, though potent in careful hands, is still more likely to mislead than it is to enlighten.

Of the schools of thought outlined above, spacepower requires the most attention here, though the schools focused upon the use of information will also be discussed because they can occupy the same theoretical space and may appear to be competitors to a spacepower revolution.

'DELTA-V': THE HIGHEST FLANK

Though dramatized in its human dimension by the heroic role of astronauts, a role highlighted by the Saturn programme of the 1960s which culminated in the flights to the moon and, for the drama truly ready for prime-time television, the epic tale of *Apollo 13*, space activities have tended to be conducted in the shadows. Military space ventures have been inherently adjunct, supportive, and ancillary to the main terrestrial action of modern strategy.[100] Even by military standards, space programmes have been heavily classified.[101] This continuing fact discourages innovative theoretical treatment of spacepower. When, for example, much of what is suspected to be 'owned' by the US National Reconnaissance Office, and tasked by the Central Intelligence Agency, cannot be confirmed by a theorist, it is easy to appreciate the appeal of more accessible fields of strategic theoretical endeavour than space. A problem has been that those who really knew about the evolution of spacepower both were prohibited by law from talking about it, and typically were people with a strong technical tilt that was rarely married to an inclination to venture into broad *strategic* theory.

Spacepower has been approached as science, as science fiction, as engineering, as human drama, as symbol of national or ideological prowess, as an increasingly important adjunct to 'strategic' (nuclear) war-fighting forces, and as a prime source of military information. In fact, spacepower has been approached as almost everything except what it is most truly: the military exploitation of a new geographical medium, a medium that needs to be understood on its own

---

[99] Sun Tzu would be intellectually very much at home with most of the contributors to John Arquilla and David Ronfeldt (eds.), *In Athena's Camp: Preparing for Conflict in the Information Age* (Santa Monica, Calif., 1997).

[100] John M. Collins, *Military Space Forces: The Next 50 Years* (Washington, DC, 1989); Lyn Dutton et al., *Military Space* (London, 1990); Oberg, *Space Power Theory*; Stephen J. Lambakis, *The Future of American Spacepower: A Book of Basic Questions*, forthcoming.

[101] William E. Burrows, *Deep Black: Space Espionage and National Security* (New York, 1986); Jeffrey T. Richelson, *America's Secret Eyes in Space: The U.S. Keyhole Spy Satellite Program* (New York, 1990); Curtis Peebles, *The Corona Project: America's First Spy Satellites* (Annapolis, Md., 1997).

technical, tactical, and operational terms, if it is to produce maximum strategic effectiveness. Although we are now in the sixth decade of a space age that can be dated from the first test flight of a German V-2 rocket in 1942, there is still next to no broad theoretical literature on spacepower.[102]

Most dimensions of national security are explained by too much theory. In the nuclear realm, for the most prominent case, theory eventually—after a slow start—far outstripped evidence and common sense. Theories of sea- and airpower of dubious quality have also flourished. Spacepower suffers from an unusual malady: an acute shortage of space-focused strategic theory and the lack of a binding organizing concept to aid understanding of what it is all about. The situation today is that spacepower—in the sense adapted from 'Billy' Mitchell on airpower of 'anything that reaches orbit'—was subject to huge acceleration (a political 'delta-v' in fact)[103] in the late 1950s and the 1960s as an instrument of Cold War competition. The spacepower that matured in the 1970s and 1980s comprised a set of military 'enabling' capabilities cued preeminently to the putative demands of high policy and of the armed forces most important for the conduct of general nuclear war.[104] Since the 1980s, and especially since the Gulf War of 1991, US spacepower has pragmatically become ever better appreciated as a team player in joint operations of war.[105] New organizations have been created, and some new doctrine has been written, designed to help integrate military spacepower into the warriors' world. Despite all this impressive practical endeavour, however, spacepower itself, and the unique environment in which it functions, remains curiously conceptually underexamined and underdeveloped. One could try to argue that 'spacepower is whatever space systems do', and that as a consequence actual military needs and behaviour will lead along the road to spacepower theory. Alternatively, one might claim that, as the ultimate among machine-dependent

[102] Oberg, Space Power Theory, and Lambakis, Future of American Spacepower, contribute useful steps towards the provision of a theory of spacepower. There is some merit in Lupton, On Space Warfare; Dana J. Johnson, Scott Pace, and C. Bryan Gabbard, Space: Emerging Options for National Power, MR-517 (Santa Monica, Calif., 1998); Robert D. Newberry, Space Doctrine for the Twenty-first Century (Maxwell AFB, Ala., Oct. 1998). Although the needs of policy, strategy, and tactics fuel the writing of theory and doctrine, those needs have a way of sidelining the quest for understanding in favour of identifying definite answers to the problems of the day

[103] 'Delta-v' is the change in acceleration required for orbital manoeuvre. For relatively non-technical explanation, see Dutton et al., Military Space, ch. 3; Alan R. Washburn, 'Orbital Dynamics for the Compleat Idiot', Naval War College Review, 52 (1999), 120–9; Oberg, Space Power Theory, 23–41, app. 1; Everett C. Dolman, 'Geography in the Space Age: An Astropolitical Analysis', Journal of Strategic Studies, 22 (1999), special issue on 'Geopolitics, Geography, and Strategy', forthcoming. For full technical treatment of the relevant astrodynamics, see James R. Wertz and Wiley J. Larson (eds.), Space Mission Analysis and Design (Dordrecht, 1991), esp. chs. 6 and 7; Michael J. Muolo, Space Handbook, ii: An Analyst's Guide, AU-18 (Maxwell AFB, Ala., Dec. 1993), ch. 2.

[104] Lambeth, 'Synergy of Air and Space'.

[105] Thomas S. Moorman, Jr., 'Space: A New Strategic Frontier', in Shultz and Pfaltzgraff, Future of Air Power, 235–49; Howell M. Estes III, 'Space and Joint Space Doctrine', Joint Force Quarterly, 14 (1996–7), 60–3; W. E. Jones, 'Air Power in the Space Age', in Stuart Peach (ed.), Perspectives on Air Power: Air Power in Its Wider Context (London, 1998), 196–218.

strategic instruments, 'spacepower is whatever technology provides'. This author is unpersuaded by those ideas. Instead, I believe that both 'operational pull' from the warrior community of 'shooters' and 'technology push' from the scientists and engineers need to be shaped by a strategic theory of spacepower.

Writing about a synergistic way forward for airpower and spacepower, Benjamin S. Lambeth advises: 'One fail-safe way of helping to ensure that the right choices [options among capabilities for possible acquisition] get made will be to have a disciplined space road map that begins with clear concepts of operations and lets these drive requirements, rather than giving technology the lead.'[106] At century's end a landmark road-map existed in the form of US Space Command's March 1998 *Long Range Plan*. However, much work remains to be done with reference to 'clear concepts of operations' and, especially, to a general grasp of the strategic possibilities and limitations of the space environment.

In book II, chapter 2 of *On War*, Clausewitz rails against scholastic theorizing, but he praises theory as properly understood and employed. He argues that theory is not a direct guide to action, but rather it can educate the mind so that useful order can be imposed upon an apparently disorderly universe.[107] A theory of spacepower should help us recognize errors when they appear, show how one thing relates to another—a point of no small importance given the complexity of war—and separate important issues from the unimportant. In the absence of a body of rigorous strategic theory, appeals to conceptual authority vanish into a void. Spacepower needs to be integrated into the mainstream of strategic thought. Unlike Alfred Thayer Mahan's unduly naval classic, *The Influence of Sea Power upon History, 1660–1783*,[108] works of theory explaining spacepower should explore the interconnectedness, indeed the interdependence, of the different geographical environments. Spacepower is of little interest *per se*. Strategic interest lies in the consequences of its application for deterrence and the conduct of war as a whole, within a context lit by steady recognition of the authority of the principle that the land matters most.

Pending the arrival of a coherent theory of spacepower, one could do worse than reflect upon the meaning of some of Clausewitz's ideas for the future of space-age warfare.[109] A beginning to theory-building for spacepower can be made with the following Clausewitzian ideas:

- War has a grammar, but not a policy logic, of its own.[110] War in space has its

---

[106] Lambeth, 'Synergy of Air and Space', 13.

[107] Clausewitz, *On War*, 578.

[108] Alfred Thayer Mahan, *The Influence of Sea Power upon History, 1660–1783* (Boston, 1890). My criticism of its lack of a truly 'joint' perspective does not contradict the view expressed earlier that Mahan was wiser than most of his critics, with reference both to seapower and to strategic matters more broadly.

[109] Donald R. Baucom, *Clausewitz on Space War: An Essay on the Strategic Aspects of Military Operations in Space*, AU-ARI-CPSS-91-13 (Maxwell AFB, Ala., June 1992), is interesting.

[110] Clausewitz, *On War*, 605.

own distinctive characteristics that policy must know and respect, but such war has meaning only for the purposes of policy.

- Countries have 'centres of gravity' key to their functioning.[111] A country's or coalition's ability to wage war successfully can be negated if those centres of gravity are menaced, damaged, or taken. Space forces can greatly enhance the ability of other kinds of military power to locate, threaten, harass, and destroy such centres.
- War is the realm of chance, uncertainty, and friction; the fog of war blinds the commander.[112] Spacepower assults some of the friction that impairs terrestrial military performance, but is itself subject to the workings of friction.
- War is a unity.[113] Spacepower is an essential team player, probably due to become the team player who adds the greatest value for lethality in combat in the twenty-first century.
- Policymakers and military commanders need to understand what the military instrument can accomplish under particular conditions.[114] The emergence of spacepower adds to the burden of comprehension by military professional and civilian layperson alike.
- As the Just War tradition maintains, there needs to be a unity of character and intensity of political purpose with the scale and kinds of military means: the principle of proportionality.[115] Contemplation of the military implications of a maturing spacepower has to accommodate appreciation of the value to policy of an unprecedentedly discriminate military instrument, without being captured by techno-military fantasies.
- Success in battle flows from the achievement of overwhelming strength at the 'decisive point'.[116] This maxim is as sound for space operations as it is for other kinds of military activity.
- Defence is the stronger form of waging war (on land).[117] In space, defence is probably the stronger form of waging war in high- and medium-earth orbit (HEO and MEO), but probably not in low-earth orbit (LEO). There is some safety in sheer distance (equal to time, provided speed-of-light-directed energy weapons are not relevant).[118]

In piecemeal fashion, many of the elements for a theory of spacepower already have been collected via raids on the existing theories of seapower and airpower. The concept of space control is a direct borrowing, while discussion of blockade

[111] Clausewitz, *On War*, 595–7.
[112] Ibid. 119–21.
[113] Ibid. 607.
[114] Ibid.
[115] Ibid. 88, 579.
[116] Ibid. 204.
[117] Ibid. 359.
[118] HEO extends beyond 35,000 km in altitude; MEO extends from 800 to 35,000 km; LEO extends from 150 to 800 km.

and 'choke points' similarly have naval origins.[119] There is a large literature on space policy, space technology, anti-satellite weapons, space-based weapons for ballistic missile defence (and particularly for what used to be known as the Strategic Defense Initiative, SDI), and arms control for 'strategic stability' in orbit.[120] Effectively, however, there is no body of high-quality writing which attempts to explain in broad terms what spacepower is and how it will work as a pervasive, technologically dynamic influence upon strategic history in ways complementary to land-, sea-, and airpower.

Because of the relative unfamiliarity of strategic theory for spacepower, it is useful if the point of view of this text, especially the most vital assumptions, are made thoroughly explicit.

- In all strategic essentials, spacepower is akin to landpower, seapower, and airpower.
- The strategic history of spacepower is likely to follow the pattern already traced by seapower and airpower.[121]
- Geographically, space is distinctive, but then so is the land, the sea, the air, and even cyberspace.
- People have only one natural environment, the land. To function in any other geography, they require technological support. The vacuum of space

---

[119] Aadu Karemaa, 'What Would Mahan Say about Space Power?', U.S. Naval Institute *Proceedings*, 114 (1998), 48–9; Tom Blow, *Defending against a Space Blockade*, AU-ARI-CP-89-3 (Maxwell AFB, Ala., Dec. 1989). Space has its prospective choke-points, just as do the maritime and land environments. Low earth orbit and geosynchronous orbit (36,000 km) are particularly attractive for, indeed are essential to, many military space missions (though not for navigation, for which semisynchronous polar orbits are most appropriate). There is a specific choke-point for any space launch in that every satellite must pass over the precise antipode of its launch site in the course of its first revolution around the earth, regardless of the shape (i.e. eccentrically elliptical, or circular) or size of its orbit. Therefore, every launch site on Earth has its precisely precalculable antipodal choke-point for the potential interception of satellites. Also, there are the Lagrange points, named after the eighteenth-century mathematician Joseph Lagrange, comprising five locations in space where offsetting (i.e. neutralizing) gravitational fields allow for satellite 'parking' with the expenditure of relatively little energy to maintain station. Three of these points are on a line with the earth and the moon, while the other two are respectively 60° ahead of, and behind, the moon in its orbit. These are not the only possible choke-points relevant to space warfare, but they are the leading candidates. This note has discussed the space equivalents to the Straits of Gibraltar, the Cape of Good Hope, the Malacca Straits, the Cumberland Gap, and the Khyber Pass.

[120] Effectively, this remains a Cold War era literature. Alas, the attitudes of many people towards spacepower were frozen in place by the challenges perceived in those years. Bhuyendra Jasani (ed.), *Space Weapons and International Security* (Oxford, 1987), and Kenneth Luongo and W. Thomas Wander (eds.), *The Search for Security in Space* (Ithaca, NY, 1980), are superior examples of a way of thinking about space that has endured long beyond its sell-by date.

[121] For many decades to come spacepower will continue to be represented very largely by unmanned vehicles in orbit. This means that the tactical handling, or 'doing', of space warfare typically will be performed by people ordering delta-vs from terrestrial command posts. Naval warriors fight at sea, and air warriors fight in the air, but space warriors, with very few exceptions, will not themselves fight in orbit. This quite startling difference between space and the other environments (apart from cyberspace) should have no bearing on my point that the space environment, for all its geophysical distinctiveness, is subject to a strategic logic common to all geographies.

admittedly is exceptionally hostile to human life, but it does not differ basically in character from the sea and the air: all these geographies can tolerate human presence only when that presence is supported by machines.

- Because people live only on the land, and belong to security communities organized politically with territorial domains, military behaviour, no matter what its tactical form, ultimately can have strategic meaning only for the course of events on land. It follows that seapower, airpower, and now space-power function strategically as enabling factors. The outcome of a war may be decided by action at sea, in the air, or in space, but the war must be concluded on land and usually with reference to the land.

- The logic of strategy is geographically universal and temporally eternal. Different strategic cultures may 'do it their way', but only if that way is consistent with the laws of physics, *inter alia* (willpower is only hot air, if the engineering is unsound).

- The unique geography of space must find expression in unique technology, operations, and tactics. That unique geography does not, however, point the way to some unique logic of strategy, let alone a unique irrelevance of strategy.

The development of airpower was accelerated massively by the outbreak of a great war only eleven years after the Wright brothers defeated gravity. With the Cold War over, in the 1990s much of the urgency departed from the debate about spacepower and strategy for war in space. That was understandable, but unfortunate, because the proliferation of missile (including space-launch) prowess around the world,[122] married to an electronic excellence far from confined to the United States, means that the space age of war is surely coming.

Spacepower refers to the ability in peace, crisis, and war to exert prompt and sustained influence in and from space.[123] Just as power in the air is power to use and to deny use of the air, so power in space can be positive and negative. The positive and negative benefits of spacepower are not identical. To be able to use space does not necessarily imply the ability to deny such use to an enemy, while the ability to deny the use of space to an enemy certainly does not mean that *ipso facto* space can be used by friendly forces. Following the elegant example set by Mahan in the first chapter of his *Influence of Sea Power upon History*, one can affirm that spacepower has both 'elements' and 'conditions'. The former constitute its vital constituent parts, the latter the context within which it will flourish or languish. Mahan speculated that trade, colonies, and a fighting navy were the elements most vital to a nation's seapower, while geographical position, physical conformation, extent of territory, number of population, national character, and especially character of the

---

[122] An excellent comprehensive review is Commission to Assess the Ballistic Missile Threat to the United States ('Rumsfeld Commission'), *Executive Summary*, and *Report, app. 3: Unclassified Working Papers* (Washington, DC, 15 July 1998). Donald H. Rumsfeld was chairman of the Commission.

[123] These words are adapted from the definition of landpower in William T. Johnsen, *Redefining Land Power for the 21st Century* (Carlisle Barracks, Pa., 7 May 1998), 6.

government constituted the six most important conditions influencing the growth of that seapower. Analysis of spacepower, following Mahan, has barely begun.[124]

Popular television programmes like *Star Trek* notwithstanding, the concept and reality of spacepower remains generally unfamiliar; for that reason, sea and airpower analogies are useful. Spacepower indeed is different, yet it ought not to be considered any more different from seapower and airpower than these latter concepts are from each other. While respectful of the distinctiveness of each geographical environment, still one must say that spacepower has well begun the process of transforming the terms of war and the grammar of strategy, just as had airpower by the middle decades of the twentieth century. Spacepower will shift the terms of war in most conflicts in ways different from the overall accomplishment of airpower, but a grasp of the latter bequeaths the beginning of understanding of the former. As each great change in strategy's grammar (military revolution, possibly) is layered upon, and pervades, what persists from before, so the older military elements are altered. Spacepower augments the effectiveness of air, sea, and landpower,[125] just as airpower augmented the potency of sea and landpower, and as airpower and seapower worked synergistically and jointly to enable landpower to terminate conflicts with territorially defined foes.

The military effectiveness of armed forces is influenced significantly by distinctive geographies. Technology advances, but the land, sea, air, and now space environments each shape military contributions unique to themselves. The logic of strategy, however, is common to armed forces in all environments. Spacepower has defining characteristics, identified immediately below, but it is not governed by a distinctive strategic logic.

First, space is but the latest variant of the 'high ground' that doctrine often advises military commanders to seize and hold. As with forces on all kinds of high ground, space systems look down on friend and foe and are relatively difficult to reach and grasp. To attack uphill has never been easy; to attack up earth's gravity

---

[124] But Oberg, *Space Power Theory*, ch. 2, makes a useful beginning. Terrestrial geography is highly significant for relative ease or difficulty of national access into orbit. For example, the weight of fuel necessary to be carried at launch in order for a rocket to achieve orbital velocity, and hence the residual weight available for mission-useful 'payload', depends vitally upon the vector of the launch and the latitude of the launch site. A space launch towards the East from the equator benefits to the extent of a 1600-kph momentum imparted by the speed of the Earth's rotation at that latitude, towards the 28,000 kph necessary to attain orbit. Kane, 'Space Age Geopolitics', 929–30; Dolman, 'Geography in the Space Age'.

[125] Lambeth, 'Technology Revolution', 80; id., 'Synergy of Air and Space'. Lambeth shows very well the growing synergy between air and space forces, but at the expense of understating the geographical, and therefore technological, tactical, and operational differences between the air and space environments. The uniqueness of the space environment is emphasized in Bruce M. DeBlois, 'Ascendant Realms: Characteristics of Airpower and Space Power', in Meilinger, *Paths of Heaven*, esp. 570–1. Although DeBlois is not persuasive when he advocates perpetuation of a sanctuary status for space ('Space Sanctuary'), he is convincing on the undesirability of airpower effecting a conceptual and organizational marriage with spacepower. Aerospace power is a geographical impossibility, though militarily interesting analogically with amphibious power.

well would continue that military condition. Second, the high ground of space is both global and of all but infinite military depth. The country or coalition which can operate at will in space is able thereby to operate from the highest of vantage points. And finally, space power, obedient to Keplerian laws of orbital motion, translates as satellites that can be available globally as either a regularly repeating or a constant overhead presence.[126]

For all the uncertainties of the future, there is a possible analogy between 1918-vintage airpower as a harbinger of airpower in 1939–45 and 1991-vintage space-power in Desert Storm, and the use of spacepower in deterrence and war in the future. Analogy is a powerful tool that can, of course, do harm if applied uncritic-ally, or with reference to unsound history. Several significant differences between the cases of airpower and spacepower have to be noted to avoid potential problems.

The development and use of airpower in 1918 was unhindered by legal or cus-tomary regimes organized to serve the concept of stability by disarming the air environment.[127] Military planners in 1916–18 sought to apply the rapidly emerging technical possibilities of airpower in the ways most likely to generate strategic utility. The practical limits were formidable, but those constraints were not sup-plemented by any theory or practice of arms control. Also, it was easier to use the air to practise airpower in 1918 than it is to use earth orbit to practise spacepower today. The air is fundamentally more friendly to humans than is space. Next, there were fewer military alternatives to airpower in 1918 than there are today to space-power.[128] The principal alternative to reconnaissance from the air in 1918 was

[126] Dutton et al., *Military Space*, 13–17; Wertz and Larson, *Space Mission Analysis and Design*, 113–23. Johannes Kepler's three laws of planetary motion comprise the core principles of astrodynamics: his laws also apply to earth satellites. Lightly adapted, the First Law states that the orbit of a satellite forms an ellipse with the centre of the earth at one focus. The Second Law states that as a satellite moves around its orbit, an imaginary line (radius) joining it to the centre of the earth sweeps out equal areas in equal amounts of time. Just as the First Law gives the shape and the inclination (relative to the plane of the equator) of an orbit, so the Second Law describes the speed of a satellite relative to its orbital position at any point in time. Kepler's Third Law, again suitably rephrased, states that the square of the orbital period is proportional to the cube of the semi-major axis. In plainer English, the period (i.e. the length of time a body takes to complete one revolution around the central body) of a satellite is dictated by the size, not the shape, of its orbit. The major axis of an orbit passes through the longer diameter of the ellipse, and the minor axis through the shorter diameter. The semi-major axis is the parameter that equals half the distance of the major axis.

[127] John Robert Ferris, *Men, Money, and Diplomacy: The Evolution of British Strategic Policy, 1919–26* (Ithaca, NY, 1989). On the persistence of official British interest in air disarmament, except in relation to 'imperial policing', of course, see Uri Bialer, *The Shadow of the Bomber: The Fear of Air Attack and British Politics, 1932–1939* (London, 1980). Advocates of air disarmament could not cope with the technical-tactical fact that in order to abolish military aviation, it would be necessary to abolish civil aviation also. J. M. Spaight, *Air Power in the Next War* (London, 1938), ch. 4, 'The Attempt to Strangle Air Power', is a powerful contemporary comment by an airpower advocate, while George H. Quester, *Deterrence before Hiroshima: The Airpower Background of Modern Strategy* (New York, 1966), ch. 5, is characteristically percep-tive and has stood the test of time.

[128] For a range of views on the relative importance of airpower to the course and outcome of the First World War, see Richard P. Hallion, *Rise of the Fighter Aircraft, 1914–1918* (Baltimore, 1988), 149; Kennett, *First Air War*, 217–26; Morrow, *Great War in the Air*, 344.

reconnaissance by the cavalry, typically a non-alternative in the battlespace of the Western Front.[129] Today, manned and unmanned air-breathing vehicles can do just about anything that space vehicles can do, but they often cannot do them as well. The fact that there are alternative, if generally inferior, ways of seeing 'over the hill', providing navigational assistance, and so forth is important to the development of spacepower.

Finally, the entry-level and the sustainment costs of new ventures in airpower were relatively cheaper in 1916–18 than are costs today for new military space enterprises. Nonetheless, the future of airpower was clearly discernible in 1918, as the future of spacepower is discernible today.

In 1918 airpower lacked the unit effectiveness that could enable it, even when employed in great quantity, to achieve decisive results under the governing military conditions of the day for war between great powers. Recall that the lack of strategic success in the war in the West, except eventually by attrition, derived from a lack of operational success attributable to two systemic tactical deficiencies.[130] First, the armies of the period could not be commanded centrally in real time because they lacked tactical radio or other means of reliable communication. Second, contemporary armies lacked the mobility in attack and particularly the mobility in the all-important front-breaker, the artillery, to transform a break-in to an enemy's position into a true breakthrough that could be exploited to operational depth. By 1917–18, the BEF could 'bite and hold', but it lacked the tactical means to exploit rapidly for decisive operational manoeuvre. The airpower of 1918 helped alleviate these deficiencies, but it could not offset them totally.

The future was demonstrated by airpower in 1918. Airpower performed strategic bombing,[131] interdiction campaigns, close ground support, and it fought for air superiority and engaged in maritime reconnaissance and patrol. Airpower also carried supplies to troops advancing in the field, spied behind enemy lines, and carried messages. Above all else, it observed events from the overhead flank. In 1918, airpower did not demonstrate that it could decide who would win a war, but it did demonstrate its potential. Whether or not there were significant operational limitations characteristic to airpower itself, or limitations likely to be exploited by the foes of airpower, remained to be seen.

In 1991, spacepower demonstrated that it could enable combat arms of all kinds

---

[129] Stephen Badsey, 'Cavalry and the Development of Breakthrough Doctrine', in Paddy Griffith (ed.), *British Fighting Methods in the Great War* (London, 1996), 138–74.

[130] John Terraine, *White Heat: The New Warfare, 1914–18* (London, 1982), ch. 5.

[131] Albeit unimpressively by the Independent Air Force (of the RAF). 'The first independent bombing campaign was a failure. In 1919 a bombing survey team arrived in Germany to judge the value of the Independent Force. Its conclusions were largely negative': Richard Overy, *Bomber Command, 1939–1945* (London, 1997), 13. Contemporary German analysis of the past effectiveness of, and future prospects for, 'strategic' bombing were equally negative. James S. Corum, *The Roots of Blitzkrieg: Hans von Seeckt and German Military Reform* (Lawrence, Kan., 1992), 145–6.

to be much more lethal than otherwise would be the case.[132] Spacepower showed that it enhanced the fighting power of all military elements prepared technically, doctrinally, and organizationally to exploit its services. Spacepower did not win, or even decide who would win, the Gulf War; but then airpower did not win, or decide who would win, the Great War in 1918. The uniqueness of each strategic historical context means that the practical operational limitations upon a kind of military power will always be disputable. After all, technological progress and better understanding of how to use new military capabilities properly should enhance the benefits to be derived from those capabilities. Richard P. Hallion is correct in asserting: 'An air force without doctrine is always uncertain about what it is doing and why it is doing it. An air force with outdated doctrine can, in effect, imprison itself, intrinsically limiting its ability to project air power.'[133] Hallion would be no less correct were he to substitute space for air in those sentences.

Spacepower has several limitations. The high cost of transportation into orbit (i.e. launch costs) limits the pace of advance of military, scientific, and commercial space systems. Launch costs have not declined noticeably over the past twenty years. The cost remains in the range $10,000–$30,000 per kilogram of payload (depending upon the launch vehicle used and the orbital parameters required).[134] Next, the laws of orbital motion that govern celestial bodies are a permanent constraint upon the flexibility with which spacepower can be employed; those laws can be overridden to a degree, but only with a virtual attrition in payload imposed by the fuel necessary to achieve some anti-Keplerian agility. The gravitational pulls that command the laws of motion are the equivalent for spacepower of the landforms (maritime defiles) and weather conditions that restrict free passage of ships at sea. The only way to defeat gravity for a while and to change altitude is by a change in velocity of the space vehicle, or 'delta-v'. NASA's Mission Control has developed the 'rule of thumb' for orbital manoeuvres called the '2:1 Rule': a velocity change ('delta-v') of two feet per second produces a change in the far side of the orbit of approximately one nautical mile in altitude above the earth.[135] Predictability 'on orbital station', or predictable orbital passage, is both a blessing and a vulnerability. The orbital task calculated by us to provide the necessary terrestrial support is also calculable by the anti-satellite weapon

[132] Secretary of Defense William J. Perry wrote: 'Space forces are fundamental to modern military operations. They are playing a central role in the ongoing revolution in warfare because of their unique capabilities for gathering, processing, and disseminating information. As demonstrated during the Persian Gulf War of 1991, space systems can directly influence the course and outcome of war. For example, space systems helped confer a decisive advantage upon United States and friendly forces in terms of combat timing, operational tempo, synchronization, maneuver, and the integrated application of fire power. These inherent strengths of space forces will contribute directly to the deterrent effectiveness of U.S. armed forces': *Annual Report to the President and the Congress* (Washington, DC, Feb. 1995), 233.

[133] Hallion, 'Air Power Past, Present and Future', 10.

[134] Oberg, *Space Power Theory*.

[135] Ibid.; Wertz and Larson, *Space Mission Analysis and Design*, 128–35.

systems of the foe. It is in the nature of spacepower to be distant from terrestrial events. Although it is the distance overhead that is militarily beneficial, still distance from earth is an important limitation.

Although limits to the strategic value of spacepower cannot be estimated with confidence, space plainly has the greatest growth potential for military utility among all the geographically distinctive elements of power. The potential marginal return in military and strategic effectiveness to scarce monies expended is higher from investment in space than in the older forms of military power.[136]

Two major classes of constraint upon the evolution of spacepower need emphasis. First, the persisting relatively high costs of space launch and operation encourage development of alternatives to spacepower, as well as technologically radical alternative to rocket motors for access to orbit. In peacetime, at least, cost–benefit analysis in the military field tends to focus more heavily upon the certain financial costs than upon the uncertain benefits to security. Second, the precept that weapons in space should be regarded differently from weapons on land, at sea, or in the air is a political reality that inhibits development of space-based weapons. The idea of space weaponization arouses unusual political opposition.

Spacepower must always be useful, but its precise roles and actual strategic utility will be distinctive to each class and case of conflict. For example, the wars in Afghanistan and the Falklands were contemporary events, but seapower was irrelevant in the former and literally all-important in the latter. Superior airpower could decide which side would win the 1991 Gulf War, but it could not decide the outcome of the low-intensity conflict waged throughout the 1980s in El Salvador. Because war is a whole enterprise with many parts working synergistically, clear evidence for the influence of a specific type of military power can be difficult to find. If and when spacepower actually decides the course and outcome of a war, the proof most probably will lie in the combat prowess of land, sea, and air forces, whose potency will have been augmented by information gathered or disseminated by space systems.

Functioning in enabling, supporting or adjunct roles, spacepower is manifested in satellite systems vital for communications, for navigation by friendly forces (and their weapons), for reconnaissance and surveillance, for early warning of missile attack, and for geodesy and meteorology.[137] Eventually, 'full-service' space forces will carry weapons for terrestrial bombardment and weapons designed to thwart the capabilities for long-range bombardment by foes.[138]

Because of the distinctive strengths and limitations of each element of the armed forces, success or failure in deterrence and war itself must be a joint responsibility. It follows necessarily that war ultimately must bear upon

---

[136] Though one must not forget the authority of the law of diminishing marginal returns.

[137] Dutton et al., *Military Space*.

[138] Space weaponization is envisaged in Estes, 'Space and Joint Space Doctrine'; Space Command, *Long Range Plan*, 42–7, 59–70.

terrestrial values. Exceptions to this prediction can be identified. For example, if one state or coalition could secure and hold truly exclusive 'command of space', the enemy might elect to surrender as a direct consequence (space could be blockaded against passage by an enemy's missiles), though in principle it might be able to find modes of war wherein disadvantage in space would not be critical. Spacepower, in common with sensible approaches to seapower and airpower, can and should aspire to make the critical strategic difference in war. But it would not be sensible to aspire to the ability to wage and win wars independently by space-oriented action. Long-standing military principles decree the general superiority of joint over single-service solutions to strategic problems.

Both seapower and airpower have played extensive adjunct and complementary roles to landpower.[139] Because mankind lives on the land and is politically organized into territorial polities, it is inevitable that belligerents usually need to come to grips with each other on the ground. If one describes spacepower as playing an adjunct, or supporting, role, that role has long-standing and distinguished precedents in the history of seapower and airpower. If space forces are denied weaponization and are unable directly to engage enemies on earth, then a strictly supporting, or non-shooting adjunct, status is mandated for them. Even if space forces are equipped with weapons to fight for space control, or to defeat ballistic missiles whose trajectories render them briefly spacecraft, their roles in war overall still could be confined to those adjunct to land, sea, and air forces.

At least until the still dawning era of information power, systems that gather, process, and provide information did not themselves fight the enemy. Ultra intelligence in World War II, whose potency as an enabling influence is beyond question, itself did not sink submarines or destroy aircraft.[140] The NAVSTAR Global Positioning System (GPS) permits economies of force in mission planning, but itself puts no weapons on target.[141] It is not always obvious where spacepower begins and ends when information from satellites augments the potency of terrestrial military operations. Can spacepower be the leading edge in a conflict?

As the leading edge of overall combat potency, spacepower will decide the course and outcome of some conflicts, even though space forces may not themselves be combat forces. To decide a conflict, a capability does not have to be directly used in combat. If it is so used, it certainly does not need to be able to conclude hostilities without the assistance of other kinds of forces. All that is

---

[139] Charles E. Callwell, *Military Operations and Maritime Preponderance: Their Relations and Interdependence*, ed. Colin S. Gray, repr. of 1905 edn. (Annapolis, Md., 1996); George Aston, *Sea, Land, and Air Strategy: A Comparison* (London, 1914).

[140] Ralph Bennett, *Behind the Lines: Intelligence in the War with Germany, 1939–45* (London, 1994).

[141] The NAVSTAR global positioning system (GPS) comprises 24 satellites, with 4 satellites deployed in semisynchronous circular orbits at 22,200 km to each of 6 orbital planes inclined at 55° to the equator. The system is designed to allow military users to secure unprecedented all-weather location (longitude, latitude, and altitude) and velocity information. The GPS tells forces or weapons exactly where they are in relation to a precisely mapped (probably by satellite-based sensors) enemy location.

claimed is that the leading-edge military capability is the most potent source of military effectiveness.

In Desert Storm, spacepower demonstrated the potential to achieve the status of leading edge in war. Whether or not that occurs soon depends upon decisions on the development of spacepower for joint warfare, and upon the prowess of those other armed forces that must exploit the advantages granted by space systems. The influence of spacepower—as of landpower, seapower, and airpower—will be characteristic of its unique nature and specific to each particular class, perhaps even instance, of conflict. A leading-edge capability for spacepower (indeed for airpower) may be exploited more readily in the open conditions of desert warfare, or in war at sea, than in heavily urban combat, for example. Just because spacecraft can overfly all scenes of terrestrial conflict, it does not follow that invariably they must yield decisive military advantage.

If the characteristic grammar of contemporary strategy as practised by the greatest power of the era is a grammar of precision in targeting,[142] it is well to enquire about the source of that precision. The grammar of information-led warfare is a grammar of precise registration of enemy location, and precise navigation by friendly forces. This precision comes from superior 'observation', which should enable superior 'orientation' in Colonel John Boyd's 'OODA loop'.[143] That superior observation can be achieved by sensors on the ground, at sea, and in the air, but for the most fundamental reasons of geography and geostrategy it comes increasingly from vehicles in earth orbit, satellites.

The Friedmans do not exaggerate wildly when they assert: 'Control of space, and particularly control of strategic sectors of space, is becoming the foundation of military operations of the post European epoch.'[144] A little earlier they had explained:

As space-based reconnaissance is perfected, and the flow of data is integrated with weapons systems able to strike at targets on land and sea, command of space will come to mean command of the earth. Any nation wishing to defend itself against a powerful military opponent will have to try to deny the enemy the use of space—it will have to destroy or paralyze the enemy's satellites and, with them, the ability to see globally and to use intercontinental weapons.[145]

The Friedmans' bold prose points to a significant pattern in the dynamic grammar of modern strategy. Just as airpower added combat prowess to landpower and seapower, so today a technically and doctrinally still only adolescent spacepower is acting more and more pervasively as an essential force multiplier for friendly

---

[142] For some historical perspective, see Donald MacKenzie, *Inventing Accuracy: A Historical Sociology of Nuclear Missile Guidance* (Cambridge, Mass., 1993); Stephen L. McFarland, *America's Pursuit of Precision Bombing, 1910–1945* (Washington, DC, 1995).

[143] John R. Boyd, 'A Discourse on Winning and Losing' (MS, Aug. 1987).

[144] Friedman and Friedman, *Future of War*, 355–6.

[145] Ibid. 333.

elements on land, at sea, and in the air. Between, say, 1918 and 1941, airpower changed from being a useful and important adjunct to ground and sea forces to being a literally indispensable adjunct.[146] In 1991 in the Gulf War, spacepower was already a strategic team player solidly located in the column of 'useful and important' assets, but today, let alone ten or twenty years from now, it has advanced its role to that of indispensable adjunct. The US Army already acknowledges that its future strategic effectiveness requires reliable assistance from space systems.[147] It plans to fight as a space-dependent force in the future.

If the army will be space dependent, how much more space dependent should one expect the navy and air force to become? After all, land, let alone ground, warfare, is severely fenced in by the constraints of terrain. Much of the potency claimed plausibly enough for tomorrow's sea and air forces must derive critically from the value added by information collected, or distributed, by vehicles in orbit. Wide-area surveillance at great distances can only be provided from sensors on space platforms. The relationship between spacepower and seapower and airpower is not quite analogous to that between airpower and landpower and seapower, because airpower, unlike spacepower, has always been licensed to shoot. When spacepower comes to include weaponization for terrestrial bombardment, in addition to weaponization for satellite, missile, and air defence, then the parallels just outlined will be far more regular.

THE ANTI-GEOGRAPHY OF CYBERSPACE

The subject of spacepower has been overtaken in debate, even to a degree preemptively sidelined, by the myriad claims for a variously defined RMA keyed to the military exploitation of information technologies. Two comments are necessary. First, as asserted in Chapter 1, information (and intelligence) is a permanent dimension of strategy and war. Second, the general information revolution 'discovered' by those inveterate popularizers, the Tofflers,[148] is keyed to an exploitation of the electromagnetic spectrum (EMS) which, commercially if not militarily, effectively is 100 years old. Readers willing to extol the extraordinary military virtues of the degree of mastery of the EMS that, say, Admiral William Owens is advocating with his 'system of systems' are invited to reconsider their views in light of the whole electronic stratum of modern strategic history. In

---

[146] Gray, *Explorations in Strategy*, 102.

[147] Briefing by Maj.-Gen. Robert H. Scales, Jr., USA, London, 25 June 1996; US Army Space and Missile Defense Command, *Vision 2010* (Huntsville, Ala., Oct. 1997), esp. 1–4. I am grateful to Steven Lambakis of the National Institute for Public Policy for bringing this document to my attention. For useful technical and socio-political context, see Brian Nichiporuk and Carl H. Builder, *Information Technologies and the Future of Land Warfare* (Santa Monica, Calif., 1995); Robert J. Bunker, *Five-Dimensional (Cyber) Warfighting: Can the Army after Next Be Defeated through Complex Concepts and Technologies?* (Carlisle Barracks, Pa., 10 March 1998).

[148] Alvin Toffler, *The Third Wave* (New York, 1990); id. and Heidi Toffler, *War and Anti-War: Survival at the Dawn of the 21st Century* (Boston, 1993).

common with the land, sea, air, and space environments, the electronic realm of cyberspace is a combat zone. The 'infosphere',[149] the 'global information infra-structure', the 'sum of the globe's communication links and computation nodes', or, more poetically, simply 'cyberspace'[150] is the final 'geographical' zone for the grammar of strategy to be considered here.

Information warfare can be defined as the offensive and defensive use of information and information systems to exploit, corrupt, or destroy an adversary's information and information systems, while protecting one's own.[151] The general unfamiliarity of the concept of cyberspace, and the unknown technical and tactical terms of engagement there, is offset by the familiarity of the logic of strategy that rules that (anti-)'geography', as it does every other one. Electronic combat can be considered within the same intellectual framework that rules the relevant geographies for land, sea, air, and space warriors. Of course, cyberspace is different, and cyberpower can directly wreak damage only in cyberspace. But the general arguments advanced at the beginning of Chapter 8 as guiding lights for this discussion of the grammar of strategy apply no less to the movement of electrons through cyberspace than they do to spacecraft in orbit, or to soldiers hemmed in by terrain and foliage in some jungle defile.

Cyberassault could be difficult to identify for certain, and even more difficult to trace to its author. Information power through cyberspace is inherently limited in its direct manifestations. The power of electronically managed information will be felt through the agency of armies, navies, air forces, and space forces, but it will not be felt, tangibly, through 'information forces'. Each form of military power contributes strategic effectiveness of kinds, and in ways characteristic to its distinctive geography (or anti-geography, in this case). To date, space has been extensively militarized, but not weaponized. There is nothing about the space environment, however, that inherently precludes weaponization. Cyberspace, by contrast, inherently can bear warfare only within cyberspace. It is true that cyberspace embraces essential support (communications, intelligence, navigation, targeting, and so forth) for all other environments, but it is also true that, unlike, say, the air or the sea, inherently it cannot bear the traffic of war with 'bombs and bullets'.

Cyberwar in cyberspace for information dominance (exploitation or denial) must be waged according to its own electronic grammar of strategy. Actions in cyberwar will include efforts to deny, destroy, capture, or alter information.

[149] David Lonsdale, 'Information Power: Strategy, Geopolitics, and the Fifth Dimension', *Journal of Strategic Studies*, 22, special issue on 'Geopolitics, Geography, and Strategy', (1999).

[150] For similar definitions, see John I. Alger, 'Introduction' to Winn Schwartau (ed.), *Information Warfare, Cyberterrorism: Protecting Your Personal Security in the Electronic Age*, 2nd edn. (New York, 1996), 12–13.

[151] 'Cyberspace' first appears in William Gibson's novel *Neuromancer* (New York, 1984). 'Cyber' derives from the Greek *kybernan*, 'to steer'. Arquilla and Ronfeldt, 'Cyberwar Is Coming!', 162, n. 7, provides useful explanation.

Cyberwarriors will conduct cybercombat to attack enemy information networks, especially the connectivity of its internetted nodes, to insert malicious viruses into computer software, to deny network service, and to destroy databases.[152] Viewed overall, cyberwar, in common, say, with air war, will be conducted at every relevant level of enemy activity or vulnerability. Command and control warfare will be waged to disrupt command channels. So-called 'strategic' information warfare will be attempted against the information infrastructure of an enemy's state and society. Targets could include financial markets, government records, the computer programs used to control public transportation, and the national power grid.

The relevance and strategic effectiveness of information warfare clearly must vary from historical case to case. As with seapower, airpower, and spacepower, the potential strategic value of cyberpower will depend upon the character of the belligerents and the kind and intensity of conflict in question. Nonetheless, the prophets and advocates of information warfare are pushing at an open door. If spacepower today is approximately where airpower was in the 1920s, then information power as a new form of war—to be waged in cyberspace—is back, by analogy, in 1911 with the first use of aircraft in war (by Italy against Turkey). We are in that era of speculation for a new geographically focused form of war, wherein super-threats are conceived. Popular novelists make money by fuelling the strategic anxiety occasioned by the advertisement of new threats.[153]

The exact forms and precise consequences of information warfare conducted in cyberspace are both unknown and unknowable at present. That necessary confession of ignorance carries a graver concern than does the like, and no less necessary, confession of ignorance about the exact form and precise consequences of future warfare on land, at sea, in the air, and in space. Certainly we know a great deal more about the terms of engagement and likely consequences of war on land, at sea, and in the air than we do about war either in space or in cyberspace.

It is difficult to know quite what to say at this early date about the grammar of strategy that will be manifested in information warfare. Two propositions must suffice as dominant working assumptions. First, although cyberspace is both nowhere and everywhere,[154] most of what needs to be understood about it, and the meaning of cybercombat, can best be comprehended via the general model of strategic effectiveness that treats each geographical environment for war as conceptually parallel. Think strategically of cyberspace as one thinks of the land, the

---

[152] Schwartau, *Information Warfare*; Martin C. Libicki, *What Is Information Warfare?* (Washington, DC, Aug. 1995); Arquilla and Ronfeldt, *Advent of Netwar*; Molander et al., *Strategic Information Warfare*; Andrew Rathmell, 'Cyber-Terrorism: The Shape of Future Conflict', *RUSI Journal*, 142 (1997), 40–5; Freedman, *Revolution in Strategic Affairs*, ch. 4; James Adams, *The Next World War* (London, 1998); Peter D. Feaver, 'Blowback: Information Warfare and the Dynamics of Coercion', *Security Studies*, 7 (1998), 88–120.

[153] e. g. Tom Clancy, *Debt of Honor* (London, 1994).

[154] Libicki, 'Emerging Primacy of Information'.

sea, the air, and space, and the relative unimportance of the glaring technical-tactical-logistical differences is suitably underlined.

Second, Andrew Vallance probably is correct when he argues:

Information warfare is unlikely to prove a stand-alone strategic option, particularly when crisis degenerates into conflict. Like electronic warfare, it is essentially a supporting strategy; its role is to supplement rather than to displace force employment strategies.[155]

When a new form of war is analysed and debated, it can be difficult to persuade prophets that prospective efficacy need not be conclusive, and detractors that some weaknesses and limitations need not be fatal. The advocates of pure information warfare point to some of the actual and potential vulnerabilities of our world to cyberassault. Such commentaries are not dissimilar in kind, historically or strategically, from the rhetoric of the theoreticians of strategic airpower in the 1920s and 1930s concerning the vulnerability of the modern urban world to the 'knock-out blow' from the air.[156] Contemporary alarmist literature about threats in cyberspace bear more than a trivial resemblance to the popular view of the pre-radar (and pre-integrated air defence system) 1930s that 'the bomber will always get through'. Would-be prophetic cyberwarriors need to correct their strategic navigation by reference to Edward Luttwak's 'paradoxical logic' of conflict and strategy.[157] Folly persists in human affairs. But the strategic theorist who assumes a particular, persisting pattern in folly is all but certain to be embarrassed by events. To translate: some cyberassault will succeed, but much will not.[158] Moreover, the cyberassaulted, and other interested parties will learn rapidly from the embarrassment.

CONTINUITY IN CHANGE

A great source of confusion in strategic affairs lies in misunderstanding of the implications of technical and tactical change. The form and character of strategy and war altered in a cumulatively revolutionary manner in the twentieth century. This much is not in question. It is my contention, however, that enormous changes in the tactical and operational grammar of strategy matter not at all for the nature and function of war and strategy.[159] The underlying message is that

[155] Vallance, 'Changing Nature of Air Warfare', p. xix.

[156] Bialer, *Shadow of the Bomber.*

[157] Edward N. Luttwak, *Strategy: The Logic of War and Peace* (Cambridge, Mass., 1987).

[158] Rathmell, 'Shape of Future Conflict', and Freedman, *Revolution in Strategic Affairs*, ch. 4, are sensibly sceptical of the more alarmist claims for cyber-peril.

[159] It is disconcerting to find expert commentators casually confusing the enduring with the transient. For example, what excuse can there be for Andrew Vallance writing about 'The Changing *Nature* of Air Warfare' (emphasis added)? Air warfare has a permanent 'nature' dictated by its geographical parameters, but an evolving 'character' driven by technological change. What could be plainer? No less an intellectual warrior than General Sir Michael Rose—commander of the UN Protection Force in Bosnia-Hercegovina—is sufficiently confused to say that 'since the end of the cold war the nature of conflict has changed', *Times Higher Education Supplement*, 23 Apr. 1999, 20. The character of conflict may have changed, but not its nature.

although the tactical grammar of modern strategy has witnessed continuous revolution, modern strategy is the same as ancient strategy. To the person who seeks to understand the process of change with continuity, it is a challenge to learn how to distinguish evolving, even radically altering, forms from persisting structures.

The history of twentieth-century warfare was a history of friction and fusion among the environmentally specialized modes of combat. In the first decade of the century, the problems of land–sea cooperation defined the dilemma. Prior even to 1914, a few prescient theorists began to consider the 'joint' challenges posed by the addition of airpower to the traditional difficulties of coordination between landpower and seapower.[160] An Olympian observer of twentieth-century strategy would have noticed in succession a focus upon land–sea cooperation, upon land–sea–air cooperation, and most recently upon land–sea–air–space–cyberspace cooperation, with uncomfortably tangential nuclear and irregular conflict offshoots. Strategy and war have had to accommodate the military exploitation of new geographies.

A Clausewitzian perspective upon the twentieth century remains authoritative. One should recall that the great man distinguished clearly between the 'logic' and the 'grammar' of war. Chapters 8 and 9 support his contention that war (and strategy) has an enduring nature that technological, social, and political changes cannot alter.[161] Whether the political and social dimensions of war require action to be effected by professional armies, or by armies of variably enthusiastic amateurs, does not much matter for strategy. Strategic performance should be directed by the logic of policy, however sensible that policy may be. Policy must govern the grammar of strategy, though that grammar will dispose of what is proposed by political guidance. The twentieth century witnessed a great expansion in the geographical domain, and hence complexity, of strategy, but that is no measure of progress. Excellence in strategy, unlike, say, excellence in aeronautical engineering, is not a quality upon which one can build cumulatively and reliably. The reasons for the essential constancy in range of quality of strategic performance lie in the complexity and diversity of the dimensions whose changing values and interactions constitute the subject of strategic history. Even if strategy were a science that, when understood 'correctly', guaranteed positive results, human, organizational, and political players would frustrate application of 'scientific' strategic knowledge.[162]

Although the story of the grammar of modern strategy provides a narrative almost unmanageably rich in diverse detail, bloody action, and periodic apparent transformations in tactical relationships, little of real consequence has changed

[160] Preeminently, Aston, *Sea, Land, and Air Strategy*.

[161] Clausewitz, *On War*, 593.

[162] Bernard Brodie: 'Strategy as a Science', *World Politics*, 1 (1949), 476–88; id., 'The Scientific Strategists', in Robert Gilpin and Christopher Wright (eds.), *Scientists and National Policy-Making* (New York, 1964), 240–56; id., *War and Politics* (New York, 1973), ch. 10.

for the statesperson and strategist. These are fighting words, I recognize, for those who believe that large-scale regular, largely symmetrical warfare is set for effective abolition, along, perhaps, with the Westphalian states' structure that created the recurring demand for that warfare. If not a paradox, at least there is a stark contrast between the changing tactical detail of strategy's grammar—the zone of real action wherein people live and die in combat, or under its menace—and the timelessness of the function, nature, and structure of strategy and war.

The realm of strategy today would be thoroughly comprehensible to strategic thinkers throughout history.[163] The political, grand strategic, operational, tactical, and logistic difficulties faced by Hannibal Barca in the Second Punic War are generically timeless.[164] The problems of joint and combined warfare, of sustaining political (and financial and logistic) support from home when a war becomes protracted, of seeking fresh allies and detaching the allies of the foe, are modern topics in the making and practice of strategy, regardless of changes in weapons technology or of fashions in political ideologies. The writings of Sun Tzu, Thucydides, the Emperor Maurice, Machiavelli, and Clausewitz have persisting merit precisely because much of their subject-matter is above the tactical detail that is strategy's grammar.

[163] e.g., to Lt.-Gen. Rudolf von Caemmerer of the German General Staff, whose excellent book, *The Development of Strategical Science During the 19th Century*, trans. Karl von Donat (London, 1905), provides a 'forethought' to this book.

[164] J. F. Lazenby, *Hannibal's War* (Warminster, 1978); Nigel Bagnall, *The Punic Wars: Rome, Carthage and the Struggle for the Mediterranean* (London, 1999).

Chapter 10

SMALL WARS AND OTHER SAVAGE VIOLENCE

The subject of this chapter is the threat or use of force in all conflicts other than those between regular military units. From revolutionary people's war to terrorism, from the conduct of small wars for empire through wars of national liberation, any threat or use of force *for political purposes* is salient to this discussion. Overall, Chapter 10 draws upon the general themes of the book, and especially upon the propositions that practice inspires theory and that all modes of actual or menaced warfare generate strategic effect. The analysis begins by contrasting the largely virtual world of major 'regular' force with the historically all-too-actual realm of 'irregular' violence. The discussion proceeds to explain how theory and practice, as always, intertwine in the pragmatic world of strategy. Chapter 10 also develops the thesis that, notwithstanding the political prominence, even briefly fashionable status, of guerrilla warfare, probably the most lasting footprint to be left in the sands of history by this violent behaviour will be in the creation of permanently established special operations forces. Guerrilla tactics are as old as strategic history; dedicated special operations forces were an innovation of the twentieth century. The argument proceeds to explain the key detail in the formal theory of guerrilla warfare advanced for the edification of modern strategy.

The chapter concludes with an overview of the twentieth-century experience of 'small wars and other savage violence' which emphasizes the historically sequenced prominence of classic small wars, imperial policing, revolutionary guerrilla, terrorist, and now allegedly civilizational/cultural wars. Attention is drawn in particular to the attractions of terrorism. The chapter, *in toto*, affirms the unity of all strategic experience.

This discussion of irregular conflict shows how durable has been much of the theory about the conduct of 'small wars', even as the technological and political contexts have been transformed. The challenge of how to bring an irregular foe to accept battle is a systemic problem for the regular combatant in 'small wars'. 'Small wars' is a term of art employed in the sense outlined a century ago by Charles E. Callwell. He wrote that such wars are 'all campaigns other than those where both the opposing sides consist of regular troops'.[1] A 'small war', defined thus, need not be war waged on a small scale.

---

[1] Charles E. Callwell, *Small Wars: A Tactical Textbook for Imperial Soldiers*, repr. of 1906 edn. (London, 1990), 21. Callwell advises that 'small war is a term which has come largely into use of late years, and

VIRTUAL WAR AND REAL VIOLENCE

Warfare varies in scale, weaponry, geographical medium, and measure of symmetry between foes, but it does not vary in intensity from context to context. For people at the sharp end of war, a location that for nuclear combat includes everybody, there is only one level of intensity, the one that threatens life and limb. To be a warrior, or to be an intended or accidental target of a warrior, is to be in peril of one's life. As the fictional US Marine Corps Colonel Nathan Jesop in the movie *A Few Good Men*, when asked if a particular soldier was in 'grave danger', replied: 'Is there another kind?' There is no little irony in the fact that military pedagogy in the West often draws absurd distinctions among so-called high-, medium-, and low-intensity conflicts. These distinctions inform us that if we are victims trapped in a cellar with a crowd of drunken, rape-minded Bosnian Serbs, we are in a condition of low-intensity conflict, whereas had we been line-of-communication troops far from the action in some major regional quarrel, our conflict condition would have been one of medium intensity. Scarcely less ironic is the fact that my next two chapters are devoted to what tactically, though not strategically, has been the strictly virtual world of nuclear conflict, while just one chapter is dedicated to the all too real world of 'small wars and other savage violence'.

Strategic theorists and the governments they advise have committed extraordinarily large resources to worrying about nuclear issues, essentially for the same reason that airbags and anti-lock brakes are options worth buying for a car. People are prepared to invest in expensive safety equipment that they may well never need. Up to a point, at least, enormity of prospective peril dominates the prediction that one will never actually be in such dire straits. Some dangers command attention because of their awesome scale and conclusiveness, even if the likelihood of occurrence is judged very low.

A danger can be too terrible to consider seriously: a nuclear war that triggers a 'nuclear winter', a collision with Earth by a large asteroid, or an earthquake that could move a substantial fraction of southern California out under the ocean are examples of this phenomenon. In the case of a possible nuclear winter, the predictors of doom found themselves frustrated politically by the fact that the attentive public already subscribed wholeheartedly to the proposition that nuclear war would be catastrophic.[2] There was no scope for political exploitation of the nuclear winter hypothesis when the public was convinced already. To argue for

which is admittedly somewhat difficult to define'. In addition to Callwell, I am pleased to acknowledge a debt for the title of this chapter to Rudyard Kipling. 'Take up the White Man's burden—the savage wars of peace': 'The White Man's Burden' (1899), in *The Works of Rudyard Kipling* (London, 1994), 324.

[2] US Congress, House of Representatives, Committee on Science and Technology, Subcommittee on Natural Resources, Agriculture Research and Environment, and Committee on Interior and Insular Affairs, Subcommittee on Energy and the Environment, *Nuclear Winter*, Joint Hearing, 99th Cong., 1st sess. (Washington, DC, 14 Mar. 1985); Carl Sagan and Richard Turco, *A Path Where No Man Thought: Nuclear Winter and the End of the Arms Race* (London, 1990).

the possibility of a nuclear winter was to move into a redundant realm wherein disaster would befall those already dead.

The virtual combat of the 'nuclear gamesmen' is the subject of Chapters 11 and 12,[3] but the topic here is the savage world of desperately real warfare. By entitling this chapter 'small wars and other savage violence' I mean to bracket, as it were, the relevant theory and practice of strategy in the twentieth century. Two soldier-scholars, one British, Colonel Charles E. Callwell, and one American, Lieutenant-Colonel Ralph Peters, writing a century apart, have each in their way captured theoretically the core matter of this discussion.

First, Charles E. Callwell of the British Army, writing at the end of the nineteenth century, provided what for several decades was the 'textbook for imperial soldiers'.[4] In a book first published in 1896 which, though not official, was officially endorsed, Callwell theorized on the basis of the extensive colonial campaign experience of several imperial powers.[5] He wrote about 'small wars'— wars waged between regular and irregular (i.e. tribal, partisan, possibly religiously inspired, local) forces. In essence, Callwell was writing about asymmetrical, uncivilized, even savage warfare. The distinction was clear enough to his contemporaries at home in Britain, in France, Spain, Russia, Germany, and the United States (remember the Little Big Horn?). There was European or 'civilized warfare' among similar states, societies, and armed forces, and there was uncivilized or savage warfare conducted to spread civilization, advance the Christian religion, make money, provide adventure, and all the other motives that help make for military action. European armies prepared assiduously for *der Tag* of a renewal of civilized warfare on the grand scale, but the actual military action for decade after decade was seen, for example, by the men of France's *Armée d'Afrique*, and by the British and partially British-officered 'native' regiments that served on India's North-West Frontier.[6] Callwell was a superior theorist and an excellent

[3] McGeorge Bundy referred pejoratively to 'the refined calculations of the nuclear gamesmen' in 'To Cap the Volcano', *Foreign Affairs*, 48 (1969), 13.

[4] The explanatory subtitle added to the 1990 repr. of the 3rd ed. (1906) of *Small Wars—A Tactical Textbook for Imperial Soldiers*—is guilty of understating Callwell's intention and achievement. *Small Wars* is a work of empirically based *strategic* theory.

[5] Callwell's earlier literary forays on the subject of 'small wars' included 'Notes on the Tactics of Our Small Wars', *Proceedings of the Royal Artillery Institution*, 12 (1881–4), 531–52; 'Notes on the Strategy of Our Small Wars', *Proceedings of the Royal Artillery Institution*, 13 (1885), 403–20; 'Lessons to Be Learnt from the Campaigns in Which British Forces Have Been Employed since the Year 1865', *Journal of the Royal United Service Institution*, 31 (1887), 357–412.

[6] On France, see Douglas Porch, *The Conquest of Morocco* (New York, 1982); id., *The Conquest of the Sahara* (New York, 1984); id., 'Bugeaud, Galliéni, Lyautey: The Development of French Colonial Warfare', in Peter Paret (ed.), *Makers of Modern Strategy: From Machiavelli to the Nuclear Age* (Princeton, NJ, 1986), 376–407; Anthony Clayton, *France, Soldiers and Africa* (London, 1988). On Britain, see Brian Bond (ed.), *Victorian Military Campaigns* (London, 1967); id., *The Victorian Army and the Staff College, 1854-1914* (London, 1972); Charles Chevenix Trench, *The Frontier Scouts* (London, 1985); T. R. Moreman, ' "Small Wars" and "Imperial Policing": The British Army and the Theory and Practice of Colonial Warfare in the British Empire', *Journal of Strategic Studies*, 19 (1996), special issue on 'Military Power: Land Warfare in Theory and Practice', 105–31; id., *The Army in India and the Development of Frontier Warfare, 1849-1947* (London, 1998).

intelligence and staff officer, but also had taken a heavy gun battery up the Khyber Pass to Kabul during the Second Afghan War in 1879, had served—without seeing action—in the First Boer War of 1880-1, nearly participated in Kitchener's expedition up the Nile to Omdurman in 1898, and commanded a small column that chased Boer farmer-soldiers in South Africa in 1900-1.[7]

Second, from the leading theorist of the conduct of small war *c.*1900, we move on a century to the most insightful contemporary theorist of 'constant conflict', 'winning against warriors', and 'the culture of future conflict'. In a series of vividly written essays, Ralph Peters performed the same service for the close of the twentieth century that Callwell did for its opening.[8] Each has penetrated, and explained plausibly *and to practicable effect*, the core of the range of 'small war' issues of his day. Some scholars question whether strategy can operate outside the modern Western Clausewitzian world, with its trinitarian elements of war. Peters, for example, rejects the Clausewitzian trinity, but not, at least not always, the relevance of strategy.[9] If there is no state, as we understand the concept, how can there be policy that is served strategically by the doings of an army? Byzantium in late antiquity had to cope tactically and strategically both with a Persian Empire that was a great power similar in many respects to itself and with different hordes of distinctly uncivilized barbarians.[10] Similarly, Callwell's British Empire and Peters's informal American empire had and have to be effective strategically against both 'civilized' and 'savage' menaces. In Callwell's words:

But the conditions of small wars are so diversified, the enemy's mode of fighting is often so peculiar, and the theatres of operations present such singular features, that irregular warfare must generally be carried out on a method totally different from the stereotyped system. The art of war, as generally understood, must be modified to suit the circumstances of each particular case. *The conduct of small wars is in fact in certain respects an art by itself, diverging widely from what is adapted to the conditions of regular warfare,* but not so widely that there are not in all its branches points which permit comparisons to be established.[11]

---

[7] Colin S. Gray, 'Introduction' to Charles E. Callwell, *Military Operations and Maritime Preponderance: Their Relations and Interdependence*, ed. Gray, repr. of 1905 edn. (Annapolis, Md., 1996), esp. pp. xxvi-xxxiii, 457-62.

[8] Ralph Peters, 'The New Warrior Class', *Parameters*, 24 (1994), 16-26; id., 'After the Revolution', *Parameters*, 25 (1995), 7-14; id., 'The Culture of Future Conflict', *Parameters*, 25 (1995-6), 18-27; id., 'Our Soldiers, Their Cities', *Parameters*, 26 (1996), 43-50; id., 'Winning against Warriors', *Strategic Review*, 24 (1996), 12-21; id., 'Constant Conflict', *Parameters*, 27 (1997), 4-14; id., 'Our New Old Enemies', in Lloyd J. Matthews (ed.), *Challenging the United States Symmetrically and Asymmetrically: Can America Be Defeated?* (Carlisle Barracks, Pa., July 1998), 215-38; id., 'The New Strategic Trinity', *Parameters*, 28 (1998-9), 73-9. These items fairly represent the Peters canon. He is also the prolific author of eight superior popular adventure novels, to date.

[9] Peters, 'New Strategic Trinity'. See also Martin van Creveld, *The Transformation of War* (New York, 1991); id., 'The Fate of the State', *Parameters*, 26 (1996), 4-18; id., 'What Is Wrong with Clausewitz?', in Gert de Nooy (ed.), *The Clausewitzian Dictum and the Future of Western Military Strategy* (The Hague, 1997), 7-23.

[10] Emperor Maurice, *Maurice's 'Strategikon': Handbook of Byzantine Military Strategy*, trans. George T. Dennis (Philadelphia, 1984).

[11] Callwell, *Small Wars*, 23 (emphasis added).

US marines in Beirut in 1983, and even US army rangers in Somalia in 1993,[12] for all their élite qualities, were the functional military successors of British (and German) 'redcoats' in the French and Indian Wars and later in the Revolutionary War. The Huron, the Hezbollah, and General Aideed's militiamen did not take prisoners after the fashion of 'civilized' forces.

'Small wars and other savage violence' challenge the strategic theorist with a seductive diversity. Both Callwell and Peters menace the integrity of some of the organizing themes of this book. If the theory of modern strategy flows from the interpretations of Napoleonic practice made by Clausewitz and Jomini, how can that theory apply to warfare as a way of life in some tribal societies,[13] or indeed to those broad acres of notably savage violence that extend from individual terroristic acts to community-wide endeavours in forcible 'ethnic cleansing'? As a strategic theorist writing a book on modern strategy, I confess to a sense of challenge in approaching the subject of this chapter. The reason for my unease may be gleaned from these characteristically direct words of Ralph Peters:

For a generation, and probably much longer, we [the United States] will face no military peer competitor. Our enemies will challenge us by other means. The violent actors we encounter often will be small, hostile parties possessed of unexpected, incisive capabilities or simply of a stunning will to violence (or both). Renegade elites, not foreign fleets, should worry us. The urbanization of the global landscape is a greater threat to our operations than any extant or foreseeable military system. We will not deal with wars of Realpolitik, but with conflicts spawned of collective emotions, sub-state interests, and systemic collapse. *Hatred, jealousy, and greed—emotions rather than strategy—will set the terms of struggles.*[14]

If torture is exciting, rape is fun, and looting is profitable for these 'violent actors', it can be hard to find a role for strategy. 'War' for fun is not really war; it is a form of recreational brigandage.[15] Both Callwell and Peters, though especially the latter, indicate that the world of force extends down into social and individual depths that escape capture by any plausible theory of strategy. At the heart of some of the writings of Ralph Peters lies the thesis that around the world there is a 'new warrior class' committed to violence for reasons that are astrategic.[16] In a sense, Peters is correct. Much of the potential cannon-fodder in conflicts from Afghanistan to Liberia fights for motives no more strategic than food, self-respect, greed, lust, ambition, and boredom. However, the world's soldiery has rarely fought for benefits more ambitious than these—more noble, perhaps, but not more

---

[12] Thomas K. Adams, *US Special Operations Forces in Action: The Challenge of Unconventional Warfare* (London, 1998), 258–66.

[13] John Keegan, *A History of Warfare* (London, 1993); id., *War and Our World* (London, 1998).

[14] Peters, 'Constant Conflict', 9 (emphasis added).

[15] I am grateful to James Wirtz for his persuasive interpretation of this point.

[16] Peters, 'New Warrior Class'.

'strategic'.[17] Political leaders may have strategic intentions, though, and their soldiers will fight to strategic effect, no matter how pathetic, venal, or otherwise astrategic individual soldiers' combat motivation may appear.

Contrary to Peters's thesis, the realm of strategy, understood in its proper Clausewitzian sense, can and should make sense of the apparently chaotic world of small wars and other savage violence. As always, there will be warriors who fight for entirely personal rewards, though the consequences of their actions will have some strategic effect. But, in common with Peters, I accept that some of the action perpetrated as sub-state activity, even if it must have strategic effect, happens for reasons that call no strategy master.

The character of small wars and other acts of savage violence can vary as much from the character of contemporary 'regular' warfare as regular warfare in, say, 1914, varied from that of 1918, 1945, or even 1991. It should follow that if strategy and war do not change their nature among different historical periods, so small wars, other forms of organized (or semi-organized, given the relativity of the quality of organization) violence, and regular warfare should be capable of analysis within the same conceptual framework.

Paradoxically, the severity of the challenge to strategy posed both by nuclear weapons and by highly asymmetrical small wars does not show strategy the door, but rather commands the strategist to work harder. As we will see, speculation on the implications of the threat or actual use of nuclear force drew strategic thinkers deeply into the twilight of increasingly refined deterrence theory. Even the appalling proposition that security may reside in the orchestration of nuclear 'threats that leave something to chance'[18] is—notwithstanding Lawrence Freedman's denial of this point[19]—a strategic judgement, which is to say a consequentialist judgement about the strategic effect of beliefs about particular risks upon the course and outcome of events. In common with the nuclear challenge, the force and threats of force employed in small wars by regulars and irregulars alike tend to be unusually rigorous in their interrogation of strategic capacity. Similarly, when a dominant landpower fights a dominant seapower, it can be difficult for either side to pursue practicable paths to victory.[20] In small wars, as Callwell explains, the overriding military-operational problem for the regular side is to

[17] The question of combat motivation remains unsettled by scholarship and anecdote. Notwithstanding the historical unity and universality of the terms and conditions of 'the face of battle', no general theory available to date is to be trusted. Mark Grimsley, 'In Not So Dubious Battle: The Motivations of American Civil War Soldiers', *Journal of Military History*, 62 (1998), 175–88, and Eliot Cohen, 'What Combat Does to Man: *Private Ryan* and Its Critics', *National Interest*, 54 (1998/9), 82–8, cover much of the ground economically and well. S. L. A. Marshall, *Men against Fire* (New York, 1947), John Keegan, *The Face of Battle* (London, 1976), and Omer Bartov, *Hitler's Army: Soldiers, Nazis, and War in the Third Reich* (New York, 1991), are all essential reading.

[18] Thomas C. Schelling, *The Strategy of Conflict* (Cambridge, Mass., 1960), ch. 8.

[19] Lawrence Freedman, *The Evolution of Nuclear Strategy*, 2nd edn. (New York, 1989), 433.

[20] Colin S. Gray, *The Leverage of Sea Power: The Strategic Advantage of Navies in War* (New York, 1992), chs. 2 and 3.

find some way to bring an elusive foe to battle.[21] Irregular, guerrilla, partisan, other unconventional warfare is the choice of the militarily weaker party. If trial by major battle must mean defeat, then only minor battle can be offered. If the enemy's army cannot be assaulted in a single 'decisive battle', what is needed is some alternative theory of victory that identifies sources of strategic effect that can be tapped by the irregulars. The point is that although, as Clausewitz insists, '[e]verything in strategy is very simple, but that does not mean that everything is very easy',[22] the difficulties are extraordinarily testing of human and organizational talent in the fields of nuclear conflict and small wars.

The domain of strategic effect, purposeful or otherwise, is not confined to 'civilized', as contrasted with 'savage', warfare. There are two principal errors to avoid. The first is to regard the realm of real war and 'real soldiering' as coterminous with symmetrical conflict, at least as roughly identical to the experience of regular forces fighting regular forces. This error can promote the idea that 'small wars', in Callwell's meaning, are irrelevant, perhaps dangerously irrelevant, diversions from the mainstream requirement to prepare for real war (i.e. *grande guerre*).[23] Armed forces that decline to take small wars seriously as a military art form with their own tactical, operational, and political—though not strategic—rules invite defeat.[24] The second error is to regard small wars and other forms of savage violence as the wars of the future that will largely supplant the allegedly old-fashioned state-centric 'regular' wars of a Westphalian world. There are some grounds for identifying a contemporary 'transformation of war' that favours irregular forces and violence, just as there are some grounds for claiming that the state, at least in the forms promoted by Westphalia, is in sharp decline, even if it is not quite ready to fall.[25]

The errors cited immediately above are errors only of emphasis. Small wars can detract from the readiness of regular forces to take the field against other regular forces. Good tactical habits for frontier warfare in Waziristan can be lethal if carried over to the killing-fields of Flanders. Furthermore, the would-be

---

[21] Callwell, *Small Wars*, 93, 125.

[22] Carl von Clausewitz, *On War*, trans. Michael Howard and Peter Paret (Princeton, NJ, 1976), 178.

[23] As Robert M. Utley has written of the US Army: 'For a century the army fought Indians as if they were British or Mexicans or Confederates. Each Indian war was expected to be the last, and so the generals never developed a doctrine or organization adapted to the special problems posed by the Indian style of fighting': *Cavalier in Buckskin: George Armstrong Custer and the Western Military Frontier* (Norman, Okla., 1988), 206. See also id., *Frontiersmen in Blue: The United States Army and the Indian 1848–1865* (Lincoln, Neb., 1967); id., *Frontier Regulars: The United States Army and the Indian, 1866–1891* (New York, 1973). At least one American general understood how to fight Indians: Charles R. Lummis, *General Crook and the Apache Wars* (Flagstaff, Ariz., 1966), esp. 17–21. The realities of Indian fighting are well conveyed in General Nelson A. Miles, *Personal Recollections and Observations*, repr. of 1896 edn. (2 vols., Lincoln, Neb., 1992).

[24] Sam C. Sarkesian, *America's Forgotten Wars: The Counterrevolutionary Past and Lessons for the Future* (Westport, Conn., 1984); A. Hamish Ion and E. J. Errington (eds.), *Great Powers and Little Wars: The Limits of Power* (Westport, Conn., 1993).

[25] Van Creveld, *Transformation of War*; id., 'Fate of the State'.

practitioner of a small war, on either side of the combat, would do well to study the closest approximation to the (fairly) modern bible on the subject, Mao Tse-tung's (and collaborators) *corpus classicus* on guerrilla warfare and related topics.[26] Mao is crystal-clear on the complementarity of irregular and regular forces and irregular and regular warfare. Indeed, he reminds any candidate romantics about guerrilla warfare, those who are seduced into the folly of what can be called 'guerrilla-ism' where guerrilla warfare is practiced and valued almost as an end in itself, that such a character of struggle is only instrumental.[27] Writing in 1934 about the anti-Japanese struggle, though with the Nationalist foe in mind, the Maoist school observed that 'if we view the war as a whole, there can be no doubt that our regular forces are of primary importance, because it is they who are alone capable of producing the decision'.[28] Moreover, some elements among regular forces can operate as guerrillas, though not if they function in regular ways— irregular war is a state of mind, an approach, as well as a set of tactical skills[29]— and they can operate in an anti-guerrilla mode. Regular armed forces today are not being atavistic when they resist political pressure literally to 'lighten up' for duty focused on the lower end of the scale of violence. There is much that regular forces trained and equipped for 'heavy' regular warfare can do to adapt to the demands of small wars. By way of contrast, regular armed forces scaled back in equipment and mass to cope with operations other than war (including peacekeeping duties), and small wars proper, would be all but useless if confronted suddenly with a requirement from policy to wage major regional combat. Given the lead time for procurement of ships and aircraft, that argument applies even more strongly to navies and air forces than it does to armies.

The second error, the heralding of a transformation in war with most belligerents comprising sub- or trans-state groups, is an error only if one exaggerates the evident contemporary trend away from state-to-state conflicts. The 'trend' is real, but it may prove short-lived. Small wars of various kinds are preoccupying many military professionals today because these conflicts are extant and appear most probable for the next few years. There was a notable 'trend' towards peace, even political peace, in the 1920s. Contemporary trends in favour of sundry forms of violence between 'civilizations',[30] and—to take a further example—in favour of a nuclear taboo that delegitimizes nuclear coercion,[31] are both possibly the

[26] Mao Tse-tung [attrib.], *On Guerrilla Warfare*, trans. Samuel B. Griffith (New York, 1961); Mao Tse-tung, *Selected Military Writings* (Peking, 1967). In Chapter 3, n. 38 above, I explain that *On Guerrilla Warfare* was written by close collaborators of Mao.

[27] Mao, *Selected Military Writings*, 246.

[28] Mao [attrib.], *On Guerrilla Warfare*, 56.

[29] Colin S. Gray, *Explorations in Strategy* (Westport, Conn., 1998), ch. 7.

[30] Samuel P. Huntington, *The Clash of Civilizations and the Remaking of World Order* (New York, 1996).

[31] Richard Price and Nina Tannenwald, 'Norms and Deterrence: The Nuclear and Chemical Weapons Taboos', in Peter J. Katzenstein (ed.), *The Culture of National Security: Norms and Identity in World Politics* (New York, 1996), 114–52; Colin S. Gray, *The Second Nuclear Age* (Boulder, Colo., 1999), ch. 4.

products of passing contexts only. Although small wars and other variants of savage violence are widespread today and seem likely to enjoy a healthy future, they are only one strand in future strategic history.

Small wars, terrorism, and other low-level nastiness demonstrate the interplay between theory and practice. They are a set of options (sometimes available) within the growing complexity of modern war. They illustrate just how difficult it is to register superior strategic performance. They share hallmarks throughout strategic history, even as the technology of war has changed. These savage 'peacetime' wars can present political demands for guardianship of a peace with security scarcely less challenging than is the menace of more regular, militarily symmetrical aggression.

SMALL WARS AND STRATEGIC THEORY

Fortunately for them, Geronimo and his Apaches did not read Jomini, but they understood, as did their nemesis, General George Crook, that, in the immortal words of Mao Tse-tung, '[t]here is in guerrilla warfare no such thing as a decisive battle'.[32] Many of the world's warriors have been unschooled in formal military theory. With respect to violent action, as contrasted with preparation for the conduct of such action, the subjects of this chapter and the next ones stand in the starkest of relief. The realm of the nuclear warrior to date has been (excepting August 1945) the twilight zone of refined calculation and more or less elegant speculation. In sharp contrast, the realm of the guerrilla and counter-guerrilla, the terrorist and counter-terrorist, has been a universe of actual deeds and misdeeds relatively unblessed by powerful, let alone sacred, texts of theory. There are, of course, two stunning exceptions to that generalization: the writings of T. E. Lawrence and of the Mao Tse-tung school. It is to these, and indeed to the whole field of relevant ideas, that the analysis now turns.

IDEAS FOR PRACTICE

To develop theories of revolutionary war, guerrilla war, terrorism, and intended antidotes to the same is to risk discovering the desperately obvious, much as did Alfred Thayer Mahan with his theory of seapower. Civil and military technologies change, but the Roman Empire would have learnt little from twentieth-century theories of counter-insurgency and counter-revolutionary warfare. Similarly, terrorism and counter-terrorism is a field of strategic interest which, though variable in its popularity, punctuates the entire historical record of strategic experience.[33]

---

[32] Mao [attrib.], *On Guerrilla War*, 52; Lummis, *General Crook and the Apache Wars*.

[33] For historical perspective on irregular warfare, including terrorism, see Walter Laqueur (ed.), *The Terrorism Reader: A Historical Anthology* (London, 1979); Robert B. Asprey, *War in the Shadows: The Classic History of Guerrilla Warfare from Ancient Persia to the Present*, rev. edn. (London, 1994); John Arquilla (ed.), *From Troy to Entebbe: Special Operations in Ancient and Modern Times* (Lanham, Md., 1996); Walter Laqueur, *Guerrilla Warfare: A Historical and Critical Study* (New Brunswick, NJ, 1998).

The twentieth century provided some novel twists to the old story of small wars: for instance, the emergence of a trans-national (Marxist-Leninist, then Maoist) political ideology helping to fuel a formal theory of guerrilla and revolutionary warfare. But there is less novelty here than meets the eye. The lore of irregular warfare most typically reappears as repeated discovery of the logic of the strategic situation that pits the weak against the strong, and vice versa. The details of weaponry alter, but in terms of fundamental skills and attitudes Major Robert Rogers's Rangers in the Seven Years War (1756–63)[34] and Britain's twentieth-century Special Air Service (SAS)[35] were both in the same business and could have learnt little from each other.

It is virtually a cliché to refer to the sheer diversity of irregular conflicts, and then to observe that that diversity precludes theory, doctrine, or dominant plans. The root of that judgement is a conclusion such as this: 'The reality is that there is no single terrorism, only separate and distinctive terrorisms.'[36] Defence planning and military thought at all levels are greatly complicated when the strategic realm is not conveniently organized by a single dominant problem: for example, 'contain Soviet power and influence within Eurasia', 'prepare to wage a great naval battle (and campaign) against the Imperial Japanese Navy in East Asian waters on the approaches to the Philippines', or 'prepare an expeditionary force to join the French Army in the field to oppose a German invasion of Belgium and France'.[37] Nonetheless, as the master theme of this book insists, strategy is strategy, regardless of specific tactical and operational detail. Indeed, most of the subject-matter of this chapter, no matter that each historical case may be unique, lends itself to general comprehension. For example, the techniques of rural and urban guerrilla and counter-guerrilla warfare are universal and timeless.

Strategic theory is the child of strategic practice and malpractice. Ideas in modern strategy on the tactical, operational, strategic, and political conduct of small wars have been stimulated by the diverse experience of colonial conquest, of resistance to that conquest, of colonial policing once conquest has nominally been secured, of national anti-colonial wars of liberation, of politically revolutionary wars, and of wars of national liberation conducted in concert with the regular forces of major allies. The modern strategic history of small wars offers a sad

[34] See Kenneth Roberts's novel, *Northwest Passage* (New York, 1937).

[35] Tony Geraghty, *Who Dares Wins: The Story of the Special Air Service, 1950–1982*, rev. edn. (London, 1983); and, with a focus on Northern Ireland, Mark Urban, *Big Boys' Rules* (London, 1992); Ken Connor, *Ghost Force: The Secret History of the SAS* (London, 1998). John Newsinger, *Dangerous Men: The SAS and Popular Culture* (London, 1997), is an occasionally perceptive, unfriendly critique of the SAS.

[36] Trevor N. Dupuy (ed.), *International Military and Defense Encyclopedia* (6 vols., Washington, DC, 1993), vi: T–Z, 2724.

[37] Respectively on Cold War policy and planning, on American war planning, and on British planning for continental war, see Melvyn P. Leffler, *A Preponderance of Power: National Security, the Truman Administration, and the Cold War* (Stanford, Calif., 1992); Edward S. Miller, *War Plan Orange: The U.S. Strategy to Defeat Japan, 1897–1945* (Annapolis, Md., 1991); John Gooch, *The Plans of War: The General Staff and British Military Strategy c.1900–1916* (London, 1974).

abundance of evidence. For special note one would single out the Second Boer War of 1899–1902, General Paul von Lettow-Vorbeck's guerrilla struggle in German East Africa against British imperial forces from 1914 to 1918, T. E. Lawrence's experience with the Arab Revolt against the Turkish Empire (though no less against French ambitions in Syria) in 1917–18, Mao Tse-tung's leadership of the anti-Japanese and anti-Nationalist struggles in the 1930s and 1940s, the campaign conducted in the 1940s by Zionist terrorists against the British Mandate in Palestine, and finally the Latin American brand of (Maoist) revolutionary guerrilla warfare as articulated by the Argentinian Che Guevara and the French Régis Debray.[38]

The subject here is the politically purposeful use of force in all cases other than the clash of regular armed forces. The plenitude of actual violence contrasts sharply with a dearth of profound theory. There are only three, arguably four, theorists of the first rank on the subject of this chapter: Charles E. Callwell, T. E. Lawrence, Mao Tse-tung (and his school), and—just possibly— Ralph Peters.[39] Close reading of their texts affords a grasp of the principles that govern irregular conflict, much as a reading of the better writings of Bernard Brodie, Albert Wohlstetter, and Thomas C. Schelling opens the door to understanding the mindset of America's nuclear Cold War warriors.

POLITICS RULES

Below the political waterline of state-to-state conflict, we are in the realm that political theorists label the 'essentially contestable'. What is the difference between a brigand, a terrorist, and a freedom fighter? If national and even international law condemns the first two, who is to say authoritatively that the third category does not apply? Of all the topics in modern strategy treated in this book, it is in this chapter that the perils of political subjectivity threaten most severely. One is almost, but only almost, tempted to acknowledge the possibility of some merit in recent writings on 'critical theoretical' approaches to security studies.[40]

[38] Deneys Reitz, *Commando: A Boer Journal of the Boer War*, repr. of 1932 edn. (London, 1982); Charles Miller, *Battle for the Bundu: The First World War in East Africa* (London, 1974); T. E. Lawrence, *Seven Pillars of Wisdom: A Triumph*, repr. of 1935 edn. (New York, 1991); Mao, *Selected Military Writings*; Menachem Begin, *The Revolt: Story of the Irgun* (Jerusalem, 1977); Che Guevara, *Guerrilla Warfare* (Lincoln, Neb., 1985); Régis Debray, *Revolution in the Revolution?* (London, 1968).

[39] Ralph Peters, whose work I admire greatly even when I disagree with it, owes the world and posterity an extended statement of his arguments, in addition to the brief, albeit frequently brilliant, essays that he has provided to date. This is not to confuse quality with quantity or mode of publication. On nuclear matters, for example, although he never wrote a book, '[p]robably no civilian strategic analyst has had more influence in the nuclear age than Albert Wohlstetter': Richard Rosecrance, 'Albert Wohlstetter', in John Baylis and John Garnett (eds.), *Makers of Nuclear Strategy* (New York, 1991), 57. The welcome sight of a book by Peters is offset heavily by the fact that it is a collection of his essays. *Fighting for the Future: Will America Triumph?* (Mechanicsburg, Pa., 1999).

[40] Keith Krause and Michael C. Williams (eds.), *Critical Security Studies: Concepts and Cases* (London, 1997). Bradley S. Klein, *Strategic Studies and World Order: The Global Politics of Deterrence* (Cambridge, 1994), and Gearóid Ó Tuathail, *Critical Geopolitics: The Politics of Writing Global Space* (Minneapolis, 1996), also are relevant, though their specialist jargon does require some deconstructing.

Perhaps, to some degree and inadvertently, we construct reality by the words and ideas we choose to employ.

The relevant record of the twentieth century is a story of anti-colonial resistance, of imperial policing, of wars of national liberation, and of irregular combat of every conceivable kind. It is important to distinguish military technique from political motive. The imperial conduct of small wars, imperial policing, guerrilla and counter-guerrilla warfare, and terrorism and counter-terrorism are all subjects for, and subject to, expert knowledge; expert knowledge, that is, without reference to personal political belief.

Sun Tzu, Thucydides, Machiavelli, Clausewitz, and Jomini can be studied and quoted with scant obeisance to current political niceties, but the strategic world of 'small wars and other savage violence' risks embroiling one in matters that can detract from objectivity. For example, dissent from the view put forward by Henry Kissinger in 1957 that nuclear weapons could be used in limited war did not *ipso facto* threaten one's credentials as a truly professional yet patriotic defence theorist.[41]

The political judgements pertaining to small wars, however, are of a different league from those relevant to regular warfare. By definition, conflict other than regular-to-regular war requires serious consideration of the claims of would-be political units that have yet to be blessed by sufficient international fora. Much of the literature on small wars and related unpleasantness is more *engagé* than is prudent, if understanding is to be advanced. This quality of concern is entirely natural for a practical subject like strategy. Just as the more powerful works of relevant theory have tended to grow out of the practical experience of soldier-theorists with the Arab Revolt, the Chinese, Vietnamese, and Cuban revolutions, so the more impressive works of theory on the more regular side have also had their inspiration in specific contexts. By way of British illustration of the point, Charles Callwell at the turn of the century, Sir Charles Gwynn in the 1930s, and Sir Robert Thompson and Colonel Frank Kitson in the 1960s all wrote practical books for practical soldiers and soldier-administrators.[42] Callwell wrote in good part about imperial soldiering on the strategic offensive in small wars. Gwynn wrote about soldiering for empire on the strategic defensive largely in policing roles. Thompson explained how best to counter communist revolutionary warfare. Kitson focused on the low-intensity operations characteristic of imperial strategic retreat.

All war must have a political dimension, but that dimension typically is far more pervasively important for the behaviour under discussion in this chapter

---

[41] Henry A. Kissinger, *Nuclear Weapons and Foreign Policy* (New York, 1957), ch. 6. James King, 'Nuclear Plenty and Limited War', *Foreign Affairs*, 35 (1957), 238–56, is a potent critique.

[42] Callwell, *Small Wars*; Charles W. Gwynn, *Imperial Policing* (London, 1934); Robert Thompson, *Defeating Communist Insurgency: Experiences from Malaya and Vietnam* (London, 1966); Frank Kitson, *Low Intensity Operations: Subversion, Insurgency, and Peacekeeping* (London, 1971).

than it is for other kinds of conflicts. Small wars on any scale are apt to be *about* polities rather than between polities, as usually is the case with regular warfare. This distinction should not be overdrawn, because there are many historical instances wherein the process of regular conflict in some important sense 'made the nation or polity'. The quasi-myth of the national struggle in a Great Patriotic War lent a measure of domestic legitimacy to the USSR that had been missing;[43] or consider how Australia, New Zealand, and Canada 'discovered', perhaps forged, their distinctive political identities respectively at Gallipoli and on Vimy Ridge.[44] Another distinction that should not be overdrawn is that between categories of violence on the spectrum of conflict. What can be called 'option purity' in style among military choices is rare. In World War II, for example, the major belligerent powers all engaged in regular warfare and in irregular warfare, including resort to terrorism. Indeed, many among the anti-colonial 'freedom fighters' of the 1940s, 1950s, and 1960s had learnt the trade of guerrilla tactics and terrorism from Allied 'special warfare' instructors in the World War. When fighting the French Empire and then the United States and its local allies, General Vo Nguyen Giap periodically, and in 1975 conclusively, waged open regular, even some positional, warfare. He conducted guerrilla-style operations, and he made systematic use of the methods of terrorism.[45] It is scarcely more surprising that many forms of regular and irregular warfare should be waged simultaneously by the same belligerent than that land, sea, air, space, and cyberspace should not constitute meaningful boundaries among conflicts. The world of strategy is a whole one.

Theorists and practitioners of modern strategy have not agreed on conceptual labels for the phenomena under discussion here. Unlike the case of most instances of regular warfare, the political status of the weaker party in irregular warfare is generally an important stake in the conflict and itself can have significant strategic effect. Is a member of the Provisional IRA a soldier or simply a terrorist-criminal? Efforts by the UN to define 'terrorism' thus far have ranged from formulae that were unduly empathetic to those actually sympathetic to 'terrorists'.[46]

---

[43] David M. Glantz and Jonathan House, *When Titans Clashed: How the Red Army Stopped Hitler* (Lawrence, Kan., 1995), 289–90.

[44] For the context, see Glen St J. Barclay, *The Empire Is Marching: A Study of the Military Effort of the British Empire, 1800–1945* (London, 1976).

[45] Cecil B. Currey, *Victory at Any Cost: The Genius of Viet Nam's Gen. Vo Nguyen Giap* (Washington, DC, 1997). In his *Selected Military Writings*, the intellectual *corpus classicus* behind Giap, Mao is entirely flexible as to which military style should be used and when. Although he was the victor in two wars—and it seems perverse, if not uncharitable, to argue with success—Giap seems to me to have been considerably overpraised as a strategist. Several times (e.g. 1951, 1965, 1968, 1972) he moved prematurely into regular open warfare and was saved ultimately only by the extreme folly of his French, then American, enemies. I am grateful to Martin Alexander of the University of Salford for encouraging a serious seed of doubt in my mind about the military genius of General Giap. At the very least, Giap is long overdue a serious balanced biography.

[46] Bruce Hoffman, *Inside Terrorism* (London, 1998), 31–2. Grant Wardlaw, *Political Terrorism: Theory, Tactics, and Countermeasures* (Cambridge, 1990), ch. 1, also provides a superior overview of the pertinent issues.

Irregular warfare, on both sides, tends to marry especially low conduct with characteristically high-minded motives. An important reason for this was expressed by T. E. Lawrence: 'while opinions were arguable, convictions needed shooting to be cured.'[47] In the rough world of strategy, to know, even to understand, people is not to love them. Civil wars of all varieties are usually about hearth, home, and, not infrequently, political ideas. The forces of *counter*-revolution, *counter*-insurgency, and *counter*-terrorism do not wish to diminish their own authority and legitimacy by extending legal belligerent rights to a domestic foe. It is no accident that, even by the appalling standards of warfare, violence tends to be more savage on all sides in the asymmetrical conflicts internal to states.

Names matter. The literature of strategic theory most relevant to this chapter offers works on small wars, revolutionary warfare, people's war, insurgency, insurrection, guerrilla warfare, internal war, unconventional war, irregular war, terrorism, and low-intensity conflict. There are some empirical differences among the categories isolated by these labels. Of these terms, only 'revolutionary warfare' (and its negation) and 'people's revolutionary war' (it does tend to have a particular political association, as with People's Democracy) carry specific political baggage; the remainder are politically neutral. It is true that 'insurgency', even 'guerrilla warfare', imply strong political motivation, but strictly they refer only to modes of conflict. Guerrilla warfare, for example, is an equal-opportunity toolkit of military method. Regular forces can fight irregularly.

SPECIAL FORCES AND UNCONVENTIONAL MINDS

The last point is one that strategic historians should be careful not to miss. For all the celebration and condemnation that attached to the phenomena of irregular forms of warfare conducted (largely) by irregulars in the twentieth century, notice also needs to be taken of the extraordinary growth in the irregular activities of the regulars. Historically assessed, the small-war story of modern strategy is unremarkable. After all, there is nothing modern about belligerencies between regular forces and the weak. Guerrilla warfare, whose principles were outlined so brilliantly by T. E. Lawrence and Mao Tse-tung, is the military, perhaps paramilitary, *modus operandi* of the weak; it has always been so. What has not always been so is manifestation of the seeming paradox of regular troops organized, trained, equipped, and directed to wage war unconventionally in what have come to be known as 'special operations'.[48]

Though regular military professionals who function in cooperation with,

---

[47] Lawrence, *Seven Pillars of Wisdom*, 190.

[48] The literature on special operations is deeply unsatisfactory. Most works on the subject are entirely uninterested in strategic relevance; instead they tend to offer adventurous narratives, or anecdotes, of daring deeds, and colourful regimental histories. Even when authors do raise their sights to issues of strategic consequence, they are apt to focus narrowly upon the unique challenges to the special operations forces of *their country*. Prominent among the better studies are M. R. D. Foot, 'Special

indeed as force multipliers for, conventional forces, the special warriors of, say, the Third Reich's Brandenburg Regiment, the Russian Spetsnaz, the British SAS, or the US Army's Delta Force are obliged to operate as 'guerrillas in uniform'. The SAS may rank high among the finest military professionals in the world, but their strategic effectiveness is keyed to their limitations. Special warriors, like irregulars everywhere and at all times, have to follow an approximation of the Chinese tactical precept 'Sheng Tung, Chi Hsi', or 'Uproar [in the] East; Strike [in the] West'.[49] Because they must confound an enemy superior in overall military mass and firepower, the warriors of modern special forces must function as guerrillas. To be more specific:

In guerrilla warfare, select the tactic of seeming to come from the east and attacking from the west; avoid the solid, attack the hollow; attack; withdraw; deliver a lightning blow, seek a lightning decision. When guerrillas engage a stronger enemy, they withdraw when he advances; harass him when he stops; strike him when he is weary; pursue him when he withdraws. In guerrilla strategy, the enemy's rear, flank, and other vulnerable spots are his vital points, and there he must be harassed, attacked, dispersed, exhausted and annihilated. Only in this way can guerrillas carry out their mission of independent guerrilla action and coordination with the effort of the regular armies.[50]

Unlike the practitioners of revolutionary or people's war, special operations forces will not swim like fish in the sea of the people. Instead they will act in small units, in clandestine, covert, or even overt ways, to fulfil unorthodox missions in unconventional modes. The units will also operate in conditions of exceptionally high risk in quest of significant political or military objectives.[51] Special operations forces are an example of the classic military principle of economy of force. Recall how Captain David Stirling of the Scots Guards was licensed by General Claude Auchinleck to form his small private army of the SAS, because he promised

Operations /1', and 'Special Operations /2', in Michael Elliott-Bateman (ed.), *The Fourth Dimension of Warfare, i: Intelligence, Subversion, Resistance* (Manchester, 1970), 19–34, 35–51; Frank R. Barnett, B. Hugh Tovar, and Richard H. Shultz (eds.), *Special Operations in US Strategy* (Washington, DC, 1984); Rod Paschall, *LIC 2010: Special Operations and Unconventional Warfare in the Next Century* (Washington, DC, 1990); Lucien S. Vandenbroucke, *Perilous Options: Special Operations as an Instrument of U.S. Foreign Policy* (New York, 1993); William H. McRaven, *SPEC OPS, Case Studies in Special Operations Warfare: Theory and Practice* (Novato, Calif., 1995); Arquilla, *Troy to Entebbe*; Susan L. Marquis, *Unconventional Warfare: Rebuilding U.S. Special Operations Forces* (Washington, DC, 1997); Thomas K. Adams, *U.S. Special Operations Forces in Action: The Challenge of Unconventional Warfare* (London, 1998). I have pursued general understanding in my *Explorations in Strategy*, pt. 3, and in 'Handfuls of Heroes on Desperate Ventures: When Do Special Operations Succeed?', *Parameters*, 29 (1999), 2–24.

   [49] Griffith, 'Introduction' to Mao [attrib.], *On Guerrilla Warfare*, 26.

   [50] Mao [attrib.], *On Guerrilla Warfare*, 4. See also Mao, *Selected Military Writings*, esp. 151–85, 'Problems of Strategy in Guerrilla War Against Japan'.

   [51] I am in debt to Maurice Tugwell and David Charters for their identification of the defining characteristics of special operations. 'Special Operations and the Threats to United States Interests in the 1980s', in Barnett et al., *Special Operations in U.S. Strategy*, 35. Also, there is merit in John Arquilla's claim that special operations are 'that class of military (or paramilitary) actions that fall outside the realm of conventional warfare during their respective time periods': 'Introduction' to *Troy to Entebbe*, pp. xv–xvi.

great military consequences with huge strategic effect upon the desert war for the hazard of only tens of men.[52] Many politicians, and some generals who, on occasion, dare to be different (e.g., General Allenby, who licensed T. E. Lawrence in World War I, and General Auchinleck in World War II), find the promise of the strategic equivalent of the free lunch irresistible.[53] One might not really believe that David Stirling with sixty-six men would be able to cripple the Luftwaffe on the ground by deep raids against airfields, but with the price of the gamble so low, why not roll the dice?

The conduct of special operations is a skill. Any army can select its élite soldiers and train the élite of the élite to be effective as 'special warriors' fighting in a guerrilla mode. But competence in military technique is not sufficient for the winning of wars. Guerrilla warfare produces political effect rather than military decision. Since politics rules, this is a happy conclusion for those attracted to the guerrilla mode of fighting. J. Bowyer Bell, in his innovative assault upon 'the myth of the guerrilla', reminds us in his commentary upon Lawrence and the Arab Revolution of the true character of the strategic effect achievable by guerrilla warfare. He claims, credibly, that the key to guerrilla warfare 'was not so much in the techniques of hit-and-run, hide-and-seek, quick ambushes and long periods of somnolence, but in the erosion of the will of the stronger—a victory to be won in Turkish hearts or Turkish judgment, not over Turkish troops'.[54]

'Special warfare', whether (strategically) independent or (operationally) adjunct (to regular operations) activities, has added a layer of complexity to the widening gyre of 'things strategic'. In the 1914–18 war, the British, French, and German armies had no special operations forces: the German *Stosstruppen* of 1918 were élite, assault infantry, not special forces.[55] In the 1939–45 war the British had, if anything, too many special warriors, organized into élite private armies,[56] while the Germans had too few, organized and led too late to make much of a difference. SS Colonel Otto Skorzeny was a genius of a 'special warrior', but the Third Reich

---

[52] For an adventure story, see Virginia Cowles, *The Phantom Major: The Story of David Stirling and the S.A.S.* (London, 1958), 21–2; for scholarly positive appraisal, see John W. Gordon, *The Other Desert War: British Special Forces in North Africa, 1940–1943* (New York, 1987), 79 ff.; for the standard biography, see Alan Hoe, *David Stirling* (London, 1992); and for the predictable attempt at demolition, see Newsinger, *Dangerous Men*, 5–7, 'The Founding Myth'.

[53] Eliot A. Cohen, *Commandos and Politicians: Elite Military Units in Modern Democracies* (Cambridge, Mass., 1978).

[54] J. Bowyer Bell, *The Myth of the Guerrilla: Revolutionary Theory and Malpractice* (New York, 1971), 6–7. A more recent book by Bell is also highly pertinent: *The Dynamics of the Armed Struggle* (London, 1998).

[55] Wilhelm Balck, *Development of Tactics: World War*, trans. Harry Bell (Fort Leavenworth, Kan., 1922), esp. chs. 9 and 12; Pascal M. H. Lucas, *The Evolution of Tactical Ideas in France and Germany during the War of 1914–1918*, trans. P. V. Kieffer (Paris, 1923), ch. 6; Bruce I. Gudmundsson, *Stormtroop Tactics: Innovation in the German Army, 1914–1918* (New York, 1989); Norman L. Kincaide, ' "Sturmabteilung" to "Freikorps": German Army Tactical and Organizational Development, 1914–1918' (Ph.D. thesis, Tempe, Ariz., Dec. 1989).

[56] Viscount Slim, *Defeat Into Victory* (London, 1986), 546–9; Julian Thompson, *The Imperial War Museum Book of War Behind Enemy Lines* (London, 1998), ch. 1, and 'Tailpiece'.

was beyond help, especially by a handful of Nazi heroes, in the years 1943–5.[57] The manifest failure of the orthodox British military effort in 1940, in the geostrategic context of continental exclusion after Dunkirk, energized British eccentricity to find unorthodox military outlets. The success of orthodox German military units in 1939–41 did not yield a political-military climate permissive of high-risk special operations. Also, so high a standard of military effectiveness was demanded and expected of most regular formations in the German Army that even the idea of super-élite units was contrary to the prevailing military culture.[58]

Regardless of their narrowly tactical affinity to guerrilla warfare, special operations are a permanent additional element increasing the complexity of modern war and strategy.[59] If the twentieth century began with war only on land and at sea, it concluded with the geographical additions of war in the air, in space (somewhat anti-geographically), in cyberspace, and in nuclear and 'special' regions. Modern strategy has not invented 'special warfare', but after 1939 it invented special forces geared (ideally, if not always in practice) to secure strategic effect through an unconventional style. The invention of distinctive special operations forces in and after World War II is historically comparable to the 'invention' of a light infantry specialized for the skirmishing role in the late eighteenth century.[60]

One has to be impressed with the theory and sometimes successful practice of revolutionary people's war. But the people's war that loomed so menacingly in the 1950s and 1960s, is probably of less significance than is the regularization of guerrilla technique in the manuals of unconventional regular warriors. Outstanding though it is, the strategic theory of Mao Tse-tung and Chu-Teh is massively derivative from Chinese classical military writings, and has obvious geographical and socio-political limitations of applicability. The realm of modern strategy should be prepared to take more (or at least as much) note of the skills of the special warrior than of the revolutionary activist. The painful era of decolonization was, inexorably, the era of wars of national liberation to which theories of

---

[57] Otto Skorzeny, *Skorzeny's Secret Missions: War Memoirs of the Most Dangerous Man in Europe* (New York, 1950); Charley Foley, *Commando Extraordinary* (London, 1954); Franz Kurowski, *The Brandenburgers: Global Mission* (Winnipeg, 1997); for an exciting popular overview, see James Lucas, *Kommando: German Special Forces of World War Two* (New York, 1986).

[58] Martin van Creveld, *Fighting Power: German and U.S. Army Performance, 1939–1945* (Westport, Conn., 1982); Jürgen E. Förster, 'The Dynamics of *Volkegemeinschaft*: The Effectiveness of the German Military Establishment in the Second World War', in Allan R. Millett and Williamson Murray (eds.), *Military Effectiveness, iii: The Second World War* (3 vols.; Boston, 1988), esp. 204–12. Van Creveld's unfavourable judgement on the fighting power of American, as contrasted with German, soldiers, needs to be modified with reference to the different assessment in Michael D. Doubler, *Closing with the Enemy: How GIs Fought the War in Europe, 1944–1945* (Lawrence, Kan., 1994).

[59] On the range of tasks that special operations forces can undertake, see Gray, *Explorations in Strategy*, ch. 9.

[60] Gunther E. Rothenberg, *The Art of Warfare in the Age of Napoleon* (Bloomington, Ind., 1980); Russell F. Weigley, *The Age of Battles: The Quest for Decisive Warfare from Breitenfeld to Waterloo* (Bloomington, Ind., 1991), ch. 11; Rory Muir, *Tactics and the Experience of Battle in the Age of Napoleon* (New Haven, Conn., 1998), chs. 4 and 5.

patriotic revolutionary, or patriotic revolutionary people's war, most obviously applied.

Although revolutionary war, like terrorism, is as old as strategic history, plainly both broad bands of behaviour registered surges in the twentieth century. Revolutionary warfare was popular as the several old-fashioned forms of colonialism beat their retreats. Terrorism, an ancient and medieval scourge as well as a modern one, assumed a new prominence after Zionist success in the 1940s and then again after the Six-Day War of 1967 in the Middle East. Ironically the terrorist scourge was a vehicle for Palestinian frustration at the repeated failure of the Arab front-line states to deal with Israel. The law of unintended consequences worked ironically in that the Jewish terrorists of the 1930s and 1940s 'showed the way' to Palestinian terrorists in the late 1960s and beyond.[61] In contrast to the specifically political roots for the small-war activities of revolutionary and terroristic combat, special operations forces should be viewed as a historically significant and widespread addition to the grand-strategic and military options available to policy. Special operations capability constitutes a permanent option in the locker of statecraft and strategy. But people's revolutionary war and terrorism, though also methods of war, require a permissive political context that sets them apart from special operations. This is not to deny that the expertise and mindset required of a 'special' force if it is to be effective at counter-terrorism obliges it to function as a unit of 'terrorists in uniform'. The point has been made already that special forces' warriors have to function as 'guerrillas in uniform'.

There is a great deal of tactical doctrine for special forces,[62] but virtually no relevant strategic theory or history. There is a large literature on variants of 'how to be a special warrior'—for example, in Major Rogers's standing orders for Rogers's Rangers in 1759, and in an immense library of colourful narratives of stirring deeds in special warfare. But strategic history which explains the effect of special operations on the course and outcome of events is not available. Similarly, the strategic theory that would help explain what 'handfuls of special warfare heroes' can accomplish, and would help educate potential clients about the services provided by special operations forces, is rudimentary.[63] The history of the twentieth century is strewn with cases of the misuse of unduly large bodies of special forces as élite shock troops, as well as with opportunities for special operations arguably lost because no one, including the special warriors themselves, were sufficiently unconventional in their thinking. The conduct of unconventional warfare carries heavier demands than the wearing of green, grey, black, or red berets and the mastery of unusual firearms. Unconventional war is a state of mind as well as a mission and a distinctive set of tactics.

---

[61] The point is argued forcefully in Hoffman, *Inside Terrorism*, chs. 2 and 3.

[62] e.g. Bob Newman, *Marine Special Warfare and Elite Unit Tactics* (Boulder, Colo., 1995); id., *Guerrillas in the Mist: A Battlefield Guide to Clandestine Warfare* (Boulder, Colo., 1997).

[63] Gray, 'Handfuls of Heroes'.

POLITICAL PURPOSE AND GUERRILLA SPIRIT

Readers will have their own most favoured theorists on the conduct of small wars. For tactical precepts, it would be difficult to improve on Colonel Rogers (e.g. 'If somebody's trailing you, make a circle, come back onto your own tracks and ambush the folks that aim to ambush you'),[64] while for an operational canon, T. E. Lawrence is incomparable, though admittedly not to everyone's taste.[65]

... suppose they [the Arabs] were an influence, a thing invulnerable, intangible without front or back, drifting about like a gas. Armies were like plants, immobile as a whole, firm-rooted, nourished through long stems to the head. The Arabs might be a vapour, blowing where they listed. It seemed that a regular soldier might be helpless without a target.[66]

Most wars are wars of contact, both forces striving to keep in touch to avoid tactical surprise. The Arab war should be a war of detachment: to contain the enemy by the silent threat of a vast unknown desert, not disclosing themselves till the moment of attack.[67]

The Turkish army was an accident, not a target. Our true strategic aim was to seek its weakest link, and bear only on that till time made the mass of it fall.[68]

Success was certain, to be proved by paper and pencil as soon as the proportion of space and number had been learned. The contest was not physical, but moral, and so battles were a mistake.[69]

The Arabs had nothing material to lose, so they were to defend nothing and to shoot nothing. Their cards were speed and time, not hitting power, and these gave them strategical rather than tactical strength. Range is more to strategy than force.[70]

It is significant that Callwell had advanced approximately the same arguments in his *Small Wars*, though from the point of view of the imperial soldier fighting the tribal guerrilla. The regular force *should* be tactically invincible in formal battle, which is why the irregular warrior ought to fight only on his own terms.

In character these operations [of the Arab Revolt] were like naval warfare, in their mobility, their ubiquity, their independence of bases and communications, in their ignoring of ground features, of strategic areas, of fixed directions, of fixed points.[71]

[64] Dupuy, *International Military and Defense Encyclopaedia*, vi. 2811.

[65] Kingsley Widmer, 'The Intellectual as Soldier', in Jeffrey Meyers (ed.), *T. E. Lawrence: Soldier, Writer, Legend* (London, 1989), 28–57, offers a complicated portrait and not wholly friendly assessment. Konrad Morsey, 'T. E. Lawrence: Strategist', in Stephen E. Tabachnick (ed.), *The T. E. Lawrence Puzzle* (Athens, Ga., 1984), 185–203, is much more flattering to its subject and, in my opinion, more accurate. Morsey concludes: 'Lawrence's romantic personality may undoubtedly have helped increase his attractiveness, but this fact does not impair the basic validity of his theory and achievement any more than his literary talent does. As a strategist, "Lawrence of Arabia" deserves his ornament of honor' (200).

[66] T. E. Lawrence, 'Guerrilla Warfare', in Gérard Chaliand (ed.), *The Art of War in World History: From Antiquity to the Nuclear Age* (Berkeley, Calif., 1994), 883. This essay was contributed by Lawrence to the *Encyclopaedia Britannica* and was first published in 1929. See also Lawrence, *Seven Pillars of Wisdom*, ch. 33.

[67] Lawrence, 'Guerrilla Warfare', 885.

[68] Ibid. 886.

[69] Ibid.

[70] Ibid. 887.

[71] Ibid.

The tactics were always tip and run; not pushes [Lawrence is writing to contrast his guerrilla ethos with the 'big pushes' of regular warfare on the Western Front], but strokes. The Arab army . . . used the smallest force in the quickest time at the farthest place.[72]

The value of the Arab army depended entirely on quality, not on quantity. The members had to keep always cool, for the excitement of a blood-lust would impair their science, and their victory depended on a just use of speed, concealment, accuracy of fire. Guerrilla warfare is far more intellectual than a bayonet charge.[73]

Lawrence was sufficiently confident, perhaps arrogant, as to write of 'the exact science of guerrilla warfare' that '[i]n 50 words':

Granted mobility, security (in the form of denying targets to the enemy), time, and doctrine (the idea to convert every subject to friendliness), victory will rest with the insurgents, for the algebraical factors ['known invariables, fixed conditions, space and time, inorganic things like hills and climates and railways, with mankind in type-masses too great for individual variety . . . '] are in the end decisive, and against them perfections of means and spirit struggle quite in vain.[74]

If Lawrence captures the operational spirit of the guerrilla warrior better than any other theorist-practitioner, Mao Tse-tung is the best strategic theorist-practitioner of small wars. Mao understood that guerrilla warfare, like regular warfare and indeed like terrorism (a pejorative term not favoured by the theorists of any strategic culture), is simply a mode of warfare. Guerrilla warfare becomes strategically lethal when it is transformed by political content into revolutionary, or people's war. Mao Tse-tung and his contemporaries had sensible things to say about guerrilla warfare, but when stripped of their rural Chinese content they were not at all extraordinary. Bearing in mind that guerrilla warfare was a global phenomenon in the twentieth century (as it was in the nineteenth also—consider the 'native' resistance on all continents to imperial conquest), and that it was waged in the forest, in jungles, in desert, on steppes, and in urban 'terrain', one needs to be ready to translate an operational ethos into the tactical doctrine most suitable for a specific contingency.

As a strategic theorist of the initially disadvantaged side in small wars, Mao Tse-tung has three preeminent claims to fame.[75] First, he emphasized the need to build a political organization around a guerrilla movement. In other words, as a good Clausewitzian (we know also that Mao was a suitably dutiful admirer of Sun Tzu), he appreciated the vitality of the linkage between political purpose, in this case as institutionalized in the Party and its Programme, and military means. Second, with his elemental categorization of revolutionary warfare in three

---

[72] Lawrence, 'Guerrilla Warfare', 887.

[73] Ibid. 890.

[74] Ibid.

[75] I am grateful for the excellent contribution by Rod Paschall on 'Guerrilla Warfare', in Robert Cowley and Geoffrey Parker (eds.), *The Osprey Companion to Military History* (London, 1996), 192–4.

parts—phase I, political organization; phase II, guerrilla operations; and phase III, transition to regular operations of war to defeat the enemy in decisive battle— Mao suggests that guerrilla warfare alone cannot deliver victory. Third, he explains that the 'people' in people's revolutionary war must be prepared to wage protracted conflict.[76] Given that most of us are attracted to the prospects of swift rewards for effort today, it is easy to see how truly heroic is Mao's message of eventual success through the conduct of protracted revolutionary warfare. His theory, and practice, of protracted war is a theory and practice of 'blood, tears, toil, and sweat'; it is a theory of victory for the weak, who are obliged to do things the long and hard way.

A VIOLENT CENTURY

The use of organized force for political purposes is a concept simultaneously Clausewitzian, quintessentially strategic, eternal in applicability, and clear enough to be useful. Moreover, the realm of war and strategy is not the world of inter-state politics alone. Various forms of intra- and trans-state warfare coexist with the relatively rare occurrence of armed conflicts between states. It is true that the greatest theorist on war of all time, Carl von Clausewitz, wrote state-centrically from his experience and study of what to him was the contemporary strategic experience of Napoleonic warfare and statecraft. He also emphasized the importance of being very strong at the 'decisive point' so as to secure victory in battle.[77] It would be wrong to claim, however, that there could be a 'fundamental problem with the Clausewitzian account of war, which is that it may be *culturally specific*'.[78] Victor Davis Hanson suggests plausibly that there has been a culturally distinctive Western way of war which contrasts sharply with an Eastern way keyed to guerrilla tactics.[79] That suggestion bears not at all upon the universal authority of Clausewitz's theory.

'Small wars and other savage violence' are part of the same empirical and intellectual universe of strategy which includes Western strategic experience. There is not, on the one hand, a culturally narrow Western world which has *On War* as its strategic bible, and on the other hand a non-Western world which rejects the Clausewitzian enlightenment. Although Clausewitz was impressed by the political consequences of a 'decisive battle', *à la* Leuctra, Manzikert, Hattin, Jena, or Waterloo, the range, reach, and grasp of his theory of war is far greater than are the conditions of the grammar of war in his own time. Whether one is a steppe

---

[76] Mao, *Selected Military Writings*, 187–266, 'On Protracted War'.

[77] Clausewitz, *On War*, 204.

[78] Chris Brown, *Understanding International Relations* (London, 1997), 116 (emphasis original).

[79] Victor Davis Hanson, *The Western Way of War: Infantry Battle in Classical Greece* (London, 1989). The social and political context of military style is recreated admirably in Antonio Santosuosso, *Soldiers, Citizens, and the Symbols of War: From Classical Greece to Republican Rome, 500–167 B.C.* (Boulder, Colo., 1997).

raider, an Athenian hoplite, a German stormtrooper, a US marine, or a Serbian 'ethnic cleanser', one lives in a world of strategic effect, in a world of strategy.

Terrorists are no more isolated from the world of strategy than are tribal warriors, peasant part-time revolutionaries, or professional soldiers.[80] By definition, terrorists are politically motivated, even if some of their acts (e.g. bank robbery, kidnapping, exemplary beatings) are indistinguishable from organized crime. Terrorists are people who seek political ends through behaviour that deliberately induces fear.[81]

Terroristic behaviour is not, of course, the prerogative of a political underclass. A classic study of Stalin's USSR, after all, is justly entitled *The Great Terror*.[82] Governments also can seek power and influence through fear. Most of the strategic action in the twentieth century occurred within states for domestic political reasons. Most of the wars and other cases of noticeably savage violence were internal conflicts, and most of the human victims of politically organized violence met their fate in internal wars. By far the bloodiest conflict in the world in the nineteenth century was the wholly domestic Taiping Rebellion in China.[83] The bloodiest war in US history was the massively uncivil civil war of 1861–5.

The end of the colonial period and its concommitant phase of retreat, the process of global urbanization, and the growth in governmental military and paramilitary mobility, striking power, and reliable near-real-time intelligence have been factors that shifted the action in 'small wars' in the twentieth century to the terrorist end of the spectrum of savage violence. The 'small-war' record of the century recorded overlapping periods.

- *Classic small wars* of imperial acquisition and consolidation, and attempts to resist such acquisition and consolidation, c.1900–c.1936 (from the Transvaal to Abyssinia).
- *Imperial policing* and resistance to imperial rule, c.1919–1966 (from Amritsar to Aden City).
- *Revolutionary guerrilla warfare* and its obverse, c.1917–c.1990 (from Arabia to the end of the Apartheid era in South Africa).
- *Terrorism* and counter-terrorism, c.1945 to the present (from Jewish terror for a state of Israel to Islamic extremist and 'general expressive' outrages).
- *'Civilizational', cultural, ethnic, and other tribal violence*, c.1991 to the present (from

---

[80] In vital senses, of course, terrorism is apt of necessity to be a way of life, and those among its practitioners who survive for any length of time are both expert and, in effect, professional 'soldiers', albeit not in uniform: Lawrence Freedman, 'Terrorism and Strategy', in Freedman et al., *Terrorism and International Order*, Chatham House Special Paper (London, 1987), is outstanding.

[81] Hoffman defines terrorism as 'the deliberate creation and exploitation of fear through violence or the threat of violence in the pursuit of political change': *Inside Terrorism*, 43.

[82] Robert Conquest, *The Great Terror: A Reassessment* (New York, 1990).

[83] Jonathan Spence, *God's Chinese Son: The Taiping Heavenly Kingdom of Hong Xiuquan* (London, 1996). Between 1850 and 1864 probably 20 million people died in, or as a result of, the Taiping Rebellion.

the collapse of the Soviet imperium to the eventual emergence of some new balance of power).

The outline is not offered as candidate history, but is tendered to suggest the shifting centre of gravity of the 'irregular' action over the course of a century. One of the general themes of this book is the interplay between strategic theory and practice. All the leading theorists of 'small wars and other savage violence' have written in response to one or other of these overlapping foci.

Walter Laqueur is plausible when he suggests that a terrorist

is not a guerrilla, strictly speaking. There are no longer any guerrillas, engaging in Maoist-style liberation of territories that become the basis of a counter-society and a regular army fighting the central government—except perhaps in remote places like Afghanistan, the Philippines, and Sri Lanka.[84]

In addition, many people will agree with Laqueur when he says:

Thus at one end of the scale, the lone terrorist has appeared, and at the other, state-sponsored terrorism is quietly flourishing in these days when wars of aggression have become too expensive and too risky. As the century draws to a close, terrorism is becoming the substitute for the great wars of the 1800s and early 1900s.[85]

As with classic guerrilla warfare, terrorism can work by wearing down the will to rule of the authorities. Neither guerrillas nor terrorists should seek, or can win, military victories *per se*. Guerrilla and terror tactics are the tactics of the belligerent unable in mass and firepower to stand and fight a regular battle or campaign with a reasonable prospect of success; they are the tactics of the weak.

The distinction between guerrilla warfare and terrorism is clear, but easily confused. Terrorism, the endeavour for political motives to spread fear by what are intended to be exemplary, even symbolic, acts of violence, is a tool of the guerrilla warrior which also can be used by the regular soldier. It is standard fare for strategic theorists to observe both that terrorism is the mode of operation of the desperately weak and that typically it fails to deliver strategic success. Although the history of modern terrorism does not record many successes (the early ending of the British Mandate in Palestine remains the 'flagship' success of a terror campaign), one needs to remember the unusually problematic nature of the relevant evidence of strategic effect. After all, terrorists, in common with the very 'regular' practitioners of nuclear deterrence, seek to act upon the will of their foes. Terrorist success cannot be registered in territory secured or in body-counts. Terrorists succeed when governments react or overreact with brutal measures that alienate the politically target population. Terrorists win when they provoke a government into defeating itself. Terrorists also can succeed by so sapping the political will of the authorities that a process of rolling concession is set in train, witness the

[84] Walter Laqueur, 'Postmodern Terrorism', *Foreign Affairs*, 75 (1996), 26.   [85] Ibid. 34.

behaviour and limited but real strategic success of the Provisional IRA in the 1990s.

Attempts to understand terrorism in strategic terms highlight the unity of all strategic experience. Terrorism is different in its actions, and menace of actions, from regular military conquest or attrition of the enemy's military strength, but then guerrilla warfare and nuclear deterrence also are different. But all these types of military conduct generate strategic effect. That effect can be produced upon the mind, the military muscle, or both, of the foe, but in either case there has to be a transition from the use of force, from violent acts and the threat thereof, to political consequences. Mao, the quintessential practitioner-theorist, claims bluntly: 'Guerrilla hostilities are the university of war.'[86] In other words, strategic theory, to help strategic practice, can be forged only in the light shone by understanding strategic experience. With reference to my theme of the unity of all strategic experience, a theme that respects the key Clausewitzian distinction between the grammar and the policy logic of war, Mao argues:

Though the strategy of guerrillas is inseparable from war strategy as a whole, the actual conduct of these hostilities differs from the conduct of orthodox operations. Each type of warfare has methods peculiar to itself, and methods suitable to regular warfare cannot be applied with success to the special situations that confront guerrillas.[87]

The character and conduct of war and strategy must vary with time and opponents, but their nature and function are permanent.

[86] Mao [attrib.], *On Guerrilla Warfare*, 73.   [87] Ibid. 95.

Chapter 11

SECOND THOUGHTS ON NUCLEAR WEAPONS

There is a considerable danger that the making of nuclear strategy and the practice of nuclear deterrence will be misjudged by historians who lack empathy in
their scholarly forays into the nuclear archives. The explanation and analysis provided in this chapter and the next should not be read as a prolonged apologia. I am
appalled at the scale and character of the contingent nuclear threats that the US
government embraced as its evolving nuclear strategy during the Cold War. But I
find nonetheless that there was method in the apparent madness, and that 'just'
intentions hovered behind the contingent emergency action messages (EAMs—
the signals for nuclear action).[1]

These two nuclear chapters share purpose with John Keegan's classic, *The Face of
Battle*, albeit in distinctly lower voice.[2] No nuclear battle concluded the great Cold
War. But in the protracted virtual war of nuclear standoff, theorists did battle with
their brutal vu-graphs, and chose to live the professional lives that gave them
responsibilities that many scholars based in universities and think-tanks neglect
to recognize. There is no nuclear strategy that in execution would not entail costs,
and pose risks, that any sane and sober person would far prefer not to run. But the
official world of modern strategy had no practicable choice other than to try to
cope with weapons that could not reliably be tamed for good Clausewitzian
purpose as tools of high policy.

The purposes of this chapter are to introduce the important subject of how the
realm of strategy coped, or failed to cope, with nuclear weapons, and to encourage
strategic historical empathy on the part of the reader.[3]

The argument here reaffirms the master theme of the book, which claims an
essential unity for all strategic experience—in this case extending even to

---

[1] Robert W. Tucker, *The Just War: A Study in Contemporary American Doctrine* (Baltimore, 1960); James
Turner Johnson, *Can Modern War Be Just?* (New Haven, Conn., 1984); Joseph S. Nye, Jr., *Nuclear Ethics* (New
York, 1986).

[2] John Keegan, *The Face of Battle* (London, 1976).

[3] The title of this chapter both promises second thoughts on the part of the author—who has been
researching and writing about nuclear topics for 30 years—and is intended to suggest the desirability
in general of a second look at the nuclear age of the Cold War. For a few 'first thoughts' on nuclear
weapons, see Colin S. Gray, 'Nuclear Strategy: The Debate Moves On', *RUSI Journal*, 121 (1976), 44–50; id.,
'Nuclear Strategy: The Case for a Theory of Victory', *International Security*, 4 (1979), 54–87; id., 'Nuclear
Strategy: A Regrettable Necessity', *SAIS Review*, 3 (1983), 13–28; id., 'Nuclear Strategy: What Is True, What
Is False, What Is Arguable?', *Comparative Strategy*, 9 (1990), 1–32.

embrace experience with nuclear weapons (and other weapons of mass destruction). It is argued in this chapter that much, certainly enough, of what Western security communities believed about the USSR in the Cold War proves to have been substantially true. Whatever one believes today about the USSR, however, the military establishments of the superpowers generally behaved prudently and with great professional correctness as they sought to manage the novel challenges posed by nuclear weapons. Whether or not the policy and strategy results of such management retrospectively warrant description as a kind of madness, both sides to the Cold War conflict were in the grip of strong influence by strategic historical necessity. To those people now convinced that the military history of the Cold War should be viewed as a form of collective insanity at worst, and gross irresponsibility at best, I offer the thought that to the *ex post facto* strategic revisionist of nuclear-era history nothing may seem impossible.[4] This chapter and the next one, however, tell a different story.

A SECOND LOOK

Modern strategists have been shaped by the challenges posed by nuclear weapons. For more than forty years the nuclear issue all but defined the domain of (Western) strategic studies.[5] The intellectual heroes of modern strategic thought have been individuals who sought to make strategic sense of nuclear weapons. Bernard Brodie, Albert Wohlstetter, Thomas C. Schelling, Herman Kahn, and—with reservations—Henry A. Kissinger were soon recognized as giants not only because of the quality of their theorizing but also because they tackled the most pressing security problems of the era.[6]

The history of nuclear weapons is fraught with guesswork about their strategic value. Much of what strategic theorists believe they know about the influence of nuclear weapons on strategic history from the 1940s until the late 1980s, they do not really know at all. As the veil that obscured erstwhile Soviet nuclear thought, policy, and behaviour is partially lifted, it is appropriate to ask whether humankind survived the decades of East–West Cold War more by luck than by strategic prudence. By analogy, in the first great struggle of the twentieth century, from 1914 to 1918, the politicians and other military professionals of the *Entente*

---

[4] There is much of factual merit in David Miller, *The Cold War: A Military History* (London, 1998).

[5] Colin S. Gray, *Strategic Studies and Public Policy: The American Experience* (Lexington, Ky., 1982); Lawrence Freedman, 'The First Two Generations of Nuclear Strategists', in Peter Paret (ed.), *Makers of Modern Strategy: From Machiavelli to the Nuclear Age* (Princeton, NJ, 1986), 735–77; Ken Booth, 'Strategy', in A. J. R. Groom and Margot Light (eds.), *Contemporary International Relations: A Guide to Theory* (London, 1994), 109–27.

[6] John Baylis and John Garnett (eds.), *Makers of Nuclear Strategy* (New York, 1991). A less flattering assessment is offered in Fred Kaplan, *The Wizards of Armageddon* (New York, 1983). The reservations about Henry Kissinger pertain to his characteristic role as popularizer, rather than innovator, of strategic ideas.

Powers—with an abundance of amateur, but eventually expert civilian assistance and sacrifice[7]—performed well enough to secure a victory that was distinguishable from defeat. But should one be more impressed by the Allied ability ultimately to generate sufficient strategic effect to win than by the costs of that success? Was success in the Cold War, including the fact that success was not purchased at violent, nuclear-led cost, on balance a triumph of Western statecraft and strategy? Is veteran nuclear policy adviser J. J. Martin correct when he trumpets:

Americans can look back with pride on the cold war years. We crafted a strategy and developed military systems that brought us successfully through a complex set of nuclear dangers, with no global catastrophes; we preserved both world order and Western interests against a determined, nuclear-armed competitor; and we are now in the process of reducing the large and destructive nuclear forces that both sides built up during the cold war.[8]

Did we not do well? Alternatively, did the war remain virtual as much despite as because of the all-but-belligerents' ideas and practices? These apparently idle, even academic, speculative questions both express a lasting challenge to historical judgement and have profound implications for future generations. The principal challenge, of course, lies in the perennial difficulty of finding satisfactory explanations for a non-event.

Few people can approach nuclear weapons dispassionately. Indeed, even to appear dispassionate in the analysis of nuclear matters can invite charges of immorality or amorality.[9] Categorization of nuclear weapons—along, say, with the Third Reich, Saddam Hussein, the Spanish Inquisition, and the Black Death—as thoroughly 'Bad Things', as Sellar and Yeatman would insist in their comic parody,[10] provides some emotional and intellectual satisfaction, but inhibits understanding. Even today, the worthy attitude of many people that the best nuclear arsenal is the least nuclear arsenal promotes a triumph of emotion over reason.[11]

The military impracticality of most forms of nuclear warfare, which appears to

---

[7] George MacDonald Fraser, in his war memoirs, makes the interesting point that 'Fourteenth Army weren't professionals. They were experts': *Quartered Safe Out Here: A Recollection of the War in Burma* (London, 1995), 87.

[8] J. J. Martin, 'Dealing with Future Nuclear Dangers', *Comparative Strategy*, 16 (1997), 253.

[9] Anatol Rapoport, *Strategy and Conscience* (New York, 1964); Philip Green, *Deadly Logic: The Theory of Nuclear Deterrence* (New York, 1968).

[10] W. C. Sellar and R. J. Yeatman, *1066 and All That* (London, 1960).

[11] Jack Steinberger, Bhalchandra Udgaonkar, and Joseph Rotblat (eds.), *A Nuclear-Weapon-Free World: Desirable, Feasible?* (Boulder, Colo., 1993); Canberra Commission on the Elimination of Nuclear Weapons, *Report* (Canberra, Aug. 1996); National Academy of Sciences, Committee on International Security and Arms Control, *The Future of U.S. Nuclear Weapons Policy* (Washington, DC, 1997); Jonathan Schell, *The Gift of Time: The Case for Abolishing Nuclear Weapons Now* (London, 1998). A contrasting view pervades Michael Quinlan, *Thinking about Nuclear Weapons*, RUSI Whitehall Paper (London, 1997); Keith B. Payne, *The Case Against Nuclear Abolition And For Nuclear Deterrence* (Fairfax, Va., Dec. 1997); Colin S. Gray, *The Second Nuclear Age* (Boulder, Colo., 1999), ch. 4.

cast lethal doubt upon the strategic value of nuclear weapons, in fact has exactly the opposite effect in the wonderful world of statecraft. The awesome brutality of prospective nuclear use, though hard to tame for intended military effect, serves superbly as an instrument of political reassurance as the *ultima ratio regis*. So deeply is this subject mired in ethical, military-operational, and historical controversies that it is unusually difficult to explore the 'second thoughts' advertised as this chapter's title. Unlike strategy for space and information forces, strategy for nuclear weapons is an issue area beset by too many thickets of beliefs, prejudices, and principles for ease of analytical passage.

Neither policy-oriented nor historical scholarship alone can probe what most needs probing. The achievement of ever more robust historical comprehension of nuclear policy and strategy is important. That comprehension, however, needs to be informed by answers to questions that professional historians are not well equipped to frame or pursue. Unlike, say, 'the Dreadnought era', the defining weaponry of the nuclear era is not self-evidently vulnerable to technical-tactical ambush by technological advance.[12] In keeping with the general themes of this text, nuclear weapons, notwithstanding their undeniable raw potency, are considered on the one hand as more fuel for strategic history as usual, and on the other hand at least as a candidate challenge to the very integrity of the strategic function itself. Several questions are key to the analysis which follows.

First, as a matter of relatively uncontentious historical record, to what purposes have nuclear weapons been applied in modern strategy? Second, in practice what has been the influence in strategic effect of these weapons? Third, how could the generally well-funded, analytically fairly sophisticated, and assuredly civilian controlled military establishments of the United States and the Soviet Union construct what amounted to a global death machine? Fourth, if there was great folly in competitive armament with tens of thousands of nuclear weapons that could not be employed on a large scale except to self-defeating effect, wherein lay the roots, and what were the dynamics, of that bilateral superpower folly?[13]

---

[12] A partial exception to this claim would be successful development of active defences against the ballistic and air-breathing missiles that constitute the leading, though far from only, means of nuclear delivery. On 23 Mar. 1983 President Ronald Reagan spoke as follows: '[I] call upon the scientific community in our country, who gave us nuclear weapons, to turn their great talents now to the cause of mankind and world peace, to give us the means of rendering these nuclear weapons impotent and obsolete': Reagan, 'Launching the SDI', in Zbigniew Brzezinski (ed.), *Promise and Peril: The Strategic Defense Initiative* (Washington, DC, 1986), 49.

[13] Colin S. Gray, *The Soviet–American Arms Race* (Lexington, Mass., 1976); Miroslav Nincic, *The Arms Race: The Political Economy of Military Growth* (New York, 1982); Craig Etcheson, *Arms Race Theory: Strategy and Structure of Behavior* (Westport, Conn., 1989); Patrick Glynn, *Closing Pandora's Box: Arms Races, Arms Control and the History of the Cold War* (New York, 1992); Grant T. Hammond, *Plowshares into Swords: Arms Races in International Politics, 1840–1991* (Columbia, SC, 1993); Barry Buzan and Eric Herring, *The Arms Dynamic in World Politics* (Boulder, Colo., 1998). Colin S. Gray, 'Arms Races and Other Pathetic Fallacies: A Case for Deconstruction', *Review of International Studies*, 22 (1996), 323–35, challenges the integrity of the concept of arms race.

The analogy is far from perfect, but there is some parallel to be drawn between the apparently murderous absurdity of tactics and operational artistry in the First World War and the even more potentially murderous absurdity of what has been termed 'nuclear strategy'. How could self-styled strategists, people of conscience and political sophistication—some with powerful minds—have contemplated with the appearance of equanimity strategic processes that all too easily might have yielded casualty rates that could be matched only by an asteroid strike on planet earth? Or, is there something wrong with the way the question is framed? Might it be the case that, as with many of the politicians and generals of 1914–18, strategists in the great Cold War performed about as well as people can perform when they lack the advantages of accurate foresight that flow from hindsight? Recall that the military leaders of 1914–18 took approximately three years to become expert in their trade and to acquire, equip, and train armies reliably capable of achieving battlefield success.[14] Although the strategists of the Cold War had forty years to master their trade, the inference of success from non-events could not yield evidence for education on a par with the bloody actualities of 1914–17.

At some risk of appearing to defend the indefensible, I suggest that the Western Alliance in the Cold War, more often than not, adopted an approach to nuclear weapons that, even when plainly questionable in retrospect, arguably was wrong for many of the right reasons. The arguments of some scholarly and policy-oriented critics of Western nuclear strategy in the Cold War can read plausibly, case by case, point by point, but characteristically they lack empathy for the base of knowledge, prevailing assumptions, and realistic available alternatives at the time. For example, it is clever to argue that '[t]he development of nuclear strategy represented an attempt at a Jominian solution to a problem that was essentially Clausewitzian in nature'.[15] But, what else could be done? The author of this insightful judgement is claiming that nuclear strategists inappropriately sought 'correct' military operational answers to questions that truly allowed of none such. How could American and Soviet strategists possibly eschew the search for the correct, or correct enough, *military* roles for nuclear weapons? The politicians and generals of 1914–18 were never confronted with a discreet cost/risk–benefit choice. Neither Herbert Asquith nor David Lloyd George was ever asked to decide whether denial of German hegemony in Europe was 'worth' nearly a million British Empire dead. Similarly, neither American nor Soviet politicians decided to build nuclear arsenals *certain* to have literally cataclysmic consequences if ever unleashed in anger. Nonetheless, the British Empire suffered very nearly one million fatalities in the war of 1914–18, and the superpowers did construct the most fearful death machine in human history. Perspective is still

[14] Jonathan Bailey, *The First World War and the Birth of the Modern Style of Warfare*, Occasional Paper 22 (Camberley, 1996).

[15] John J. Weltman, *World Politics and the Evolution of War* (Baltimore, 1995), 152.

desperately lacking, but the time for second thoughts on nuclear matters is plainly due.

THE REALM OF NECESSITY

Talented theorists as far apart in age and dates of authorship as Bernard Brodie and Robert Jervis have written persuasively of the nuclear revolution.[16] As time passes, however, the revolutionary implications of nuclear weapons can fade somewhat in assessed significance. It will not have escaped readers' notice, I am sure, that the organization of this book appears to treat nuclear weapons and the nuclear revolution as *just another* domain wherein the grammar of strategy seeks to make sense of ideas, resources, and behaviour for the logic of policy. It is my contention that the practice and malpractice of modern strategy can indeed be approached usefully by means of a holistic appreciation that keeps in view war on land, at sea, in the air, in space, in cyberspace, on asymmetrical terms (small wars), and with nuclear weapons. Admittedly, categories are mixed in this array. Specifically, modern strategy is treated by geographical (and even anti-geographical, with cyberspace) environment, by type of weapons, and by character of belligerents. So be it. The message here is that the nuclear revolution has occurred in the stream of strategic history, and that despite the 'prospect of Armageddon', as Jervis's subtitle so accurately reminds us, this revolution has signalled neither the end of (strategic) history nor even a dead end for strategy. However, it is significant that nuclear weapons are the only class of weapon allowed to be the focus of chapter-length—in fact two-chapter-length—attention. Strategy for nuclear weapons is still strategy, but these are weapons uniquely capable of cancelling the strategic effect of all other weapons.

The case for a nuclear revolution in military and security affairs is paradoxically unanswerable, but not unarguable. Emphatically arguable is the scope of the revolutionary change supposedly wrought by the arrival of mature nuclear arsenals, which is to say of nuclear forces judged survivable. As Jervis asserts, 'it is mutual second-strike capability and not nuclear weapons per se that has generated the new situation'.[17] Nuclear weapons have not retired strategy, but strategic reasoning has certainly helped to confine the writ of those weapons in defence plans. Lawrence Freedman, following an earlier idea of Bernard Brodie, was not entirely correct in his suggestion that 'strategic thought . . . may have reached a dead end', because of the nuclear fact which commands a context wherein 'stability depends on something that is more the antithesis of strategy than its apotheosis'.[18] But

---

[16] Bernard Brodie (ed.), *The Absolute Weapon: Atomic Power and World Order* (New York, 1946); Robert Jervis, *The Meaning of the Nuclear Revolution: Statecraft and the Prospect of Armageddon* (Ithaca, NY, 1989).

[17] Ibid. 9.

[18] Lawrence Freedman, *The Evolution of Nuclear Strategy*, 2nd edn. (New York, 1989), 433.

Freedman did express the essence of the strategic problem with exemplary clarity. There is significant merit in his 1989 claim that '[n]o operational nuclear strategy had yet been devised that did not carry an enormous risk of degenerating into a bloody contest of resolve or a furious exchange of devastating and crippling blows against the political and economic centres of the industrialized world'. He proceeds: 'In 1981 the Reagan administration made a final attempt to square the circle.'[19] Freedman's judgements are not unreasonable; indeed, they are sensible. The problem is that inadvertently they may help lead people away from achieving that empathy with policy and strategy-makers that is a prerequisite for understanding.

Bernard Brodie, and then—much later—Robert Jervis and Lawrence Freedman, to cite only three of the more cogent theorists, all write eloquently about the implications of *the* central organizing feature of the nuclear age. Specifically, nuclear weapons can transform the character of war and strategy because of their inability to deliver military victory at bearable cost to the 'victor'.[20] In addition, nuclear weapons could deny the validity of the rule of classical strategy which holds that the enemy's armed forces, in one or several geographical mediums, have to be overcome before victory can be secured. Nuclear armed aircraft or missiles could coerce or actually destroy an enemy at home, even if that enemy's traditional hard military shell of armies, naval and air forces had barely been engaged in combat. Classical strategy ruled the military practice of the twentieth century. German U-boats, in repeated campaigns, could not defeat the enemy's war effort while ignoring that enemy's fighting strength at sea.[21] Similarly, so-called 'strategic' bombardment from the air has yet to demonstrate effectiveness while attempting to ignore the active air defences of competent foes.[22]

It is the unprecedented efficiency in energy release potential—most typically expressed as energy yield in tons of TNT—in relation to weight of ordnance that has effected the nuclear revolution.[23] The revolution in the nuclear revolution lay quintessentially in the awesome fact that a single delivery vehicle—an aircraft, a cruise or ballistic missile, a freighter in a harbour, a delivery van—could wreak as

---

[19] Ibid. 395.

[20] Jervis, *Meaning of the Nuclear Revolution*, 4–8.

[21] John Terraine, *Business in Great Waters: The U-Boat Wars, 1916–1945* (London, 1989); Richard Compton-Hall, *Submarines and the War at Sea, 1914–18* (London, 1991); Paul G. Halpern, *A Naval History of World War I* (London, 1994). Peter Padfield, *Dönitz: The Last Führer: Portrait of a Nazi War Leader* (New York, 1984), 229, emphasizes 'the extraordinary amateurishness of the German war effort: Dönitz was conducting a campaign of vital importance . . . with a staff of half a dozen young U-boat men!'

[22] Noble Frankland, *The Bombing Offensive against Germany: Outlines and Perspectives* (London, 1965); Stephen L. McFarland and Wesley Phillips Newton, *To Command the Sky: The Battle for Air Superiority over Germany, 1942–1944* (Washington, DC, 1991); Horst Boog (ed.), *The Conduct of the Air War in the Second World War: An International Comparison* (Providence, RI, 1992).

[23] Trevor N. Dupuy, *The Evolution of Weapons and Warfare* (Indianapolis, 1980), ch. 27; Martin van Creveld, *Technology and War: From 2000 B.C. to the Present* (New York, 1989), ch. 17; Charles C. Grace, *Nuclear Weapons: Principles, Effects and Survivability* (London, 1994).

much or more destruction in a single sortie as previously would have required sorties by several hundred aircraft or by thousands of artillery tubes. As the nuclear arsenals of the superpowers climbed from single digits to tens of thousands, and as the physical effects of nuclear weapons were better appreciated and sensibly feared, so the scope of the strategic challenge became all too apparent both to superpowers and to most of their security dependants.[24]

Viewed in long retrospect, the following pronouncement by Bernard Brodie in 1946 appears uncannily prescient: 'Thus far the chief purpose of our military establishment has been to win wars. From now on its chief purpose must be to avert them. It can have almost no other useful purpose.'[25] This early celebration of the overwhelming importance of deterrence scores high on the scale of accurate focus on the greatest of problems, but it missed the mark in other respects. Some of the historical commentary today on strategy in the Cold War is scarcely wiser with the advantage of hindsight than was Brodie, who was very largely in the realm of speculation in 1946. What are the leading difficulties with much of what may, perhaps not unfairly, be called the Brodie–Jervis–Freedman approach to nuclear strategy? My argument is that readers of those three outstanding theorists are likely to be at risk of undervaluing certain facts, principles of prudence, and considerations that shaped the course of modern strategic history.[26]

The more closely one looks at assessments of nuclear strategic performance in the Cold War, the stronger the sense of *déjà vu*. Some historians would appear to know more about Sir Arthur Wellesley's army in the Peninsula than he did, and certainly more about the BEF in the First World War than did Sir Douglas Haig. Similarly, many young and even some middle-aged 'Turks' today appear confident in their ability to wage the virtual conflict of the great Cold War more effectively than did the responsible people at the time. Hindsight is wonderful, but it is neither the moral equivalent of foresight nor free of distinctive biases. No scholar can judge the wisdom shown by a historical figure with complete fairness, because the scholar is both blessed and cursed with hindsight/foresight. That thought is especially apposite to commentary upon the course of theory and policy towards the strategic utility of nuclear weapons in the Cold War. *We know* that

---

[24] From 9 nuclear warheads in 1946, the US total ascended possibly to as high as 26,000 by 1983. By 1985, the Soviet nuclear arsenal may well have comprised in excess of 40,000 weapons of all kinds: Thomas B. Cochrane, William M. Arkin, and Milton M. Hoenig, *Nuclear Weapons Databook, i: U.S. Nuclear Forces and Capabilities* (Cambridge, Mass., 1984), 15; Thomas B. Cochrane et al., *Nuclear Weapons Databook, iv: Soviet Nuclear Weapons* (New York, 1989), 25. Between 1950 and 1960, the US nuclear weapon stockpile increased from 450 to 18,500. In that same period the Soviet stockpile grew from zero (or several, at most) to somewhere in the range 1710–4520.

[25] Brodie, 'Implications for Military Policy', in *Absolute Weapon*, 76.

[26] In the case of Bernard Brodie, I refer here only to his 1946 writing in *Absolute Weapon*. As well as the comments in Chapter 3 above, see Ken Booth, 'Bernard Brodie', in Baylis and Garnett, *Makers of Nuclear Strategy*, 19–56; Barry H. Steiner, *Bernard Brodie and the Foundations of American Nuclear Strategy* (Lawrence, Kan., 1991). Note the starring role properly given to Brodie in Kaplan, *Wizards of Armageddon*, and Gregg Herken, *Counsels of War* (New York, 1985).

the East–West Cold War concluded with a whimper and not a bang, and *we know* that the earnest hunt for militarily profitable nuclear strategy ultimately was probably not well rewarded.[27] Our knowledge now of these facts or near-facts is not particularly interesting or important. In contrast, what is both interesting and important for a practical field like strategy is how and why strategic choices were made, given the unavailability of reliable crystal balls. With reference to judgement in strategic history, there is no small merit in Jac Weller's admittedly unrealistically uncompromising advice: 'In order to appreciate fully a general's capacities, the reader should not know more at any point than the commander himself knew at the time.'[28] Weller was writing in criticism of the omniscience that historians Sir Charles Oman and Sir John Fortescue employed in order to wage the Peninsular campaigns more effectively than did Sir Arthur Wellesley.

There are two reasons why the temptation to play God at the final judgement as strategic historian should be resisted. First, it is simply unjust, and probably immoral, to criticize historical figures with direct or indirect reference to matters that those figures could not possibly know and had no reason to predict. The historian cannot help but know that a nuclear Third World War did not conclude the Cold War. Equally, those on both sides who ran the statecraft and strategy of that famous struggle had no way of knowing that there was not a nuclear war in their near or medium-term future. Second, historians, even some justly renowned historians, can forget that strategy is a practical subject, and that strategy's practitioners are always in the same unenviably ignorant condition as the historians' historical subjects. The strategist is never able to decide on a course of action with the hindsight/foresight available to later critics of his choices. Much can be learnt from strategic experience, but that wisdom is not in the same league as the hindsight available to scholars. Unlike the strategic historian, even the excellent strategic historian, the strategist and those who must advise him inhabit a world wherein the future has yet to happen, where information is often horribly uncertain, and, indeed, where all of Clausewitz's contributors to friction work overtime.

In short, I am troubled lest historians provide distorted judgement on the past for reason of their superior knowledge. As the Cold War recedes into history, and 'nuclear history' projects proliferate, so the subfield long known as nuclear

[27] Michael J. Hogan (ed.), *The End of the Cold War: Its Meaning and Implications* (Cambridge, 1992); Mike Bowker and Robin Brown (eds.), *From Cold War to Collapse: Theory and World Politics in the 1980s* (Cambridge, 1993); Richard Crockatt, *The Fifty Years War: The United States and the Soviet Union in World Politics, 1941–1991* (London, 1995); John Lewis Gaddis, *We Now Know: Rethinking Cold War History* (Oxford, 1997). To combine some of these titles, Cold War warriors would have been delighted to know—really to know—that the conflict would be of 50 years' duration and would conclude with the collapse of the USSR. None of this could be known at the time. Early in 1951, for example, there were some quite authoritative fears in Washington, DC, that the Cold War might have only a few months further to run before it became red-hot. For another example, in October 1962 some US cabinet officers in Washington believed that the Cold War most probably would terminate in a very large bang within a week.

[28] Jac Weller, *Wellington in the Peninsula, 1808–1814* (London, 1992), p. xiv.

strategy more and more comes under the historiographical hammer. The shift from policy advice and 'policy science' to the realm of history would be more welcome than it is were there not some potentially lethally incorrect implications that well-meaning scholars may draw from the unique course of nuclear-era strategic history to date. It is interesting when historians disagree about the implications of the great Byzantine military defeat at Manzikert in 1071.[29] But when historians differ on the merit or otherwise in the United States adopting a strategic forces triad in the Cold War, or developing limited nuclear options for the war plans of the 1970s and 1980s,[30] the strategic consequences of their debate include annihilation if foolish views find their way into policy and strategy. The subject of this book really matters. If strategy is done badly, humans can die in large numbers.

I challenge readers briefly to try and set aside their current wisdom on nuclear issues and think with some empathy about the problems posed to statecraft and strategy in the Cold War. Although that war was concluded in 1989, the nuclear era most definitely rolls on. Nuclear weapons are no longer fashionable, but they have not gone away. In fact, the strategic history of the twenty–first century begins with the systemic problem that the much-heralded information revolution in military affairs is not able to retire, operationally and therefore strategically, the problems posed by the still-breathing nuclear revolution.[31] Five observations about the nuclear revolution are especially important.

NOT QUITE AN 'ABSOLUTE WEAPON'

Neither the atomic bomb nor even the hydrogen bomb was 'the absolute weapon'. That negative claim is not contradicted by the fact that thus far nuclear weapons have had the strategically unusual potential of being able to defeat a foe without first defeating that foe's armed forces. Furthermore, no less unusually, defeat of the foe could not guarantee that his undefeated armed forces would be unable or unwilling to deliver a fatal (nuclear) counterblow in retaliation. That, of course, is the familiar logic of mutual deterrence in the context of mutual assured destruction, or MAD. There is some sense in the proposition that holds that between the superpowers in the Cold War, MAD was simply a fact of military-technical life: it was neither policy nor strategy.[32] Without seeking to contradict that proposition entirely at this juncture, it is important to note that an existential claim on behalf of an alleged absolute quality to nuclear arms is, strictly, fallacious. Nuclear

[29] J. C. Cheynet, 'Manzikert: un désastre militaire?', Byzantion, 50 (1980), 410–38; Alfred Friendly, The Dreadful Day (London, 1981).

[30] Lynn Etheridge Davis, Limited Nuclear Options: Deterrence and the New American Doctrine, Adelphi Paper 121 (London, winter 1975–6).

[31] T. V. Paul, Richard J. Harknett, and James J. Wirtz (eds.), The Absolute Weapon Revisited: Nuclear Arms and the Emerging International Order (Ann Arbor, Mich., 1998).

[32] For opposing views of MAD, see Donald G. Brennan, 'The Case for Missile Defense', Foreign Affairs, 43 (1969), 633–48, and Wolfgang K. H. Panofsky, 'The Mutual Hostage Relationship between America and Russia', Foreign Affairs, 52 (1973), 109–18. Each of these seminal articles was a tour de force.

weapons do not represent the end of strategic history. Quite the contrary: the raw physical potency of nuclear arms has stimulated energetic endeavours to sideline or 'marginalize' such arms.[33] The arrival of atomic armament in 1945 opened a new chapter in strategic history, it did not write *finis* to strategy. When Brodie, and later Freedman, speculated to the effect that strategy had hit a 'dead end' with the age of nuclear plenty, their plausible claims had a rather narrow strategic writ.[34] Specifically, the superpowers discovered that large-scale employment of nuclear weapons would most probably prove self-defeating, in fact would sunder the rational connection between military power and political purpose that lies at the core of strategy. The American defence establishment sought to come to terms with this astrategic implication between approximately 1955 and 1965;[35] the Soviet defence establishment grappled with its recognition of this same inconveniently astrategic fact between 1972 and 1982.[36] Tactically, nuclear weapons could be rendered less than absolute by other nuclear, as well as by ever more precisely delivered conventional, weapons. Operationally, the potentially absolute character of nuclear weaponry may be evaded by provision of massive disincentives to nuclear war. Finally, politically, one may so set the stage that some mix of taboos, 'lore', and net military and political disadvantage renders nuclear use all but unthinkable.[37]

STRATEGIC HISTORY MOVES ON

Purported strategic philosophical truths should not be permitted to float free of all reference to the course of strategic history. For example, the great truth that a 'nuclear war cannot be won and must never be fought' (a mantra of the 1980s) connects to different strategic realities.[38] Nuclear war must always be a terrible event. But there are degrees of terrible, and those degrees could matter. A World War III in 1948–9, occasioned by Western determination to break the Soviet blockade of Berlin, would have seen the use of 50–250 US atomic weapons. For the human race, for planet earth, for the United States, and even for Europe, that would have been a deeply regrettable but survivable catastrophe. However, had World War III occurred as a result of Nikita Khrushchev's maladroit Berlin diplomacy in 1961, over US misinterpretation of the Soviet nuclear alert (which was not

[33] Edward N. Luttwak, *Strategy: The Logic of War and Peace* (Cambridge, Mass., 1987), 168–74; Lawrence Freedman, 'Nuclear Weapons: From Marginalization to Elimination?', *Survival*, 39 (1997), 184–9.

[34] Bernard Brodie, 'Strategy Hits a Dead End', *Harper's*, 211 (1955), 33–7; Lawrence Freedman, 'Has Strategy Reached a Dead-End?' *Futures*, 11 (1979), 122–31.

[35] Gray, *Strategic Studies and Public Policy*; Freedman, *Evolution of Nuclear Strategy*.

[36] John G. Hines, Ellis M. Mishulovich, and John F. Shull, *Soviet Intentions, 1965-1985, i: An Analytical Comparison of U.S.–Soviet Assessments During the Cold War*; (2 vols., McLean, Va., 22 Sept. 1995); Andrei A. Kokoshin, *Soviet Strategic Thought, 1917-91* (Cambridge, Mass., 1998); William E. Odom, *The Collapse of the Soviet Military* (New Haven, Conn., 1998), 66–71.

[37] These matters are exceptionally well aired in Paul et al., *Absolute Weapon Revisited*.

[38] Ronald Reagan, *National Security Strategy of the United States* (Washington, DC, Jan. 1988), 15.

detected in the USA) called at the time of the Czech crisis of 1968, or for reason of misinterpretation of nuclear release exercise behaviour in the early 1980s, the result would most probably have been terminal for 'civilization as we know it'.[39]

Given the blessed absence of historical evidence of nuclear use in battle after 1945, it is difficult to discipline theoretical discourse with regard to particular periods. Suffice it to say for now that much of the alleged strategic wisdom that supposedly explains state behaviour during the Cold War is distinctly ahistorical with reference to the military balance or, in Soviet terms, the correlation of forces. Nuclear weapons, like nuclear wars, come in a wide range of different possibilities, and the differences could matter profoundly.

MILITARY BALANCE AND MILITARY COMPETITION

It is commonplace today to claim that for much of the Cold War the strategic balance between the superpowers was meta-stable. One feels most comfortable with this view, however, with either the advantage of hindsight or the luxury of lack of responsibility. Variants of the existential conviction that nuclear weapons deter, regardless of military-technical and tactical detail, have long been popular, even among many people who offered policy advice apparently in contradiction to that conviction.[40] This is one of the several zones either of genuine miscommunication between reasonable people or, possibly no less genuinely, of cultural incapacity to communicate. In short, this commonplace view is strategically wrong.

Neither American nor Soviet officials could assume that a militarily and therefore politically useful advantage was unattainable by vigorous arms competition. Given the novelty of the atomic, then hydrogen, bombs, and of cruise and ballistic missiles, how could a prudent official in either superpower have assumed otherwise? Each side believed that the other was motivated to seek and use whatever technical, tactical, operational, strategic, or political advantage came its way. In 1950, 1951, and so forth, the future course of the strategic arms competition was strictly a matter for speculation. Critics today of US or Soviet policy and strategy in the late 1940s and the 1950s need to challenge their happy strategic-historical certainties and ask themselves which principles *they* might have endorsed for the guidance of competitive behaviour in, say, 1950, 1960, or 1970, had they been entrusted with the keys to the kingdom at those times.

---

[39]   See Cochrane et al., *U.S. Nuclear Forces and Capabilities*, 15, for approximate stockpile numbers.

[40]   Robert Jervis, 'Why Nuclear Superiority Doesn't Matter', *Political Science Quarterly*, 94 (1979), 617–33; id., *The Illogic of American Nuclear Strategy* (Ithaca, NY, 1984); McGeorge Bundy, 'Existential Deterrence and its Consequences', in Douglas MacLean (ed.), *The Security Gamble: Deterrence Dilemmas in the Nuclear Age* (Totowa, NJ, 1984), 3–13; Kenneth N. Waltz, 'Nuclear Myths and Political Realities', *American Political Science Review*, 84 (1990), 732–45.

THE NUCLEAR-ARMED ADVERSARY

Nuclear strategy is not a game of solitaire. The great truths of existential nuclear deterrence have to stand examination with reference to actual historical players. Today, oral history has confirmed what prudence commanded during the Cold War. The Soviet Union did not believe with any confidence that nuclear war could be waged and won; language to that effect was either simply atavistic—for example, when endorsed by strategic dinosaurs such as Marshal Andre Grechko (USSR Minister of Defence, 1967-76)—or ideologically mandated. But the Soviet General Staff quite genuinely 'considered the nuclear balance to be unstable, because technological advances and increases in the size of the arsenal could significantly augment the power of one side relative to the other, thereby upsetting the balance'.[41] As the yield, accuracy, and number of weapons altered, so did the overall nuclear power of the state. Whatever American strategic thinkers judged to be the deeper truths of nuclear deadlock, the practical issue was not 'What is true?', but rather 'What do Soviet (or American) strategists believe to be true?' The problem of evidence was inevitably severe, but the case for prudence was unanswerable. It was only prudent to assume that the Soviet (or American) adversary believed a strategically usable military advantage lurked in the nuclear competition.

In retrospect, several Western schools of thought about nuclear forces, strategy, and war were correct. Centre-left critics of American nuclear strategy certainly were correct in pointing to the suicidal character of the belligerent possibilities in nuclear combat, though this was scarcely a stunning insight. The centre-right was correct in affirming a need to meet strategic challenges strategically, notwithstanding the embarrassing fact that plausible schemes for military success were hard to design and explain.[42] Much as it pains me to acknowledge the fact, the great on-off-on nuclear debate of the 1970s and 1980s was distinctly akin to the

---

[41] Hines et al., *Soviet Intentions, 1965-1985*, i: 17.

[42] The exciting title invented by editorial staff for an article of mine in 1980, and deployed without my prior knowledge, did not much assist intelligent debate. Colin S. Gray and Keith B. Payne, 'Victory Is Possible', *Foreign Policy*, 39 (1980), 14-27. This article, and others of its ilk (e.g. my 'Nuclear Strategy'), were not—contrary to appearances—intended as gung-ho propaganda for the thesis that 'a nuclear war can be won'. My purpose, rather, was to urge a genuinely 'strategic' approach to policy and strategy for nuclear weapons. In company with what Luttwak was to write in his master-work on *Strategy*, I believed—then and now—that 'nuclear weapons are fully subject to the same logic of strategy that applies to all other weapons' (ibid. 174). The logic of mutual assured destruction, if allowed to guide practice, is a logic of strategic paralysis. It has always seemed to me to be foolish to forswear possible military, and hence strategic and political, advantage from nuclear threats or actual use, *if nuclear weapons are a vital, rather than merely supporting, element in your strategy*. In the 1970s, as in the 1980s and 1990s, I did not believe that the US government took sufficiently seriously its obligation to protect its homeland. As well as constituting a political and moral point, that belief was also an arguable item with strategic implications for the effectiveness of foreign policy. In retrospect, I failed to convince, and I probably all but invited misunderstanding. See Michael Howard, 'On Fighting a Nuclear War', *International Security*, 5 (1981), 3-17, and Leon Wieseltier, *Nuclear War, Nuclear Peace* (New York, 1983), 47-53. On the range of choice among 'nuclear strategies', see Colin S. Gray, *Nuclear Strategy and National Style* (Lanham, Md., 1986), ch. 9. Then, as now, I endorsed what I called 'damage limitation for deterrence and coercion (classical strategy)'.

hypothetical struggle by a group of blind people to comprehend tangibly the scope, character, and purpose of the anecdotal elephant. Then, as today, the practical problem was not to come to terms with the full potential awfulness of nuclear war. Defence professionals understandably, if sometimes uncomfortably and ungraciously, gave short shrift to protesters who were moved morally by the conviction that nuclear war would be an intolerable abomination. The practical problem, then as now, is to decide what to do about the challenge of nuclear peril.

It so happens that the deeply professional strategic analysts of the Soviet General Staff believed almost exactly as prudent American (and other NATO) strategic thinkers were obliged to assume. In a fascinating and generally convincing oral history, Colonel-General Andrian A. Danilevich of the Soviet General Staff has explained why the Soviet military establishment did not really endorse the idea of a 'strategic balance'.

In the late 1970s we talked about reaching a strategic balance. In reality, there was not and could not be a real military balance, because you [the United States] had advantages in certain systems; we had advantages in others. You were ahead in SSBNs, in control systems, in protection means. In weapon yield, in the land groupings of nuclear weapons we held the advantage, in early warning systems there was rough parity. But with the massive potential we both had, all these distinctions tended to lose their meaning. So one could talk about a strategic balance, meaning that under any set of conditions, each side could cause unacceptable damage to the other. So in this context one could draw conclusions about strategic parity-equal capabilities for mutual destruction. *But the fact is that these were all theoretical conclusions. In practice it often happens differently, especially in wars.* You could simply look at the correlation of forces, make some calculations and tell your opponent, 'we outnumber you 2:1, victory is ours, please surrender'. But in reality you could outnumber your opponent 3:1 and still suffer a crushing defeat, like Hannibal defeated the Romans, or like the German victories over us in 1941. So *the correlation of forces is significant, but there is also a sea of specific, subjective factors, or even random events, which reduce these objective factors to nil.* Therefore, in theory we may have the possibility to totally destroy the US and vice versa. But in practice this may not happen. In practice the result could be completely unexpected. Because perhaps not all of these forces you have would be used. Because in the end you might not find the man who will press that button. That depends on many, many things. In the military art it is impossible to make predictions because things may go otherwise than you had planned. Although with nuclear weapons everything is subject to analysis, calculations, you can say exactly what damage there will be, etc. But in practice, things may go otherwise. And it is the fear of that 'otherwise' that forces us to modernize nuclear weapons, the control systems, to develop various options for their use, etc.[43]

Notwithstanding the rambling element typical of oral testimony, it would be

---

[43] Col.-Gen. (Ret.) Andrian A. Danilevich, testimony in Hines et al., *Soviet Intentions, 1965–1985, ii: Soviet Post-Cold War Testimonial Evidence*, 30 (emphasis added). Danilevich was a General Staff officer from 1964 to 1990, eventually a very senior one indeed, and was a confidant of the high command. Most definitely he was in a position to know. I am grateful to Professor John Erickson of Edinburgh University for his advice on Danilevich and related matters of Soviet nuclear strategy.

difficult to exaggerate the importance of Danilevich's logic. He refuses to deny, at least to rule out, an art to war, even nuclear war, that in practice might upset what McGeorge Bundy once called derisively 'the refined calculations of the nuclear gamesmen'.[44] Following Clausewitz, Danilevich insists that war, including nuclear war, is the realm of chance, risk, uncertainty, and—in a word—friction. There are good reasons to believe that Danilevich's views are authoritatively illustrative of the military professionals of the Soviet General Staff.[45] One can see readily enough, therefore, how prudent conservative officials on both sides of the strategic arms competition earnestly believed themselves obliged to assume that skill, surprise, technical breakthroughs, and chance might deliver useful advantage or perilous disadvantage. Barring the creation of a literal 'doomsday machine', destruction, let alone mutual destruction, cannot possibly literally be 'assured'.[46] An unsound affirmation of faith in the concept of military certainty has been provided by the US Navy with its unhappy reported invention of the idea of 'assured conventional destruction'.[47] The quest for reliability of strategic effect is as persistent as it is ill-advised.

During the Cold War each side knew that the other was seeking military

[44] McGeorge Bundy, 'To Cap the Volcano', *Foreign Affairs*, 48 (1969), 13.

[45] As well as being senior special assistant to the chief of the Main Operations Directorate of the General Staff in the 1970s, Danilevich served as assistant for doctrine and strategy to Chiefs of the General Staff Marshal Akhromeev and General Moiseev from 1984 until 1990. Furthermore he was Director of the General Staff project which produced a top-secret three-volume study on *Strategy and Deep Operations* (1977–1986), 'the basic reference document for Soviet strategic and operational nuclear and conventional planning for at least the last decade of the Soviet state': Hines et al., *Soviet Intentions, 1965–1985, ii*: 20.

[46] A true 'doomsday machine' would be a military system that *automatically* escalated from any use of nuclear weapons against the homeland to a nuclear response of such magnitude as to menace all life on earth. That nuclear response would not need to be 'delivered' against the enemy; very large and 'dirty' (e.g. cobalt-encased) nuclear devices could be buried in one's own homeland. The world's weather system would ensure eventual global catastrophe: Herman Kahn, *On Thermonuclear War*, 2nd edn. (New York, 1969), 144–53. It is possible, indeed probable, that in the 1970s the USSR constructed a form of doomsday machine which it called 'Dead Hand' (*Mertvaia Ruka*). 'Dead Hand' allegedly entailed the automatic launch of command missiles when sensors decided that an attack was under way. The command missiles were designed and programmed to transmit nuclear-release messages to groups of ICBMs. 'Dead Hand' was not entirely automatic, in that it had to be switched on in time of crisis. Also, this variant of a doomsday command arrangement was built to ensure missile launch against the United States, not simply to produce limitless catastrophe. The best evidence for 'Dead Hand' is in Hines et al., *Soviet Intentions, i*: 19–21, and *ii*: 100–1. Notwithstanding direct oral testimony by Vitalii Leonidovich Kataev (senior adviser to the chairman of the Central Committee Defence Industry Department) claiming that 'Dead Hand' was operational 'by the early 1980s' (ibid. *ii*: 101), doubt remains as to whether this really was so. The US version of this Soviet system, in the form of ERCS (Emergency Rocket Communications System)—dedicated Minuteman ICBMs—differed in several vital respects from 'Dead Hand'. Most importantly, US ERCS missiles could not be launched as an automatic response to the sensing of weapons effects, and they transmitted voice messages to ICBM launch control crews, not directly to the missiles without human intervention: Blair, *Logic of Accidental Nuclear War*, 304–5, n. 60.

[47] As reported in Alan D. Zimm, 'Deterrence: Basic Theory, Principles, and Implications', *Strategic Review*, 25 (1997), 48–9.

advantage, could not be certain that that quest would prove chimerical, and could only guess how willing the foe would be to take risks. Exactly how each superpower also made its military calculations was yet another area of potentially significant uncertainty. We know now, for example, that Soviet and American defence analysts differed over the proper way to calculate ICBM survivability.[48] Much that is clear today was, however, opaque at the time. On balance, it is now reasonably certain that from late 1975 until 1982 the Soviet ship of state did not really have a captain: Brezhnev was alive, but following his heart attack in Vladivostok in 1975 was not functioning as a political or strategic leader. Similarly, it is now quite well known that the real drive behind the Soviet nuclear arms programmes of the 1970s and early 1980s was provided by the defence industry's urge for regular production. The political interests of Brezhnev's cronies, rather than operational requirements derived from strategic war planning conducted by the General Staff, was the major impetus behind the 'strategic' arms build-up.[49] But US watchers of matters Soviet did not, and most probably could not, know these facts at the time. Moreover, even if there was no malevolent grand design from Moscow intending to acquire the military-technical means to wage and win World War III, the 'strategic' weapons did exist, indeed were created with a promiscuous disregard to almost everything except production norms. In addition, the General Staff subscribed quite genuinely to what in the West was labelled a 'war-fighting' approach to deterrence.[50] We know that the unlovely USSR of late Cold War vintage filed for political reorganization with a whimper, rather than sought to resolve its domestic and imperial problems with a 'bang'. Not only was that welcome process of political and strategic demise unpredictable in, say, 1980; it may

---

[48] Hines et al., *Soviet Intentions*, ii: 150–1. In the late 1960s and early 1970s, Soviet officials were convinced that US silo-housed ICBMS were first-strike weapons because they were not capable of riding out an attack, according to Soviet measures of effectiveness (MOEs) deriving from uniquely Soviet models of missile survivability developed by Dr Vitali N. Tsygichko, a mathematician and colonel of artillery who served with the General Staff from 1964 until 1977. American officials were unaware that because their ICBMs and ICBM launch control centres failed *Soviet* standards of survivability, it was assumed quite rationally in the USSR that US ICBMs must be governed by a firing doctrine either of launch on strategic warning (preventive strike) or of launch on tactical warning (preemptive strike). Soviet MOEs for a functional 'kill' against a US ICBM included the jamming of a silo's door, the rupturing of the fuel system, or launch-control disruption. Between 1972 and 1979 Dr Tsygichko also modelled the consequences of large-scale nuclear war in Europe. His analytical results, though not disputed, were not politically acceptable and were suppressed by 'overclassification and severe restrictions on dissemination': ibid. 139–40.

[49] Ibid. ch. 4.

[50] Ibid. *passim*; Colin S. Gray, 'War Fighting for Deterrence', *Journal of Strategic Studies*, 7 (1984), 5–28. This misleading pejorative term is employed to denote a school of thought that, allegedly, believes that a nuclear war could be fought and won, an approach that mandates the targeting of a foe's military forces and strategic command. That charge aside, the concept of nuclear 'war fighting' is an obvious linguistic nonsense. To fight a nuclear war is to fight a nuclear war, regardless of which among the enemy's assets are targeted. Colin S. Gray, 'Targeting Problems for Central War', in Desmond Ball and Jeffrey Richelson (eds.), *Strategic Nuclear Targeting* (Ithaca, NY, 1986), 171–93, presents the kind of analysis that incites the ireful 'war fighting' charge.

not even have been foreordained. Several alternative USSRs may well have lurked in some different, if fortunately only virtual, histories of the 1980s.[51]

The point is not to claim that Western strategists were correct in their determination to wage great arms competition with vigour in the 1980s. Rather, the argument is that Western strategists from the 1960s to the mid-1980s were obliged, on the evidence available, to assume that the USSR was a formidable foe ready, willing, and able to take advantage of any slackening of will and effort on the part of the Western Alliance.[52]

THE OPERATIONAL PERSPECTIVE

The historical figures who conducted nuclear policy during the Cold War did so for reasons, and eventually according to all but codified principles and assumptions, that are surprisingly resilient to criticism from hindsight. If there was a higher bilateral insanity about the nuclear arms competition, it was constructed of rational, in the Soviet case political-structural, building-blocks. The competition was not fuelled by insatiable ambitions or collective paranoia in either superpower. Quite the contrary: it was propelled from outset to conclusion by tolerably accurate perceptions of political antagonism. Each side's military professionals did what they were told to do, which generally happened to be what was in their nature. The professionals prepared for war, as their civilian masters commanded, and naturally enough they prepared as best they could to wage war as effectively as they would be able. It so happens that the hypothetical war in question would have been variably, but massively, nuclear.

Military establishments are not debating societies: they are the executive agents of the societies they protect. The military establishments of the superpowers had both to think strategically about nuclear weapons and to make operational preparations for their contingent employment. There is ample scope for dispute over the wisdom of particular choices among weapons options, and certainly over choices in quantities produced[53]—to the limited degree to which these are known

---

[51] The thesis that the USSR not only fell, but was pushed hard, is advanced in a robustly partisan manner in Jay Winik, *On the Brink: The Dramatic, Behind the Scenes Saga of the Reagan Era and the Men and Women Who Won the Cold War* (New York, 1996). The author deserves high praise for truth-in-advertising, as well as some praise for a fairly plausible tale well told.

[52] This was the assumption that provided the political context wherein Ronald Reagan could unseat Jimmy Carter after only one term of office. Colin S. Gray, 'The Most Dangerous Decade: Historic Mission, Legitimacy, and Dynamics of the Soviet Empire in the 1980s', *Orbis*, 25 (1981), 13–28, would prove to be unduly alarmist. But this article can be read today as an honest and even prudent 'period piece'.

[53] e.g. Fen Osler Hampson, *Unguided Missiles: How America Buys Its Weapons* (New York, 1989); Theo Farrell, *Weapons Without a Cause: The Politics of Weapons Acquisition in the United States* (London, 1997); David H. Dunn, *The Politics of Threat: Minuteman Vulnerability in American National Security Policy* (London, 1997). Though scholarly in method and tone of argument, these studies amount to exercises in the examination of weapon procurement pathologies. For a little historical perspective, consider what Daniel A. Baugh has to say about the most powerful navy of the eighteenth century. 'Venality and neglect were so

for the Soviet case—but the scope, scale, and broadly the course of the nuclear arms competition make strategic historical sense, though a sense on the Soviet side heavily propelled by domestic politics.

Given the political hostility in East–West relations mandated by a malign mixture of ideology and realpolitik, given the dynamism of mid-twentieth-century civilian and military technologies, and given the nature of the responsibilities of military professionals, it is difficult to see how the makers and executors of modern strategy could have behaved very differently towards nuclear arms—though on the American side more effort could and should have been devoted to active defence.[54] It is not a canonical truth to claim that nuclear war could not be won during the Cold War. Of course, the risks would have been appalling, but Danilevich is right: any outcome is possible, depending upon the unique circumstances of the time. Victory with nuclear arms was a distinct possibility, even probability, for the United States in the 1950s, 1960s, and perhaps later, given the fragility of Soviet strategic command and control.[55]

In his excellent book *The Pursuit of Victory*, Brian Bond chides me for some of my writings wherein, in his view, I criticized some views of mutual nuclear deterrence as being defeatist and suggested that the United States could have won a nuclear war in the 1950s and early 1960s. What I wrote was certainly impolitic, though it may well have been correct. It is interesting that Bond misses the point that I am striving to make in this chapter when he writes: 'The fact remains that responsible Western leaders did not believe that a meaningful military victory over the Soviet Union could be achieved.'[56]

That may be true, but it was the duty of military professionals to do their best, even in unpromising circumstances. As Bond wrote about the military at the turn of the nineteenth century:

extensive in the eighteenth-century navy that an administrative historian, if he did not know in advance that the British navy was by far the strongest and most consistently victorious navy of the period, could easily end with a catalogue of reasons for British naval collapse. In fact, one historian who investigated the British navy in the early eighteenth century [Ruth Bourne, *Queen Anne's Navy in the West Indies*, 1939] was so appalled by what she found that she concluded the empire must have been won by trade, for it could not have been won by the navy': *British Naval Administration in the Age of Walpole* (Princeton, NJ, 1965), 2. Among many scholars there is a like reluctance today to allow US military power in the 1970s and 1980s much retrospective responsibility for the fall of the Soviet empire.

[54] For the reasons laid out so cogently in Brennan, 'Case for Missile Defense', and implied in the worrying title of Fred Charles Iklé, 'Can Nuclear Deterrence Last Out the Century?', *Foreign Affairs*, 51 (1973), 267–85.

[55] This is a judgement from the imagined realm of virtual strategic history that no archive, oral history, memoir, or exercise transcript can validate. It is my best estimate deriving from all the sources at my command over more than 30 years; sources including a host of anecdotal detail from American officials and warriors who were in the trade of practising nuclear deterrence and preparing for the conduct of nuclear war. Among the more useful guides to thought on this subject, see Kahn, *On Thermonuclear War*; Richard K. Betts, *Nuclear Blackmail and Nuclear Balance* (Washington, DC, 1987); Bruce G. Blair, *The Logic of Accidental Nuclear War* (Washington, DC, 1993); and, above all others, the Danilevich testimony in Hines et al., *Soviet Intentions*, i: 19–69.

[56] Brian Bond, *The Pursuit of Victory: From Napoleon to Saddam Hussein* (Oxford, 1996), 175.

But while some foolish statements were certainly made, for example by the then Colonel Foch in asserting that every improvement in fire-power would be to the advantage of the attacker, by and large the professional experts were acutely aware of the difficulties of securing Napoleonic-style decisive victories on the modern battlefield. *Since great conflicts would surely occur, the professionals' task was to consider how to win them*: they could not afford to appear defeatist. In any case, the situation did not seem hopeless.[57]

Those words do not fit the nuclear case perfectly, but they contain more than a germ of relevance. The military professionals of the Cold War were acutely aware of the tactical and operational, hence the strategic and political, problems with nuclear weapons. They were not optimistic, let alone confident, in their assessments of the prospects for large-scale military success. But significant military advantage might be secured—and anyway it was their duty to do their best.

None of this is to deny for a moment the terrible moral, ecological, and other implications of nuclear war. But viewed in narrowly military operational terms, victory in a nuclear war periodically appeared as a possibility to planners and to intelligence analysts charged with giving an estimate of the opponent's view of the world. Since a nuclear-armed power must devise strategic guidance for its nuclear armament, and since military professionals must plan, equip, and train to fight with the weapons of the age, generic critics of nuclear strategy need to exercise caution lest they stray into an astrategic world of make-believe. If nuclear weapons exist, and a country tells its military establishment to prepare for war, albeit in hope of war prevention, then the practical domain of the issue reduces to some variant of 'which strategy'. All strategy, even all nuclear strategy, has to be 'war-fighting' strategy. The military establishments of East and West during the Cold War could do no other than make operational preparation to wage war, including nuclear war, as effectively as they could. The wonder lies not in the necessary military historical facts of operational preparation for war, but rather in the amazing phenomenon of a protracted nuclear stand-off, wherein the contradictory principles of readiness to fight and security against inadvertent or accidental combat were both followed well enough.[58]

MISSING CHOICES

Statesmen and strategists of the nuclear era are trapped in the existential conundrum that they may be obliged to wage a form of war—nuclear war—that they believe unlikely to have any outcome other than bilateral disaster. Many people shared a deep sense of foreboding in 1914 and, again, in 1939. But in neither case did polities go to war with their leaders convinced that the conflict upon which they were embarking would almost certainly fail to solve the most pressing problems of national and international security. Had an East–West war occurred in the 1970s or 1980s, it would have been difficult to find a senior person on either side

[57] Brian Bond, *The Pursuit of Victory: From Napoleon to Saddam Hussein* (Oxford, 1996), 80 (emphasis added).
[58] Blair, *Logic of Accidental Nuclear War*.

who would have subscribed to any version of the more responsible prevalent attitudes of 1914 or 1939—'painful but necessary', and the like. After the mid-1960s, the political leaders and the military professionals of East and West were appalled by the monster of nuclear armament that they had created. They realised that nuclear war, though not nuclear weapons, could not, *après* Clausewitz, be a rational instrument of state policy.[59] That is to say, nuclear war writ large, waged on a great scale, most probably could not deliver useful strategic effect in support of political interests. Nonetheless, nuclear deadlock might have proved a temporary condition, at least in the calculations of one side's war planners. It is not easy to convey to readers the full domain of the realm of necessity that engulfed the strategic theorists, defence analysts, and officials of East and West. The world of the American and Soviet nuclear strategists in the years of Cold War was one wherein politics, not weaponry, framed the basic context of strategic life. East and West were ideologically, geopolitically, and geostrategically at odds, and the military establishments had to make the best of what political skill in grand strategy, economic resources for defence functions, and technical prowess could deliver.

No matter what one may believe should suffice to maximize the prospects for success in deterrence, the armed forces of East and West had no practical choice other than to prepare to conduct war with nuclear weapons. It is no criticism of scholarly theorists of strategy to note that their responsibilities are confined to the intellectual, the moral, and perhaps the policy-advisory. Functioning within the realm of necessity and executive responsibility, military establishments, benefiting or otherwise from such political guidance as they could extract from generally reluctant civilian leaders,[60] had to plan, equip, and train to wage nuclear war. It may well be true to object that there are no attractive nuclear strategies on offer,[61] but that objection cannot mitigate the responsibility to seek the best among the bad in the realm of necessity in real strategic history.

---

[59] Col.-Gen. Danilevich of the Soviet General Staff informs us that 'before the 1960s we had a different point of view. We thought that if there were ever a nuclear exchange, we would have an advantage: more territory, less concentration of industry, of population, certain spiritual arguments—we thought that in the event of an equal exchange the U.S would be destroyed but we would survive. But by the 1970s we had concluded that there was no chance in hell that we would survive. *By the 1980s we concluded further that we would be destroyed by our strike, so that we could not strike at all.* As our nuclear arsenal grew, the political environment changed and our views changed': testimony in Hines et al., *Soviet Intentions, ii:* 64 (emphasis added).

[60] Janne E. Nolan, *Guardians of the Arsenal: The Politics of Nuclear Strategy* (New York, 1989); Blair, *Logic of Accidental Nuclear War*, esp. chs. 3 and 4; Danilevich testimony in Hines et al., *Soviet Intentions, ii*. Hines reports on Danilevich's testimony that '[h]e repeated what he had said in earlier interviews, that after the 1972 high-level exercise [on nuclear war] in which Brezhnev and the Politburo participated [and which scared them profoundly], the political leadership, including even Minister of Defense Ustinov, ignored strategy. "They never really asked what we [or the General Staff] were doing", after that experience. This did not change under Andropov, Chernenko, or Gorbachev' (69). So much for a hands-on attention to nuclear strategy at the highest level in the USSR.

[61] Freedman, 'First Two Generations of Nuclear Strategists', 778.

One may believe that every accessible potential path in nuclear use would lead to a history-ending catastrophe. If that is so, what choices does one have? In nominal practice, the choices reduce firstly to lobbying for a better world wherein the realm of strategic necessity does not mandate a small series of 'choices', all of which lead to catastrophe. Second, one may choose the best that one can, because, as Danilevich affirms, the unexpected could occur. In practice, at least for societies as a whole, there is truly no choice. As the nuclear arsenals matured and expanded from decade to decade, so the practicable alternatives reduced in fact to planning, equipping, training, and commanding either for a certainty of holocaust, or providing potential 'speed bumps' through flexibility in operational strategy on what all too obviously could prove to be a slide or gallop to global disaster.[62]

The strategists of East and West sought to tame their burgeoning nuclear arsenals to derive such strategic effectiveness from them as might be gleaned. At the time, and even more in retrospect, the schemes and hopes for nuclear strategy in the middle and later decades of the Cold War can appear absurdly ambitious and all but criminally dangerous. But what other course was realistically open to the actual historical polities in, say, the 1960s and 1970s? In some senses an individual can opt out of the arms competition, though not out of the potential consequences thereof—if popular views on the perils of competitive armament are sound[63]—but a polity as a whole usually cannot. Granting that hopes for control in nuclear war, and for a less than utterly catastrophic outcome to such a conflict, are probably vain, what if the practicable alternative is a certainty of lack of control and the occurrence of utter catastrophe?

Debates over nuclear strategy have long been plagued by the posing of false alternatives. The defence professionals of East and West in the Cold War, at least after the mid-1950s in the West and the mid-1960s in the East, harboured no serious illusions about the winnability of nuclear war, or, possibly, about the difficulty of controlling nuclear use.[64] The actual choices available, however, were not

[62] Herman Kahn, *On Escalation: Metaphors and Scenarios* (New York, 1965); Richard Rosecrance, *Strategic Deterrence Reconsidered*, Adelphi Paper 116 (London, spring 1975); Warner R. Schilling, 'U.S. Strategic Nuclear Concepts in the 1970s: The Search for Sufficiently Equivalent Countervailing Parity', *International Security*, 6 (1981), 48–79; Freedman, *Evolution of Nuclear Strategy*, ch. 25. Thanks to Danilevich, we now know that the USSR did 'plan' on selected nuclear strikes, but '[h]e said that most General Staff officers most closely associated with such planning had no idea whether "we could really do it", whether any of it would work or how it would turn out', testimony in Hines et al., *Soviet Intentions, ii*: 68.

[63] For a sceptical analysis of purported causal connections between competitive armament and war, see Gray, 'Arms Races and Other Pathetic Fallacies'. A less sceptical view pervades the excellent historical case study, David Stevenson, *Armaments and the Coming of War: Europe, 1904–1914* (Oxford, 1996). See the judicious judgement in Michael Howard, *The Lessons of History* (New Haven, Conn., 1991), ch. 5, 'The Edwardian Arms Race'.

[64] Neither superpower invested as early or prudently redundant in its strategic command and control as probably it ought. Paul Bracken, *The Command and Control of Nuclear Forces* (New Haven, Conn., 1983), was a minor public revelation when it appeared; Bruce G. Blair, *Strategic Command and Control: Redefining the Nuclear Threat* (Washington, DC, 1985), identified the possible, or probable,

driven by great moral or philosophical truths. The strategists of both sides were locked into a realm of necessity wherein contingency plans for the use of nuclear armed forces were judged essential if deterrence was to be done. To deter or not to deter was believed not to be a practical matter for choice.

malperformance of the strategic command system as the most real threat; Ashton B. Carter, John D. Steinbruner, and Charles A. Zraket (eds.), *Managing Nuclear Operations* (Washington, DC, 1987), was comprehensive and deeply expert; while the titles of Blair, *Logic of Accidental Nuclear War*, and Scott D. Sagan, *The Limits of Safety: Organizations, Accidents and Nuclear Weapons* (Princeton, NJ, 1993), speak eloquently for the messages in the books.

Chapter 12

NUCLEAR WEAPONS IN STRATEGIC HISTORY

What sense is the strategic historian and the chronicler of strategic thought to make of nuclear weapons? In this second chapter on the nuclear experience in modern strategy I offer an overview of what nuclear weapons to date have meant for the theory and practice of strategy. The analysis in Chapter 11 provided context to help make sense of nuclear weapons in strategic history. Here I provide a strategic accounting of the 'first nuclear age' that was the East–West Cold War.[1] The analysis has as its centrepiece the thesis that the two massively diverse strategic cultures of the United States and the erstwhile USSR agreed on some major issues of nuclear forces and strategy.

The argument in this chapter and the previous one is not intended as a paean of praise for Western statecraft and strategy. Indeed, this author is troubled lest ill-merited self-satisfaction should mislead us about our mastery of nuclear matters into believing that we have forged an iron cage that can contain nuclear peril reliably. Nonetheless, there are some grounds for satisfaction. Western, particularly American, statecraft in the Cold War bears very favourable comparison with, say, British and French statecraft in the 1900s and 1930s.[2] The scope and scale of US strategic success since 1945 is too easily taken for granted. A country unprepared, certainly underprepared, for international leadership helped organize and then sustained an historically unprecedentedly effective coalition for collective defence;[3] it deterred well enough whatever of great moment needed deterring; and it coped more than adequately with the novelty of the strategic challenge posed by weapons of mass destruction. No polity, super or otherwise, performs

---

[1] Colin S. Gray, *The Second Nuclear Age* (Boulder, Colo., 1999), esp. ch. 2.

[2] Notwithstanding doubts about causation, the facts are that in the Cold War the US and its NATO allies secured peace with security, and eventually a bloodless triumph, whereas in 1914 and 1939 Britain and France twice secured war with protracted insecurity. Of course, attitudes towards war differed among the 1900s, 1930s, and post-1945 years, in part because of the 'crystal ball effect' provided by nuclear weapons regarding war's probable costs: Joseph S. Nye, Jr., 'Old Wars and Future Wars: Causation and Prevention', in Robert I. Rotberg and Theodore K. Rabb (eds.), *The Origin and Prevention of Major Wars* (Cambridge, 1989), 11. To be fair to the French concerning World War I, it was no small triumph of diplomacy to fight Germany with Russia, Britain, Italy, and eventually even the US as allies. In 1870–1, France had been diplomatically isolated by Otto von Bismarck.

[3] Nicholas Henderson, *The Birth of NATO* (London, 1982); Don Cook, *Forging the Alliance: NATO, 1945 to 1950* (London, 1989).

flawlessly. Recall that a theme of this book is the inherent difficulty of sustaining excellence in the conduct of strategy.

The credulous citizens of imperial Athens succumbed to the hubris of power and were seduced by foolish leaders into undertaking the disastrous Sicilian Expedition.[4] Imperial Rome periodically overreached in perilous campaigns against its superpower rival, Persia.[5] Imperial Britain, though in the end militarily victorious, for a while was humiliated as a consequence of its determination to subdue the Boer Republics in Southern Africa.[6] The American war in South-East Asia, particularly South Vietnam, was neither well conceived as an expression of high policy nor well conducted by US armed forces in the theatre.[7] The war, if war there had to be, should have been waged by the Kennedy administration in the early 1960s primarily for Laos, not by the Johnson administration in the mid- and late 1960s in South Vietnam. In Laos, the North Vietnamese had few systemic advantages: in South Vietnam they had advantages on a scale that rendered success for American policy and strategy improbable, though not impossible. The point is that the United States made some substantial mistakes in statecraft and strategy during the Cold War, the limiting of the war largely to Vietnam being only the most obvious.

The story here, however, is generally not one of failure and folly. Most imperial or hegemonic powers have a 'Sicilian Expedition' or two on their record. Critics of US statecraft might gain useful perspective by recalling Britons in Pretoria, French soldiers at Dien Bien Phu and in Algiers, and Russians in Kabul and Grozny.[8] This chapter reveals the typically successful application of a Clausewitzian approach to nuclear weapons. I explain that the nuclear era has manifested itself in two fairly distinctive 'ages' to date, and I argue that nuclear weapons have helped to keep the peace. The discussion regards the nuclear arms competition as the equivalent of war,[9] and suggests that although not much actually can be done with nuclear weapons, that which can be done is critically important for good and potentially for ill.[10] Despite the half century-plus of experience with the nuclear era, and notwithstanding the fact that the discipline of modern strategic studies was

---

[4] Donald Kagan, *The Peace of Nicias and the Sicilian Expedition* (Ithaca, NY, 1981).

[5] Arther Ferrill, *The Fall of the Roman Empire: The Military Explanation* (London, 1986).

[6] Thomas Pakenham, *The Boer War* (New York, 1979).

[7] H. R. McMaster, *Dereliction of Duty: Lyndon Johnson, Robert McNamara, The Joint Chiefs of Staff, and the Lies That Led to Vietnam* (New York, 1997); Jeffrey Record, *The Wrong War: Why We Lost in Vietnam* (Annapolis, Md., 1998).

[8] Bernard B. Fall, *Street Without Joy* (New York, 1972), on the French adventure in Indochina; Anthony H. Cordesman and Abraham R. Wagner, *The Lessons of Modern War, iii: The Afghan and Falklands Conflicts* (Boulder, Colo., 1990), ch. 2; Anton Lieven, *Chechnya: Tombstone of Russian Power* (New Haven, Conn., 1998).

[9] Samuel P. Huntington, 'Arms Races: Prerequisites and Results', in Carl J. Friedrich and Seymour E. Harris (eds.), *Public Policy, 1958* (Cambridge, Mass., 1958), 40–86.

[10] Robert Jervis, 'The Political Effects of Nuclear Weapons: A Comment', *International Security*, 13 (1988), 80–90.

forged in response to nuclear-related challenges, we know little reliable about the *strategic* effect of nuclear weapons. The problem, of course, is that the jewel in the crown of successful strategic performance in the nuclear era, deterrence, 'manifests' itself only negatively in actions not taken.

Every one of the themes that bind this text are illustrated and tested by these chapters on nuclear experience. For example, the revolution in military affairs (assuredly the military-technological revolution) effected by nuclear weapons calls into question the continuing relevance of the Clausewitzian canon. No less an authority than Raymond Aron was moved to pose the matter thus directly: 'Do nuclear analysts merit the title of neo-Clausewitzians?'[11] His answer was notably opaque, but it is significant that he deemed the question worthy of extended consideration. Could the *corpus classicus* of strategic theory serve the nuclear-armed modern world of strategic practice?[12] For a further example of the salience of these nuclear chapters to my central themes, the persisting fact of great difficulty in the conduct of strategy is exceedingly tested by the emergence of 'weapons' whose military utility is likely to prove self-defeating on several of strategy's dimensions in most contexts.

CLAUSEWITZ AND 'THE BOMB'

An important criterion for the plausibility of claims for a 'just war' has always been a right intent. Perhaps after the fashion of premodern doctors who did their best, though hampered by ignorance, many modern strategists did their best to cope with nuclear weapons and new means of weapon delivery. As Lawrence Freedman noticed, modern strategy failed to tame 'the bomb', at least to tame 'the bomb' in a way militarily recognizable to previous generations of theorists. Freedman wrote that 'the position we have reached is one where stability depends on something that is more the antithesis of strategy than its apotheosis—as threats that things will get out of hand, that we might act irrationally, that possibly through inadvertence we could set in motion a process that in its development and conclusion would be beyond human control and comprehension'. He concludes his brilliant indictment with the damning rhetorical flourish: 'C'est magnifique, mais ce n'est pas la stratégie.'[13] But, one might ask, what is 'la stratégie'? In the view of many generic critics of nuclear strategy, the issue is whether or not a Clausewitzian strategic approach to nuclear weapons is appropriate.

[11] Raymond Aron, *Clausewitz: Philosopher of War*, trans. Christine Booker and Norman Stone (London, 1983), 345. 'Neo-Clausewitzian' is not always a label intended to confer eponymous approbation. See Anatol Rapoport, 'Introduction', to Carl von Clausewitz, *On War*, abridged edn. (London, 1968), 11–80. See also Rapoport, *Strategy and Conscience* (New York, 1964), pp. xvii–xxiii.

[12] Michael Howard, 'The Classical Strategists', in Institute for Strategic Studies, *Problems of Modern Strategy*, pt. 1, Adelphi Paper 54 (London, Feb. 1969), 18–32.

[13] Lawrence Freedman, *The Evolution of Nuclear Strategy*, 2nd edn. (New York, 1989), 433.

If strategy is about 'the use of engagements for the purpose of the war',[14] does the very character of nuclear weapons preclude strategic roles for them? Can nuclear weapons be 'used'? If, as Bernard Brodie insisted, nuclear weapons have utility only in 'nonuse', is that utility still a strategic utility?[15]

Clausewitz's teaching on strategy confounds even Freedman's reasonable-sounding Parthian shot, let alone the unsympathetic critiques of theorists to whom the adjective 'strategic' has strongly pejorative connotations. Strategy is about the threat or use of force for political purposes. Strategic effect is the influence of that threat or use of force upon the course of events. The fact that by the late 1960s a large-scale bilateral nuclear war could not serve reasonable political purposes does not deny nuclear weapons classification as weapons, nor does it deny that nuclear weapons are a truly strategic instrument. Paradoxically, perhaps, the arguably astrategic destructive power of nuclear weapons itself is a potent source of strategic influence.[16]

As one of the strategic theorists whom Freedman criticized, I find his arguments simultaneously variably persuasive. He is correct, but perhaps insufficiently empathetic, when he criticizes the result of efforts at strategically rational operational nuclear strategy, while he is incorrect in focusing his critique upon an unduly literally Clausewitzian view of what is strategic.

Overall, I contend that the theorists of nuclear strategy, when wrong, tended to be wrong for the right reasons, and were wrong because they were obliged by political and professional prudence to attempt what had to be attempted.[17] Also, I believe that the theorists of nuclear strategy were right about the strategic utility of nuclear weapons, when the Clausewitzian language of 'the engagement' is interpreted to encompass 'deterrence "action"', which is to say threats and latent menaces at work in the minds of those intended to be deterred.

It is commonplace, and wrong, to argue that the nuclear revolution effected an incompatibility, a fatal chasm, between (nuclear, or conventional escalating to nuclear) military power and political purpose. Quite the contrary: nuclear weapons proved a strategist's delight. Understandably and inalienably, the armed forces of East and West made militarily authoritative plans for contingent nuclear employment, as was their duty. Those plans, in action, just might have delivered politically recognizable victory, though most probably they would not have done

[14] Carl von Clausewitz, *On War*, trans. Michael Howard and Peter Paret (Princeton, NJ, 1976), 128.

[15] Bernard Brodie, *War and Politics* (New York, 1973), ch. 9.

[16] Robert Jervis, *The Meaning of the Nuclear Revolution: Statecraft and the Prospect of Armageddon* (Ithaca, NY, 1989).

[17] It has always been my position that although there is some vital strategic merit in the threat to punish a foe with nuclear strikes, it is gratuitously dangerous, and subversive of intended deterrent effect, deliberately to eschew efforts at damage limitation: Colin S. Gray, *Nuclear Strategy and National Style* (Lanham, Md., 1986), ch. 9. The judgements in the text on 'the theorists of nuclear strategy', unless otherwise specified, are pitched at a level above the fray of debate among theorists concerning 'which nuclear strategy'.

so. That, however, cannot be the point for this discussion. The point here is that the armed forces of all nuclear weapon states are both professionally obliged and prudently advised to approach nuclear weapons as weapons. One wonders about the fundamentals of a non-Clausewitzian approach to nuclear weapons. If, again by analogy, nuclear weapons could not function as a military instrument of victory like, say, airpower, that does not have to mean that these weapons could not function strategically. Perhaps Freedman's plaintive condemnatory cry, 'C'est magnifique, mais ce n'est pas la strategie', falls at the hurdle of that old harasser of theories, the level-of-analysis problem? Could it be that, although nuclear weapons do not appear likely to score highly at the tactical and operational levels of military endeavour, nonetheless they can register impressive scores in the realm of grand strategy and upon policy itself? Nuclear weapons can work directly on the source of the real action in world politics, in the minds of policymakers. To win this 'engagement' can be to win the war; thus are Clausewitz and nuclear weapons strategically reconciled, even when the nuclear war plans seem to offer far less assurance than was tendered to the German government by its General Staff in 1914. This is not to suggest that undifferentiated threats simply to effect a nuclear catastrophe, regardless of consequences to the would-be deterrer, will deter. But critics of nuclear strategy should be careful of their analytical level of targeting.

NUCLEAR AGES

Strategic history to date has registered two quite distinctive nuclear ages, and even a third can be hypothesized plausibly. The ages in question are distinguishable by political structure, not by weapons technology. In summary form, the first nuclear age covered the years 1945–89, and was coterminous with the onset and duration of the Cold War. The second nuclear age is the post-Cold War period to date.

In the first nuclear age there was a dominant strategic nuclear relationship—between superstates and their respective security dependants—and the war that most exercised the minds of 'the best and the brightest' in East and West alike was the war that, by the 1960s, might have ended civilization. Today's nuclear lore was overwhelmingly developed in response to the challenges of potential *grande guerre* between two very great polities and their formal and informal empires. Strategic theory for nuclear weapons was adapted from classical models, with reference to a putatively cataclysmic World War III.[18] This is not to claim that all the nuclear weapons built from 1945 until 1989 were built with *der Tag* of an East–West World War III in mind. Plainly, the variably modest nuclear arsenals of Britain, France, China, Israel, India, and Pakistan were acquired for local and regional reasons related only indirectly to the central East–West contest. Nonetheless, all nuclear

[18] Freedman, *Evolution of Nuclear Strategy*, chs. 1–3.

problems of the 1945–89 period were dominated by the Soviet–American strategic relationship.

By contrast, the demise of the Soviet imperium in 1989, and then even of the USSR itself in 1991, retired politically the salience of a (nuclear) East–West World War III. Nuclear problems remain for national and international security, but they are not the problems of the 1945–89 period of the first nuclear age.[19] The political structure of the problems of nuclear strategy changed radically with the end of the Cold War. Instead of refining yet more foolishly apolitical models of strategic stability in superpower nuclear relations,[20] American defence analysts have had to worry both about asymmetric confrontations between the United States and regional nuclear proliferants and about possible crises and wars between regional rivals who are nuclear armed.[21] It is not by any means certain that international society—admittedly a difficult contestable concept[22]—enjoys the services of a body of well-tested deterrence theory deriving from the strategic historical experience of the first nuclear age.[23] But whatever the level of confidence in our understanding of nuclear matters in the era of cold war, confidence is lower in the identity and quality of ideas claimed as relevant to nuclear issues in this second nuclear age.

History can be made to show what an author wishes it to show. Nonetheless, history would seem to show that deterrence is exceedingly unreliable.[24] One

[19] From a large and growing literature, see Lawrence Freedman, 'Great Powers, Vital Interests and Nuclear Weapons', Survival, 36 (1994–5), 35–52; Fred Charles Iklé, 'The Second Coming of the Nuclear Age', Foreign Affairs, 75 (1996), 119–28; Keith B. Payne, Deterrence in the Second Nuclear Age (Lexington, Ky., 1996); Godfried van Benthem van den Bergh, 'The Nuclear Revolution into Its Second Phase', in Jorn Gjelstad and Olav Njolstad (eds.), Nuclear Rivalry and International Order (London, 1996), 22–39; Robert A. Manning, 'The Nuclear Age: The Next Chapter', Foreign Policy, 109 (1997–8), 70–83; T. V. Paul, Richard J. Harknett, and James J. Wirtz (eds.), The Absolute Weapon Revisited: Nuclear Arms and the Emerging International Order (Ann Arbor, Mich., 1998); Center for Counterproliferation Research (National Defense University) and Center for Global Security Research (Lawrence Livermore National Laboratory), U.S. Nuclear Policy in the 21st Century: A Fresh Look at National Strategy and Requirements, Final Report (Washington, DC, 1998); Gray, Second Nuclear Age; John Baylis and Robert O'Neill (eds.), Alternative Nuclear Futures (Oxford, 1999).

[20] e.g. Glenn A. Kent, Randall J. DeValk, and David E. Thayer, A Calculus of First-Strike Stability (A Criterion for Evaluating Strategic Forces), RAND Note N-2526-AF (Santa Monica, Calif., June 1988); Dean Wilkening et al., Strategic Defenses and Crisis Stability, RAND Note N-2511-AF (Santa Monica, Calif., Apr. 1989).

[21] John Arquilla, 'Bound to Fail: Regional Deterrence after the Cold War', Comparative Strategy, 14 (1995), 123–35; Dean Wilkening and Kenneth Watman, Nuclear Deterrence in a Regional Context (Santa Monica, Calif., 1995); Graham E. Fuller and John Arquilla, 'The Intractable Problem of Regional Powers', Orbis, 40 (1996), 609–21; Payne, Deterrence in the Second Nuclear Age, esp. ch. 2.

[22] C. A. W. Manning, The Nature of International Society (London, 1962); Hedley Bull, The Anarchical Society: A Study of Order in World Politics (New York, 1977); Hedley Bull and Adam Watson (eds.), The Expansion of International Society (Oxford, 1985).

[23] Richard Ned Lebow and Janice Gross Stein, We All Lost the Cold War (Princeton, NJ, 1994); Payne, Deterrence in the Second Nuclear Age.

[24] Raoul Naroll, Vern L. Bullough, and Frada Naroll, Military Deterrence in History: A Pilot Cross-Historical Survey (Albany, NY, 1975). John J. Mearsheimer, Conventional Deterrence (Ithaca, NY, 1983), remains useful, while William R. Thompson, 'Anglo-German Rivalry and the 1939 Failure of Deterrence', Security Studies, 7 (1997/8), 58–89, offers insight into the true complexity of the possible historical causes of recorded effects.

important reason why historiographical combat over understanding of the strategic history of the Cold War really matters is that attitudes towards future nuclear strategy are likely to rest upon contestable interpretations of the first nuclear age. Is it true to argue, as did Sir Michael Howard, that '[w]hat is beyond doubt . . . is that we effectively deterred the Soviet Union from using military force to achieve its political objectives'? He proceeds to challenge the gods with the claim: 'We have become rather expert at deterrence.'[25] In support, John Keegan states unequivocally that 'it was the balance of terror throughout the Cold War which prevented nuclear war'; while Emanuel Adler asserts, 'To a large extent, these expectations [of the outcome and efficacy of war with nuclear weapons] help explain why the Cold War stayed and ended cold.'[26] These claims may be true, but they exceed the evidence. If anything, indeed, scholarship suggests that we were more lucky than skilful in the avoidance of a cataclysmic conclusion to the Cold War.

The leading security problems of the first nuclear age were the deterrence of possible imperial adventure by a superpower, and how to arrange to employ a force that grew to 10,000–12,000 nuclear weapons efficiently in a single integrated operational plan (SIOP). In contrast, the security problems of the second nuclear age focus instead, illustratively, upon possibly 'loose nukes' in the former USSR,[27] the discouragement of nuclear proliferation to what Western, indeed G-8, polities have learnt to call 'rogue states',[28] and the deterrence of, and defence against, weapons of mass destruction (including biological, toxin, and chemical weapons) in the hands both of 'rogues' and of other regional and extra-state players.[29]

Strategic history is dependent upon the course of political history. Military expertise offers only a second-order enlightenment on the differences that distinguished the 1990s from the 1970s and 1980s. The great difference for strategic history between the 1980s and the 1990s was the presence, or absence, of the Soviet super state. The political architecture of world power was transformed when the USSR collapsed. As Clausewitz might well have written, had he been a

[25] Michael Howard, 'Lessons of the Cold War', *Survival*, 36 (1994–5), 161, 164.

[26] John Keegan, *War and Our World* (London, 1998), 64; Emanuel Adler, 'Condition(s) of Peace', *Review of International Studies*, 24, special issue (1998), 182.

[27] Kurt M. Campbell et al., *Soviet Nuclear Fission: Control of the Nuclear Arsenal in a Disintegrating Soviet Union*, CSIA Studies in International Security 1 (Cambridge, Mass., Nov. 1991); William Potter, *Nuclear Threats from the Former Soviet Union*, CTS-39-93 (Livermore, Calif., 16 Mar. 1993); Graham Allison et al., *Cooperative Denuclearization: From Pledges to Deeds*, CSIA Studies in International Security 2 (Cambridge, Mass., Jan. 1993); Graham T. Allison et al., *Avoiding Nuclear Anarchy: Containing the Threat of Loose Russian Nuclear Weapons and Fissile Material*, CSIA Studies in International Security 12 (Cambridge, Mass., 1996); John C. Baker, *Non-Proliferation Incentives for Russia and Ukraine*, Adelphi Paper 309 (London, 1997).

[28] Michael Klare, *Rogue States and Nuclear Outlaws: America's Search for a New Foreign Policy* (New York, 1995).

[29] The distinctive, and not so distinctive, challenge posed by biological, toxin, and chemical weapons is discussed at the end of this chapter.

graffiti artist: 'politics rules!' But political history has a way of repeating the same broad range of challenges to statesmen and strategists, even as the detail alters radically. The theorists and practitioners of modern strategy must consider the strong possibility that this second nuclear age, which features a single super-power, a still descending, heavily nuclear-armed, geopolitically much truncated, ex-superpower, and a short list of regionally troublesome rogue states, is but a passing phase in history.[30]

I believe a sound historical, not futurological, understanding of modern strategy will equip people to deal well enough with the future. Nonetheless, it may be useful to break with the rule and speculate that beyond the second nuclear age of today there lies most probably a third nuclear age which would resemble in its security architecture the first nuclear age of 1945–89. This bold hypothesis is more political than strategic; indeed, the strategic implications follow inexorably from the political assumptions. Specifically, it is plausible to postulate a new, third nuclear age wherein, yet again, a particular strategic relationship would dominate the course of history.[31] The most serious candidate for US opponent in this hypo-thetical third nuclear age is the People's Republic of China. One might be misled by expressions of genuine Great Russian rage, frustration, and nostalgia for superpower status into believing that there is a Russian super-threat in our future. Many things are possible, but fewer are probable. A Russian return in the near term to the status of major menace to the balance of power in Eurasia is unlikely.

My prediction is that the current second nuclear age, which is dominated by the problems of proliferation among regional polities, will be succeeded within two decades by a bipolar security architecture that pits American against Chinese power and influence. This hypothesised third nuclear age, though offering a rich mixture of cultural and geostrategic asymmetries, would nonetheless eventually provide near enough a balance in geostrategic weight between protagonists, certainly in the Asia-Pacific region.

WORLD POLITICS

The arrival of gunpowder may have facilitated the growth of the modern Euro-pean state, while eventually it enabled first the Portuguese and then the Spanish, Dutch, French, British, Russians, Americans, and Germans, to seize and hold great

---

[30] A thesis of Gray, *Second Nuclear Age*.

[31] Of course, there is no law of world order requiring recurrent restructuring to fit an iron necessity for bipolarity. The twenty-first century may witness the transformation of the current condition of unipolar US hegemony into a tripolar or even multipolar international system. Geoffrey Parker, *Geo-politics: Past, Present, and Future* (London, 1998), is a sound review of alternative geostrategic geometries, while Randall L. Schweller, *Deadly Imbalances: Tripolarity and Hitler's Strategy of World Conquest* (New York, 1998), is a pertinent, if unpersuasive, case study.

seaborne or continental empires.[32] One looks in vain for comparable consequences for the organization of world politics that flowed from the nuclear revolution. If, in a crude military-technical sense rather than necessarily strategically, nuclear weapons and their means of delivery obviously all but defined superior armament through most of the second half of the twentieth century, what difference did they make to the 'game of nations'?

The strategic history of the nuclear era has yet to show that the defining weapon of this era either creates or undoes empires. In some strategically significant ways at least, militarily the most powerful weapon of the period did not make its possessors more powerful. Potential tactical and actual strategic effects were sharply out of step. These comments sceptical of the net influence of nuclear weapons should not be misinterpreted as endorsement of any proposition suggesting an 'essential irrelevance' of those weapons to statecraft and strategy.[33] Still less does this text endorse the position that the lack of state or coalition advantage that can be garnered from nuclear possession demonstrates the folly of such possession. Nothing could be further from the truth.

A combination of unrestricted access to science and technology, delegitimizing nuclear taboo,[34] and plain old strategic prudence has thus far served to tame the military atom as a mover and shaker of world politics. The structure of international order after 1945 owed little to the Manhattan Project. The United States and the USSR were superpowers both by virtue of the traditional sources of state strength and because World War II eliminated all rivals.[35] The British Empire looked like a superpower in the 1920s and 1930s, and Germany was a superpower in 1940–2.[36] But by 6 August 1945, only two superpolities remained on the board, though their strengths were hugely asymmetrical.

American policy towards nuclear weapons was not responsible for the onset of the Cold War, speculations by revisionist historians notwithstanding.[37] But those

[32] Geoffrey Parker, *The Military Revolution: Military Innovation and the Rise of the West, 1500–1800* (Cambridge, 1988); Brian M. Downing, *The Military Revolution and Political Change: Origins of Democracy and Autocracy in Early Modern Europe* (Princeton, NJ, 1992); Bert S. Hall, *Weapons and Warfare in Renaissance Europe: Gunpowder, Technology, and Tactics* (Baltimore, 1997).

[33] John Mueller, 'The Essential Irrelevance of Nuclear Weapons: Stability in the Postwar World', *International Security*, 13 (1988), 55–79; id., 'Nine Propositions about the Historical Impact of Nuclear Weapons', in Gjelstad and Njolstad, *Nuclear Rivalry and International Order*, 55–74; id., 'The Escalating Irrelevance of Nuclear Weapons', in Paul et al., *Absolute Weapon Revisited*, 73–98.

[34] T. V. Paul, 'Nuclear Taboo and War Initiation in Regional Conflicts', *Journal of Conflict Resolution*, 39 (1995), 696–717. Gray, *Second Nuclear Age*, ch. 4, finds the nuclear taboo dangerously unreliable. Though not bereft of all value for international security, this taboo is, alas, commanding only for the policy of those insufficiently motivated to flout it. The concept of a nuclear taboo is not so much incorrect as misleading, if people believe it to be very useful to help control the truly hard cases wherein necessity knows no law or taboo.

[35] William T. R. Fox, *The Super-Powers* (New York, 1944).

[36] Anthony Clayton, *The British Empire as a Superpower, 1919–39* (Athens, Ga., 1986); Richard Overy, *Why the Allies Won* (London, 1995), ch.1.

[37] Gar Alperovitz, *Atomic Diplomacy: Hiroshima and Potsdam* (New York, 1965); Gregg Herken, *The Winning Weapon: The Atomic Bomb in the Cold War, 1945–1950* (New York, 1980). James G. Hersberg,

weapons did assuredly influence the course and the outcome of that great protracted struggle. Historians will never be able to tell for certain whether nuclear weapons kept the Cold War cold. Nothing in the archives, and no-one's oral testimony, can transform the 'virtual history' of an imagined non-nuclear post-1945 world into a source of reliable guidance on the strategic influence of nuclear weapons in the only, actual, history that we have. Modern great war, especially modern great war on the scale of totality waged by the USSR from 1941 to 1945, was known to be so terrible that there was scant need for reinforcement of that appreciation by yet a new layer of horror. That said, it is still plausible to suggest that World War III would have erupted at some point between the late 1940s and the mid-1980s had nuclear weapons not provided an inhibition to policy of a character unique in strategic history.

The grim continent-wide experience of war in 1914–18 did not encourage military romanticism in 1939, yet the second great war occurred. Norman Angell, among others, predicted before 1914, and again before 1939, that the modern world could not afford to fight large-scale and protracted wars.[38] He was right, but Europe went to war anyway on a heroic scale, not once, but twice within a quarter-century. Experience of great war appears to teach that no costs, in anticipation, can strike the sword of war as a policy instrument from the hands of statesmen. Such a view fuelled pessimism in the late 1940s and 1950s—it was commonplace for would-be leaders of public opinion to assert the inevitability of nuclear war (recall the slogan 'better Red than dead')—not without good cause, one should add. Bernard Brodie and the others who defined the atomic bomb as 'the absolute weapon' in 1946 were at least half correct. For the first time in strategic history, the human race had created a weapon which, when advanced technically into the 'super' league of the hydrogen bomb,[39] and when procured in the thousands, would be absolutely unusable in action in pursuit of strategic advantage, and useful in pursuit of prevention of strategic disadvantage only insofar as it remained a threat.

In strategic effect, nuclear weapons function as a counter-deterrent to the nuclear weapons of others. They also discourage the large-scale conduct of military operations of any kind because of the fear of accident, of inadvertent

'Reconsidering the Nuclear Arms Race: The Past as Prelude?', in Gordon Martel (ed.), *American Foreign Relations Reconsidered, 1890–1993* (London, 1994), 187–210, is, in my opinion, insufficiently empathetic to the difficulties facing policymakers, but it is exceptionally useful as a guide to the literature. Vojtech Mastny, *The Cold War and Soviet Insecurity: The Stalin Years* (New York, 1996), and Vladislav Zubok and Constantine Pleshakov, *Inside the Kremlin's Cold War: From Stalin to Khrushchev* (Cambridge, Mass., 1996), help set the record straight. Superior histories with a pervasive nuclear theme include Marc Trachtenberg, *History and Strategy* (Princeton, NJ, 1991), and David Holloway, *Stalin and the Bomb: The Soviet Union and Atomic Energy, 1939–1956* (New Haven, Conn., 1994).

[38] Norman Angell, *The Great Illusion: A Study of the Relation of Military Power in Nations to Their Economic and Social Advantage*, 3rd edn. (London, 1911); id., *The Great Illusion—Now* (London, 1938).

[39] Samuel R. Williamson, Jr. and Steven L. Rearden, *The Origins of U.S. Nuclear Strategy, 1945–1953* (New York, 1993); Richard Rhodes, *Dark Sun: The Making of the Hydrogen Bomb* (New York, 1995).

escalation, or even of purposeful escalation once combat gathers momentum. Although the Cold War was the product of history, geopolitics, ideology, and per-sonalities, at times military, and especially military nuclear, competition seemed to hold political centre stage in East–West relations.[40] The so-called nuclear arms race played only a supporting role in a security drama scripted by politics on a stage provided by geography.[41] Nonetheless, the lines of political demarcation between the virtual belligerents and their dependent imperia were frozen in part by near-universal appreciation of the risks of adventurous policies. Official and public attention came to focus upon the nuclear engines of destruction. After 1969, arms control, and nuclear arms control in particular, was the only available field for active bilateral East–West statecraft. The protracted process of the Stra-tegic Arms Limitation Talks (SALTs I and II), though nominally about whatever the spokesperson meant by strategic stability and the like, was actually surrogate war. The nuclear arms competition and a negotiating process dealing in weapons that could not be employed in battle were the only competitions that the powers dared wage with nuclear weapons.

It is probably not true to argue that nuclear weapons prolonged the political life of the Soviet Union and of the Cold War. It is probably correct, however, to argue that the nuclear revolution had a significant and positive strategic influence upon the course of postwar history. We can never know whether or not a World War III would have been triggered in the crises of 1948, 1956, 1968, 1973, and 1983,[42] had nuclear weapons not existed in ever larger numbers to influence cost-benefit policy calculations. But the existence of these weapons must have helped tilt the scales against war, at least in contexts where tolerably rational strategic choices were made.[43]

Nuclear weapons may not be militarily very useful, but they are essential if a

[40] See Albert Wohlstetter, *Legends of the Arms Race*, USSI Report 75-1 (Washington, DC, 1975), on the existential issue of an arms race, and Barry Buzan and Eric Herring, *The Arms Dynamic in World Politics* (Boulder, Colo., 1998), for a much broader analysis. It is noteworthy, and encouraging, that Buzan and Herring adopt the concept of 'arms dynamic—that is, the entire set of pressures that make actors (usually states) both acquire armed forces and change the quantity and quality of the armed forces they possess' (5; emphasis original). The concept of 'arms race' has been challenged recently: Colin S. Gray, 'Arms Races and Other Pathetic Fallacies: A Case for Deconstruction', *Review of International Studies*, 22 (1996), 323–35.

[41] Colin S. Gray, *The Geopolitics of Super Power* (Lexington, Ky., 1988).

[42] If a 'crisis' in international politics requires two parties, then 1983 cannot well qualify. The crisis, though real, existed in Soviet perceptions and was unknown to Western policymakers at the time. A fairly standard form of NATO nuclear release exercise ('Able Archer', 2–11 Nov. 1983) was monitored by a Soviet intelligence community extraordinarily alert to possible signs of an impending nuclear attack (Operation RYAN, the Russian acronym for nuclear missile attack). RYAN (1981–4) read 'Able Archer' as evidence that NATO might be about to attack. The result was a war scare in Moscow. Robert M. Gates, *From the Shadows: The Ultimate Insider's Story of Five Presidents and How They Won the Cold War* (New York, 1996), 270–7; Ben B. Fischer, *A Cold War Conundrum: The 1983 Soviet War Scare*, CSI 97-10002 (Langley, Va., Sept. 1997).

[43] The qualification is significant. Iklé, 'Second Coming of the Nuclear Age'; Payne, *Deterrence in the Second Nuclear Age*. Thoughtful, detailed revisionist treatments of Cuba 1962 and the Middle East 1973

nuclear (and possibly biologically and chemically) armed foe is to be confronted and confounded.[44] One should add that there is global consensus upon the strategic value of nuclear weapons as the *ultima ratio regis*. Thus far, these weapons have not shown much value as instruments for coercion in muscular diplomacy, but their prospective capacity to 'save the country in the last resort' is appreciated in every nuclear-weapon state, and in every state that would like to acquire nuclear arms. Nuclear weapons raise the stakes of conflict precipitately, whether or not they are keyed into well-designed and well-executable targeting plans. Existential deterrence is aided by adding the latent menace posed by weapons of mass destruction to whatever conventional and unconventional (e.g. terroristic) options may be available. Indeed, terrorists armed with weapons of mass destruction translate as the awesome novel possibility of 'catastrophe terrorism'.[45]

Little can be done with nuclear weapons, but that little is important. To be nuclear-armed probably does not add to a country's influence in the world, except, that is, where it really matters. A country's nuclear arms will discourage extreme security challenges from an adversary who is well armed conventionally, while those nuclear arms mean that one is largely immunized against intimidation by the nuclear arms of others. In Michael Quinlan's words, 'a nuclear state is a state that no-one can afford to make desperate'.[46] A superpower's nuclear arsenal helps discourage nuclear proliferation. It can, with variable plausibility, extend deterrence to protect friends and allies who might otherwise elect to 'go nuclear', and it should discourage the use of chemical, biological, or conventional weaponry against them. These significant but still minimal benefits of nuclear weapons do not dominate the subject of nuclear weapons in world politics with total assurance. The benefits to deterrence provided by nuclear arms are offset somewhat by the perils of technical accident, of political error (inadvertent war), and of potential wilful adventure by some nuclear-armed Hitler or Saddam. Overall, the subject of the influence of nuclear weapons in world politics is an exercise in attempting to understand a realm of necessity—the weapons exist and cannot safely be banished entirely—not of policy discretion, at least for players with serious duties for international order or for those whose external security is menaced severely.[47]

dominate Lebow and Stein, *We All Lost the Cold War*. Elli Lieberman, *Deterrence Theory: Success or Failure in Arab–Israeli Wars*, McNair Paper 45 (Washington, DC, Oct. 1995), is a powerful critique of Lebow and Stein.

[44] This opinion finds strong expression in Michael Quinlan, *Thinking about Nuclear Weapons*, RUSI Whitehall Paper (London, 1997); Keith B. Payne, *The Case Against Nuclear Abolition and For Nuclear Deterrence* (Fairfax, Va., 1997); Robert G. Joseph and John H. Reichart, 'The Case for Nuclear Deterrence Today', *Orbis*, 42 (1998), 7–19.

[45] Martin Shubik, 'Terrorism, Technology, and the Socioeconomics of Death', *Comparative Strategy*, 16 (1997), 399–14; Richard K. Betts, 'The New Threat of Mass Destruction', *Foreign Affairs*, 77 (1998), 26–41.

[46] Quinlan, *Thinking about Nuclear Weapons*, 19.

[47] Gray, *Second Nuclear Age*, ch. 3. Mitchell Reiss, *Bridled Ambition: Why Countries Constrain Their Nuclear Capabilities* (Washington, DC, 1995), and Scott D. Sagan, 'Why Do States Build Nuclear Weapons? Three Models in Search of a Bomb', *International Security*, 21 (1996/7), 54–86, cover most of the motivational ground in question.

NUCLEAR FORCES AND NUCLEAR STRATEGY

The nuclear World War III between the United States and the USSR failed to occur, notwithstanding cataclysmic predictions advanced by some self-styled experts on the future. A result of that happily non-war history is that there is a residual and ultimately irreducible indeterminacy about the influence of nuclear strategy in the first nuclear age.[48] 'Nuclear strategy' embraces both intellectual history and the politically contingent plans of nuclear weapon states and coalitions. What are the leading problems of evidence that inhibit scholarly judgement, though encouraging scholarly exploration and speculation?

NOT PROVEN: A PROBLEM OF EVIDENCE

First, the absence of bilateral nuclear war between East and West meant that the essentially practical realm of strategy had to function without a field test. One might object that nuclear strategy truly was field-tested for its contributions to both general and immediate deterrence throughout the course of the Cold War.[49] But every claim for the strategic effect of intended deterrence requires careful judgement.[50] In fact, two leaps of faith are required in this instance: one needs to leap both from the assumed relevance of a calculated military relationship and from the assumed relevance of the details of that relationship. Nuclear weapons should matter for deterrence; they can hardly help but shape perceptions of the intensity of risk, but do perceived details of nuclear strategy (i.e. beliefs about the adversary's targeting plans and military capabilities) matter very much?

Second, not only has strategic history yet to yield evidence of bilateral nuclear combat, but also our reliable knowledge of authoritative, operational nuclear war plans is at best incomplete in the American case, largely missing in the Soviet, British, and French regard, and totally missing in inaction for China, Israel, India, Pakistan, and North Korea.

Third, as Field Marshal Helmuth Graf von Moltke wrote famously as a matter of common lore, 'No plan of operations extends with certainty beyond the first contact with the enemy's main strength.'[51] This idea can be adapted to the nuclear era by rephrasing as the claim that no nuclear war plan survives first contact with a statesman's fears. This third problem of lack of evidence adds to the difficulties for judgement posed by the absence of nuclear battle and the lack of access to authoritative nuclear plans. Both sides would probably have tried to wage nuclear war as an ad hoc expression of high policy. Contrary to what many in the West

---

[48] The most penetrating discussion to date is Payne, *Deterrence in the Second Nuclear Age*.

[49] Patrick Morgan, *Deterrence: A Conceptual Analysis* (Beverly Hills, Calif., 1977), ch. 2.

[50] Gordon Craig and Alexander George, *Force and Statecraft: Diplomatic Problems of Our Time*, 3rd edn. (New York, 1995), 195, comment appropriately on the evidence problem with the possible influence of nuclear threats.

[51] Daniel J. Hughes (ed.), *Moltke on the Art of War: Selected Writings*, trans. Hughes and Harry Bell (Novato, Calif., 1995), 45.

believed in the Cold War about a putative 'Soviet way' in great war, subsequent evidence suggests that if any side were likely to have proceeded rigidly to implement 'the Plan', most probably it would have been the United States, with its iconic SIOP.[52] Military historians will recall the irony in the fact that in both World War I and World War II Anglo-American tactical theorists were wont to presume a military flexibility for Anglo-American soldiers, as contrasted with a largely presumptive teutonic inflexibility, which was the reverse of the truth. Among the leading armies of the twentieth century, the German was persistently in the forefront in delegating tactical authority to the people at the sharp end (*Auftragstaktik*, or 'mission-oriented command system').[53]

It is not unusual for theorists and commentators to be chided by government 'insiders' for confusing strategic ideas with operational military intentions. For example, Bruce Blair, a former missile launch officer in the Strategic Air Command, complains: 'As assured destruction attracted endorsements across the spectrum of opinion, its adherents inflated it from a procurement norm to a norm for wartime planning.'[54] Plausible though this charge is, Blair himself is not entirely innocent of what one might call the 'expert's fallacy'. If the operationally untutored are susceptible to seduction by strategic ideas, the operationally expert are at risk of capture by the logic of routines that may well be upset in practice by the human intervention of desperately fearful politicians. In his outstanding study, *Logic of Accidental Nuclear War*, Blair explains persuasively why preemptive nuclear response was politically impracticable, but he is less compelling when he advises that prompt ICBM launch, or launch under attack (LUA, what insiders used to call the 'Midnight Express' of missile launch on *tactical* warning), was the real, the operational, US military intention.[55] Subsequent studies have come to adopt Blair on LUA as gospel.[56] Allegedly, so we are told, the US Air Force did not really care about ICBM survivability in the late 1970s and early 1980s, because—*après* Bruce Blair—the birds would already have flown, launched under attack on receipt of warning by the North American Air Defense Command (NORAD) of radar and infrared tactical notice of an incoming Soviet missile assault.

There was much to be said in favour of ICBM LUA (indeed, I said some of it in

[52] Bruce G. Blair, *The Logic of Accidental Nuclear War* (Washington, DC, 1993), esp. chs. 3 and 4; testimony of Col.-Gen. (Ret.) Andrian A. Danilevich, in John G. Hines, Ellis M. Mishulovich, and John F. Shull, *Soviet Intentions, 1965–1985, ii: Soviet Post-Cold War Testimonial Evidence* (McLean, Va., 22 Sept. 1995), 19–69; Andrei A. Kokoshin, *Soviet Strategic Thought, 1917–91* (Cambridge, Mass., 1998).

[53] Martin van Creveld, *Fighting Power: German and U.S. Army Performance, 1939–1945* (Westport, Conn., 1982), 36. But see Russell F. Weigley, *Eisenhower's Lieutenants: The Campaign of France and Germany, 1944–1945* (Bloomington, Ind., 1981), and Michael D. Doubler, *Closing with the Enemy: How GIs Fought the War in Europe, 1944–1945* (Lawrence, Kan., 1994).

[54] Blair, *Logic of Accidental Nuclear War*, 176.

[55] Ibid. 185–95.

[56] Theo Farrell, *Weapons Without a Cause: The Politics of Weapons Acquisition in the United States* (London, 1997), 38–42; David H. Dunn, *The Politics of Threat: Minuteman Vulnerability in American National Security Policy* (London, 1997), 212–13.

1985),[57] but Blair's commentary notwithstanding, it placed requirements upon the policymaking process that appear reasonable only when contrasted with the Homeric demands of prevention or preemption (or launch on *strategic* warning — which is to say, launch on the intelligence spectrum from what one believes to be advance notice through to strong suspicion). Blair's superb studies of nuclear command and control, in company with a handful of like treatises,[58] opened a window on the practice of nuclear strategy that was sorely needed. Controversialists addicted to debate on the grand abstractions — stability, assured destruction, MAD, stable deterrence, flexibility in response — can only benefit from a powerful dose of Blair and the rest of his school on the once-understudied subject of command stability. There are problems for students of nuclear strategy, however, in knowing how seriously to treat the arguments advanced by such a scholar-practitioner as Bruce Blair. One needs to remember that nobody has *any* experience of the actual conduct of bilateral nuclear combat. The genuinely expert nuclear warriors of the Cold War era, some of whom have deployed their nuclear credentials as the basis of a claim for special knowledge of nuclear war, happily were genuinely expert only in planning and training for nuclear conflict. Strategic futurology is no more proof against error than is any other kind. A four-star general, even if he is commander-in-chief of the Strategic Air Command (SAC), or Supreme Allied Commander, Europe (SACEUR), has no campaign ribbons for nuclear combat.[59] The history of nuclear strategy in the Cold War is the chronicle

---

[57] Colin S. Gray, 'ICBMs and Deterrence: The Controversy over Prompt Launch', *Journal of Strategic Studies*, 10 (1987), 285–309.

[58] Bruce G. Blair, *Strategic Command and Control: Redefining the Nuclear Threat* (Washington, DC, 1985); id., *Logic of Accidental Nuclear War*; id., *Global Zero Alert for Nuclear Forces* (Washington, DC, 1995). See also Paul Bracken, *The Command and Control of Nuclear Forces* (New Haven, Conn., 1983); Daniel Ford, *The Button: The Pentagon's Strategic Command and Control System* (New York, 1985); Ashton B. Carter, John H. Steinbruner, and Charles A. Zraket (eds.), *Managing Nuclear Operations* (Washington, DC, 1987); Kurt Gottfried and Bruce G. Blair (eds.), *Crisis Stability and Nuclear War* (New York, 1988); Paul B. Stares, *Command Performance: The Neglected Dimension of European Security* (Washington, DC, 1991); Peter Douglas Feaver, *Guarding the Guardians: Civilian Control of Nuclear Weapons in the United States* (Ithaca, NY, 1992); Scott D. Sagan, *The Limits of Safety: Organizations, Accidents, and Nuclear Weapons* (Princeton, NJ, 1993); Shaun R. Gregory, *Nuclear Command and Control in NATO: Nuclear Weapons Operations and the Strategy of Flexible Response* (London, 1996).

[59] Former CinCSAC Gen. George Lee Butler was particularly prominent in the public campaign in the 1990s to promote the elimination, at least delegitimization, of nuclear weapons. For example, Gen. Butler served both on the Canberra Commission on the Elimination of Nuclear Weapons, and on the Committee on International Security and Arms Control of the (US) National Academy of Sciences. Gen. Butler and former SACEUR, Gen. Andrew Goodpaster, registered no objection to, nor did they seek to qualify, their being jointly introduced as follows at a National Press Club Luncheon on 4 Dec. 1996: 'During their long and honored careers, these officers had vast arsenals of nuclear weapons under their command. Few people have a better understanding of the threat posed by these weapons of mass destruction than they. They are here today to tell us why the United States and the world must rid itself of all nuclear weapons': National Press Club Speakers Series, *Transcript*, 2. Military people with experience of command of nuclear armed forces will be exceptionally well informed about nuclear weapons and plans for their use. However, whatever authority they wield as experts is an authority based only on peacetime experience of nuclear operations.

of plans and planning processes for targeting, of the procurement of forces, and of the training and prewar operational practices of those forces. The real action in nuclear strategy from 1945 until 1989 occurred in the minds of would-be deterrers and intended deterrees. Virtual history is fun, and it can be exciting as well as interesting and educational, but it is not quite history.[60] Expertise on virtual nuclear combat is virtual expertise only.

MODERN STRATEGIC STUDIES

Cold War strategic studies were the product of the nuclear revolution. Those studies enjoyed what appeared for a while to have been a 'golden age'—approximately from 1955 to 1966—when three streams of theory were articulated: ideas on deterrence, limited war, and arms control.[61] The typical modern strategic theorist has been American, civilian, male, social scientific in professional affiliation, and lacking in serious (i.e. life-threatening) personal military experience.[62] The appearance in 1989 of a revised edition of Lawrence Freedman's excellent study, *Evolution of Nuclear Strategy*, spares me the task of telling the story of nuclear strategy in the Cold War. My differences with Freedman are differences of interpretation, not of historical record.

Skill bias as well as superpower arrogance yielded a corpus of nuclear-era strategic theory from the United States that had significant weaknesses. Until recently, American strategic theory has had too many authors trained in economics, mathematics, and a rational-choice approach to political science, and too few trained in anthropology and history. The result has been a canon of purportedly strategic precepts ill-supported by actual strategic history, all but indifferent to the dilemmas of real people, and naïvely rationalistic in assessment of motivation.[63]

Accepting the risk of seeming eccentrically disagreeable, some of the canon lore of modern strategic truth that I was taught in the 1960s was either wrong or at least perilously flawed, because incomplete. The three streams of strategic theory which created the main supporting pillars of modern Western strategic studies—

---

[60] Herman Kahn, *On Thermonuclear War*, 2nd edn. (New York, 1969), chs. 7–12; Harold Deutsch and Dennis E. Showalter (eds.), *What If? Strategic Alternatives of WWII* (Chicago, 1997); Niall Ferguson (ed.), *Virtual History: Alternatives and Counterfactuals* (London, 1997).

[61] Colin S. Gray, *Strategic Studies and Public Policy: The American Experience* (Lexington, Ky., 1982), ch. 4.

[62] John Keegan has ventured the opinion that '[s]trategic and war studies have failed as university subjects because they have indeed been taught in universities by people who have been nowhere but universities. They know nothing of the realities of their subject, nor can they; in consequence, their students learn nothing either': 'Towards a Theory of Combat Motivation', in Paul Addison and Angus Calder (eds.), *Time to Kill: The Soldier's Experience of War in the West, 1939–1945* (London, 1997), 11 (emphasis original).

[63] For essentially 'friendly' critiques, see Hedley Bull, 'Strategic Studies and Its Critics', *World Politics*, 20 (1968), 593–605; Bernard Brodie, *War and Politics* (New York, 1973), ch. 10; Colin S. Gray, *Strategic Studies: A Critical Assessment* (Westport, Conn., 1982); Stephen M. Walt, 'The Renaissance of Security Studies', *International Studies Quarterly*, 35 (1991), 211–39; Richard K. Betts, 'Should Strategic Studies Survive?' *World Politics*, 50 (1997), 7–33.

deterrence, limited war, and arms control—were each noticeably in some error. To consider first the realms of lesser immediate danger, limited war and arms control, the American strategic literature on both failed basic tests of strategic cultural domain. In other words, just because an idea plays well in Cambridge, Massachusetts, that does not mean that it will handle the relevant policy traffic in Moscow or Baghdad. The American theory of limited war in the nuclear period, a theory developed to explain what occurred in, and mercifully failed to occur over, Korea from 1950 until 1953 as a source of possible precedent for future conflicts,[64] in effect elevated technique or operational virtuosity over politics. During their intellectually most focused decade, American theorists speculated extensively about limited war. Although the core inspiration was limited conventional war as in Korea, theory ventured into the zones of tactical nuclear war and even limited 'strategic' nuclear war.[65] As representation of a problem-solving culture, as optimists confident that almost any mission is feasible—if tackled competently—and as people comfortingly reassured by their interpretation of Clausewitz on real, or limited, war, American strategic theorists wrote for a while as if the idea of limited war would cure all strategic ills.

The American literature of 1955–63 on limited war is by no means all foolish. Given that both nuclear weapons and political conflicts are persisting facts of international life, it is only sensible to consider how force can be used with non-suicidal consequences. Where the literature tended to stray from the path of prudence, however, was in its working assumption that a reliable common grammar of limited war could be applied that would dominate both the logic of policy and tame many of the problems of friction. With respect to the use of nuclear weapons, by the 1970s Soviet experts came to share American beliefs about the necessity for extreme care.[66] Nonetheless, the prospective dynamics of conflict rendered aspirations for profitable superpower resort to nuclear weapons little more than a gambler's throw; never had Clausewitz's cautionary words, 'In the whole range of human activities, war most closely resembles a game of cards', been more apposite.[67] Similarly, his insistence that it is in the nature of war to tend towards an absolute expression of violence presaged perfectly the fear over unwanted escalation which came to dominate strategic theory and practice in the 1960s and 1970s. Clausewitz wrote:

War is an act of force and there is no logical limit to the application of that force. Each side,

---

[64] William W. Kaufmann, 'Limited Warfare', in Kaufmann (ed.), *Military Policy and National Security* (Princeton, NJ, 1956), 102–36; Robert E. Osgood, *Limited War: The Challenge to American Strategy* (Chicago, 1957); Bernard Brodie, *Strategy in the Missile Age* (Princeton, NJ, 1959), ch. 9; Morton H. Halperin, *Limited War in the Nuclear Age* (New York, 1963).

[65] Henry Kissinger, *Nuclear Weapons and Foreign Policy* (New York, 1957); id., *The Necessity for Choice* (New York, 1961); Klaus Knorr and Thornton Read (eds.), *Limited Strategic War* (London, 1962).

[66] Hines et al, *Soviet Intentions*, ii.

[67] Clausewitz, *On War*, 86.

therefore, compels its opponent to follow suit: a reciprocal action is started which must lead, in theory, to extremes.[68]

The American theory of limited war required a cooperative, even a symmetrical, foe. Since war is not a game with agreed rules, the limits in limited war always must be asserted and, if possible, defended. In the real world of diverse polities, distinctive personalities, differences in intensity of polity motivation to fight, as well as differences in feasible styles of war, frequently threaten to make a mockery of ideas for limited war. Also, limited war is a perilously civilized concept. The American theorists of limited war had little to offer on the topics of fanatically committed enemies, incompetent people, or Western societies unwilling to sacrifice in 'rationally' limited ways for limited political purposes. The American experience of combat in Vietnam from 1965 to 1973 was not the limited war that had been envisaged.[69] But that awful experience demonstrated with brutal clarity some of the reasons why the modern American theory of limited war was flawed. It is one thing sensibly to wage war in a limited way in support of limited objectives; it is quite another to wage such war to a successful outcome.

If the American theory of limited non-nuclear war was missing in action in South-East Asia, and if ideas on the limited use of nuclear weapons were not tested in the field, what can be said about another intellectual and policy realm close to nuclear strategy: the American rediscovery of arms control? The core notion underpinning efforts to achieve negotiated measures of arms control is the insight that potential enemies share a common interest in preventing unwanted war and suffering high levels of damage in war.

As noted earlier, theory poses rival paradoxes. On the one hand, political enemies need to cooperate because they are enemies, and hence might fight. On the other hand, political enemies cannot cooperate precisely because they are enemies.[70] Strategic history has a way of frustrating the scholar by declining to

---

[68] Clausewitz, *On War*, 77. Although Clausewitz thus powerfully identifies the bilateral dynamic of the conflict process that is war, I stand by the judgement offered in Chapter 4 above that he does not discuss 'the enemy' and the interactive dynamic of war anywhere near as extensively as the subject merits. See also Stephen J. Cimbala, *Clausewitz and Escalation: Classical Perspectives on Nuclear Strategy* (London, 1991).

[69] Stephen Peter Rosen, 'Vietnam and the American Theory of Limited War', *International Security*, 7 (1982), 83–113.

[70] Colin S. Gray, *House of Cards: Why Arms Control Must Fail* (Ithaca, NY, 1992). Other works sceptical of the value in arms control include Malcolm Wallop and Angelo Codevilla, *The Arms Control Delusion* (San Francisco, 1987), and Kerry M. Kartchner, *Negotiating START: Strategic Arms Reduction Talks and the Quest for Strategic Stability* (New Brunswick, NJ, 1992). The majority position by a wide margin is generically friendly to the theory and attempted practice of arms control. Illustrative flag-carriers for the majority camp include Albert Carnesale and Richard N. Haas (eds.), *Superpower Arms Control: Setting the Record Straight* (Cambridge, Mass., 1987); Emanuel Adler (ed.), *The International Practice of Arms Control* (Baltimore, 1992); Ashton B. Carter, William J. Perry, and John D. Steinbruner, *A New Concept of Cooperative Security*, Brookings Occasional Papers (Washington, DC, 1992); Stuart Croft, *Strategies of Arms Control: A History and Typology* (Manchester, 1996); Nancy W. Gallagher (ed.), *Arms Control: New Approaches to Theory and Policy* (London, 1998). If wisdom is indicated by numbers, the 'ayes' for arms control definitely have it.

provide reliable tests for ideas, but with regard to the theory of arms control, for once the evidence is plain and conclusive. During the Cold War nothing military-technical was negotiable between the superpowers, or between East and West, that would have much of a beneficial impact upon the prospects for avoidance of a great nuclear war. The reason why this should be so is not hard to identify. The causes of war did not lie in the military machines of East and West, or even in difficulties of real-time communication between the political owners of those machines. To modify that claim slightly, to the degree to which there may have been some military-technical 'logic of accidental nuclear war' lurking as a ghost in the machines,[71] nothing of much note negotiated in 'structural' (e.g. SALT and START) or even 'operational' (i.e. the 'hot-line' agreement of 1963, or the 'incidents at sea' agreement of 1972) arms control could work as an exorcist. As with limited war, the problem with arms control was the small matter that in the practical field of modern strategy it simply did not work. This negative judgement may not apply to all arms control endeavours, but it certainly applied to the perceived problems of instability in the strategic relations of the superpowers. A few theorists were right to be sceptical at the time: the large Western intellectual, political, and bureaucratic investment in arms control in the Cold War was effort very largely wasted.

It seems almost churlish to venture criticism at the third area of preeminent American strategic intellectual prowess, that of deterrence. After all, even if US performance as deterrer lacked finesse, how can one cavil at success? One must note that, for nuclear deterrence, unlike limited war and arms control, there is neither historical evidence of strategic failure nor obvious weakness in the theory *qua* theory. The principal trouble with the deterrence effect is that its causation is far more complicated than the now classic literature on nuclear-era strategy typically recognizes. Periodic thoughtful ruminations by the leading example of an empathetic theorist-practitioner, Fred Charles Iklé[72] and revisionist strategic-historical studies by scholars as politically diverse as Alexander George, Janice Gross Stein, Ned Lebow, and Keith B. Payne have emphasized what has long been widely suspected—that nuclear deterrence is unreliable.[73] When this critical literature on statecraft and strategy is overlaid with detailed studies of actual or potential command instability (on both sides of the Cold War divide), the mainstream of deterrence theory, and its variants, of the 1950s and early 1960s appears less confident.

If there is a pervasive and enduring weakness in the articulation of the theory of

[71] Blair, *Logic of Accidental Nuclear War*.

[72] Fred Charles Iklé, 'Can Nuclear Deterrence Last Out the Century?', *Foreign Affairs*, 51 (1973), 267–85; id., 'Nuclear Strategy: Can There Be a Happy Ending?', *Foreign Affairs*, 63 (1985), 810–26; id., 'Second Coming of the Nuclear Age'.

[73] Alexander George and Richard Smoke, *Deterrence in American Foreign Policy: Theory and Practice* (New York, 1974), was a major analytical audit, mid-term in the Cold War. Lebow and Stein, *We All Lost the Cold War*, and Payne, *Deterrence in the Second Nuclear Age*, are a generation later than George and Smoke.

deterrence, it is the lack of emphasis placed upon explanation of the structural point that deterrence, unlike defence, is voluntary. An intended deterree may be unwilling, or unable, to be deterred. No excellence in efforts at deterrence can guarantee successful deterrent effect. The deterree has to agree to be deterred, no matter how unwillingly. The American literature of the 1950s which addressed 'the requirements of deterrence'—to cite William Kaufmann's path-breaking analysis[74]—carried, at least appeared to carry, the message that deterrence was a problem that could be solved scientifically by application of the correct solution. In short, meet the requirements and stable deterrence is yours. Regarded prudently, however, more than half a century of strategic experience in the nuclear era suggests the advisability of a defensive backstop against the possibility of deterrence failure or irrelevance. Practical difficulties frequently render deterrence problematic. The fact that a defence good enough to be strategically useful is also problematic does not fracture my policy logic.

QUESTIONS OF INFLUENCE

There is a large and detailed literature on the course of the Cold War.[75] Not for many decades, however, will sufficient time have passed for historians to be able to offer mature judgement on the second half of the twentieth century. Today, the new-found availability of former Soviet sources of strategic information does not conclude longstanding arguments about the wisdom in US or NATO nuclear policy initiatives, but it does facilitate the task of the strategic historian. Nonetheless, the record of nuclear weapons in modern statecraft and strategy is different from the records carved by landpower, seapower, airpower, spacepower, and prospectively even cyberpower. Not only have nuclear weapons been employed only in 'nonuse', following Bernard Brodie's phrase,[76] as latent or explicit threat, but that strategic utility in nonuse, for deterrence, is inherently unprovable. Who are the heroes and heroines of nuclear deterrence? Can one refer to 'daring nondeeds' of deterrence? What are the plots for 'ripping yarns' from deterrence country?

Many scholars of modern strategy can agree that nuclear weapons have been strategically influential. As a looming virtual presence hovering over our lives,

[74] William W. Kaufmann, 'The Requirements of Deterrence', in Kaufmann (ed.), *Military Policy and National Security*, 12–38.

[75] Martin Walker, *The Cold War and the Making of the Modern World* (London, 1993), Richard Crockatt, *The Fifty Years War: The United States and the Soviet Union in World Politics, 1941–1991* (London, 1995), and David Miller, *The Cold War: A Military History* (London, 1998), are useful overviews. Also, four books by John Gaddis merit honourable mention: *Strategies of Containment: A Critical Appraisal of Postwar American National Security Policy* (New York, 1982); *The Long Peace: Inquiries Into the History of the Cold War* (New York, 1987); *The United States and the End of the Cold War: Implications, Reconsiderations, Provocations* (New York, 1992); *We Now Know: Rethinking Cold War History* (Oxford, 1997). See also the essays on the Cold War decades in Gordon Martel (ed.), *American Foreign Relations Reconsidered, 1890–1993* (London, 1994).

[76] Brodie, *War and Politics*, ch. 9.

nuclear weapons have cast a giant shadow. But beyond a latent menace, and aside from serving as symbolic items for superpower political treatment in the lengthy conclaves on 'strategic' nuclear arms control, what real influence have nuclear weapons exercised? These weapons have not won any hot wars—after 1945, at least, when two atomic bombs concluded a major war—and neither has fear of their use plausibly caused wars to be lost.[77] The superpowers certainly treated each other with great strategic respect during the Cold War, and probably that respect was enhanced by nuclear anxieties. Beyond the self-evidently correct argument that the strategic behaviour of the superpowers from 1947 to 1989, and the strategic ideas that helped shape that behaviour, was compatible with a condition of non-war—'peace' would be too ambitious a claim[78]—it is not obvious that we know very much about deterrence in the Cold War. In particular, it is difficult to relate strategic ideas and nuclear postures to the broad course of political-military events. This author, for example, engaged in a succession of debates about nuclear strategy and nuclear forces—for the United States and for NATO—but did the outcomes to those debates matter? If policymakers know that 'war is hell', and that nuclear war is an especially abominable form of hell, what justification could there be for both defence intellectuals and responsible officials seeking to render hell survivable? Was this an oxymoron?

THE RULES OF THE GAME WHEN PRUDENCE IS TRUMPS

There was a common East–West strategic enlightenment on many nuclear matters in the Cold War. For excellent reasons, notwithstanding the ultimately potentially catastrophic consequences, both superpowers acquired strategic nuclear forces postures that were similar in essential structure and philosophy of operation. It is my slightly reluctant conclusion that the superpowers did the right things for most of the right reasons in their bilateral construction of a great death machine. Readers can grapple with the finer points of this logic.

Debate on nuclear strategy and nuclear armed forces has a way of neglecting to recognize the large realm of consensus among Soviet and Western defence professionals. The practical world that 'does' nuclear strategy by and large agrees on how that strategy should be done, though, as we will see below, not what that strategy should achieve. Most specifically, as this author among others claimed at the time, the USSR never accepted any virtue in the idea of *mutual* vulnerability— though the reality of such vulnerability, of course, had to be recognized (but not

---

[77] The only case for which an argument could be made would be Vietnam. An unreasonable fear of Chinese intervention in Vietnam in the mid-1960s, an intervention that might well have required an American nuclear response, placed a fatal inhibition on the boldness of American strategic thinking about possible theories of victory in the war. Jeffrey Record, *The Wrong War: Why We Lost in Vietnam* (Annapolis, Md., 1998), 38–41, is sensible.

[78] Adler, 'Condition(s) of Peace'.

celebrated).[79] The world of modern strategy, to date, has registered only two very great nuclear-armed powers, the United States and the USSR/Russia.[80] Allowing for differences in strategic and military cultures, geostrategic context, and exact timing of competitive military-technical accomplishments, the similarities in the American and Soviet nuclear enlightenment are striking. Distinctive strategic cultures and national styles were stamped indelibly upon much of the detail of US and Soviet performance as nuclear powers, but the breadth and depth of cross-cultural agreement remains impressive. The measure of this agreement is especially notable because geography has played less of a distinctive role in shaping nuclear strategy than it has in influencing the national and coalition choices exercised over and among land, sea, and air forces. There is, though, an obvious sense in which that claim inadvertently might mislead. After all, it was precisely the geostrategic asymmetry in relations between each superpower and NATO-Europe that served as the principal influence driving US efforts to extend (nuclear) deterrence. Furthermore, the distribution of capabilities within each superpower's nuclear forces triad reflected each party's distinctive strategic geography and history.[81] But, for all their geostrategic and cultural differences, modern strategy

---

[79] Gray, *Nuclear Strategy and National Style*. See also Richard Pipes, 'Why the Soviet Union Thinks It Could Fight and Win a Nuclear War', *Commentary*, 64 (1977), 21–34; Fritz Ermath, 'Contrasts in American and Soviet Strategic Thought', *International Security*, 3 (1978), 138–55; Benjamin S. Lambeth, 'On Thresholds in Soviet Military Thought', *Washington Quarterly*, 7 (1984), 69–76. Edward L. Warner III, *Soviet Concepts and Capabilities for Limited Nuclear War: What We Know and How We Know It*, N-27-69-AF (Santa Monica, Calif., Feb. 1989), and Colin S. Gray, 'Soviet Nuclear Strategy and New Military Thinking', in Derek Leebaert and Timothy Dickinson (eds.), *Soviet Strategy and New Military Thinking* (Cambridge, 1992), 29–56, are interesting for what they reveal about the state of Western knowledge on Soviet strategy at the end of the Cold War. By far the best study available on the Soviet and Russian military transitions of the 1980s and 1990s is William E. Odom, *The Collapse of the Soviet Military* (New Haven, Conn., 1998).

[80] In the interest of highlighting what most needs to be understood, here I choose to ignore the strategic contexts of the lesser nuclear powers—Britain, France, China, Israel, India, and Pakistan. These polities can be ignored safely for my purposes because they do not exhibit a strategic logic contradictory to the superstate analysis, but rather show less of interest because their nuclear assets are less. Martin van Creveld, *Nuclear Proliferation and the Future of Conflict* (New York, 1993), suggests that new nuclear weapon states (NWSs), perhaps even 'rogue' NWSs, will not adopt new, let alone roguish, strategic nuclear doctrines.

[81] As a great continental state with a landpower preponderance traditional in its military posture, the USSR understandably deployed most of its strategic nuclear weapons under the control of the Strategic Rocket Forces, the legatee of an artillery tradition. In contrast, the US, though of continental size, geostrategically is effectively insular and at the dawn of the nuclear era inherited traditions of excellence preeminently in maritime power and airpower. The distinctive geographies, histories, distribution of influence among the different (geographically focused) military cultures, and politics of the superpowers meant that each country weighted the elements in its strategic forces' 'triad' uniquely. The USSR deployed most of its nuclear firepower on its land-based missile force, whereas the United States privileged its long-range aviation and its sea-based missile force. It is noteworthy, however, that both superpowers came to adopt—one cannot quite say 'planned'—a triadic structure for their strategic forces' posture: intercontinental ballistic missiles (ICBMs), submarine-launched ballistic missiles (SLBMs), and manned bombers. From the mid-1960s until the mid-1980s, the two polities differed noticeably, however, in both their rhetorical commitment to, and their actual investment in, active and passive defences against nuclear attack. Robert P. Haffa, Jr., *Rational Methods, Prudent Choices: Planning US Forces* (Washington, DC, 1988), ch. 2; Freedman, *Evolution of Nuclear Strategy*, 342–3; Charles L.

coped with the nuclear challenge effectively in a common way, whether that strategy was American or Soviet. The paragraphs below identify important points for policy, strategy, and defence planning, on which the superpowers *de facto* agreed. The items comprise summary judgements that apply particularly to the later years of the Cold War. The United States and the Soviet Union, historically the only two polities thus far that have been obliged to exercise significant discretion over the scale, character, and contingent *modus operandi* for employing nuclear forces, demonstrated elements of a common strategic enlightenment.

In general terms, the superpowers agreed that nuclear war would not be won, but that 'friction' could so impair enemy performance that some significant military advantage might be secured. However, pessimistic or not, policymakers and military planners had to prepare for nuclear war as best they could. The most important difference between the superpowers was in their attitudes towards homeland protection. The authors of the most authoritative Western study yet conducted of Soviet nuclear strategy concluded that the Soviet leaders 'rejected the desirability of mutual vulnerability, so they attempted to acquire the capacity to limit damage'.[82] Soviet strategists always believed that missile and air defences were important. When they accepted constraints on ballistic missile defence (BMD) in the anti-ballistic missile (ABM) defence treaty (1972) regime, and subsequently opposed American plans to proceed with President Reagan's Strategic Defense Initiative, the reason was calculation of net Soviet non-competitiveness, not strategic philosophical opposition to active defence.[83] One should not forget that only one country deployed BMD (around Moscow) in the

---

Glaser, *Analyzing Strategic Nuclear Policy* (Princeton, NJ, 1990), esp. 259–60; Scott D. Sagan, *Moving Targets: Nuclear Strategy and National Security* (Princeton, NJ, 1989); Dean Wilkening, 'Future U.S. and Russian Nuclear Forces: Applying Traditional Analysis Methods in an Era of Cooperation', in Paul K. Davis (ed.), *New Challenges for Defense Planning: Rethinking How Much Is Enough* (Santa Monica, Calif., 1994), 301–48; Miller, *Cold War*, pt. 2, esp. 88.

[82] Hines et al., *Soviet Intentions, i:* 21. This is also the view in Odom, *Collapse of the Soviet Military*, 66–72. There is merit in Sayre Stevens, 'The Soviet BMD Program', in Ashton B. Carter and David N. Schwartz (eds.), *Ballistic Missile Defense* (Washington, DC, 1984), 182–20; Keith B. Payne, *Strategic Defense: 'Star Wars' in Perspective* (Lanham, Md., 1986), ch. 4; David Yost, 'Strategic Defenses in Soviet Doctrine and Force Posture', in Fred S. Hoffman, Albert Wohlstetter, and Yost (eds.), *Swords and Shields: NATO, the USSR, and New Choices for Long-Range Offense and Defense* (Lexington, Mass., 1987), 123–57. For a post-Cold War review, see Keith B. Payne et al., '"Cold Peace" or Cooperation? The Potential for U.S.–Russian Accommodation on Missile Defense and the ABM Treaty', *Comparative Strategy*, 16 (1997).

[83] Odom cites the evidence of Col.-Gen. Nicolai Detinov—a general officer who worked with Politburo members on ABM matters: 'Initially convinced of the feasibility of an ABM system, they did not initiate a program for two reasons. First, their own technology was not yet adequate; second, it would draw resources away from and disrupt ICBM programs, which were proceeding smoothly. The U.S. proposal for an ABM treaty, therefore, came as a pleasant surprise. By ending the U.S. ABM programs, it would free the Soviets from engaging in simultaneous competition in both strategic offensive and defensive systems and permit Soviet ICBM programs to move ahead on schedule . . . According to Detinov, the logic of U.S. views on the winnability of a nuclear war and how to achieve "strategic stability" played no role at all in the Soviet acceptance of the ABM treaty.' *Collapse of the Soviet Military*, 71, 436, n. 25.

1970s and 1980s, the USSR. Nonetheless, aside from the realm of active defence of the homeland, the superpowers shared many approaches to problems of nuclear strategy, nuclear armed forces, and even nuclear war.

Here, in outline, is that common nuclear lore.

Safety in Numbers

For preference, nuclear-armed forces should be large in number. If those forces are the *ultima ratio regis*, they are not a defence effort concerning which one should take gratuitous risks. When the political stakes are as high as this, there is comfort in sheer quantity. There is no strategic virtue in being nuclear-armed lightly, as contrasted with plentifully. A larger scale of nuclear posture reassures its owner and the owner's security dependants, while discouraging aspirations for successful surprise attack by nuclear armed foes. Moreover, as Sir Michael Quinlan wisely observes, 'a structure of deterrence' requires 'genuine concepts of possible use': 'Weapons deter by the possibility of their use, and by no other route; the distinction sometimes attempted between deterrent capabilities and war-fighting capabilities has in a strict sense no meaningful basis.'[84] Numbers, preferable large numbers, of nuclear weapons are required if a polity is to be able to deploy nuclear-armed forces survivably, and to menace or strike at military, economic, or political targets discretely. If, in some moral or political sense, it is wrong to be nuclear-armed, such an error cannot be diminished by mere reduction in the scale of the arsenal. A small nuclear arsenal cannot be politically correct because of the modest number of its weapons. Nuclear-armed is nuclear-armed.

Diversity for Survivability and Effectiveness

Nuclear-armed forces should be diverse in character, will therefore be diversely deployed in different geographies, and hence should pose more, rather than fewer, problems for the would-be organizer of a surprise attack. Students of superpower nuclear strategy in the Cold War should not forget that the defence deliberations in both superstates were scarred by memories and interpretations of the national traumas suffered in 1941. It so happens, in one of those remarkable coincidences of strategic history, that the superpowers crafted their dynamic responses to the problems of the nuclear era against the backdrop of genuine near-catastrophe in the Soviet case and at least apparent disaster in the American. However, one should not rush to conclude that experience as victims of strategic surprise routinely encouraged gross examples in the nuclear era of defence-conservative planning by the two superpowers. Military reasoning, over-cautious or not,[85] was by no means consistently dominant over force acquisition in either

---

[84] Quinlan, *Thinking about Nuclear Weapons*, 15.

[85] Explaining the evolution of the US strategic nuclear force posture in the 1960s, Haffa reminds us that '[t]he strategic force that emerged was supposedly limited by a target set intended for assured destruction. But rather than dividing the mission into thirds, with each part of the triad owning a share of the required, delivered, 400 EMT [equivalent megatonnage], [Secretary of Defense Robert S.] McNamara chose, conservatively and with great uncertainty, that *each strategic arm should be capable of*

country. In the US case, poisonous inter-service rivalries,[86] and in the Soviet case, the power of personalities, the Party and especially of the defence-industrial lobby[87] could often explain more of the detail of the strategic nuclear posture than could rationales looking to strategic ideas, 'military requirements', military cultures, military-operational preferences, or arms control considerations. The superpowers agreed that national security is better served by larger nuclear forces more varied in character (ICBMs, manned bombers, SLBMs, and also long-range cruise missiles) than by smaller forces more restricted in kind (i.e. at least several thousand warheads carried by ICBMs, manned bombers, SLBMs, and cruise missiles, rather than 'merely' a few hundred). Notwithstanding that point, a domestic and international political history, as contrasted with a strategic history, of the nuclear arms competition of the superpowers would show that many decisions on weapon acquisition and force structure were taken for a mix of reasons, some of which bore scant relation to any recognizably strategic calculation.[88] In retrospect,

accomplishing assured destruction, for a potential, deliverable total of 1,200 EMT': *Rational Methods, Prudent Choices*, 27 (emphasis added). EMT is a measure of the blast surface damage of a nuclear weapon expressed in one megaton equivalents. Damage from nuclear blast declines from the point on the ground closest to the explosion—it may be an air burst—as a function of the cube root of the yield of the warhead. Therefore $EMT = NY^{\frac{2}{3}}$, where N is the number of warheads and Y their yields in megatons. The Office of the Secretary of Defense under McNamara decided as a matter of 'scientific' systems analysis that 400 EMT constituted the 'elbow' of the cost curve, showing sharply diminishing returns to military effort. For the economists' logic of the mathematics of assured destruction, see Alain C. Enthoven and K. Wayne Smith, *How Much Is Enough? Shaping the Defense Program, 1961–1969* (New York, 1971), chs. 5 and 6.

[86] Jeffrey C. Barlow, *Revolt of the Admirals: The Fight for Naval Aviation, 1945–1950* (Washington, DC, 1994); Farrell, *Weapons Without a Cause*. On the strength of the several American military cultures, see Carl H. Builder, *The Masks of War: American Military Styles in Strategy and Analysis* (Baltimore, 1989), and Williamson Murray, 'Does Military Culture Matter?', *Orbis*, 43 (1999), 27–42. The most incisive explanation of why, and how, distinctively geographically focused armed forces differ in their world-views is J. C. Wylie, *Military Strategy: A General Theory of Power Control*, ed. John B. Hattendorf, repr. of 1967 edn. (Annapolis, Md., 1989), ch. 5. Although interservice (and intraservice) rivalry is a universal phenomenon, the US armed forces have talked more about, and practised less, 'joint' planning and behaviour than anyone else. A key to the control of harmful—as contrasted with usefully competitive—interservice rivalry is the ending of the so-called 'stovepipe' procurement process. Only when the acquisition process for major items of equipment becomes truly 'joint' can the worst aspects of interservice rivalry be curtailed.

[87] Hines et al., *Soviet Intentions*, i. 48–67, is outstanding.

[88] On 'the American way' in rational defence analysis—from the dominant RAND school—see Edward S. Quade (ed.), *Analysis for Military Decisions* (Chicago, 1964); Charles J. Hitch, *Decision-Making for Defense* (Berkeley, Calif., 1965) (the author, Comptroller of the US Department of Defense from 1961-5, was the eponymous father of what came to be called admiringly (not ironically), 'Hitchcraft', from the supposedly magical effectiveness of his analytical methods); Roland N. McKean (ed.), *Issues in Defense Economics* (New York, 1967); E. S. Quade and W. I. Boucher (eds.), *Systems Analysis and Policy Planning: Applications in Defense* (New York, 1968); Enthoven and Smith, *How Much Is Enough?* If defence analytical skills could develop strategically correct quantifiable answers to problems of national security, then America should have been safe indeed from the early 1960s onwards. Unfortunately, the means assuredly adequate for that safety could not be calculated mathematically. Decisions for war, and hence the requirements of, and sometimes the relevance of, deterrence, are too complex for reduction to an equation or two. It is pertinent to ask whether quantifiable defence analysis can yield 'correct'

it is clear that the law of unintended consequences struck again over the scale and structure of superpower nuclear forces. Truly, neither side planned long in advance to deploy a 'triad' of strategic nuclear arms. But the eventual procurement of such a triad by both sides was a strategically benign consequence of substantially astrategic influences.

Invest in Control

Command, control, communications, and intelligence (C^3I) should be as capable of survival under attack as are the forces they are required to support. Both superpowers recognized that deterrence might be served well enough simply by the existence of nuclear armed forces that appeared able to evade, or ride out, a surprise attack. Nonetheless, both countries also realized that should C^3I functions be neglected (or, being conservatively prudent, even if those functions were not neglected), there could be severe problems of command and control even for the basic retaliation mission, let alone for the disciplined, purposeful conduct of a nuclear campaign. Indeed, undue confidence in some presumed existentiality of deterrence might allow a clever foe to attempt a nuclear 'decapitation' strike.[89] By the late 1970s, the superpowers agreed that the problem of C^3I for a general nuclear war could not be confined to the challenge of flashing an unmistakeable, and hopefully verified, green light to the nuclear strike forces (technically challenging though that could be while under attack).[90] Neither superpower was content to regard World War III as a single-variant Armageddon. Two very different political systems, each with its own strategic and military cultural peculiarities, decided that the path of responsible statecraft and strategy required investment in a commitment to the capability to control nuclear conflict. The fact that neither side was, or could be, confident that such a capability would make any difference in the dread event should not deny the prudence in the commitment.

Targeting Matters

The details of nuclear targeting—following the reasoning of Giulio Douhet[91]—is presumed to matter. Responsible senior officials both in the United States and the USSR rejected a fatalistic approach to nuclear war: 'après moi le déluge.'[92] The

solutions. Whether such solutions, even if calculable, are politically viable. And whether the precise answers provided to questions about the strategic force posture matter very much for decisions on peace or war.

[89] John Steinbruner, 'Nuclear Decapitation', *Foreign Policy*, 45 (1981), 16–28.

[90] So challenging did both sides expect the physical environment to be in a context of attempted launch under attack (LUA), and so short would the timelines be for executive decision, that there were understandable pressures from the military to favour early launch on 'warning': Blair, *Logic of Accidental Nuclear War*. Readers should understand that by the time unambiguous, verified 'warning' was received and acted upon, it might be too late, not to say purposeless also, to launch at all.

[91] Giulio Douhet, *The Command of the Air*, trans. Dino Ferrari, repr. of 1942 edn. (New York, 1972), 50.

[92] Richard Lee Walker, *Strategic Target Planning: Bridging the Gap between Theory and Practice*, National Security Affairs Monograph Series 83-9 (Washington, DC, 1983); William C. Martel and Paul L. Savage, *Strategic Nuclear War: What the Superpowers Target and Why* (Westport, Conn., 1986); Desmond Ball and

paradox is quite startling. Few officials or politicians in the era of Cold War could have believed that nuclear war waged on a large scale would be survivable for themselves, their state, or their society. Nonetheless, the war-planning machinery of both sides, albeit in their separate ways, converged on the belief that the details of nuclear targeting mattered. Defence professionals as individual citizens, family people and the like, may well typically have subscribed to the view that 'nuclear war is nuclear war', both for the purposes of intended deterrent effect and in cataclysmic consequences. But citizens as responsible defence professionals cannot help but notice that there is a night-and-day difference between a nuclear 'war' wherein tens, perhaps hundreds, of weapons are used against geographically fairly isolated military targets and a nuclear 'war' wherein thousands of weapons turn enemy society into a 'smoking radiating ruin'.[93] The most practical of differences between the two mindsets is that the former would preclude the kind of planning for weapons and C³I survivability that might allow a great nuclear war not to be quite so great, while the latter would not. It seems imprudent to this defence professional literally to programme unlimited catastrophe in the event of nuclear war.

Although it was the American defence community, and then a reluctant NATO,[94] that lauded strategic flexibility, with regard to nuclear war 'planning' it was the USSR that most closely approached a flexible spirit. If the ghost of Alfred von Schlieffen, as he has been traditionally viewed, haunted defence planners anywhere, it was in the United States. Bruce Blair is persuasive when he records:

US strategic forces had to be prepared to inflict severe, comprehensive damage to the array of targets in the former Soviet Union in four distinct categories formally established by national guidance. *Target coverage constituted the critical variable in the US command system during a crisis.* It was the raison d'être of the strategic nuclear organization of the United States.[95]

Blair explains:

Unlike the US system, which tended to invoke spontaneously a pre-established objective (comprehensive target coverage) and plan (the single integrated operational plan, or SIOP) at the onset of a crisis, the Soviet system assumed that preplanned options had a short shelf life. The system considered them so perishable in a crisis that the organization's highest priority was to tailor a new menu of options to suit the particulars of the situation.[96]

Jeffrey Richelson (eds.), *Strategic Nuclear Targeting* (Ithaca, NY, 1986); Theodore Postol, 'Targeting', in Carter et al., *Managing Nuclear Operations*, 373–406; Sagan, *Moving Targets*; Desmond Ball and Robert C. Toth, 'Revising the SIOP: Taking War-Fighting to Dangerous Extremes', *International Security*, 14 (1990), 65–92.

[93] David Alan Rosenberg, 'A Smoking, Radiating Ruin at the End of Two Hours: Documents on American Plans for Nuclear War with the Soviet Union, 1954–1955', *International Security*, 6 (1981/2), 3–38.

[94] Helga Haftendorn, *NATO and the Nuclear Revolution: A Crisis of Credibility, 1966–1967* (Oxford, 1996).

[95] Blair, *Logic of Accidental Nuclear War*, 32 (emphasis added).

[96] Ibid. 34.

American pre-planned 'flexibility' could have proved catastrophically unresponsive to the strategic demands of policy facing unexpected unfolding events, while the Soviet anticipation of ad hoc targeting could have been massively frustrated by nuclear command disconnection. What matters most for this discussion, however, is not to debate questions about the relative operational wisdom of participants in the Cold War. What matters is the need to recognize that the defence planning machine of neither superpower was willing to abandon all hope for the control of nuclear combat. On the strategic folly of large-scale nuclear war, all could agree. Moreover, since the nexuses between small- and large-scale nuclear war were unknown, inclinations to nuclear adventure for coercion were rare.

This element of agreement between the superpowers constituted a convention of prudence. In reality, the superpowers in the later years of the Cold War wrote, programmed, and trained constraints into their systems of nuclear action overwhelmingly because even merely the modest possibility of a controllable nuclear war was infinitely preferable to a military context wherein the only option for action would be a 'wargasm'.[97] As we try to make sense of the experience of modern strategy with nuclear weapons, we have to ask how officials in the superpowers could have acted prudently otherwise.

Details Count

The military-technical details of nuclear force deployment and operation are assumed, again prudently, to matter for the prospects for peace or war. But, does it really matter whether nuclear warheads are 'mated' with their delivery rockets on a regular basis, or only in times of crisis? How important is it that the US Strategic Air Command should 'fail safe', as contrasted with 'fail deadly', in the event that reliable communication is cut off between nuclear-armed planes aloft and the National Command Authorities (NCA)?[98] Does it matter if US or Soviet ICBMs cannot ride out a missile attack? If one expects to preempt—the authoritative Soviet view through the early 1970s—then virtually any character of ICBM deployment will be good enough. Similarly, if one expects to LUA on tactical warning (by dual phenomenology from infrared sensors on early-warning satellites and ground-based radar), why should the details of missile basing be of much interest? American military professionals could be no more certain that they would be allowed to LUA their ICBM force than Soviet military professionals could rely on timely orders to preempt with theirs.

Lurking none too far beneath the details of nuclear force deployment and oper-

---

[97] 'Wargasm' is what Herman Kahn meant by a 'spasm theory of war', according to which a polity 'simply launches out suddenly, almost blindly doing the greatest possible destruction to the enemy without asking specifically, How does any particular part of this destruction aid one to achieve his final goal?': *On Thermonuclear War*, 308.

[98] Herman Kahn, *Thinking about the Unthinkable* (New York, 1964), 43; Albert Wohlstetter, 'Continuing Control as a Requirement for Deterring', in Carter et al., *Managing Nuclear Operations*, 166–7.

ation is the topic of the causes of war. Might the nuclear-armed forces intended by their political owners to deter war, instead actually provoke it? On the Soviet side of the equation, a genuine belief—*après* Marx and Lenin—in the deep-seated political, in this case imperialist, roots of war discouraged acute concern about possible US misinterpretation of particular events in force acquisition or behaviour. On the American side, the strategic cultural authority of an engineering approach to security problems inclined officials to seek national safety in technical fixes. In this perspective, the difference between peace and war might be the choice of horizontal, as contrasted with vertical, shelters for MX ICBMs.[99]

ULTIMA RATIO REGIS

The experience of the superpowers with nuclear weapons in the Cold War cannot be the experience of all nuclear weapon states. But that joint superpower record is significant for strategic history because the two polities in question were obliged to cope with novel nuclear facts. Furthermore, because both states could spend heavily upon defence, they moved in policy, strategy, operations, and tactics from a condition of acute nuclear scarcity to one of almost embarrassing nuclear abundance. This analysis would appear much the same regardless of the identity of the state pairs in a great nuclear-shadowed Cold War. The broad items of nuclear-related strategic agreement specified above should describe the practicable conclusions of any adversary pair of large nuclear powers in the late twentieth century.

Chapters on nuclear strategy in a book on modern strategy should not simply ignore non-superpower nuclear players. Suffice it to observe that there remains a uniquely absolute quality to nuclear menace that is vastly reassuring to polities that otherwise could worry about the potency of late-model conventional threats. Strategic cultures as diverse as those of Britain, France, China, Israel, India, Pakistan, North Korea, and many 'wannabes', agree that what nuclear acquisition means for modern strategy is that the national territory and political independence of nuclear-armed states is not to be violated or challenged, for sensible fear of the possible consequences.

STRATEGY RUMBLES ON

On balance we did well to avoid allowing a World War III to terminate the Cold War. The non-war outcome was probably attributable at least as much to luck as to good political and strategic judgement, but still the occasions for possible folly were strewn with almost liberal abundance through the first two decades of the conflict. Some historians would have us believe that there was little worth fighting

[99] Colin S. Gray, *The MX ICBM and National Security* (New York, 1981), ch. 5; Dunn, *Politics of Threat*, ch. 7.

about between the United States and the USSR, but that argument is rather silly.[100] At stake in the early crises of the Cold War, say until Berlin 1961, was the reputation of each superstate as a protecting power. I challenge scholars who doubt the proximity of a World War III to the political-military events of 1947–89 to reconsider their judgement in the light of Thucydides' arguments about 'fear, honour, and interest' as put into the mouths of the Athenian ambassadors to the Spartans in 432 BC.[101] Given the historical novelty of the nuclear challenge, the superpowers, their nuclear-armed allies, and other nuclear-weapon states have done well to reach this time of writing without triggering a nuclear war.

The lack of actively nuclear history in recent decades has induced a widespread inclination to belittle the strategic significance of nuclear weapons. The enormity of the damage that East and West might have wrought upon each other, upon bystanders, and indeed upon the Earth itself now appears so disproportionate to the intensity of conflict between the values at stake that a condition of nuclear incredulity has set in. If those who held the commanding heights of the USSR could defend their system no more vigorously and effectively than in 1989–91, how can one believe that the USSR would have 'gone to war' à outrance nucléaire in the 1960s, 1970s, or early 1980s? This line of thought is not so much blind to the strengths of the USSR in those years as simply incredulous that any system that allowed itself to die by political euthenasia was really a long-term candidate for nuclear belligerency on the largest of scales.

This sense of nuclear incredulity contributes also to practical disbelief in nuclear menace from nuclear-proliferant powers. Notwithstanding the known physical reality of, say, Israeli, Indian, and Pakistani nuclear weapons—as well as the better-attested nuclear arsenals of Britain, France, and China—not until there is a nuclear war somewhere around the several arcs of crisis beloved by geo-political theorists will these weapons descend from abstraction into the zone of pressing problems. The ever wider proliferation of ballistic and cruise missiles, and of weapons of mass destruction (WMD), as yet has spurred only a leisurely pace in development and deployment of active missile defences. The leading reason is because nuclear danger today, rather like the similarly substantial and technically not unrelated challenge of terrestrial assault by asteroids, though recognized, is largely ignored. In the absence of a hideous nuclear or extra-terrestrial assault 'event', there are more pressing problems on which to spend scarce assets.

I have emphasized the difficulty for the strategic theorist posed by the welcome fact of the all-but-total lack of evidence on nuclear combat. In the Cold War, deterrent effect was sought—of course one cannot be sure that deterrence was actually 'done'—by people, machines and organizations that planned, procured, and trained. But all thought and writing about nuclear strategy and nuclear war

---

[100] John Mueller, *Retreat from Doomsday: The Obsolescence of Major War* (New York, 1989).

[101] Robert B. Strassler (ed.), *The Landmark Thucydides: A Comprehensive Guide to 'The Peloponnesian War'*, trans. Richard Crawley, rev. edn. (New York, 1996), 43.

can refer thus far strictly to the realm of theory. Even those few scholar-participants who were professional servants of the nuclear would-be deterrent of a superpower, be they a missile launch officer like Bruce Blair or a senior defence planner and policymaker such as Fred Charles Iklé, do not know, and cannot discover, how a nuclear war between East and West would have been conducted. Blair, among others, informs us that in the 1970s and 1980s US ICBMs would have had time to launch and to escape safely from attack once ground-based radars confirmed the warning of Soviet ICBM or SLBM (submarine-launched ballistic missile) launches.[102] But, would the NCA have used the very short, though admittedly probably adequate, time available that this launch tactic required? Perhaps—but, scarcely less likely, perhaps not.

The Clausewitzian idea that strategy teaches 'the use of engagements for the object of the war' can help integrate nuclear weapons into a general framework of strategic comprehension. Because all kinds of military, indeed grand strategic, power have strategic effect, the technical singularity of nuclear weapons matters not really at all. It is perhaps unusually difficult to assess the strategic effect of weapons whose 'engagements' after 1945 have all been virtual. It is hard to demonstrate just what deterrence was 'done' by explicit or latent nuclear menace. However, with strategic effect as the common coin of the strategic realm, one has to exercise judgement about the relative leverage even of seapower or airpower. Strategic effect can be generated whether or not the forces in question engage in battle. Furthermore, with reference to the direct behaviour towards each other of the virtual combatants in the Cold War, it was not only the engines of nuclear destruction that were not committed to real fighting; the conventionally equipped elements of the armies, navies, and air forces were similarly restricted to competition rather than combat.

If modern strategists, and the organizations and processes through which they operated, are judged to have performed poorly or well in coping with the novel challenge posed by nuclear weapons, who or what is the appropriate strategic historical standard? Are the political leaders, their occasionally attentive publics, and most of the defence experts in the nuclear weapon states wrong to find residual strategic merit in national nuclear capabilities? It may be unlikely that a general East–West nuclear war in the 1970s or 1980s could have been disciplined by measures for the attempted control of escalation, but does it follow that the superpowers should have programmed a single Armageddon option—truly an 'extinction event'—in lieu of what have traditionally been called war plans? The strategists of East and West did not discern practicable choices for the achievement of equal or superior security at much lower force levels. Disarmament follows, it does not cause, political peace.

To close these chapters on the grammar of strategy for the nuclear challenge, let

---

[102] Blair, *Logic of Accidental Nuclear War*, 185–95.

us reconsider the interesting thought quoted already from John Weltman: 'The development of nuclear strategy represented an attempt at a Jominian solution to a problem that was essentially Clausewitzian in nature.'[103] He is not so much wrong as misleading and ungenerous. Weltman reminds us that, following Jomini, there has been a quest for the correct nuclear strategy. In addition, Welt-man suggests that the real challenge has been, not to find an ever better oper-ational nuclear strategy, but rather to find some plausible way to harness the militarily all but useless nuclear arsenal to the political purposes of the state and coalition. It seems reasonable to argue that, although nuclear tragedy has always been possible, modern strategy has accommodated nuclear weapons amazingly well. The Clausewitzian problem to which Weltman alludes has been resolved as defence communities around the world have learnt just how limited, though vital, are the political missions that nuclear weapons can serve.

Whether or not the Clausewitzian problem of reconciling military power with state purpose can be resolved satisfactorily for nuclear weapons, there remains an operational grammar to strategy for these weapons that has to be sought, refined, and applied by defence establishments. Existential or 'virtual' nuclear arsenals may require no strategists, no strategy, no war plans, and indeed no seriously functioning nuclear-military establishment;[104] but those ideas, attractive or not, are idle conceptual toys and not propositions that could be entertained by people who must seek to behave responsibly.

AN AFTERWORD ON OTHER WEAPONS OF MASS DESTRUCTION

Nuclear weapons are not the only weapons of mass destruction (WMD). They are, however, the WMD that are technically and tactically mature, and whose strengths and weaknesses for strategic effectiveness are long and best appreci-ated. The strategic literature addressing nuclear WMDs is abundant indeed. In sharp contrast, such other possible WMDs as biological, toxin, and chemical weapons, though the subject of much scientific, technical, and some tactical and doctrinal (for chemical weapons), investigation, and writing, feature scarcely at all in genuinely strategic theory (a fact for which we should possibly be grateful).[105]

[103] John J. Weltman, *World Politics and the Evolution of War* (Baltimore, 1995), 152.

[104] Michael J. Mazarr (ed.), *Nuclear Weapons in a Transformed World: The Challenge of Virtual Nuclear Arsenals* (London, 1997).

[105] US Congress, Office of Technology Assessment, *Proliferation of Weapons of Mass Destruction: Assessing the Risks*, OTA-ISC-559 (Washington, DC, Aug. 1993), and id., *Technologies Underlying Weapons of Mass Destruction*, OTA-BP-ISC-115 (Washington, DC, Dec. 1993), provide so excellent a basic guide that they might jointly warrant description as a would-be WMD proliferant's 'bible'. For more basics, see Hugh D. Crone's useful work, *Banning Chemical Weapons: The Scientific Background* (Cambridge, 1992). As noted in the text, science, arms control, tactics, and history, but not strategy, figure prominently in the literature on 'other WMD'. Edward M. Spiers, *Chemical Warfare* (London, 1986); id., *Chemical and Biological*

These other, non-nuclear WMD are today the focus of intense interest by defence communities globally. The reasons for this draw inspiration from that pervasive law of unintended consequences to which reference has already been made. Strategic interest in non-nuclear WMDs flows fairly directly, and with impeccable logic, from the nuclear, information technology, and irregular warfare stories already told here. Irregular combat—terrorism, to take a leading example—is an option attractive to the weak. Non-nuclear WMDs represent a basket of options for polities or sub-state groups who need to offset the nuclear and information-led conventional prowess of powerful enemies.[106]

The technical-tactical grammar of strategy for other WMDs is hugely variable, though the strategic meaning of these weapons probably is not. The term 'other WMDs' embraces the living organisms of biological warfare, which must incubate to multiply and attack their human hosts; the chemical toxins from living agents, which can kill instantly; and the dead manufactured chemical agents that, again, can kill or incapacitate at once. These are the weapons of choice for the militarily very weak. The possibilities that they may offer to the desperate and the dedicated constitute a challenging new subject for strategic speculation.

Strategic history records biological warfare in the form of the catapulting of the bodies of plague victims over the walls of besieged cities, and the deliberate spreading of diseases (e.g. measles and smallpox) to native populations not protected by natural immunities. Chemical warfare has long been familiar in the form of the offensive and defensive use of noxious smoke to blind and incapacitate a foe. Modern chemical warfare (with chlorine gas) was initiated by Germany at Ypres in April 1915. Scientific and technical descriptions of these other WMDs are not in short supply, and neither are analyses of the distinctive challenges posed to actual and putative arms control regimes. At present, the Biological and Toxin and the Chemical Weapons conventions (respectively of 1972 and 1995) both lack plausible provision for verification, let alone enforcement. A major reason for that fact is because biological and toxin weapon development can be concealed readily in apparently innocent medical and pharmaceutical research facilities. Furthermore, the precursor materials necessary for chemical weapons happen generally to be 'dual-use' for thoroughly mundane industrial and agricultural

---

Weapons: A Study of Proliferation (London, 1994); Susan Wright (ed.), *Preventing a Biological Arms Race* (Cambridge, Mass., 1990); Victor Utgoff, *The Challenge of Chemical Weapons: An American Perspective* (New York, 1991); Stockholm International Peace Research Institute, *The Problem of Chemical and Biological Warfare, i: The Rise of CB Weapons* (New York, 1971); M. Dando, *Biological Warfare in the 21st Century: Biotechnology and the Proliferation of Biological Weapons* (New York, 1994); Leonard A. Cole, *The Eleventh Plague: The Politics of Biological and Chemical Warfare* (New York, 1997); Richard M. Price, *The Chemical Weapons Taboo* (Ithaca, NY, 1997).

[106] Stuart E. Johnson (ed.), *The Niche Threat: Deterring the Use of Chemical and Biological Weapons* (Washington. DC, Feb. 1997); Paula A. DeSutter, *Denial and Jeopardy: Deterring Iranian Use of NBC Weapons* (Washington, DC, Sept. 1997); Shubik, 'Terrorism, Technology, and the Socioeconomics of Death'; Betts, 'New Threat of Mass Destruction'.

purposes. The better insecticides are actually nerve agents, and anyone with a fertilizer factory has already the basis for a chemical weapons facility.

This discussion of non-nuclear WMDs is appended as an 'afterword' to the extensive analysis of nuclear WMDs, not as an afterthought, but because thus far these weapons have lain on the margins of strategic relevance. Should this book one day appear in a revised edition, I hope I will not then have pressing reasons to accord 'other WMDs' a chapter of their own. Suffice it for now to record three points about this technically diverse category.

First, although other, non-nuclear WMDs are the weapons of the weak and militarily challenged, the relative ease of their nominal acquisition (and conceal-ment) is not matched by any ease of reliable employment in action for huge strategic effect. Nuclear weapons, let alone information-led conventional weapons, are predictable in their operation and effects; 'other WMDs' by and large are not. Biological agents are difficult to keep alive, difficult to deliver to their victims, and potentially strategically fatally slow in acting. Chemical, unlike bio-logical, weapons are physically robust for, say, explosive aerosol delivery by shell or rocket, but they are vulnerable to 'rain-out', adverse winds, and natural and manmade terrain that inhibits the spread of lethal dosage. However, the newer bio-toxins provide a hellish combination of chemical robustness and instant biological fatality.

Second, there may be a growing consensus supporting the proposition that biological and chemical weapons are the moral and political equivalent of nuclear weapons. This matter of equivalence is strategically significant, because the lead-ing powers for international order have all foresworn development and posses-sion of biological and chemical arms. To deter, or retaliate against, the use of 'other WMDs' by militarily much weaker players obliges the G-8 world to affirm the principle that all WMDs are created, and will be regarded as, strategically equal. Nonetheless, grave uncertainty does surround the question of whether or not it would be prudent or legitimate to respond to, say, a biological assault, arguably asymmetrically with a nuclear strike.[107] In practical terms it could be difficult to identify, let alone prove the identity of, the perpetrator of a bio-logical offensive whose effects would manifest themselves only after a period of weeks, months, or even years of successful human incubation of the hostile agents.

Third and finally, discussion of 'other WMDs' plainly belongs here because strategy rules for this awful instrument of man's political will, as it does for the other instruments already analysed. It is true that the topic of 'other WMDs' is most worrisome in its potential to enable acts of expressive or 'catastrophe terror-ism'.[108] One might be tempted to exclude such a possibility from the rational consequentialist realm of strategic means and ends. Unfortunately, a bid to

[107] Lawrence Freedman, *The Revolution in Strategic Affairs*, Adelphi Paper 318 (London, Apr. 1998), 45–7.
[108] Shubik, 'Terrorism, Technology, and the Socioeconomics of Death'.

achieve 'catastrophe', to be effected, say, by a contagious and untreatable viral disease, could be a wholly rational, albeit wholly unreasonable, act of 'policy'. Strategic theory is morally and politically neutral. It is an equal opportunity body of reasoning and lore.

Chapter 13

STRATEGY ETERNAL

This exploration and explanation of the grim world of modern strategy has been both long and complex. The story that emerges, however, is by no means complicated. The difficulty with strategy lies in its performance rather than its permanent nature or even its changing character. At the outset of this enquiry a set of six questions were posed, shaped, and directed by the organizing proposition that there is an essential unity to all strategic experience in all periods of history because nothing vital to the nature and function of war and strategy changes. This concluding chapter revisits those basic general questions in order to see how best they should be answered in light of the whole record of modern strategy.

REVISITING THE QUESTIONS

Strategy and strategic history are eternal. The threat or use of politically motivated force is structural to the human social condition. I am not wholly unsympathetic to, but ultimately am unpersuaded by, the suggestion by Chris Brown that 'we need to pay serious attention to the implications of the view that knowledge is constructed, not found, that it rests on social foundations and not upon some bedrock of certainty'.[1] That postmodern thought has a way of encouraging scholars to play self-indulgent word games, neglect empirical enquiry, surrender to a rudderless relativism, and generally to gallop up blind alleys. To continue with Brown's metaphor, provided one maintains a properly Clausewitzian respect for the potential authority of chance, risk, and chaos,[2] it is useful to conceive of strategic scholarship as roughly akin to Michelangelo's approach to sculpture; he understood his task as finding the form immanent in the marble. One can think of strategic study as education, defined strictly as deriving from the Latin *educere*—a 'leading out' of what is there to be found. If this sounds monstrously positivist, I should hasten to add that much of what the strategist–sculptor–educator discovers, as contrasted with constructs, will not appear with a wholly persuasive guarantee of authenticity. It is true that strategic theory must organize, select, make judgements on probable causalities, and thereby 'construct' strategic reality. But it is also true that the process of strategic theory-making is in constant dialogue with the behaviour which moves

[1] Chris Brown, *Understanding International Relations* (London, 1997), 119.
[2] Carl von Clausewitz, *On War*, trans. Michael Howard and Peter Paret (Princeton, NJ, 1976), 85–6.

strategic history onwards (though alas only upwards in a crudely geographical sense).

The first of the six general questions posed at the beginning of this book was: How do the theory and practice of strategy interact? Strategic ideas and theory must define, organize, and explain for the practical world wherein threats or deeds have strategic consequences. More often than not, the production of strategic theory in most of its guises is stimulated by the demands of policy or military practice for solutions to problems. Strategic ideas on seapower, on nuclear weapons, and on counter-insurgency, for instance, were in each case triggered by the needs of practitioners.[3] Even when the world of theory pre-dates actual manifestation of a strategic problem, as with aircraft, theorists are moved by the conviction that the solution to a practical problem will be needed in the future. The need variably recognized by security communities today to make strategic sense of spacepower, information power, and biological and chemical weapons will predictably trigger a phase of theory-building in each of these areas. The wiser theorists will appreciate that they should construct a new superstructure for, say, spacepower on the basis of the eternal lore of strategy.

Scholars should not allow either their research agendas or their conclusions to be dictated by officials. It also is essential that scholars of strategy understand that theirs is not a fine art free-floating beyond strategic history. Scholarly theorists — unlike, say, generals in World War I or US and Soviet policymakers in the 1970s and early 1980s — are gripped by a necessity that is intellectual, and may be professional. Theory for action, however, as opposed to theory strictly for glory of scholarly reputation and for career, has to allow for unwelcome constraints. The dangers of nuclear strategy, any nuclear strategy, are almost too obvious to be worth citing. So, given those dangers, what is one's nuclear strategy to be? What can the camp of theory offer to the politicians, civil servants, and soldiers who are not prudently at liberty to 'construct' a new post-nuclear strategic reality more to their liking? If strategic, perhaps anti-strategic, ideas take scant notice of the calls of prudence in coping with a world of frequently grim necessity (e.g. imperial Germany must be disciplined, or there has to be a strategy for nuclear weapons), then they move into a zone of absurdity, of practical irrelevance for a vital subject that is inherently practical in its referents.

The second general question of the book asks what the growing complexity of defence preparation and war means for strategy. This question is almost paradoxical when considered against all of modern strategic history. The near-paradox lies in the fact that, although the multi-layering of new concerns for the strategist

---

[3] This was the case both for Alfred Thayer Mahan and for Sir Julian Corbett: Jon Tetsuro Sumida, *Inventing Grand Strategy and Teaching Command: The Classic Works of Alfred Thayer Mahan Reconsidered* (Washington, DC, 1997); Eric Grove, 'Introduction', to Julian S. Corbett, *Some Principles of Maritime Strategy*, ed. Grove, repr. of 1911 edn. (Annapolis, Md., 1988), pp. xi–xiv; Bernard Brodie, *War and Politics* (New York, 1973), ch. 10; Mao Tse-tung, *Selected Military Writings* (Peking, 1967).

has proceeded apace, with the air, the depths of the sea, outer space, the electromagnetic spectrum (and cyberspace)—as well as nuclear weapons and irregular warfare—adding complication upon complication, nothing essential about war and strategy has changed. Chapter 1 introduced no fewer than seventeen dimensions of strategy. Every item in this set of dimensions could play in every strategic historical event regardless of period, opponents, and technology. To understand the ingredients of war and strategy in 2000 is to understand them for 1900, or indeed for 500 BC.

If, as argued here, strategy has a permanent set of dimensions, albeit with each (politics, culture, technology, command, and so forth) playing to greater or lesser effect at different times, that permanence carries a virus potentially lethal to a contemporary thesis on revolutions in military affairs (RMA). If strategy for war—as for peace with security—is a whole enterprise with many dimensions, then signal advantage in one or even several of those dimensions is likely to be held strategic hostage by quality of performance elsewhere.[4] By analogy, in the man-machine system that is a car on the road, the effect on total system performance of a huge boost in engine power is hostage to the performance of brakes, tyres, steering, gears, and the skill of the driver.

Question 3 asks why strategy is so difficult. This question can suggest implicitly that the growing complexity of modern strategy has increased effective strategic performance. The armies that marched from their railheads to war in August 1914 were primitive organisms indeed when compared even with their successors in 1917–18, let alone in 1944–5 or 1991. It seems to be a law of strategic effect, however, that for every improvement in the military, or adjunct civilian, tools available to the strategist there is some compensating friction or other impediment that places a new limit on the strategic effectiveness of forces. For example, a major reason why nuclear weapons delivered so much less than absolute strategic utility was that other polities also acquired them. Each new wonder of military art and science arrives with its own distinctive technical-tactical weaknesses, and requires mastery of new equipment and tactics. It is also difficult to keep ownership of innovations in friendly hands. Radio, radar, aircraft, submarines, nuclear weapons, and computers would be so much more useful if only we could monopolize their ownership. Not for nothing did the eastern Romans in the fifth century try to keep advanced armament out of the hands of the barbarians north of the Danube.[5]

In the golden words of General Samuel B. Griffith, USMC, 'There are no mechanical panaceas.'[6] Griffith was commenting specifically on the merit in fuel–air explosives for counter-guerrilla operations, but his strategic nugget is a general

    [4] Colin S. Gray, 'RMAs and the Dimensions of Strategy', *Joint Force Quarterly*, 17 (1997–8), 50–4.
    [5] E. A. Thompson, *The History of Attila and the Huns* (Oxford, 1948), 180.
    [6] Samuel B. Griffith, 'Introduction', to Mao Tse-tung [attrib.], *On Guerrilla Warfare*, trans. Griffith (New York, 1961), 31.

truth. British and German soldiers blundered into each other at Mons on 21 August 1914, with both parties labouring under a pall of ignorance at the level of operational intelligence. But it should not be imagined that strategic performance will be greatly improved in an age of information abundance which allows information warriors to conduct information-led warfare in digitized battlespace.[7] There is a filter of strategic judgement that must act as a two-way transmission belt linking military power with political purpose. It is no easier to be a strategist today than it was a century ago, despite the availability of machines that can see over the other side of the hill, can allow all but instant global communications, and can strike at the speed of light. Strategic performance was difficult for both sides in World War I, but then so it was in the Gulf War of 1991 and in the Balkan wars that studded the rest of that decade. The military victor in each case did not obviously win the peace, i.e. did not unambiguously succeed in using successful engagements to secure desired political goals.

The fourth thematic question is whether it is probable that superiority in only one or even several of strategy's dimensions can deliver victory. Modern strategic history illustrates the persisting truth in Clausewitz's insistence that war be approached holistically.[8] Every chapter here attests to the pattern of multiple reciprocal dependencies that interconnect, indeed bind, strategy's many dimensions. It was always so. The increased complexity of strategy's military 'grammar' in modern times means only that there are more nexuses, more interdependencies, than ever before. Particular dimensions will play more significantly in particular conflicts—the social or the geographical, for example—but the passage of a century of strategic experience reveals no definitive retirement of any one among them. People continue to matter most, regardless of the march of technological achievement in the potential for war-making. Whether a conflict is great or minor, regular or irregular, it is always a 'team' event wherein each dimension counts for something. Modern strategic history does not show that 'technology rules', or 'logistics rules', or even that 'politics rules'—though the latter always reigns—at least, in the absence of careful qualification of claims.

The story of modern strategy is one of complex relations, any of which could be vital, among the dimensions. Wherever one looks, there is a jointness, at least a mutuality in support, which confounds any foolish quest for a single golden key to understanding. Nazi Germany did not lose World War II because *inter alia* it was poorly led, lacked the material and human resources to be strategically competitive, or was in some blatant as well as subtle way truly an evil regime. Germany lost for all of those mutually reinforcing reasons, and others besides.[9] As

---

[7] Barry D. Watts, *Clausewitzian Friction and Future War*, McNair Paper 52 (Washington, DC, Oct. 1996); id., 'Ignoring Reality: Problems of Theory and Evidence in Security Studies', *Security Studies*, 7 (1997/8), 115–71; Williamson Murray, 'Does Military Culture Matter?', *Orbis*, 43 (1999), 27–42.

[8] Clausewitz, *On War*, 607.

[9] R. J. Overy, *Why the Allies Won* (London, 1995).

Clausewitz wrote, 'in war more than in any other subject we must begin by look-ing at the nature of the whole'.[10] Problems of national security cannot be reduced, for example, to correct investment choices among emerging technologies, to operational artistry, to the combat skills of warriors, or to excellence in the sci-ence of supplying and moving troops. Each is important, but none reliably can offset serious deficiencies elsewhere.

Question 5 asks what changed in the twentieth century and what did not. I choose to answer the question primarily with critical reference to the continuing merit in Clausewitz's theory of war. If *On War*, providing a general theory of its subject, speaks as meaningfully to strategic conditions in 2000 as it did to those in 1900 or 1800, then it is a safe bet that the book will speak as sensibly to 2100 also. The strategist as theorist, as planner, or as executive, has found that the past century delivered a poisoned chalice of changes. Every apparent gain in effective-ness was matched or even overmatched by an offsetting loss. The electron is har-nessed for war, but—alas—by foes also. It is wonderful to be able to see over the hill, but—again—enemies too acquire the ability to do that. I could devote much of this concluding chapter—perhaps better a hefty appendix—to a chronicling of the myriad changes, great and not so great, that merit mention in the column of 'what has changed' over the course of the past century. Any temptation one might feel to produce such a list should be terminated by recognition that one would be focusing only on second-order matters. Of course, the routinization of invention by industrious societies will generate new machines, even new kinds of machines, employed as part of novel systems on behalf of institutions that are either new-born or eventually transformed. But no matter how expertly detailed the chron-icle provided on strategy-oriented change, the end result must be only illustration of my master theme—that nothing essential changes because there is a unity to all strategic historical experience. It really does not matter whether strategy is 'done' by 'foot, horse, and guns', or by cruise missiles, spacecraft, and cyber-assault. The tools change with technology, as must the dependent tactics. But strategy uses 'the engagement', and the military tools employed in it, at a level that is indifferent to the evolving terms of combat.

The most basic reason why strategy appears, alas, to be eternal lies in our human nature. I do not mean to imply that human beings, either individually or as security communities, are in some essential way incapable of learning 'the ways of peace'. Many, perhaps most, people can and do 'construct peace' by doing it, which is to say by acting and thinking in a cooperative rather than a conflictual mode.[11] The fatal problem is that history as we know it yields no grounds for optimism that a positive kind of peace can be constructed to a degree which precludes the appearance of objective threats to security. As the aphorism has it: we have seen the problem and it is us.

[10] Clausewitz, *On War*, 75.
[11] Emanuel Adler, 'Condition(s) of Peace', *Review of International Studies*, 24, special issue (1998), 165–91.

Clausewitz's theory of war, indeed any general theory of war, must explain and help understanding of a timeless phenomenon. Rather than summarize changes in the character of modern strategy and war, the argument of this book is better concluded by a critical reaffirmation of the unchanging nature and function of our subject. Because strategy does not, indeed cannot, change, it does not follow that Clausewitz is all we need. He left considerable terrain untrod and he was not infallible. The weaknesses in his theory that stemmed principally from his place in time and culture mean that his ideas need periodic amendment and clarification if they are to continue to inspire and elucidate.

I do not confuse *On War* with a sacred book, but its authority survives even potent attacks. I am much attracted to Ken Booth's charge:

For many years, and still today in part, international relations [and strategic studies] teaching has been more like Sunday school than university education. Set questions elicited set answers. Choice quotations were learned from the sacred books. The quality of thinking was judged by the extent to which it replicated the canons of the past.[12]

Booth is right, and wrong, and perceptive in both respects. He is right in that Clausewitzian statements and aphorisms are frequently offered as a mantra in place of reasoned argument and judgement. But the perils of underexamined orthodoxy granted, still Clausewitz offers the most persuasive of intellectual road-maps to the nature and function of strategy and war. He was a theorist anchored by time, place, and therefore culture, and (as explained in Chapter 4) his theorizing was by no means immaculate. Nonetheless, person of his historical context as he had to be, the star of Clausewitz's genius as a theorist of war shone at least as brightly at the close of the twentieth century as it did at its beginning.[13] As a general theorist, Clausewitz has historically distant and also flawed competitors in Sun Tzu and Thucydides, but no plausible peers after his death in 1831.

For all his genius and continuing relevance, there are at least two important areas in which Clausewitz fails to offer much useful guidance: 'the face of battle' itself and, scarcely less surprisingly, the political-military battlespace of strategy.

There is an inescapable human dimension to strategy, especially to its 'doing' in combat, that often evades scholarly notice. On the one hand, civilians, and indeed many soldiers not of a warrior kind, can be uncomfortable discussing that which they have not experienced personally. On the other hand, veterans of combat are uncomfortable discussing danger, fear, discomfort, noise, smells, and pain with those whose acquaintance with the battlefield level of these 'nasties' is strictly

---

[12] Ken Booth, 'Dare Not to Know: International Relations Theory versus the Future', in Booth and Steve Smith (eds.), *International Relations Theory Today* (Cambridge, 1995), 329–30.

[13] Nearly a century ago, Lt.-Gen. Rudolf von Caemmerer of the Great General Staff of the German Army wrote as follows: 'We Germans look upon Clausewitz as indisputably the deepest and acutest thinker on the subject of war; the beneficial effect of his intellectual labours is universally recognised and highly appreciated': *The Development of Strategical Science during the 19th Century*, trans. Karl von Donat (London, 1905), 95.

vicarious. One should note that nuclear war and strategy, as an extension in major key of the 'strategic' bombing of World War II, was a democratizing menace. A sociologically and psychologically significant reason why relatively young civilian theorists could play 'expert' in the realm of nuclear strategy was precisely because that realm had no past, no bemedalled warriors, no fund of practical experience. Common ignorance is a great leveller.

Despite, perhaps because of, his extensive personal knowledge of combat, Clausewitz keys his great work to the importance of battle and pulls no punches in advising readers that '[t]he decision by arms is for all major and minor operations in war what cash payment is in commerce'.[14] That is insightful, useful to understanding, and well expressed. It is less useful, perhaps, in that 'battle' becomes rather abstract. Why do people fight? What motivates people sufficiently to induce them to deny elemental urges towards behaviour likely to preserve their lives? For all the bloody rhetoric about battle and the marvellous borrowing from mechanical science of the compound concept of friction, Clausewitz's battle is not very persuasively human. In John Keegan's words:

> There was nothing about rum in Clausewitz, or about commanding officers having nervous breakdowns, or about one sort of warrior being better than another, or about officers bullying their subordinates. The warrior in Clausewitz was a sort of cipher—a being subject to fear and fatigue and capable of bravery—but faceless, unindividualistic and asocial, for all that Clausewitz had to say about the enthusiasm of popular armies.[15]

I emphasize the human dimension of strategy at this late juncture in part in attempted atonement for my deliberate neglect of the face of battle through most of the text. The explanation is easy enough and is conclusive. A book that is Clausewitzian in its focus upon 'the use of engagements for the object of the war' strictly has no need to descend into the emotion, pain, and discomfort of actual combat. In other words, this text can hide from the face of battle, the tactical doing of strategy, behind its high level of analysis. It is eminently reasonable for a work that seeks to understand strategy to eschew other than mere, though not just token, recognition of the vital role of those who must 'do strategy', tactically (i.e. personally). Nonetheless, I admit to some discomfort with an analysis which blanks out people and is obliged to treat them as cipher-like combatants in the engagements that strategy must use for the political object of war. An obvious reason why Clausewitz had no need to dwell upon the human face of battle was because he was writing primarily for a military readership who he could assume would be intimately familiar with combat's nastier realities.

Another terrain upon which Clausewitz chose not to tread was that of the working of strategy. The great man tells us: 'Everything in strategy is very simple, but

---

[14] Clausewitz, *On War*, 97.

[15] John Keegan, 'Towards a Theory of Combat Motivation', in Paul Addison and Angus Calder (eds.), *Time to Kill: The Soldier's Experience of War in the West* (London, 1997), 4–5.

that does not mean that everything is very easy.' He has told us also that 'strategy is the use of engagements for the object of the war'. He talks of friction, and about war being 'a remarkable [and ever variable] trinity' of passion, chance, and reason.[16] But this amounts to a brilliant statement of the fairly obvious. The most significant land upon which Clausewitz declined to tread was that of the actual practice of strategy. One can excuse his decision not to discuss in detail the different purposes of war that should lead to different characters of military efforts, but it is less easy to excuse a decision to halt analysis at the point of stating that strategy is difficult. Clausewitz's most powerful claim to fame is that he spoke more eloquently than anyone else about the difficulties of his subject. It is standard to praise him for his determination not to offer a cookbook on war, a manual for the practical soldier. Such self-abnegation is certainly praiseworthy. The fact remains that he left the most difficult terrain of his subject almost wholly unmapped, let alone untilled. If 'war is simply a continuation of political intercourse, with the addition of other means',[17] why is it so difficult for strategists to perform competently? The third general question of this book, the difficulty of securing superior strategic performance, pointed to a permanent problem that even the greatest of strategic theorists only registered.

Strategy is an extraordinarily difficult enterprise primarily because it is a bridging function between unlike elements. In the same way that the accumulation of personal wealth need not bring happiness, so the achievement of military success need not bring security—though military failure is likely to bring insecurity. Clausewitz's analysis in *On War*, for all its insight, ingenuity, and adherence to fundamentals in its more mature chapters, leaves much work to be done on the persisting problems with strategy. Neither the grammar of war and strategy nor the logic of policy truly are 'given'. The 'object of the war' will not often be cast in concrete. War aims frequently fluctuate with the political implications of the strategic effect generated by tactical and operational success. Probably it is unjust to criticize a theorist, especially a theorist of Clausewitz's stature, for helping us only to know how to think about strategic difficulties, rather than for addressing the problems with strategy more directly. He did not attempt the latter. It is a mark of esteem for his genius, and a tribute to his unchanging relevance, that we can feel so acutely the loss of what he chose not to attempt to explore or explain.

The last among the general questions posed in the Introduction asked what the strategic experience of the twentieth century might tell us about the future. The concluding section at least provides a guide to an answer.

---

[16] Clausewitz, *On War*, the quotations and references pertain respectively to 178, 128, 119–21, 89.
[17] Ibid. 605.

THE DEADLY GAME CONTINUES: FROM THE TWENTIETH CENTURY TO THE TWENTY-FIRST

There is an essential unity to all strategic experience, because nothing that would make for structural change in the nature or function of strategy and war has altered radically. Weakness on some of war's dimensions eventually settled Hannibal's fate in the Second Punic War, as they did Hitler's in World War II.[18] Recall the words of Clausewitz: 'But war, though conditioned by the particular characteristics of states and their armed forces, must contain some more general—indeed, a universal—element with which every theorist ought above all to be concerned.'[19] There is universality even amidst great diversity. Strategy and strategic effect do not differ from war to war, among geographical environments, or among culturally distinctive belligerent polities.

'Bad times' recur in world politics.[20] Strategic history is dynamic and kaleidoscopic in its changing forms and character, but it is not normatively progressive. For example, the Hague Conventions (1899 and 1907) codified a requirement for the humane treatment of prisoners of war, *inter alia*, but such treatment has been the norm in 'civilized' warfare for centuries.[21] Strategy is, of course, highly variable in its salience in different historical periods. This book has identified different modes in warfare, some keyed to the constraints and demands of distinctive geographies (land, sea, air, space, cyberspace), some that transcend individual environments (irregular, unconventional, or special operations), and some that are associated with particular weapon or transportation technologies (e.g. nuclear and missile warfare). There has been nothing static about the detailed content of modern strategy.

Every chapter, in its own way, has opened a different window upon a modern strategy that changes its form and character, but not its nature, function, or degree of difficulty in performance. There are two distinctive aspects to the proposition that bad times recur. The first is that, although active demands for military security certainly ebb from time to time, thus far they have always flowed again. The second is that, viewed globally, bad times are always present for some fraction of humanity.

The spirit of this pessimistic claim is pervasive throughout the text, though one

---

[18] Like the Germans in the twentieth century, Hannibal's mercenary army was unparalleled in its combat prowess, but incapable of generating sufficient total strategic effect for victory in war. To be good at fighting is important, but rarely sufficient. J. F. Lazenby, *Hannibal's War: A Military History of the Second Punic War* (Warminster, 1978).

[19] Clausewitz, *On War*, 593.

[20] Colin S. Gray, *Villains, Victims, and Sheriffs: Strategic Studies and Security for an Inter-War Period* (Hull, 1994).

[21] Adam Roberts, 'Land Warfare: From Hague to Nuremberg', in Michael Howard, George J. Andreopoulos, and Mark R. Shulman (eds.), *The Laws of War: Constraints on Warfare in the Western World* (New Haven, Conn., 1994), 116–39; John Keegan, *War and Our World* (London, 1998), 52–3.

may be inclined to give praise for a modern strategic history that plainly has not unfolded anywhere near as catastrophically as many people expected. The idea that bad times return, at least for those who generally enjoy good times of peace with security, strengthens and develops the master theme of the book which points to an essential unity for all strategic experience. Bad times return on a scale that is approximately equivalent throughout history.

Periodically, though fortunately irregularly, super threats to peace with security emerge.[22] Both Hitler's Germany and, possibly (to risk mixing sources of menace), the nuclear arms acquired for the strategic conduct of the Cold War were extraordinary threats to human welfare. Even when one descends from the super league of 'bad times', one finds that there are always large numbers of people for whom 'normal' security conditions are not benign. More often than not, the bad times that threaten to return take the form of domestic repression, and of terroristic and other violent actions by the domestically disgruntled. The strategic history of the twentieth century unfolded on a spectrum of scale and character of violence, actual and threatened, active and latent. At any point in time, 1900, 1918, 1935, or whenever, strategic behaviour on that spectrum emphasized specific options. Modern strategic history has banished the possibility of the use of mounted soldiers for shock action, scouting, and troop mobility, but it has not seen the demise of the relevance of shock action, intelligence-gathering by light forces, and mobility for infantry. Doctors can eradicate some diseases; alas, strategists can perform no like miracles. The authority of political motives and processes renders the challenges posed to the art, and *social* science, of strategy, far more intractable than the problems attacked by medical science.

I do not believe that it is 'ideologizing the supposedly "objective"'[23] to observe, empirically, that bad times on any reasonable definition have had a way of returning for many people throughout the entire course of historical experience accessible to us. It is sadly ironic that the two wars which 'framed' the twentieth century— the Boer War and the Kosovo phase of the Balkan wars of the 1990s— both saw the pitiful displacement of whole civilian populations. The argument about the recurrence of bad times, when enhanced by consideration of a permanent spectrum and kaleidoscope of conflict and violence—albeit with changing detail—should encourage scepticism about claims for radical change for the better in the terms of security. Although technology has evolved rapidly, war forms have not. Guerrilla warfare, or terrorism, or nuclear menace, or large-scale conventional war, are discounted by the bold futurologist as yesterday's phenomena. But one suspects, nonetheless, that the full spectrum of conflict, though dressed in the latest techno-tactical clothes, will continue to confound the arrogantly prophetic and the naïvely hopeful.

[22] Colin S. Gray, *Weapons Don't Make War: Policy, Strategy, and Military Technology* (Lawrence, Kan., 1993), 95–9.
[23] Booth, 'Dare Not to Know', 330.

To understand modern strategy is to understand it in all ages. The purposes for which humans contend will change, but the deadly game endures. This is not a book of prediction, except insofar as it claims that understanding of the past provides theoretical tools for prudent guesswork about the future. It would be agreeable to conclude this exploration with a message of hope. The closest I can come to an inspirational conclusion is the thought that the *grandes guerres* of the twentieth century could, each of them, have ended both differently and very much worse.

The Allied victory in 1918 set the stage for the more radical replay which opened in 1939, but the alternative of a German triumph in 1918 must have had tragic consequences also. The victory of the Grand Alliance in 1945 was compromised from the outset by its massive indebtedness to the Soviet contribution. Nonetheless, Hitler's Third Reich was a rogue regime in a mercifully tiny class of historical offenders that had to be defeated at any cost. Moving on, historically, there is much to lament about the great Cold War, but also there is much to celebrate. From the perspective of civilization, the right side won, won clearly, and won at a socially, politically, and even ethically bearable cost.

In his role as sage, Alexander Solzhenitsyn has something important to say when he writes:

In the Computer Age we still live by the law of the Stone Age: the man with the bigger club is right. But we pretend this isn't so. We don't notice or even suspect it—why, surely our morality progresses together with our civilization.[24]

Modern strategy is neither a morality tale nor is it a tale of moral progress. The dynamic character of strategy and war has, however, persuaded some people of the illusion that strategy is a planet in yesterday's political universe. Change in form is ever confused with change in kind. Possible revolutions in the character *of* warfare are mistaken for revolutions in the nature of, or even *from*, warfare.

Is the glass of strategic achievement half-empty or half-full? Should we be appalled that the twentieth century recorded no fewer than three great wars, or should we be agreeably surprised that the 'better—perhaps not quite good—guys and gals' won each round? Those who respect strategic history must be restrained in optimism for the future. It is always possible that the twenty-first century will be different, but readers are invited to cast their minds back. From the perspectives of, say, 1700, 1800, and 1900, how did the history of the succeeding centuries proceed? Is there an overwhelming reason to believe that strategic history is about to turn some historically or morally dramatic corner into a zone of irrelevance? I think not. In historical fact, we have done quite well in modern strategy. By luck and some judgement the German Problem was forcibly and correctly resolved, and then Soviet geopolitical and ideological pretensions were outlasted and defeated. In an imperfect world it would be impious to ask for more.

[24] Alexander Solzhenitsyn, 'The March of the Hypocrites', *The Times*, 21 Aug. 1997, 16.

REFERENCES

ADAMS, J., *The Next World War* (London, 1998).

ADAMS, T. K., *U.S. Special Operations Forces in Action: The Challenge of Unconventional Warfare* (London, 1998).

ADDISON, P., and CALDER, A. (eds.), *Time to Kill: The Soldier's Experience of War in the West, 1939-1945* (London, 1997).

ADLER, E. (ed.), *The International Practice of Arms Control* (Baltimore, 1992).

—— 'Condition(s) of Peace', *Review of International Studies*, 24 (1998), 165-91.

AGRE, P. E., 'Yesterday's Tomorrow: The Advance of Law and Order into the Utopian Wilderness of Cyberspace', *Times Literary Supplement*, 3 July 1998, 3-4.

ALEXANDER, B., *Lost Victories: The Military Genius of Stonewall Jackson* (Edison, NJ, 1996).

ALGER, J. A., 'Introduction', to W. Schwartau (ed.), *Information Warfare, Cyberterrorism: Protecting Your Personal Security in the Electronic Age*, 2nd edn. (New York, 1996), 8-14.

ALGER, J. I., *The Quest for Victory: The History of the Principles of War* (Westport, Conn., 1982).

—— *Definitions and Doctrine of the Military Art: Past and Present* (Fort Wayne, NJ, 1985).

ALLISON, G. T., *Essence of Decision: Explaining the Cuban Missile Crisis* (Boston, 1971).

—— et al., *Cooperative Denuclearization: From Pledges to Deeds*, CSIA Studies in International Security 2 (Cambridge, Mass., Jan. 1993).

—— et al., *Avoiding Nuclear Anarchy: Containing the Threat of Loose Russian Nuclear Weapons and Fissile Material*, CSIA Studies in International Security 12 (Cambridge, Mass., 1996).

ALPEROVITZ, G., *Atomic Diplomacy: Hiroshima and Potsdam* (New York, 1965).

ANDERSON, C. R., *The Grunts* (San Rafael, Calif., 1976).

ANGELL, N., *The Great Illusion: A Study of the Relation of Military Power in Nations to Their Economic and Social Advantage*, 3rd edn. (London, 1911).

—— *The Great Illusion—Now* (London, 1938).

ARON, R., *Peace and War: A Theory of International Relations* (Garden City, NY, 1966).

—— 'The Evolution of Modern Strategic Thought', in Institute for Strategic Studies (ed.), *Problems of Modern Strategy* pt. 1, Adelphi Paper 54 (London, Feb. 1969), 1-17.

—— *Clausewitz: Philosopher of War*, trans. C. Booker and N. Stone (London, 1983).

ARQUILLA, J., 'The Strategic Implications of Information Dominance', *Strategic Review*, 22 (1994), 24-30.

—— 'Bound to Fail: Regional Deterrence after the Cold War', *Comparative Strategy*, 14 (1995), 123-35.

—— (ed.), *From Troy to Entebbe: Special Operations in Ancient and Modern Times* (Lanham, Md., 1996).

—— and RONFELD, D., 'Cyberwar is Coming!', *Comparative Strategy*, 12 (1993), 141-65.

—— —— *The Advent of Netwar*, MR-789-OSD (Santa Monica, Calif., 1996).

—— —— (eds.), *In Athena's Camp: Preparing for Conflict in the Information Age* (Santa Monica, Calif., 1997).

ASPREY, R. B., *War in the Shadows: The Classic History of Guerrilla Warfare from Ancient Persia to the Present*, rev. edn. (London, 1994).

ASTON, G., 'Combined Strategy for Fleets and Armies; or "Amphibious Strategy"', *Journal of the Royal United Service Institution*, 51 (1907), 984-1004.

ASTON, G., *Sea, Land, and Air Strategy: A Comparison* (London, 1914).

AVANT, D. D., *Political Institutions and Military Change: Lessons from Peripheral Wars* (Ithaca, NY, 1994).

BACEVICH, A. J., 'Preserving the Well-Bred Horse', *National Interest*, 37 (1994), 43–9.

—— and SULLIVAN, B. R. (eds.), *The Limits of Technology in Modern War*. Forthcoming.

BADSEY, S., 'Cavalry and the Development of Breakthrough Doctrine', in P. Griffith (ed.), *British Fighting Methods in the Great War* (London, 1996), 138–74.

BAER, G. W., *One Hundred Years of Sea Power: The U.S. Navy, 1890–1990* (Stanford, Calif., 1994).

BAILEY, J. B. A., *Field Artillery and Firepower* (Oxford, 1989).

—— 'British Artillery in the Great War', in P. Griffith (ed.), *British Fighting Methods in the Great War* (London, 1996), 23–49.

—— *The First World War and the Birth of the Modern Style of Warfare*, Occasional Paper 22 (Camberley, 1996).

BAKER, J. C., *Non-Proliferation Incentives for Russia and Ukraine*, Adelphi Paper 309 (London, 1997).

BALCK, W., *Development of Tactics: World War*, trans. H. Bell (Fort Leavenworth, Kan., 1922).

BALDWIN, D. A., 'The Concept of Security', *Review of International Studies*, 23 (1997), 5–26.

BALL, D., 'The Development of the SIOP, 1960–1983', in D. Ball and J. Richelson (eds.), *Strategic Nuclear Targeting* (Ithaca, NY, 1986), 57–83.

—— and RICHELSON, J. (eds.), *Strategic Nuclear Targeting* (Ithaca, NY, 1986).

—— and TOTH, R. C., 'Revising the SIOP: Taking War-Fighting to Dangerous Extremes', *International Security*, 14 (1990), 65–92.

BARCLAY, G. ST. J., *The Empire Is Marching: A Study of the Military Effort of the British Empire, 1800–1945* (London, 1976).

'BARFLEUR' (pseud. for R. CUSTANCE), *Naval Policy: A Plea for the Study of War* (Edinburgh, 1907).

BARLOW, J. C., *Revolt of the Admirals: The Fight for Naval Aviation, 1945–1950* (Washington, DC, 1994).

BARNABY, F., *The Automated Battlefield* (London, 1986).

BARNETT, C., *Britain and Her Army, 1509–1970: A Military, Political and Social Survey* (London, 1970).

—— *Engage the Enemy More Closely: The Royal Navy in the Second World War* (New York, 1991).

—— 'The Consequences of the Great War', *RUSI Journal*, 143 (1998), 70–1.

BARNETT, F. R., TOVAR, B. H., and SHULTZ, R. H. (eds.), *Special Operations in US Strategy* (Washington, DC, 1984).

BARNETT, J. R., *Future War: An Assessment of Aerospace Campaigns in 2010* (Maxwell AFB, Ala., Jan. 1996).

BARNETT, R. W., 'Grasping 2010 with Naval Forces', *Joint Force Quarterly*, 17 (1997–8), 25–31.

BARNHART, M. A., *Japan Prepares for Total War: The Search for Economic Security, 1919–1941* (Ithaca, NY, 1987).

BARTLETT, M. L. (ed.), *Assault from the Sea: Essays on the History of Amphibious Warfare*. (Annapolis, Md., 1983).

BARTOV, O., *Hitler's Army: Soldiers, Nazis, and War in the Third Reich* (New York, 1991).

BASSFORD, C., *Clausewitz in English: The Reception of Clausewitz In Britain and America, 1815–1945* (New York, 1994).

—— 'John Keegan and the Grand Tradition of Trashing Clausewitz: A Polemic', *War in History*, 1 (1994), 319–36.

—— 'Landmarks in Defense Literature: On War, by Carl von Clausewitz', *Defense Analysis*, 12 (1996), 267–71.

BATHURST, R. B., *Intelligence and the Mirror: On Creating an Enemy* (London, 1993).

BAUCOM, D. R., *Clausewitz on Space War: An Essay on the Strategic Aspects of Military Operations in Space*, AU-ARI-CPSS-91-13 (Maxwell AFB, Ala, June 1992).

BAUGH, D. A., *British Naval Administration in the Age of Walpole* (Princeton, NJ, 1965).

BAYLIS, J., and GARNETT, J. (eds.), *Makers of Nuclear Strategy* (New York, 1991).

—— and O'NEILL, R. (eds.), *Alternative Nuclear Futures* (Oxford, 1999).

—— and SMITH, S. (eds.), *The Globalization of World Politics: An Introduction to International Relations* (Oxford, 1997).

BEAUFRE, A., *An Introduction to Strategy*, trans. R. H. Barry (London, 1963).

BECKETT, I. F. W., 'Total War', in C. McInnes and G. D. Sheffield (eds.), *Warfare in the Twentieth Century: Theory and Practice* (London, 1988), 1–23.

BEGIN, M., *The Revolt: Story of the Irgun* (Jerusalem, 1977).

BELL, A. C., *A History of the Blockade of Germany and of the Countries Associated with Her in the Great War, Austria-Hungary, Bulgaria, and Turkey, 1914–1918* (London, 1937).

BELL, C., *The Conventions of Crisis: A Study in Diplomatic Management* (London, 1971).

BELL, J. B., *The Myth of the Guerrilla: Revolutionary Theory and Malpractice* (New York, 1971).

—— *The Dynamics of the Armed Struggle* (London, 1998).

BELLAMY, C., *The Future of Land Warfare* (New York, 1987).

—— *The Evolution of Modern Land Warfare: Theory and Practice* (London, 1990).

BENBOW, T., 'Naval Aviation', in E. Grove and P. Hore (eds.), *Dimensions of Sea Power* (Hull, 1998), 70–86.

BENNETT, R., *Behind the Battle: Intelligence in the War with Germany, 1939–45* (London, 1994).

BERGERUD, E. M., *Red Thunder, Tropic Lightning: The World of a Combat Division in Vietnam* (New York, 1994).

BERKOWITZ, B. D., *Calculated Risks: A Century of Arms Control, Why It Has Failed, and How It Can Be Made to Work* (New York, 1987).

BERNSTEIN, R., and MUNRO, H. R., *The Coming War with China* (New York, 1997).

BEST, G., *Humanity in Warfare* (New York, 1980).

—— *War and Law Since 1945* (Oxford, 1994).

BETTS, R. K., *Surprise Attack: Lessons for Defense Planning* (Washington, DC, 1982).

—— *Nuclear Blackmail and Nuclear Balance* (Washington, DC, 1987).

—— 'Should Strategic Studies Survive?', *World Politics*, 50 (1997), 7–33.

—— 'The New Threat of Mass Destruction', *Foreign Affairs*, 77 (1998), 26–41.

BIALER, U., *The Shadow of the Bomber: The Fear of Air Attack and British Politics, 1932–1939* (London, 1980).

BIDWELL, S., and GRAHAM, D., *Fire-Power: British Army Weapons and Theories of War, 1904–1945* (London, 1982).

BLACK, J., *Why Wars Happen* (London, 1998).

—— and WOODFINE, P. (eds.), *The British Navy and the Use of Naval Power in the Eighteenth Century* (Leicester, 1988).

BLACKBOURN, D., *Fontana History of Germany, 1780–1918: The Long Nineteenth Century* (London, 1997).

BLAINEY, G., *The Causes of War* (London, 1973).

BLAIR, B. G., *Strategic Command and Control: Redefining the Nuclear Threat* (Washington, DC, 1985).

—— *The Logic of Accidental Nuclear War* (Washington, DC, 1993).

—— *Global Zero Alert for Nuclear Forces* (Washington, DC, 1995).

BLAIR, C., Jr., *Silent Victory: The U.S. Submarine War Against Japan* (New York, 1976).

BLAKER, J. R., *Understanding the Revolution in Military Affairs: A Guide to America's 21st Century Defense*, Progressive Policy Institute, Defense Working Paper 3 (Washington, DC, Jan. 1997).

BLAXLAND, G., *Amiens: 1918* (London, 1968).

BLOW, T., *Defending Against a Space Blockade*, AU-ARI-CP-89-3 (Maxwell AFB, Ala., Dec. 1989).

BOGGS, M. W., *Attempts to Define and Limit 'Aggressive' Armament in Diplomacy and Strategy*, University of Missouri Studies 16 (Columbia, Mo., 1941).

BOHEC, Y. LE, *The Imperial Roman Army* (New York, 1994).

BOND, B. (ed.), *Victorian Military Campaigns* (London, 1967).

—— *The Victorian Army and the Staff College, 1854–1914* (London, 1972).

—— *Liddell Hart: A Study of His Military Thought* (New Brunswick, NJ, 1977).

—— *British Military Policy between the World Wars* (Oxford, 1980).

—— (ed.), *The First World War and British Military History* (Oxford, 1991).

—— *The Pursuit of Victory: From Napoleon to Saddam Hussein* (Oxford, 1996).

BOOG, H. (ed.), *The Conduct of the Air War in the Second World War: An International Comparison* (Providence, RI, 1992).

—— et al., *Germany and the Second World War, iv: The Attack on the Soviet Union* (Oxford, 1998).

BOOTH, K., *Navies and Foreign Policy* (London, 1977).

—— *Strategy and Ethnocentrism* (London, 1979).

—— 'Bernard Brodie', in J. Baylis and J. Garnett (eds.), *Makers of Nuclear Strategy* (New York, 1991), 19–56.

—— 'Strategy', in A. J. R. Groom and M. Light (eds.), *Contemporary International Relations: A Guide to Theory*, (London, 1994), 109–27.

—— 'Dare Not to Know: International Relations Theory versus the Future', in K. Booth and S. Smith (eds.), *International Relations Theory Today* (Cambridge, 1995), 328–50.

—— 'Discussion: A Reply to Wallace', *Review of International Studies*, 23 (1997), 371–7.

—— 'Security and Self: Reflections of a Fallen Realist', in K. Krause and M. C. Williams (eds.), *Critical Security Studies: Concepts and Cases* (London, 1997), 83–119.

BORASTON, J. H. (ed.), *Sir Douglas Haig's Despatches (December 1915–April 1919)*, repr. of 1919 edn. (London, 1979).

BORDEN, W. L., *There Will Be No Time: The Revolution in Strategy* (New York, 1946).

BOULDING, K., *Conflict and Defense: A General Theory* (New York, 1962).

BOURNE, R., *Queen Anne's Navy in the West Indies* (New Haven, Conn., 1939).

BOWKER, M., and BROWN, R. (eds.), *From Cold War to Collapse: Theory and World Politics in the 1980s* (Cambridge, 1993).

BOYD, J. R., 'A Discourse on Winning and Losing' (MS, Aug. 1987).

BOYER, M. A., *International Cooperation and Public Goods: Opportunities for the Western Alliance* (Baltimore, 1993).

BOZEMAN, A. B., *Politics and Culture in International History* (Princeton, NJ, 1960).

BRACKEN, P., *The Command and Control of Nuclear Forces* (New Haven, Conn., 1983).

BREEMER, J. S., *The Burden of Trafalgar: Decisive Battle and Naval Strategic Expectations on the Eve of the First World War*, Newport Paper 6 (Newport, RI, Oct. 1993).

BRENNAN, D. G., 'The Case for Missile Defense', *Foreign Affairs*, 43 (1969), 633–48.

BREWER, J., *The Sinews of Power: War, Money and the English State, 1688–1783* (New York, 1989).

BRODIE, B. (ed.), *The Absolute Weapon: Atomic Power and World Order* (New York, 1946).

—— 'Implications for Military Policy', in B. Brodie (ed.), *The Absolute Weapon: Atomic Power and World Order* (New York, 1946), 70–107.

—— 'War in the Atomic Age', in B. Brodie (ed.), *The Absolute Weapon: Atomic Power and World Order* (New York, 1946), 21–69.

—— 'Strategy as a Science', *World Politics*, 1 (1949), 476–88.

—— 'Strategy Hits a Dead End', *Harper's*, 211 (1955), 33–7.

—— *Strategy in the Missile Age* (Princeton, NJ, 1959).

—— 'The Scientific Strategists', in R. Gilpin and C. Wright (eds.), *Scientists and National Policy-Making* (New York, 1964), 240–56.

—— *War and Politics* (New York, 1973).

—— 'The Continuing Relevance of *On War*', in C. von Clausewitz, *On War*, trans. M. Howard and P. Paret (Princeton, NJ, 1976), 45–68.

—— 'A Guide to the Reading of *On War*', in C. von Clausewitz, *On War*, trans. M. Howard and P. Paret (Princeton, NJ, 1976), 641–711.

—— 'Technological Change, Strategic Doctrine, and Political Outcomes', in K. Knorr (ed.), *Historical Dimensions of National Security Problems* (Lawrence, Kan., 1976), 263–306.

—— 'The Development of Nuclear Strategy', *International Security*, 2 (1978), 65–83.

BROWN, C., *Understanding International Relations* (London, 1997).

BRZEZINSKI, Z. (ed.), *Promise and Peril: The Strategic Defense Initiative*. (Washington, DC, 1986).

BUCHOLZ, A., *Hans Delbrück and the German Military Establishment: War Images in Conflict* (Iowa City, 1985).

—— *Moltke, Schlieffen, and Prussian War Planning* (New York, 1991).

BUILDER, C. H., *The Masks of War: American Military Styles in Strategy and Analysis* (Baltimore, 1989).

—— *The Icarus Syndrome: The Role of Air Power Theory in the Evolution and Fate of the U.S. Air Force* (New Brunswick, NJ, 1994).

—— 'Keeping the Strategic Flame', *Joint Force Quarterly*, 14 (1996–7), 76–84.

—— and DEWAR, J. A., 'A Time for Planning? If Not Now When?', *Parameters*, 24 (1994), 4–15.

BULL, H., 'Strategic Studies and Its Critics', *World Politics*, 20 (1968), 593–605.

—— 'The Theory of International Politics, 1919–1969', in B. Porter (ed.), *The Aberystwyth Papers: International Politics, 1919–1969* (London, 1972), 30–55.

—— *The Anarchical Society: A Study of Order in World Politics* (New York, 1977).

—— and WATSON, A. (eds.), *The Expansion of International Society* (Oxford, 1985).

BUDERI, R., *The Invention That Changed the World: The Story of Radar from War to Peace* (New York, 1996).

BUNDY, M., 'To Cap the Volcano', *Foreign Affairs*, 48 (1969), 1–20.

—— 'Existential Deterrence and Its Consequences', in D. MacLean (ed.), *The Security Gamble: Deterrence Dilemmas in the Nuclear Age* (Totowa, NJ, 1984), 3–13.

BUNKER, R. J., *Five-Dimensional (Cyber) Warfighting: Can the Army after Next be Defeated through Complex Concepts and Technologies?* (Carlisle Barracks, Pa., 10 Mar. 1998).

BURCHILL, S., 'Realism and Neo-realism', in S. Burchill, and A. Linklater et al., *Theories of International Relations* (London, 1996), 67–92.

BURDICK, C., and Jacobsen, H.-A. (eds.), *The Halder War Diary, 1939–1942*, abridged version of 1962–4 edn. (Novato, Calif., 1988).

BURKE, P., *Popular Culture in Early Modern Europe*, rev. edn. (Aldershot, 1994).

BURROWS, W. E., *Deep Black: Space Espionage and National Security* (New York, 1986).

BUZAN, B., *People, States and Fear: An Agenda for International Security Studies in the Post-Cold War Era*, 2nd edn. (Boulder, Colo., 1991).

—— and HERRING, E., *The Arms Dynamic in World Politics* (Boulder, Colo., 1998).

BUZAN, B., WAEVER, O., and WILDE, J. DE, *Security: A New Framework for Analysis* (Boulder, Colo., 1998).

BUZZANCO, R., *Masters of War: Military Dissent and Politics in the Vietnam Era* (Cambridge, 1996).

BYMAN, D., and EVERA, S. VAN, 'Why They Fight: Hypotheses on the Causes of Contemporary Deadly Conflict', *Security Studies*, 7 (1998), 1–50.

CABLE, J., *Gunboat Diplomacy, 1919–1991* (London, 1994).

—— *The Political Influence of Naval Force in History* (London, 1998).

CAEMMERER, Lt.-Gen. R. VON, *The Development of Strategical Science During the 19th Century*, trans. K. von Donat (London, 1905).

CALDWELL, W., Jr., 'Promises, Promises', Naval Institute *Proceedings*, 122 (1996), 54–7.

CALLWELL, C. E., 'Notes on the Tactics of Our Small Wars', *Proceedings of the Royal Artillery Institution*, 12 (1881–4), 531–52.

—— 'Notes on the Strategy of Our Small Wars', *Proceedings of the Royal Artillery Institution*, 13 (1885), 403–20.

—— 'Lessons to Be Learnt from the Campaigns in Which British Forces Have Been Employed since the Year 1865', *Journal of the Royal United Service Institution*, 31 (1887), 357–412.

—— *Military Operations and Maritime Preponderance: Their Relations and Interdependence*, ed. C. S. Gray, repr. of 1905 edn. (Annapolis, Md., 1996).

—— *Small Wars: A Tactical Textbook for Imperial Soldiers*, repr. of 1906 edn. (London, 1990).

CAMPBELL, K. M., et al., *Soviet Nuclear Fission: Control of the Nuclear Arsenal in a Disintegrating Soviet Union*, CSIA Studies in International Security 1 (Cambridge, Mass., Nov. 1991).

CANBERRA COMMISSION ON THE ELIMINATION OF NUCLEAR WEAPONS, *Report* (Canberra, Aug. 1996).

CARNEGIE ENDOWMENT FOR INTERNATIONAL PEACE, *Report of the International Commission to Inquire into the Causes and Conduct of the Balkan Wars* (Washington, DC, 1914).

CARNESALE, A., and HAAS, R. N. (eds.), *Superpower Arms Control: Setting the Record Straight* (Cambridge, Mass., 1987).

CARTER, A. B., and SCHWARTZ, D. N. (eds.), *Ballistic Missile Defense* (Washington, DC, 1984).

—— STEINBRUNER, J. D., and ZRAKET, C. A. (eds.), *Managing Nuclear Operations* (Washington, DC, 1987).

—— PERRY, W. J., and STEINBRUNER, J. D., *A New Concept of Cooperative Security*, Brookings Occasional Papers (Washington, DC, 1992).

CARVER, Field Marshal Lord, *The Apostles of Mobility: The Theory and Practice of Armoured Warfare* (London, 1979).

CASTEX, R., *Strategic Theories*, trans. and ed. E. C. Kiesling (Annapolis, Md., 1994).

CECIL, H., and LIDDLE, P. H. (eds.), *Facing Armageddon: The First World War Experienced* (London, 1996).

Center for Counterproliferation Research (National Defense University) and Center for Global Security Research (Lawrence Livermore National Laboratory), *U.S. Nuclear Policy in the 21st Century: A Fresh Look at National Strategy and Requirements, Final Report* (Washington, DC, 1998).

CHANDLER, D., *The Campaigns of Napoleon* (London, 1967).

—— (ed.), *The Military Maxims of Napoleon*, trans. Lt.-Gen. Sir G. C. D'Aguilar (New York, 1987).

CHEYNET, J. C., 'Manzikert: un désastre militaire?', *Byzantion*, 50 (1980), 410–38.

CHURCHILL, W. S., *The World Crisis* (2 vols., London, 1938).

CIMBALA, S. J., *Clausewitz and Escalation: Classical Perspective on Nuclear Strategy* (London, 1991).

—— *Coercive Military Strategy* (College Station, Tex, 1998).

CLANCY, T., *Debt of Honor* (London, 1994).

CLAUSEWITZ, C. VON, *On War*, trans. M. Howard and P. Paret (Princeton, NJ, 1976).

—— *The Campaign of 1812 in Russia*, repr. of 1843 edn. (London, 1992).

—— *Historical and Political Writings*, trans. and ed. P. Paret and D. Moran (Princeton, NJ, 1992).

CLAYTON, A., *The British Empire as a Superpower, 1919–39* (Athens, Ga., 1986).

—— *France, Soldiers and Africa* (London, 1988).

CLODFELTER, M., *The Limits of Air Power: The American Bombing of North Vietnam* (New York, 1989).

COCHRANE, T. B., ARKIN, W. M., and HOENIG, M. M., *Nuclear Weapons Databook, i: U.S. Nuclear Forces and Capabilities* (Cambridge, Mass., 1984).

—— et al., *Nuclear Weapons Databook, iv: Soviet Nuclear Weapons* (New York, 1989).

COHEN, E. A., *Commandos and Politicians: Elite Military Units in Modern Democracies* (Cambridge, Mass., 1978).

—— (director), *Gulf War Air Power Survey*, 5 vols. and summary (Washington, DC, 1993).

—— 'The Mystique of U.S. Air Power', *Foreign Affairs*, 73 (1994), 109–24.

—— 'The Meaning and Future of Air Power', *Orbis*, 39 (1995), 189–200.

—— 'A Revolution in Warfare', *Foreign Affairs*, 75 (1996), 37–54.

—— 'What Combat Does to Man: *Private Ryan* and Its Critics', *National Interest*, 54 (1998/9), 82–8.

—— and GOOCH, J., *Military Misfortunes: The Anatomy of Failure in War* (New York, 1990).

COHEN, S. B., *Geography and Politics in a Divided World* (London, 1964).

COHEN, W. S. (Secretary of Defense), *Annual Report to the President and the Congress* (Washington, DC, 1998 and 1999).

COLE, L. A., *The Eleventh Plague: The Politics of Biological and Chemical Warfare* (New York, 1997).

COLE, M., *Cultural Psychology: A Once and Future Discipline* (Cambridge, Mass., 1996).

COLIN, J. *The Transformations of War*, trans. L. H. R. Pope-Hennessy (London, 1912).

COLLINS, J. M., *Military Space Forces: The Next 50 Years* (Washington, DC, 1989).

—— *Military Geography for Professionals and the Public* (Washington, DC, 1998).

COLSON, B., *La Culture stratégique américaine: l'influence de Jomini* (Paris, 1993).

Commission on Integrated Long-Term Strategy, *Discriminate Deterrence* (Washington, DC, 11 Jan. 1988).

Commission to Assess the Ballistic Missile Threat to the United States, *Executive Summary* (Washington, DC, 15 July 1998).

—— *Report; Appendix III: Unclassified Working Papers* (Washington, DC, 15 July 1998).

COMPTON-HALL, R., *Submarines and the War at Sea, 1914–18* (London, 1991).

CONNAUGHTON, R., *The War of the Rising Sun and Tumbling Bear: A Military History of the Russo-Japanese War, 1904–5* (London, 1988).

CONQUEST, R., *The Great Terror: A Reassessment* (New York, 1990).

COOK D., *Forging the Alliance: NATO, 1945 to 1950* (London, 1989).

COOX A. D., 'The Effectiveness of the Japanese Military Establishment in the Second World War', in A. R. Millett and W. Murray (eds.), *Military Effectiveness, iii: The Second World War* (Boston, 1988), 1–44.

CORBETT, J. S., *The Campaign of Trafalgar* (London, 1910).

—— *Some Principles of Maritime Strategy*, ed. E. Grove, repr. of 1911 edn. (Annapolis, Md., 1988).

—— *England in the Seven Years' War: A Study in Combined Strategy*, repr. of 1918 edn. (2 vols., London, 1973).

CORDESMAN, A. H., and WAGNER, A. W., *The Lessons of Modern War, i: The Arab–Israeli Conflicts, 1973–1989* (Boulder, Colo., 1990).

CORUM, J. R., *The Roots of Blitzkrieg: Hans von Seeckt and German Military Reform* (Lawrence, Kan., 1992).

—— *The Luftwaffe: Creating the Operational Air War, 1918–1940* (Lawrence, Kan., 1997).

COSTELLO, J., *The Pacific War* (New York, 1982).

COWLES, V., *The Phantom Major: The Story of David Stirling and the S.A.S.* (London, 1958).

CRAIG, G. A., *Germany, 1866–1945* (New York, 1978).

—— and GEORGE, A., *Force and Statecraft: Diplomatic Problems of Our Time*, 3rd edn. (New York, 1995).

CRANE, C. C., *Bombs, Cities, and Civilians: American Airpower Strategy in World War II* (Lawrence, Kan., 1993).

CREASEY, E., *The Fifteen Decisive Battles of the World: From Marathon to Waterloo*, repr. of 1851 edn. (Royston, Herts., 1996).

CREVELD, M. VAN, *Supplying War: Logistics from Wallenstein to Patton* (Cambridge, 1977).

—— *Fighting Power: German and U.S. Army Performance, 1939–1945* (Westport, Conn., 1982).

—— *Command in War* (Cambridge, Mass., 1985).

—— 'The Eternal Clausewitz', in M. Handel (ed.), *Clausewitz and Modern Strategy* (London, 1986), 35–50.

—— *Technology and War: From 2000 B.C. to the Present* (New York, 1989).

—— *The Transformation of War* (New York, 1991).

—— *Nuclear Proliferation and the Future of Conflict* (New York, 1993).

—— with CANBY, S. L., and BROWER, K. S., *Air Power and Maneuver Warfare* (Maxwell AFB, Ala., July 1994).

—— 'The Fate of the State', *Parameters*, 26 (1996), 4–18.

—— 'What is Wrong with Clausewitz?', in G. de Nooy (ed.), *The Clausewitzian Dictum and the Future of Western Military Strategy* (The Hague, 1997), 7–23.

CRISS, P. J., and SCHUBERT, D. J., *The Leading Edge: Air Power in Australia's Unique Environment*, Canberra Papers on Strategy and Defence 62 (Canberra, 1990).

CROCKATT, R., *The Fifty Years War: The United States and the Soviet Union in World Politics, 1941–1991* (London, 1995).

CROFT, S., *Strategies of Arms Control: A History and Typology* (Manchester, 1996).

CRONE, H. D., *Banning Chemical Weapons: The Scientific Background* (Cambridge, 1992).

CROWL, P., 'Alfred Thayer Mahan: The Naval Historian', in P. Paret (ed.), *Makers of Modern Strategy: From Machiavelli to the Nuclear Age* (Princeton, NJ, 1986), 444–77.

CURREY, C. B., *Victory at Any Cost: The Genius of Viet Nam's Gen. Vo Nguyen Giap* (Washington, DC, 1997).

CUSTANCE, R., *A Study of War* (Boston, 1924).

DANCHEV, A., 'On Specialness', *International Affairs*, 72 (1996), 737–50.

—— *Alchemist of War: The Life of Basil Liddell Hart* (London, 1998).

DANDO, M., *Biological Warfare in the 21st Century: Biotechnology and the Proliferation of Biological Weapons* (New York, 1994).

DAVID, S. R., 'Internal War: Causes and Cures', *World Politics*, 49 (1997), 552–76.

DAVIS, L. E., *Limited Nuclear Options: Deterrence and the New American Doctrine*, Adelphi Paper 121 (London, winter 1975–6).

DAVIS, P. K. (ed.), *New Challenges for Defense Planning: Rethinking How Much Is Enough* (Santa Monica, Calif, 1994).

DAVIS, W. C., *The Cause Lost: Myths and Realities of the Confederacy* (Lawrence, Kan., 1996).

DEBLOIS, B. M., 'Ascendant Realism: Characteristics of Airpower and Space Power', in P. S. Meilinger (ed.), *The Paths of Heaven: The Evolution of Airpower Theory* (Maxwell AFB, Ala., 1997), 529–78.

—— 'Space Sanctuary: A Viable National Strategy', *Airpower Journal*, 12 (1998), 41–57.

DEBRAY, R., *Revolution in the Revolution?* (London, 1968).

DELBRÜCK, H., *History of the Art of War, iv: The Dawn of Modern Warfare* (Lincoln, Neb, 1985).

DESCH, M. C., 'Culture Clash: Assessing the Importance of Ideas in Security Studies', *International Security*, 23 (1998), 141–70.

DESUTTER, P. A., *Denial and Jeopardy: Deterring Iranian Use of NBC Weapons* (Washington, DC, Sept. 1997).

DEUTSCH, H., and SHOWALTER, D. E. (eds.), *What If? Strategic Alternatives of WWII* (Chicago, 1997).

DEVEREUX, T., *Messenger Gods of Battle: Radio, Radar, Sonar: The Story of Electronics in War* (London, 1991).

Director of Central Intelligence, *Soviet Capabilities for Strategic Nuclear Conflict, 1982–92, National Intelligence Estimate: 1, Key Judgments and Summary*, NIE 11–3/8–82 (Top Secret), decl. 19/2/93 (Washington, DC, 15 Feb. 1983).

DOCKRILL, S., *Eisenhower's New-Look National Security Policy, 1953–61* (London, 1996).

DOLMAN, E. C., 'Geography in the Space Age: An Astropolitical Analysis', *Journal of Strategic Studies*, 22 (1999).

DOUBLER, M. D., *Closing with the Enemy: How GIs Fought the War in Europe, 1944–1945* (Lawrence, Kan., 1994).

DOUGHTY, R. A., *The Seeds of Disaster: The Development of French Army Doctrine, 1919–1939* (Hamden, Conn., 1985).

—— *The Breaking Point: Sedan and the Fall of France* (Hamden, Conn., 1990).

DOUHET, G., *The Command of the Air*, trans. D. Ferrari, repr. of 1942 edn. (New York, 1972).

DOWER, J. W., *War Without Mercy: Race and Power in the Pacific War* (New York, 1986).

DOWNING, B. M., *The Military Revolution and Political Change: Origins of Democracy and Autocracy in Early Modern Europe* (Princeton, NJ, 1992).

DOYLE, A. C., *Sherlock Holmes: The Complete Short Stories* (London, 1928).

DUFFIELD, J. S., *Power Rules: The Evolution of NATO's Conventional Force Posture* (Stanford, Calif., 1995).

DULL, P. S., *A Battle History of the Imperial Japanese Navy (1941–1945)* (Annapolis, Md., 1978).

DUNN, D. H., *The Politics of Threat: Minuteman Vulnerability in American National Security Policy* (London, 1997).

DUPUY, T. N., *The Evolution of Weapons and Warfare* (Indianapolis, 1980).

—— (ed.), *International Military and Defense Encyclopedia* (6 vols., Washington, DC, 1993), vi: T–Z.

DUTTON, L., et al., *Military Space* (London, 1990).

EARLE, E. M. (ed.), *Makers of Modern Strategy: From Machiavelli to Hitler* (Princeton, NJ, 1941).

EDMONDS, M., 'Land Warfare', in R. Carey and T. C. Salmon (eds.), *International Security in the Modern World* (London, 1996), 179–206.

ELLIS, J., *Brute Force: Allied Strategy and Tactics in the Second World War* (New York, 1990).

—— 'Reflections on the "Sharp End" of War', in P. Addison and A. Calder (eds.), *Time to Kill: The Soldier's Experience of War in the West, 1939–1945* (London, 1997), 12–18.

EMME, E. M. (ed.), *The Impact of Air Power: National Security and World Politics* (Princeton, NJ, 1959).

EMMETT, P., 'Information Mania: A New Manifestation of Gulf War Syndrome', *RUSI Journal*, 141 (1996), 19–26.

ENGLISH, J. A., *A Perspective on Infantry* (New York, 1981).

ENTHOVEN, A. C., and Smith, K. W., *How Much Is Enough? Shaping the Defense Program, 1961–1969* (New York, 1971).

ERICKSON, J. (ed.), *The Military-Technical Revolution: Its Impact on Strategy and Foreign Policy* (London, 1966).

ERICKSON, J. (ed.), *The Road to Stalingrad: Stalin's War with Germany* (London, 1975).

—— *The Road to Berlin: Continuing the History of Stalin's War with Germany* (Boulder, Colo., 1983).

ERMATH, F., 'Contrasts in American and Soviet Strategic Thought', *International Security*, 3 (1978), 138–55.

ESTES, H. M., III, 'Space and Joint Space Doctrine', *Joint Force Quarterly*, 14 (1996–7), 60–3.

ETCHESON, C., *Arms Race Theory: Strategy and Structure of Behavior* (Westport, Conn., 1989).

EVANGELISTA, M., *Innovation and the Arms Race: How the United States and the Soviet Union Develop New Military Technologies* (Ithaca, NY, 1988).

EVANS, M. H. H., *Amphibious Operations: The Projection of Sea Power Ashore* (London, 1990).

EVERA, S. VAN, 'Offense, Defense, and The Causes of War', *International Security*, 22 (1998), 5–43.

FADOK, D. S., *John Boyd and John Warden: Air Power's Quest for Strategic Paralysis* (Maxwell AFB, Ala., Feb. 1995).

—— 'John Boyd and John Warden: Airpower's Quest for Strategic Paralysis', in P. S. Meilinger (ed.), *The Paths of Heaven: The Evolution of Airpower Theory* (Maxwell AFB, Ala., 1997), 357–98.

FALL, B. B., *Street Without Joy* (New York, 1972).

—— *Hell in a Very Small Place: The Siege of Dien Bien Phu* (New York, 1985).

FALLS, C., *The Nature of Modern Warfare* (London, 1941).

—— *A Hundred Years of War* (London, 1953).

FARRAR-HOCKLEY, A., *Death of an Army* (London, 1967).

FARRELL, T., 'Figuring Out Fighting Organizations: The New Organizational Analysis in Strategic Studies', *Journal of Strategic Studies*, 19 (1996), 122–35.

—— 'Making Sense of Doctrine', in M. Duffy, T. Farrell, and G. Sloan (eds.), *Doctrine and Military Effectiveness*, Strategic Policy Studies 1 (Exeter, 1997), 1–5.

—— *Weapons Without a Cause: The Politics of Weapons Acquisition in the United States* (London, 1997).

—— 'Culture and Military Power,' *Review of International Studies*, 24 (1998), 407–16.

FEAVER, P. D., *Guarding the Guardians: Civilian Control of Nuclear Weapons in the United States* (Ithaca, NY, 1992).

—— 'Blowback: Information Warfare and the Dynamics of Coercion', *Security Studies*, 7 (1998), 88–120.

FEHRENBACH, T. R., *This Kind of War: The Classic Korean War History* (Washington, DC, 1994).

FERGUSON, N., 'The Kaiser's European Union: What if Britain Had "Stood Aside" in August 1914?', in N. Ferguson (ed.), *Virtual History: Alternatives and Counterfactuals* (London, 1997), 228–80.

—— (ed.), *Virtual History: Alternatives and Counterfactuals.* (London, 1997).

—— *The Pity of War* (London, 1998).

FERGUSSON, B., *The Watery Maze: The Story of Combined Operations* (London, 1961).

FERRILL, A., *The Origins of War: From the Stone Age to Alexander the Great* (London, 1985).

—— *The Fall of the Roman Empire: The Military Explanation* (London, 1986).

FERRIS, J. R., *Men, Money, and Diplomacy: The Evolution of British Strategic Policy, 1919–26* (Ithaca, NY, 1989).

FEST, J. C., *Hitler* (New York, 1975).

FISCHER, B. B., *A Cold War Conundrum: The 1983 Soviet War Scare*, CSI 97–10002 (Langley, Va., Sept. 1997).

FOLEY, C., *Commando Extraordinary* (London, 1954).

FOOT, M. R. D., 'Special Operations /1', in M. Elliott-Bateman (ed.), *The Fourth Dimension of Warfare, i: Intelligence, Subversion, Resistance* (Manchester, 1970), 19–34.

—— 'Special Operations /2', in M. Elliott-Bateman (ed.), *The Fourth Dimension of Warfare, i: Intelligence, Subversion, Resistance* (Manchester, 1970), 35–51.

FOOT, R., *The Wrong War: American Policy and the Dimensions of the Korean Conflict* (Ithaca, NY, 1985).

FORD, D., *The Button: The Pentagon's Strategic Command and Control System* (New York, 1985).

FÖRSTER, J. E., 'The Dynamics of *Volkegemeinschaft*: The Effectiveness of the German Military Establishment in the Second World War', in A. R. Millett and W. Murray (eds.), *Military Effectiveness, iii: The Second World War* (Boston, 1988), 180–220.

FOSTER, G. D., 'On Strategic Theory and Logic: Review of Edward N. Luttwak, *Strategy: The Logic of War and Peace*', *Strategic Review*, 15 (1987), 75–80.

—— 'Research, Writing, and the Mind of the Strategist', *Joint Force Quarterly*, 14 (1996–7), 111–15.

FOX, W. T. R., *The Super-Powers* (New York, 1944).

FRANCE, J., *Victory in the East: A Military History of the First Crusade* (Cambridge, 1994).

FRANK, R. B., *Guadalcanal: The Definitive Account of the Landmark Battle* (New York, 1992).

FRANKEL, B. (ed.), 'Roots of Realism', *Security Studies*, 5 (1995).

—— (ed.), 'Realism: Restatements and Renewal', *Security Studies*, 5 (1996).

FRANKLAND, N., *The Bombing Offensive Against Germany: Outlines and Perspectives.* (London, 1965).

FRASER, D., *And We Shall Shock Them: The British Army in the Second World War* (London, 1983).

—— *Knight's Cross: A Life of Field Marshal Erwin Rommel* (London, 1993).

FRASER, G. M., *Quartered Safe Out Here: A Recollection of the War in Burma* (London, 1995).

FREEDMAN, L., 'Has Strategy Reached a Dead-End?', *Futures*, 11 (1979), 122–31.

—— 'The First Two Generations of Nuclear Strategists', in P. Paret (ed.), *Makers of Modern Strategy: From Machiavelli to the Nuclear Age* (Princeton, NJ, 1986), 735–77.

—— 'Terrorism and Strategy', in L. Freedman et al., *Terrorism and International Order*, Chatham House Special Paper (London, 1987), 56–76.

—— *The Evolution of Nuclear Strategy*, 2nd edn. (New York, 1989).

—— 'Great Powers, Vital Interests and Nuclear Weapons', *Survival*, 36 (1994–5), 35–52.

—— 'Nuclear Weapons: From Marginalization to Elimination?', *Survival*, 39 (1997), 184–9.

—— *The Revolution in Strategic Affairs*, Adelphi Paper 318 (London, Apr. 1998).

—— (ed.), *Strategic Coercion: Concepts and Cases* (Oxford, 1998).

—— and KARSH, E., *The Gulf Conflict, 1990–1991: Diplomacy and War in the New World Order* (Princeton, NJ, 1993).

FRENCH, D., *British Economic and Strategic Planning, 1905–1915* (London, 1982).

—— *British Strategy and War Aims, 1914–1916* (London, 1986).

—— 'The Meaning of Attrition, 1914–1916', *English Historical Review*, 103 (1988), 385–405.

—— *The British Way in Warfare, 1688–2000* (London, 1990).

—— *The Strategy of the Lloyd George Coalition, 1916–1918* (Oxford, 1995).

FRIEDMAN, G., and FRIEDMAN, M., *The Future of War: Power, Technology, and American World Dominance in the 21st Century* (New York, 1996).

FRIEDMAN, N., *The US Maritime Strategy* (London, 1988).

FRIENDLY, A., *The Dreadful Day* (London, 1981).

FRITZ, S. G., '*Frontsoldaten*': The German Soldier in World War II* (Lexington, Ky., 1995).

FRY, R. G., 'End of the Continental Century', *RUSI Journal*, 143 (1998), 15–18.

FUKUYAMA, F., *The End of History and the Last Man* (New York, 1992).

FULLER, G. E., and ARQUILLA, J., 'The Intractable Problem of Regional Powers', *Orbis*, 40 (1996), 609–21.

FULLER, J. F. C., *Armament and History: A Study of the Influence of Armament on History from the Dawn of Classical Warfare to the Second World War* (London, 1946).

—— *A Military History of the Western World, iii: From the American Civil War to the End of World War II* (New York, 1957).

FURSENKO, A., and NAFTALI, T., *'One Hell of a Gamble': Khrushchev, Castro, Kennedy, and the Cuban Missile Crisis, 1958–1964* (London, 1997).

FUSSELL, P., *The Great War and Modern Memory* (New York, 1975).

GABRIEL, R. A., and BOOSE, D. W., Jr., *The Great Battles of Antiquity: A Strategic and Tactical Guide to Great Battles That Shaped the Development of War* (Westport, Conn., 1994).

GADDIS, J. L., *Strategies of Containment: A Critical Appraisal of Postwar American National Security Policy* (New York, 1982).

—— *The Long Peace: Inquiries into the History of the Cold War* (New York, 1987).

—— *The United States and the End of the Cold War: Implications, Reconsiderations, Provocations* (New York, 1992).

—— *We Now Know: Rethinking Cold War History* (Oxford, 1997).

GALLAGHER, N. W. (ed.), *Arms Control: New Approaches to Theory and Policy* (London, 1998).

GALLOIS, P., *The Balance of Terror: Strategy for the Nuclear Age* (Boston, 1961).

GAT, A., *The Origins of Military Thought: From the Enlightenment to Clausewitz* (Oxford, 1989).

—— 'Liddell Hart's Theory of Armoured Warfare: Revising the Revisionists', *Journal of Strategic Studies*, 19 (1996), 1–30.

—— 'British Influence and the Evolution of the Panzer Arm: Myth or Reality?, Part 1', *War in History*, 4 (1997), 150–73.

—— 'British Influence and the Evolution of the Panzer Arm: Myth or Reality?, Part 2', *War in History*, 4 (1997), 316–38.

—— *Fascist and Liberal Visions of War: Fuller, Liddell Hart, Douhet, and Other Modernists* (Oxford, 1998).

GATES, R. M., *From the Shadows: The Ultimate Insider's Story of Five Presidents and How They Won the Cold War* (New York, 1996).

GEORGE, A., and SMOKE, R., *Deterrence in American Foreign Policy: Theory and Practice* (New York, 1974).

—— and SIMONS, W. E. (eds.), *The Limits of Coercive Diplomacy* (Boulder, Colo., 1994).

GERAGHTY, T., *Who Dares Wins: The Story of the Special Air Service, 1950–1982*, rev. edn. (London, 1983).

GIAP, V. N., *People's War, People's Army* (New York, 1962).

GIBBON, E., *The History of the Decline and Fall of the Roman Empire*, ed. J. B. Bury (7 vols., London, 1909).

GIBBS, N. H., *History of the Second World War: Grand Strategy, i: Rearmament Policy* (London, 1976).

GLANTZ, D. M., and HOUSE, J., *When Titans Clashed: How the Red Army Stopped Hitler* (Lawrence, Kan., 1995).

GLASER, C. L., *Analyzing Strategic Nuclear Policy* (Princeton, NJ, 1990).

—— and KAUFMANN, C., 'What Is the Offense–Defense Balance and Can We Measure It?', *International Security*, 22 (1998), 44–82.

GLOCK, J. R., 'The Evolution of Air Force Targeting', *Airpower Journal*, 8 (1994), 14–28.

GLYNN, P., *Closing Pandora's Box: Arms Races, Arms Control and the History of the Cold War* (New York, 1992).

GOERLITZ, W., *History of the German General Staff, 1657–1945* (New York, 1953).

GOLDHAGEN, D. J., *Hitler's Willing Executioners: Ordinary Germans and the Holocaust* (London, 1996).

GOLDMAN, E. O., *Sunken Treaties: Naval Arms Control Between the Wars* (University Park, Penn., 1994).

—— 'Thinking about Strategy Absent the Enemy', *Security Studies*, 4 (1994), 40–85.

GOLDRICK, J., and HATTENDORF, J. B. (eds.), *Mahan Is Not Enough: The Proceedings of a Conference on the Works of Sir Julian Corbett and Admiral Sir Herbert Richmond* (Newport, RI, 1993).

GOLDSTEIN, E., *Winning the Peace: British Diplomatic Strategy, Peace Planning, and the Paris Peace Conference, 1916–1920* (Oxford, 1991).

GOLLIN, A., *No Longer an Island: Britain and the Wright Brothers, 1902–1909* (London, 1984).

GONG, G. W., *The Standard of 'Civilization' in International Society* (Oxford, 1984).

GOOCH, J., *The Plans of War: the General Staff and British Military Strategy c.1900–1916* (London, 1974).

—— 'Soldiers, Strategy and War Aims in Britain, 1914–18', in B. Hunt and A. Preston (eds.), *War Aims and Strategic Policy in the Great War, 1914–1918* (London, 1977), 21–40.

—— (ed.), *The Origins of Contemporary Doctrine*, Occasional Paper 30 (Camberley, Sept. 1997).

GOODERSON, I., *Air Power at the Battlefront: Allied Close Air Support in Europe, 1943–45* (London, 1998).

GORDON, A., *The Rules of the Game: Jutland and British Naval Command* (London, 1996).

GORDON, J. W., *The Other Desert War: British Special Forces in North Africa, 1940–1943* (New York, 1987).

GORDON, M. R., and TRAINOR, B. E., *The Generals' War: The Inside Story of the Conflict in the Gulf* (Boston, 1995).

GOTTFRIED, K., and BLAIR, B. G. (eds.), *Crisis Stability and Nuclear War* (New York, 1988).

GRACE, C. C., *Nuclear Weapons: Principles, Effects and Survivability* (London, 1994).

GRAFFIS, J. M., 'Strategic: Use with Care', *Airpower Journal*, 8, special edn. (1994), 4–10.

GRAHAM, D., and BIDWELL, S., *Coalitions, Politicians and Generals: Some Aspects of Command in Two World Wars* (London, 1993).

GRANT, C., 'The Use of History in the Development of Contemporary Doctrine', in J. Gooch (ed.), *The Origins of Contemporary Doctrine*, Occasional Paper 30 (Camberley, Sept. 1997), 7–17.

GRANT, U. S., *Personal Memoirs* (2 vols., New York, 1994).

GRAY, C. S., 'The Defence Policy of the Eisenhower Administrations, 1953–1961' (D.Phil. thesis, Oxford, 1970).

—— 'Nuclear Strategy: The Debate Moves On', *RUSI Journal*, 121 (1976), 44–50.

—— *The Soviet-American Arms Race* (Lexington, Mass., 1976).

—— *The Future of Land-Based Missile Forces*, Adelphi Paper 140 (London, winter 1977).

—— 'Nuclear Strategy: The Case for a Theory of Victory', *International Security*, 4 (1979), 54–87.

—— *The MX ICBM and National Security* (New York, 1981).

—— 'The Most Dangerous Decade: Historic Mission, Legitimacy, and Dynamics of the Soviet Empire in the 1980s', *Orbis*, 25 (1981), 13–28.

—— 'National Style in Strategy: The American Example', *International Security*, 6 (1981), 21–47.

—— *American Military Space Policy: Information Systems, Weapon Systems, and Arms Control* (Cambridge, Mass., 1982).

—— *Strategic Studies: A Critical Assessment* (Westport, Conn., 1982).

—— *Strategic Studies and Public Policy: The American Experience* (Lexington, Ky., 1982).

—— 'Nuclear Strategy: A Regrettable Necessity', *SAIS Review*, 3 (1983), 13–28.

—— 'Space Is Not a Sanctuary', *Survival*, 25 (1983), 194–204.

—— 'War Fighting for Deterrence', *Journal of Strategic Studies*, 7 (1984), 5–28.

—— 'Defense Planning and the Duration of War', *Defense Analysis*, 1 (1985), 21–36.

—— *Nuclear Strategy and National Style* (Lanham, Md., 1986).

—— 'Targeting Problems for Central War', in D. Ball and J. Richelson (eds.), *Strategic Nuclear Targeting* (Ithaca, NY, 1986), 171–93.

—— 'ICBMs and Deterrence: The Controversy over Prompt Launch', *Journal of Strategic Studies*, 10 (1987), 285–309.

GRAY, C. S., 'Nuclear Strategy: What Is True, What Is False, What Is Arguable?', *Comparative Strategy*, 9 (1990), 1–32.

—— *War, Peace and Victory: Strategy and Statecraft for the Next Century* (New York, 1990).

—— 'Defense Planning for the Mystery Tour: Principles for Guidance in a Period of Nonlinear Change', *Airpower Journal*, 5 (1991), 18–26.

—— 'The Holistic Strategist', *Global Affairs*, 7 (1992), 171–82.

—— *House of Cards: Why Arms Control Must Fail* (Ithaca, NY, 1992).

—— *The Leverage of Sea Power: The Strategic Advantage of Navies in War* (New York, 1992).

—— 'Soviet Nuclear Strategy and New Military Thinking', in D. Leebaert and T. Dickinson (eds.), *Soviet Strategy and New Military Thinking* (Cambridge, 1992), 29–56.

—— 'Arms Control Does Not Control Arms', *Orbis*, 37 (1993), 333–48.

—— 'Force, Order, and Justice: The Ethics of Realism in Statecraft', *Global Affairs*, 8 (1993), 1–17.

—— *Weapons Don't Make War: Policy, Strategy, and Military Technology* (Lawrence, Kan., 1993).

—— *The Navy in the Post-Cold War World: The Uses and Value of Strategic Sea Power* (University Park, Pa., 1994).

—— 'Strategy in the Nuclear Age: The United States, 1945–1991', in W. Murray, M. Knox, and A. Bernstein (eds.), *The Making of Strategy: Rulers, States, and War* (Cambridge, 1994), 579–613.

—— *Villains, Victims and Sheriffs: Strategic Studies and Security for an Inter-War Period* (Hull, 1994).

—— 'Sea Power for Containment: The U.S. Navy In The Cold War', in K. Neilson and E. J. Errington (eds.), *Navies and Global Defense: Theories And Strategy* (Westport, Conn., 1995), 181–207.

—— 'Arms Races and Other Pathetic Fallacies: A Case for Deconstruction', *Review of International Studies*, 22 (1996), 323–35.

—— 'The Continued Primacy of Geography', *Orbis*, 40 (1996), 247–59.

—— *Explorations in Strategy* (Westport, Conn., 1996).

—— 'The Influence of Space Power upon History', *Comparative Strategy*, 15 (1996), 293–308.

—— 'Introduction', to Charles E. Callwell, *Military Operations and Maritime Preponderance: Their Relations and Interdependence*, ed. C. S. Gray, repr. of 1905 edn. (Annapolis, Md., 1996).

—— *The American Revolution in Military Affairs: An Interim Assessment*, Occasional Paper 28 (Camberley, 1997).

—— 'RMAs and the Dimensions of Strategy', *Joint Force Quarterly*, 17 (1997–8), 50–4.

—— 'Handfuls of Heroes on Desperate Ventures: When Do Special Operations Succeed?', *Parameters*, 29 (1999), 2–24.

—— *The Second Nuclear Age* (Boulder, Colo., 1999).

—— 'Fuller's Folly: Technology, Strategic Effectiveness, and the Quest for Dominant Weapons', in A. J. Bacevich and B. Sullivan (eds.), *The Limits of Technology in Modern War*. Forthcoming.

—— 'Amphibious Operations', in R. Holmes (ed.), *The Oxford Companion to Military History*. Forthcoming.

—— and PAYNE, K. B., 'Victory Is Possible', *Foreign Policy*, 39 (1980), 14–27.

GRAZIA, S. DE, *Machiavelli in Hell* (New York, 1994).

GREEN, P., *Deadly Logic: The Theory of Nuclear Deterrence* (New York, 1968).

GREGORY, S. R., *Nuclear Command and Control in NATO: Nuclear Weapons Operations and the Strategy of Flexible Response* (London, 1996).

GRIFFITH, P., *Battle Tactics of the Western Front: The British Army's Art of Attack, 1916–18* (New Haven, Conn., 1994).

—— (ed.), *British Fighting Methods in the Great War* (London, 1996).

GRIFFITH, S., 'Introduction', to Mao Tse-tung [attrib.], *On Guerrilla Warfare*, trans. S. Griffiths (New York, 1961), 3–34.

GRIMSLEY, M., 'In Not so Dubious Battle: The Motivations of American Civil War Soldiers', *Journal of Military History*, 62 (1998), 175–88.

GROVE, E., 'Introduction', to J. S. Corbett, *Some Principles of Maritime Strategy*, ed. E. Grove, repr. of 1911 edn. (Annapolis, Md., 1988).

—— *The Future of Sea Power* (Annapolis, Md., 1990).

GUDMUNDSSON, B. I., *Stormtroop Tactics: Innovation in the German Army, 1914–1918* (New York, 1989).

—— *On Artillery* (Westport, Conn., 1993).

GUEVARA, C., *Guerrilla Warfare* (Lincoln, Neb., 1985).

GUILMARTIN, J. F., Jr., *Gunpowder and Galleys: Changing Technology and Mediterranean Warfare at Sea in the Sixteenth Century* (Cambridge, 1974).

GUINN, P., *British Strategy and Politics, 1914–1918* (Oxford, 1965).

GWYNN, C. W., *Imperial Policing* (London, 1934).

HAFFA, R. P., Jr., *Rational Methods, Prudent Choices: Planning US Forces* (Washington, DC, 1988).

HAFFNER, S., *The Meaning of Hitler* (London, 1997).

HAFTENDORN, H., *NATO and the Nuclear Revolution: A Crisis of Credibility, 1966–1967* (Oxford, 1996).

HALL, B. S., *Weapons and Warfare in Renaissance Europe: Gunpowder, Technology, and Tactics* (Baltimore, 1997).

HALL, E. T., *Beyond Culture* (Garden City, NY, 1977).

HALLION, R. P., *Rise of the Fighter Aircraft, 1914–1918* (Baltimore, 1988).

—— *Strike from the Sky: The History of Battlefield Air Attack, 1911–1945* (Washington, DC, 1989).

—— *Storm over Iraq: Air Power and the Gulf War* (Washington, DC, 1992).

—— 'Introduction: Air Power Past, Present and Future', in R. P. Hallion (ed.), *Air Power Confronts an Unstable World* (London, 1997), 1–11.

HALPEN, P. G., *A Naval History of World War I* (London, 1994).

HALPERIN, M. H., *Limited War in the Nuclear Age* (New York, 1963).

HAMMOND, G. T., *Plowshares into Swords: Arms Races in International Politics, 1840–1991* (Columbia, SC, 1993).

HAMPSON, F. O., *Unguided Missiles: How America Buys Its Weapons* (New York, 1989).

HANDEL, M. I. (ed.), *Intelligence and Military Operations* (London, 1990).

—— 'The Evolution of Israeli Strategy: The Psychology of Insecurity and the Quest for Absolute Security', in W. Murray, M. Knox, and A. Bernstein (eds.), *The Making of Strategy: Rulers, States, and War* (Cambridge, 1994), 534–78.

—— *Masters of War: Classical Strategic Thought*, 2nd edn. (London, 1996).

HANNAH, N. B., *The Key to Failure: Laos and the Vietnam War* (Lanham, Md., 1987).

HANSON, V. D., *The Western Way of War: Infantry Battle in Classical Greece* (London, 1989).

HARDIN, R., et al. (eds.), *Nuclear Deterrence: Ethics and Strategy* (Chicago, 1985).

HARLEY, J. A., 'Information, Technology, and the Center of Gravity', *Naval War College Review*, 50 (1997), 66–87.

HARRIS, J. P. with BARR, N., *Amiens to the Armistice: The BEF in the Hundred Days' Campaign, 8 August–11 November 1918* (London, 1998).

HARRIS, M., *Cultural Materialism: The Struggle for a Science of Culture* (New York, 1979).

HARRIS, T., 'Problematizing Popular Culture', in T. Harris (ed.), *Popular Culture in England, c.1500–1850* (London, 1995).

HARTCUP, G., *The War of Invention: Scientific Developments, 1914–18* (London, 1988).

—— *The Silent Revolution: The Development of Conventional Weapons, 1945–85* (London, 1993).

HASTINGS, M., *Bomber Command* (New York, 1979).

HATTAWAY, H., and JONES, A., *How the North Won: A Military History of the Civil War* (Urbana, Ill., 1983).

HATTENDORF, J. B. (ed.), *The Influence of History on Mahan: The Proceedings of a Conference Marking the Centenary of Alfred Thayer Mahan's 'The Influence of Sea Power upon History, 1660–1783'* (Newport, RI, 1991).

HECKSCHER, E. F., *The Continental System: An Economic Interpretation*, repr. of 1922 edn. (Gloucester, Mass., 1964).

HEINL, R. D., *Victory at High Tide: The Inchon–Seoul Campaign* (London, 1972).

HENDERSON, N., *The Birth of NATO* (London, 1982).

HENNESSY, M. A., *Strategy in Vietnam: The Marines and Revolutionary Warfare in I Corps, 1965–1972* (Westport, Conn., 1997).

HERBIG, K. L., 'Chance and Uncertainty in *On War*', in M. I. Handel (ed.), *Clausewitz and Modern Strategy* (London, 1986), 95–116.

HERKEN, G., *The Winning Weapon: The Atomic Bomb in the Cold War, 1945–1950* (New York, 1980).

—— *Counsels of War* (New York, 1985).

HERMAN, M., *Intelligence Power in Peace and War* (Cambridge, 1996).

HERSBERG, J. G., 'Reconsidering the Nuclear Arms Race: The Past as Prelude?', in G. Martel (ed.), *American Foreign Relations Reconsidered, 1890–1993* (London, 1994), 187–210.

HERWIG, H. H., *The First World War: Germany and Austria-Hungary, 1914–18* (London, 1997).

HEUSER, B., *NATO, Britain, France and the FRG: Nuclear Strategies and Forces for Europe, 1949–2000* (London, 1997).

HEWITT, H. J., *The Organization of War under Edward III, 1338–62* (Manchester, 1996).

HEZLET, A., *Aircraft and Sea Power* (New York, 1970).

HILLEN, J., 'Must U.S. Military Culture Reform?', *Orbis*, 43 (1999), 43–57.

HINES, J. G., MISHULOVICH, E. M., and SHULL, J. F., *Soviet Intentions, 1965–1985* (2 vols., McLean, Va., 22 Sept. 1995).

HITCH, C. J., *Decision-Making for Defense* (Berkeley, Calif., 1965).

HITCHCOCK, W. T. (ed.), *The Intelligence Revolution: A Historical Perspective* (Washington, DC, 1991).

HOBKIRK, M. D., *Land, Sea or Air? Military Priorities, Historical Choices* (London, 1992).

HOE, A., *David Stirling* (London, 1992).

HOFFMAN, B., *Inside Terrorism* (London, 1998).

HOFFMAN, F. G., 'Joint Vision 2010: A Marine Perspective', *Joint Force Quarterly*, 17 (1997–8), 32–8.

HOGAN, M. (ed.), *The End of the Cold War: Its Meaning and Implications* (Cambridge, 1992).

HOLBROOKE, R., 'America, a European Power', *Foreign Affairs*, 74 (1995), 38–51.

HOLLIS, M., and SMITH, S., *Explaining and Understanding International Relations* (Oxford, 1990).

HOLLOWAY, D., *Stalin and the Bomb: The Soviet Union and Atomic Energy, 1939–1956* (New Haven, Conn., 1994).

HOOKER, R. D., Jr. (ed.), *Maneuver Warfare: An Anthology.* (Novato, Calif., 1993).

HOUGH, R., *The Great War at Sea, 1914–1918* (Oxford, 1983).

HOWARD, M., 'The Classical Strategists', in Institute for Strategic Studies (ed.), *Problems of Modern Strategy*, pt. 1, Adelphi Paper 54 (London, Feb. 1969), 18–32.

—— *The Continental Commitment: The Dilemma of British Defence Policy in the Era of the Two World Wars* (London, 1972).

—— 'The Influence of Clausewitz', in C. von Clausewitz, *On War*, trans. M. Howard and P. Paret (Princeton, NJ, 1976), 27–44.

—— 'The Forgotten Dimensions of Strategy', *Foreign Affairs*, 57 (1979), 976–86.

—— (ed.), *Restraints on War: Studies in the Limitation of Armed Conflict* (Oxford, 1979).

—— 'On Fighting a Nuclear War', *International Security*, 5 (1981), 3–17.

—— 'Reassurance and Deterrence: Western Defense in the 1980s', *Foreign Affairs*, 61 (1982/3), 309–24.

—— *The Causes of Wars and Other Essays* (London, 1983).

—— *Clausewitz* (Oxford, 1983).

—— 'Empire, Race and War in pre-1914 Britain', in *The Lessons of History* (New Haven, Conn., 1991), 63–80.

—— *The Lessons of History* (New Haven, Conn., 1991).

—— 'Lessons of the Cold War', *Survival*, 36 (1994–5), 161–6.

—— 'Out of the Trenches', *Times Literary Supplement*, 13 Nov. 1998, 3–4.

—— ANDREOPOULOS, G. A., and SHULMAN, M. R. (eds.), *The Laws of War: Constraints on Warfare in the Western World* (New Haven, Conn., 1994).

HUGHES, D. J. (ed.), *Moltke on the Art of War: Selected Writings*, trans. D. J. Hughes and H. Bell (Novato, Calif., 1993).

HUGHES, T. A., *Over Lord: General Pete Quesada and the Triumph of Tactical Air Power in World War II* (New York, 1995).

HUGHES, W. P., Jr., *Fleet Tactics: Theory and Practice* (Annapolis, Md., 1986).

—— 'The Strategy-Tactics Relationship', in C. S. Gray and R. W. Barnett (eds.), *Seapower and Strategy* (Annapolis, Md., 1989), 47–73.

HUNT, B. D., *Sailor-Scholar: Admiral Sir Herbert Richmond, 1871–1946* (Waterloo, Ont., 1982).

HUNTINGTON, S. P., 'Arms Races: Prerequisites and Results', in C. J. Friedrich and S. E. Harris (eds.), *Public Policy, 1958* (Cambridge, Mass., 1958), 40–86.

—— *Political Order in Changing Societies* (New Haven, Conn., 1968).

—— *The Clash of Civilizations and the Remaking of World Order* (New York, 1996).

HURLEY, A. H., and EHRHART, R. C. (eds.), *Air Power and Warfare* (Washington, DC, 1979).

HUSSEY, J., 'The Flanders Battleground and the Weather in 1917', in P. H. Liddle (ed.), *Passchendaele in Perspective: The Third Battle of Ypres* (London, 1997), 140–58.

HYNES, S., *The Soldier's Tale: Bearing Witness to Modern War* (New York, 1997).

IGNATIEFF, M., *The Warrior's Honor: Ethnic War and the Modern Conscience* (London, 1998).

IKE, N. (ed.), *Japan's Decision for War: Records of the 1941 Policy Conferences* (Stanford, Calif., 1967).

IKLÉ, F. C., 'Can Nuclear Deterrence Last Out the Century?', *Foreign Affairs*, 51 (1973), 267–85.

—— 'Nuclear Strategy: Can There Be a Happy Ending?', *Foreign Affairs*, 63 (1985), 810–26.

—— 'The Role of Character and Intellect in Strategy', in A. W. Marshall, J. J. Martin, and H. S. Rowen (eds.), *On Not Confusing Ourselves: Essays on National Security Strategy in Honor of Albert and Roberta Wohlstetter* (Boulder, Colo., 1991), 312–16.

—— 'The Second Coming of the Nuclear Age', *Foreign Affairs*, 75 (1996), 119–28.

ION, A. H., and ERRINGTON, E. J. (eds.), *Great Powers and Little Wars: The Limits of Power* (Westport, Conn., 1993).

ISELY, J. A., and CROWL, P. A., *The U.S. Marines and Amphibious War: Its Theory, and Its Practice in the Pacific* (Princeton, NJ, 1951).

JABLONSKY, D., 'Why Is Strategy Difficult?', in G. L. Guertner (ed.), *The Search for Strategy: Politics and Strategic Vision* (Westport, Conn., 1993), 3–45.

JACOBSEN, C. G. (ed.), *Strategic Power: USA/USSR* (New York, 1990).

JAMES, D. C., 'American and Japanese Strategies in the Pacific War', in P. Paret (ed.), *Makers of Modern Strategy: From Machiavelli to the Nuclear Age* (Princeton, NJ, 1986), 703–32.

—— *Refighting the Last War: Command and Crisis in Korea, 1950–1953* (New York, 1993).

JASANI, B. (ed.), *Space Weapons and International Security* (Oxford, 1987).

JERVIS, R., 'Why Nuclear Superiority Doesn't Matter', *Political Science Quarterly*, 94 (1979), 617–33.

—— *The Illogic of American Nuclear Strategy* (Ithaca, NY, 1984).

—— 'The Political Effects of Nuclear Weapons: A Comment', *International Security*, 13 (1988), 80–90.

—— *The Meaning of the Nuclear Revolution: Statecraft and the Prospect of Armageddon* (Ithaca, NY, 1989).

JOHNSEN, W. T., *Redefining Land Power for the 21st Century* (Carlisle Barracks, Pa., 7 May 1998).

JOHNSON, D. J., PACE, S., and GABBARD, C. B., *Space: Emerging Options for National Power*, MR-517 (Santa Monica, Calif., 1998).

JOHNSON, J. T., *Can Modern War Be Just?* (New Haven, Conn., 1984).

JOHNSON, J. L., 'The Navy in 2010: A Joint Vision', *Joint Force Quarterly*, 14 (1996–7), 17–19.

JOHNSON, S. E. (ed.), *The Niche Threat: Deterring the Use of Chemical and Biological Weapons* (Washington, DC, Feb. 1997).

—— and LIBICKI, M. C. (eds.), *Dominant Battlespace Knowledge*, rev. edn. (Washington, DC, Apr. 1996).

JOHNSTON, A. I., *Cultural Realism: Strategic Culture and Grand Strategy in Chinese History* (Princeton, NJ, 1995).

—— 'Thinking about Strategic Culture,' *International Security*, 19 (1995), 32–64.

—— 'Cultural Realism and Strategy in Maoist China', in P. J. Katzenstein (ed.), *The Culture of National Security: Norms and Identity in World Politics* (New York, 1996), 216–68.

JOMINI, A. H. DE, *The Art of War*, repr. of 1862 edn. (London, 1992).

JONES, A., *The Art of War in the Western World* (Urbana, Ill., 1987).

JONES, J. F., Jr., 'General Douhet Vindicated: Desert Storm 1991', *Naval War College Review*, 45 (1992), 97–101.

JONES, R. V., *Most Secret War: British Scientific Intelligence, 1939–1945* (London, 1978).

JONES, W. E., 'Air Power in the Space Age', in S. Peach (ed.), *Perspectives on Air Power: Air Power in Its Wider Context* (London, 1998), 196–218.

JOSEPH, R. G., and Reichart, J. H., 'The Case for Nuclear Deterrence Today', *Orbis*, 42 (1998), 7–19.

'A. Jurist' (pseud. for F. J. P. VEALE), *Advance to Barbarism* (London, 1948).

KAGAN, D., *The Peace of Nicias and the Sicilian Expedition* (Ithaca, NY, 1981).

—— *The Fall of the Athenian Empire* (Ithaca, NY, 1987).

—— *On the Origins of War and the Preservation of Peace* (New York, 1995).

KAHAN, J. H., *Security in the Nuclear Age: Developing U.S. Strategic Arms Policy* (Washington, DC, 1995).

KAHN, D., 'Clausewitz and Intelligence', in M. I. Handel (ed.), *Clausewitz and Modern Strategy* (London, 1986), 117–26.

KAHN, H., *Thinking About the Unthinkable* (New York, 1964).

—— *On Escalation: Metaphors and Scenarios* (New York, 1965).

—— *On Thermonuclear War*, 2nd edn. (New York, 1969).

KAISER, D., *Politics and War: European Conflict from Philip II to Hitler* (Cambridge, Mass., 1990).

KANE, F. X., 'Space Age Geopolitics', *Orbis*, 14 (1971), 911–33.

KANE, T., 'Getting It There: The Relationship between Military Logistics and Strategic Performance' (Ph.D. thesis, Hull, 1998).

KAPLAN, F., *The Wizards of Armageddon* (New York, 1983).

KAPLAN, M. A. (ed.), *Strategic Thinking and Its Moral Implications* (Chicago, 1973).

KAPLAN, R. D., *Balkan Ghosts: A Journey through History* (New York, 1993).

KAREMAA, A., 'What Would Mahan Say about Space Power?', US Naval Institute *Proceedings*, 114 (1998), 48–9.

KARTCHNER, K. M., *Negotiating START: Strategic Arms Reduction Talks and the Quest for Strategic Stability* (New Brunswick, NJ, 1992).

KAUFMAN, R. G., *Arms Control during the Pre-Nuclear Era: The United States and Naval Limitations between the Two World Wars* (New York, 1990).

KAUFMANN, W. W., 'Limited Warfare', in W. W. Kaufmann (ed.), *Military Policy and National Security* (Princeton, NJ, 1956), 102–36.

—— 'The Requirements of Deterrence', in W. W. Kaufmann (ed.), *Military Policy and National Security* (Princeton, NJ, 1956), 12–38.

KAVANAGH, D., *Political Culture* (London, 1972).

KEANEY, T. A., and COHEN, E. A., *Gulf War Air Power Survey: Summary Report* (Washington, DC, 1993).

KEEGAN, J., *The Face of Battle* (London, 1976).

—— *Six Armies in Normandy: From D-Day to the Liberation of Paris, June 6th–August 25th, 1944* (New York, 1982).

—— *The Mask of Command* (New York, 1987).

—— (ed.), *Churchill's Generals* (New York, 1991).

—— 'Peace by Other Means?', *Times Literary Supplement*, 11 Dec. 1992, 3–4.

—— *A History of Warfare* (London, 1993).

—— 'Towards a Theory of Combat Motivation', in P. Addison and A. Calder (eds.), *Time to Kill: The Soldier's Experience of War in the West* (London, 1997), 3–11.

—— *War and Our World* (London, 1998).

KEELEY, L. H., *War Before Civilization* (New York, 1996).

KEENAN, E. L., 'Muscovite Political Folkways', *Russian Review*, 45 (1986), 115–81.

KEMP, A., *The Maginot Line: Myth and Reality* (New York, 1982).

KENNEDY, P. M., *The Rise and Fall of British Naval Mastery* (New York, 1976).

—— *The Rise of the Anglo-German Antagonism, 1860–1914* (London, 1980).

—— *The Realities behind Diplomacy: Background Influences on British External Policy, 1865–1980* (London, 1981).

—— *The Rise and Fall of the Great Powers: Economic Change and Military Conflict from 1500 to 2000* (New York, 1987).

—— 'Military Effectiveness in the First World War', in A. R. Millett and W. Murray (eds.), *Military Effectiveness, i: The First World War* (Boston, 1988), 329–50.

KENNETT, L., *The First Air War, 1914–1918* (New York, 1991).

KENT, G. A., DEVALK, R. J., and THAYER, D. E., *A Calculus of First-Strike Stability (A Criterion for Evaluating Strategic Forces)*, RAND Note, N-2526-AF (Santa Monica, Calif., June 1988).

KERSHAW, I., *Hitler, 1889–1936: Hubris* (London, 1998).

KHALILZAD, Z. M., and Ochmanek, D. A. (eds.), *Strategy and Defense Planning for the 21st Century* (Santa Monica, Calif., 1997).

KIER, E., *Imagining War: French and British Military Doctrine between the Wars* (Princeton, NJ, 1997).

KIESLING, E. C., 'Introduction', to Raoul Castex, *Strategic Theories*, trans. and ed. E. C. Kiesling (Annapolis, Md., 1994), pp. xi–xliv.

—— *Arming against Hitler: France and the Limits of Military Planning* (Princeton, NJ, 1997).

KINCAIDE, N. L., ' "Sturmabteilung" to "Freikorps": German Army Tactical and Organizational Development, 1914–1918' (Ph.D. thesis, Tempe, Ariz., 1989).

KING, J., 'Nuclear Plenty and Limited War', *Foreign Affairs*, 35 (1957), 238–56.

KIPLING, R., 'The White Man's Burden' (1899), in *The Works of Rudyard Kipling* (London, 1994), 323–4.

KISSINGER, H. A., *Nuclear Weapons and Foreign Policy* (New York, 1957).

—— *The Necessity for Choice* (New York, 1961).

—— *Diplomacy* (New York, 1994).

KITSON, F., *Low Intensity Operations: Subversion, Insurgency, and Peacekeeping* (London, 1971).

KLARE, M., *Rogue States and Nuclear Outlaws: America's Search for a New Foreign Policy* (New York, 1995).

KLEIN, B. S., *Strategic Studies and World Order: The Global Politics of Deterrence* (Cambridge, 1994).

KLUCKHOHN, C., and KELLY, W. H., 'The Concept of Culture', in C. C. Hughes (ed.), *Custom-Made: Introductory Readings for Cultural Anthropology*, 2nd edn. (Chicago, 1976), 187–203.

KNORR, K., and READ, T. (eds.), *Limited Strategic War* (London, 1962).

KNOX, M., *Mussolini Unleashed, 1939–1941: Politics and Strategy in Fascist Italy's Last War* (Cambridge, 1982).

—— 'Conclusion: Continuity and Revolution in the Making of Strategy', in W. Murray, M. Knox, and A. Bernstein (eds.), *The Making of Strategy: Rulers, States, and War* (Cambridge, 1994), 614–45.

KNUTSEN, T. L., *A History of International Relations Theory* (Manchester, 1992).

KOKOSHIN, A. A., *Soviet Strategic Thought, 1917–91* (Cambridge, Mass., 1998).

KOHOUT, J J., III, et al., 'Alternative Grand Strategy Options for the United States', *Comparative Strategy*, 14 (1995), 361–420.

KRAUSE, K., and WILLIAMS, M. C. (eds.), *Critical Security Studies: Concepts and Cases* (London, 1997).

KREPINEVICH, A. F., Jr., *The Army and Vietnam* (Baltimore, 1986).

—— 'Cavalry to Computer: The Pattern of Military Revolution', *National Interest*, 37 (1994), 30–42.

KUROWSKI, F., *The Brandenburgers: Global Mission* (Winnipeg, 1997).

LAFFIN, J., *British Butchers and Bunglers of World War One* (Gloucester, 1988).

LAMBAKIS, S. J., *The Future of American Spacepower: A Book of Basic Questions*. Forthcoming.

LAMBETH, B. S., 'On Thresholds in Soviet Military Thought', *Washington Quarterly*, 7 (1984), 69–76.

—— 'The Uses and Abuses of Air Power', *Wall Street Journal*, 27 July 1995.

—— 'The Technology Revolution in Air Warfare', *Survival*, 39 (1997), 65–83.

—— 'The Synergy of Air and Space', *Airpower Journal*, 12 (1998), 4–14.

LANCHESTER, F. W., *Aircraft in Warfare: The Dawn of the Fourth Arm* (London, 1916).

LAQUEUR, W. (ed.), *The Terrorism Reader: A Historical Anthology* (London, 1979).

—— 'Postmodern Terrorism', *Foreign Affairs*, 75 (1996), 24–36.

—— *Guerrilla Warfare: A Historical and Critical Study* (New Brunswick, NJ, 1998).

LASSWELL, H. D., *Politics: Who Gets What, When, How* (New York, 1950).

LAVELLE, A. J. C. (ed.), *The Tale of Two Bridges and the Battle for the Skies over North Vietnam* (Maxwell AFB, Ala., 1976).

LAWRENCE, T. E., *Seven Pillars of Wisdom: A Triumph*, repr. of 1935 edn. (New York, 1991).

—— 'Guerrilla Warfare', in G. Chaliand (ed.), *The Art of War in World History: From Antiquity to the Nuclear Age* (Berkeley, Calif., 1994), 880–90.

LAZENBY, J. F., *Hannibal's War: A Military History of the Second Punic War* (Warminster, 1978).

LEBOW, R. N., and STEIN, J. G., *We All Lost the Cold War* (Princeton, NJ, 1994).

LEFFLER, M. P., *A Preponderance of Power: National Security, the Truman Administration, and the Cold War* (Stanford, Calif., 1992).

LEGGE, J. M., *Theater Nuclear Weapons and the NATO Strategy of Flexible Response*, R-2964-FF (Santa Monica, Calif., Apr. 1983).

LEONARD, R., *The Art of Maneuver: Maneuver-Warfare Theory and AirLand Battle* (Novato, Calif., 1991).

LEPINGWELL, J. W. R., 'The Laws of Combat? Lanchester Reexamined', *International Security*, 12 (1987), 89–127.

LEVY, J. S., 'The Offensive/Defensive Balance of Military Technology: Theoretical and Historical Analysis', *International Studies Quarterly*, 28 (1984), 219–38.

—— 'The Causes of War: A Review of Theories', in P. E. Tetlock et al. (eds.), *Behavior, Society, and Nuclear War* (New York, 1989), i. 290–333.

LEWIS, S. J., *Forgotten Legions: German Army Infantry Policy, 1918–1941* (New York, 1985).

LIEBERMAN, E., *Deterrence Theory: Success or Failure in Arab–Israeli Wars*, McNair Paper 45 (Washington, DC, Oct. 1995).

LIBICKI, M. C., *The Mesh and the Net: Speculations on Armed Conflict in a Time of Free Silicon* (Washington, DC, Aug. 1995).

—— *What Is Information Warfare?* (Washington, DC, Aug. 1995).

—— 'The Emerging Primacy of Information', *Orbis*, 40 (1996), 261–74.

LIDDELL HART, B. H., *The British Way in Warfare* (London, 1932).

—— *The Revolution in Warfare* (London, 1946).

—— (ed.), *The Rommel Papers* (London, 1953).

—— 'Foreword', to G. Ritter, *The Schlieffen Plan: Critique of a Myth* (London, 1958), 3–10.

—— *Great Captains Unveiled* (Freeport, NY, 1967).

—— *Strategy: The Indirect Approach* (London, 1967).

LIEVEN, A., *Chechnya: Tombstone of Russian Power* (New Haven, Conn., 1998).

LINDERMAN, G. F., *The World within War: America's Combat Experience in World War II* (New York, 1997).

LLOYD, A. B. (ed.), *Battle in Antiquity* (London, 1996).

LONSDALE, D., 'Information Power: Strategy, Geopolitics, and the Fifth Dimension', *Journal of Strategic Studies*, 22 (1999).

LORD, C., 'American Strategic Culture', *Comparative Strategy*, 5 (1985), 269–93.

LOWE, C. J., and Dockrill, M. L. (eds.), *The Mirage of Power: British Foreign Policy, 1902–22, iii: The Documents* (London, 1972).

LUCAS, J., *War on the Eastern Front, 1941–1945: The German Soldier in Russia* (London, 1979).

—— *Kommando: German Special Forces of World War Two* (New York, 1986).

LUCAS, P. M. H., *The Evolution of Tactical Ideas in France and Germany during the War of 1914–1918*, trans. P. V. Kieffer (Paris, 1923).

LUDENDORFF, E., *My War Memories, 1914–1918*, 2nd edn. (2 vols., London, n.d.).

LUKACS, J., *The Hitler of History* (New York, 1998).

LUMMIS, C. R., *General Crook and the Apache Wars* (Flagstaff, Ariz., 1966).

LUONGO, K., and WANDER, W. T. (eds.), *The Search for Security in Space* (Ithaca, NY, 1980).

LUPTON, D. E., *On Space Warfare: A Space Power Doctrine* (Maxwell AFB, Ala., June 1998).

LUTTWAK, E. N., *The Political Uses of Sea Power*, Studies in International Affairs 23 (Washington, DC, 1974).

—— *The Grand Strategy of the Roman Empire: From the First Century A.D. to the Third* (Baltimore, 1976).

—— 'The Problems of Extending Deterrence', in *The Future of Strategic Deterrence*, pt. 1, Adelphi Paper 160 (London, autumn 1980), 31–7.

—— *Strategy: The Logic of War and Peace* (Cambridge, Mass., 1987).

LUTTWAK, E. N., 'The Air War', in A. Danchev and D. Keohane (eds.), *International Perspectives on the Gulf Conflict, 1990–91*, (London, 1994), 224–58.

—— 'Toward Post-Heroic Warfare', *Foreign Affairs*, 74 (1995), 109–22.

LUVAAS, J., 'Student as Teacher: Clausewitz on Frederick the Great and Napoleon', in M. I. Handel (ed.), *Clausewitz and Modern Strategy* (London, 1986), 150–70.

LYNN, J. A., 'The History of Logistics and *Supplying War*', in J. A. Lynn (ed.), *Feeding Mars: Logistics in Western Warfare from the Middle Ages to the Present* (Boulder, Colo., 1993), 9–27.

LYNN-JONES, S. M., 'Offense–Defense Theory and Its Critics', *Security Studies*, 4 (1995), 660–91.

MACHIAVELLI, N., *The Art of War*, trans. E. Farnsworth (Indianapolis, 1965).

McCAUSLAND, J., *The Gulf Conflict: A Military Analysis*, Adelphi Paper 282 (London, Nov. 1993).

McCULLY, N. A., *The McCully Report: The Russo-Japanese War, 1904–05*, repr. of 1906 report (Annapolis, Md., 1977).

McFARLAND, S. L., and NEWTON, W. P., *To Command the Sky: The Battle for Air Superiority over Germany, 1942–1944* (Washington, DC, 1991).

—— *America's Pursuit of Precision Bombing, 1910–1945* (Washington, DC, 1995).

McINNES, C., *Hot War, Cold War: The British Army's Way in Warfare, 1945–95* (London, 1996).

MacISAAC, D., 'Voices from the Central Blue: The Air Power Theorists', in P. Paret (ed.), *Makers of Modern Strategy: From Machiavelli to the Nuclear Age* (Princeton, NJ, 1986), 624–47.

McKEAN, R. N. (ed.), *Issues in Defense Economics* (New York, 1967).

MacKENZIE, D., *Inventing Accuracy: A Historical Sociology of Nuclear Missile Guidance* (Cambridge, Mass., 1993).

McKERCHER, B. J. C., 'Of Horns and Teeth: The Preparatory Commission and the World Disarmament Conference, 1926–1934', in B. J. C. McKercher (ed.), *Arms Limitation and Disarmament: Restraints on War, 1899–1939* (Westport, Conn., 1992), 173–201.

MACKINDER, H. J., *Democratic Ideals and Reality* (New York, 1962).

MACKSEY, K., *Invasion: The German Invasion of England, July 1940* (London, 1981).

McMASTER, H. R., *Dereliction of Duty: Lyndon Johnson, Robert McNamara, the Joint Chiefs of Staff, and the Lies That Led to Vietnam* (New York, 1997).

McNAMARA, R. S., *In Retrospect: The Tragedy and Lessons of Vietnam* (New York, 1995).

McPHERSON, J. M., *Battle Cry of Freedom: The Civil War Era* (New York, 1988).

McRAVEN, W. H., *SPEC OPS, Case Studies in Special Operations Warfare: Theory and Practice* (Novato, Calif., 1995).

MADARIAGA, S. DE, *Disarmament* (New York, 1929).

MAGYAR, K. P., and DANOPOULOS, C. P. (eds.), *Prolonged Wars: A Post-Nuclear Challenge* (Maxwell AFB, Ala., 1994).

MAHAN, A. T., *The Influence of Sea Power upon History, 1660–1783*, repr. of 1890 edn. (London, 1965).

—— *The Influence of Sea Power upon the French Revolution and Empire, 1793–1812* (2 vols., Boston, 1892).

—— *The Life of Nelson: The Embodiment of the Sea Power of Great Britain*, 2nd edn. (London, 1899).

—— *Retrospect and Prospect: Studies in International Relations, Naval and Political* (London, 1902).

—— *Naval Strategy, Compared and Contrasted with the Principles and Practice of Military Operations on Land*, repr. of 1911 edn. (Boston, 1919).

—— *Mahan on Naval Strategy: Selections from the Writings of Rear Admiral Alfred Thayer Mahan*, ed. J. B. Hattendorf (Annapolis, Md., 1991).

MAIER, K. A. et al., *Germany and the Second World War, ii: Germany's Initial Conquests in Europe* (Oxford, 1991).

MANDELBAUM, M., 'Is Major War Obsolete?', *Survival*, 40 (1998–9), 20–38.

MANNING, C. A. W., *The Nature of International Society* (London, 1962).

MANNING, R. A., 'The Nuclear Age: The Next Chapter', *Foreign Policy*, 109 (1997-8), 70-83.

MAO TSE-TUNG, [attrib.], *On Guerrilla Warfare*, trans. S. B. Griffith (New York, 1961).

—— *Selected Military Writings* (Peking, 1967).

MARDER, A. J., *From the Dreadnought to Scapa Flow: The Royal Navy in the Fisher Era, 1904-1919, v: Victory and Aftermath (January 1918-June 1919)* (London, 1970).

MARQUIS, S. L., *Unconventional Warfare: Rebuilding U.S. Special Operations Forces* (Washington, DC, 1997).

MARSHALL, S. L. A., *Men against Fire.* (New York, 1947).

MARTEL, G. (ed.), *American Foreign Relations Reconsidered, 1890-1993* (London, 1994).

MARTEL, W. C., and SAVAGE, P. L., *Strategic Nuclear War: What the Superpowers Target and Why* (Westport, Conn., 1986).

MARTIN, J. J., 'Dealing with Future Nuclear Dangers', *Comparative Strategy*, 16 (1997), 253-61.

MASTNY, V., *The Cold War and Soviet Insecurity: The Stalin Years* (New York, 1996).

MATHEWS, J. T., 'Power Shift', *Foreign Affairs*, 76 (1997), 50-66.

MATTHEWS, L. J., *Challenging the United States Symmetrically and Asymmetrically: Can America Be Defeated?* (Carlisle Barracks, Pa., July 1998).

MAURICE, *Maurice's Strategikon: Handbook of Byzantine Military Strategy*, trans. G. T. Dennis (Philadelphia, 1984).

MAZARR, M. J. (ed.), *Nuclear Weapons in a Transformed World: The Challenge of Virtual Nuclear Arsenals* (London, 1997).

MEARSHEIMER, J. J., *Conventional Deterrence* (Ithaca, NY, 1983).

—— *Liddell Hart and the Weight of History* (Ithaca, NY, 1988).

MEILINGER, P. S. (ed.), *The Paths of Heaven: The Evolution of Airpower Theory* (Maxwell AFB, Ala., 1997).

MENON, R., *Maritime Strategy and Continental Wars* (London, 1998).

MERTSALOV, A., 'The Collapse of Stalin's Diplomacy and Strategy', in J. Erickson and D. Dilks (eds.), *Barbarossa: The Axis and the Allies* (Edinburgh, 1994), 134-49.

MIDDLEBROOK, M., and EVERITT, C., *The Bomber Command War Diaries: An Operational Reference Book, 1939-1945* (London, 1985).

MIERZEJEWSKI, A. C., *The Collapse of the German War Economy, 1944-1945: Allied Air Power and the German National Railway* (Chapel Hill, NC, 1988), 180.

MILES, N. A., General, *Personal Recollections and Observations*, repr. of 1896 edn. (2 vols., Lincoln, Neb., 1992).

MILLER, C., *Battle for the Bundu: The First World War in East Africa* (London, 1974).

MILLER, D., *The Cold War: A Military History* (London, 1998).

MILLER, E. S., *War Plan Orange: The U.S. Strategy to Defeat Japan, 1897-1945* (Annapolis, Md., 1991).

MILLETT, A. R., and MASLOWSKI, P., *For the Common Defense: A Military History of the United States of America*, rev. edn. (New York, 1994).

—— and MURRAY, W. (eds.), *Military Effectiveness* (3 vols., Boston, 1988).

MITCHELL, W., *Winged Defense: The Development and Possibilities of Modern Air Power, Economic and Military*, repr. of 1925 edn. (New York, 1988).

MOLANDER, R. C., RIDDILE, A. S., and WILSON, P. A., *Strategic Information Warfare: A New Face of War*, MR-661-OSD (Santa Monica, Calif., 1996).

MOMYER, W. W., *Air Power in Three Wars* (Washington, DC, 1983).

MOORMAN, T. S., Jr., 'Space: A New Strategic Frontier', in R. H. Shultz, Jr., and R. Pfaltzgraff (eds.), *The Future of Air Power in the Aftermath of the Gulf War* (Maxwell AFB, Ala., July 1992), 235-49.

MOREMAN, T. R., ' "Small Wars" and "Imperial Policing": The British Army and the Theory and Practice of Colonial Warfare in the British Empire', *Journal of Strategic Studies*, 19, special issue on 'Military Power: Land Warfare in Theory and Practice' (1996), 105–31.

MOREMAN, T. R., *The Army in India and the Development of Frontier Warfare, 1849–1947* (London, 1998).

MORGAN, D., *The Mongols* (Oxford, 1986).

MORGAN, P., *Deterrence: A Conceptual Analysis* (Beverly Hills, Calif., 1977).

MORROW, J. H., Jr., *The Great War in the Air: Military Aviation from 1909 to 1921* (Washington, DC, 1993).

MORSEY, K., 'T. E. Lawrence: Strategist', in S. E. Tabachnick (ed.), *The T. E. Lawrence Puzzle* (Athens, Ga., 1984), 185–203.

MUELLER, J., 'The Essential Irrelevance of Nuclear Weapons: Stability in the Postwar World', *International Security*, 13 (1988), 55–79.

—— *Retreat from Doomsday: The Obsolescence of Major War* (New York, 1989).

—— 'The Impact of Ideas on Grand Strategy', in R. Rosecrance and A. A. Stein (eds.), *The Domestic Bases of Grand Strategy* (Ithaca, NY, 1993), 48–62.

—— 'The Perfect Enemy: Assessing the Gulf War', *Security Studies*, 5 (1995), 77–117.

—— 'Nine Propositions about the Historical Impact of Nuclear Weapons', in J. Gjelstad and O. Njolstad (eds.), *Nuclear Rivalry and International Order: Nuclear Arms and the Emerging International Order* (Ann Arbor, Mich., 1998), 55–74.

—— 'The Escalating Irrelevance of Nuclear Weapons', in T. V. Paul, T. J. Harknett, and J. J. Wirtz (eds.), *The Absolute Weapon Revisited: Nuclear Arms and the Emerging International Order* (Ann Arbor, Mich., 1998), 73–98.

MUIR, R., *Tactics and the Experience of Battle in the Age of Napoleon* (New Haven, Conn., 1998).

MÜLLER, R.-D., and UEBERSCHÄR, G. R., *Hitler's War in the East, 1941–1945: A Critical Reassessment* (Providence, RI, 1997).

MUOLO, M. J., *Space Handbook, ii: An Analyst's Guide*, AU-18 (Maxwell AFB, Ala., Dec. 1993).

MURRAY, W., *The Change in the European Balance of Power, 1938–1939: The Path to Ruin* (Princeton, NJ, 1984).

—— 'The Influence of Pre-War Anglo-American Doctrine on the Air Campaigns of the Second World War', in H. Boog (ed.), *The Conduct of the Air War in the Second World War* (New York, 1992), 235–53.

—— *Air War in the Persian Gulf* (Baltimore, 1995).

—— 'The 1996 RMA Essay Contest', *Joint Force Quarterly*, 15 (1997), 6–7.

—— 'Thinking about Revolutions in Military Affairs', *Joint Force Quarterly*, 16 (1997), 69–76.

—— 'Clausewitz Out, Computers In: Military Culture and Technological Hubris', *National Interest*, 48 (1997), 57–64.

—— 'Does Military Culture Matter?', *Orbis*, 43 (1999), 27–42.

—— and GRIMSLEY, M., 'Introduction: On Strategy', in W. Murray, M. Knox, and A. Bernstein (eds.), *The Making of Strategy: Rulers, States, and War* (Cambridge, 1994), 1–23.

—— KNOX, M., and BERNSTEIN, A. (eds.), *The Making of Strategy: Rulers, States, and War* (Cambridge, 1994).

—— and MILLETT, A. R. (eds.), *Calculations: Net Assessment and the Coming of World War II* (New York, 1992).

—— —— (eds.), *Military Innovation in the Interwar Period* (Cambridge, 1996).

NADIN, T., and MAPEL, D. R., (eds.), *Traditions of International Ethics* (Cambridge, 1992).

NAFTALI, T., 'A New Cold War History' (review of J. L. Gaddis, *We Now Know: Rethinking Cold War History*, 1997), *Survival*, 39 (1997), 151–7.

NAROLL, R., BULLOUGH, V. L., and NAROLL, F., *Military Deterrence in History: A Pilot Cross-Historical Survey* (Albany, NY, 1975).

National Academy of Sciences, Committee on International Security and Arms Control, *The Future of U.S. Nuclear Weapons Policy* (Washington, DC, 1997).

NAVEH, S., *In Pursuit of Military Excellence: The Evolution of Operational Theory* (London, 1997).

NELSON, H., 'Space and Time in *On War*', in M. I. Handel (ed.), *Clausewitz and Modern Strategy* (London, 1986), 134–49.

NEUFELD, M. J., *The Rocket and the Reich: Peenemünde and the Coming of the Ballistic Missile Era* (Cambridge, Mass., 1995).

NEWBERRY, R. D., *Space Doctrine for the Twenty-First Century* (Maxwell AFB, Ala., Oct. 1998).

NEWMAN, B., *Marine Special Warfare and Elite Unit Tactics* (Boulder, Colo., 1995).

—— *Guerrillas in the Mist: A Battlefield Guide to Clandestine Warfare* (Boulder, Colo., 1997).

NEWSINGER, J., *Dangerous Men: The SAS and Popular Culture* (London, 1997).

NICHIPOROK, B., and BUILDER, C. H., *Information Technologies and the Future of Land Warfare* (Santa Monica, Calif., 1995).

NINCIC, M., *The Arms Race: The Political Economy of Military Growth* (New York, 1982).

NOLAN, J. E., *Guardians of the Arsenal: The Politics of Nuclear Strategy* (New York, 1989).

—— (ed.), *Global Engagement: Cooperation and Security in the 21st Century* (Washington, DC, 1994).

NYE, J. S., Jr., *Nuclear Ethics* (New York, 1986).

—— 'Old Wars and Future Wars: Causation and Prevention', in R. I. Rotberg and T. K. Rabb (eds.), *The Origin and Prevention of Major Wars* (Cambridge, 1989), 3–12.

—— and OWENS, W. A., 'America's Information Edge', *Foreign Affairs*, 75 (1996), 20–36.

OBERG, J. E., *Space Power Theory* (Washington, DC, 1999).

O'CONNELL, R. L., *Sacred Vessels: The Cult of the Battleship and the Rise of the U.S. Navy* (New York, 1991).

O'HANLON, M., 'Can High Technology Bring U.S. Troops Home?', *Foreign Policy*, 113 (1998–9), 72–86.

OLSON, W. C., and GROOM, A. J. R., *International Relations Then and Now: Origins and Trends in Interpretation* (London, 1991).

OSGOOD, R. E., *Limited War: The Challenge to American Strategy* (Chicago, 1957).

—— and TUCKER, R. W., *Force, Order, and Justice* (Baltimore, 1967).

O TUATHAIL, G., *Critical Geopolitics: The Politics of Writing Global Space* (Minneapolis, 1996).

OVERY, R. J., *The Air War, 1939–1945* (New York, 1981).

—— *Why the Allies Won* (London, 1995).

—— *Bomber Command, 1939–1945* (London, 1997).

OWENS, W. A., 'The Emerging System of Systems', US Naval Institute *Proceedings*, 121 (1995), 35–9.

—— 'The American Revolution in Military Affairs', *Joint Force Quarterly*, 10 (1995–6), 37–8

—— 'Introduction', to S. E. Johnson and M. C. Libicki (eds.), *Dominant Battlespace Knowledge*, 2nd edn. (Washington, DC, Apr. 1996), 1–14.

PADFIELD, P., *Dönitz, The Last Führer: Portrait of a Nazi War Leader* (New York, 1984).

PAKENHAM, T., *The Boer War* (New York, 1979).

PALMER, B., Jr., *The 25-Year War: America's Military Role in Vietnam* (Lexington, Ky., 1984).

PANOFSKY, W. K. H., 'The Mutual Hostage Relationship between America and Russia', *Foreign Affairs*, 52 (1973), 109–18.

PAPE, R. A., *Bombing to Win: Air Power and Coercion in War* (Ithaca, NY, 1996).

PAQUETTE, L., 'Strategy and Time in Clausewitz's *On War* and in Sun Tzu's *The Art of War*', *Comparative Strategy*, 10 (1991), 37–51.

PARET, P., *Clausewitz and the State* (New York, 1976).

—— 'The Genesis of *On War*', in C. von Clausewitz, *On War*, trans. M. Howard and P. Paret (Princeton, NJ, 1976), 3–25.

—— 'Revolutions in Warfare: An Earlier Generation of Interpreters', in B. Brodie, M. D. Intriligator, and R. Kolkowicz (eds.), *National Security and International Stability* (Cambridge, Mass., 1983), 157–69.

—— 'Clausewitz', in P. Paret (ed.), *Makers of Modern Strategy: From Machiavelli to the Nuclear Age* (Princeton, NJ, 1986), 186–213.

—— (ed.), *Makers of Modern Strategy: From Machiavelli to the Nuclear Age* (Princeton, NJ, 1986).

—— 'Napoleon and the Revolution in War', in P. Paret (ed.), *Makers of Modern Strategy: From Machiavelli to the Nuclear Age* (Princeton, NJ, 1986), 123–42.

—— *Understanding War: Essays on Clausewitz and the History of Military Power* (Princeton, NJ, 1992).

PARIS, M., *Winged Warfare: The Literature and Theory of Aerial Warfare in Britain, 1859–1917* (Manchester, 1992).

PARKER, G., *The Military Revolution: Military Innovation and the Rise of the West, 1500–1800* (Cambridge, 1988).

PARKER, G., *Geopolitics: Past, Present, and Future* (London, 1998).

PARRY, J. H., *The Spanish Seaborne Empire*, 2nd edn. (London, 1967).

PASCHALL, R., *LIC 2010: Special Operations and Unconventional Warfare in the Next Century* (Washington, DC, 1990).

—— 'Guerrilla Warfare', in R. Cowley and G. Parker (eds.), *The Osprey Companion to Military History* (London, 1996), 192–4.

PAUL, T. V., 'Nuclear Taboo and War Initiation in Regional Conflicts', *Journal of Conflict Resolution*, 39 (1995), 696–717.

—— HARKNETT, R. K., and WIRTZ, J. J. (eds.), *The Absolute Weapon Revisited: Nuclear Arms and the Emerging International Order* (Ann Arbor, Mich., 1998).

PAYNE, K. B., *Strategic Defense: 'Star Wars' in Perspective* (Lanham, Md., 1986).

—— *Deterrence in the Second Nuclear Age* (Lexington, Ky., 1996).

—— *The Case Against Nuclear Abolition and For Nuclear Deterrence* (Fairfax, Va., Dec. 1997).

—— et al., ' "Cold Peace" or Cooperation? The Potential for U.S.-Russian Accommodation on Missile Defense and the ABM Treaty', *Comparative Strategy*, 16 (1997).

PEABODY, D., *National Characteristics* (Cambridge, 1985).

PEEBLES, C., *The Corona Project: America's First Spy Satellites* (Annapolis, Md., 1997).

PERRETT, G., *A Country Made by War: From the Revolution to Vietnam – the Story of America's Rise to Power* (New York, 1989).

PERRY, W. J. (Secretary of Defense), *Annual Report to the President and the Congress* (Washington, DC, 1995).

—— 'Defense in an Age of Hope', *Foreign Affairs*, 75 (1996), 64–79.

PETERS, R., 'The New Warrior Class', *Parameters*, 24 (1994), 16–26.

—— 'After the Revolution', *Parameters*, 25 (1995), 7–14

—— 'The Culture of Future Conflict', *Parameters*, 25 (1995–6), 18–27.

—— 'Our Soldiers, Their Cities', *Parameters*, 26 (1996), 43–50

—— 'Winning against Warriors', *Strategic Review*, 24 (1996), 12–21

—— 'Constant Conflict', *Parameters*, 27 (1997), 4–14.

—— 'Our New Old Enemies', in L. J. Matthews (ed.), *Challenging the United States Symmetrically and Asymmetrically: Can America Be Defeated?* (Carlisle Barracks, Pa., July 1998), 215–38.

—— 'The New Strategic Trinity', *Parameters*, 28 (1998–9), 73–9.

—— *Fighting for the Future: Will America Triumph?* (Mechanicsburg, Pa., 1999).

PIPES, R., 'Why the Soviet Union Thinks It Could Fight and Win a Nuclear War', *Commentary*, 64 (1977), 21–34.

PORCH, D., *The Conquest of Morocco* (New York, 1982).

—— *The Conquest of the Sahara* (New York, 1984).

—— 'Bugeaud, Galliéni, Lyautey: The Development of French Colonial Warfare', in P. Paret (ed.), *Makers of Modern Strategy: From Machiavelli to the Nuclear Age* (Princeton, NJ, 1986), 376–407.

POSEN, B. R., *The Sources of Military Doctrine: France, Britain, and Germany between the World Wars* (Ithaca, NY, 1984).

—— and ROSS, A. L., 'Competing Visions for U.S. Grand Strategy', *International Security*, 21 (1996/7), 5–53.

POSSONY, S. T., and MONTOUX, E., 'Du Picq and Foch: The French School', in E. M. Earle (ed.), *Makers of Modern Strategy: Military Thought from Machiavelli to Hitler* (Princeton, NJ, 1941), 206–33.

POSTOL, T., 'Targeting', in A. B. Carter, J. D. Steinbruner, and C. A. Zraket (eds.), *Managing Nuclear Operations* (Washington, DC, 1987), 373–406.

POTTER, W., *Nuclear Threats from the Former Soviet Union*, CTS-39-93 (Livermore, Calif., 16 Mar. 1993).

POWERS, B. D., *Strategy Without Slide-Rule: British Air Strategy, 1914–1939* (London, 1976).

PRADOS, J., *The Hidden History of the Vietnam War* (Chicago, 1995).

—— and STUBBE, R. W., *Valley of Decision: The Siege of Khe Sanh* (New York, 1993).

PRICE, R. M., *The Chemical Weapons Taboo* (Ithaca, NY, 1997).

—— and TANNENWALD, N., 'Norms and Deterrence: The Nuclear and Chemical Weapons Taboos', in P. J. Katzenstein (ed.), *The Culture of National Security: Norms and Identity in World Politics* (New York, 1996), 114–52.

PRINS, G., 'The Four-Stroke Cycle in Security Studies', *International Affairs*, 74 (1998), 781–808.

PRIOR, R., and WILSON, T., *Command on the Western Front: The Military Career of Sir Henry Rawlinson, 1914–18* (Oxford, 1992).

—— *Passchendaele: The Untold Story* (New Haven, Conn., 1996).

PRYOR, J. H., *Geography, Technology, and War: Studies in the Maritime History of the Mediterranean, 649–1571* (Cambridge, 1988).

QUADE, E. S. (ed.), *Analysis for Military Decisions* (Chicago, 1964).

—— and BOUCHER, W. I. (eds.), *Systems Analysis and Policy Planning: Applications in Defense* (New York, 1968).

QUESTER, G. H., *Deterrence before Hiroshima: The Airpower Background of Modern Strategy* (New York, 1966).

—— *Offense and Defense in the International System* (New York, 1977).

QUINLAN, M., *Thinking about Nuclear Weapons*, RUSI Whitehall Paper (London, 1997).

RAPOPORT, A., *Strategy and Conscience* (New York, 1964).

—— 'Introduction', to C. von Clausewitz, *On War*, abridged edn. (London, 1968), 11–80.

RATHMELL, A., 'Cyber-Terrorism: The Shape of Future Conflict', *RUSI Journal*, 142 (1997), 40–5.

REAGAN, R. (President), *National Security Strategy of the United States* (Washington, DC, Jan. 1988).

RECORD, J., *Hollow Victory: A Contrary View of the Gulf War* (Washington, DC, 1993).

—— 'Vietnam in Retrospect: Could We Have Won?' *Parameters*, 26 (1996–7), 51–65.

—— *The Wrong War: Why We Lost in Vietnam* (Annapolis, Md., 1998).

REID, B. H., 'Introduction', *Journal of Strategic Studies*, 19, special issue on 'Military Power: Land Warfare in Theory and Practice' (1996), 1–9.

REID, B. H., *Studies in British Military Thought: Debates with Fuller and Liddell Hart* (Lincoln, Neb., 1998).

REISS, E., *The Strategic Defense Initiative* (Cambridge, 1992).

REISS, M., *Bridled Ambition: Why Countries Constrain Their Nuclear Capabilities* (Washington, DC, 1995).

REITZ, D., *Commando: A Boer Journal of the Boer War*, repr. of 1932 edn. (London, 1982).

RENWICK, R., *Fighting with Allies: America and Britain in Peace and at War* (New York, 1996).

REYNOLDS, C. G., *The Fast Carriers: The Forging of an Air Navy* (New York, 1968).

—— *Command of the Sea: The History and Strategy of Maritime Empires*, 2nd edn. (2 vols., Malabar, Fla., 1983).

RHEINGOLD, H., *The Virtual Community* (New York, 1993).

RHODES, R., *Dark Sun: The Making of the Hydrogen Bomb* (New York, 1995).

RICHELSON, J. T., *America's Secret Eyes in Space: The U.S. Keyhole Spy Satellite Program* (New York, 1990).

RICHMOND, H., *Statesmen and Sea Power* (Oxford, 1946).

RIPER, M. VAN, and HOFFMAN, F. G., 'Pursuing the Real Revolution in Military Affairs: Exploiting Knowledge-Based Warfare', *National Security Studies Quarterly*, 4 (1998), 1–19.

RITTER, G., *The Schlieffen Plan: Critique of a Myth* (London, 1958).

ROBERTS, A., 'Land Warfare: From Hague to Nuremberg', in M. Howard, G. J. Andreopoulos, and M. R. Shulman (eds.), *The Laws of War: Constraints on Warfare in the Western World* (New Haven, Conn., 1994), 116–39.

ROBERTS, K., *Northwest Passage* (New York, 1937).

ROBERTSON, G. (Secretary of State for Defence), *The Strategic Defence Review* (London, July 1998).

ROBERTSON, J. I., Jr., *Stonewall Jackson: The Man, the Soldier, the Legend* (New York, NY, 1997).

RODGER, N. A. M., 'Introduction', to N. A. M. Rodger (ed.), *Naval Power in the Twentieth Century* (Annapolis, Md., 1996), pp. xvii–xxiv.

—— *The Safeguard of the Sea: A Naval History of Great Britain, i: 660–1649* (London, 1997).

ROGERS, C. J. (ed.), *The Military Revolution Debate: Readings on the Military Transformation of Early Modern Europe* (Boulder, Colo., 1995).

ROSE, G., 'Neoclassical Realism and Theories of Foreign Policy', *World Politics*, 51 (1998), 144–72.

ROSE, J. H., *Man and the Sea: Stages in Maritime and Human Progress* (Cambridge, 1935).

ROSECRANCE, R., *Strategic Deterrence Reconsidered*, Adelphi Paper 116 (London, spring 1975).

—— 'Albert Wohlstetter', in J. Baylis and J. Garnett (eds.), *Makers of Nuclear Strategy* (New York, 1991), 57–69.

ROSEN, S. P., 'Vietnam and the American Theory of Limited War', *International Security*, 7 (1982), 83–113.

—— *Winning the Next War: Innovation and the Modern Military* (Ithaca, NY, 1991).

ROSENBERG, D. A., 'A Smoking Radiating Ruin at the End of Two Hours: Documents on American Plans for Nuclear War with the Soviet Union, 1945–1955', *International Security*, 6 (1981–2), 3–38.

—— 'U.S. Nuclear War Planning, 1945–1960', in D. Ball and J. T. Richelson (eds.), *Strategic Nuclear Targeting* (Ithaca, NY, 1986), 35–56.

ROSKILL, S. W., *The Strategy of Sea Power* (London, 1962).

ROSS, S. T., *American War Plans, 1945–1950* (London, 1996).

ROTBERG, R. I., and RABB, T. K. (eds.), *The Origin and Prevention of Major Wars* (Cambridge, 1989).

ROTHENBERG, G. E., *The Art of Warfare in the Age of Napoleon* (Bloomington, Ind., 1980).

RUSSETT, B., *A Post-Thucydides, Post-Cold-War World*, Panteoin University Institute of International Relations, Occasional Research Papers, Special Issue (Athens, Dec. 1992).

SAGAN, C., and TURCO, R., *A Path Where No Man Thought: Nuclear Winter and the End of the Arms Race* (London, 1990).

SAGAN, S. D., 'Nuclear Alerts and Crisis Management', *International Security*, 9 (1985), 99–139.

—— *Moving Targets: Nuclear Strategy and National Security* (Princeton, NJ, 1989).

—— *The Limits of Safety: Organizations, Accidents, and Nuclear Weapons* (Princeton, NJ, 1993).

—— 'Why Do States Build Nuclear Weapons? Three Models in Search of a Bomb', *International Security*, 21 (1996/7), 54–86.

SAMUELS, M., *Command or Control? Command, Training and Tactics in the British and German Armies, 1888–1918* (London, 1995).

SANTOSUOSSO, A., *Soldiers, Citizens, and the Symbols of War: From Classical Greece to Republican Rome, 500–167 B.C.* (Boulder, Colo., 1997).

SARKESIAN, S. C., *America's Forgotten Wars: The Counterrevolutionary Past and Lessons for the Future* (Westport, Conn., 1984)

SAWYER, R. D. (trans.), *The Seven Military Classics of Ancient China* (Boulder, Conn., 1993).

SCALES, R. H., Jr., *Firepower in Limited War*, rev. edn. (Novato, Calif., 1995).

SCAMMELL, G. V., *The World Encompassed: The First European Maritime Empires, c.800–1650* (London, 1981).

SCHAFFER, R., *Wings of Judgment: American Bombing in World War II* (New York, 1985).

SCHELL, J., *The Gift of Time: The Case for Abolishing Nuclear Weapons Now* (London, 1998).

SCHELLING, T. C., *The Strategy of Conflict.* (Cambridge, Mass., 1960).

—— *Arms and Influence* (New Haven, Conn., 1966).

—— and HALPERIN, M. H., *Strategy and Arms Control* (New York, 1961).

SCHILLING, W. R., 'U.S. Strategic Nuclear Concepts in the 1970s: The Search for Sufficiently Equivalent Countervailing Parity', *International Security*, 6 (1981), 48–79.

SCHLESINGER, A., Jr., 'Back to the Womb? Isolationism's Renewed Threat', *Foreign Affairs*, 74 (1995), 2–8.

SCHRAM, S., *The Thought of Mao Tse-tung* (Cambridge, 1989).

SCHREIBER, G., STEGEMANN, B., and VOGEL, D., *Germany and the Second World War, iii: The Mediterranean, South-east Europe, and North Africa, 1939–1941* (Oxford, 1995).

SCHULZINGER, R. D., *A Time for War: The United States and Vietnam, 1941–1975* (New York, 1997).

SCHURMAN, D. M., *Julian S. Corbett, 1854–1922: Historian of British Maritime Policy from Drake to Jellicoe* (London, 1981).

SCHWARTAU, W., 'The Fourth Force', in W. Schwartau (ed.), *Information Warfare, Cyberterrorism: Protecting Your Personal Security in the Electronic Age*, 2nd edn. (New York, 1996), 469–72.

SCHWARTZ, D. N., *NATO's Nuclear Dilemmas* (Washington, DC, 1983).

SCHWEIZER, P., *Victory: The Reagan Administration's Secret Strategy That Hastened the Collapse of the Soviet Union* (New York, 1994).

SCHWELLER, R. L., *Deadly Imbalances: Tripolarity and Hitler's Strategy of World Conquest* (New York, 1998).

SEATON, A., *The Russo-German War, 1941–45* (New York, 1971).

SEGAL, G., 'Strategy and "Ethnic Chic"', *International Affairs*, 60 (1983–4), 15–30.

—— (ed.), *New Directions in Strategic Studies: A Chatham House Debate*, RIIA Discussion Paper 17 (London, 1989).

SELLAR, W. C., and YEATMAN, R. J., *1066 and All That* (London, 1960).

SEVERSKY, A. P. DE, *Victory through Air Power* (New York, 1942).

SHEFFIELD, G. D., 'The Shadow of the Somme: The Influence of the First World War on British

Soldiers' Perceptions and Behaviour in the Second World War', in P. Addison and A. Calder (eds.), *Time to Kill: The Soldier's Experience of War in the West, 1939–1945* (London, 1997), 29–39.

SHERRY, M. S., *The Rise of American Air Power: The Creation of Armageddon* (New Haven, Conn., 1987).

SHERWIG, J. M., *Guineas and Gunpowder: British Foreign Aid in the Wars with France, 1793–1815* (Cambridge, Mass., 1969).

SHUBIK, M., 'Terrorism, Technology, and the Socioeconomics of Death', *Comparative Strategy*, 16 (1997), 399–414.

SHUE, H. (ed.), *Nuclear Deterrence and Moral Restraint: Critical Choices for American Strategy* (Cambridge, 1989).

SIMPKIN, R., *Race to the Swift: Thoughts on Twenty-First Century Warfare* (London, 1985).

SIMPSON, H. R., *Dien Bien Phu: The Epic Battle America Forgot* (Washington, DC, 1994).

SIMPSON, K., 'The Reputation of Sir Douglas Haig', in B. Bond (ed.), *The First World War and British Military History* (Oxford, 1991), 141–62.

SIMS, J. E., *Icarus Restrained: An Intellectual History of Nuclear Arms Control, 1945–1960* (Boulder, Colo., 1990).

SINGH, A., 'Time: The New Dimension in War', *Joint Force Quarterly*, 10 (1995–6), 56–61.

SHY, J., 'Jomini', in P. Paret (ed.), *Makers of Modern Strategy: From Machiavelli to the Nuclear Age* (Princeton, NJ, 1986), 143–85.

SIXSMITH, E. K. G., *British Generalship in the Twentieth Century* (London, 1970).

SKORZENY, O., *Skorzeny's Secret Missions: War Memoirs of the Most Dangerous Man in Europe* (New York, 1950).

SLATER, J., 'The Maritime Contribution to Joint Operations', *RUSI Journal*, 143 (1998), 20–4.

SLIM, Viscount, *Defeat Into Victory.* (London, 1986).

SMART, I., *Advanced Strategic Missiles: A Short Guide*, Adelphi Paper 63 (London, Dec. 1969).

SMITH, J. T., *Rolling Thunder: The American Strategic Bombing Campaign Against North Vietnam, 1964–68* (Walton-on-Thames, 1994).

SMITH, M., *British Air Strategy between the Wars* (Oxford, 1985).

SMITH, P. A., Jr., *On Political War* (Washington, DC, 1989).

SMUTS, J. C., ' "Magna Carta" of British Air Power', in E. M. Emme (ed.), *The Impact of Air Power: National Security and World Politics* (Princeton, NJ, 1959), 33–7.

SNIDER, D. M., 'An Uninformed Debate on Military Culture', *Orbis*, 43 (1999), 43–57.

SNYDER, C. (ed.), *The Strategic Defense Debate: Can 'Star Wars' Make us Safe?* (Philadelphia, 1986).

SNYDER, J. L., *The Soviet Strategic Culture: Implications for Limited Nuclear Operations*, R-2154-AF (Santa Monica, Calif., Sept. 1977).

SOKOLOVSKIY, V. D., *Soviet Military Strategy*, ed. H. Dinerstein, L. Gouré, and T. Wolfe (Englewood Cliffs, NJ, 1963).

SOLZHENITSYN, A., 'The March of the Hypocrites', *The Times*, 21 Aug. 1997, 16.

SPAIGHT, J. M., *Air Power in the Next War* (London, 1938).

SPECTOR, R. H., *Eagle against the Sun: The American War with Japan* (New York, 1985).

—— *After Tet: The Bloodiest Year in Vietnam* (New York, 1993).

SPEIER, H., 'Ludendorff: The German Concept of Total War', in E. M. Earle (ed.), *Makers of Modern Strategy: From Machiavelli to Hitler* (Princeton, NJ, 1941), 306–21.

SPENCE, J., *God's Chinese Son: The Taiping Heavenly Kingdom of Hong Xiuquan* (London, 1996).

SPIERS, E. M., *Chemical Warfare* (London, 1986).

—— *Chemical and Biological Weapons: A Study of Proliferation* (London, 1994).

STARES, P. B., *Command Performance: The Neglected Dimension of European Security* (Washington, DC, 1991).

STEIGER, R., *Armour Tactics in the Second World War: Panzer Army Campaigns of 1939–41 in German War Diaries* (New York, 1991).

STEINBERGER, J., UDGAONKAR, B., and ROTBLAT, J. (eds.), *A Nuclear-Weapon-Free World: Desirable, Feasible?* (Boulder, Colo., 1993).

STEINBRUNER, J., 'Nuclear Decapitation', *Foreign Policy*, 45 (1981), 16–28.

STEINER, B. H., *Bernard Brodie and the Foundations of American Nuclear Strategy* (Lawrence, Kan., 1991).

STEVENS, S., 'The Soviet BMD Programs', in A. B. Carter and D. N. Schwartz (eds.), *Ballistic Missile Defense* (Washington, DC, 1984), 182–220.

STEVENSON, D., *Armaments and the Coming of War: Europe, 1904–1914* (Oxford, 1996).

STEWART, J. T. (ed.), *Airpower: The Decisive Force in Korea* (Princeton, NJ, 1957).

Stockholm International Peace Research Institute, *The Problem of Chemical and Biological Warfare, i: The Rise of CB Weapons* (New York, 1971).

STONE, N., *The Eastern Front, 1914–1917* (London, 1975).

STRACHAN, H., 'The British Way in Warfare Revisited', *Historical Journal*, 26 (1983), 447–61.

—— 'The British Way in Warfare', in D. Chandler (ed.), *The Oxford Illustrated History of the British Army* (Oxford, 1994), 417–34.

—— 'Germany in the First World War: The Problem of Strategy', *German History*, 12 (1994), 237–49.

—— 'The Battle of the Somme and British Strategy', *Journal of Strategic Studies*, 21 (1998), 79–95.

—— 'Economic Mobilization: Money, Munitions, and Machines', in H. Strachan (ed.), *The Oxford Illustrated History of the First World War* (Oxford, 1998), 134–48.

STRASSLER, R. B. (ed.), *The Landmark Thucydides: A Comprehensive Guide to 'The Peloponnesian War'*, trans. R. Crawley, rev. edn. (New York, 1996).

Strategy and Force Planning Faculty (US Naval War College) (ed.), *Strategy and Force Planning* (Newport, RI, 1995).

STRAUSS, B. S., and OBER, J., *The Anatomy of Error: Ancient Military Disasters and Their Lessons for Modern Strategists* (New York, 1990).

STROMSETH, J., *The Origins of Flexible Response: NATO's Debate over Strategy in the 1960s* (London, 1988).

STUART, R. C., *War and American Thought: From the Revolution to the Monroe Doctrine* (Kent, OH, 1982).

SUGANAMI, H., *On the Causes of War* (Oxford, 1996).

SULLIVAN, B. R., 'The Future Nature of Conflict: A Critique of "The American Revolution in Military Affairs" in the Era of Jointery', *Defense Analysis*, 14 (1998), 91–100.

SUMIDA, J. T., *Inventing Grand Strategy and Teaching Command: The Classic Works of Alfred Thayer Mahan Reconsidered* (Washington, DC, 1997).

SUMMERS, H. G., Jr., *On Strategy: A Critical Analysis of the Vietnam War* (Novato, Calif., 1982).

—— *On Strategy, ii: A Critical Analysis of the Gulf War* (New York, 1992).

—— *The New World Strategy: A Military Policy for America's Future* (New York, 1995).

SUMMERTON, N. W., 'The Development of British Military Planning for a War Against Germany, 1904–1914' (Ph.D. thesis, London, 1970).

SUN TZU, *The Art of War*, trans. R. D. Sawyer (Boulder, Colo., 1994).

TATE, M., *The United States and Armaments* (Cambridge, Mass., 1948).

TAYLOR, T., *The March of Conquest: The German Victories in Western Europe, 1940* (Baltimore, 1991).

TEDDER, LORD, *Air Power in War* (London, 1947).

TERRAINE, J., *The Smoke and the Fire: Myths and Anti-Myths of War, 1861–1945* (London, 1980).

—— *To Win a War: 1918, The Year of Victory* (New York, 1981).

TERRAINE, J., *White Heat: The New Warfare, 1914–18* (London, 1982).

—— *A Time for Courage: The Royal Air Force in the European War, 1939–1945* (New York, 1985).

—— 'Indirect Fire as a Battle Winner/Loser', in C. Barnett et al., *Old Battles and New Defences: Can We Learn from Military History?* (London, 1986), 7–31.

—— *Business in Great Waters: The U-Boat Wars, 1916–1945* (London, 1989).

—— 'The Substance of the War', in H. Cecil and P. H. Liddle (eds.), *Facing Armageddon: The First World War Experienced* (London, 1996), 3–15.

THOMPSON, E. A., *The History of Attila and the Huns* (Oxford, 1948).

THOMPSON, J., *The Lifeblood of War: Logistics in Armed Conflict* (London, 1991).

—— *The Imperial War Museum Book of War behind Enemy Lines* (London, 1998).

THOMPSON, R., *Defeating Communist Insurgency: Experiences from Malaya and Vietnam* (London, 1966).

THOMPSON, W. R., 'Anglo-German Rivalry and the 1939 Failure of Deterrence', *Security Studies*, 7 (1997/8), 58–89.

THORPE, G. C., *Pure Logistics: The Science of War Preparation*, repr. of 1917 edn. (Washington, DC, 1986).

TILL, G., 'Airpower and the Battleship in the 1920's', in B. Ranft (ed.), *Technical Change and British Naval Policy, 1860–1939* (London, 1977), 108–22.

—— *Maritime Strategy and the Nuclear Age* (London, 1982).

—— 'Adopting the Aircraft Carrier: The British, American and Japanese Case Studies', in W. Murray and A. R. Millett (eds.), *Military Innovation in the Interwar Period* (Cambridge, 1996), 191–226.

—— FARRELL, T., and GROVE, M. J., *Amphibious Operations*, Occasional Paper 31 (Camberley, 1997).

TOFFLER, A., *The Third Wave* (New York, 1980).

—— and TOFFLER, H., *War and Anti-War: Survival at the Dawn of the 21st Century* (Boston, 1993).

TOWLE, P. A., 'The Evaluation of the Experience of the Russo-Japanese War', in B. Ranft (ed.), *Technical Change and British Naval Policy, 1860–1939* (London, 1977), 65–79.

—— *Pilots and Rebels: The Use of Aircraft in Unconventional Warfare, 1918–1988* (London, 1989).

—— 'The Distinctive Characteristic of Air Power', in A. Lambert and A. C. Williamson (eds.), *The Dynamics of Air Power* (Bracknell, Berks., 1996), 3–17.

TRACHTENBERG, M., *History and Strategy* (Princeton, NJ, 1991).

TRAVERS, T., *The Killing Ground: The British Army, the Western Front and the Emergence of Modern Warfare, 1900–1918* (London, 1987).

—— *How the War Was Won: Command and Technology in the British Army on the Western Front, 1917–1918* (London, 1992).

TRENCH, C. C., *The Frontier Scouts* (London, 1985).

TRENCHARD, H. M., *Air Power* (London, Dec. 1946).

TUCHMAN, B. W., *The March of Folly: From Troy to Vietnam* (New York, 1984).

TUCKER, R. W., *The Just War: A Study in Contemporary American Doctrine* (Baltimore, 1960).

TUGWELL, M., and CHARTERS, D., 'Special Operations and the Threats to United States Interests in the 1980s', in F. R. Barnett, B. H. Tovar, and R. H. Shultz (eds.), *Special Operations in U. S. Strategy* (Washington, DC, 1984), 27–43.

UK Ministry of Defence, *British Defence Doctrine*, Joint Warfare Publication (JWP) 0–01 (London, 1996).

ULLMAN, H. K., and WADE, J. P., *Shock and Awe: Achieving Rapid Dominance* (Washington, DC, 1996).

URBAN, M., *Big Boys' Rules* (London, 1992).

US Congress, House of Representatives, Committee on Science and Technology, Subcommittee on Natural Resources, Agriculture Research and Environment, and Committee on Interior and Insular Affairs, Subcommittee on Energy and the Environment, *Nuclear Winter, Joint Hearing*, 99th Cong., 1st sess. (Washington, DC, 14 Mar. 1985).

—— Office of Technology Assessment, *Proliferation of Weapons of Mass Destruction: Assessing the Risks*, OTA-ISC-559 (Washington, DC, Aug. 1993).

—— *Technologies Underlying Weapons of Mass Destruction*, OTA-BP-ISC-115 (Washington, DC, Dec. 1993).

US Joint Chiefs of Staff, ' "Joint Vision 2010": America's Military—Preparing for Tomorrow, *Joint Force Quarterly*, 12 (1996), 34–49.

US Marine Corps, *Warfighting* (New York, 1994).

US Navy and US Marine Corps, . . . *From the Sea: Preparing the Naval Service for the 21st Century* (Washington, DC, 1992).

US Space Command, *Long Range Plan* (Peterson AFB, Colo., March 1998).

US Strategic Bombing Survey, *The Effects of Strategic Bombing on the German War Economy* (Washington, DC, 31 Oct. 1945).

—— *The Effects of Strategic Bombing on German Transportation*, 2nd edn. (Washington, DC, Jan. 1947).

UTGOFF, V., *The Challenge of Chemical Weapons: An American Perspective* (New York, 1991).

UTLEY, J. G., *Going to War with Japan, 1937–1941* (Knoxville, Tenn., 1985).

UTLEY, R. M., *Frontiersmen in Blue: The United States Army and the Indian, 1848–1865* (Lincoln, Neb., 1967).

—— *Frontier Regulars: The United States Army and the Indian, 1866–1891* (New York, 1973).

—— *Cavalier in Buckskin: George Armstrong Custer and the Western Military Frontier* (Norman, Okla., 1988).

VALLANCE, A. G. B., *The Air Weapon: Doctrines of Air Power Strategy and Operational Art* (London, 1996).

—— 'The Changing Nature of Air Warfare', in R. P. Hallion (ed.), *Air Power Confronts an Unstable World* (London, 1997), pp. xiii–xxiii

VAN DEN BERGH, G. VAN B., 'The Nuclear Revolution into Its Second Phase', in J. Gjelstad and O. Njolstad (eds.), *Nuclear Rivalry and International Order* (London, 1996), 22–39.

VANDENBROUCKE, L. S., *Perilous Options: Special Operations as an Instrument of U.S. Foreign Policy* (New York, 1993).

VAT, D. VAN DER, *The Pacific Campaign: World War II, The U.S.-Japanese Naval War, 1941–1945* (New York, 1991).

—— *Stealth at Sea: The History of the Submarine* (Boston, 1995).

VEGETIUS, *Vegetius: Epitome of Military Science*, trans. N. P. Milner (Liverpool, 1993).

VERBRUGGEN, J. F., *The Art of Warfare in Western Europe during the Middle Ages: From the Eighth Century to 1340*, 2nd edn. (Woodbridge, Suffolk, 1997).

VILLACRES, E. J., and BASSFORD, C., 'Reclaiming the Clausewitzian Trinity', *Parameters*, 25 (1995), 9–19.

VLAHOS, M., 'A Crack in the Shield: The Capital Ship Concept under Attack', *Journal of Strategic Studies*, 2 (1979), 47–82.

—— 'The War after Byte City', *Washington Quarterly*, 20 (1997), 41–72.

WALKER, M., *The Cold War And the Making of the Modern World* (London, 1993).

WALKER, R. L., *Strategic Target Planning: Bridging the Gap between Theory and Practice*, National Security Affairs Monograph Series 83–9. (Washington, DC, 1983).

WALLACE, W., 'Truth and Power, Monks and Technocrats: Theory and Practice in International Relations', *Review of International Studies*, 22 (1996), 301–21.

WALLOP, M., and CODEVILLA, A., *The Arms Control Delusion* (San Francisco, 1987).

WALT, S. M., 'The Renaissance of Security Studies', *International Studies Quarterly*, 35 (1991), 211–39.

WALTON, C. D., 'Victory Denied: The Myth of Inevitable American Defeat in Vietnam' (Ph.D. thesis, Hull, 1999).

WALTZ, K. N., *Man, the State and War: A Theoretical Analysis* (New York, 1959).

—— 'Nuclear Myths and Political Realities', *American Political Science Review*, 84 (1990), 732–45.

WALZER, M., *Just and Unjust Wars: A Moral Argument with Historical Illustrations* (New York, 1977).

WARDEN, J. A., III, *The Air Campaign: Planning for Combat* (Washington, DC, 1989).

—— 'Employing Air Power in the Twenty-first Century', in R. H. Shultz, Jr., and R. L. Pfaltzgraff, Jr. (eds.), *The Future of Air Power in the Aftermath of the Gulf War* (Maxwell AFB, Ala., July 1992), 57–82.

—— 'Success in Modern War: A Response to Robert Pape's *Bombing to Win*', *Security Studies*, 7 (1997–8), 172–90.

WARDLAW, G., *Political Terrorism: Theory, Tactics, and Countermeasures* (Cambridge, 1990).

WARK, W. K., *The Ultimate Enemy: British Intelligence and Nazi Germany, 1933–1939* (Ithaca, NY, 1985).

WARLIMONT, W., *Inside Hitler's Headquarters, 1939–45*, repr. of 1962 edn. (Novato, Calif., n.d.).

WARNER, E. L., III, *Soviet Concepts and Capabilities for Limited Nuclear War: What We Know and How We Know It*, N-27-69-AF (Santa Monica, Calif., Feb. 1989).

WASHBURN, A. R., 'Orbital Dynamics for the Compleat Idiot', *Naval War College Review*, 52 (1999), 120–9.

WATKINS, J. D. et al., *The Maritime Strategy* (Annapolis, Md., Jan. 1986).

WATSON, B. W. (ed.), *Military Lessons of the Gulf War* (London, 1991).

WATTS, B. D., *Clausewitzian Friction and Future War*, McNair Paper 52 (Washington, DC, Oct. 1996).

—— 'Ignoring Reality: Problems of Theory and Evidence in Security Studies', *Security Studies*, 7 (1997/8), 115–71.

WAVELL, A., *Generals and Generalship* (New York, 1943).

WEBSTER, C., and FRANKLAND, N., *The Strategic Air Offensive against Germany, 1939–1945* (4 vols., London, 1961).

WEGENER, W., *The Naval Strategy of the World War*, trans. H. H. Herwig (Annapolis, Md., 1989).

WEIGLEY, R. F., *The American Way of War: A History of United States Military Strategy and Policy* (New York, 1973).

—— *Eisenhower's Lieutenants: The Campaign of France and Germany, 1944–1945* (Bloomington, Ind., 1981).

—— *The Age of Battles: The Quest for Decisive Warfare from Breitenfeld to Waterloo* (Bloomington, Ind., 1991).

WEINBERG, G., *A World at Arms: A Global History of World War II* (Cambridge, 1994).

—— *Germany, Hitler, and World War II* (Cambridge, 1995).

WEISS, S., *Allies in Conflict: Anglo-American Strategic Negotiations, 1938–44* (London, 1996).

WELLER, J., *Wellington in the Peninsula, 1808–1814* (London, 1992).

WELLS, H. G., *The War in the Air* (London, 1908).

WELTMAN, J. J., *World Politics and the Evolution of War* (Baltimore, 1995).

WERTZ, J. R., and LARSON, W. J. (eds.), *Space Mission Analysis and Design* (Dordrecht, 1991).

WHALEY, B., *Codeword Barbarossa* (Cambridge, Mass., 1973).

WHEELER-BENNETT, J. W., *The Disarmament Deadlock* (London, 1934).

WHITE, C. M., *The Gotha Summer: The German Daytime Air Raids on England, May–August 1917* (London, 1986).

WHITE, L. A., *The Concept of Cultural Systems: A Key to Understanding Tribes and Nations* (New York, 1975).

WHITEHOUSE, S., and BENNETT, G. B., *Fear Is the Foe: A Footslogger from Normandy to the Rhine* (London, 1995).

WIDMER, K., 'The Intellectual as Soldier', in J. Meyers (ed.), *T. E. Lawrence: Soldier, Writer, Legend* (London, 1989), 28–57.

WIESELTIER, L., *Nuclear War, Nuclear Peace* (New York, 1983).

WILKENING, D., 'Future U.S. and Russian Nuclear Forces: Applying Traditional Analysis Methods in an Era of Cooperation', in P. K. Davis (ed.), *New Challenges for Defense Planning: Rethinking How Much is Enough* (Santa Monica, Calif., 1994), 301–48.

—— et al., *Strategic Defenses and Crisis Stability*, RAND Note N-2511-AF (Santa Monica, Calif., Apr. 1989).

—— and WATMAN, K., *Nuclear Deterrence in a Regional Context* (Santa Monica, Calif. 1995).

WILLEMS, E., *A Way of Life and Death: Three Centuries of Prussian-German Militarism, An Anthropological Approach* (Nashville, Tenn., 1986).

WILLIAMS, R., *Culture and Society: 1780–1950* (New York, 1983).

—— 'The Analysis of Culture,' in J. Storey (ed.), *Cultural Theory and Popular Culture: A Reader* (Hemel Hempstead, Herts., 1994), 56–64.

WILLIAMSON, S. R., Jr., *The Politics of Grand Strategy: Britain and France Prepare for War, 1904–1914* (Cambridge, Mass., 1969).

—— 'Joffre Reshapes French Strategy, 1911–1913', in P. M. Kennedy (ed.), *The War Plans of the Great Powers, 1880–1914* (London, 1979), 133–154.

—— and REARDEN, S. L., *The Origins of U.S. Nuclear Strategy, 1945–1953* (New York, 1993).

WILLMOTT, H. P., *The Barrier and the Javelin: Japanese and Allied Pacific Strategies, February to June 1943* (Annapolis, Md., 1983).

WILSON, P., 'The Transformation of Military Power, 1997–2027', paper presented at the 1997 Pacific Symposium, Honolulu, Hawaii, 28–9 Apr. 1997.

WINIK, J., *On the Brink: The Dramatic, Behind the Scenes Saga of the Reagan Era and the Men and Women Who Won the Cold War* (New York, 1996).

WINTERS, H. A., *Battling the Elements: Weather and Terrain in the Conduct of War* (Baltimore, 1998).

WINTON, J., *Ultra at Sea* (London, 1988).

WOHL, R., *The Generation of 1914* (London, 1980).

WOHLSTETTER, A. J. et al., *Selection and Use of Strategic Air Bases*, R-266 (Santa Monica, Calif., Apr. 1954).

—— et al., *Protecting U.S. Ability to Strike Back in the 1950s and 1960s*, R-290 (Santa Monica, Calif., Apr. 1956).

—— 'The Delicate Balance of Terror', *Foreign Affairs*, 37 (1959), 211–34.

—— 'Illusions of Distance', *Foreign Affairs*, 46 (1968), 242–55.

—— *Legends of the Arms Race*, USSI Report 75-1 (Washington, DC, 1975).

—— and BRODY, R., 'Continuing Control as a Requirement for Deterring', in A. B. Carter, J. D. Steinbruner, and C. A. Zraket (eds.), *Managing Nuclear Operations* (Washington, DC, 1987), 142–96.

WOODWARD, D. R., *Lloyd George and the Generals* (Newark, Del., 1983).

WRIGHT, Q., *A Study of War* (2 vols., Chicago, 1942).

WRIGHT, S. (ed.), *Preventing a Biological Arms Race* (Cambridge, Mass., 1990).

WYLIE, J. C., *Military Strategy: A General Theory of Power Control*, ed. J. B. Hattendorf, repr. of 1967 edn. (Annapolis, Md., 1989).

YOST, D., 'Strategic Defenses in Soviet Doctrine and Force Posture', in F. S. Hoffman, A. J. Wohlstetter, and D. Yost (eds.), *Swords and Shields: NATO, the USSR, and New Choices for Long-Range Offense and Defense* (Lexington, Mass., 1987), 123–57.

ZIMM, A. D., 'Deterrence: Basic Theory, Principles, and Implications', *Strategic Review*, 25 (1997), 42–50.

ZUBER, T., 'The Schlieffen Plan Reconsidered', *War in History*, 6 (1999), 262–305.

ZUBOK, V., and PLESHAKOV, C., *Inside the Kremlin's Cold War: From Stalin to Khrushchev* (Cambridge, Mass., 1996).

INDEX

nuclear alerts and crisis management 62
nuclear peril 187
offence and defence 180–1
and Russian culture 134
seapower 219
see also nuclear weapons
Colin, J. vii
combined operations, definition 240n
command 39–40
command, control, communications and
   intelligence (C³I) 344
communications, civil and military authorities
   59, 101
complexity
   and dominance of partial theories 124–7
   as factor for paucity of modern strategists 115–6
   and simplicity, as category of strategic culture
   149
control 159–62
conventional warfare, in nuclear era 197–99
Corbett, Julian S. 80
   compared to Clausewitz 85
   general theory 126
   limitations 89
   seapower 217, 219, 223
Corum, James S. 33n
coup d'oeil 108
Creasey, Edward 38
Creveld, Martin van 84
   on Clausewitz 112
   information-led combat 236–7
   new nuclear weapon states 340
   politics 29
crisis resolution 183
Crook, General George 281
Crowl, Philip 80n
Cuba 62, 198
cultural activity, war as 8
culture 28–9
   as context 129–51, 155
   military 146
   politicians and generals 59
   see also ethics; strategic culture
Custance, Admiral Sir Reginald 1, 81, 86, 90,
   116
cyberwar 191, 209, 244
   anti-geography 267–70
   as revolution in military affairs 248–9

Danchev, Alex 2
Danilevich, Colonel-General Andrian A. 310–11,
   314, 316n, 317
'Dead Hand' 311n
DeBlois, Bruce M. 260

Debray, Régis 283
deception, and warfare 35
decisive points 97–8, 108
   see also centre of gravity
decolonization 289
defence
   and offence 99–100, 110, 176, 179–81
   and offence in sea warfare 220
   and offence in space warfare 257
defence planning, and war 4–5
Delbrück, Hans 2
Delta Force 287
delta-v 254–67
demodernization, *Wehrmacht* in Russia 27
Desch, Michael 135, 136n
Desert Storm *see* Gulf War
determinism, and strategic culture 134
deterrence 169, 190, 324–5, 337–8
   nuclear 78–9
Dieppe 61
Dill, Sir John 70
disarmament, popular hopes for 192
distributed manoeuvre 2–3n
doctrine, and strategic theory 35–7
doomsday machine 311
Douhet, General Giulio 89, 208, 230,
   344
   general theory 126
   targeting in aerial warfare 233–4
Dulles, John Foster 78
Dunkirk 39, 148
duration 172–4

economic warfare 162
economics
   and logistics 31–3
   and war 192–3
Edmonds, Martin 19
Eisenhower, Dwight D. 7, 78, 99
El Salvador 264
electromagnetic spectrum (EMS) 5, 40, 164
electronic warfare 187, 240
Emergency Rocket Communications System
   (ERCS) 311n
enemy
   will of 103–4
   see also adversaries
Enigma 38–9
Entente, economic warfare 162
environment 163–5
Epstein, Robert M. 2–3n
equivalent megatonnage (EMT) 342–3n
Erickson, John 154
essentialism, danger of 56–7